Patterns of Authority:
A Structural Basis for Political Inquiry

Comparative Studies in Behavioral Science:
A WILEY SERIES

Robert T. Holt and John E. Turner, *Editors*
Department of Political Science
University of Minnesota

The Logic of Comparative Social Inquiry
by Adam Przeworski and Henry Teune

The Analysis of Subjective Culture
by Harry C. Triandis

Comparative Legislative Behavior: Frontiers of Research
edited by Samuel C. Patterson and John C. Wahlke

Mass Political Violence: A Cross-National Causal Analysis
by Douglas A. Hibbs, Jr.

Cross-Cultural Research Methods
by Richard W. Brislin, Walter J. Lonner, and Robert M. Thorndike

Unity and Disintegration in International Alliances
by Ole R. Holsti, P. Terrence Hopmann, and John D. Sullivan

Comparative Social Research: Methodological Problems and Strategies
edited by Michael Armer and Allen D. Grimshaw

Planning and Budgeting in Poor Countries
by Naomi Caiden and Aaron Wildavsky

Politics and Social Equality: A Comparative Analysis
by Robert W. Jackman

Measurement and Analysis of Political Systems: A Science of Social Behavior
by Stephen Coleman

Patterns of Authority: A Structural Basis for Political Inquiry
by Harry Eckstein and Ted Robert Gurr

Patterns of Authority: A Structural Basis for Political Inquiry

HARRY ECKSTEIN
Princeton University

TED ROBERT GURR
Northwestern University

A WILEY-INTERSCIENCE PUBLICATION

JOHN WILEY & SONS New York • London • Sydney • Toronto

Library of Congress Cataloging in Publication Data:

Eckstein, Harry.
Patterns of authority.

(Comparative studies in behavioral science)
"A Wiley-Interscience publication."
Includes bibliographical references and index.
1. Authority. I. Gurr, Ted Robert, 1936– joint author. II. Title.

JC571.E34 301.15'52 75-19003
ISBN 0-471-23076-6

Printed in the United States of America

10 9 8 7 6 5 4 3 2 1

To the Memory of Peter Woodward

SERIES PREFACE

The last decade has witnessed the burgeoning of comparative studies in the behavioral sciences. Scholars in specific disciplines have come to realize that they share much with experts in other fields who face similar theoretical and methodological problems and whose research findings are often related. Moreover, specialists in a given geographic area have felt the need to look beyond the limited confines of their region and to seek new meaning in their research results by comparing them with studies that have been made elsewhere.

This series is designed to meet the needs of the growing cadre of scholars in comparative research. The emphasis is on cross-disciplinary studies, although works within the perspective of a single discipline are included. In its scope, the series includes books of theoretical and methodological interest, as well as studies that are based on empirical research. The books in the series are addressed to scholars in the various behavioral science disciplines, to graduate students, and to undergraduates in advanced standing.

Robert T. Holt
John E. Turner

University of Minnesota
Minneapolis, Minnesota

Preface

This book proposes a new approach to the scope of "political" studies: it equates political analysis with the study of authority patterns in any and all social units. At the same time it reports some of the research conducted in this framework by members of the Workshop in Comparative Politics at Princeton University between 1966 and 1971. It may be quixotic to propose a new focus for political inquiry, and it was not really our original intention to do so. The first author established the Workshop in Comparative Politics as a means for conducting collaborative research on a theoretical issue that could not be studied adequately by a single scholar with the help of a few research assistants.[1] The objective was to make a set of intensive, country-case studies of authority patterns that would provide a strong test of his "congruence" theory of political performance. The gist of this theory is that high performance by any political system requires that the authority patterns of governmental institutions closely resemble those of less inclusive social units, notably those that socialize citizens and recruit and train political cadres and elites.[2] The research design envisioned a complex division of labor. The theoretical and conceptual foundations of the enterprise were developed by the first author and then revised and translated into operational procedures in a cooperative effort that engaged all members of the Workshop. Student members then conducted field studies in countries of their choice, hoping that, in addition to achieving dissertations, they would find sufficient information to assess congruence in that country. The second author of this book joined the Workshop shortly after its inception to

[1] The assumption was that social theory must be tested with a substantial number of cases. An alternative view, suggested in part by the experience of the Workshop, is proposed in Harry Eckstein, "Case Study and Theory in Political Science," in Fred I. Greenstein and Nelson W. Polsby, Eds., *Handbook of Political Science, Vol. 7: Strategies of Inquiry* (Reading, Mass.: Addison-Wesley, 1975).

[2] The fullest and most recent statement of this theory is Harry Eckstein, "Authority Relations and Governmental Performance," *Comparative Political Studies*, Vol. 2 (October 1969), pp. 269–325.

provide general methodological skills, to undertake comparative assessment of governmental performance, and to help coordinate field research and analysis of data.

The original objective of the Workshop could not be realized for one fundamental reason: its information requirements proved to be far beyond our collective capacity to satisfy. An analytic scheme for systematic description of authority relations was devised, but once reduced to operational specifications, a full description of the authority patterns of any one type of social unit in a society was recognized as being a formidable task even in the most favorable circumstances for fieldwork. Moreover, the secondary literature, on which we had hoped to rely for some material, was woefully inadequate to the purpose. The work of other scholars provided tantalizing glimpses of authority patterns in diverse social units, but rarely had sufficient conceptual precision or empirical scope to substitute for fieldwork. The Workshop members who attempted fieldwork thus could not hope to characterize overall "congruence" in a society; instead they focused on the study of one or a few kinds of social units. Most often these were secondary schools, while in some instances they were families, elementary schools or universities, political parties, and bureaucracies.

Suffice to say that for some student members the description of authority patterns became an end in itself while for others it was a means to different and diverse theoretical objectives which, unlike congruence theory, could be sought through the analysis of one kind of social entity in a single society. Those of us who were not engaged in fieldwork meanwhile turned our attention to characterizing the performance and authority patterns of a large number of national political systems, by means of systematic coding of secondary sources. Like the field studies this work proved to have considerable intrinsic value, both for empirical generalization and for testing of hypotheses. But it could not sufficiently contribute to testing congruence theory as originally conceived.

The scope of the empirical research done under the auspices of the Workshop is displayed in the following list of field and documentary studies of authority and performance carried out beginning in 1967. Note that research topics are not necessarily listed by titles their authors attach to them. The dates in parentheses are those of dissertations, reports, papers, and publications through 1975. Most of these are referred to with full citations in subsequent chapters.

Field Studies

Gurston Dacks: Authority Patterns, Bureaucracy, and Negotiations in Canadian Federal-Provincial Relations (1972).

Robert Friedman: Participation in Sweden: A Study of Families, Schools, and the National Ministry of Education (1972[2]).

Philip Goldman: The Congruence of Authority in Catholic, Protestant, and Secular Secondary Schools in the Netherlands (1972).

Craig MacLean: Authority Patterns in Philippine Families, Schools, and Public Agencies.

Donald A. Newman: Transforming Authority Relations in a Modernizing Society: Tunisia.

Joel Prager: Spanish Authority Patterns and Political Stability (1972[2]).

Rafael Rivas: Authority Patterns in the Liberal and Conservative Parties of Colombia.

Ronald Rogowski: Social Structure and Stable Rule in Germany: Secondary Schools and Political Parties (1970, 1971).

William R. Schonfeld: Youth and Authority in France: A Study of Secondary Schools and the National School of Administration (ENA) (1970, 1971, 1975).

Lois Wasserspring: Authority Norms and Practices in Post-Revolutionary Mexico: Secondary Schools, the PRI, and Economic Interest Groups (1971).

Peter Woodward: Political Culture and Pressure Group Politics: A Comparison of Political Authority Relations in French- and English-speaking Canada.

Susan Woodward: Training for Self-Management: A Study of Yugoslav Secondary Schools (1973, 1974).

Alan Zuckerman: Hierarchical Social Division and Political Groups: Factions in the Italian Christian Democratic Party (1971).

Documentary Studies

Harry Eckstein: The Evaluation of Political Performance: Problems and Dimensions (1971).

Ted Robert Gurr: Persistence and Change in Political Systems, 1800–1971 (1973, 1974).

Ted Robert Gurr and Muriel McClelland: Political Performance, A Twelve-Nation Study (1971).

Muriel McClelland: Inequality in Industrial Authority (1969).

One fateful conclusion emerged from the conceptual and empirical work reviewed above: the analysis of authority relations has been a crucial but badly neglected field of study. This was our primary motivation for writing this book—to provide a rationale, concepts, methods, illustrative data, and theoretical justifications for further, systematic research into the subject. We do not, alas, report the conclusive testing of a single theory—though the first author hopes to do so in the future. Instead, we wish to stimulate fresh research on a subject that is relevant to a broad range of theoretical issues. Part I of the book evaluates critically some other, prevailing notions of political study and gives a rationale for treating the general study of authority as a special field, more comprehensive than conventional political science. Part II presents a conceptual scheme for the analysis of patterns of authority. Its six chapters discuss ten dimensional properties that can be identified in all authority relations and can be used for precise description and comparison of authority patterns in social units as diverse as schools, voluntary associations, and the state. These concepts, as stated, were translated into operational techniques and used in field research between 1967 and 1971 in European and Third World countries. The chapters in Part III summarize the resultant methodological experience and show how the concepts proposed in Part II can be and have been applied in different settings.

The last two parts of the book deal with substantive and theoretical issues in the study of authority patterns. Part IV outlines a rigorous approach to developing typologies, argues that typologies have theoretical as well as descriptive uses, and then employs the technique of progressive differentiation to make a series of increasingly fine distinctions among types of authority patterns. Finally, Part V advances some new theoretical arguments about, first, the kinds of social conditions that influence patterns of authority and, second, the relevance of authority variables for the analysis of some of the most important problem areas of contemporary political science: political socialization, conflict and cohesion, the performance of political systems, and problems of institutional persistence and change.

Our most optimistic hope for this book is that it will serve as a "foundation" study. It is comparable in intent, though not at all in content, to such works as David Easton's *The Political System*[3] and Robert A. Dahl and Charles E. Lindblom's *Politics, Economics and Welfare.*[4] There is little point in speculating whether it will be any more or less influential than these or analogous works by Catlin, Lasswell, and Downs. But we claim three advantages over most such foundation studies: the approach proposed has been fully elaborated, is worked out with both conceptual and operational rigor, and has already been applied in a substantial number of case and comparative studies. Thus it should prove useful in a variety of ways for other scholars, whether or not they accept our claims about the importance of studying authority relations in nongovernmental as well as governmental settings—for a field of "archology" instead of conventional "political science."

The analytic scheme and operational procedures certainly are eminently suited to the descriptive analysis of the state organizations that have always been the central focus of political inquiry. Used in conjunction with the tentative typology proposed in Part IV, they should sensitize researchers to crucial differences among and within institutions that are often glossed over. In particular, they demonstrate the inadequacy of dichotomous distinctions between "democratic" and "authoritarian" political arrangements and provide a basis for more discriminating analyses.

[3] Easton, *The Political System* (New York: Knopf, 1953).

[4] Dahl and Lindblom, *Politics, Economics and Welfare* (New York: Harper and Row, 1953).

No "new" methodologies are proposed, but we argue for a multimethod strategy of research called "triangulation" that has general applicability. Specific multimethod strategies for studying some of the central dimensions of authority relations also are described, not only in the abstract but with reference to specific field applications. These procedures should be useful for case and comparative studies of authority irrespective of the user's paradigmatic assumptions and theoretical interests.

The theoretical arguments advanced in Parts II and V can be evaluated, and can stimulate further theoretical work on quite different premises than those assumed here. The relevance of authority variables for explaining numerous puzzles in such subjects as political socialization and political development is sketched in Part II. It is proposed in Part V that authority patterns are chiefly a function of a society's system of stratification and differentiation; the argument suggests some new synthesizing perspectives on arguments advanced by theorists as diverse as Marx and Durkheim, among others. In the final chapter of Part V the importance of authority variables for the "performance" and durability of social institutions is argued in detail and it is suggested *inter alia* that congruence theory implies limitations on the size and complexity of viable political institutions. These theoretical arguments remain speculative in a way that the conceptual and methodological elements of the book are not, and can be examined critically and empirically from a variety of perspectives. They provide a large agenda for problem-solving.

Ultimately this book may not need any more justification than the fact that the approach it presents has already been very productive of empirical research, for us and our students, and has stimulated us to many challenging theoretical ideas. We hope that it will do as much for others.

Because of the scope and duration of the Workshop many acknowledgments are in order. The study was funded during its first three years by a basic research contract from the Advanced Research Projects Agency of the Department of Defense and thereafter by grants from the National Science Foundation. The second author's work on the study was facilitated by a Ford Foundation Faculty Fellowship in 1970 and a Guggenheim Fellowship in 1972–1973. Significant support of every kind has been provided throughout by Princeton University's Center of International Studies, the official "home" of the Workshop.

Most of the student members of the Workshop are cited in the listing of field research topics. At almost every turn this book bears the stamp of their ideas and evidence. Without their spirited and dedicated participation neither the Workshop nor this book would have been possible.

Muriel McClelland served as the Workshop's principal research assistant, later research associate, from 1966 through 1970. Several research assistants also contributed more briefly but substantially to different Workshop projects: Mary Fosler, Erika B. K. Gurr, James Testa, and Thomas Reepmeyer. The list of credits would be seriously incomplete without a special word of thanks to June Traube of Princeton University, who capably and cheerfully disposed of the intricate secretarial tasks and administrative details of the Workshop for nearly a decade, and to Jane McDowall, who kept financial order.

Part I appeared, as Eckstein's work, in the *American Political Science Review,* Vol. LXVII, No. 4 (December 1973), and is reprinted here, somewhat revised, by permission of the *Review's* editor.

Every coauthored work involves a certain division of labor. In this case Eckstein drafted Parts I and II, Gurr Part III, and both of us different segments of Parts IV and V. We jointly reviewed, and often revised, every sentence, paragraph, and idea and jointly assume responsibility for the whole.

HARRY ECKSTEIN
TED ROBERT GURR

Princeton, New Jersey
Evanston, Illinois
April 1975

CONTENTS

Patterns of Authority:
A Structural Basis for Political Inquiry

PART ONE

Introduction: Authority Patterns and the Scope of Political Science

CHAPTER ONE

Political Inquiry as the Study of Authority Patterns

At the most fundamental level, every field of inquiry rests on an implicit or explicit conception of its "scope"—that is, a conception of the nature of its subject matter and a delimitation of that subject from others. To be sure, overlaps and linkages can usually be found among any set of academic fields, particularly among "sister disciplines," like the social sciences. Nevertheless, prevalent conceptions of the scope of a field generally imply more than just an arbitrary, subjective interest in particular phenomena. They also imply that a subject matter differs so greatly from others that it justifies or indeed requires considerable autonomy, in the sense of a distinct set of disciplinary tools and products: special descriptive concepts, methods of inquiry, general theoretical perspectives and approaches, and empirical generalizations.

Political scientists' conceptions of the scope of their field have tended toward two extremes: on one hand, a very narrow conception centered on "state-organizations"; on the other, a very broad one encompassing all asymmetric human relationships. Both conceptions have important flaws, either as definitions of subjective interests or as delineations of a subject matter in terms of disciplinary considerations. Awareness of these flaws accounts for one of the more peculiar facets of contemporary political studies: the remarkably numerous and various attempts by political scientists to define explicitly what they study[1]—something normally taken for granted, therefore left implicit, in academic fields. This discussion presents one more such attempt, justified by lack of consensus on the matter and failure (as it seems to us) to work out a satisfactory delimitation of the field's scope.

Politics as State-Organizations

Until quite recently, the predominant (for a long time, in fact, fully consensual) conception of political phenomena was that they had to do with "governments" or "state-organizations," as we know them in the modern West, together with organizations subsumed to them, like local governments, or directly impinging on them, like political parties. Most political scientists saw little need to worry about the precise meaning of terms like "government" and "the state." Hence the prevalent approach resembled the predominant stance in contemporary studies of modernization: modernity is what exists in Western Europe and North America. Differences in meaning, mostly implicit, were many;[2] but mainly these were shades and nuances around a common and familiar core. State-organizations were thought of as those formally organized structures of societies that specialize in the exercise of "sovereignty," as that term has been understood roughly since the early seventeenth century: specialized organizations that make laws and implement them, resolve conflicts arising under them, and have a uniquely "legitimate" right to do so.

One basis for the foregoing conception of the scope of politics was certainly the subjective interests of political scientists—what they wanted to know about. Another, made explicit only when the conception was attacked, was that sovereign states and their organizations are *sui generis* among social structures, thus constituting a subject matter best kept separate from others. This argument was based on various grounds: (1) the state's supposedly unique membership structure (i.e., since it is not associational, one cannot join or resign at will or at low cost); (2) its supposedly unique scope (ability to regulate subsidiary units without being regulated by a superior one); (3) its supposedly unique functions (above all, integrating the various groups of society, or mediating among them); or (4) the supposedly unique instrumentality it uses to perform its tasks (legitimate coercion). A certain view of history, or perhaps cultural arrogance, also lay behind the emphasis on the formal organizations of sovereign states. This was the view that the sovereign state-organization, as developed in the modern West, was the natural destiny of all societies—not a remote end, but one achieved as soon as a modicum of "civilization" was attained. Thus it was that the kinds of polities described by such early anthropologists as Maine and Fraser could be dismissed as simply "prepolitical."[3]

It is true that political scientists have long been concerned with all kinds of organizations and activities that impinge on states but are not formal parts of them. However, their concerns with such phenomena initially derived from and were circumscribed by their very identification of politics with state-organizations. Attacks on that identification can be traced only to about 1930 and became common only in the 1950s.[4] The chief factor that made the objections common, then and now, involves the broadening geographic interests of political scientists: their new and growing concern with the politics of "developing" societies. In such societies, a search for specialized formal organizations exercising the attributes of sovereignty and displaying the supposedly unique characteristics of states, sometimes reveals nothing at all or, more commonly, a façade behind which political realities are rather ineffectively hidden. This is most obvious, of course, in still largely tribal societies, where functionally diffuse structures based on primordial identifications remain the focus of social regulation, regardless of whether imitation-states (or, rather, capitals) have been superimposed on them; and between these and modern Western state-organizations runs an extensive continuum on which lie different approximations to what we know as statehood. The narrow traditional notion of political phenomena did not serve subjective interests in such societies, nor did it prevent the feeling that in some sense they had a "political" life like other polities, even at the most primitive levels of social organization.[5]

Once doubts about the narrow conventional conception of politics had been thus engendered, it became manifest that the conception was unserviceable even for an extensive interest in the politics of Western societies. The focus on state-organization restricts study to Western societies roughly after the Peace of Westphalia (no exact data can be given, of course). If we go back much farther we find the work of sovereign state-organizations performed by a hodgepodge of diffuse, imperfectly differentiated, more or less autonomous institutions: royal dynasties, ecclesiastical structures, municipal councils, guilds, merchant companies, land-owning nobles, and universities. We find no "constitutions" as formal organizational blueprints, only charters, compacts, bills (and sometimes so-called Constitutions, like those of Clarendon) as contractual agreements or explicit statements of usage among competitive and overlapping *potentias*. We find no monopolies, actual or pretended, of legitimate coercion. Instead, there is a long and slow fashioning of sovereignty and its instruments as a gradual process of "political expropriation"[6] that seems more closely tied to special historical circumstances than to the universal attributes of civilized life. Yet one has the sense that "politics" antedates that process and went on throughout its unfolding; and political scientists anxious for light on political development in non-Western societies turn, not unnaturally, to the earlier histories of Western polities themselves.

As the boundaries between state-organizations and other structures for carrying on government and politics weakened, another objection against the focus on state-organizations emerged. This criticism involved a view occasionally advanced earlier[7] (e.g., by Merriam): that apart from possibly unimportant variables like size, there is not a great deal of difference between "public" governments and "private" ones—not enough, at any rate, to warrant a generic distinction on which to rest disciplinary divisions and all they entail.[8] This view is quite different from one admitting the study of "private" groups into the field as influences on public power and policy. The latter view treats the groups as related to political systems through boundary exchange; the former admits them as political systems in their own right. It thus implies that in excluding private governments, political science deprives itself of much material useful for building empirical theories, while at the same time failing to make an optimum contribution to the general understanding of social life.[9]

The Functional Conception of Politics

The principal response to the difficulties associated with the notion of politics centered on state-organizations has been a tendency to define politics in terms of certain social functions rather than social structures.[10] The essential purpose of the functional conceptions has been to raise the traditional focus of political study to a more general level, at which equivalence between sovereign state-organizations and other structural modes of carrying on what is sensed to be political activity becomes apparent.

The logic behind the functional conceptions seems impeccable. Since political structures differ widely in space and time, the identification of politics with any special structural arrangement unduly restricts and handicaps the field. But different structures can perform the same functions (i.e., can be functional "equivalents"). Hence the field's scope can be broadened and yet remain clearly defined in relation to nonpolitical phenomena, if one identifies the functions of state-organizations and then studies whatever performs those functions where such organizations do not exist or are ill developed.

Neat as this logic may seem, the functional revision creates large difficulties of its own. The foremost is that the functions of political structures are hard to identify; indeed, almost no functional conception of what is "political" coincides exactly with any other. To be sure, we can discern a latent consensus among the conceptions, but it is on a notion of the "political" function that seems, in the final analysis, to identify nothing in particular—to make politics into the study of "the whole of social life in all its facets," as Bentley put it. Some people may not object to this. But it is hardly what the functionalists intend; it may impose intolerable burdens in political research; it has tended to lead—although not of necessity—to theories so general and imprecise (because concerned with such a diversity of phenomena) that they are trivial and uninformative; and if politics becomes equated with social life, we will no doubt want to carve it into separate fields, as we now carve up social studies, thus returning to our starting point.

The function on which the various functional conceptions converge is that of "maintaining social order"—not in the narrow sense of "law and order," but in the very broad sense of assuring the continuity (viability) of society through its harmonious and efficient operation. That function, as functional sociologists like Parsons make clear, is really a large and diverse (indeed all-encompassing) complex of functions. Parsons lists them under four categories, which will do as well as any: (*a*) pattern-maintenance (roughly, imparting to members the society's general norms of behavior and special norms pertaining to its special roles, and getting commitment to them); (*b*) integration (coordinating the elements of social life to make them mutually supportive, or at least not mutually destructive); (*c*) goal-attainment (defining and achieving social ends and purposes); and (*d*) adaptation (generating an appropriate level of social resources, distributing them in ways perceived as just, and mobilizing them to the attainment of social goals). It should be apparent that all institutions of society, in one way or another, to one degree or another, are involved in the performance of these functions. It is also evident that all the functions must be performed in all social institutions if these are to be "viable"—a point that functionalists gleefully emphasize rather than conceal.

Functional definitions of politics thus converge on a view that broadens the scope of the field at the cost of virtually eliminating its boundaries. For this reason, they hardly define the political scientist's subjective interests, however much broader now than formerly; and although all social phenomena might be usefully analyzed in terms of the order-maintaining function at a high level of generality, it does not follow that disciplinary distinctions beneath that level are unimportant. We note in this connection that functional approaches to special subjects, like politics and economics, have been mainly advanced by sociologists in quest of overarching theories,[11] and that over a span of about a decade and a half such approaches in politics have hardly gone beyond the initial definitional level of conceptualization.[12]

The obvious way to save the functional alternative from this difficulty is to identify politics with a single "political" function in whose performance modern state-organizations specialize. But this also raises large problems. One, as stated, is to identify the function. Two views of this are common (and others are possible or occasionally advanced). Politics is concerned with "goal-attainment" (Parsons), or politics is concerned with "integration" (Almond). That difficulty might be resolved by a synthesis, in the manner of Bourricaud and Spiro: politics is concerned with "integrating conflicting views about social goals."[13] However, that would still leave a major research difficulty. Functions are abstractions, not concrete entities. The first task of any political analysis would therefore be to identify the structures—or, worse, aspects of structures—that have something to do with the performance of the functions, which might be all or any in a society.

Parsons puts his finger on the intricacy of that task in a rather offhand footnote: "The polity in (my) sense is *not* identical with government, which we interpret to be a complex of *organizations*. Government has other than political functions, and other organizations participate in the polity."[14] People like Parsons, who steer clear of empirical work on concrete phenomena, can get around this. But what does one do when descending from the rarefied air of conceptualization? What aspects of American government, for example, are, or are not, political? What aspects of American business, trade unions, schools, professions? The critical point is that on such a basis, we still find ourselves studying "the whole of social life in all its facets," quite as much as with the broader functional alternative. In one case, we do so because everything is political, in the other because everything has, or might have, political aspects. And the burden this entails is magnified by having to identify the political aspects without structural guidelines to the task—no guidelines other than that the aspects investigated must have to do with goal-attainment or integration. No one has ever done this or anything like it; and no wonder.

The moral is that functional conceptions of a subject matter are, in their very nature, to be avoided if satisfactory structural ones, directing attention immediately to concrete phenomena, are available. But is it really possible to devise a structural conception of politics that avoids the main shortcomings of the traditional conception of the field—a conception that does not define the subject in narrowly culture-bound terms, nor make too sharp and rigid the distinction between public governments and private ones?

Politics as Asymmetric Relationships

Attempts to redefine the subject matter of politics antedate by many years recent interests in underdeveloped, developing, and historic polities. The earlier attempts (mainly of the 1930s) were in fact structural, not in the least culture-bound, and virtually oblivious to distinctions between public and private governments. If nothing else, they demonstrate that the functionalist's way of delimiting the field is not the only alternative to the conventional structural conception.

The object of the earlier redefinitions was to make politics a "discipline" rather than to accommodate expanding subjective interests, save perhaps for an embryonic interest in private groups as political orders in themselves (rather than because of their boundary exchanges with "polities"). In gist, their object was to make it possible for political science to be scientific in some serious sense of the term, and in that respect, among others, those who advanced the redefinitions were precursors of contemporary "behavioralism" in the field. The prevalent conception of the scope of politics seemed to them the first and foremost impediment to the achievement of a "science" of politics, in part because of its very narrowness, in part because the phenomena considered to be political seemed too complex and various to serve as the subject matter of a science. In a sense, the very "uniqueness" used to justify the autonomous study of state-organizations furnished the main ground for the attack on the conventional delimitation of politics as a discipline.

A typical argument to this effect is Catlin's.[15] Science, according to Catlin, induces generalization from "simple" phenomena that are "commonplace and frequent of occurrence"; states have been and are few in number, and they are also quite "uniquely" constituted (i.e., complex and variable on many dimensions); hence nothing can safely be induced from their study. The problem is readily translatable into statistical language: it is difficult or impossible to generalize if one has small n and large variance. The solution must be to find a far simpler subject matter embodying many more instances. That subject matter must certainly be of the essence in state-organizations; but just as certainly, it must also be found in many other contexts.

Note that the problem discerned was not that of finding "equivalents" of state-organizations in premodern cultures. The problem was to find something to replace the focus on the state in *all* cultures.[16]

Despite differences in language, the solutions proposed, like those of the functionalists, converged on a common point. In essence, it was proposed that politics be equated with what might be called "asymmetric" human relationships. All the early revisionists started with the same question: what are (in Catlin's chemical metaphor) the "elements" from which all political complexes, as thought of conventionally, are compounded—or, in different metaphors, the particles or cells of "bodies" politic? The answer was derived from what seemed (and no doubt is) an obvious truth: governments are *complexes* of rule and hierarchy (of κράτος and -ἀρχή). Hence the elementary relations constituting them must be *items* of power, or control, by some men over others. These items consist of interactions in which abilities to produce intended effects and derive benefits are unequally distributed. This is precisely what is meant by "asymmetric" relations; as Lasswell might put it in his pungent way, they are relations in which someone affects more than he is affected, controls more than he is controlled, and/or receives more of what is allocated. Such asymmetries manifestly occur in virtually all human relationships, everywhere and on all social levels. They certainly are intrinsic to state-organizations, but states are just particularly large, complex, well-patterned, persistent, and (more questionably) "pure"[17] complexes of them. Asymmetric relations thus provide just the kind of simple, frequent, and commonplace units of analysis that seem to be presupposed by inductive science.

So the argument went—and it surely is not, prima facie, unpersuasive. It would be hard to argue that asymmetry is not inherent in governments of all types and at all social levels, or that anything of great consequence about the governments of states would be missed by considering them large and complex networks of power and control relations. Easton does point out that "goals"—the purposes to which power and control are put—also matter.[18] He is right; but nothing precludes analysis of the substance as well as process of politics, no matter how politics is conceived. After all, nothing prevented those concerned with state-organizations from analyzing their policies. Nor does the conception of politics as asymmetric relations (*pace* moral critics like Franz Neumann) necessarily have misanthropic implications. It does not imply, as Neumann argued it did, that all human collectivities are ultimately controlled by brute coercion, that there are no absolute moral laws, that democracy and constitutional government are impossible, that no qualitative differences of any consequence exist among polities, or even that asymmetry is always strongly weighted in favor of nominal rulers.

To separate the study of politics from that of modern state-organizations, then, a functional conception of politics was not required; a plausible structural alternative was available. Nevertheless, one may have important reservations about the early structural redefinition. It seems better regarded as a large first step toward a serviceable conception of the field's subject than as a definitive delimitation of its scope.

Most important, the equation of politics with asymmetric relations delimits very little. Like the functional conception of politics as the order-maintaining aspects of society, it broadens the field by virtually eliminating its boundaries. To be sure, there are social relationships that are symmetric, or almost so. One thinks of buyer-seller exchange relations (under free-market conditions), affective relations among friends or spouses, or interactions on collegial decision-making bodies that are not just nominally collegial. But although such relations frequently occur, they "characterize" few social units; they do so less and less as the notion of symmetry is more strictly defined; they are almost nonexistent in many societies and subsidiary units; and they are more likely to occur in ephemeral interactions than in organized or institutional collectivities. Certainly it would be difficult to say that any concrete institution or relationship in any society is automatically excluded from the scope of politics defined as the universe of asymmetric relations.[19]

From this difficulty others follow. One involves our subjective interests. Easton (see pp. 33–35) rejects the equation of politics with asymmetric relations mainly because of this consideration: political scientists are interested simply in "political" asymmetries, not all social asymmetries. A general theory of power would help them, he argues, but would still have to be shaped to the special phenomena of political power, conceived in some narrower sense.[20] More important is the question whether conceiving politics more narrowly (but not in the very narrow sense of state-organization) is advisable also on "disciplinary" grounds—that is, whether a general theory of asymmetric relations, even if useful, would help much. A strong argument to the effect that it would not can certainly be made.

The crux of this argument is that since the world of asymmetric relations varies extremely on many dimensions, the classification of human relations into symmetric and asymmetric ones would not be very informative for description or theory. Asymmetric relations vary, for example, on the basis of numbers of people involved in them (from two to just about all human beings). They vary with respect to continuity and regularity of interaction—asymmetries exist in continuous and regular interactions in a persistent social collectivity (teacher and pupil, in school), or in regular but hardly continuous interaction (doctor and patient), or in ephemeral interaction (criminal and victim, or the slow driver and the drivers he slows down). They vary in regard to the nature of the "actors" involved in asymmetric interactions, who may be single individuals or more or less complex collective individuals. They vary in regard to degree and direction of asymmetries; that is, in different degrees they may involve unidirectional or multidirectional flows of power and control (in certain, probably most, respects, bosses control their secretaries; in others, secretaries run their bosses). And so on, along many more criteria of discrimination, any of which might be consequential for one theoretical purpose or another.

It is possible to cover all this diversity and more with generalizations of some description, and no doubt some people's interests will run to such an extreme level of generality, or beyond. But the distinction between symmetric and asymmetric relations surely discriminates no more than the first and simplest distinction biologists make among members of that extremely heterogeneous class, the animal "kingdom": protozoa (one-celled animals) and metazoa (many-celled animals). For most purposes, a field so broadly delimited would have to be subdivided into many virtually autonomous subdisciplines. Thus, as with the functional alternative, we return to our starting point: trying to find a delimitation of "political" asymmetries that seems to be defensible on disciplinary grounds and at least approximates special subjective interests.

Delimiting the Scope of "Politics" as a Problem in Classification

Working out a reasonable delimitation of the scope of political phenomena is, of course, a matter of classification: arriving at the defining traits of a special class of cases to which the label "political" is sensibly applied. What we have uncovered to this point is a rather familiar problem in the construction of taxonomies (familiar, at any rate, in fields that take classifications more seriously, and construct them less arbitrarily, than political scientists do). To clarify that problem and point the way to a reasoned solution of it, we now digress briefly on the subject of constructing classificatory categories.

Taxonomies that are more than mere arbitrary labeling can be constructed by numerous methods, which could be treated fully only in a separate work. However, the best of these methods for most purposes, as well as the most widely used where classification is regarded as an important intellectual enterprise (e.g., in biology), is a procedure that might be called "progressive differentiation" (our term). That method happens to be especially useful if one has the dilemma of being either excessively restrictive or excessively extensive in one's conception of a class of cases—precisely the difficulty uncovered here.

"Progressive differentiation" proceeds, in gist, as follows:

1. One begins with a very broad and heterogeneous subject matter, whose units perhaps have only a single attribute in common (e.g., they are "organisms": material entities capable of reproducing themselves).
2. One asks on what basis that subject matter can be subdivided into two (or at any rate a very small number of) very populous subsets, so that (*a*) all instances of the subject matter fall into one subset or the other and (*b*) all cases in a subset share one characteristic in addition to that of the whole subject matter, which (*c*) is not found in any case in the other subset(s). (That initial cut, in biology, is made between plants and animals, on the basis of ability to produce "food" by processing inorganic matter.)
3. One then asks the same question of the subsets (e.g., animals, as stated, are divided into protozoa and metazoa), continuing to differentiate until a compelling stopping point is reached—the most compelling being the point at which differentiations can be made sensibly only by singling out particular individuals, not sets of them.

The process involves the systematic use of "branching." Each offshoot, at every level, is a member of a more inclusive branch but has at least one characteristic different from all other offshoots from the same branch. Figure 1.1 portrays the process graphically (using biological categories, somewhat simplified, to identify levels of differentiation).

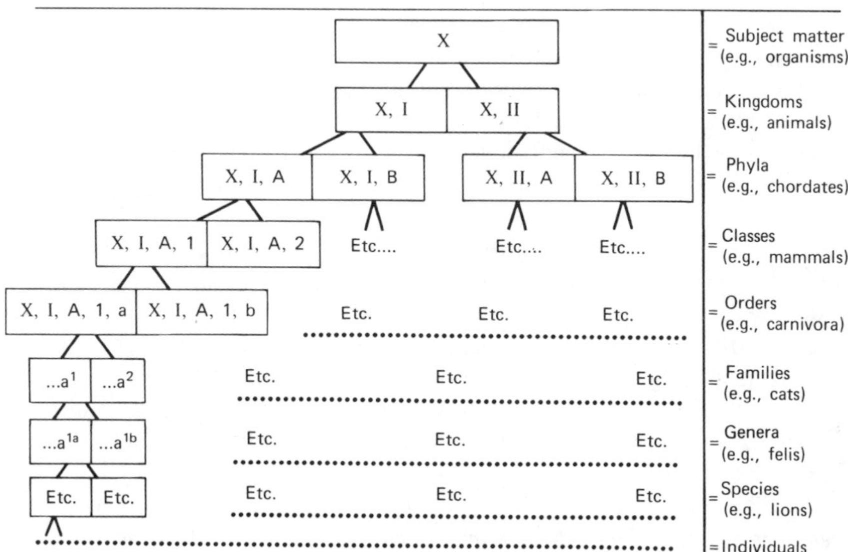

Fig. 1.1 The method of progressive differentiation.

Classificatory schemes constructed by progressive differentiation have several characteristics that such schemes ought to have if used as bases of general propositions. They leave nothing "residual" (unclassifiable), and they preclude both ambivalence (i.e., having equally good reasons for classifying a case under two or more sets) and ambiguity (difficulty in deciding to what set a case belongs). Even more important here, it should be evident that at the upper levels of a classificatory ladder thus constructed, cases will be very numerous and very heterogeneous, whereas at the lower levels they will become progressively more homogeneous—similar or identical on many dimensions—and more limited in number. Consequently, although generalizations are possible at any level, those that cover the more inclusive (less differentiated) categories can provide only limited information about the less inclusive classes, and sometimes hardly any of the information one subjectively wants about them. In that sense, they will be "vacuous." On the other hand, a class may be so narrowly defined that subjectively sought information becomes available only at a price that is disproportionate in relation to the possibilities of induction or validation of theories arrived at by any means whatever. In such a case, one is compelled to seek a tradeoff between the extensiveness and homogeneity of the classes. Even if the compulsion is not absolute, any large gain in extensiveness is to be preferred if the cost in loss of homogeneity is small—not just because of the requisites of inductive methods but because of the parsimony of theories about a subject, in the sense of ratio between cases covered and information provided.

Our criticism of others' ways of delimiting the scope of political study can now be restated in a more compact manner. In addition, the tack to take to solve the problem we have uncovered seems clearly to emerge from this note on methodical taxonomy.

1. *The conventional delimitation of the scope of the field sacrifices too much extensiveness for the sake of homogeneity.* This is true not just because state-organizations are rather few in number, but also because they are insufficiently different from other structures to make the gain in homogeneity large. This is not to mention the nonmethodological fact, certainly admissible as a supplementary argument, that our subjective interests no longer are confined to so exclusive a subject matter, although they surely continue to include it.

2. *The early revisionist conception of politics as the study of asymmetric relations sacrifices too much homogeneity for the sake of extensiveness.* It does so chiefly because Catlin and like-minded writers seem to assume that typological categories should have a single defining characteristic, "commonplace and frequent of occurrence." Obviously categories may have any number of defining characteristics, so long as the mix between subjective interests and disciplinary imperatives remains reasonable. In fact, the broad structural conception of politics itself has at least three: (*a*) *Homo sapiens*, (*b*) in relationships, that (*c*) are asymmetric.

3. *The later "functional" revision has the same result, compounded by difficulties that always arise when one emphasizes functions rather than structures.* It proceeds, implicitly, from the right question: to what more numerous, if less homogeneous, class can "states" be considered to belong? But the answers provided lead to the same overextensiveness and excessive heterogeneity as do the earlier revisions; still worse, they direct attention to elusive abstractions from concrete observables.

4. *Our problem then is to find a reasonable tradeoff between the homogeneity of the conventional conception of the scope of the field and the inclusiveness of proposed revisions, without incurring avoidable costs in our ability to identify pertinent phenomena.* To avoid vagueness, we want a "structural" conception of political phenomena. For the sake of homogeneity, we do not want to include all asymmetric relations, although political phenomena are intended to be a distinct subset of such relations. For inclusiveness, we do not want the conception to be limited to state-organizations, although such organizations should be a distinct subset of the class.

This clearly calls for adding structural criteria of discrimination to that of "asymmetry." The full set of traits must be characteristic of state-organizations and also of much else, yet still delimit a rather homogeneous and precisely identifiable set of cases.

Here we can leave criticism, and turn to the constructive part of the argument.

Political Relations as a Subset of Asymmetric Relations

Our position is that three criteria in addition to asymmetry can be used to define political phenomena in a manner that reconciles our subjective interests with disciplinary requirements. Stepwise, they delimit successively narrower "populations" suitable to increasingly informative empirical theory—populations that increasingly resemble the phenomena central to the traditional subjective interests of political scientists, but are not in the least culture-bound, nor so intrinsically limited in number or widely various that rigorous inductive procedures are ruled out.[21]

1. *Asymmetric relations may or may not occur in social units, among people acting in their capacities as members of the units. Those that do thus occur may be considered political, others not.*

This criterion subtracts from all power and control relations a large number and variety that are especially far removed from the common-sense conception of politics, often quite amorphous, and if not subtracted or distinguished, likely to make theories vacuous. Examples are the power of a criminal over his victim or the slow driver over the queues in his wake. Such relations are clearly asymmetric and satisfy formal definitions of control (or power), such as that of Dahl and Lindblom:[22] "B is controlled by A to the extent that B's responses are dependent on A's acts in an immediate and direct functional relationship." But they do not occur in social units, or do so only in a trivial sense (e.g., in that they occur among members of the same nation).

To avoid ambiguity, and the definitional carping it begets, we had better be precise about what a "social unit" is (although readers no doubt have an immediate feel for the term).

(*a*) Social units are not mere aggregates of persons but, so to speak, collective individuals. That is, they have a certain identity of their own, separate from the identities of their members—a property generally ratified by special proper names (the United States, New Jersey, Princeton University, the Woodrow Wilson School, etc.). They thus persist despite turnover in members, often having legal status quite apart from that of the individuals that constitute them. They are, in the medieval sense, "corporations" (i.e., bodies or entities in their own right).

(*b*) In such collective individuals, interactions are recurrent and patterned; that is, they occur continuously, or at least very frequently, and can be generalized about with rather high predictability. They are not sporadic or isolated encounters—not, for example, the kind of relationship that exists between buyer and customer but the kind that employers have with their employees.

(*c*) However much the unit may be identified by its members, the members also identify themselves in terms of the unit; in one degree or another, their personal identity is perceived by themselves as that of the larger entity. One does not "identify" oneself by saying: "I am the person held up at gunpoint last January 24"; one does think of oneself as "a professor at Princeton University," and the like. The strengths of such personal identifications with collectivities vary, but some tendency to define the self by the collectivity can always be found in "social units."

(*d*) As corporate entities, social units have goals distinct from those of individual members and individuals. Indeed, individual satisfaction, like individual identity, is itself defined in some degree by collective goal-attainment. In the case of families like those Banfield studied in Southern Italy,[23] that definition is extreme, but it exists in virtually all families. As societies "develop," however, the identification of self-satisfaction with collective goals seems to become focused increasingly on larger-scale units, including the "state" and organizations like political parties. By and large, old equations between self and collectivity remain, but others (hence other social "units") are superadded. (We leave aside the vexing question of whether there are "rational" collective goods. Empirically detectable nonrational ones suffice.)

(*e*) As in other "bodies" there exists in social units a more or less specific, or differentiated, set of roles—a division of labor—attuned to the unit's goals, together with definitions of tasks, duties, responsibilities, and rights appropriate to the roles. This, again, is as manifest in small-scale units like families as in states or corporations. Someone is charged with the shopping, the cooking, the cleaning up, the bill paying, much as roles are devised to legislate, administer, adjudicate, lobby, or aggregate votes. The allocation may vary among members almost daily, and also may be quite uninvidious, but generally it both exists and remains fairly fixed, if only because of variations in capacity to perform tasks or because of expertise acquired in performing them.

By confining the field to social units thus conceived, we clearly eliminate many of the problems, subjective and disciplinary, raised by the broad conception of politics as social asymmetry. Most of all, we avoid the undesirable state of arriving at uninformative generalizations that cover both asymmetry in social units and in encounters among individuals outside them—generalizations perhaps as vacuous as "the controller tends to command a greater stock of 'pertinent values' (force, position on a highway, etc.) than the controlled."

2. *Asymmetric relations may or may not occur among hierarchically ordered segments or members of a social unit, and they may or may not manifestly affect relations among such segments. Those that occur among hierarchically ordered segments, or manifestly affect their relations, may be considered political, others not.*

Segments of a unit are hierarchically ordered if any of them are thought of as "superior" to others—literally, at a higher level—giving the unit the appearance of "stratiformity." (The term is borrowed from geology, to avoid the probably invidious connotations of the more familiar term "stratification.") In formal organizations, stratiformity appears on organization charts and often through ranking by title: permanent secretary, undersecretary, assistant secretary, and so on. In other cases, it is simply a matter of implicit perceptions (e.g., of parents or teachers by children and by themselves).

Stratiformity, in the foregoing sense, is surely a characteristic of governments (as conventionally conceived) and of most other social units. On the other hand, there (probably) are social units in which stratiformity is deliberately avoided. More important, there are many interactions within a social unit that occur on the same level of its hierarchy and do not manifestly affect relations among the hierarchic levels. Examples are social relations among legislators or bureaucrats, or in a small-scale unit, certain interactions, unnecessary to specify, between spouses or children in families. Very indirectly, these may, of course, affect relations among the levels (cocktail parties in Washington may promote voting coalitions, or children's quarrels may turn mild parents into temporary tyrants). But these are usually remote and highly unpredictable effects, like those that encounters outside social units might cumulatively have on more comprehensive units in which they occur. They certainly do not "manifestly" affect between-level relations in the sociologists's sense of the term (i.e., in the sense of having intended and recognized effects on social relations).[24] They are thus not in the least like interactions among nominal peers, such as members of a board of directors, who are intended to make rules for a social unit and are recognized to do so.

The second criterion of discrimination thus narrows the field by subtracting interactions within social units that most resemble encounters outside them, which seems desirable for disciplinary reasons. It also narrows the field, although not extremely, in a direction dictated by the focus of our subjective interests.

3. *Asymmetric relations within social units, occurring among or*

manifestly affecting between-level relations, may or may not be concerned with the direction of the units. Those concerned with their direction may be considered political, others not.

The "direction" of a social unit refers to four matters that are indivisible but distinguishable and, in any event, have to be discussed seriatim. One involves a cluster of activities, the second a set of role incumbents, the third a set of instruments by which the role incumbents perform the activities, the fourth the activation of a set of sentiments toward the activities, instruments, and role incumbents.

(*a*) Direction as *activity* involves the general management of the unit: defining its goals and means to attain them; specifying proper conduct within it and, in a sense, "policing" members to assure that their conduct conforms to specification; allocating roles within the unit, together with special tasks, duties, or rights associated with the roles; and coordinating roles and conduct to achieve effective performance in regard to goals or, in a more diffuse sense, to minimize conflict and confusion.

(*b*) Conceivably all members of a social unit might participate equally in performing these activities on a continuing basis. However, such utopian "communal" arrangements rarely if ever exist, nor are they even closely approximated. (In any case, they would not be "asymmetrical.") In virtually all cases, special *role incumbents* have assigned or assumed rights or responsibilities to see to the unit's "management," in the various senses of the term. Such role incumbents may be called the unit's "directors." Their activities in the unit are partly analogous to the mechanisms of control in organic "systems" that keep the organism in equilibrium under stress or prevent stresses from arising in the first place. They are also partly analogous to the activities of engineers who define the objectives of mechanical systems and generate or manipulate structural capabilities and other resources to attain them.

By virtue of their special rights or responsibilities, incumbents of such special roles are always superiors of others. However, the term "superordinates" seems to be a better label. The obvious reason is that a superior may be thought of simply as higher in status than other unit members without in any sense being a director in the unit—general status levels and levels of direction need not coincide and ought not to be equated by definition. A superior becomes a superordinate when, in addition to nominal superiority, he exercises considerable actual control over the unit. Here too, however, a modification especially stressed by Dahl and Lindblom[25] is in order. Flows of control between directors and those who are directed need not be and in fact rarely are entirely unidirectional. By any formal definition of control, the actions of subordinates can control those of superordinates no less than vice versa, either in latent effect or because manifestly meant to do so (i.e., meant to influence the superordinates' actions). Subordinate actions concerned with directives other than those that merely carry out what superordinates ordain are thus also part of a unit's structure of direction. Such actions may, of course, matter more or less. But even when they are of great import, superordinates have a special role in the determination of the unit's network of direction, in the sense of quite autonomous power inherent in their roles, or in the sense of aggregating, selecting, or otherwise processing inputs from subordinates, or both.

(*c*) Direction is carried out by means of *directives*: prescriptions potentially backed by sanctions if disregarded by unit members. Directives may take the form of petty commands, broad rules, or implanting in members internalized norms reinforced by the use of deprivations to punish noncompliance. The term "directive" is sometimes used by sociologists and psychologists to denote any guide to action that compels particular choices among alternatives or limits the range of perceived alternatives, thus reducing the possibility of "anomie" as a psychic condition.[26] Here the sense of the term is narrower: not any guide to action, including all habits and sentiments of morality and propriety, but explicit guides to action within social units, or sometimes interactions with other units in one's capacity as member of a unit.

(*d*) However, an important aspect of direction, the roles of directors and the perception of directives, is precisely that they do evoke special sentiments of morality or propriety; specifically, they activate perceptions of *legitimacy*. Such perceptions can be either diffuse or specific. When diffuse, they involve general perceptions of the rightfulness or justice of the overall constitution of a pattern of direction, hence its worthiness of being supported. When specific, they involve sentiments of obligation to comply with directives because invested with a special moral quality derived from that diffuse sense of rightful constitution, therefore of the propriety of punitive sanctions in cases of noncompliance which, otherwise employed, would be perceived as immoral. The perceptions need not be positive. All that is stated here is that, positive or negative, they are evoked. It is inconceivable that they might not be where obligations are prescribed, where ability to prescribe them is differentially allocated, and where the behavior used to police and enforce prescriptions is not regarded as morally rightful in any relationship, under all circumstances.

The third criterion of discrimination thus focuses attention on a special cluster of between-level relations within social units. It subtracts relations that are not concerned with their direction in the senses just named, which are probably the great majority. The reasons for the subtraction again are both disciplinary and subjective. From the disciplinary standpoint, the important points are that "rule" in any form must have to do with rules or their obvious equivalents, and interactions that are not concerned with rules are both extremely heterogeneous (even within units, between levels of stratiformity) and lack attributes of those that are. The most obviously lacking attribute is legitimacy: they do not activate perceptions of it, but only arouse general sentiments of morality that are modified, in one degree or another, when the quality of legitimacy is discerned. As for subjective interests, the essential point is that "direction," in all the senses given here (the management of a social unit, the existence of superordinate roles, the prescription and policing of directives, and the perception of special moral qualities that justify rights, privileges, and punitive behavior otherwise deemed immoral or amoral) is intrinsic to common-sense notions of government.

The Nature of Authority Patterns: A Summary

The special class of asymmetric relations delimited by these criteria of discrimination may be called *authority patterns*.

Figure 1.2 portrays how the class was worked out as an exercise in progressive differentiation.[27] It clearly implies that some generalizations about social relationships as such should also pertain to "politics," as should some generalizations about all asymmetric relationships, as well as within-unit and between-level asymmetries. Thus as we pass down the branch points, an increasing number of generalizations about more inclusive subjects become pertinent to politics; however, the theoretical understanding of politics should also require a good many generalizations about the less inclusive class alone.

The case for delimiting the scope of politics at the indicated level of discrimination still has to be made; so far only groundwork has been provided. Before we proceed to that most critical part of the argument, however, three brief sets of remarks are required. First, to prevent confusion, our notion of the nature of authority patterns should be contrasted with other uses of the term "authority;" second, to make an extensive argument succinct, it should be more directly and summarily stated; and third, what may appear to be (but is not) a qualification of the emphasis on "asymmetry" as a defining trait of authority patterns should be briefly introduced.

1. The concept of "authority," like other similar notions (power, control, influence) has had a checkered definitional history in social studies.[28] The term is probably used most widely as Weber meant it.[29] Weber never appeared to offer a detailed formal definition of authority, and his use of the concept is ambivalent in certain senses.[30] However, he consistently used

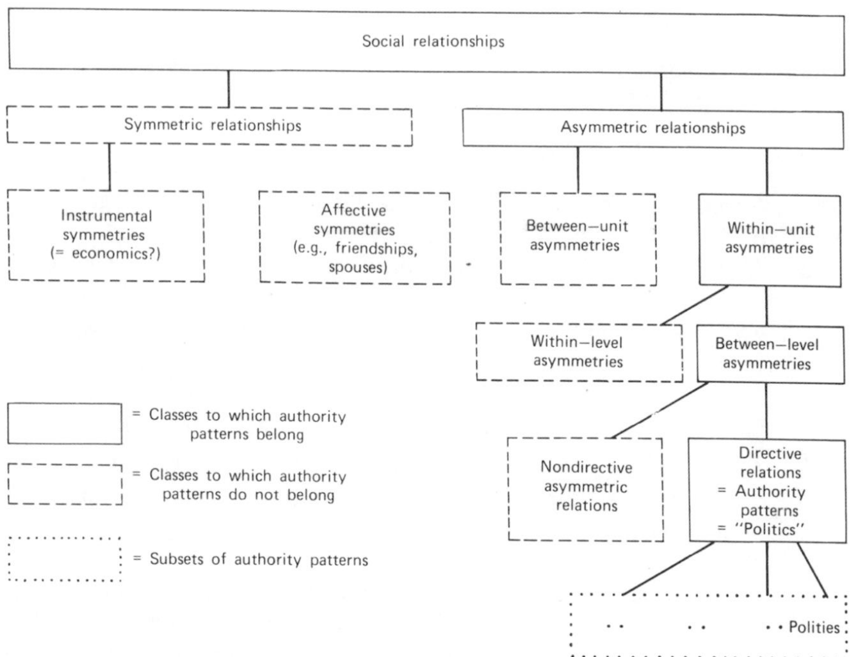

Fig. 1.2 The place of authority patterns in a taxonomy of social relationships.

it in one way that differs from our usage. Weber understood authority as a special quality that an exercise of "imperative control" (in our terminology, direction) might or might not have: *positive* legitimacy. We use it as a label for a structure in which activities, roles, and instruments evoke legitimacy sentiments, *positive or negative*. This avoids some knotty problems eminently worth avoiding: how to measure levels of positive legitimacy; at what level of positive legitimacy "power" (or control, or what have you) becomes authority; whether directors can be "authorities" to some people but not others in the same unit, in regard to some directives but not others, at one point in time but not another; whether the absence of negative legitimacy perceptions equals the presence of positive ones—and many others with which no one has yet managed to come to grips. It is surely enough to know that perceptions of legitimacy are evoked to know also that one is in a special universe of asymmetric relations different from others (for which terms like "power" or "control" are quite serviceable).

2. The proposed conception of an authority pattern can be summarized in a general formal definition, elaborated in more specific definitions that are needed to make sense of the general conception:

General definition

An *authority pattern* is a set of asymmetric relations among hierarchically ordered members of a social unit that involves the direction of the unit.

Subsidiary and additional definitions

(a) *Social units* are collectivities of individuals that may be regarded as collective individuals (as discussed earlier).

(b) *Hierarchic order* exists where members of a unit are perceived as ranked in levels of superiority and inferiority.

(c) *The direction* of a social unit involves the definition of its goals, the regulation of conduct of its members, and the allocation and coordination of roles within it. Direction is carried out through directives prescribed by incumbents of superordinate roles in the unit.

Directives are prescriptions of conduct that evoke legitimacy sentiments. Such sentiments raise the question of whether prescriptions of conduct ought to be regarded as obligatory and rightfully backed by sanctions.

Superordinates are any unit superiors who are assigned, or assume, special responsibility for arriving at directives and seeing to it that they are carried out. (In Dahl and Lindblom's terminology, they are both superiors in the unit and, to a substantial extent at least, its actual "controllers.")

Subordinates are, residually, any other unit members. It should be noted, however, that in cases of complex stratiformity a member may be both superordinated and subordinated vis-à-vis different other members. Sometimes, in cases of complex differentiation along functional lines, a member may be both a "super" and a "sub" vis-à-vis the same other members, in regard to different activities—an ambiguity that disappears if role incumbents rather than concrete individuals in all their aspects are treated as a unit's "members."

(d) *Super-sub relations* (a self-explanatory term) are at the core of any authority pattern: there is no direction of a unit without a flow of directives and actions enforcing them from supers to subs, and cases in which subs do not try to influence supers in some degree and manner are probably very rare. But since supers generally interact in arriving at directives, either as peers or in a special stratiform structure of superordination, *super-super relations,* insofar as they "manifestly" concern a unit's direction, are also an aspect of authority patterns. And since subs may interact in trying to influence the directives of the superordinates, those *sub-sub relations* manifestly concerned with doing so may be considered a further aspect.

3. To anticipate a point dealt with more extensively later (pp. 30–33) we concede that "symmetrical" relations of certain kinds sometimes play a role in authority patterns. They occur—in the form of bargaining, vote trading, side payments, and the like—in competition for superordinated positions or, among superordinates, for policy outcomes. This statement in no way reneges on the position that symmetry and asymmetry are critical dividing lines among social phenomena, at a very high level of generality. It merely means that like almost all subjects of inquiry, symmetry and asymmetry intersect at certain points.

The Case for Equating "Politics" with Authority Patterns

Our argument is that authority patterns, as delimited and defined in the two preceding sections, are a sensible point at which a decent tradeoff between inclusiveness and homogeneity can be struck, and subjective interests can be reconciled with disciplinary considerations. That argument rests on three main bases. Each of these is addressed to particular difficulties and advantages of conceptions of the field's scope that have been proposed by others—plus some supplementary considerations emphasizing the signal importance of studying authority patterns, regardless of whether taken as defining the subject matter of the field.

1. *The conception of political study as the study of authority patterns is sufficiently broad (deals with phenomena sufficiently commonplace and frequent of occurrence) to serve as a proper basis for inductive science.* That is, the conception serves the purpose of those who first attacked the narrow traditional delimitation of the field's scope, without incurring the disadvantages of the alternatives they proposed.

"Societies"—a term that refers simply to the most inclusive "collective individuals"—consist of very large numbers of such patterns in every case, some very simple and small-scale (e.g., nuclear families), others much more complex and extensive. True, authority patterns at their simplest are not as simple as "acts of control," being clusters of such acts. But nothing prevents "analyzing" them into simpler component units, in any of the ways by which any entity can be broken down into components clustered in a certain manner: by distinguishing "dimensions" on which they vary, "elements" of which they consist, or smaller-scale "particles" to which they are reducible. It clearly is unnecessary for inductive science to deal always with the most simple and irreducible phenomena that cluster in entities. In fact, virtually all the very "simple" phenomena of science (cells, chemical elements, molecules; atoms) turn out to be clusters of still simpler phenomena, and failure to arrive at the end of the chain of simplicity—if indeed there is an end—has not handicapped other fields of inquiry. The main requirement surely is that numbers be sufficient to offset problems arising from range of variability (as argued previously), and it is hard to see a priori why in the study of authority any serious difficulties should arise on that score.

2. *Defining the scope of the field as the study of authority patterns does not make it so broad that we are taken far beyond the range of subjective interests, or confronted with phenomena so heterogeneous that informative theory becomes unlikely or elaborate disciplinary tools for special types of authority patterns are required.* That is, the definition retains the principal advantages of the traditional narrow conception of the field's scope, without incurring its manifest liabilities.

The methodological reasons for including far more within the scope of the field than state-organizations (and very near equivalents) are important, but by no means definitive. If such organizations were in fact as unique as some consider them, it would be self-defeating to subsume them under a more numerous set of cases: what is gained methodologically would perforce be lost in knowledge of the subject matter. But state-organizations and near equivalents are not unique. They differ from other authority patterns, but only on a very limited number of variables, whose import for methods and products of inquiry is unlikely to be large.

For one thing, the idea of sovereignty is just that: an idea—and an idea more normative than empirical. The idea characterized well the pretensions of sovereigns as expropriators of authority, and sometimes it justified their successes; it also served the longings for peace and harmony of those caught in struggles between competitive, overlapping authorities. But even if indivisible in principle (we leave that to political philosophers), it has never really been undivided in practice—certainly not if taken to involve the autonomous power to make laws perceived as binding and to enforce them with coercion perceived as morally permissible. Appearance on official statute books or civil and criminal codes is not all that makes directives appear obligatory. Virtually every social unit has its own set of directives, mostly unchecked by more inclusive authority, and each unit enforces it own set with more or less severe punitive sanctions, often of a kind considered impermissible among individuals outside the unit. And the activity is little changed even if there exists appeal to higher authority. Normative theorists, like the "pluralists," were the first to perceive this, wishing to deny any unique normative position to the state; empirical theorists ought to follow suit, to deny it any claim to autonomy as subject matter for a discipline.

When comparing state-organizations and other authority patterns subsumed under them by the idea of sovereignty, we find that the dimensions on which they vary largely coincide. An "analytic scheme" for the less inclusive patterns serves well as an analytic scheme for the more inclusive; a typology of them is serviceable as a typology of "states" as well. We see this in subsequent chapters, devoted to the analysis of authority patterns into constituent dimensions and an attempt to synthesize the analytic elements into clusters serviceable as typology. But we already know from the way the conception of authority patterns was worked out that state-organizations belong to the same "family" (or class, or genus) as other authority patterns at a rather high level of differentiation. It is hard to think of a (nonfanciful) criterion of discrimination that would differentiate further, aside from extensiveness—territory and number of members—and the probably related variable of complexity. Whether these factors make much difference in regard to disciplinary considerations (concepts, methods, problems, theories) is at least an open question that ought not to be settled by definition, especially by a definition that brings manifest handicaps to inductive science. Besides, states and near equivalents vary considerably in extensiveness and complexity, and some "private" governments are certainly larger and more complex than many public ones. Size and complexity thus seem more useful as potential explanatory variables than as defining characteristics of a field.

If this position is correct, both parts of the foregoing general argument follow: we do not go far beyond the focus of subjective interests in dealing with authority patterns, nor define a subject that is vastly heterogeneous, or even significantly more so than the original basis of the field—taking heterogeneity in the literal sense: not "different" (any concrete individual differs from all others) but "belonging to different genera."

3. *The conception of political phenomena as authority patterns helps to identify the equivalents of state-organizations where such organizations do not exist or are not highly developed.* That is, the conception serves the purpose of the functional alternatives to the traditional structural conception of the scope of the field, while avoiding the liabilities of purely functional conceptions.

In a sense, all authority patterns are "equivalents" of state-organizations (i.e., belong to a class to which the latter also belong and which, although numerous, discriminates a great deal because it excludes most human relationships, symmetric or asymmetric). Authority patterns are equivalents of state-organizations even in the various functional senses that have been proposed: they maintain order, integrate, define, and try to attain goals. Moreover, if scale as such is the critical variable that distinguishes "states" from social units included in them, no difficulty arises in answering the question that the functionalists take as their point of departure: what is the nearest equivalent of state-organization in societies where it does not exist—in, say, Nuer society or among the Mayas? No need at all to resort to "functional" equivalents, an obvious structural one being available: the nearest equivalent is the authority pattern of the most inclusive (or extensive) social unit (which may, in some cases, be smaller than the "anthropological" unit). We can, in fact, take this as a simple general definition of all "polities" (or "governments") as subsets of the class "authority patterns," thus avoiding dubious elements of their definition (e.g., that they are sovereign wielders of authority, or monopolize legitimate conercion, or alone perform order-maintaining functions in societies).[31]

There is nothing wrong with making a specialty of the study of polities in that sense or of other subsets of the more inclusive class. Definitions of scope are intended for disciplines a whole, not for any and all who work in them. What is regrettable is not specialization within a field but equating the whole of the field with the specialty, so that avoidable liabilities are incurred and closely similar subjects neglected.

4. *Neglecting the study of nongovernmental authority patterns not only leaves unstudied much that is interesting and important in itself, but also leaves the study of "polities" (however defined) uniformed by much that can be extremely useful for understanding them.* That is, even if authority patterns were not taken to define and delimit politics as a discipline, there would be weighty reasons for political scientists to extend their scope of attention to such patterns in all forms. Some of these reasons, however, would not be as weighty as they seem if governments as a special category were far more different from other authority patterns than we consider them to be.

It has often been argued that "private governments" should receive much wider and more intensive study. The reason generally given is not that they are sufficiently like "public governments" to form a subject matter for a single discipline. It is simply pointed out that they exist; that they are interlaced with public authority; and that they are highly consequential—not least for the network of governmental directives that constrain individual lives, provide privileges and rights, and impose obligations, duties, deprivations. The argument, unfortunately, has not been widely acted on in practice. There are exceptions in political science, but they are out of the ordinary.[32] There are more in other social sciences, particularly in family and industrial sociology, but they too are hardly commensurate with the extensiveness and import of the subject.[33] The consequence, needless to say, is conceptual, methodological, and theoretical retardation. Indeed, there seems to be a growing tendency to consider the neglect part and parcel of a conspiracy to conceal the networks of power and privilege that dominate supposedly "liberal" societies. Maybe so; but no demons are needed to explain the void. Just as likely is another possibility—namely, that areas of disciplinary overlap may engender voids as well as duplications. According to this hypothesis, political scientists neglect private governments because they are concerned with public ones and do not like to wander far outside their boundaries; other social scientists neglect them because their interests are broader, because they have no specialized competence to analyze them, or because they consider them to fall within the political scientist's domain. One can expect that the current sense of a "crisis of authority" in all institutions in all advanced societies—plus the sense that nebulous powers dominate them in uncharted ways—will lead to studies that decrease the void. On the evidence, however, studies with normative axes to grind are as likely to retard or divert disciplinary advances as to promote them, and they are most fruitful when informed by study conducted from a more neutral basis.

As long as systematic studies of nongovernmental authority patterns are few and crude, we are deprived also of knowledge that has great potential use for making sense of governmental patterns, in at least three ways. (*a*) Despite pitfalls when imputing traits from small-scale to large-scale entities, there is much to be learned about macrocosms from microcosms.[34] The smaller units, moreover, often accomodate better methods of study and are more accessible to investigation than the larger ones. (*b*) Given Easton's undisputable statement that political study could profit from a general theory of power, the field could profit even more from a general theory of authority patterns—not, in this case, by imputation from one level to another, but by the partial application to less general phenomena of theories about more extensive ones.* (*c*) Even if governmental authority patterns are separated from less extensive ones, the latter are likely to be important explanatory variables for aspects of governmental authority—for example, on the basis of learning processes, or because they provide links in other senses (mediate between) governmental and strictly nonpolitical variables, such as economic ones, social status, or mobility. Eckstein has made an extensive case for using nongovernmental authority patterns as explanatory variables (in theories of stability in democracies or, in a more general sense, performance levels of all kinds of government) in other publications (see Chapter 16), and we refer readers to these for a full statement of his argument. The general point, however, does not rest only on his hypotheses. Nongovernmental authority patterns have been used, implicitly, as explanatory variables for governmental ones in hosts of works and have been so used explicitly at least as far back as Montesquieu, or indeed Confucius.

Note that this delimitation of "politics" is not wholly unprecedented. There is at least one (implicit) anticipation of it in the modern history of political thought. It is mentioned at this point partly to avoid misimpressions about claims to originality and partly because, indirectly, it adds

* Easton's sense of "political study" is discussed briefly in the Appendix to this chapter.

to the force of our argument. The anticipation occurs in the works of the so-called pluralists (Figgis, Laski, Cole) of an earlier period. The pluralists argued, in gist, that the state's claim to sovereignty did not give it a special *moral* status relative to other social structures. It is true that they were not concerned with the scope of politics as a field of study. They were normative philosophers. Besides, political science hardly existed as a special "field" when these authors first wrote. However, their arguments rested on doubt about the very existence of something properly considered "sovereign" or, better, doubt that the special attributes of structures claiming sovereignty made much or any moral difference.

How does this reinforce our argument? Simply because if the same moral problems (e.g., of rights, obligations, liberty) are raised in a variety of social units, it is probable that descriptive similarities among them also will be great. Put differently: if apparently diverse phenomena pose largely the same problems, moral or otherwise, we may take this as a powerful indication of their being, despite appearances, members of a common taxonomic class.

Politics, International Relations, and "Political Economy"

Objections to our position are less likely to concern what it adds to the conventional scope of political study than what it seems to subtract. Two apparently subtracted subjects are especially likely to be cited: (1) relations among polities, and (2) the nonauthoritative, in general symmetric, processes central to "economic" analyses of politics, such as political bargaining, political coalition formation, and the adjustment of governmental programs and party positions to voters' preferences.[35]

These are certainly among the more common subjective interests in political science departments. Moreover, a reasoned case for including both in the political scientist's field of attention can certainly be made. It seems to us, however, that their elimination from "politics" here is either more apparent than real or else inconsequential. This needs elaboration.

1. We all know that the study of *international relations* has long played a major role in political science departments. Reasons for this, as long as polities are central to our concerns, are not hard to find; above all, it is arguable that linkages between the internal affairs of polities and relations among them are such that neither can be properly understood without the other.[36] The argument is somewhat intricate, but the basic position is obvious.

The first point to note by way of rebuttal is that nothing said here rules out the study of international relations. Anyone interested in that special subject can still pursue it.

Beyond this, aspects of international relations, as conventionally conceived, are not excluded by the proposed delimitation of politics—particularly two in which "linkages" are ignored at most obvious peril. One is the study of supranational integration. Authority patterns above the national level fall within the field's scope no less than those below it. In addition, the study of authority patterns can certainly accomodate studies of how the patterns are formed. Every field theorizes about statics and dynamics, and the study of political dynamics is fundamentally concerned with the processes by which political units come into being or cease to exist. Processes of international integration surely are processes that develop directive, asymmetrical relations, within embryonic social units, out of relations falling into other taxonomic categories. (That applies to the formation of nation-states themselves no less than processes that, some argue, are now taking us "beyond the nation-state.") The second aspect still manifestly included in politics is, of course, foreign policy, especially insofar as it has directive consequences for members of polities.

Nevertheless, other aspects of international relations clearly cannot be squeezed into the proposed delimitation without procrustean distortion. They fall outside it because they are symmetric in character—more akin to economic market relations than to authority relations; or because they involve between-unit asymmetries; or, farthest removed from our conception of politics, because they involve only indirect impingements rather than "relationships" in the sense of interactions. These aspects of international relations are also "linked" to within-unit affairs, and vice versa; and it is in regard to the latter that potential disciplinary losses (not losses in status and the like) become serious.

There is reason to think that the losses would not be large on either side. The disciplinary boundaries between politics and economics, after all, have not prevented studies that link political and economic factors or political studies using economic postulates and methods. Neither have those between politics and sociology, politics and psychology, and politics and anthropology, prevented the development of political sociology, studies of political socialization, or studies of primitive political systems. Moreover, economists study markets and sociologists study corporations, without very deleterious consequences. Serious scholars who feel compelled to cross disciplinary boundaries do so, paying the price in time and effort. In the case of studies of polities and their relations, the price will certainly not be as great as in many others: neither area at present requires mastery of exotic skills or peculiar talents. Indeed, on the evidence, interdisciplinary programs can be useful substitutes for departmental identities, and they have the advantage of allowing one to choose by reasoning rather than brute convention among the disciplines to be related.

Here we come to gains that may offset any losses if departmental divorces occur. It is by no means certain that specialists in international relations are best served as general political scientists. At the student or even faculty levels, they might better devote more time and other resources to studying international relations as such. They might also learn more that would help them make sense of their subject from other fields (e.g., economics, anthropology) than they presently do from various subdivisions of political science—many of which are forced by departmental rules and teaching loads on undergraduates, graduate students, and teachers. Given the manifest taxonomic differences between polities and international systems, and the resemblances of the latter to other phenomena, this is very likely to be the case. By the same token, as already argued, those who study polities may learn more from studying authority patterns at lesser levels than from the study of international relations. (We say "may" because we do not know enough to say "will." Just for that reason, however, choices should be open, not foreclosed.)

One is struck by the paucity of theories, or even theoretical approaches or frameworks, that apply both to polities and to their relations (as distinguished from their linkages), except at very general and uninformative levels. This is precisely what would be expected if taxonomic differences were considerable. And yet, simply because scholarly convention and administrative habit identify international relations and politics, people continue to devote themselves to distracting exercises that might justify the habit. They search for definitions of politics that might cover both international and intranational affairs (not hard to do, but also not very useful). They look for any signs in international activities indicating that these are not absolutely different from intranational activities (also easy, since, of course, they are not). They try to develop perspectives of inquiry, theoretical approaches, and theories that might apply to both sets of phenomena (more difficult, but certainly also possible at a sufficiently inclusive, and heterogeneous, level). The results are often trivial or embarrassing. It would seem less wasteful, on the face of it, simply to work with one's materials, allowing any correspondences to emerge naturally from the work, than to strain after commonalities simply to have habit appear as reason.

2. Objections to the possible elimination from "politics" of *symmetric relations that figure in the making of directives* (as well as in processes of recruitment to superordinate roles) should be taken more seriously. For one thing, such relations are what "politics" is often taken to mean (e.g., when distinguished from government or administration). More important, the

relations involved do not just play a momentous role in state-organizations; they can occur in any and all authority patterns, and probably do in most.

To disarm objections on this score, it should suffice to say that the study of the direction of social units clearly includes the study of processes by which directives are arrived at, carried out, and observed or defied, as well as processes by which those who carry out direction are recruited to their roles. The notion of asymmetry merely provides the first of several criteria of discrimination by which the concrete phenomena of the field are identified. If symmetric relations occur among members of concrete units identified by these criteria, *and if these relations are manifestly concerned with the direction of the units* (in short, intrinsic to authority), they fall within (or, better, intersect with) the boundaries here delimited—just as asymmetric relations among members that are "nonauthoritative" fall outside them.

The elaboration of the general definition of authority patterns points to two aspects of the patterns likely to involve symmetries. One is certain relations among superordinates (*super-super relations*). Superordinates may work out directives by vote trading and other modes of bargaining to form winning coalitions.[37] Such collaboration is not always corrupt or cynical, or even just utilitarian. There are cultures in which particular value is attached to collegial behavior and consensual decisions—Norway, Eckstein has argued, is a case in point—where symmetry among superordinates is a general end rather than a means for optimizing particular utilities. (It is manifest also that the more a social unit's tacit or explicit decision-rules require assent by numerous participants, the greater the number and significance of symmetries in decision-processes will be.) Symmetries may, of course, also occur in *sub-sub relations* intended to "influence" direction. This does not refer to equal power to influence superordinates. It refers chiefly to exchanges and compromises among subordinates for the sake of forming cohesive influential groups.

Despite all this, it must be granted that the inclusion of symmetric relations in "political" study introduces an element of dissonance or impurity into the proposed conception of politics. Symmetries remain symmetries, no matter how well justified their inclusion in studies of asymmetric relations and no matter how often one says that they must affect asymmetries of a particular kind. The conceptual dissonance can be tolerated. But it should be realized that relations in authority patterns that are not themselves authoritative will at least require theories different from those that are.[38]

It is altogether likely that the theories required will substantially resemble or coincide with those of economics—the field preeminently concerned with "instrumental symmetries" in social relations. (They may also resemble certain theories of international relations, if and when properly formulated.[39]) The adaptations of economic theories to political relations are, in fact, already well-developed in a new "political economy" that better merits the label than the old (see note 35). These theories link two fundamentally different but intertwined aspects of organized or institutionalized human relations: those in which humans are equals and exchange, and those in which they are hierarchically ordered and direct or are directed.

Proponents of economic theories of politics often justify their work on grounds begging questions that need not be begged. They claim that "human nature" is inherently Hobbesian or in some more benign sense value- maximizing, hence that politics and economics must be governed by the same laws. Or they suggest that methodological imperatives (parsimony, the deductive derivation of propositions, predictive or explanatory power) somehow compel working with economists' methods on economists' postulates. All this is probably untrue, and surely unnecessary. The political economists need only claim that concrete political structures and processes contain relations of the kind that economic theories are designed to handle; thus such theories are a useful basis (prefabricated, as it were) for partial accounts of politics. How partial or comprehensive these accounts can be is best left to be settled a posteriori by competition between contending approaches.

This argument has several further implications of consequence:

It implies without ambiguity that the contemporary political economists' fixation with state-organization and processes intimately associated with the state (e.g., party competition) is ill advised. Their theories pertain to processes that may occur in any and all authority patterns.

A second implication is that we should start to develop theories of asymmetric relations—particularly those that occur within social units, between levels, and involve "direction"—as rigorous and fertile as those of instrumental symmetry. Such a counterpart to economic theory certainly does not presently exist even in embryonic form, and the failure of political scientists to define their subject matter surely goes far to explain why this is the case. In turn, the lack of a powerful "pure" theory of politics helps to explain why contemporary political economy is so much more economic than political.

A third implication is related to this point. Our argument implies that "political economy" should be thought of in two ways, and that one should work toward much greater symmetry of emphasis between these modes. There is, on one hand, the economics of politics: the study of symmetries in authority patterns. On the other hand, we have the politics of economics: the study of authority in symmetric relations. We do not refer here to Dahl's still largely unheeded call for the political analysis of business firms as "political orders."[40] The subject is much larger and more subtle. It entails study of the ways authority impinges on symmetry in any and all social units and relations—not excluding economic markets themselves. Except for economists' theories of monopoly and oligopoly, that subject has been much less explored than have economic theories of politics. Assuming that the necessary theoretical tools are developed, a political Downs roaming through the economists' domain might conceivably bring in some eyebrow-raising results.

We hold, in essence, that there are two fundamental sciences of society: one dealing with symmetrical social relationships, the other concerning asymmetric ones in social units—"economics" and "politics." Between these, since they intersect, a comprehensive science of social interaction must build bridges, as must many particular explanations of particular social occurrences. Since the science of symmetrical interaction is well developed (and suitable to what are generally considered "hard" methods of thought and inquiry), a recent tendency has been to develop "economic" theories applicable to political phenomena. This is a useful tendency. But it would be useful also if a concomitant effort were made to develop "political" theories of economics—and of politics.

Appendix

A Note on Easton's Conception of the Political System

The point of this chapter—that authority patterns should define and delimit political study—is not claimed to be wholly original, only persuasive. As well as being anticipated by normative philosophers, and following up arguments for studies of "private" governments as important influences on public ones or as not greatly dissimilar from the latter in nature or impact on individuals, it is also in line with suggestions of many contemporary critics of liberal democracies—especially their argument that liberal governmental institutions conceal oppressive networks of power that act through them or directly constrain individuals. In effect, it simply makes explicit what is largely implicit in all these views, and rests the case for equating political inquiry with the study of all authority patterns less on normative grounds than on "disciplinary" considerations.

Even in this regard, the argument might appear to have been developed previously by David Easton, in the *The Political System*. Some comments on points of difference between Easton's position and ours are therefore in order.

Easton defines "political acts" as those that "*authoritatively* allocate values in a society."[41] A social structure, therefore, is political if it engages in the authoritative allocation of values. The operative term "authoritative" corresponds to ours, and Easton's position, like ours, was worked out by criticism of the very narrow and very broad structural conception of the subject-matter of the field, to some extent on similar grounds. (The "functional" alternative was not considered by Easton, since it had not become current when he wrote—although he also ignores it in his later work.)

If our argument only restated, in a somewhat different way, Easton's position, it could be justified on the ground that Easton's influence on the conception of the field has hardly been great—except for the mouthing of definitions—and bears repetition and reinforcement. Actually, however, resemblances between Easton's position and ours are illusory. Easton's conception of politics (as distinguished from his systems approach to political study) has had no discernible impact on what political scientists do, for the good and simple reason that it only presents a new verbal way to characterize the conventional conception of the field.

That Easton's position remains closely tied to the notion of political structures as state-organizations, or very near equivalents, is evident in this crucial passage:

> ". . . in spite of the fact that for the members of [organizations that are not society-wide] their policies carry the weight of authority, it is at once apparent that political science does not undertake to study these policies for their own sake. Political science is concerned rather with the relation of the authoritative policies, made in such groups as associations, to other kinds of policies, those that are considered authoritative for the whole society. In other words, political research seeks first and foremost to understand the way in which values are authoritatively allocated . . . for the whole society."[42]

Processes of direction, directive roles, and internal directives in less comprehensive groups thus remain beyond the disciplinary pale. They are considered only as substantive inputs into "polities" (as defined earlier)—as parts of the "super-sub" relationships of the most inclusive authority patterns, or matters of boundary exchange between polities and nonpolitical structures.

Why does Easton delimit the field in a manner so closely tied to a conception of it that he attacks? Because, in the final analysis, he takes into account only our conventional subjective interests, not any disciplinary considerations, except when he attacks alternatives. Wherever his restrictive conception is stated, he invokes as support for it only the observation that political scientists are "not concerned" with a more broadly defined subject-matter. This is an explanation of what they do, but hardly a reason for doing nothing else. Besides, it is manifestly untrue, because some investigators are concerned with more, and Easton says nothing about what their concerns ought to be. Values are allocated by the "policies" of all groups;[43] indeed, one can go further and hold that values are allocated in some sense not just by "policies" but in all social relations (asymmetrically or otherwise). Therefore, the part of Easton's definition of the subject of the field that refers to value allocation is clearly gratuitous. Since all policies of all groups may be "authoritative," that part of the definition of politics also delimits nothing specifically political—a point that should have given Easton pause about making "society-wide" relations the only attribute that discriminates between political and nonpolitical phenomena.

It is not widely realized that the operative part of Easton's delimitation of politics is society-wide relations, nothing else. More attention has been paid to the redundant parts—which *appear* to say more than the crucial part of the definition. But Easton's own subsequent work confirms our argument: nowhere has he concerned himself with anything other than governments in the conventional sense. Our position can thus be taken as one to which much of Easton's preliminary argument about the nature of political phenomena leads, although Easton himself never reaches it. In that sense, it does not reiterate his views but extends them over a rather similar route toward a different destination.

Readers might note, in this connection, a curious point about Easton's use of sources. In two places, he cites Sir George Cornewall Lewis' *A Treatise on the Methods of Observation and Reasoning in Politics*, published in 1852—a book that precociously anticipates many current methodological issues in political science. He does not cite Lewis' *The Influence of Authority in Matters of Opinion*, published three years earlier, which attempts to demonstrate that authority pervades all of social life, all groups (as DeGrazia puts it)[44] having their own "small common goods" and "small authorities" that "envelop us at birth and clothe us throughout life." Easton may simply have neglected that work. It is not hard to miss it, for its influence has been virtually nil. Nevertheless, it comes closer to what we argue than does Easton's position itself.

Notes

1. For a list of 10 such definitions (a sample, not an inventory) see Harry Eckstein, "The Concept 'Political System.'" Paper presented at the 1963 Annual Meeting of the American Political Science Association.

2. Charles H. Titus has claimed to have identified no fewer than 145 definitions of the term "state." See his "A Nomenclature in Political Science," *American Political Science Review*, Vol. 25 (February 1931), pp. 45–61.

3. For a choice example of this view, see William Archibald Dunning, *A History of Political Theories* (New York: Macmillan, 1902).

4. We are ignoring here certain much earlier normative political philosophers who are discussed below. The reason for ignoring them at this point is stated in the later passages.

5. See the very large literature on "primitive" political systems: for example, M. Fortes and E. E. Evans-Pritchard, *African Political Systems* (London: Oxford University Press, 1940); I. Schapera, *Government and Politics in Tribal Societies* (London: Watts, 1956); A. I. Richards, Ed., *East African Chiefs* (London: Faber, 1960); and Lucy Mair, *Primitive Government* (Harmondsworth: Penguin Books, 1962).

6. Max Weber, *From Max Weber: Essays in Sociology* (New York: Oxford University Press, 1946), p. 83.

7. Charles Merriam, *Public and Private Governments* (New Haven, Conn.: Yale University Press, 1944).

8. See especially Robert A. Dahl, "Business and Politics: An Appraisal of Political Science," *American Political Science Review*, Vol. 53 (March 1959), pp. 1–35.

9. For a more extensive critique of the traditional conception of politics, see David Easton, *The Political System* (New York: Knopf, 1953).

10. Examples are Gabriel A. Almond, "Comparative Political Systems," *Journal of Politics*, Vol. 18 (August 1956), pp. 391–409; Almond and James S. Coleman, Eds., *The Politics of the Developing Areas* (Princeton, N.J.: Princeton University Press, 1960); Talcott Parsons, "'Voting' and the Equilibrium of the American Political System," in *American Voting Behavior*, Eugene Burdick and Arthur J. Brodbeck, Eds. (New York: Free Press, 1960); and David E. Apter, "A Comparative Method for the Study of Politics," *American Journal of Sociology*, Vol. 64 (1958), pp. 221–237.

11. For example, Talcott Parsons and Neil J. Smelser, *Economy and Society* (New York: Free Press, 1956).

12. This criticism does not apply to works that do not define politics functionally but urge a functional approach to the subject otherwise defined. For example, Almond's widely influential functional approach to the study of political systems is mainly tied to a conception of politics that stresses, à la Weber, an instrument of action rather than a social function: legitimate coercion. In his definition of 1956, legitimate coercion (plus territorial jurisdiction) is all that is advanced; in the definition of 1960, functional language is merely added to the original notion—probably to make the definition of the subject look as functional as the approach to its study. (See note 10 for references.)

13. Burricaud: political structures have the task of forging a common will out of conflicting wills in a society. Spiro: political structures are those institutions of a society that "process" their "issues." See François Bourricaud, "Science politique et sociologie," *Revue Française de Science Politique*, Vol. 8 (June 1958), and Herbert J. Spiro, "Comparative Politics: A Comprehensive Approach," *American Political Science Review*, Vol. 25 (September 1962), pp. 577–596.

14. Parsons, *Structure and Process in Modern Societies*, p. 42.

15. George E. G. Catlin, *A Study of the Principles of Government* (London: Allen and Unwin, 1930).

16. Catlin was by no means the only man to perceive the problem or try to solve it. His contributions were in fact overshadowed by those along similar lines of Harold Lasswell.

17. "Pure" means "unmixed with symmetric interactions" here. This is questionable for reasons outlined below.

18. Easton, *The Political System,* p, 117.

19. Catlin was quite aware of this problem. (See *A Study of the Principles of Politics*, p. 66.) He specifically counsels that politics as a discipline must not concern itself with "all the life of the coummunity," only with the activities in it that are, somehow, political. On the other hand, recognizing that little remains clearly nonpolitical by his definition, he also advises Aristotelian wholism in holding that politics is present in all social relationships. Easton rightly extends this view to Lasswell's conception of politics, although not to his substantive work. (See *The Political System*, pp. 119–124.)

20. Easton, p. 123.

21. It is probable that the criteria will seem "obvious" when stated. If so, all the better—and all the more reason for making them explicit. Points obvious when stated, after all, are not always obvious when not stated. The unfortunate tacks others have taken in exercises of this kind attest to that.

22. Robert A. Dahl and Charles E. Lindblom, *Politics, Economics, and Welfare* (New York: Harper and Row, 1953).

23. Edward Banfield, *The Moral Basis of a Backward Society* (New York: Free Press, 1958).

24. Marion J. Levy, Jr., *The Structure of Society* (Princeton, N.J.: Princeton University Press, 1952).

25. *Politics, Economics, and Welfare*, p. 94.

26. Sebastian De Grazia, *The Political Community* (Chicago: University of Chicago Press, 1948).

27. We are aware that as a taxonomy of social relationships, Figure 1.2 (and the argument it represents) is incomplete. The reason is that at this point, we are not concerned with all social relationships, only with the place of political ones among them. No doubt, however, this involves a weakness: a full, methodical taxonomy of social relationships conceivably might, but probably will not, look different.

28. For a sense of the confusion surrounding the term, see Robert L. Peabody, *Organizational Authority* (New York: Atherton Press, 1964), Chps. 1 and 2, and Carl J. Friedrich, Ed., *Authority* (Cambridge, Mass.: Harvard University Press, 1958).

29. Max Weber, *The Theory of Social and Economic Organization* (New York: Oxford University Press, 1947), p. 153.

30. Note, for example, the following ambivalence in Weber's use of the concept. (1) Authority is held to exist in *many* types of "corporate groupes" (i.e., in our terms, social units) and to involve "the legitimate exercise of imperative control." An aspect of such control is the use of coercion regarded as rightfully exercised. (2)

The *state* is defined by its "monopoly of legitimate coercion." Clearly statement 2 contradicts statement 1, unless the latter is confined to "stateless" societies. The ambivalence arises, in our view, from the wish—more typical of political scientists than of sociologists—to make overly rigid distinctions between polities and other social units.

31. The notion of extensiveness in fact figures in some definitions of political systems. The most explicit example is Apter's: polities are the *most generalized membership units* of societies with defined responsibility for maintaining the societies and enjoying a monopoly of coercive power. Other definitions imply the same more awkwardly. For examples, one of Almond's definitions includes the notion of an "autonomous society;" the much earlier one of MacIver includes the notion of a "territorially demarcated community (among numerous other definitional attributes); also, there is Dahl and Lindblom's notion that government has "the last word" over other organizations in an "area." See Apter, "A Comparative Method for the Study of Politics"; Almond and Coleman, *The Politics of the Developing Areas;* Robert M. MacIver; *The Modern State* (London: Oxford University Press, 1926),p. 22; Dahl and Lindblom, *Politics, Economics, and Welfare,* p. 42.

32. See Dahl, "Business and Politics," for documentation in one area of private authority.

33. We refer here to studies mainly concerned with the systematic study of authority patterns—such as that of Peabody. Authority being ubiquitous, references to authority patterns, or potentially relevant materials, may be found in virtually all studies of social institutions, but chiefly in their interstices, between the lines, in connection with other matters, without special emphasis on systematic treatment.

34. A useful work to consult on both points is Sidney Verba, *Small Groups and Political Behavior: A Study of Leadership* (Princeton, N.J.: Princeton University Press, 1961). To avoid possible confusion of terms, it should be noted that microcosms and macrocosms are not quite the same as micro- and macro-levels. The micro-level of any entity consists of entities that constitute the larger unit; microcosms, on the other hand, are macrocosms writ small: much like the latter, except in regard to scale. Thus individual persons, or relations among them, are at the micro-level of societies, but not—unless rather farfetched analogies hold—microcosms of them; families, however, are (or may be) both.

35. Much of the recent literature on this subject is summarized in R. L. Curry, Jr., and L. L. Wade, *A Theory of Political Exchange* (Englewood Cliffs, N.J.: Prentice-Hall, 1968), and some of its anticipations are summarized in James M. Buchanan and Gordon Tullock, *The Calculus of Consent* (Ann Arbor: University of Michigan Press, 1962), pp. 323–340. In a sense, most of the literature on political competition, anyway in democracies, is concerned with the subject, even if economic postulates or methods of reasoning are not explicitly used.

36. See, for example, James N. Rosenau, *Linkage Politics: Essays on the Convergence of National and International Systems* (New York: Free Press, 1969).

37. For a list of such possible "exchanges," see William H. Riker, *The Theory of Political Coalitions* (New Haven, Conn.: Yale University Press, 1962), pp. 108–114.

38. This, in turn, should not be bothersome. No one has ever held that theories of politics can avoid all nonpolitical factors.

39. If theories resemble both those of economics and international relations, these two bodies of theory should resemble each other. In this connection, note that "entrepreneurial" (i.e., economic) theories of international relations are now beginning to emerge. A good example is Norman Frohlich and Joe A. Oppenheimer, "Entrepreneurial Politics and Foreign Policy," *World Politics*, Vol. 24 (Supplement, 1972), pp. 151–178.

40. Dahl, "Business and Politics," pp. 3–9.

41. Easton, *The Political System*, p. 134 (italics added).

42. *Ibid., loc. cit.*

43. Ibid. p. 130.

44. Sebastian De Grazia, *The Political Community*, p. 330.

45. Ten years ago Eckstein wrote an essay on the development of "comparative politics," from its remote ancestry in the works of Aristotle to the present. [See "A Perspective on Comparative Politics," in *Comparative Politics: A Reader*, Eckstein and Apter, Eds. (New York: Free Press, 1963), pp. 3–32] The essay concluded with a problem to which no solution had then been worked out. As long as political studies emphasized formal-legal aspects of state-organizations, they had a certain focus and simplicity. The tendency in the field, for good reasons, was to deemphasize that subject -matter. But the result of this practice was loss of focus and simplicity—thus a loss of bearings in regard to what the field was all about, especially as a field of *specialization*. Political scientists often did not practice what they preached: they continued, in their work, to deal chiefly with state-organizations, while disavowing the reasons for doing so (in the manner of Easton). Or, if they did follow their own prescriptions, they seemed to equate politics with "the whole of social life in all its phases." The problem, then, was to find a different but still focused and relatively simple conception of the subject of the field. The present essay presents an answer to that problem.

PART TWO

Description: The Elements of Authority Patterns

Systematic Description and Analytic Concepts

To study authority patterns, certain indispensable tools must be developed. The most basic are concepts for systematically describing patterns of authority in detail and with a view toward generalizing about them. Part II presents a scheme of such concepts.

The scheme allows us to examine six aspects of patterns of authority: influence relations among superordinates and subordinates, inequalities among them, certain "static" aspects of structures of superordination (their conformation, or "anatomy"), certain "dynamic" aspects of such structures (their processes, or "physiology"), the manner in which members of social units are recruited into superordinated positions, and the bases of legitimacy perceptions.

The word "scheme" is used with intent—to denote that the concepts presented and discussed are not an arbitrary list, but based on reasoning. To see in what sense this is so, as well as for proper judgment and understanding of the concepts, several general introductory points should be kept in mind throughout.

Generality of the Concepts

The concepts are intended to apply to authority patterns in any and all social units, regardless of variations that do not directly involve authority relations (such as size, complexity, or function) and regardless of whether the units exhibit great or little overall asymmetry between superordinates and subordinates. No doubt some aspects of authority patterns will seem more worth stressing in studies of certain social units than in others (see

Chapter 8) or more germane to certain theoretical purposes than others. No doubt also, some selection among aspects of authority will be compelled by problems of data gathering and other limitations on the scope of research. These, however, are matters for particular judgments of prudence and significance that can best be made when a comprehensive set of common elements of authority patterns has been identified.

The general study of authority patterns obviously requires general descriptive concepts, but we have other reasons for attempting to develop such concepts here, including the following: (1) If it can be shown that a considerable battery of descriptive concepts applies to authority patterns of all kinds, the critical argument of Chapter 1—that such patterns constitute a highly numerous subject matter (unlike "states"), yet still a quite homogeneous one (unlike all asymmetric relations)—will be supported, or at least illustrated. (2) The concepts will elaborate and will further identify the traits of authority patterns as a taxonomic class, thus helping to delimit the class from others. (3) Authority patterns are presently studied, from a variety of points of view and with a variety of conceptual tools, by psychologists, sociologists, anthropologists, organization theorists, and political scientists. A general scheme of descriptive concepts should help cross-disciplinary communication and promote the ability to use work on authority relations cumulatively, by introducing order where there is at present great diversity. (4) Such a scheme should also promote our ability to extrapolate macro-theory about authority from micro-studies—indeed, to use the findings of studies of authority in any context to help make sense of it in others, or in general. (5) Some theoretical purposes are not only indirectly facilitated by the ability to compare authority in quite different contexts, but absolutely require that ability. An example is Eckstein's contention[1] that levels of political performance vary with overall "congruence" between governmental and certain nongovernmental authority patterns. (6) By the same token, new theoretical propositions about the relations between authority patterns, or aspects of them, in different social units might emerge if comparability among such patterns were great.

Generality on the level aimed at is unlikely to be attained unless two precepts are observed in working out the concepts. First, since comparison is an objective and since authority patterns in social units are highly variable (even in units of the same kind, let alone of very different kinds), the concepts should identify a limited set of "dimensions" on which the patterns vary, and these dimensions should, if possible, be continua on which different units can be differently located. The alternative is to identify qualitatively different "elements" that constitute particular cases in the whole class of authority patterns. But this would hinder ability to compare and would make for an insupportably complex set of concepts. (For example, comparison and economy are both promoted by being able to locate cases on a continuous "Participation" dimension, varying from a maximum to a minimum value. Both are hindered by identifying a dozen or more qualitatively different acts of participation, even if these are reduced, by suitable statistical devices, to a few more general categories, as by Verba, Nie, and Kim.[2] In many cases, to be sure, overall location on a dimension will be a composite measure of qualitatively distinguishable measures. But this is a matter of putting dimensions operationally to work, not a problem at the initial stages of conceptualization. If a dimension clearly entails a set of quite different subdimensions, these should of course be identified, as should any aspect of authority that defies location on a continuous dimension.

A second "rule" that follows from the aim to develop very general concepts is that each dimension should be derived from the very definition of authority patterns or its elaboration in subdefinitions. This can be done by showing that the dimensions are either directly contained in the definitions or indirectly implied by them. Only in this way can one be sure that all authority patterns will occupy positions on each dimension and will not cause the problems that can arise when dimensions are tailored to individual cases or limited types; in addition, the dimensions will involve authority, not other broad aspects of social units. For less general purposes, the set of dimensions can be reduced or augmented readily; for additional richness of detail, the schematic concepts can be supplemented by as much ordinary description as seems advisable.

Systematic Description

Descriptions presented in general concepts having the foregoing characteristics inevitably sacrifice some richness of detail for other values and will, to an extent, be couched in unconventional terminology—technical language to those who see a need for it, jargon to others. Both are inevitable where "systematic description" is the objective, as it is here. Therefore, we must be explicit in defining systematic description, as opposed to unsystematic ways of portraying observations.

The fundamental hallmark of systematic description is simply that portraiture as such is not its end. It is, instead, an instrument for the quintessential purpose of inquiry in a discipline: arriving at generalizations about sets of cases. In terms common in German philosophy a century ago and anthropology now, its end is nomothetic, not idiographic, study. Consequently, some descriptive considerations that loom large where one is concerned with individuals *qua* individuals—bringing out their peculiarities, making a subject "vivid" by faithful depiction or subtle caricature—are subordinated to considerations that promote ability to generalize: above all, comparability (discovering sets of cases to treat as homologous or dissimilar) and cumulativeness (having descriptive data "add up" for inductive purposes).

For the sake of these considerations, systematic description has at least three distinctive characteristics. (*a*) It is always carried out on the basis of a *preconstructed scheme of concepts,* applied to cases in a standardized manner. Like any other disciplinary tool or product, such a scheme will certainly have to be revised as research unfolds. But the scheme always explicitly precedes substantive inquiry, has an existence separate from it, and guides decisions about what and how to investigate. If not, cumulative results are unlikely except as happy accidents, and questions of comparability, hence generalizability or fit between generalizations and pertinent cases, will be difficult to resolve. (One consequence is, of course, that systematic description is always stereotyped and constricted—certainly more so than, say, felicitous portraiture by a novelist or journalist.) (*b*) Conceptual schemes for systematic description also are constricting because they necessarily *select limited attributes of phenomena* from all possible ones. Hence the loss of the shades and nuances of phenomena. Evidently, not even the most meticulous "clinical" report can tell everything about a case. In systematic description, however, decisions about what to spotlight are not made on the basis of the observer's sense of the observed case but on the basis of attributes emphasized for explicit or implicit purposes of generalization in his conceptual scheme. (*c*) Particular emphasis is put on the *precision of concepts* in such schemes: careful verbal and/or operational definitions. Ambiguities and ambivalences in description work against cumulation and generalization no less than the ad hoc improvisation of conceptual equipment or the idiosyncratic spotlighting of quite different aspects of different cases.

The extent to which concepts for systematic description restrict detail should not be exaggerated. The scheme presented here does permit descriptions of authority patterns in great detail—in fact, greater detail than any we have found in existing accounts of authority. This is because the concepts are intended potentially to serve a large variety of theoretical purposes (see Chapter 14). Nevertheless, the point of the scheme is to promote "nomothetic" studies, not "idiographic" ones, and this involves both advantages and costs.

Inadequacies of Available Concepts for Describing Authority Patterns

Existing studies of authority relations can certainly help in the construction of a conceptual scheme for the systematic description of authority patterns. We will in fact make much use of them here. In the main, however, the methodical construction of such a scheme is still unfinished business on the agenda of the social sciences. Individually and collectively, descriptions of authority relations are flawed by several inadequacies that severely constrict their usefulness for our purpose.

In the most general terms, the problem with the literature is this: There is no lack of labels for describing authority patterns, technical or otherwise. But descriptive concepts used in studies of authority have not been pulled together in a thoughtfully devised conceptual scheme that can be uniformly applied for purposes of comparison and cumulativeness; similar concepts are used in a promiscuous manner (undefined, or with a bewildering variety of meanings, or with matters that ought to be explicit and precise left implicit and vague); and many concepts are not used in ways applicable to all social units. These general difficulties have several particular sources.[3]

1. The literature of political science is undoubtedly the most likely source of concepts for the systematic description of authority patterns, polities being such patterns and (if we are right) not hugely different from other varieties of them. However, at least two shortcomings make the political science literature less than fully serviceable for the purpose. No one has attempted to construct a comprehensive analytic scheme for the systematic description of polities alone (extraordinary as that may seem in this age of "behavioral" exactitudes). At most, our descriptive schemes identify selected dimensions on which polities vary, leaving the description of how they vary to ad libbing; and even the general dimensions differ a great deal from one case to another because they are intended to elaborate a variety of "theoretical approaches." Examples are Almond's familiar "functional" and "capabilities" dimensions[4] and Lasswell's[5] dimensions for analyzing influence and power. In addition, many descriptive concepts defined and used with some precision in political science are so defined with reference to polities as special social units only, not in a manner useful for broader purposes—no doubt because of the traditional focus on state-organizations and their near equivalents. An example is the common operational definition of "participation" in terms of voting, which simply does not occur in many social units, or in terms of discussion of "political" issues, activism in campaigns, and the like;[6] another is the Dahl-Lindblom conception of polyarchy, which, despite its ostensibly more general purpose, also emphasizes voting.

2. Most descriptions of authority relations (including those of polities) use only, or mainly, "improvisation." Labels are undefined or, worse, applied with highly various definitions. Aspects of authority are intuitively (it often seems randomly) selected for emphasis; thus little "adds up" and avoidable problems of comparability arise. There is, on the whole, greater emphasis on vividness of description than on disciplinary considerations, espe-

cially on peculiarities of unique cases rather than the features that would most readily identify the sets to which they belong. This applies to studies of polities no less than nongovernmental authority patterns (even if not quite to the same extent). Thus existing descriptions furnish mainly raw material for a systematic scheme of concepts and information that might be restated using the concepts of such a scheme.

3. Descriptive concepts not only tend to lack explicit definitions and uniform usage, they generally make very broad and crude distinctions, which are not useless, but provide little information. Rarely does anyone go beyond the distinction between "democratic" and "authoritarian" patterns. Rarely does anyone make explicit just what clusters of attributes these broad classificatory terms distinguish. Probably the best elucidation of attributes is that of Lewin, White, and Lippitt; but their concepts were constructed for experimental studies of the effects of styles of adult supervision on children, and therefore are tailored mainly to exercises of authority in face-to-face relationships, not more general use.[7]

4. When research into authority patterns is conducted with systematic methods, the conceptual bases for the research instruments used are either crude or nonexistent. Method is thus stressed over content. For example, Peabody[8] managed to get his data on organizational authority in two public service agencies and a school with an interview schedule of 18 questions (at least 7 of which have nothing to do with authority at all), even though "description," not theory, was claimed to be the purpose of his work[9] and no circumstances compelling so brief a research instrument are cited. Moreover, most of Peabody's questions asked about very general attitudes toward leaders and supervisors; the "variables" they are supposedly based on were few (acceptance of authority, level of position in a hierarchy, individual satisfaction, organizational goals) and undefined, and their derivation was mysterious. Moreover, only the first two variables have anything to do with the description of authority patterns as such—that is, what they *are*, not what they *do* or how well they *perform*. And Peabody's book is unusual for being rather fastidious about the general concept of authority and its facets.

The overall picture that emerges (exceptions granted) is one of concepts that discriminate only crudely; that are often not defined at all, or if defined, are ambiguous and ambivalent; that only lend themselves to the description of particular social units, like polities, or particular relations, like face-to-face interaction; and that vitiate good methods of research with bad tools for identifying subjects for inquiry and reporting. We can say without exaggerating greatly that except for the ubiquitous democratic-authoritarian dichotomy (and perhaps including it), the literature teems with classificatory concepts that convey little more precise information than patent medicine labels. Furthermore, the concepts are sometimes blatantly intended to make cases attractive or repugnant to those lacking detailed knowledge of the situations. And classifiers often first coin their labels, then try to give them meaning (which surely is to work from back to front). Hunch and arbitrariness thus predominate, and the resultant roster of imprecise terms is vast: totalitarian, oligarchic, liberal, libertarian, laissez-faire, participatory, directive, polyarchic, hierarchic, charismatic, tyrannical, despotic, feudal, traditional, rational, legal, rational-legal, constitutional, pluralist, elitist, system-dominant, subsystem-dominant, representative, dictatorial, parochial, civic, competitive, semicompetitive, caesaristic, and so on and on.

The Nature of "Analytic" Concepts

The cavalier treatment of definitions aside, terms of this kind convey little information about what they purport to describe fundamentally because they are *synthetic* concepts, not based upon the use of *analytic* ones. If one grasps the kinds of concepts involved, the following points should be apparent: (*a*) analytic and synthetic concepts are the only kinds that can be used in systematic description; (*b*) concepts of the synthetic variety are informative only to the extent that they make use of analytic ones; (*c*) in the development of concepts, the analytic must therefore have priority over the synthetic.

Analytic concepts are used to identify the constituent parts of complex entities—the proximate or ultimate "elements" combined in them—and an "analytic scheme" is a comprehensive set of concepts for characterizing complex phenomena. (The term "analysis" is used here in a manner conforming to its Greek origin, as is its counterpart, "synthesis." The terms are not used to distinguish abstract ideas and concrete phenomena, or general principles underlying observations and the observations themselves.)

Some familiar examples of analytic concepts are the phonemes combined in words, chemical elements combined in compounds, simple tones combined in complex musical sounds, and colors combined in compound light. Such schemes of analytic concepts can consist of qualitatively different elements or of elements that are "dimensional" in character (i.e., they can quantitatively identify measured locations on continuous scales—height, length, weight, mass, force, density, etc.). Whether one or the other kind of scheme is used depends on purposes and abilities. In any event, the difference between them, although not inconsequential, is less than absolute, since qualitative analytic distinctions (e.g., colors) can usually be turned into dimensional ones (e.g., wavelength), at least theoretically.

Analytic schemes can be worked out in numerous ways. There are no set rules for constructing them, only ways that have been successful. Sometimes it is possible to split complex entities into component material substances, as in the chemist's laboratory. Sometimes elements can be otherwise "isolated," as in producing the components of complex musical sounds. Sometimes (as in the case of most social phenomena), the elements of entities can only be "abstracted" (not actually isolated), since they are not discrete material entities separable from the compounds they constitute. In such a case, the procedure generally used, and certainly useful, is precisely that recommended previously for achieving "generality." One asks on what distinguishable dimensions, inherent in the conception of a subject (and/or potentially significant for theory about it), phenomena vary, and how they appear to vary, logically or on the basis of previous observations, on the dimensions. The resultant variations then constitute the analytic scheme used to describe individual cases.

A simple example of such social "analysis"—perhaps too simple, since it dichotomizes continuous variables—is Parsons' scheme of "pattern variables" for the description of social roles, as portrayed in Table 1.[10] In this case the pattern variables, or dimensions, were derived logically (at least so it is claimed) from the notion of roles as systems of "action," the variations by reflecting on the basic dilemmas that must be resolved in any course of action (e.g., whether to make emotional evaluations of objects or action, what kind of normative standards to apply in acting).

Synthetic concepts identify similar sets of complex entities as such. In some cases (as in chemical formulas) they may tell us all there is to know about the constituent elements of the cases. More often they provide information only about their distinctive traits. It is not really necessary for synthetic concepts to do more, but to the extent that they do not, descriptions by synthetic concepts must always be partial and usually needs to be supplemented by using analytic concepts (or ad lib depiction) to portray individuals in detail.

Table 1 Parsons' Analytic Scheme for Describing Social Roles

Dimension (or Pattern Variable)	Variations on Dimension	
Role of "cathexis" in action	Neutrality	Affectivity
Moral standards governing actions	Self-orientation	Other-orientation
Scope of the role	Specificity	Diffuseness
Treatment of objects of action	Universalism	Particularism
Valued attributes in objects	Achievement	Ascription

The attributes used to characterize sets of complex entities always implicitly constitute a potential analytic scheme or part of one. For example, the Dahl-Lindblom conception of polyarchy (one of four alleged types of "sociopolitical process") involves variations on six dimensions that could readily be elaborated into a full set of analytic concepts for the description of any and all sociopolitical processes.[11] The dimensions are: opportunity of participants in the processes to vote freely for leaders, weighting of votes, relations of elected and nonelected officials, the role of elections in the recruitment of leaders, availability of sources of information, and ability to put up rival candidates freely for leadership roles. To constitute a comprehensive analytic scheme, the elaboration would have to be considerable, particularly since the same dimensions are not used to characterize the other types, despite the obvious possibility of doing so. The utility of the exercise, if done, should also be manifest: ability to describe any sociopolitical process in detail and by rather broad labels, and in a way that allows comparable categories and subcategories to emerge and information to be cumulative. It should now be evident that synthetic concepts are used chiefly for broad descriptions in which a good deal of information is omitted (an example is the statement that a musical sound is a "C-major chord"). This is not criticism of such concepts, for the omission may be deliberate and useful. More important, it should be evident that "systematic description" starts best with analytic concepts. This is because analytic concepts allow the construction of synthetic ones, are implied in them anyway, and can provide more detail about cases, if more detail is wanted. Even if one starts at the other end, which is permissible, one should be precise and consistent about the dimensions, and variations on dimensions, on the basis of which synthetic distinctions are made. But starting at the other end has no particular advantages and, on the basis of the record (for reasons that are surely evident), the practice invites the same conceptual sloppiness that afflicts studies of authority. Moreover, definitions of the labels used in synthetic concepts refer, willy-nilly, to analytic elements. If these are left imprecise or primitive (undefined), the labels may move us emotionally and convey a variety of intuitive images, but they cannot furnish reliable information and are unlikely to afford extensive enlightenment.

A Note on Procedure

For the reasons just given, the following chapters deal only with analytic concepts for describing authority patterns. These are supplemented (in Part IV) by speculations about synthetic concepts—a subject that depends on "analysis," data, and the solution of certain theoretical problems, and thus can be treated only very tentatively here (see Chapters 12 and 13).

Both the nature of the analytic concepts and the manner of presenting them follow from these preliminary remarks. The basic concepts are continuous "dimensions" on which each case can occupy a particular measured position. The dimensions, of course, are defined and their derivation from the definition of authority patterns (or definitions that elaborate it) is discussed. The derivations are obvious in most cases—hopefully, at least, since the derivations are supposed to be contained in, or clearly implied by, the definition. Consequently also, a rationale for including dimensions in the scheme is not lavishly furnished in each instance but sometimes covers sets of related dimensions. Variations on the dimensions are then discussed. The treatment of the variations brings out instances in which a dimension can or must be divided into subdimensions, so that locating cases on it requires summary measures or a set of locations on the subdimensions should be independently reported.

To give concrete content to abstract conceptual discussions, illustrations from pertinent cases are then given; these should aid comprehension of the abstract discussion. The cases may be familiar but generally are taken from available field studies of authority. The illustrations are frequently accompanied by interpretative speculations or the elucidation of puzzles they seem to pose. Thus the potential use of data about authority patterns in the construction of theory can also be exemplified. All this is done sparingly, because conceptualization, not the presentation and interpretation of data, is our central concern; theory is discussed separately in Part V.

We only begin to come to grips here with the problem of how to describe authority patterns systematically. A great deal that is required for the purpose is omitted: how to obtain data pertinent to the dimensions, how to process data into standard measures and locate cases on the dimensions with some minimal precision, how to aggregate measures obtained on subdimensions, and so on. We have extensive ideas on all these matters, presented in Part III; but we prefer, first, to set forth the scheme of concepts to which they pertain.[12]

Notes

1. Harry Eckstein, *Division and Cohesion in Democracy* (Princeton, N.J.: Princeton University Press, 1966), Appendix B, and "Authority Relations and Governmental Performance," *Comparative Political Studies*, Vol. 2, No. 3, (October 1969), pp. 269–325.

2. Sidney Verba, Norman H. Nie, and Jae-On Kim, *The Modes of Democratic Participation: A Cross-National Comparison* (Beverly Hills, Calif.: Sage Professional Papers in Comparative Politics, No. 01-013, 1971). See also Verba and Nie, *Participation in America: Political Democracy and Social Equality* (New York: Harper & Row, 1972), Chs. 3–4.

3. No attempt is made here to review in detail the whole literature touching on authority relations—which, given the ubiquity of such relations in social units, almost coincides with that on societies and social groups. The discussion is, of course, based on wide reading of works that give authority relations particular attention. To check on its validity, readers should consult a comprehensive bibliography, like that of Peter M. Blau and W. Richard Scott, *Formal Organizations: A Comparative Approach* (San Francisco: Chandler, 1962); or a selective but extensive, one, like that in Robert L. Peabody, *Organizational Authority: Superior-Subordinate Relationships in Three Public Service Organizations* (New York: Atherton Press, 1964); or a reader, like William A. Glaser and David L. Sills, *The Government of Associations* (Totowa, N.J.: Bedminster Press, 1966).

4. Gabriel A. Almond and G. Bingham Powell, Jr., *Comparative Politics: A Developmental Approach* (Boston: Little, Brown, 1966).

5. Harold Lasswell, *Politics: Who Gets What, When, How* (New York: McGraw-Hill, 1936), and Lasswell and Abraham Kaplan, *Power and Society: A Framework for Political Inquiry* (New Haven, Conn.: Yale University Press, 1950).

6. A notable step forward in regard to this has been taken by Verba and his associates; see note 2.

7. R. White and R. Lippitt, "Leader Behavior and Member Reaction in Three Social Climates," in D. Cartwright and A. F. Zander, Eds., *Group Dynamics: Research and Theory* (New York: Row, Peterson, 1953), and K. Lewin and R. Lippitt, "An Experimental Approach to the Study of Autocracy and Democracy," *Sociometry*, Vol. 1 (1938).

8. See note 3.

9. Page 46.

10. Talcott Parsons and Edward A. Shils, Eds., *Toward A General Theory of Action* (Cambridge, Mass.: Harvard University Press, 1954), pp. 76–91.

11. Dahl and Lindblom, *Politics, Economics, and Welfare*, pp. 277–278.

12. For the record, we add a brief review of how the concepts were actually worked out. The process by which they crystallized differed somewhat from what it should have been. (1) Our chief reason for attempting to devise analytic concepts for describing authority patterns was a theoretical interest that required the systematic comparison of such patterns. Since existing concepts seemed to be too vague and crude for that purpose, an attempt was made to devise a better set. (2) Initially that attempt was more "intuitive" than systematic, although systematic description for comparison and cumulation was the objective. We proposed dimensions and variables on them on the basis of hunches about how an authority pattern might be dissected, plus extrapolation of concepts from existing literature (what others had looked at in describing such patterns) and some reflection on the logical implications of the definition of authority patterns. (3) The results were intensively discussed and criticized in a group of graduate students at Princeton, leading to considerable elaboration of the concepts and some revisions. (4) Further revisions were made as a result of two considerations: greater emphasis on the logical defensibility of the dimensions and on their applicability in the widest variety of contexts, for a wide va-

riety of purposes. (5) In addition, some changes were made after a kind of "simulated field research": trying to see how well the scheme could be used to chart the universes of authority presented in a number of novels and anthropological and sociological case studies. (6) Finally, attempts to "operationalize" the concepts—in the sense of devising directions for collecting data pertinent to them and aggregating pertinent data in specific and summary scores—further affected the concepts, by feedback from conceptions of manageable observations. (7) In this process, the original set of concepts underwent many marginal changes (as it did also in the preparation of this book), but not wholesale alteration. In that sense we remain principally responsible for the scheme outlined here. However, many hands have by now played a role in concocting the concepts. (For a list of the main participants, see the Preface.)

CHAPTER TWO

S-s Relations: Dimensions of Influence[1]

Relations among superordinates and subordinates (hereafter "supers" and "subs," or *S* and *s*, for short) are central to any authority pattern; the notion of "direction" obviously implies people who direct and are directed, and their interactions. The four dimensions discussed here all involve flows of "influence" among supers and subs: attempts to affect behavior and the actual effects of the attempts. These are not the only dimensions on which *S-s* relations can be characterized, but they will probably seem most important for most purposes. Our labels for them are *Directiveness, Participation, Responsiveness,* and *Compliance.*[2]

Directiveness

General Discussion

Directiveness refers to the extent to which activities in a social unit are subject to directives, rather than being left to the free discretion of members. The variable is plainly contained in the notion of authority patterns, for although all such patterns by definition involve the direction of social units, the definition leaves open the extent of direction. Moreover, Directiveness is the aspect of authority most commonly emphasized in studies of the subject and at the heart of most synthetic labels for varieties of it.

Conceived as an aspect of influence relations, Directiveness can be defined as the extent to which supers attempt to influence the behavior of members of a social unit by means of directives. Their *success* in influencing behavior is not fully covered by the dimension; it obviously depends on a great many more factors than "attempt to influence" (including other dimensions of authority patterns). In the first instance, however, the *extent* of supers' influence depends on how "directive" they are: how much the supers attempt to regulate by directives and, as we see presently, on how many levels beyond the mere issuing of directives they make the attempt to influence subs.

Directiveness is plainly a continuum: its poles are readily identified (see Fig. 2.1) and, potentially, social units can be located between the poles by interval measures as discriminating as desired. Directiveness is at a maximum when everything done in a social unit is dealt with, in every detail, by rigidly enforced directives. Units near that extreme—it is almost inconceivable that any unit in real life should actually be located at the extreme—can be labeled "totalitarian," or, since that term has been used rather loosely and tendentiously and seems to have incurred disrepute, "regimented." (The military term is apt because military units—and prisons—probably come closer to the maximal pole of the variable than any others.) The minimal extreme is somewhat harder to characterize. A total lack of directives means that there is no authority pattern at all, and it would be vacuous to say that Directiveness is at its lowest when only one directive governs activity in a unit. Perhaps one can best think of minimal Directiveness as a tendency to issue directives only insofar as the existence of the unit clearly requires it. This may be a generally specifiable level, in the manner of "functional requisites," or it may be a level that varies with specific external pressures on social units and their internal purposes. In any case, saying that Directiveness is minimal if all avoidable directives are avoided should not cloud the broad meaning intended. Units approaching that extreme can be labeled "permissive," since all benefit of doubt is given in them to "free" behavior and wide choices of behavior are thus allowed.

Although the general notion of Directiveness seems simple, it can and should be dissected into several components:

1. Most fundamentally, of course, direction requires the existence of orders (commands, imperatives, rules, statutes, etc.) emanating from superordinates. The extent to which items of behavior are dealt with by supers' orders may be termed the *coverage* aspect of Directiveness.[3] In the extreme case of regimentation, this is comprehensive; at the permissive extreme, it is

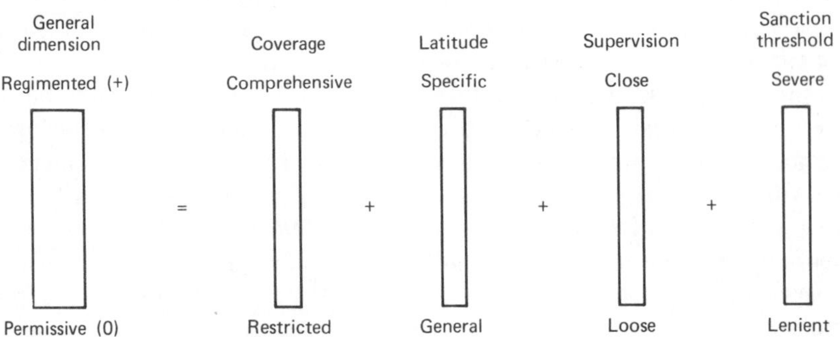

Fig. 2.1. The Directiveness dimension.

restricted to bare essentials. However, orders are not equally consequential for behavior—in fact, the mere existence of orders does not necessarily make them operative directives at all.

2. In assessing Directiveness we not only want to know whether an area of behavior is "covered" by directives but also whether it is covered in greater or lesser detail. An order may leave great *latitude* to members of a unit or it may not: that is, there may be a greater or smaller number of ways of behaving that are in compliance with an order. Since choices are left open by *s*-latitude (i.e., leaving room for discretion to subs), the effect is similar to lack of directives. Latitude may result from vagueness or from the precise setting of wide boundaries. In many cultures, for example, the loose directive "students must be neat in appearance" leaves wide room for choice, whereas the directive "students must wear the school uniform" leaves no such discretion. We thus know little about Directiveness unless we know how general or specific directives are.

3. If Directiveness is measured by the extent to which choices of actions are narrowed, one must also take into account the extent to which *supervision* is used to detect failures to comply. If supervision is lax or absent, members of a unit at least may decide whether to take advantage of the condition. In many cases, no doubt, the very existence of a directive, and any remote possibility of being found in noncompliance, will have a constraining influence—more, of course, if one is greatly attached to the unit and its superordinates than if one is not. Nevertheless, lack of supervision always opens possibilities, always reduces the probability that noncompliance will be costly, and sometimes denotes that an order is merely nominal—in desuetude.

4. If level of Directiveness is judged by effects on behavior, not just treated as supers' wishful intentions, we must deal with the threshold at which *sanctions* are used and their severity when invoked. Directives imply sanctions by definition; but to the extent that sanctions are merely potential choices or implicitly left open, and to the extent that sanctions are lenient when applied, cost-benefit calculations may have the same effect.

Each of these aspects of Directiveness may, for certain purposes, be treated as a distinct dimension. At any rate, all are clearly "dimensional." However, it seems more sensible to treat them in a "value-added" manner: there is a certain logical order among them from the standpoint of their probable behavioral consequences. Coverage narrows choice; latitude narrows it more, supervision still more, and sanction threshold and severity more again.

Two other matters of lesser import (but both possible sources of confusion) should be mentioned briefly. First, it is possible that directives in a social unit will attempt to influence behavior outside the unit as well as in it (e.g., school directives regarding conduct outside the school or military directives prescribing behavior off base). In such cases, one may speak of an *overspill* of authority. Second, Directiveness does not always depend on explicit instructions. Most people in most social units act in accordance with a larger or smaller set of internalized imperatives for conduct, instilled by all the usual processes that make for "conventions." These are generally recognizable to observant outsiders and are nearly always recognizable when behavior is uniform despite a lack of explicit instructions, especially when sanctions are brought into play, by superordinates or peers, against deviations. One could, in fact, make the *explicitness* of directives a separate subdimension of Directiveness; but it is hard to see why explicit prescriptions should have weightier behavioral consequences than implicit conventions. Sometimes they do; often they do not. Incidentally, it is important not to confuse such conventions with what sociologists call "internalized norms." The two often coincide. However, one can be aware of a convention as a directive that is not one's own norm (just as an explicitly prescribed directive may or may not correspond with personal norms), and internalized norms may not be at all akin to directives, but just private conceptions of proper conduct. In actual cases, distinguishing between direct orders, "standing" orders, implicit directives, and internalized norms may cause some difficulties, but the abstract distinctions should be clear enough.

Illustration: Directiveness in German and British Lower-Class Families

A set of German novels set in the late Imperial and Weimar periods was examined for data on authority patterns prevalent in higher- and lower-class families during these periods (by Reepmeyer).[4] The main methodological assumption underlying the exercise was that since novelists tend to be gifted observers who generalize personal experience, the careful reading of fiction can serve as a reasonable substitute for field studies when such activities cannot be carried out. An ancillary assumption was that the risks in treating any novel as a data source can be reduced by using novels as checks on one another and other risky sources of information as checks on overall results.

It was found that in wealthy and aristocratic families, Directiveness by parents in regard to children was remarkably low. Because of this, the switch from quite permissive homes to highly regimented boarding schools was depicted as involving strain and shock—including, for example, an attempted suicide.[5] There was strong contrast between what the novels depict and stereotyped beliefs about German families. Middle-class families (especially "old" middle-class families) fit the stereotype somewhat better. They exhibited comprehensive coverage of children's activities, by specific directives with close supervision; however, the parent actually in charge, the mother—a bit unexpectedly in "Fatherland"—was seldom quick to invoke sanctions, nor was she severely punitive when sanctions were used. In working-class families, however, virtually all the children's activities were "covered," and enforcement was often peremptory and violent: directives were almost always "specific" (not "help your mother" but "wash the dishes," "get some potatoes") and generally supplied even when children had no intention of doing anything else. Parents seemed to assume that noncompliance would follow from lack of constant reinforcement of their directives or from failure to accompany directives with rather explicit threats of physical punishment.

There is reason to think that the German working-class family was far from unique. Even in that paragon of "stable democracies," Great Britain, the close study of lower-class families discloses a kind of Directiveness similar to the German. An example is provided by Josephine Klein's description of family life in Ashton, a coal-mining town.[6] In Ashton, the husband regiments the wife (in regard to his own comforts, not in regard to such other family matters as bringing up the children), in every sense except that of immediate and constant supervision. Apart from insistence on a petty and regular routine in the household, there is an aura of violent retribution in husband-wife relations. The wife compensates by regimenting the children (i.e., making all their activities into daily "routine"[7] or, in some cases, making drastic swings between extreme permissiveness and regimentation[8]).

If relations between supers and subs in working-class families are indeed ubiquitously "regimented," some interesting puzzles may be solved and others posed. For example, we may have a simple and novel explanation of the general finding that members of the "lower strata," supposedly beneficiaries of the libertarian loosening of political restraints (political in the conventional sense), "are relatively more authoritarian, . . . more attracted to an extremist movement . . . and, once recruited . . . not alienated by its lack of democracy."[9] This is most often explained by different levels of education and "sophistication,"[10] either explicitly or by insinuation, on the assumption that the more a person knows, the more he values "democratic" traits. The association leaves a lot of unexplained variance and seems snobbish. A less haughty alternative that needs exploration is furnished by the possibly general existence of regimentation in the most intimate experiences of lower-class persons, and the consequent sheer lack of familiarity with permissive relationships, or bewilderment and discomfort when placed in them. This explanation would be powerful if at least two conditions hold (as seems to be the case). First, it should be true that lower-class families do, in general, regiment their members more than families in other strata. Second, one should be able to explain the greater frequency of regimentation in such families by the peculiarities of the situations in which members of the lower class find themselves (e.g., the discipline necessitated by scarcity and an unusually high domestic workload, crowded conditions in the home, or the transference to the family of workplace experiences). The explanation would become still more powerful if it could be shown that it is the more regimented lower-class members (not the less frequently found members who experience domestic permissiveness) who tend most toward authoritarian values and/or extremist rebelliousness; and it would become nearly irrefutable if regimented members of other classes could be shown to exhibit similar dispositions. The outcome of research into these questions is not a foregone conclusion. At the very least, however, domestic attitudes and behavior in regard to authority have, prima facie, a less mystifying relation to authority elsewhere than variables like "sophistication."

What is likely to occur if supers who come from permissive backgrounds direct subs who come largely from regimented ones? And what can be expected if the opposite occurs? For cases that can suggest answers, one might study Britain's "secondary modern" schools, in which most pupils are lower-class and most teachers not; or the Weimar Republic, in which largely middle-class rulers presided, in a highly libertarian system, over a rapidly growing working class; or American community colleges and free-admission universities, in which the social composition of the student bodies differs vastly from that of the faculty. It would seem that many phenomena that social scientists have attributed to "marginality" might in fact result from contrasts in the class origins of people thrown together in social units and their different experiences with authority in the intimate units that form them.

The question, of course, arises why the British lower classes should not have imperiled democracy while their German equivalents did (anyway, helped to do so). One might find an answer in other dimensions of authority; Directiveness, after all, is not the only component of authority relations. One might also find an answer in greater apathy in particular segments of the British working class, or in the supposed frequency of "deference" to the traditional British ruling class. We do not suggest a solution of this puzzle, but it should be noted that if the proposed solution of the first (working-class authoritarianism) works, the second becomes more mystifying.

Illustration: Directiveness in French Schools

Schonfeld reports that an "authority-laden syndrome" is common throughout the lower grades of the French educational system.[11] An essential ingredient of the syndrome is a high degree of regimentation in the present sense. This includes, in Schonfeld's terminology, a high level of "task, instrumental, and comportmental coverage": in school and out, pupils' time is filled with study requirements; these are defined by detailed national curricula further detailed by school administrators, "senior teachers," and particular instructors. The work is defined in great detail, and so is the manner of doing it (pen to be used, size of margins to be left on pages, etc.); comportment in class is also prescribed with petty precision.[12] There is, in addition, "continuous supervision and a relatively low threshold at which moderately strong sanctions are administered"[13] (e.g., by *surveillants*—proctors, *carnets de correspondance*—weekly evaluations of the child's work and behavior, and *cartes de conduite*—reports especially devoted to matters of misconduct); thus sanctions can emanate from parents as well as teachers.

As pupils enter the higher grades, explicit coverage gradually gives way to "assumed" coverage (i.e., coverage by implicit rules or, as Schonfeld calls it, "internalized direction"). Fewer and fewer directives, especially petty ones, are issued. However, pupils do not perceive this change as involving any marked lessening of coverage. On a scale of 1 to 5, pupils aged 12 to 13 averaged 3.44 in regard to coverage perceptions, and those aged 17 to 18, 3.47.[14] This illustrates exactly the difference between implicit (conventional) directives and internalized norms; the directives are not externally issued but are nevertheless perceived as if they were. However, the shift is associated with other changes. In particular, regimentation in the lower grades is accompanied by the *chahut*, a particular nasty form of rebellious ragging of teachers and disrupting of classes, whereas behavior in the higher grades is markedly less delinquent. Whether this is a consequence of internalization is not clear. Even in the lower grades, teachers who evoke "caesaristic legitimacy"—that is, are perceived as powerful, strong, forceful—tend to be spared the *chahut*, and such teachers may be more common in the higher grades; in addition, Schonfeld suggests that such pure utility calculations as doing well on examinations become more pronounced as pupils become more conscious of the relation between school performance and future careers; thus mischievous impulses are subdued.[15]

Can one deduce a governmental model to match the pattern described by Schonfeld? It would certainly look something like the historic pattern often presented by specialists in French government: a tendency to oscillate between relatively "authoritarian" rule by caesaristic figures and parliamentary near-anarchy, punctuated by rebellion, while the bureaucracy and the petty rules it administers remain highly immobile constants. Schonfeld, indeed, has argued that not only the general outlines of modern French political history but the narrower outlines of the development of the Fifth Republic, and indeed the student rebellion of May 1968, can be matched with (if not in every detail deduced from) the pattern of the educational system. And if this is so, the probability arises that educational authority patterns are a particularly crucial determinant of governmental patterns—a probability already broached in Hyman's pioneering inventory of the literature on "political socialization".[16]

In addition, if educational patterns are generally similar to the French in one respect—in that explicit Directiveness declines with progress through the grades—we may further explain without class snobbery the very common finding that the more highly educated generally exhibit more libertarian preferences and expectations than the less educated. The usual insinuation, as stated, is that these attitudes are due to levels of intelligence and sophistication per se: smarter people have permissive preferences and other admirable biases. But educational patterns may reinforce the less tendentious possibility already raised by characteristics of Directiveness in families: that nothing more invidious than familiarity with less regimented (or less explicitly regimented) patterns of authority is at work. If this is true, associations between nonlibertarian attitudes and educational levels would decline if early education were less regimented or if more people had the chance to pass through the higher levels of education.

In this connection, a country like Sweden might furnish a crucial test case. Friedman's study of "participation" in the schools of that country suggests a pattern quite different from the French (and, I suspect, most others) in the lower grades.[17] There *is* a tendency for patterns to loosen in the libertarian direction in that country too, but from a much more libertarian base. Hence one might well find that less-educated Swedes exhibit tendencies similar to those of better-educated people elsewhere—in which event the less invidious interpretation would be powerfully supported.

Participation

General Discussion

Subordinates need not be merely passive recipients of direction, and they seldom are. Some of them generally attempt to influence the directive activities of supers. Acts by which subs attempt to wield such influence are acts of participation, and Participation as a dimension of authority patterns refers to overall characteristics and measures of such acts in social units.[18]

The dimension is derivable from the definition of authority patterns in two ways. Most simply, although acts of participation are not acts of direction, they do "concern" the direction of social units, thus plainly fall within the scope of the definition. Obviously, describing only what the supers do would be to give a partial account of acts that concern a unit's direction. In addition, it is essential to know about Participation to assess degrees of asymmetry between subs and supers. Asymmetry is inherent in the very notion of superordination but degree is not: it depends on the extent to which supers act in accordance with or contrary to subs' explicit preferences—hence, in large part, their Participation.

Participation is plainly a continuous dimension (see Figure 2.2). As in the case of Directiveness, social units exhibit more or less of it, and distinctions regarding it can potentially be made as discriminating as seems useful.

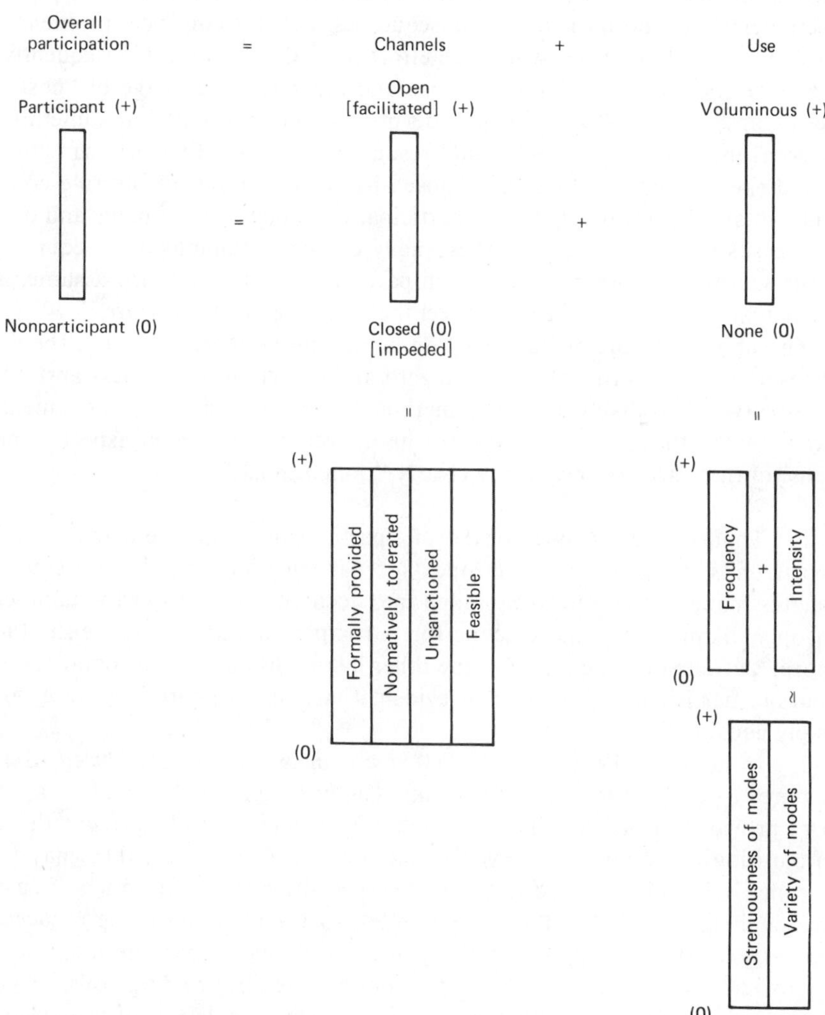

Fig. 2.2. The Participation dimension.

There is, however, a difficulty in specifying the poles of the continuum—also as in the case of Directiveness, but with the difference that in dealing with Participation it is the high extreme that resists exact specification. At the low extreme, Participation is simply zero: all subs are "nonparticipant." The high extreme, on the other hand, lies at (or near) infinity. More Participation is nearly always possible in terms of numbers of subs who participate, numbers of acts of participation, intensity of the acts, or extensiveness of matters one seeks to influence. The upper extreme of Participation could of course be specified by finding a level of it beyond which increments have no measurable consequences; but this empirical problem is probably insoluble or not worth the effort needed to solve it. Consequently, we leave the matter to common sense and imagery. The image of "costs" seems apt: extreme "participants" devote to their participation something approaching the maximum "liquid" resources for action that they can command (i.e., resources other than those absorbed by unavoidable role commitments). This means that their participation is highly continuous and that it consists of a variety of activities, many of them strenuous (i.e., requiring large sacrifices of other values); such participation, one can also assume, is particularly likely to make supers feel that they are under pressure.[19]

The upper extreme of Participation is not elusive merely because the dimension varies in principle between zero and (near) infinity. A less abstract reason (which is likely to cause methodological, especially measurement, problems) is that the dimension can be dissected into several aspects, and some of these are not themselves clearly "dimensional."

1. To begin, when one speaks of "participant" and "nonparticipant" social units, both the *channels* open for participation and the *use* subordinates make of them must be taken into account. The greater the number of open channels, the more scope for participation and, in that sense, the more "participant" the unit. On the other hand, although open channels encourage participation,[20] it is also evident that equal opportunity does not imply equal use.

2. In addition, determining whether channels are *open* or *closed* itself requires a series of separate judgments. Channels may be "formally" open (i.e., provided, or at least not proscribed) by explicit formal rules like those in constitutions or by-laws. Even if not proscribed, however, they may be "normatively" disapproved in the unit (especially by supers), in which case the significance of what the formal rules provide is bound to be reduced; similarly, normative approval will open channels more than the mere lack of formal proscription, or it may counterweigh proscriptions. Two "practical" considerations also matter. One is whether the use of proscribed channels, or failure to use open ones, leads to sanctions. The other is the

feasibility of using apparently open channels. For example, a professor who holds his office hours when students are normally in class, or bed, is in fact closing a channel, not opening it.

Although these four matters (formal rules, prevalent norms, likelihood of sanctions, feasibility) are separable, it should not be insuperably difficult to aggregate them. All, at any rate, relate to the question of the extent to which participatory activities by subs are facilitated or impeded, which is certainly "dimensional." Ultimately, it is a matter reducible to costs: the greater the impediments, the more costly is participation. Friedman thus rightly speaks of "subsidies" to participation, and we could as aptly speak of imposts or tolls on it.[21]

Channels of participation always exist and never can be absolutely abolished by supers who try to prevent participation: even slaves can plead, rebel, or make known their wishes by recalcitrance. Hence to say that channels are open or closed is to use a metaphor for "highly facilitated" or "highly impeded," and the four considerations outlined earlier tell us to what extent facilitation or impediment occurs.

3. Just as the openness of channels requires a series of separate judgments, the extent to which they are used requires that one distinguish two matters. The first is the *frequency* of use: participant acts may be isolated and sporadic, or they may be frequent and continuous. Frequency of participation, however, leaves in doubt the question of how *intensively* subs participate—in effect, how much, not just how often, they "invest" resources in acts of participation and, by extension, how intensely they value what they seek to accomplish by participating and how much "pressure" they exert on supers. Intensity and frequency of participation are usually associated; but they are not the same and should be separately evaluated, if possible.

4. In both describing and using channels of participation, one must bear in mind that acts of participation are qualitatively quite various. This raises difficulties of two kinds. Certain acts of participation occur only in certain kinds of social units (e.g., voting, especially in formal elections, and "campaigning"); consequently, for general purposes, specific acts associated with special units must be subsumed to broader categories applicable to all. In addition, acts of participation differ in the "investments" they entail and in the consequences they are likely to have; thus they must be given different weights in any assessment of a unit's position on the overall Participation dimension.

The first problem seems to be soluble by distinguishing four general types of participatory activity. The first may be called *group actions*; its essence is that participants either form cooperative associations for the purpose of influencing supers or join already established groups to achieve their ends by attempting to influence supers through the groups' actions. The second is *direct personal actions*: dealing directly with supers through individual contacts (e.g., personal representations or letters). The third is *indirect personal actions*: using media likely to come to supers' attention (e.g., letters to newspapers). The fourth is *impersonal actions*: activities in which the participant remains anonymous, his actions simply adding a numerical increment to a more general activity (e.g., voting or depositing unsigned criticisms in the suggestion box).[22]

It is, of course, possible to confine general comparisons of social units to such qualitative categories. On reflection, however, it should be apparent that they contain an underlying "dimension"—namely, intensity of participation. They are related to intensity in two senses. First, group actions make by far the greatest demands on participants, impersonal actions by far the least, and between them, direct personal actions are more strenuous than indirect ones. If intensity of preference is related to willingness to incur costs (as it must be, the alternative being unthinkable), we can readily order the types of participant acts on a dimension, even solving an additional problem that has rarely been well handled in political and other studies: how to obtain an objective indicator of intensity. Second, we can assume that intense participants not only use the more demanding modes of participation (which are also more likely to make supers feel "pressured") but a variety of modes, particularly if these include the more strenuous ones. Other things being equal, therefore, the variety of participant activities thus can be used as another means for making the qualitative modes of participation dimensional and obtaining objective indicators of intensity.

Illustration: The Transition from Individual to Group Participation in Swedish Schools

Friedman's study of several Swedish schools presents evidence that between grades 4 and 12 the level of participation changes little if one simply takes into account the proportion of pupils who have "participated" (i.e., tried to influence teachers or school administrators) in some fashion.[23] About nine out of ten pupils actually participated in grade 4 and nearly all did in grade 12; their normative valuation of nonparticipation was close to zero throughout; and the change in willingness to complain to teachers in five hypothetical (loaded) cases was from approximately three-fourths to almost all.[24] If we knew nothing more, we might hypothesize that "participants" are chiefly made in the family at an early age, and include a very large proportion of the population in a country notable for stable democratic government and rather "democratic" relations in other social institutions.

However, the modes of participation become more variegated as pupils progress through school, chiefly by the increasing use of the most demanding mode, group action. Direct individual actions remain virtually constant, at a very high level. Indirect personal actions decline in regard to use of parents as intermediaries but increase in regard to use of other pupils, and change is rather small in both cases. Group action is another matter. The proportion of those who have ever formed groups to influence teachers rises from 4% in grade 4 to 79% in grade 12. Some of this increase is no doubt due to accretion; this always occurs when one asks successively older respondents whether they have "ever" done something (as Friedman did). What makes the increase significant is that a marked jump occurs at grade 10 and continues to grade 12 (38 to 79%), but there is none to speak of between grades 7 and 10 (39 to 38%). Much the same thing occurs in normative valuation of group actions, except that the jump in actual group activity in the last two grades is preceded by a marked increase (which continues in the later grades) in corresponding norms in the previous three. It may also be noteworthy that normative approval of group actions tends to increase sharply before normative disapproval markedly decreases. That is, the increase of normative approval occurs first among pupils who initially neither approve it nor disapprove it; only thereafter are pupils converted away from disapproval.

These findings are not surprising. The family provides little scope for groupist participation; only larger and more complex social units do. And one would not expect to see the automatic use of group activity as soon as children are placed in a context that makes it possible, since group activity presupposes skills that probably must be learned gradually—as well as, apparently, presupposing the prior acquisition of favorable norms regarding it. The school thus seems critical for the development of "variegated" and "strenuous" modes of participating, hence also for overall participation levels and their probable effects. It seems especially critical at ages when dependence on and attachment to the family generally weaken.

The five-nation study of "political" participation by Verba et al. strongly bears this out.[25] Level of education has path coefficients of .23 and .20 to two kinds of groupist participation—"communal" activity (which is virtually identical with our notion of group action) and electoral "campaigning." However, the path coefficient to "particularized contacts" (= direct personal action) is only .11 and that to voting (= impersonal action) is an infinitesimal .01.

Here we have a clue to why, in all cases investigated, those who feel high "civic competence" (namely, ability to influence governmental authorities) increase with level of education and "similar educational groups compared cross-nationally resemble one another at least as much as, and perhaps more than, do different educational groups within the same nation."[26] The clue is: (*a*) that effective participation increases the perception of ability to affect; (*b*) that a greater variety and strenuousness of participatory acts increases pressure on supers, thus also, even if not in perfect proportion, effective influence; and (*c*) that schools, especially at the higher levels of secondary education, are generally crucial for developing tendencies toward high Participation in the composite sense suggested here.

It should be emphasized that schools do not necessarily perform that critical task just by having the requisite conformation. They do so quite dramatically in Sweden. However, Almond and Verba's findings show that in Mexico and Germany (as of 1959) there actually was less willingness to form groups to attain a governmental objective (change a local regulation) among those with "some secondary education" than those with none.[27] Their evidence leaves something to be desired from our point of view: they only ask about unspecified "local regulations," which simply may not loom large in many cases. Nevertheless, it bears out the obvious—that there is nothing automatic about the apparent impact of Swedish schools on modes of participation.

What then makes for that impact? Perhaps it is wrong to look only to the schools themselves for explanation. Friedman's study turns up a curious fact that might be taken to imply that the family, as a cell of society, also plays a vital if rather indirect role. Friedman distinguishes participatory acts along a universality-particularity dimension; in gist, acts are "universal" if they concern the whole unit (e.g., the time when school starts), "particular" when they only concern the individual, and something in between when they concern special segments of the unit to which the participating individual belongs (e.g., the scheduling of an exam). We might expect close correspondence between group actions and universal ends, individual actions and particular purposes; but there is no such correspondence. Willingness to participate for purely "particular" ends starts in grade 4 at 28% and increases by grade 12 to 79%; the figures for "segmental" ends are 34 and 100%, those for "unit ends" 40 and 67%, respectively.[28] More fourth graders thus are willing to participate for unit ends than more particular (selfish) ones. Friedman is so startled by this finding that he dismisses it as "noise." Possibly, perhaps, his astonishment reflects an American cultural bias. Young children in Sweden may have instilled in them a higher concern for overall social units than particular segments and individuals and, as a general group, may discover particular, especially selfish, interests only after a process of "socialization." Families may strongly instill in them a sense of the supremacy of collective over selfish interests, whereas in other societies the opposite seems to occur. Schools, in such a case, while supporting that sense of "unity" (literally speaking), would heighten the sense of segmentation and individuality by using obvious segmental distinctions (by grade) and constant judgments of individual achievement.

A host of further implications can be read into this conjecture. The one that matters here is that preschool experiences and experiences while children are very young may provide dispositions highly conducive to the development of group participation when the context for such participation is appropriate. If family life is laissez-faire, or if the parents are despotic in their individual interests, this would not be the case. It also would be unlikely if the family exhibits "amoral familism"[29]—that is, if it does not instill a sense of being intimately bound to other family (and other) units in the intricate whole that children first encounter when they go to school; there is not much difference between looking out only for oneself and caring only about one's own.

Responsiveness

General Discussion

The complement of the participant sub is the responsive super. Participant subs seek to influence the way supers direct social units; responsive supers are disposed to be influenced by them and to seek out "inputs" from them. Since the extent of being so disposed determines the actual effects of Participation no less than amount of pressure exerted, Responsiveness is an intrinsic aspect of authority patterns for exactly the same reasons that Participation is. Besides, to make sense of the latter one clearly needs to know about the former, since Responsiveness can be a critical "subsidy" granted to or withheld from Participation.[30]

The polar extremes of Responsiveness may be labeled by the familiar term *autocratic*—literally, self-sustained power—and a neologism (for there is no conventional antonym of autocracy), *alterocracy* (see Figure 2.3). Polar autocrats simply disregard all participation by subs or inhibit its occurrence in the first place. They define their own problems and issues, keep their own counsel, issue whatever directives they please, implementing them as they see fit, and ignore or block off "feedback," except for information required to sanction noncompliance. Polar alterocrats exhibit the opposite characteristics; they act in all cases according to what they perceive to be the "public opinion" of social units, counting their own preferences no greater than any others. In both cases, the essential attitudes and dispositions to act involve the perception of a certain identity between superordinates and social units. The difference is that autocrats perceive social units as collective extensions of themselves, and alterocrats see themselves as personal extensions of social units.

Both extremes should be regarded as "limiting cases"—that is, they define the end points of a dimension but are not themselves on it. This is logically necessary in the case of alterocracy. If alterocracy is absolute, there is no effective asymmetry between supers and subs, hence no authority—only a vacuous "superiority" without "control." The case is "limiting" also in an empirical sense, since absolute alterocracy presupposes

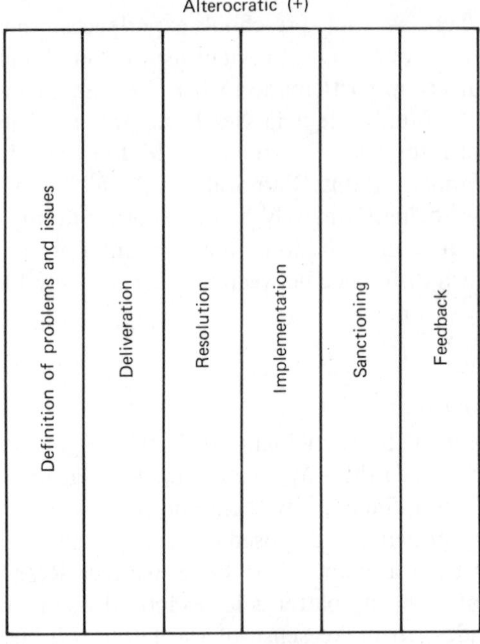

Fig. 2.3. The Responsiveness dimension.

a condition that is wildly implausible: absolutely identical preferences by subs about all matters that arise at all phases of a process of direction. If this condition is not satisfied, supers must at least decide what preferences to entertain and treat as "public opinion"; or they must engineer unanimity out of divergent preferences or work out acceptable tradeoffs and exchanges among them; or they must act where subs lack clear-cut preferences, if action is imperative—all of which leaves scope for control as well as superiority.

Absolute autocracy is a "limiting" case solely for empirical reasons. Absolute autocrats are certainly authorities, but it is virtually inconceivable that instances of such absolutism would be found to be characteristic of social units rather than ephemeral occurrences (i.e., characteristic of isolated supers during transient periods). If nothing else, the dependence of virtually all supers on the services of "lieutenants" makes the case wholly improbable.

In actuality, then, supers will be located along a continuum between being absolutely responsive and unresponsive. That continuum, moreover, poses no complications of the kind that appeared under Directiveness and Participation. The only factor that might complicate locating cases along an undifferentiated Responsiveness dimension is the divisibility of the process of direction into certain phases; Spiro[31] identifies these as the recognition of problems to be dealt with, the definition of "issues" (in effect, contending courses of action), deliberation, and resolution. If we were concerned with direction rather than just policy making, we would of course add implementation, sanctioning, and the reception and processing of feedback from subs. Responsiveness can be high at some phases and low at others. But the qualitative differences involved concern phases of direction and not qualitative aspects of Responsiveness itself, which should reduce the problem of locating units on a single Responsiveness dimension.

Illustration: Responsiveness as a "Subsidy" to Participation in French and Swedish Schools

The French schools studied by Schonfeld present a striking contrast between pupils' norms of Participation and their behavior: the great majority attach high value to Participation but actually participate very little. They see this situation as resulting from the failure of teachers to provide channels for Participation, and Schonfeld's data on Responsiveness bear them out. High Responsiveness is greatly valued by pupils, but teachers are perceived as mainly unresponsive: most are perceived either as "totally" unresponsive or only "mildly" responsive, and this remains constant by grade. The pupils' views accord with how teachers perceive themselves. Asked whether they were totally unresponsive, or mildly, moderately, highly, or totally responsive, the teachers agreed most (almost perfectly) with the second option.[32] Under the circumstances, there is little point in participating, but some point in the mischievous *chahut*.

It would have been interesting to compare data on Responsiveness and Participation among adults in the schools: teachers and their own superordinates. Metraux and Mead's study of French "culture patterns,"[33] suggests a conflicting pattern in the French *foyer*. Husbands are, supposedly, highly responsive to clearly subordinated wives—"the husband is king, but he always asks the advice of his wife and *takes* this advice in the foyer and in business . . .". But neither parent seems responsive to children. It is distinctly possible that adult relations thus inculcate (by example) favorable attitudes toward Responsiveness, whereas generational divisions prevent the attitudes from becoming behavior in certain contexts. It is also possible that this might militate against certain coalitions (e.g., between students and workers).

In distinct contrast, Friedman's Swedish teachers "subsidize" participation. Even in regard to teaching methods, in which teachers might claim special expertise, about one-fourth say they would *always* seek out pupils' views and only one-fourth that they would not. The rest would do so if the matter is "important" or if they themselves were "unsure." More than one-fourth would seek out pupils' advice on any matter whatsoever, and only 4% say they would never do so on any matter.

It will be remembered that Friedman incredulously dismissed the finding that younger Swedish pupils expressed a particularly great willingness to participate where collective rather than personal ends are concerned—matters involving the whole school or classes (which themselves can be considered social units, not special segmental interests, as we generally think of them). We suggested that the cultivation of a sense of collective over personal values might account for this. The data on teachers' Responsiveness strikingly fit this speculation. Teachers particularly expressed a strong valuation of advice by pupils on unit problems: 76% for the school as a unit, 93% for the class, as against only 42% for purely personal matters. They also seemed to value "group actions" greatly and to disvalue equally "indirect personal action" through intermediaries.

Illustration: The Impact of Economic Modernization on Responsiveness in German Families

The novels analyzed by Reepmeyer suggest a possibility that is a good deal less superficial than the stereotyped notion of Germany as a land of autocratic husbands and fathers. Apart from differences among families by class, which go beyond Directiveness, industrialization and its concomitant factors appear to have had a special impact on Responsiveness among those who grew up during the early stages of German industrialization, especially in the bourgeoisie (and, presumably, the working class).

There can be little doubt that fathers were the ultimate superordinates in traditional German families. However, this does not necessarily mean that the fathers were highly autocratic. In families not substantially disrupted by economic change (e.g., aristocratic families) male parents do not appear to have been overweening. They had the last word but apparently did not close off or necessarily disregard subs' preferences, anyway within a rather highly ordered framework of rules and routines.

In the course of rapid industrialization, however, a familiar change rapidly occurred in family life. The intimate association of household and workplace, characteristic of traditional artisanship, farming, and petty commerce, broke down. The father as breadwinner left the household, usually for long and wearisome hours, leaving the mother as substitute super. The father's primacy, however, remained substantially unchanged. Consequently, no figure who could be responsive to children was readily at hand. Inputs from children could, of course, be communicated to the father, but mainly under conditions (fatigue, preoccupation, after having been regimented at work) likely to produce indifference or anger. There appears to have resulted not an excess but a *vacuum* of authority, which is revealed especially on the Responsiveness dimension, not in coverage by directives or sanctions. The very primacy of the inaccessible super, and the rapidity of change, militated against easy and speedy adjustments to the situation.

In general, the theme of reaching out to an unresponsive mother occurs again and again in novels set in the period, often with great poignancy (see Hesse's *Demian*, Glaeser's *Class of 1902*, Carossa's *Eine Kindheit*), especially on the part of sons, since mothers had more discretion in regard to daughters. If this interpretation has merit, the generations that botched Weimar and went berserk under Nazism probably perceived authority more as a passive, implacable, disembodied force than as a tangible despotism, against which one could at least struggle. To check whether this hypothesis has merit, one would want to compare the effects of economic modernization where different family authority patterns prevail.

Compliance

General Discussion

The complement of the directive super is the compliant sub. Directive supers seek to influence the behavior of members of social units; compliant subs are disposed to behave according to their directives. Since the extent of being so disposed is a manifest determinant of the actual consequences of directives, not only for subs but also for the behavior of supers (e.g., in regard to sanctions wielded), Compliance is an intrinsic aspect of authority patterns for the same reasons that the other influence dimensions are.

In locating subs along a continuous Compliance dimension, we encounter a problem that is not posed to an important extent by the other aspects of influence. The problem involves calculations of costs and benefits. A sub may behave in accordance with a directive simply because he has a general disposition to comply with supers; perhaps, however, having weighed the advantages and disadvantages of alternative actions, he has calculated that compliant behavior benefits him most. All kinds of considerations may enter into such a calculation. The sub may calculate without taking supervision and sanctions into account, as if the directive were merely a suggestion. He may also consider the probable costs of noncompliance. Even if these are low compared to benefits, and noncompliance seems to be worth the risk, considerations of diffuse "legitimacy" may lead the sub to comply. Particular directives may, on calculation, seem to call for noncompliance, but perceptions of the net value of an overall structure of direction or set of directives may negate the calculation—or perhaps reduce the probability that any such calculation will be made in the first place.

In the final analysis, of course, anyone addicted to "economic" explanations can reduce to cost-benefit ratios any act of compliance or noncompliance, or any sentiment favorable to such acts. (An ingenious exercise in reducing all perceptions of legitimacy to such ratios is presented by Rogowski and Wasserspring.[34]) However, it should also be evident that three quite different "values" may enter into the ratios: (1) the specific value of the act, all else aside; (2) the more diffuse value of supporting or thwarting a general *S*-structure; and (3) the value of compliance or noncompliance in themselves. Whether one proceeds from economic or other postulates, these values must be identified in ranking units on a Compliance dimension.

Empirically, the matter can be handled in several ways. For example, one might assume that compliance at least denotes absence or weakness of noncompliant dispositions. It seems clear, however, that conceptually Compliance is a dimension that involves "true opposites"—that is, it varies on a continuum whose zero point is located in the middle, not at the low extreme. At the highest (+1) level, which might be called *submissiveness*, compliance as such is an overriding value: directives are complied with simply because issued by authorities. At the lowest (−1) level, which might be called *insubordination* (in the most literal sense), the value of noncompliance overrides other considerations. At the zero point, which might be called *indifference*, calculations of immediate specific costs and benefits have full play. Between the zero point and the high extreme, one can potentially identify different degrees of *allegiance*.[35] By this is meant the extent to which dispositions to comply as such, plus positive perceptions of legitimacy, keep subs from calculating the costs and benefits of compliance with specific directives in the first place, or favorably affect such calculations. At about the midpoint of that half of the overall dimension, legitimacy perceptions most outweigh general tendencies toward submission to authorities; thereafter such perceptions are gradually replaced by specific cost calculations. Below the zero point one can, potentially, identify different degrees of *opposition* on exactly the same basis.

The dimension, a bit curiously perhaps, presents us with three "limiting cases": the zero point as well as the two extremes. This is because by definition some perception of "legitimacy" is intrinsic to directives, thus to authority. The "indifference" point therefore denotes total absence of authority. One might instinctively resist the notion of three limiting cases, but it seems improbable that social units, as defined, will often or ever fall exactly at the extremes, which define systems of pure force, or in the middle, which defines a system of pure exchange relations in which power to back directives with sanctions is at most one of several currencies.

Figure 2.4 represents in rather rough fashion the considerations just discussed. Readers should particularly note two things:

1. The figure distinguishes between "dispositions" to comply and "determinants" of compliance behavior. It does so precisely because in various degrees, utilitarian calculations can determine compliance, no less than unconditional dispositions to comply or not to do so, as well as the conditional dispositions that rest on legitimacy perceptions. For this reason, assuming correspondence of subjective dispositions and actual behavior, while always risky, is particularly likely to be misleading in the case of Compliance. The dimension, in consequence, is meant to capture tendencies to comply or not to comply that do not rest on highly precarious judgments of egocentric advantage. Compliance behavior can certainly be used, cautiously, as an indi-

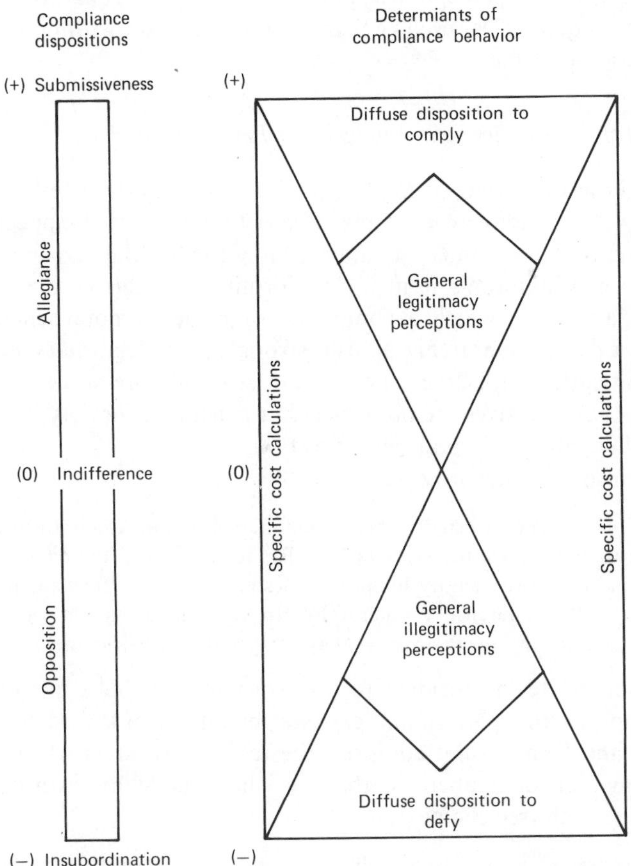

Fig. 2.4. The Compliance dimension.

cator of this: people who always comply, or never do so, or comply about as often as not, certainly will be easy and safe to locate at the limiting points of the dimension; in other cases, however, circumspection is imperative.

2. The figure is particularly rough in indicating the likely mixtures of the three determinants of compliance behavior at various points of the "dispositions" dimension. It merely shows that as the diffuse disposition to comply with supers declines, it is replaced increasingly by a mixture of specific cost calculations and legitimacy perceptions; and it demonstrates further that legitimacy perceptions themselves play first an increasing role, then a declining role, in relation to specific cost calculations, as allegiance declines to indifference. (The same, as stated, applies to the "opposition" half of the dimension.) No specific quantities should be read into the representation. For example, we do not contend that at the midpoint of allegiance, legitimacy perceptions and specific cost calculations play approximately equal roles, even though Figure 2.4 as drawn might make this interpretation possible.

Illustration: Compliance in English and French Schools

Rupert Wilkinson's study of English public schools in the late Victorian era (1870–1914)[36] provides an example of a set of units that appear to have exacted and obtained something approaching the "submissiveness" extreme of allegiance. Wilkinson's term is "conformity"; by this he means a set of behavior patterns in which a compound of rather remote benefits (being trained to rule in a hierarchic polity), strong diffuse legitimacy perceptions (i.e., identification with "the school"), not-so-subtle pressures to fit in, and a pretense that directives are not orders but general "propriety," produced a virtually thoughtless acceptance of direction.

In Wilkinson's own words:

> ". . . the public schools usually made their members want to conform to the pattern of life that the authorities prescribed. By devious ways, the education system taught the individual to identify his private desires with a mystical fondness for the community and a deference to hierarchy. In the end, it taught them to enjoy cooperation and loyalty for their own sake, irrespective of their context."

Wilkinson relates an incident in his own public school experience which both exemplifies this pattern and exposes the fallacy of the assumption that "coercion and formal rules comprise the main constraints which authority can put on individual liberties; that he who acts of his own consent invariably acts with free choice."

> "At Winchester it was frequently said—by boys as well as Masters—that membership in the Combined Cadet Force was 'non-compulsory.' This belief was

firmly, and I am sure sincerely echoed by the Master commanding the Winchester 'Corps' in his recruiting address [at which attendance was compulsory]. One part of the address went approximately as follows: 'I do want to impress upon you that the Corps is *not* compulsory. You are quite at liberty not to join. If you do not join, I don't honestly know what we'd do with you . . .[pause for thought] 'it's so seldom happened. But I'm sure we'd find something . . . digging potatoes or something.'"

Wilkinson notes that this statement was not overtly coercive, and digging potatoes not all that odious an alternative to the Corps; something more subtle was at work.

> "Quite simply [the recruiting address] stated that there was no traditionally sanctioned, socially respected alternative to service in the Corps. The argument was effective because it was not operating in a vacuum. New members of the school had quickly learned from the regular testimony of housemasters and prefects, that the Corps was a school 'Institution' and that it was a 'bad notion'—i.e. 'bad form'—not to join. In reality, it was more than a 'bad notion'; it was virtually unthinkable."

Wilkinson also reports that with the exception of the medically unfit, everyone in his House, and probably everyone at Winchester, joined the Corps when he was there.

Wilkinson argues more generally that group loyalty and commitment were fanned "by making the individual value himself only as a part of the group and as a part of the historical continuum." Only insofar as the individual

> ". . . contributed to the community and deferred to traditions did his actions carry meaning. If he failed to contribute, if he failed to defer, he was liable to be scorned by his fellows and occasionally even punished by the prefects."

One can see why such a pattern would not lead to petty cost calculations in regard to authority, but less easily why it did not produce slavish people, or tyrants. The standard explanations probably hold. The authority of the School was more institutional than personal, "identification" was cultivated more than blind obedience, and authority was mediated, or directly enforced, by peers (the prefects) through whom pupils, in a sense, "participated." Judging from novels and memoirs that deal with late Victorian public schools, mischievousness toward masters, approaching the level of the *chahut*, seems to have been common. And coverage was not provided by streams of petty directives; rather, considerable latitude was allowed. The pattern is one of conforming rigidly to the basic expectations of an institution, not petty personal tyranny.

The French schools studied by Schonfeld (including some elite institutions, somewhat analogous to the English schools, the *lycées* or *lycée* sections) exhibit a much more "utilitarian" pattern of compliance. Schonfeld discovered that "indifference" toward compliance with rules and orders is by all odds the most common norm—55% as against only 26% who value compliance and 18% who value "defiance."[37] One would deduce from such a normative foundation that, as a rule, the same students would alternately conform or be disobedient, in accordance with perceived costs and/or benefits. The evidence, although not as direct or voluminous as one might like, points exactly to such a situation. Three points are particularly apropos. (1) As students approach the final year of secondary school, when fateful examinations are scheduled and learning becomes a matter of immediate utility, the incidence of defiant disobedience as measured by frequency of the *chahut* and number of teachers subjected to it, drops abruptly. (2) Variations among teachers who are *chahuté* also suggest a highly instrumental orientation, especially as final matriculating exams approach. The largest category consists of teachers with "weak personalities"—which can be taken to mean "teachers whom it is not dangerous to cross," although Schonfeld stresses that teachers with "strong personalities" are not notable for actual punitiveness (punitive supers confronted by calculating subs rarely are). The next largest category consists of teachers with "insufficient competence"—that is, teachers not likely to contribute to one's own competence. The proportion of such teachers who are *chahuté* increases sharply as the final year is approached and most steeply of all in the final year. Next, displaying the same temporal pattern, come teachers who teach "unimportant subjects"—unimportant, that is, for final examinations. (3) The largest proportional drops in teachers who are ragged occur in regard to "newcomers," "substitute teachers," and "women," all categories unrelated to ability (or inability) to help achieve favorable results on examinations.[38]

Of course these findings describe proportions and tendencies, not absolutes. Defiant behavior also varies (slightly) with "satisfaction" with one's school, which may be either a matter of calculating advantages or a more diffuse sentiment of identification. And the more frequent ragging of "weak personalities" may be due to legitimacy sentiments, rather than a perception of low risk. Schonfeld speaks of "caesaristic legitimacy," although the evidence for its existence is the behavior described, not anything independent of it. In general, however, the findings support the supposition of a dominant utilitarian mode of behavior better than alternatives.

It is often held that Englishmen, especially of the elite, are highly pragmatic and calculating in matters of politics, whereas the French are dogmatic and impulsive. Perhaps; but if so, one wonders when and how the British come by their pragmatism, and when and how the French lose theirs.

A quite different contrast between French and English schoolboys may explain more. English pupils during the late Victorian era seemed to perceive the whole school as a "facility" for success, or otherwise admirable, but in the main, contemporary French youths reserve such perceptions for individual teachers. This is precisely the difference between reliable allegiance based on "legitimacy" and tenuous compliance based on immediate, petty cost calculations. The "caesaristic legitimacy" enjoyed by forceful individuals in the French schools should perhaps be regarded as no legitimacy, properly speaking, since it does not involve a judgment on the rightness of the overall authority pattern of a social unit. At the very least, such selective judgments of legitimacy should be distinguished from those that are more general, and thus may be extended to supers who do not live up to ideal models of worthy superordinates. People who learn early in life to perceive the legitimacy of complex organizations can be expected, as adults, to behave differently from those who learn only to perceive legitimacy in particular individuals. Specifically, it may be suggested that all legitimacy, including that of governments, will be precarious if legitimacy perceptions remain selectively "individual" during people's formative years. Britain and France certainly seem to fit this very general hypothesis.

Notes

1. The dimensions introduced in this chapter are treated less elaborately than those dealt with in subsequent chapters. The reason is that the dimensions of influence are elaborated on again in Part III, Chapter 11, to illustrate how to proceed from definitions to empirical operations.

2. Capital letters are used throughout for such conceptual labels to denote that the terms are used in special senses—although the sense of the concepts often closely corresponds to familiar usage. This is fairly standard practice in social science, to signal that familiar terms may be used in somewhat unconventional ways.

3. Supers' orders include not only those issued by incumbents of superordinate roles at the time of study but also a unit's "standing orders," so to speak: those issued in the past and still in force.

4. Thomas Reepmeyer, *Authority Relations in the German Family During the Weimar Era*, senior thesis, Princeton University, 1972.

5. Sybille Bedford, *A Legacy* (New York: Simon & Schuster, 1957), p. 74 ff.

6. Josephine Klein, *Samples from English Culture* (London: Routledge & Kegan Paul, 1965).

7. *Ibid.*, p. 116.

8. *Ibid.*, p. 470.

9. See Seymour Martin Lipset, *Political Man: The Social Bases of Politics* (Garden City, N.Y.: Doubleday, 1960), p. 101 ff. for a marshaling of the evidence for this proposition.

10. E.g., by Lipset himself.

11. William R. Schonfeld, *Youth and Authority in France: A Study of Secondary Schools* (Beverly Hills, Calif.: Sage Professional Papers in Comparative Politics, No. 01–014, 1971), p. 27 ff.

12. *Ibid.*, pp. 15–17.

13. *Ibid.*, pp. 18–19.

14. *Ibid.*, pp. 36–38.

15. *Ibid.*, p. 48.

16. Herbert H. Hyman, *Political Socialization* (New York: Free Press, 1959).

17. Robert S. Friedman, *Participation in Democracy: A Theory of Democracy and Democratic Socialization*, Ph.D. thesis, Princeton University, 1972.

18. "Attempting" to influence, it should be noted, implies intention. The dimension thus does not refer to any and all consequences that subs' behavior have on supers, and it does not correspond to some writers' notion of "control" (e.g., Dahl's). We are concerned here with direction, not causality.

19. This conception of high Participation implies that in comparing the participation of individuals, their overall resources and other unavoidable role commitments should, ideally, be taken into account. If this were done, some familiar distinctions between levels of participation by class and occupation might vanish—or at least be readily explained.

20. They are not absolute requisites for it; we all know that some people sometimes use channels of participation closed by supers, even at risk of the most severe sanctions.

21. This, like the question of "liquid" resources, raises the intriguing possibility that less absolute participation in some units is relatively more "participatory" than more of it in others, because of impediments or absence of facilities. As far as we know, the whole extensive literature on political participation makes nothing of this. The idea raises a host of (overlooked) theoretical possibilities.

22. We developed these categories independently, but they resemble those of Sidney Verba, Norman H. Nie, and Jae-On Kim in *The Modes of Democratic Participation* (Beverly Hills, Calif.: Sage Professional Papers in Comparative Politics, No. 01–013, 1971). Their categories are voting, campaign activity, citizen-initiated contacts, and communal activity. Differences between their categories and ours can be explained by noting that they are solely concerned with polities, not any and all patterns of authority.

23. Friedman, *Participation in Democracy*, Ch. III.

24. The hedging words "nearly" and "about" are due to a (remarkably small) number of "no answer" responses on questionnaires.

25. Verba et al., *The Modes of Democratic Participation*, p. 7.

26. Gabriel A. Almond and Sidney Verba, *The Civic Culture* (Princeton, N.J.: Princeton University Press, 1963), pp. 204–208.

27. *Ibid.*, p. 207.

28. Friedman, *Participation in Democracy*, Ch. III, pp. 40–46.

29. Edward C. Banfield, *The Moral Basis of a Backward Society* (New York: Free Press, 1958).

30. It seems strange that political science should have produced a vast special literature on Participation but none at all on Responsiveness. It also seems strange that the "sense of civic competence" should have been related again and again to such variables as education or socioeconomic status and not to the responsiveness of governmental structures. The most simple explanation of variations in sense of civic competence is that ability to obtain responsive results varies from polity to polity and among social segments. The usual implication is that variations in feelings of competence issue from deeper causes. Obviously this need not be so.

31. Herbert J. Spiro, *Government by Constitution* (New York: Random House, 1959), pp. 23–26.

32. Schonfeld, *Youth and Authority in France*, pp. 19–24, 58–60.

33. R. Metraux and M. Mead, *Themes in French Culture* (Stanford, Calif.: Stanford University Press, 1954).

34. Ronald Rogowski and Lois Wasserspring, *Does Political Development Exist*? (Beverly Hills, Calif.: Sage Professional Papers in Comparative Politics, No. 01–024, 1971). For a later, more elaborate, tighter treatment, see also Rogowski, *Rational Legitimacy* (Princeton, N.J.: Princeton University Press, 1974).

35. Note that in Chapter 16 we treat "allegiance" as dependent on authority variables, whereas we treat it here as one of those variables. There is no contradiction, since aspects of authority can causally depend on others, and since this aspect of authority patterns can also be considered an aspect of how well they "perform"—the subject of Chapter 16.

36. Rupert Wilkinson, *The Prefects: British Leadership and the Public School Tradition* (London: Oxford University Press, 1964). The quotations below appear, respectively, on pages 38, 177, 177–178, 178, and 42.

37. Schonfeld, *Youth and Authority in France*, p. 29.

38. *Ibid.*, p. 56.

CHAPTER THREE

S-s Relations: Dimensions of Inequality

Nature and Derivation of the Inequality Dimensions

By definition, superordinates are both "superiors" and "controllers" in social units. Purely nominal superiors are not superordinates; generally they merely symbolize the existence of social units, latently promote identification with them, and perform ceremonial functions. Controllers who are not superiors wield force, power, or influence, or are simply causal agents; they do not exercise authority.

The influence dimensions, broadly speaking, tell us about the extent of supers' *control* in the units they direct: the amount of control they attempt to exert and the amount actually exerted (when compliance is taken into account), modified by due consideration of subs' own participation in the processes by which they are directed and supers' responsiveness to their inputs. The inequality dimensions, on the other hand, allow us to investigate the extent of supers' *superiority:* the steepness of the "hierarchical order" that separates supers and subs. It should be noted immediately that this does not refer to the "nature" (or "shape") of hierarchical order in social units—that is, the characteristics of organizational blueprints and the like, or the number of ordinal grades between those who occupy the highest and lowest positions in a unit. These matters are covered by another dimension (Conformation) under another general heading. Rather, the inequality dimensions are concerned with the actual space, so to speak, that separates supers from subs. The vertical lines on organization charts and their equivalents indicate only that such space exists, not how much.

The notion of inequality is intrinsic to that of hierarchic order, thus is as plainly contained in the definition of authority patterns as are the influence dimensions. One possible objection to treating *S-s* inequality separately, or at all, should be disarmed at the outset. There can be little doubt that normally degrees of inequality and influence are closely associated; nor is there any doubt that researchers generally have a greater interest in and attach greater importance to influence relations. However, the close association of the two, let alone their identity, cannot be taken for granted. It is conceivable that high control will be associated with low superiority, or the reverse; and cases in point are not hard to produce. In any event, all questions of association are empirical, not a priori; thus they can be established only by separate study. Moreover one cannot assume that influence will always count for more than inequality; most certainly it cannot be supposed that discrepancies between influence and inequality will be negligible to know about.

In gist: the definition of authority patterns abstractly justifies the inclusion of *S-s* inequalitites in their study; the probability that inequality and influence will be imperfectly associated makes such inclusion advisable in practice; and the possibility that high and low correlations between influence and inequality will have important consequences makes their separate study all but mandatory for many purposes.

At a minimum, inequality between supers and subs consists of the very fact that they *are* supers and subs. Nothing more may be involved; and even that fact may count for next to nothing if supers occupy their positions transiently and on a random basis (e.g. by lot, in frequent and regular rotation). Generally, however, more is entailed. How much more, and in what senses, is largely captured in the dimensions that follow.

Inequality Perceptions: Distance

General Discussion

Distance refers to the perception of differentials in the general worthiness (standing, station, estimability) of supers and subs. To gauge distance, physical or subjective, one must compare the location of two or more points on a scale. In the case of "general worthiness" the scale involves diffuse perceptions of the kind one makes in ranking (usually stereotyping) people or groups, not perceptions of specific traits, like physical strength, intelligence, character, and beauty. Specific perceptions to be sure, can, govern diffuse ones, but they are simply criteria or bases for evaluations that remain diffuse. (The difference is that between considering a person intelligent and considering him admirable, regardless of whether admiration depends on level of intelligence.) It should be evident that if supers rank high on such a scale, Distance between them and subs need not be great—it depends on how subs are ranked. Ditto, of course, for low or middling rank.

Distance is always a continuum along which cases can be located by making distinctions as fine as one deems useful and possible (see Figure 3.1). The low extreme of any Distance continuum obviously is no distance at

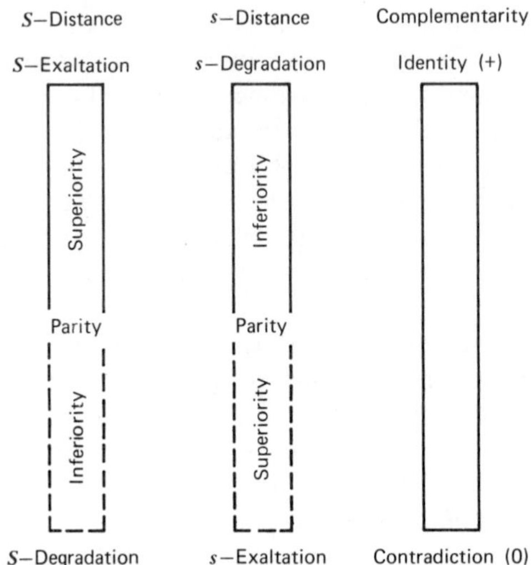

Fig. 3.1 The Distance dimensions. *S*-Distance is the distance that supers perceive between themselves and subs; *s*-Distance is that which subs perceive between themselves and supers. The dotted lines indicate "Distance inversion." Complementarity is absolute if *S-s* and *s-S* perceptions fall at identical points on the two dimensions, as shown. Degrees of complementarity can be ascertained by comparing the points at which the two sets of perceptions fall.

all—in this case, the perception that supers and subs are equally worthy. That extreme may be labeled *parity*. The term seems more apt, although less conventional, than equality, since the facts of being superordinated and subordinated inherently entail an inequality of sorts. But although that inequality is always hierarchic, and generally is recognized as such, superordination, at parity, will tend to be perceived as similar to a merely functional distinction—an aspect of a unity's division of labor, and no more.

The high extreme of any distance scale lies in infinity; what needs to be clarified is the kind of perception that is tantamount to "infinity" in the diffuse evaluations human beings make of one another. Infinite social distance is less abstract than infinite arithmetic distance. It surely exists when a group of people are regarded by another as so sublime, or so debased, that they do not belong on a common scale of worthiness, thus cannot be individually compared with one another in the first place. In such a situation a set of people perceive equal distance between the highest and lowest of their own group and any member of the other. Perceptions of this kind are common when groups regard others as belonging to different orders of being: as subhuman or superhuman, beasts or divinities. The sentiment exists in slave societies. It is approached in theocracies. It generally divides tribal conquerors and those they conquer and rule. And it is the very essence of caste systems: in "pure" caste systems there is an ordinal jump, irreducible to comparative quantities, between each caste, even if each caste is ranked as higher or lower in relation to every other in the overall system.

The opposite pole of *S-s parity* thus is the *degradation* of subs and the *exaltation* of supers. Both labels fit literally: they denote being beneath gradation (in biology "degrading" means reducing to a lower form of life) or being qualitatively above it.

To say that Distance involves diffuse perceptions means that it is intrinsically a simple scale, not compounded of a number of distinguishable scales. Nevertheless, there are aspects of Distance that it is either advisable or necessary to deal with separately.

One of these is the *bases* of Distance already mentioned. For purposes of rich description, as well as certain comparisons and theories, we may want to know about these no less than amount of Distance as such; for example, we usually want to know about them to understand *why* Distance is great or small. The bases on which Distance perceptions may rest are not themselves reducible to a dimension; they are qualities potentially as various as the traits of human beings. However, one can expect Distance to be greater when the decisive qualities on which perceptions of it rest are "ascribed" (i.e., not capable of being achieved, but intrinsically part of a person by birth or upbringing) than when they are "acquired." Certainly it is hard to think of cases at or near the extremes in which ascriptive bases do not play an exclusive or dominant role, or of cases at parity in which they do.

A more important point, which is essential for correct (not just rich) description, is the *two-dimensionality* of Distance. Two separate measures must always be reported: supers' perception of Distance between themselves and subs (*S*-Distance) and subs' perceptions of it in relation to Supers (*s*-Distance). Any simple aggregation of the two sets of evaluations in a single overall measure will be misleading, and in the most extreme case will be absolutely misleading. Suppose, for example, that one assigns a positive value (say, +1) to exaltation and the same negative value (−1) to degradation; and suppose that supers and subs both regard themselves as exalted and the others as degraded. Then an aggregate measure would report overall distance at absolute parity—a perfect misrepresentation of the case. Something is "equal" in it—namely, disdain—but that kind of equality surely is not parity in our sense. Such an extreme situation is perhaps inconceivable (although the case of the gypsies, discussed below, seems to be an instance of it); but it does show why *S*- and *s*-Distance are entirely separate matters.

It is also important to note that *both* the *S* and *s* perceptions of Distance can run all the way from the low to the high extremes—as the hypothetical example indicates. We might think that both would stop at parity, and no doubt in the great majority of cases supers at least do not perceive themselves as less estimable than subs or subs perceive themselves as more estimable than supers. But nothing compels this. Distance perceptions may be *inverted*, in that the superiority intrinsically entailed by superordination will be confined to a perception of formal hierarchy in functional units, without being extended beyond this to a more general sense of worthiness.[1]

Distance inversion is only likely where two separable aspects of the perceptions of Distance become entangled. These may be called *unit-specific* and *general social* Distance. Unit-specific Distance is that perceived between roles in functionally narrow segments of society (e.g., between teachers and pupils, *qua* teachers and pupils, in schools); general social Distance involves perceptions of whole persons in the broadest social contexts. Differences between the two aspects of Distance depend, of course, on the clear-cut functional differentiation of societies and the concomitant ability fully to distinguish special "roles" from general "positions."[2] Consequently, it is seldom possible to disentangle these aspects of Distance absolutely, particularly since either kind of Distance perception can enhance or diminish the other—which is not to say that the attempt to distinguish them is not worthwhile.

Distance-inversion is *most* likely where the bases of perceiving general social Distance are largely ascriptive and those for unit-specific Distance largely of the achieved variety. Implicitly, then, Distance inversion is likely to be found, and to be significant, in imperfectly "modernized" societies—either those in transition or those that join "modern" and "traditional" forms in some sort of symbiosis. Even in such societies it is likely to be confined to certain social units and certain members of the units, that is, units that are narrowly specific in function and in which some subs are likely to be recruited from strata above those from which supers generally originate.

Although the *S* and *s* aspects of Distance must always be dealt with separately, there is one way in which they can be used to report a single measure of Distance. By comparing the two aspects, a measure of their *complementarity* can be arrived at, and this itself is a continuous dimension with readily specifiable extremes.[3] Complementarity is absolute (at "identity") if *S*-Distance equals *s*-Distance (e.g., if both perceive parity); lesser complementarity is simply the difference between one set of perceptions and the other; and the low extreme ("contradiction") occurs if there is mutual disdain and self-glorification, as in the hypothetical case given earlier. Measures, or decent estimates, of complementarity are advisable because of the likely impact of the phenomenon on the operation of authority—not least, its characteristics on the four influence dimensions.

Illustration: Distance and Bureaucratization in an American Factory

In two studies,[4] Alvin Gouldner reports on work relations during the period 1948–1951 at a General Gypsum plant in a small, midwestern American town. The plant consisted of a mine and a surface installation; in both places *s-S* perceptions of Distance seem to have been very near "parity" and, during the earlier part of the period, almost "identical" between subs and even the highest superordinate, the plant manager. The lack of perceived Distance is evident in terminology used by both subs and supers. Doug (the plant manager) was called "intimate" with the men; the men felt they could get "close" to him; the production manager considered himself "no better than any of the plant workers." On the whole, parity was even more closely approximated in the mine than on the surface. Gouldner observes that the surface men preferred to keep a certain distance (his term) from foremen, treating them as impartial "fathers," whereas miners treated their supervisors as "brothers." The whole plant was redolent of small-town American informality and intimacy—the "one big happy family" of American rhetoric. Acting like a "big shot," "showing who was boss," being formal in any way (particularly, insisting on the use of bureaucratic channels and observance of the company's formal rules), were regarded as breaches of propriety, especially by subs, but apparently also by supers.

This pattern was violated when a new plant manger, one Peele, was installed. By insisting on observance of the company's bureaucratic rules, Peele created a much more formal, "business-like" atmosphere. He was apparently respected and does not seem to have been markedly despotic or conceited. But he introduced bureaucratic impersonality and, with it, Distance, at least in the sense that it exists on formal organization charts. The resultant decrease of complementarity in perceived Distance (as it appeared to the workers) poisoned the atmosphere in the plant, even between subs and lesser supers. In 1950 matters came to a head in a wildcat strike, whose the immediate cause clearly involved change on the Distance dimension. The strike was precipitated by a supervisor who swore at one of the men. In itself, swearing was not considered intolerable—only if it was "serious." In determining what made swearing serious, the men drew a distinction between friendly, egalitarian invective and the kind that implies diffuse distance. In the words of one worker: "If a guy is ugly he swears to agitate you. *To show you he's better than you.*" Swearing, moreover, carried a latent implication of invidiousness on the surface, where the strike broke out: it was particularly associated with the "groundhogs" or "low-caste" miners working below ground. (Working below ground seems to imply inferiority even in highly egalitarian societies, just as being high up—the penthouse—has an aura of superiority.) The strike can thus be viewed as withdrawal of compliance in retaliation for change in a long-accustomed pattern of high complementarity at a very low level of Distance.

One must be very cautious in drawing object lessons from the case. Gouldner seems to treat it as a basis for attacking increased bureaucratization as responsible for increasing Distance, reducing complementarity, thus adversely affecting the performance of industrial units. No doubt this holds for the General Gypsum plant. However, it should be plain that bureaucratization can have effects on perceptions of Distance, hence also on their consequences, precisely opposite to those described by Gouldner. If complementarity is low at the outset, the strict observance of bureaucratic forms on both sides will surely tend to increase it. There also is no reason to suppose that bureaucratization will always heighten perceived Distance. Nonbureaucratized social units may well operate like intimate families, but they can also operate as systems of castes or estates. Bureaucratization at least puts people on the same map, inhibiting arbitrary despotism no less than informal leniency.[5]

Illustration: Distance Perceptions in Swedish Families and Schools

If low Distance between rulers and ruled is a requisite of highly participatory democracy, the extreme importance of Swedish schools in the development of attitudes requisite to such democracy again emerges in Friedman's study. So also does a point that bears (indirectly) on the argument that attitudes normally associated with bureaucratization can lessen subs' perception of Distance vis-à-vis supers.

At grade 4, Distance in the Swedish family seems rather high, and about equally high in schools. (This does not imply that Swedish parents are cold and remote; in fact, as we shall see, just the opposite underlies the perception of Distance by children.) About 90% of the children Friedman studied "look up" very much or rather much to parents (both of them) and about 80% to teachers. It is tempting to treat this attitude as inherent in age differences and dependency, but plausible as the notion is, it is wrong—at any rate less right than might be thought. It is true that as children pass through the grades of school, the Distance they perceive vis-à-vis teachers steeply and continuously declines; by grade 9 the proportion of pupils who look up a good deal to teachers is only about 20% and thereafter remains fairly constant. A decline in looking up to parents also occurs, but it is not nearly so steep: at the same ages it is at 60 to 70%, with significant decline only at a particular point in late adolescence (between grades 10 and 11). Thus it is in the schools that Swedish supers are first perceived without an aura of large "superiority," in rough parallel to increases in the variety and intensity of Participation. There is, at most, very limited spillover from the schools to the families, despite a steeper decline in dependency on parents, which makes this all the more significant.

Searching for factors that might account for these different developmental tendencies, one notices that parents can count on two "bases" for favorable overall perceptions (age aside), but teachers can command only one of them. Parents are perceived as "empathetic": that is, as having intimate knowledge of the child and being able and willing to help with problems; they are also perceived as having a kind of general "expertise" (special knowledge, wisdom, experience). Teachers, we may assume, command only the second basis, anyway to the same extent as parents; thus their superiority might be considered more vulnerable, as well as especially conditional on continuous proof.

The matter, however, is not so simple. The expertise children perceive in their parents (e.g., on questions of politics or religion) declines very sharply and approaches nil in late adolescence, rather unlike the expertise of teachers. Empathy, on the other hand, remains consistently high, and changes in it parallel changes in overall perceived Distance—not absolutely, but in fairly close association. This is worth noting, first, because it suggests that two bases of Distance do not necessarily make for more Distance than one; it depends on what the bases are. Second, and more important, it implies that specific, achieved bases of Distance are more tenuous than rather diffuse, ascriptive ones. Since Distance involves diffuse perceptions, this is hardly surprising; but it does reinforce the point that bureaucratization can lessen Distance through the specific achievement values it entails, at least when, initially, perceptions of this factor are far removed from parity.

It appears that the increased significance of achievement values can also work toward parity from the opposite direction. In the lower grades, Schonfeld's French school children exhibited almost as much "inverse" Distance (34%) as the opposite (27%)—the rest (39%) being at or near parity. In the higher grades, however, when the "utility" of teachers becomes more important than ascriptive traits (like sex), distance inversion was much less frequent (18%) and parity much more so (56%).[6]

Illustration: Exaltation and Degradation as "Limiting Cases": Untouchables and Gypsies

In the case of intact caste systems there is virtually perfect complementarity in Distance perceived by high and low castes. The one is seen as exalted, the other as degraded, and the interactions of the two (e.g., in Baderi, a village in eastern India, as described by Bailey[7]) indicate that they do not see themselves as belonging to a single species, any more than gods and men, or humans and animals. In Baderi, for examples, food touched by the low caste is "polluted," and the low caste itself helps to ensure that members of the higher caste do not touch it. The low caste is herded into ghettos. When addressed, its members are expected to behave, and do behave, in a silly way, like children. They are always addressed in the familiar; they always reply in the honorific. They must sit or squat when a member of the high caste deals with them, and they do so. Only dirty and despicable tasks are allotted to them or done by them.

This situation is exactly reversed in the case of the gypsies. Long regarded as subhuman (dirty, childish, useless, corrupt, satanic, irrational) by people among whom they travel, they reciprocate in kind. Clébert's study of the gypsies—the only decent study done from the inside—brings out the subjects'[1] perceptions of nongypsies as degraded and only themselves as properly "human." (Their myth of man's origin, for example, treats both whites and blacks as miscreations. God, the fable goes, made a man out of clay but absentmindedly left the clay too long in the kiln, causing man to come out black. On the next attempt God overcompensated, and the underbaked man came out white. Only on the third attempt did He get man right: like a gypsy.) Consequently gypsies simply *use* nongypsies (e.g. steal their property while respecting their own) and are as squeamish and disdainful toward others as others are toward them.

Where such absolute noncomplementarity prevails, it is impossible to fuse groups in a single social unit and to order them under a single authority pattern. It is interesting to note that the opposite case exhibits the same characteristics, only in a more subtle manner. Slaves are not subsumed to *social* authority patterns but to *individual* masters. In the traditional Indian caste systems, every Pan was "somebody's nigger": a piece of personal property attached to a patron who was personally responsible for his behavior. The people conquered and brought home as *thralls* by the Vikings were similarly subject to personal, not social authority. Such people always remain "outside" social units, even if physically in them; the minimum requirement of civic incorporation—being somewhere on a common scale—is not satisfied.

In these senses, exaltation and degradation, although by no means imaginary constructs, do seem to be "limiting cases" in the study of authority patterns. At most, exalted and degraded people can "belong" jointly only to nuclear social units, and even then, it would seem, only in dyadic (one-to-one) relationships. Their relations can, of course, be gradually transformed. But readers can judge for themselves (assuming that our point is valid) the likelihood of civic incorporation, even with marked inequality, in certain multiracial societies, such as Rhodesia or South Africa. Perhaps this perspective also sheds light on why American Indians, refusing servitude, were exterminated or literally herded into reservations.

Inequality Manifestations: Deportment (and Proximity)

General Discussion

Deportment refers to differentials in the ways supers and subs observably treat one another. As in the case of Distance, such differentials always involve *S-s* and *s-S* relations separately: supers may treat one another differently from subs, and vice versa. In addition, one should keep in mind that differences between the ways people treat one another in the context of authority and how they interact informally will reveal unmistakably the effects of authority relations as such on their conduct. As in the case of Distance also, *S-s* and *s-S* Deportment may be more or less complementary, as well as the inverse of what should usually be expected: less respectful behavior toward subs than toward supers and less constraint or coldness toward one's peers than toward others.

As Figure 3.2 indicates, the behavior of supers toward subs may range from *arrogance* to *familiarity* (with perhaps a tendency, in isolated cases, to something more than familiarity: fawning on the subs). Arrogant supers are

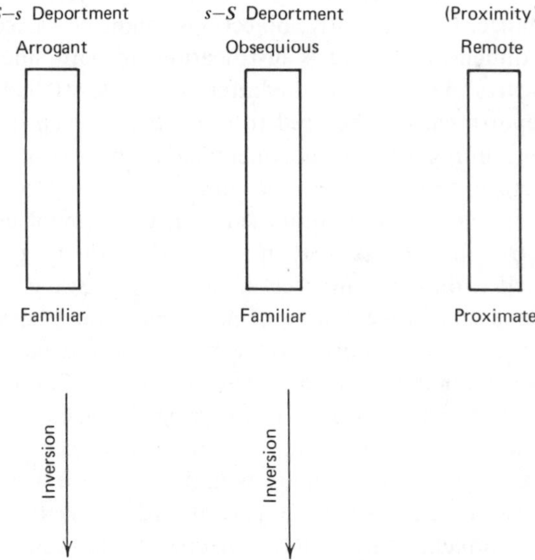

Fig. 3.2 The Deportment dimensions. The parentheses around "Proximity" denote that lack of this factor does not *necessarily* imply high inequality (or high Proximity the opposite), and the permissibility of regarding Proximity as an independent dimension, not just a special component of Deportment.

pretentious and swaggering; they put on what the British call "side." In polite cultures they tend to be cold and haughty, in impolite ones insolent or gratuitously punitive: the difference is rather inconsequential for our purpose, although the one may be found normatively congenial and the other not. It is important to emphasize, however, that coldness and discourtesy are not "arrogant" in themselves—only if they are confined to the treatment of subordinates. Familiarity simply entails treating subs as if they were one's exact equals: partners or friends. Near the middle of the continuum bounded by these two types of behavior, one should expect to find formal courtesy—neither flaunting one's superiority nor acting as if it did not exist.

The complement of the "familiar" super is, of course, the familiar sub, and the complement of arrogance by *S* is *obsequiousness* on the part of *s*. Obsequious subs in effect exaggerate inferiority into servility, whereas familiar subs behave as if superordination, as distinguished from the division of functional roles, did not exist; and here again the approximate midpoint is formally correct behavior. The obsequious sub may grovel and debase himself, or he may match a super's aloof *politesse* with excessive unctuousness; the difference again is inconsequential.

Deportment can certainly be regarded as the objective counterpart of subjective Distance. Consequently, objections might be raised to treating it as a separate dimension. There is justification on both sides. Deportment certainly "indicates" Distance. If the latter cannot be studied more directly, patterns of Deportment can be used to infer it; and even if direct study is possible, findings in regard to Deportment should be used as checks or findings as to Distance: to corroborate or question results. However, there are at least three arguments on the other side. (*a*) One cannot use Deportment as a check on Distance unless it is, in any case, studied separately. (*b*) Deportment in itself is only an imperfect indicator of Distance, more useful as a check than as a conclusive source of pertinent data. It should be evident that people who act in a formally correct manner may in fact perceive more, or less, distance than their formal behavior implies. Similarly, arrogance often increases when supers perceive shrinking Distance vis-à-vis subs. (*c*) Deportment can affect the operation and performancce of authority independently of Distance. It is especially bound to do so if a tendency toward formal correctness countervails large perceptions of Distance on either side or lack of high complementarity on the Distance dimensions.

The critical argument for giving Deportment the status of an independent dimension (interrelated with others, to be sure, but not at all the same) is, of course, the second: Deportment is not *merely* an objective manifestation of a subjective tendency. However, one special aspect of the way supers and subs observably treat one another would seem to involve distance in the most straightforward sense: physical separation. This is a facet of behavior particularly emphasized in one of the best (and most influential) interpretative case studies of authority available, Michel Crozier's *The Bureaucratic Phenomenon*:[9] the tendency to attempt to use or avoid direct face-to-face interactions between subs and supers.

Being direct or indirect in *S-s* relations is itself a continuous dimension, which may be labeled *Proximity*. (We shall see shortly why a separate label may be in order.) Supers are highly "proximate" if they let nothing interpose between themselves and subs in regard to actions involving the first two influence dimensions: they directly issue orders to subs, themselves supervise and wield sanctions, and are the immediate targets of participant acts. Beyond this, they also tend to make themselves "available" (in Kornhauser's sense of the term) by fraternizing with subs informally, which, of course, allows either party to use the occasion (lunches, coffee breaks, etc.) for business. Proximate subs reciprocate by using the opportunities supers provide for direct interaction and by circumventing anything formally interposed between levels of a unit's hierarchy. In contradistinction, "remote" supers deal with subs impersonally, through intermediaries, through memoranda, notes, and the like, and through detailed and comprehensive impersonal rules; they cultivate "channels" in the sense of sizable interspaces between themselves and subs. Remote subs reciprocate by themselves avoiding encounters in which direction might take a proximate, personal cast.

Even though Proximity involves distance in its least metaphoric meaning, it is, if anything, a less reliable indicator of Distance in the present sense than other aspects of Deportment. In the first place, it often results simply from the size and complexity of a social unit, including the possibility of the existence of many strata of superordination between the highest supers and the lowest subs. Actually this problem is rather insignificant. By emphasizing "attempts" to use or avoid proximate dealings and taking only real possibilities into account, difficulties arising from size can largely be discounted. It is more important to recognize that supers may practice remoteness for reasons other than their sense of superiority or for reasons that involve superiority in very complicated or ambiguous ways. They may act remotely for the sake of efficiency (e.g., to avoid being inundated by trivial business or to make sure that proper paper records are kept). They may also cultivate remoteness precisely because their sense of actual superiority is less than their formal status denotes: for example, to avoid having to display their relative lack of cultivation, intellectual superiority, or experience. Not least, the avoidance of face-to-face relations may signal an attempt to avoid perceptions of superiority altogether—in effect, attempting to make superordination appear to be a purely "institutional" matter. It thus could be taken to denote low *S-s* Distance quite as readily as the opposite. The problem is illustrated exactly by observing that exalted supers and degraded subs are either almost totally remote (e.g., if subs are herded in ghettos) or totally proximate (as in master-slave relationships).

Despite this, Proximity can and probably should be considered an aspect of Deportment as an inequality dimension and used as an indicator of Distance. Our point is mainly cautionary: amount of Proximity has an ambiguous relationship to both variables, and gingerly treatment is called for to prevent the misinterpreting of observations. One may suspect that the relationship in both cases is curvilinear: for example, neither arrogant nor familiar supers will cultivate remoteness but "formally correct" ones will; and the same for subs. Above all, we do not mean to suggest that Proximity is of little practical consequence—that it can be safely ignored, and all ambiguities of its relation to other matters avoided. Crozier demonstrates that Proximity may have very substantial significance, anyway in his own society.

Illustrations: Some Relations of Deportment to Distance and Proximity

Several concrete expectations can be derived from the abstract points made about the relations of Deportment to Distance and of Proximity to Deportment. One would certainly expect low Distance to be accompanied by familiar Deportment and proximate interactions among supers and subs. One would similarly expect rather arrogant and obsequious Deportment, as well as remoteness, in interactions among highly distant supers and subs. However, instances that involve subtle departures from these expectations (but not necessarily negligible ones) should also be found. The illustrations sketched below exemplify these expectations, as well as providing material for relating conceptual abstractions about Deportment to concrete cases.

Parity, Familiarity, and Proximate Interactions in an American Factory. The General Gypsum plant studied by Gouldner strikingly conforms to the expectation that perceptions of parity and familiar behavior will coincide, and that both will be associated with highly proximate interactions. For all intents and purposes, Distance was at absolute parity in the mine. This was true after, no less than before, the arrival of the new, bureaucratically inclined plant manager: workers and supervisors alike, the miners allowed themselves to be affected by the changes introduced by Peele much less than did the surface men. Familiarity in their observable behavior comes out in the prevalent, indeed exclusive, use of nicknames or jocular pseudonyms. The head of the mine was "Old Bull" to everybody; others were "Woodchuck," "Whistler," "Moonbeam," "Yo-Yo"; a worker named Jacob unaccountably was "Nick"; Benjamin Neal was always "Benjamin Neal!" As among familiars anywhere, cordiality was anything but *de rigueur.* "The miners, whether supervisors or not," writes Gouldner, "expressed their feelings about the person or thing which aroused them, in forceful and eloquent detail." Counting four-letter words, an observer might infer that supervisors were arrogant, but that would be 180° off course; as we saw before, there were two kinds of swearing at the plant. Proximity in behavior, both as norm and fact, was concomitantly great. Gouldner reports, for example, that "main office executives and top plant management ambivalently recounted stories about old miners who disregarded the company's lines of communication, and demanded to see the President of the Company directly when they had a grievance." Workers certainly often bypassed their immediate supervisors, and got away with it.

> "If a miner wished something done, he usually went directly to the man who could do it. After searching around and finding him, the miner would discuss the matter and get his consent. The miner might then go to his supervisor and get his permission, after telling him what already had been arranged. Similarly, Old Bull, the head of the entire mine, might tell a miner to go to the supply room and ask for something. The miner would go, but usually he would not mention that it was Old Bull who wanted the supplies. Nevertheless, these would be given to him without question."

At the same time, informal socializing occurred: drinking at the saloon, hunting and fishing together, bowling on the same team, and so on. The only "proximity" avoided was close, personal supervision on the job, but that entailed lack of Directiveness, not remote control.[10]

Relations on the surface were not quite as "familiar." The men liked supervisors to be friendly but not "too friendly"; they preferred the supers to be neutral foremen, not fully integrated members of their own group. That, perhaps, made the men less vulnerable to the changes introduced by Peele. Nevertheless, they perceived formal correctness and insistence on the use of bureaucratic channels as a deprivation against which, in the end, they responded aggressively. In certain senses, Peele's changes involve manifest deprivations; for example, his predecessor had allowed the men to take company supplies for their own use; Peele always charged them. But the overall impression is that the workers suffered more from the constraint of accustomed ways than the withdrawal of marginal perquisites. The critical point for us is that under these circumstances, courtesy on the part of Peele was interpreted as arrogance, and consequently as an attempt to "degrade" the workers.

This illustrates a "subtlety" in the relation of Deportment to Distance: to understand how the former leads to perceptions of the latter, one must first have a notion of the conduct expected by members of a unit, exactly as in gauging levels of "relative deprivation." Only then can one make sense of the surface men's apparent inference of arrogance and their sharp reaction to what appears superficially to have been a change less disruptive for them than it was for the miners.

It might be noted in passing that a high degree of familiarity (and parity) seems, paradoxically perhaps, to depend on a certain continuity in the formal ranking of unit members. At the General Gypsum plant, rapid passage into and out of hierarchical positions appears to have had an effect precisely opposite to what one might expect. To increase the likelihood that his reforms would actually be installed, Peele resorted to a familiar Napoleonic device: he demoted old supervisors and promoted new men from the ranks. One of the buttresses of the old equality in the plant was precisely the gradual passage of men to higher positions—gradual enough that they never forgot their origins and supervisors did not feel threatened. The new supervisors, however, handled prosperity badly. More than Peele himself, they flaunted their status, pulled rank to let the men know "who was boss;" and with the usual insecurity of parvenus, stood over the men, acted as if they expected insubordination, and stopped informal activities (bull sessions, kidding) as if endangered by them. Predictably, this conduct reached its peak when a new super controlled a former one. In that sense, there is something not quite right with the ancient idea of interchanging subs and supers for the sake of equality and effective rule; for if anything justified the men's exaggerated perception of degradation, it was precisely the behavior of the newest promotees.

Deportment and Distance: Alienation in Feudal Societies. Whereas the General Gypsum plant largely conforms to the expected association between Distance, Deportment, and Proximity, the evolution of certain feudal societies, as interpreted by Gaetano Mosca,[11] does not. Mosca demonstrates that large social Distance need not be manifested in arrogant or obsequious Deportment or in a tendency to avoid proximate interactions. In medieval England, for example, the squires, who were greatly "superior" to the peasants, nevertheless interacted with them as if familiars rather than people apart: they lodged and fed the peasants, "sat with them at their great oaken boards and . . . drank the same beer." Exactly the same thing holds for the Celtic aristocracy in Ireland, the "O's" and "Mc's," who were "one with the peasants in blood, habits, and ideas"—close to them, in a sense, by reasons of interdependence, neighborliness, and common rudeness and ignorance. The status distinction preceded the behavioral one, in these and other cases.

Even more interesting is Mosca's point that milder Deportment by supers can be associated with perceptions of enlarged Distance—and by way of these, rebelliousness. For example, the landowning Polish nobles of the Middle Ages acted in an extremely extortionate, ruthless, and violent manner toward their peasants, yet managed to avoid rebellion as long as they lived among their people, wore the same kind of clothes, exhibited the same (rude) manners, and were similarly superstitious. Rebellion became common only when the nobles became less harsh, but also "frenchified" in their behavior (polite, liberal, and agnostic) and prone to live as absentees. Mosca argues that something quite similar occurred elsewhere in Eastern Europe (e.g., in Russia).

What distorts the association between Deportment and Distance in these cases is, of course, the perception of superordinates as "aliens" or *culturally* distant people; and this is clearly reinforced if in addition to acquiring foreign ways, supers take to living as absentees, whether in another country or simply more among their own kind, in cities or suburbs, than with their inferiors. This kind of "alienation" need not be confined to agrarian and feudal societies. In the General Gypsum plant, for example, the importation of a southerner as plant board superintendent (just before the strike) led to a particular stir among the men and a sharp breakdown in friendship between workers and supervisors. Although the new superintendent was even more devoted to "efficiency at all costs" than other supers, what was perceived most acutely was precisely his coming from the South and his "not knowing how to treat the men." It is all summed up in comments by one of the workers: "He's a *slave-driver . . . used to talking to a lot of niggers,* so he acts superior."[12]

Remoteness and Lack of Complementarity in France. The ability of changes in Proximity to affect Deportment and Distance in what seem to be contradictory directions is only one of the subtleties in their relationship. In addition, "remote" interactions are often used to reduce problems arising from lack of complementarity. In that case, the very remoteness of interactions "indicates" that Distance perceptions are great on one side—but just the opposite for the other. Such a lack of complementarity appears to be a general theme in French culture and to underlie a dread of face-to-face relations in French organizations.

Crozier's study of plants in the French tobacco monopoly revealed almost as many species of uncomplementary perceptions and behavior patterns as collectors might wish. There was, in the first place, lack of complementarity between subs and supers in general. For example, the production workers (there were also "maintenance" workers who looked after the machinery) showed almost no respect for their foremen, and the foremen, as well as having little respect for the workers, blamed this state of affairs on the systematic undermining of their authority by maintenance men. The workers valued the physical presence of directors, the highest supers in each plant, and familiar, or at least warmly courteous behavior on their part; but they perceived the directors as cold and haughty: "He never says good morning," "when talking he keeps his hands in his pockets," "he does not pay attention," and so on. The desire for interaction with higher supers was great, but only a tiny fraction of the workers had *ever* said anything to their directors—and this in plants not particularly large (300–400 people).

Second, an extraordinary set of status conflicts existed among the lower supers: assistant directors, technical engineers, and comptrollers. Formally, the assistant directors were second in command. The technical engineers, however, refused to regard them as superordinates; they preferred, in fact, to think of themselves as independent of all superordination, viewing even the directors' position as largely judicial (arbitrating conflicts with impersonal rules) rather than directive. A large part of the basis for the engineers' perception was the view that the assistant directors constituted a sort of status mafia, being *polytechniciens* who see themselves as socially superior, while those without similar education disdained the airs that *polytechniciens* assume, considering the latter conspiratorial and undemocratic. In consequence, assistant directors and technical engineers saw one another as pretentious and superfluous. On one side, there was a prevalent belief that anything done by the technical engineers could be done just as well by competent foremen; on the other, the positions of the assistant directors were held to be synecures for liberally educated incompetents.

To add to the confusion, production and maintenance workers themselves had uncomplementary relationships. The maintenance men viewed themselves as superior and, in a sense, superordinates—the equals, for example, of the production foremen. The production workers sometimes did indeed regard them as "bosses" but more often resented their pretentions, and especially their higher wages and lesser workloads. We know already that the supervisors of the production workers, in consequence, believed that the maintenance men undermined their own authority.

The resulting confusion, tension, and outright quarreling need not be described. Under the circumstances, the directors' tendency to withdraw from regular personal interaction in the units surely is understandable. So is the tendency to cover conduct in the plants by a vast number of detailed, impersonal regulations, permitting superordinates to function largely in a judicial rather than executive capacity. Supers dreaded proximate interactions simply because there were indeed good reasons for being terrified. Without some insulative device, the whole operation of the plants could have been brought to a standstill by resentful subordinates; and since this was in no one's interest, the supers "retreated" (Crozier's term) behind a barrier of impersonal work rules, relying on these and occasional adjudication (or investigations without result) to keep the plants operating.[13]

One can see special reasons for the state of affairs described by Crozier in the rather peculiar circumstances of the plants he investigated. Crozier, however, considers it to be a widespread French phenomenon. He regards it as a way of reconciling two pervasive but entirely dissonant values: the desire to avoid all personal dependency and the conception of authority as general and absolute. The location of authority in impersonal regulations, rules, and channels can reconcile these values. It is hard to think of any other way, except perhaps fostering the perception of a superordinate as himself an impersonal force—an institution incarnate, so to speak. Perhaps this sheds some light on why the idea, so impenetrable to Anglo-Saxons, of an abstract General Will (and that of a capitalized Legislator) originates in French political philosophy, precisely as a device for reconciling absolute liberty with the facts of rule. Perhaps it also helps one to grasp why the most successful and authoritative of modern French heads of state cultivated a pronounced aura of impersonality in two senses: that of his remoteness and that of his character as an animate institution. It is just possible that there was a degree of calculation in the conceit.

It might be noted without elaboration that those who seek explanations of adult behavior in childhood patterns can find at least indirect corroboration of this argument in Schonfeld's study of French schools. Lack of complementarity in Distance perceptions and Deportment certainly characterizes French pupils and teachers.[14] But, despite the existence of a multitude of petty institutional regulations, proximate interactions are unavoidable in schools and the insubordinate *chahut,* which is the very inverse of obsequiousness, might be considered to be a result of that condition.

Notes

1. Distance inversion poses a minor definitional difficulty. Splitters of straws may object that it denotes absence of authority, since supers have been defined as controllers *and* superiors. Surely, however, this is niggling as long as some kind of formal superiority is recognized. The occurrence of considerable inversion is in any case unlikely, precisely because formal superiority will tend to mute it. Distance inversion also seems to be confined to subs; we know of no case in which supers manifest it—except perhaps unconsciously, by anomic or paranoid behavior. And a large amount of distance inversion by subs generally indicates that the very existence of the unit or its authority pattern is imperiled. Therefore, confining descriptions of *S-s* relations only to the influence dimensions does not suffice, definitions aside.

2. Talcott Parsons, *Essays in Sociological Theory Pure and Applied* (New York: Free Press, 1949), pp. 393–394.

3. In Parts III and V we use the term "complementarity" more broadly to denote the ways in which other aspects of supers' and subs' norms and behavior fit.

4. Alvin W. Gouldner, *Patterns of Industrial Bureaucracy* (New York: Free Press, 1954), and *Wildcat Strike* (Yellow Springs, Ohio: Antioch Press, 1954).

5. For a fuller summary of the General Gypsum studies, see Muriel McClelland, *Inequality in Industrial Authority* (Workshop in Comparative Politics, Princeton University, Technical Report 4, November 1969).

6. For the pertinent data, see Robert S. Friedman, *Participation in Demoncracy: A Theory of Democracy and Democratic Socialization,* Ph.D. thesis, Princeton University, 1972, pp. IV-27–IV-30 and VI-9–VI-18; William R. Schonfeld, *Youth and Authority in France: A Study of Secondary Schools* (Beverly Hills, Calif.: Sage Professional Papers in Comparative Politics, No. 01-014, 1971), p. 50.

7. F. G. Bailey, *Tribe, Caste, and Nation* (Manchester: Manchester University Press, 1960).

8. Jean-Paul Clébert, *The Gypsies* (London: Vista Books, 1963).

9. Chicago: University of Chicago Press, 1964, esp. p. 222.

10. For references, see Gouldner, *Industrial Bureaucracy,* pp. 39–40, 108–109, 115, 129, and 143.

11. Gaetano Mosca, *The Ruling Class* (New York: McGraw-Hill, 1939), pp. 111–114.

12. Gouldner, *Wildcat Strike,* p. 73.

13. For references, see Michel Crozier, *The Bureaucratic Phenomenon* (Chicago: U. of Chicago Press, 1964), pp. 82–83, 91, 97, 99, and 122–131.

14. Schonfeld, *Youth and Authority in France,* pp. 25 and 61–64.

CHAPTER FOUR

S-S Relations: Structures of Direction

Preliminary Discussion

The reasons for dealing with relations among superordinates (*S-S* relations) in a separate set of dimensions are simple and ought to be obvious. However, since we conventionally think of "authority" only in *S-s* terms (i.e., as wielded by supers over subs), a brief word about the obvious is advisable.

It is evident that there is no direction, hence no authority pattern, without directives. It should be equally evident that there are no directives without decisions about what they are to be, and no decisions without structures and processes for making them and carrying them out. Some of these processes involve interplay among supers and subs (Participation and Responsiveness), but still more manifestly, they involve relations among supers themselves. In effect, the *S*-side of *S-s relations* usually (not always) consists of a collectivity of persons whose interactions nearly always have something, and sometimes everything, to do with the ways in which social units are directed. Any description of an authority pattern that omits *S-S* relations is, therefore, seriously truncated (granted that practical concerns or special theoretical objectives may justify or compel the omission) and the "derivation" of some overall complex of *S-S* dimensions should not be in doubt.

One objection that might be raised against this argument is that social units sometimes operate for very long periods during which no directives are issued. Primitive and traditional societies, in fact, have general norms against deliberate innovations in regard to rules of conduct and all else that is entailed by social "direction"; and since authority in many primitive societies seems to be revealed mainly through the mediation of conflicts under the "usages" of society, even mere enforcement of conventional rules is apparently lacking. It is not necessary to resort to the old dodge of calling such cases "prepolitical" (or "stateless") to disarm the objection, even granting that there may be social units without authority patterns. The objection merely requires a clarification of what is meant by "decisions" in regard to directives.

Just as political philosophers distinguish between express and tacit consent to directives, we can distinguish between express and tacit decisions by supers in regard to them. *Express decisions* are explicit directives that replace old ones or cover previously "free" activities. *Tacit decisions* are made through activities, and sometimes inactivity, tantamount in actual effects to express decisions. For example, supers may allow previous directives to fall into disuse by not wielding supervision or sanctions to enforce them, or they may reaffirm orders or conventions by rigid enforcement. In some cases, they may, without appearing to do so, introduce new directives simply by imposing deprivations for behavior contrary to what they want. A kind of tacit decision making also occurs when subs' pressures for change are simply ignored. And we all know that supers can subtly change operative directives by reinterpreting them. "Found law" is thus often tantamount to "made law" (hardly an original point), and even in the settlement of disputes much scope for fiddling with conventional directives is usually available to chiefs, elders, judges, or arbitrators. Those who criticize the exclusive emphasis by some political scientists on express decisions by arguing that there are also "non-decisions"[1] thus are right—but they miss the point that non-decisions (preventing issues from entering the arena of decision making by supers) are merely one of several species of tacit decisions that can have effects analogous to express ones.

In many social units tacit decisions of various kinds are the primary mode of stating social directives; and in many societies express decisions typically are stated as if tacit, although no one is deluded about what is going on. But even when express decisions are commonly made, much tacit decision making generally occurs. Indeed, the mere ordering of priorities for new decisions, or the allocation by supers of resources to enforcement activities, implies, consciously or otherwise, tacit decisions regarding all the activities that go on in social units (but, of course, not their "coverage" by directives). In that sense—which is perhaps more farfetched than necessary for the present purpose—supers in all cases are continuously engaged in decision making about all facets of behavior in the units they direct.

Whether to treat *S-S* relations separately in the analytic scheme thus poses no difficulties; nor is it difficult to decide which of supers' activities do or do not concern direction. Nevertheless, the analysis of superordination raises a special problem: the determination of the facets of *S-S* relations to be included in the scheme. The problem is greater than in the case of *S-s* relations for two reasons. (1) The definition of authority patterns indicates only that the characteristics of superordination as such should *somehow* be covered in full systematic descriptions. (2) These characteristics seem immensely various: they appear to vary greatly just among states. Think, for example, of the differences between a bureaucratized, federalized, constitutional democracy like the United States and the government of, say, the Mali Republic. The characteristics of superordination seem even more various, by several orders of magnitude, if one includes polities of all types and the authority patterns of all other kinds of social units. Moreover, at first glance much of this variety is qualitative and not readily stated as quantitative differences—hence relatively difficult to compare. How can we cope with such variety to establish a limited set of dimensions, suitable to comparisons, cumulation, and generalization?

The solution proposed here consists of three dimensions, for which our labels are *Conformation, Decision-Rules,* and *Decision-Behavior.* The number of dimensions may seem small for handling such varied phenomena—even considering that the first of them comprehends a sizable number of separable subdimensions. Nevertheless, we contend that the dimensions not only permit very broad descriptions and gross comparisons but are also capable of covering many small details and nuances.

Since the rationale for selecting the dimensions to order the enormous variety in *S-S* relations is not at all self-evident, let us explain how they were arrived at.

1. To begin, one can distinguish between static and dynamic aspects of *S-S* relations. The distinction in this case does not refer to stability or change (as it commonly does in social science). Rather, it is used in an older and more catholic sense, to describe phenomena at "rest" and in action. The phenomenon at rest is the general form, or shape, of a unit's *decision structure*; descriptions of the phenomenon in action add the *decision-processes* through which the superordinates work out directives. The difference is exactly that between a machine inactive and in operation or an athletic team depicted with each player in position as against teams in the process of scoring and preventing points. We are, of course, aware that many sociologists and anthropologists use the word "structure" for both the static arrangement and the processes of social units.[2] However, there is no uniform use of the term, and ours corresponds closely to that of Nadel ("structure indicates an ordered arrangement of parts")[3] and that of Radcliffe-Brown,[4] which is virtually identical to Nadel's and particularly distinguishes the static characteristics of a structure (like the arrangement of the various components of the heart) and the dynamic processes by which a structure "functions" (in the case of the heart, pumps blood through the body). The distinction simply indicates (*a*) that one fully grasps the nature of a unit or pattern only when one has "mapped" both the arrangement of

its components and the way the components interact in the functioning of the whole; and (*b*) that the latter presupposes the former, whereas the former is uninformative without the latter.

Anyone who feels squeamish about this use of terminology may prefer to borrow from the life sciences, substituting "anatomy" for structure and "physiology" for processes. The words hardly matter, as long as the intended meaning is grasped and the point of the distinction seen.

Relations among supers in the structural sense include such matters as their "spatial" arrangement (as on blueprints or organization charts), the differentiation of tasks among them, and the lines of communication through which their activities flow and are coordinated. In processes of direction, relations among supers involve characteristics of their interactions in arriving at express or tacit decisions. (For example, baseball managers rank "above" coaches because they assign the coaches' tasks and coordinate their activities, as well as having responsibility for overall team policy; this is an aspect of the team's decision-structure. Some managers never or rarely take major decisions without first obtaining agreement from their coaches or asking for their recommendations; this involves decision-process.)

2. The distinction between the statics and dynamics of decision making by supers provides a useful, indeed probably necessary, first analytic division of the whole complex of *S-S* relations. However, decision-structures and processes are complexes of variables and obviously vary greatly. Consequently, our initial problem remains: since the definition of authority patterns does not immediately point to particular aspects of *S-S* relations, how can we nonarbitrarily select analytic concepts for the general, systematic description of such relations?

A simple solution of this problem is available. Deriving dimensions from the definition of authority or authority patterns, it will be recalled, was not an end in itself. The purpose of deriving concepts from the definition was to make sure that they would be truly general (i.e., applicable to all authority patterns in social units); and the purpose of selecting "dimensional" concepts was to make descriptions conducive to comparisons and, ultimately, theoretical generalizations. It follows that we can avoid arbitrariness by selecting concepts for characterizing *S-S* relations that can be considered to serve the same ends. Those outlined below were selected because they indeed seem to do so—although they may not exhaust all the possibilities. Since they are not directly contained in or implied by our basic definitions, greater doubts may arise about whether they are the kind of concepts wanted, but the basic rationale for their selection surely is correct.

3. There is one rather obvious way in which the selection of dimensions for describing *S-S* relations can be simplified. Supers do not all operate on the same level of superordination. There are hierarchical distinctions

between the levels, and asymmetric relations occur between them. As stated elsewhere, supers can, in effect, be both supers and subs in relation to different individuals and roles. Consequently, the dimensions that describe relations between supers and subs can also be used to describe aspects of relations among the supers.[5] If degree of asymmetry in social units is to be gauged, it is essential so to use them. In any event, distinguishing levels of superordination seems essential for structural description, and the description of decision-processes clearly requires references to the manner in which lower supers "participate" in the making of directives, the extent to which higher supers "respond" to their participation, and similar matters.

We can learn a lot about superordinates' relations in this manner. However, many of these relations are same-level relations, and there is much more to decision-structures than their division into levels. Consequently, using the *S-s* dimensions for describing relations among the superordinates is only a beginning.

4. Some readers may feel consternation when they realize that we do not make the conventional distinction between decision making and implementation; among political scientists making that distinction is almost a reflex. Eliminating the distinction here helps economize on conceptual equipment. That, however, is not the major reason for avoiding it. More important reasons are the following: (*a*) Processes of implementation are often tantamount to processes of decision making; this hardly novel observation is especially apropos if tacit decisions are equated with express ones. (*b*) Furthermore, certain aspects of the structure and process of implementation are contained in the three general dimensions. Readers should have little difficulty factoring out how the dimensions concern implementation from how they concern decision-taking. (*c*) Still further, many aspects of the process of implementing directives are manifestly covered by the *S-s* dimensions: most manifestly of all in the supervision and sanctions aspects of Directiveness. (*d*) Finally, other aspects of the process will be caught in applying the super-sub dimensions to relations among higher and lower supers, since the lower supers generally have special responsibility for implementing directives. The extent to which the activities of lower supers are themselves "directed" (covered, restricted in latitude, supervised, and sanctioned) certainly tells us a great deal about the administrative process, as will the Compliance of lower superordinates.

For all these reasons, it is pointless to introduce conceptual complexities for the sake of the separate treatment of decision-taking and implementation. Separate treatment could, in fact, be regarded as leading to "diseconomies," since the distinction between these activities generally is a good deal more apparent than real, and often obfuscates actual states of affairs.

In sum, then, the *S-S* dimensions are intended to provide a limited set of structural and (using an ugly bit of social science jargon) processual dimensions on which all authority patterns can be comparatively located and which can serve a considerable variety of theoretical purposes. As in the case of the *S-s* dimensions, additional or different detail for particular descriptive or theoretical purposes can always be generated in the usual ways: by adding "systematic" concepts or by improvised depiction.

S-S Structure: Conformation and its Subdimensions

General Discussion

The structures through which supers operate have numerous components that are both general and dimensional. Each of these can be regarded as a separate variable, and for some purposes this probably should be done. They are treated here as facets of a more comprehensive variable, Conformation, because a common "underlying" dimension can be found in all of them; moreover, that common dimension is, in all likelihood, highly significant in its own right, and it might be disregarded if the various aspects of *S-S* structure were treated altogether separately.

The overall dimension Conformation (Figure 4.1) refers to the *complexity* of decision-structures. All such structures have some degree of complexity, and although highly discriminating measures of complexity may be hard to obtain, the matter is theoretically dimensional and susceptible to fine discriminations.

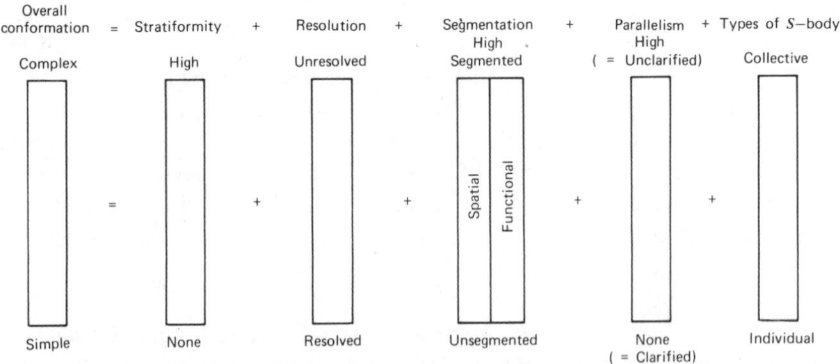

Fig. 4.1 Conformation and its aspects. "Highly segmented" means highly differentiated, overlapping, and uncoordinated. Bear in mind, however, that under conditions stated in the text, coordination may add to complexity.

One polar extreme of the dimension, *absolute simplicity*, is readily specifiable: it exists when there is a single super who exercises all direction in a social unit. The opposite pole, *maximal complexity*, is more difficult to specify, because, as in the case of Participation, it lies in "infinity."[6] Greater complexity seems always possible in some sense—for example, by increasing numbers of supers and levels of superordination, by increasing the functional differentiation of the superordinate structure, or by adding coordinating bodies. (The variety of ways in which complexity can increase will be clearer when the subdimensions are discussed.) The nature of social units clearly restricts the complexity of their *S-S* structures: there can be only a limited amount of complexity in nuclear families, but almost infinite quantities in very large-scale structures like nation-states. That, however, does not alter the lack of a clear-cut upper extreme. Nevertheless, on the basis of our subsequent discussions of the various components of complexity, it will be possible to specify the characteristics of a structure so complex that any additional complexity does not seem worth describing. Consequently we defer specific treatment of the higher extreme until the subdimensions have been dealt with. At that point also, it will be possible to argue in more detail that the overall complexity of decision-structures is likely to be at least as consequential as its various facets separately considered.

Stratiformity. One aspect of Conformation—the most obvious and most easily understood—is the *stratiformity* of the superordinate structure. Stratiformity refers to the horizontal differentiation of decision-structures: the number of levels (layers, rungs) of which the structures consist. The greater the number of such levels, the more complex a structure. In the simplest case, we find only one level of superordination: for example, parents in a nuclear family. Greater complexity in nuclear families can result from the location of, say, the mother at an intermediate level between the children and the father; and still greater complexity would result from the rank-ordering of children, by age or sex, if that ordering entails more than nominal "superiority." An authority pattern thus is stratiform to the extent that it contains levels that can be considered *both S-* and *s*-levels. This is obviously a "dimensional" matter, and every authority pattern can be located at some point of the dimension.

Resolution. Although the abstract notion of stratiformity is simple and straightforward, considerable difficulties may be encountered in identifying layers of superordination. The most likely source of such difficulties is an aspect of the Conformation of decision-structures that deserves treatment in its own right, as a generally applicable dimension having much to do with the overall complexity of such structures. Holt and Turner refer to it as the *resolution* of authority structures.[7] By this they mean the extent to which there are or are not intrinsic ambiguities or conflicts in the "rank-order of policy-making roles and structures." In the highly "resolved" structure of superordination, no disputes or obscurities arise over who is superordinated over whom: every super knows exactly who is his own immediate superordinate (if anyone), through what channels he must proceed to obtain decisions at a higher level, whom he is empowered to direct, and through whom he is to act on lower levels of superordination or on subordinates; and there is no obscurity about where the buck stops (i.e., where highest superordination rests).

Highly resolved decision-structures thus have the appearance of clear-cut echelons—not only on organization charts, which often lie, but in the actual perceptions of role incumbents and, by virtue of these, in the ways the structures actually operate. They resemble military organizations in which everyone is in place on a highly stratiform ladder running from commanders-in-chief to private soldiers.

Many factors can prevent the high resolution of decision-structures in this sense. A common and familiar cause is the distinction between line and staff personnel below the highest supers; another is the mutual convergence of two quite distinct authority patterns on a special domain of activity (e.g., that of state and church on the regulation of marriage and divorce, in certain countries). In fact, all the further aspects of Conformation treated below can increase or decrease resolution, although they also have other effects on decision structures and affect their *overall* complexity more directly than through the resolution of authority.

Segmentation. Like horizontal differentiation, the vertical differentiation of *S-S* structures into distinct subunits on the same levels adds an increment of complexity to their overall Conformation. The extent to which they are so differentiated may be called their *segmentation*. This again is clearly a "dimension" on which all authority patterns occupy one location or another.

Segmentation can be spatial, functional, or both. In the case of a federal polity, it is spatial. It is also spatial in the French tobacco monopoly, since the monopoly is divided into a large number of rather small plants, whose directors are all formally subsumed to a Central Office. Within each plant, however, segmentation is functional: between maintenance men and production workers, both of whom, as we saw, had their own supers, up to and (unresolvedly) including the assistant directors.

Both types of segmentation are familiar, and no further discussion is needed. However, extent of segmentation as such says little about the overall complexity of *S-S* structures unless two related variables, both also clearly dimensional, are considered alongside it. One of these has the effect of adding to the contribution that segmentation makes to complexity, the other tends to diminish it. (Consequently, they are subsumed under segmentation—an additional reason being that they do not occur unless segmentation exists.)

The exacerbating factor is *overlap* among segmented subunits and their supers. The functions, tasks, or jurisdictions of the segments may be sharply discrete, in the sense that none intrudes on the domain, spatial or functional, of any other. On the other hand, the boundaries of the segments, hence powers of their supers, may shade off into one another or, in the most extreme case, may for all practical purposes coincide. (For example, dozens of agencies in the executive branch of our government have something to do with the regulation of fuel and power resources, and the spatial jurisdictions or functional divisions among them are exceedingly unclear.) Spatially differentiated segments generally are highly discrete, whereas functionally differentiated ones tend more to overlap; this is not necessary but certainly is highly probable.

The alleviating factor is *coordination* among segmented supers: the extent to which means exist for concerting their activities, for clarifying confused responsibilities and jurisdictions, and for resolving disputes about these matters. Higher supers, of course, generally discharge these tasks. In highly segmented units, however, such individuals are unlikely to discharge the tasks successfully unless effective means for coordinating actions exist among the lower supers themselves.

In many cases, special bodies, with continuous existence, are created to achieve coordination, either formally by the fiat of higher supers or informally by segmented supers themselves. The creation of such bodies hardly guarantees effective coordination and the reduction of complexity; often, in fact, it simply augments complexity by adding segments with unclear tasks and jurisdictions, competing and overlapping with previously existing segments. Consequently, caution is advisable in assessing the overall effects of coordinative devices in practice, although in principle they always potentially mitigate the complexity that results from segmentation.

Coordination can also be achieved entirely informally, if segmented supers regularly interact and influence one another. Because of this, one kind of "overlap" in *S-S* structures actually lessens complexity: overlapping membership by certain supers in segmented parts of the superordinate structure. A case in point is provided by British Cabinet committees. Most Cabinet members, as well as some lesser ministers, have multiple memberships on such committees and sometimes hold more than one departmental portfolio as well. They thus "represent" numerous segmented subunits in their individual persons. Very similar effects can follow from any regular interactions among supers—and, at least in Britain, the practice seems to deal better with complexity than the use of "superministers" with multiple, but unclear, departmental responsibilities (as tried, and quickly discontinued, by the Tories some years ago).

As in the case of special coordinative bodies, there is a catch in this general argument too—namely, the assumption that interactions by supers across segments are harmonious and amicable, not discordant and self-aggrandizing. Structural facilities (in effect, channels) for regular interaction among segmented supers can be provided, from physical facilities like common-rooms to the institution of periodic luncheon meetings and the like; and *S-S* interaction, like *s-S* Participation, can also be structurally impeded. But no matter what facilities are provided, no one can assure that they will be used, or used in the proper spirit, to any great consequence. This matter, however, takes us into the domain of decision-processes, which is considered later. The point is not irrelevant to structure, but it does serve to emphasize the importance of characteristics of *both* structures (channels) and processes (use) in descriptions of *S-S* relations.

Parallelism. Horizontal and vertical differentiation are often combined. Functionally or spatially differentiated units can have their own stratiformity up to any level of superordination, including the very highest (e.g., pope and emperor in the Holy Roman Empire—if indeed that was a social unit, having an authority pattern). In that case we can speak of *parallelism* in the *S-S* structure. Parallelism is a continuous dimension, and location on it is determined by the level of superordination at which the separate hierarchies intersect (i.e., are subject to a single super or collective body of supers). The higher that level, the greater is complexity (other things equal), since all the complicating factors discussed so far—number of segmented units, overlaps of function or jurisdiction, problems of coordination by formal bodies or regular interactions—will then occur at numerous levels of the superordinate structure. In addition, the greater is parallelism, the larger will be the number of "same-level" supers, tending to create problems somewhat like those that involve the resolution of authority.

Holt and Turner refer to these as problems concerning the "clarification" of authority patterns.[8] The difference between these problems and those involving resolution is that they arise less from confusion about levels of superordination than from the condition that numerous supers operate on equivalent levels without being integrated into a collective decision-making "unit." Even if the segments do not overlap, the lack of clear-cut "superiority" can then make for conflicts, or simply "unclear" hierarchy. A familiar illustration is the parallel authority of kings and cardinals, barons and bishops, even squires and lower clergy, emanating from that of popes and emperors in Western Christendom.

Types of S-Bodies. Parallelism almost always stops at the level of the highest superordinates—that of "headship" in authority patterns. At that level, however, authority may be *individual* or *collective*, and, if collective, more or less so, thus further complicating matters. This can also occur at any lower level of stratiformity, of course; it may characterize the whole *S*-structure, not just its head. However, collective *S*-bodies are more likely to occur at the higher levels, and their occurrence is likely to be especially consequential at these levels, although the inverse is not unknown. For example, in the Fifth French Republic S_1 (the actual head) is an individual and S_2 (the next level of superordination) a collective body.

The fact that superordination is collective rather than individual is not necessarily consequential. But it is very likely to be so—again, especially at high levels of stratiformity. Collective authority offers opportunities as well as posing dangers. In highly segmented units, for example, it permits the representation and potential coordination of the segments. On the other hand, it also threatens the paralysis of the decision-structure, and if paralysis occurs at high levels, collectivity assures that only rather routine, short-range, tactical directives will be issued. However that may be, the conceptual point—that collective superordination complicates *S*-structures—should be evident enough. Whether "complicates" in this and any other sense means "less effective" (or more so) is not a question for conceptualization but for theory, and it almost certainly varies among units, according to circumstances.

Maximal Complexity. On the basis of the various components of Conformation, it is now possible to provide a notion of *maximal complexity* in *S-S* structures that can at least anchor the idea—that is, furnish an image of a structure so complex that further increments of complexity are unlikely to matter. (1) The maximally complex structure is highly stratiform: it has many levels of superordination. (2) Questions of exactly who is superordinated over whom are highly unresolved. (3) The structure is highly segmented, functionally and spatially. Moreover, there is a great deal of overlap among the segments, and means of coordination are lacking or, worse, are provided only by bodies that add segments and muddle the resolution of the structure. (4) Segmentation that overlaps and is muddled runs to the highest levels of superordination along parallel hierarchies: the structure is "unclarified" as well as "unresolved." (5) Supers at every level, or at higher levels, are collective bodies composed of numerous individuals.

If all these conditions obtain in an authority pattern, then surely marginal differences (e.g., in the precise number of differentiated segments, or in one or two more or fewer layers of superordination) will be inconsequential. In effect, although the maximal pole of the overall Conformation dimension lies in infinity, there is no great difficulty in specifying a point of complexity that can "close" the dimension at its upper extreme, for conceptual, and potentially operational, purposes.

The Significance of Overall Complexity. It is also possible now to discuss with some specificity why overall complexity matters in its own right. In the first place (and not dependent on the preceding discussion of its components), overall complexity of structure has been important in other sciences, especially the life sciences. It plays a major role, for example, in theories of evolution and in regard to generalizations about the brain, which is the higher "control" structure in certain organisms. It is likely that complexity of structure will be as important a variable in regard to social systems as it has been in the case of "living systems." It is surely reasonable to expect the level of performance of social units to depend on the complexity of their structures, particularly their own higher "control" structures (although it should be stressed that the exact nature of that relationship in social systems is at present obscure, is bound to vary with circumstances, and is unlikely to be unilinear). One may also suspect that the ability to cope with complexity as such, hence the operation of certain complex social units (perhaps anything more complex than kinship units), will depend on prior experience with or exposure to complex relationships, even if only in subordinate roles. Most important for our purposes, the complexity of superordinate structures is bound to have repercussions on the *S-s* dimensions. For example, structures of superordination may be so complex that subs will have no idea where and how to participate to good effect; thus they may not participate at all or may use only the less demanding modes of Participation; certainly as complexity grows, the costs to subs of finding out how and where to exert pressure also rise, as does the probability of misinformation and failure to achieve the desired ends. Similarly, Responsiveness may undergo an avoidable decline as complexity grows: the lower supers may be constrained in responding by their lack of real power to decide, and higher supers may be unable to decide which channels of pressures passing through lower supers to take seriously. Complexity, on the contrary, can also open channels of participation and increase the probability of Responsiveness by more accessible and, in highly segmented units, less cross-pressured supers. Similarly also, if Bagehot is right, allegiance may be imperiled by a structure of superordination so complex that it is incomprehensible to ordinary subs. Bagehot argued that the signal importance of the British monarchy was precisely that it provided a transparent personal symbol for the existence of governmental authority, a focus of identification and majesty comprehensible to ordinary minds.

Such examples could be multiplied almost indefinitely. They are not meant to imply that any of the matters mentioned are affected by overall complexity alone. Particular aspects of Conformation also matter and may often matter more. Simply stated, it is possible to treat the subdimensions separately; but they can also be subsumed to an underlying dimension, and failure to do this is likely to mean that one overlooks many important considerations. This point is supported much more specifically by the illustrations that follow.

Illustration: Conformation in Small-Scale Units: A Reflection on "Being Born to Rule"

A basic principle of biology and common sense is that size tends to be equated with complexity of structure. Consequently, we think of the Conformation of families, especially "conjugal" families, as being relatively simple. Surely this is right. However, there are different degrees of complexity even in families of the conjugal type. The amount of complexity that can exist in such families may seem trivial compared with that of macrocosmic units, like polities. However, differences in their complexity may be anything but trivial in consequence, including consequences for polities themselves. To make this point, we consider and reflect on the Conformation of German families, as depicted in the novels studied by Reepmeyer—and to some extent confirmed in the pioneering sociological studies of authority in families organized by Horkheimer.[9]

As a rule, the higher the social status of German families during the late Imperial and Weimar periods, the more complex was their Conformation. In working-class families authority remained formally patriarchal, even (as we saw) with the physical removal of the father from the household. The mother was at best an administrative lieutenant, at worst a subordinate like the children. On occasion, an element of complexity appeared when an older son, because of the association of authority with being male, occupied an ambiguous place in the hierarchy. A more important element of complexity—less in the sense of the stratiformity of the structure than in that of its "resolution"—derived from the growing likelihood that there would be several wage earners in the family. Older sons and sometimes women thus lost their basic economic dependence on the father and on this basis not infrequently asserted coequal status in the family's *S*-structure. The result, in some instances, was a struggle for power and independence, which Wittfogel (in Horkheimer) mistakes for an "equilibrated" (*ausbalancierte*) ordering of authority. More often, it seems to have led to a kind of collective headship in the family, especially between father and oldest son: fathers and sons became "comrades," sharing common goals and cooperating in their attainment.[10] Despite these shadings and nuances, the typical working-class family was as simple in Conformation as it is possible to be: a single (individual or collective) S presided over a set of subordinates. Much the same pattern apparently prevailed in peasant families, but without the nuances created by the condition of the urban lower class.

In bourgeois families, this simple Conformation was complicated by two factors. First, a layer of servants was added to the structure. Although the number of servants varied with the family's means, typically there was a cook, a nanny, and a maid; and if the father was a solid bourgeois (e.g., a higher *Beamter*) a girl or two, or even a butler, would be added. Second, during the period studied the bourgeois mother seems to have become, in some senses, an S_2 figure subordinated to the father but superordinated over everyone else; in some senses she was a coequal to the father; and in some senses, through the father's abdication of household responsibilities, even the head of the structure. In terms of the father's norms, the first seems to have been the case; in terms of the mother's, the second; in terms of actualities rather than norms, most probably the third. It should be evident that children in such a household would at least learn to perceive an element of stratiformity and that they would be more likely than lower-class children to view headship as a collective affair.

A quantum jump in complexity occurs in wealthy and aristocratic households. Even if based on a pair of spouses, such families departed widely from our usual conception of a "nuclear" family, especially as they probably were perceived by children growing up in them.

The families generally included quite a crowd of people: not only parents and children but also grandparents (far more commonly than in families of lesser status, except peasant families), assorted uncles and aunts, cousins, in-laws, nonrelations having ties of some kind to the family, and large staffs: tutors, governesses, majordomos, stewards, maids, cooks, gardeners, footmen, and handymen. Presiding over all was the family's head, others in the household being his "court," in an only slightly metaphorical sense. To that extent, the unit's authority pattern was highly "resolved," the head's unquestioned position as S_1 being buttressed by his symbolic personification of the "institutional" character of the family—the lineage or firm that tied the family to past and future and, of course, to something far more complex than the household as such. The resolution of the structure at that level, however, lessened its complexity only slightly. Stratiformity was considerable. For example, only rarely were the parents of the children of the household not subordinated to a higher level of superordination; and directives for children seldom came from the family's head, or even the subjects' parents: they came, almost always, from or through the staff. Moreover, the "resolved" role of the head was more potential than actual: an ultimate possibility rarely exercised. Toward the later part of the period, the head's wife and other highly placed females in the family became virtually independent.

They traveled a great deal on their own, usually had individual social positions and personal fortunes, and, often married for dynastic or commercial reasons, they lived in cordial separateness from their husbands. In effect, they had begun to constitute an earthbound "jet set."

An element of segmentation was involved in these women's roles as well. The male supers seem to have been mainly concerned with matters of the children's careers, the females with manners and cultivation. The regulation of day-to-day life fell chiefly to the staff, but even here segmentation is observable: the less "menial" members of the staff (e.g., tutors and governesses) represented the family to the children, especially concerning themselves with proper conduct, industry, and education; the more menial staff seems, of all things, to have taken responsibility for forming the children's sense of class distinctions and stratiform authority in the world. Identifying their own status with that of the family, it was especially the servants who impressed on children the need to act up to their station in life. The servants themselves formed hierarchies reaching up to the higher levels of the family: for example, governesses or tutors long with the family were often regarded as full-fledged members (e.g., dined with the family). Making all even more complex, there were often quite separate hierarchies of relatives alongside the core hierarchy of the family. And making all more stratiform, a special hierarchy of respect and sometimes authority passed through the line of primogeniture—from the head to his oldest son to the senior grandson.

The foregoing description is, if anything, a simplification. But it will suffice to demonstrate that in regard to complexity, the upper-class family was a world apart from others. It exhibited much greater stratiformity, much more segmentation of authority, even parallel hierarchies, to an extent, and various possibilities for unclear resolution below the level of the formal head. Perhaps a gradual increase of complexity occurred as one went up the social scale, but at or near the very highest social level, a discontinuous change in complexity seemed to set in. In any event, very few families exhibited a structure nearly as complex as that described, and they were invariably aristocratic or plutocratic families.

As in the case of Directiveness in lower-class families, there was nothing unique about the Conformation of German upper-class families. *Mutatis mutandis*, the description could fit the families of the upper crust in virtually all societies. Certainly we can find structural counterparts of higher-class German families in the United States (e.g., the Rockefellers, the Kennedys), and even more certainly, we can find them in Britain. This is precisely what gives the descriptive finding potential theoretical importance.

It is well known that members of the upper crust play an inordinately large role in the governments of many societies, including democracies that are not notable for social deference. For many reasons, aristocrats and plutocrats have demonstrated a remarkable capacity for adapting to a variety of governmental arrangements. The rich and wellborn command a disproportionate amount of convertible political resources. They can count on powerful networks of friendship and connections to help them get on. In the age of aristocracy, government (together with soldiering and the priesthood) was their special social function, and the orientation toward these historic roles is passed on through the generations. In some societies, like Britain, the upper classes still command widespread political deference.

Of all such explanations, the least credible on its face is the claim of aristocrats that they are "born to rule." Genetically, of course, that is ludicrous. And yet, perhaps the claim rests on more than arrogance or a continued orientation toward historic social roles. If ruling in the conventional sense entails operating large-scale, complex organizations, and if operating such organizations requires skills not automatically possessed by men, then aristocrats and plutocrats do seem to possess a major advantage over others by virtue of their birth. Almost from infancy, they live surrounded by complex Conformation. Simply for that reason, complexity must seem more natural and manageable to them than to people born into simpler structures. It is undoubtedly true that others acquire skill and ease in coping with complexity; individual differences here surely count for at least as much as social ones. Nevertheless, members of the upper crust always retain one advantage: they learned (or at least had the opportunity to learn) earlier—and that may count as much for political skills as for any others.

In addition to the complexity that surrounds them from birth, aristocrats and plutocrats appear to have another political advantage. They perceive the existence of impersonal, collective "institutions" earlier, their families being associated with firms and lineages that are often far-flung in time and space. If the postulates of learning theory hold at all, these circumstances must render the aristocrats less oriented than their competitors toward purely personal domination and more toward the performance of institutional roles of authority in historic collectivities: more able to wield (and to surrender) authority, with an ease bordering on instinct.

If this argument seems plausible, a study of members of higher political elites, using early exposure to complexity (in any context) as an explanatory variable, might be rewarding. And if the argument is valid, some important questions arise. What becomes of complex authority as family structure decreases in scale and becomes simple throughout all of society? Do certain new institutions function to the same effect as complex patrician families? Does a critical change occur in the nature and perhaps effectiveness of large-scale authority patterns? Or is the result simply greater equality in competition for higher superordinated roles—a lessening of privilege?

Illustration: Conformation in a Large-Scale Unit: Decision Structure in the British Welfare State

Just as biologists associate size with complexity, so they also associate complexity with the "efficiency" of organisms. The size-complexity equation seems serviceable for authority patterns as well, particularly if we think of size not as number of people or physical area but also take into account volume and variety of activities. The complexity-efficiency equation, however, probably applies to authority patterns only up to a point. The relationship between complexity and efficacy seems to be curvilinear, since beyond a certain threshold of complexity in decision structures, the capacity for arriving at well-considered decisions (indeed, perhaps for arriving at "decisions" worthy of the name at all) apparently declines.

Both these generalizations can be illustrated by the development of British governmental structure in the era of the "positive" state, especially the postwar "welfare state." That development is not at all unique. Making the necessary changes, our general points probably apply to all highly developed countries. Indeed, they probably apply not only to governments in these countries but to many "private" organizations as well—any organizations very large in scale, diverse in activity, and highly centralized (such as certain industrial conglomerates or trade unions).

Size and Complexity. The ways in which the volume and variety of governmental activities have grown in Britain during the last century, and the large jump that occurred in both during the years immediately after World War II, are familiar; in any case, Britain differs from other Western countries in this regard only in details and degree. Consequently, we can proceed directly to a discussion of the effects of growth in activity on the complexity of the British governmental structure. This saves space, of course; but even so two further shortcuts are required to keep the discussion within reasonable limits. Some basic knowledge of the structure of British government must be assumed; otherwise the illustration would quickly grow into a book. In addition, the effects of welfare state activities on every aspect of the Conformation of British government have been so great and various that only a few examples can be given here. This is advisable not only for reasons of space, it is compelled by another consideration. As a result of growth in its activities, contemporary British government has become so hugely complex that the voluminous literature about it has only begun to fathom the many details of its Conformation. Indeed, it seems unlikely that even the higher superordinates who preside over the structure are fully aware of all its facets.

1. The most obvious effect of the growth of governmental activities and functions has been a greatly increased *segmentation* of the government's structure, and the most obvious aspect of that is increased functional segmentation. Around the middle of the eighteenth century, the divisions of the central government were very few: the Chancellor and Treasury, concerned with financial administration; a Secretary of State, dealing with domestic *and* overseas matters; the Admiralty; and, performing a few miscellaneous chores, the Lord Chancellor, the Lord President, the Lord Privy Seal, and the Chancellor of the Duchy of Lancaster. These figures, and their staffs, kept domestic peace, collected revenues, carried on diplomacy and war—and did little else. Nowadays, there are usually some 30 specialized departments, grown by a series of convulsive cellular splits from this exceedingly simple structure. (The exact number sometimes is contracted, sometimes expanded, according to perceived administrative and political exigencies.) The sheer number of ministries, moreover, is deceptive on the side of simplicity, for a similar segmentation seems continuously to be taking place within many departments, especially in multipurpose departments like the Treasury. Furthermore, a vast number of other bodies has been and is being nucleated to specialize in tasks involving more than one department. Some of these are highly ephemeral (an outlandish example is the "Committee on the Spontaneous Manifestation of Personal Gratification on the Cessation of Hostilities" formed at the end of World War II); others are as permanent as the departments themselves. These are bodies engaged in coordination, but specialized units just the same; many major departments even have officials who do little but attend meetings. Some new spatial segmentation has occurred as well, although not so much. The National Health Service provides two examples: the use of a new regional structure for administering the hospital services, which is quite separate and different from the rest of the local-government structure, and the use of bodies for administering general practitioner services whose territorial division coincides with old local-government units but whose jurisdictions are independent. Parliament has resisted segmentation more than the executive structure, but specialized standing committees are now accepted in principle, and the first such committees have recently been installed.

2. Along with segmentation, *stratiformity* has also increased. The most obvious example is the development of committees of the Cabinet as a new layer of superordination between the Cabinet as such and individual ministers as heads of departments. These generally include both ministers with Cabinet rank and other ministers; thus the new structures are not

merely a new *S*-level but overlap in stratiformity with both the Cabinet and the specialized departments. Their major functions are to help the Cabinet handle the general crush of business and to provide an alternative to coordination at the Cabinet level. Before the war, the Cabinet sometimes set up ad hoc committees, but there were only two standing Cabinet committees: the Imperial Defense Committee and the Home Affairs Committee; virtually all high-level business was transacted in full Cabinet. The postwar Labour government, in contrast, used no fewer than 17 standing Cabinet committees, as well as continuing to use ad hoc committees (e.g., the Committee on the Distribution and Marketing of Meat, Fruit and Vegetables—which should convey the flavor of the setup); and most Cabinet business was effectively settled at the committee level. In addition, it is at least arguable that a new level of stratiformity has also been developed *above* the level of the Cabinet. The Prime Minister, it is often suggested, has increasingly become a presidential figure, and some very fateful decisions (e.g., the Suez intervention) have been made by a small coterie of the Cabinet intimate with the premier.

3. Since governmental activities rarely can be neatly compartmentalized, much *overlap* has resulted from increased segmentation (and, to an extent, the development of new layers of stratiformity). Under the postwar Labour government, for example, it was necessary for five major departments to collaborate before a single house could be built in Britain. Town and Country Planning had to approve sites, the Board of Trade had to provide certain raw materials, the Ministry of Labour supplied manpower, the Ministry of Works issued building licenses, and the Ministry of Health had overall responsibility for housing policy. As stated, vast numbers of interdepartmental coordinating committees have been developed at all levels of policymaking and administration to prevent work at cross-purposes, but no one has ever been able to make precise sense of the overall effects. It is certain only that the committees add more bodies that might increase complexity, that they seem to prevent really spectacular muddles, but that some activities requiring close coordination among many units (e.g., town and country planning) have bogged down in unfathomable intricacy, and indeed have been discontinued, despite the committees' work or, in part, because of it. One suspects that the factor responsible for efficient operation, especially at the lower levels of administration, is the informal network of "old-boy" relations among British officials: close personal ties and much social interaction, traceable to common educational backgrounds and similar factors.

4. As a result of all these developments, certain difficulties about the *resolution* of the structure have arisen. They are not as bad as in the premodern era, before the full development of the centralized state, but the

clear-cut stratiformity of the old cabinet system has certainly been undermined. For example, there is ambiguity about the precise ordering of superordination in regard to central economic planning among a department (the Treasury), a Cabinet committee (the Economic Policy Committee), high-level interdepartmental committees concerting the activities of the principal economic departments (e.g. Trade, Labour, Works), a body of special experts attached to the Cabinet (the Economic Planning Staff), and two special high-level interdepartmental committees (the Investment Programmes Division and the Import Programmes Division). Just how these bodies might be ordered on a ladder of stratiformity—who, that is, could override whom—seems a nearly insoluble problem. There is no question that the Cabinet as a collective body, or possibly the Chancellor of the Exchequer and Prime Minister as individuals, could say the last word about general economic policy. Just below that level, however, stratiformity is hopelessly confused.

5. The use of *collective S-bodies* has increased less dramatically than other aspects of complex Conformation. This is only to be expected, since the British have always used such bodies to a remarkable extent. In one sense, however, collective *S-bodies* have increased in complexity—or at least have become "collective" in an unprecedented sense. Since the welfare state can accomplish few objectives without the active cooperation of "private" associations (e.g., the British Medical Association, the National Farmers Union, major industrial and commercial associations like the Federation of British Industries, and the trade unions), representatives of these associations have been increasingly coopted into the executive structure itself. There they do not act merely in a consultative capacity; in many cases, it is as if they were full-fledged voting members.[11] Decisions thus have increasingly taken on the aura of negotiations between autonomous but mutually interdependent officials representing public and private authorities, on a basis that is continuous and organized, rather than sporadic and improvised.

6. *Parallelism* has increased chiefly in two ways. New hierarchies, dealing with special segmented tasks, have been developed alongside the old structure of local government. And through the development of party committees in Parliament (not to be confused with specialized committees of Parliament as such) an embryonic set of bodies parallel to the structure of the administrative departments, and capable of exerting much influence at higher decision levels, has also come into being.

Complexity and Efficacy. Our account here is a small, oversimplified sample of what has occurred, intended only to convey the general flavor of the structure. It should, however, permit us to raise an important and rather ironic theoretical possibility.

In the case of Britain, the animus behind the growth of governmental activities and functions has been to achieve the "rationalization" of social interactions, even more than a more even division of wealth and welfare.[12] The old patterns of the economic market, of autonomous hospitals and other medical services, of private housing development and the private allocation of land to industry, recreation, and farming (among many similar matters), was extremely "polycentric." Myriads of autonomous actors made independent decisions, virtually unregulated by any authority charged with promoting generally desirable outcomes. The results produced by the polycentric patterns were in fact increasingly perceived as undesirable. They were certainly perceived as "irrational": no more than unintended overall effects of vast numbers of unrelated decisions, out of which generally desired states of affairs could emerge only by fortune or the workings of some mysterious "hidden hand." The chief point of expanding governmental activities, consequently, was to achieve rational unified control, for general social benefit, over irrationally polycentric activities.

The irony is that the result has been vastly increased polycentricity within the government itself. Powers once effectively centralized in the Cabinet have been dispersed to other agencies so numerous that it is extremely difficult nowadays to affix definite responsibility for any but the very highest and the most routine activities of government (those decided either by the Prime Minister and those close to him, and those which are strictly intradepartmental and of little general consequence). The overall picture is almost as complex as that of a private market, and the old "market" forces (farmers, employers, workers, professionals) have even been coopted into segments of the structure, up to very high levels. It is as if polycentricity had merely been shifted from one level of society to another.

Whether the resulting structure is capable of making "rational" decisions, especially in the more complex areas of policy making, is open to question. One may even entertain serious doubts about whether it produces calculated "decisions" in the first place. The tendency is for different "interests" in the structure to arrive at mutual agreements by negotiations, cordial or acrimonious, in which various "currencies"—threats, persuasion, "side payments," political clout, and the like—determine the results. These, consequently, resemble more the outcomes that emerge from markets than genuine decisions.

This point, to be sure, is mainly speculative. Only speculation is possible, due to the extreme paucity of studies of how the structure operates, and the common assumption in available studies that it in fact operates as it is supposed to do. The speculation, however, is not wildly unreasonable. At least it can help explain why the more ambitious and complicated enterprises of the British welfare state, such as detailed central economic planning and close controls over urban and rural development, have been virtually discontinued. And it may also help explain why, in so many developed countries, the old pressures for rational control by increased centralization are yielding to pressures for more rational control by decentralization—not necessarily a return to unregulated private arrangements, but more diminutive, hence simpler, public ones. The process of political centralization and expropriation of "private" activities that began in the Middle Ages seems, through its effects on the complexity of overall Conformation, to have reached points of diminishing returns that are only now becoming clearly discernible.[13]

Notes

1. Peter Bachrach and Morton S. Baratz, "Decisions and Nondecisions: An Analytical Framework," *American Political Science Review,* Vol. 56, No. 4 (December 1962), pp. 947–952.

2. E.g., Marion J. Levy, Jr., *The Structure of Society* (Princeton, N.J.: Princeton University Press, 1952), pp. 57–58.

3. S. F. Nadel, *The Theory of Social Structure* (London: Cohen & West, 1957), p. 8.

4. A. R. Radcliffe-Brown, *Structure and Function in Primitive Society* (New York: Free Press, 1952), p. 9.

5. Strictly speaking, in that case we would be dealing with *s-S* relation, not *S-S* relation—although among actors who are all supers vis-à-vis others. The point should be made to avoid the appearance of inconsistency, but it is hardly of great import.

6. Infinity is in quotes because, strictly speaking, the term denotes a very large, unspecifiable number—as also in the case of the Participation dimension.

7. Robert T. Holt and John E. Turner, *The Political Basis of Economic Development* (Princeton, N.J.: Van Nostrand, 1966), p. 57.

8. *Ibid.,* p. 58.

9. Max Horkheimer, *Autorität und Familie* (Paris: Alcan, 1936).

10. *Ibid.,* p. 520.

11. For an elaboration of this point, see Harry Eckstein, "The British Political System," in Samuel H. Beer and Adam Ulam, Eds., *Patterns of Government* (New York: Random House, 1962), pp. 254–257.

12. *Ibid.,* Ch. 9.

13. All points made in this illustration, as stated, are extremely condensed: both factual and speculative points. For more detail and more intricate argument, see *ibid.,* pp. 233–261.

CHAPTER FIVE

S-S Relations: Processes of Direction

S-S Process: Decision-Rules

General Discussion

Superordinate structures in action make decisions concerning the direction of social units. Making such decisions requires that supers and subs be able to recognize when decision-processes have been concluded, especially "properly" concluded. An indispensable ingredient of the processes, therefore, is the existence of Decision-Rules that provide basic criteria under which decisions are considered to have been taken. In large-scale modern organizations, these are usually found in constitutions, charters, by-laws, and the like. More commonly they exist only in normative beliefs or conventional practices, and even codified Decision-Rules are generally modified or elaborated by such norms and practices.

To avoid possible misunderstandings, we should immediately point out two matters not included in the present notion of Decision-Rules

First, the notion of a Decision-Rule sometimes denotes a uniformity postulated or found in the ways individuals or groups make up their minds about alternative actions. An example is the postulate that people always use "rational" calculation to select from alternative courses of action that which yields for them greatest utility or least disutility. Another is the finding that the votes of individuals can be accurately predicted by assuming that they perceive a greater or lesser number of attractive and unattractive features in candidates, sum these without assigning weights to them or by weighting them in a specified manner, and then vote for the person who gets the highest score. Such postulates or findings might be better called decision-regularities, to avoid overburdening the term "rule" with disparate meanings. In any case, they are not what the present concept denotes, even though actual behavior may be the only or best evidence available for determining what Decision-Rules are in certain cases.

Second, the notion of Decision-Rules does not refer to prescriptions governing relations among supers and subs, such as formal rules about Participation. It refers to the operation of the *S*-structure only. There is, however, a marginal exception if only the members of the unit as a whole, both subs and supers, can arrive at certain valid decisions through referenda or their equivalents. In such cases, the distinction between *S* and *s* simply disappears for the particular "legislative" actions concerned.[1]

Anyone familiar with the formal legislative procedures of national parliaments, or national constitutions more generally, is aware that the Decision-Rules of social units display considerable qualitative variation. As in the case of previous variables, however, most, perhaps all, such variations can be made "dimensional" through a quantitative variable that underlies the qualitative differences. That variable is the number of supers whose assent is needed before a directive may be considered operative for the social unit.

"Assent" should here be construed rather broadly. It may refer to the need for a positive vote in favor of a directive or failure to exercise a power to veto. In this case, as in most others, acts of commission and omission may have identical consequences. Assent may also involve actions at different stages of the process of direction, as distinguished in the section on Responsiveness; being able to stop the initiation of a decision-process is equivalent to ability to prevent a decision at the stage of "resolution," which is equivalent to being able to ignore with impunity anything decided at that stage in the process of implementation. In all cases the matter to be determined is the number of supers having recognized rights to prevent directives from becoming operative in the full sense.

The notion of recognized rights is, however, a major limitation on the broadness of the meaning of "assent." In determining the extent to which Decision-Rules distribute power to decide among numerous supers, it would be foolish to take into account mere inefficiency or outright insubordination by lesser supers charged with carrying out directives. If this were done, differences among Decision-Rules would all but vanish—all supers would nearly always be able to keep directives from operating, anyway potentially.

On one extreme of the dimension, thus conceived (see Figure 5.1), are *monocratic* arrangements (a term in good standing since the seventeenth century). Such arrangements are simple in principle: a single super decides every highly consequential directive, sometimes all directives. The preferences of other supers and of subs may be taken into account or even actively solicited, but the super alone decides.

Simple as this is, a major practical complication in identifying monocracy may arise when the super is a collective body, as in most cabinet systems. To determine whether such arrangements are monocratic, a potentially tricky question must be answered: Do the individuals who constitute the S-

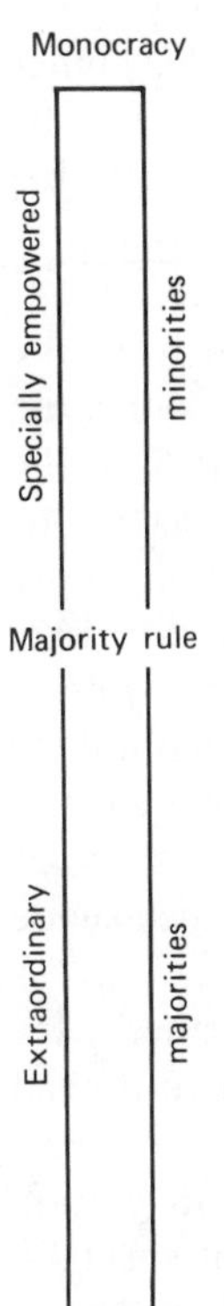

Fig. 5.1 The Decision-Rules dimension.

body operate chiefly as an undifferentiated unit or do they chiefly act in their individual or segmental capacities? If the first is true, the arrangement is monocratic; if the second, it is not. As a rule, however, the first alternative is mainly fiction or pretense. The pretense can certainly be consequential. For example, votes are almost never taken in the British cabinet, or if taken, never reported. This custom is due to the pretense that the cabinet is a real collective individual, the monarch in another form—a factor that certainly affects operation of the cabinet. But it is manifestly unlikely that a group of men drawn from different segments of social units will act as a single, undifferentiated body, even if the possibility of doing so exists.

The antitheses of monocratic arrangements are *polycratic* ones. (This neologism is unavoidable because conventional language provides no appropriate concept.[2]) In the extreme case of polycracy, unanimity by supers is required for directives to take effect. This does not necessarily mean absolutely all supers, especially not in highly complex social units. In cases of great stratiformity, we are seldom interested in more than the higher levels of superordination. In cases of great segmentation, polycracy may be considered extreme if assent is required by all supers who have a discernible corporate "interest" in directives, in the sense that segments for which they have special responsibility are likely to be directly affected by them.

Majority rule divides the polycracy segment of the continuum from the segment running toward extreme monocracy. Proceeding by logic alone, the rule that a simple majority decides should probably be located at the midpoint of the continuum. Where majority rule prevails, every assent or dissent has an exactly equal change to succeed or fail: any individual super may be "pivotal" in forming a winning coalition for or against a directive. In practical terms, however, it might be preferable to locate majority rule at a higher point: fine gradations between it and a unanimity rule are unlikely to occur, and majority rule does imply a kind of equality among supers. This is a matter we need not finally settle now; it seems sufficient to point out that majority rule is the decisive point at which Decision-Rules shade off toward monocracy and polycracy.

Between that point and the polycratic extreme, we find requirements for "extraordinary majorities" of various kinds, like those required to amend the American Constitution. Toward the opposite extreme are specially empowered minorities. Most frequently these are sets of experts in certain domains of a unit's activities, or representatives of limited sets of specially interested segments, whose assent is recognized to signify more than that of other members of the superordinate structure for directives of certain kinds.

In general, units can be located on the monocracy-polycracy dimension by determining the distribution of probabilities among supers that their preferences will be pivotal (i.e., decisive) in forming successful combinations for or against directives. This follows the conception of "power" suggested by Shapley and Shubik.[3] In essence, that conception is to determine the total number of "voting" sequences that may occur in decision-processes (which, given n "voters," is always $n!$) and the number of times any individual voter may be decisive in the sequences. The "power" of each individual voter can then be expressed as

$$P_i = \frac{m_i}{n!}$$

where m_i is his number of pivotal positions. P_i, of course, is always a proportion of unity, and the overall distribution of such proportions gives a basis for assessing location on the monocracy-polycracy continuum. (We are not here attempting to "operationalize" the dimension, even if this formulation might prove helpful in doing so. The object is to help clarify the dimension conceptually.)

Although the Decision-Rules dimension may be simple in principle, certain difficulties are bound to arise in putting it to work. These should be pointed out immediately to avoid questionable findings, exact or impressionistic, and to identify cases in which highly exact or simple descriptions are unlikely.

The most likely, and probably most vexing, source of difficulty is that some units have more than one Decision-Rule—for different types of decision, or at different stages of the decision-process, or at different levels of a unit's stratiformity. In such cases, problems usually can be avoided by concentrating on the more critical and consequential decisions, the more important phases of the decision-process (probably initiation and resolution), and the Rules prevailing at the higher *S*-levels. In some such cases, however, arriving at an overall location of the unit on the dimension will be impossible, and a complex rule set must be described instead; in addition, rough judgments must generally be made to do in lieu of exact measurements.

A second common source of difficulty is that the Decision-Rule even for a particular kind of decision may be so complex that exact and highly reliable characterizations become unlikely. For example, the Decision-Rule for passing ordinary bills in the American Congress combines majority rule in both houses, a monocratic presidential power to veto, a two-thirds majority requirement after the veto has been exercised, specially empowered minorities at the committee and joint committee stages, and a significant element of monocracy in the role of committee chairmen. In such a case, appearances can be extremely deceiving. Ambiguities and confusion are especially probable in regard to power to prevent decisions from being taken. In addition, it is easy to mistake systems of what might be called "dispersed monocracies" for cases of genuine polycracy. Something like such a system seems to have prevailed in the American legislative process. Individual chairmen of committees or small groups on the committees, especially powerful committees like Rules or Ways and Means, have been effectively able to stop legislative actions. As a result, at least until recent and possibly ephemeral reforms, they were often "bought off" through a tacit arrangement that gave them virtually monocratic power in certain areas in return for ceding it in others. This is hardly polycracy in the intended meaning of the term, although difficulties in operating a polycratic structure may be at the bottom of the arrangement—and even though the arrangement may often make necessary overwhelming sentiments in favor of a policy if positive action is to be taken. It seems unnecessary to add that Decision-Rules may be adopted precisely because they are likely to convey false impressions.

A third source of difficulty is that officially prescribed, vocally advocated, and actually practiced Decision-Rules may be at odds. This also can lead to deliberate deceptions. The American legislative process again is a case in point. There is constant talk about majority rule, but decisions are constantly prevented by minorities (even individuals), and not infrequently taken by them.

Finally, a problem arises when monocrats religiously practice consultation with other supers and are highly responsive to them or tend to anticipate reactions. This problem is not as serious as the others: monocracy remains monocracy, and differences in tendencies to take others' preferences into account appear under other dimensions (the Influence dimensions). Nevertheless, actual states of affairs in such cases may resemble polycracy (or majority rule) and may be mistaken for it.

Illustration: Polycracy in American Academic Departments

The Decision-Rules. In American academic departments, the formal, ostensible Decision-Rule for all matters typically is majority rule among those empowered to have a say. Except for decisions on academic personnel, this usually includes all faculty. Personnel decisions, strictly speaking, are not "directives" but often imply or reflect them (e.g., what is or is not to be taught in a department, how, and with what emphasis), and the participants include faculty of rank higher than and sometimes equal to the persons on whom actions are to be taken. Nowadays, representatives of students are often given voices and votes, in varying proportions to those of faculty members. As a result of the rule, the higher supers of the departments (chairmen, vice-chairmen, directors of special programs) formally have housekeeping and executive functions and serve as liaison between departments and higher university authorities. Chairmen, to be sure, can usually influence votes or indirectly affect decisions by actions on agendas or discussions. But they rarely play the monocratic role assumed by chairmen in many European universities, where the professors *ordinarius* (incumbents of departmental "chairs") usually have untrammeled power to run departments as they see fit, subject only to their own willingness to consult and take advice and to constraints by higher university authorities. (This pattern does prevail in some American universities and colleges, but it is unknown in the more prestigious institutions.)

In actual fact, the formal provisions for majority rule are highly misleading. The operative Decision-Rule is better stated as a rather complex set of rules, as follows: (1) Simple majorities suffice in matters of routine departmental housekeeping requiring collective decisions (e.g., decisions on the final standing of students on graduation), but decisions are usually unanimous anyway. (2) Extraordinary majorities are generally needed on more important matters not involving personnel; the more consequential the matter (the more people or segments of a department are likely to be affected), the larger the majority must be. Examples are decisions on the basic organization of a department by fields, on course requirements, or on innovations in the departmental curriculum entailing the phasing out of old and hiring of new faculty. The expectation in such cases is that decisions will not be made by majorities falling significantly short of unanimity. (3) All types of decisions on faculty personnel—hiring,. firing, promoting—require extraordinary majorities. (4) The more senior the person, or the more directly personnel decisions have implications for departmental policies, the closer the decision much approach unanimity. (5) Since minor decisions generally are unanimous in fact and major decisions are expected to approach unanimity in principle, it follows that the typical overall rule set approaches extreme polycracy, especially of senior faculty. This would be true even if the prevalence of unanimous votes on minor matters were discounted, precisely because departures from the polycratic arrangement may be large only in the case of relatively insignificant decisions.

Conditions of Effective Operation of the Rule Set. An important question for theorizing about Decision-Rules concerns the conditions under which such Rules (hence also the social units in which they prevail) can work effectively. These conditions can be inferred in part from the very nature of the rules; in part also, one must recognize divergences between ostensible and operative rules to arrive at them. To the description of the Decision-Rules of American academic departments, we therefore add some remarks on the conditions that enable them to work; those who participate in decision making in such departments may be only vaguely aware of these conditions, and many junior participants are probably not aware of them at all. The nine conditions listed are not exhaustive, but they cover the most essential requisites for the smooth operation of the rule set described.

1. Since the operative rules are nowhere formally stated, members of departments must be "socialized" into an implicit grasp of the rule set. A particularly critical aspect of the departmental socialization process must be to inculcate self-restraint in deliberation and voting, thus permitting the right kind of majorities to emerge. For example, unanimous or near-unanimous majorities are unlikely unless members who perceive themselves to be in the probable minority, but who feel less than absolutely in the right, are willing to give the majority the benefit of doubt and switch their preferences. For the same reason, taking a strong position off the cuff can be troublesome. Since the ego becomes strongly attached to positions vehemently taken, members must learn to practice silence or the art of speaking softly and inconclusively—practices that rarely come naturally to peda-

gogues. Because of this, problems often arise with junior faculty members who lack deference, with student representatives who are not only unsocialized but lack a long-run stake in their departments, or with senior faculty recruited from nonacademic units in which the Decision-Rules are different. Almost inevitably, members who are not fully socialized perceive the more highly socialized members of departments as temporizing, lacking in conviction, and willing to cast unprincipled votes; and they often make the "ruleful" conduct of the decision-process difficult by their own imperfect understanding of the rules and by intruding alien expectations into decision-making processes.

2. There must be much prior informal consultation, negotiating, and mediating before official discussions occur. Only thus can a sense of the probable majority emerge well in advance of the discussions. Here chairmen have special responsibilities and considerable power to influence or even rig decisions; to a lesser extent, other department members can be manipulative, too. This again is likely to be misinterpreted by those not yet fully socialized into the rules, as substituting *faits accomplis* where open deliberations should prevail.

3. The rule set operates effectively only with a good deal of log-rolling. Mutual "favors" are particularly important in regard to the most serious matters, because unanimity must be approached especially closely on these occasions. Favors are also highly important in regard to any matters on which certain members' preferences are intense, since the probability that anyone will sublimate his preferences is low. Without log-rolling the general distribution of benefits in departments would probably permanently disadvantage certain members, who would then be unlikely to help constitute extraordinary majorities. The uninitiated are likely to perceive the prevalence of mutual back-scratching as further evidence of unprincipled behavior, most of all in regard to matters that seem to call for particularly objective deliberation. In fact, however, decisions might be far more capricious if any sizable party in a department could persistently overwhelm others. Exerting power without expertise is much more likely in such cases than in others, and legitimate sectional interests are more likely to be slighted.

4. It is generally functional to the smooth operation of the rule set if log-rolling proceeds according to the rule that less intense preferences defer to more intense preferences—again, especially in regard to "serious" matters. As a corollary, the more preferences are intense, the more log-rolling is necessary if decisions are to be made effectively. Judgments of personnel generally evoke the most intense preferences, since they tend to become entangled in particularistic and emotional personal considerations. Consequently, log-rolling is most likely, and most functional, in matters of hiring, dismissal, and promotion.

5. Since contrary preferences on issues are often equally intense, there should be a tendency either to avoid or postpone decisions on a good many issues, or to engage in "tacit" decision making that bypasses regular channels. The art of determining agendas thus becomes critically important, as does that of allowing new states of affairs to "emerge." Here, of course, the chairman has a particularly delicate task. He must decide when matters are ripe or unripe for the departmental agenda (which obviously gives him some monocratic power) and by what means destructive processes of express decision making can be avoided, yet business still be transacted.

6. The rule set operates well only if there is a substantial amount of delegation to special committees and deference to their recommendations on grounds of assumed special expertise. There are two principal problems in constituting such committees. First, the log-rolling requirement must not be violated; second, the committees must be so balanced that diverse intense preferences by their members will not produce a result opposite to that intended and department members will not perceive them as representing special interests. The chairman can again have a vital indirect influence on decisions by designating the committee members and their functions.

7. There should similarly be great deference to the special expertise of certain department members in regard to the substantive divisions of a department—its subfields of specialization. Such professional deference is especially required to justify log-rolling: that is, to square it with the expectation of objective professional judgments.

8. Decisions that directly put the personal interests of department members at odds (such as the awarding of scarce leaves or the division of limited funds for salary increases) should be taken without the participation of the members concerned. Among other things, this means that a number of matters concerning senior faculty must be reserved to the chairman's powers. This, together with the more indirect influence the chairman may have on decisions and, even more, nondecisions, makes the frequent rotation of the chairmanship desirable, compensating for the loss of experience and know-how that rotation inevitably entails.

9. It hardly seems necessary to add that all these conditions will be promoted by consensus on an academic "paradigm" in the field of the department. Lacking such consensus, only wide tolerance of heterodoxy is a satisfactory substitute. It follows that the rule set functions effectively only in the more coherent or consciously heterodox fields. Between these (e.g., in departments characterized by rival orthodoxies) the rule set either functions badly or is replaced by another, such as the monocratic rule of the chairman.

Bases and Consequences of the Rule Set. A second major set of theoretical problems concerning Decision-Rules involves the reasons for their being what they are; a third, the consequences they have for the units in which they operate. What then are some of the bases and results of the rule set described, taking into account both its nature and requirements to operate it smoothly?

Whatever might be thought of the net balance of consequences of the rule set and its correlates, it should be apparent that it does serve useful, perhaps even indispensable, functions in academic units. It should also be evident that its existence can largely be explained by examining the units themselves.

One notices first that the matters expected to be decided by unanimous or near-unanimous votes are precisely those on which judgments are expected to be objectively professional, not mere leanings and opinions. Examples are the evaluation of personnel (especially senior personnel, about whom most returns are already in) and conceptions of the major specialized divisions of a field of study or the proper contents and sequences of studies to be followed in attaining professional competence in the field. On such matters one expects qualified professionals either to be of a single mind or, if no single "right" solution is available, to suspend judgment altogether. This expectation, in turn, is most conducive to two apparently (but only apparently) paradoxical Decision-Rules. One is the monocracy of a single individual, preferably the wisest or most experienced. This, as stated, is the typical rule in European departments. The other is the polycracy of all considered qualified to make properly professional judgments. The latter rule can accommodate a few deviant individuals whose judgment might be considered temporarily clouded by human fallibility. But it cannot accommodate the dominance of shifting majoritarian coalitions or less transient factions. The rule set thus sustains the fundamental myth that prevails in all academic departments and through some of its correlates (e.g., deference to specialist experts or particularly well-informed committees) actually helps to realize it.

The tendency toward expectations of unanimity is reinforced by the assumption that academics have at heart the overall academic interests of their departments rather than personal or segmental advantages. On this basis, it is assumed not only that uniquely right policies exist but that they will also be the policies preferred by department members. Whether the operation of the rule set promotes such an outlook is rather doubtful. However, the prevalence of log-rolling does at least ensure that different segmental interests, if indeed they exist, receive some degree of consideration.

One can also argue that the rule set is particularly suited to a unit in which all the higher supers have life tenure and in which, unlike the typical

European case, large numbers of peers are found at the highest rank. (Whether the latter is the case seems to determine whether the extremely monocratic or highly polycratic alternative is chosen.) Like it or not, tenured department members have to work, and to an extent live, together, and it would clearly be disastrous for any set of them to feel persistently disadvantaged vis-à-vis any other. Moreover, the behavior that accompanies the formation of majoritarian coalitions is likely to leave intolerable scars in such a situation, whatever general distribution of benefits results. If, then, tenure is functional in academic life, so are the Decision-Rules practiced in it.

A further positive consequence of the rule set is that it hinders the imposition of particular fads and hobby-horses as departmental gospel. The obstacle is not insurmountable, but to the extent that the rule set operates, it obviously is great.

By the same token, however, the rule set entails a manifest cost. It promotes *immobilisme* in departments: a tendency to resist change, especially major change. Polycracy always has that consequence, simply because the amount of agreement needed to engineer change is greater than that required to prevent it. In a limited way, this holds in cases of majority rule, where the majority is a very numerous body composed of many different segmental interests. During the last 30 years, for example, only 11% of all initiatives in Switzerland have managed to pass when put to the popular vote, and then only if supported by the national Parliament after a process of compromise in which segmental interests were taken into account; even 60% of all parliamentary decisions brought to a popular referendum have been rejected.[4] It is now generally recognized in Switzerland that the initiative and referendum, originally designed to allow the expression of public will, serve more to prevent the formation of any *positive* political will altogether. *Immobilisme* is likely to be even more pronounced if extraordinary majorities are required—as they are, for example, in the case of certain American legislative decisions. And it is most likely if particular individuals or small groups possess monocratic privileges to effectively veto decisions of special kinds, as do chairmen of Congressional committees. In such cases the price of any action not supported by overwhelming sentiment may be the delegation to strategically placed individuals of monocratic rights to decide in particular domains of action; thus in effect, polycracy is transformed into a system of dispersed monocracies. Many American academic departments are precisely such systems.

A further consequence of the rule set that seems anything but "functional" is that it gives unusual power to individuals who are stubborn, selfish, or easy to bring to the point of righteous conviction. If the rules operate, such individuals nearly always get their way over more temperate and accommodating members. The rule set thus is tailor-made for ideologues and scoundrels. It is just as likely, however, that the existence of such individuals will induce persistent rifts, animosities, and, thereby, paralysis. And the critical mass for such effects is not large: two or three senior people who fail to play by the rules and their concomitants, or try to exploit them, usually suffice.

The resulting arrangement somewhat resembles the American legislative process but usually has an even more pronounced feudal flavor. There are typically individuals or small groups acting as barons over particular departmental fiefdoms that cover special subjects, groups of students, and junior teaching staff; they are presided over by a suzerain whose special powers derive from common interests in the harmony of the whole; they generally act in concert to safeguard their special benefices; their harmony is endangered by vain, stubborn, or imperious individuals; in general, they resist change more than being capable of engineering it. Let us stop elaborating the analogy here; it is only analogy, but it certainly seems to the point.

Whether the arrangement is, on the whole, desirable in an academic context would require the examination of alternatives to it: monocracy or something closer to simple majority rule. This is not the place for such an examination. Academic readers may, however, wish to make it for themselves.

S-S Processes: Decision-Behavior

General Discussion

Decision-Behavior refers to the ways in which superordinates interact in working out directives (and in equivalent processes, such as deciding whether or how to apply sanctions against violations of directives). Since no such interactions occur in extreme monocracy, the dimension does not pertain to such cases. But extreme monocracy, although not strictly speaking a "limiting" case, is bound to be rare; hence for all practical purposes, the dimension can be regarded to be generally applicable.

The illustration we have just worked through indicates that Decision-Rules are likely to be interrelated with Decision-Behavior. The nature of such behavior would be strictly deducible from the nature of Decision-Rules if supers always and in all respects adopted modes of behavior consistent with the most effective working of the Rules. If this were the case, however, Decision-Rules would always work well, and they manifestly do not. Consequently, Decision-Behavior should be treated as a separate dimension, interrelated with other aspects of structures and processes of superordination, but imperfectly so.

Like Decision-Rules and most other aspects of authority patterns, the behavior of supers in the process of working out decisions yields a vast number of qualitatively different modes of acting. Any of these may loom large in idiographic descriptions, and, as always, they pose problems if systematic descriptions are desired for purposes of cumulation and comparison. To some degree, superordinates in every social unit no doubt follow unique ways of working out directives. Even in the same units their behavior in decision making probably varies according to who happens to occupy superordinate roles and according to types of directive being made—perhaps even from one directive to another, regardless of type. Here as elsewhere, the problem for conceptualization is to cull the essential and general from the contingent and accidental and, if at all possible, to find a continuous dimension that may be considered to "underlie" general qualitative differences.

Our solution of the problem is to characterize supers' Decision-Behavior on the basis of the extent to which they value and act out harmonious (or "concordant") modes of decision making. Three simple considerations led to the conclusion that the matter of harmony in making decisions furnishes the underlying dimension we seek.

1. Decision-Processes concerning directives occur simply because it is necessary to choose courses of action from among alternatives likely to be valued differently by those who interact in the processes—alternatives that affect differently the actors' real or perceived "interests" or those of the people represented. Even if not explicitly stated, alternative courses of action always exist and are always likely to have different effects on different people. Consensus may reduce conflicts over values, but it rarely extends beyond broad preferences that still allow scope for conflict over specifics. Homogeneity in social units may reduce the range and intensity of clashes concerning special interests. The members of homogeneous units are never identical, however, and what may appear as petty objective differences to external observers, may be differences of considerable consequence to the members of a social unit.

2. All decision-processes, therefore, have at least latently the task of harmonizing differences. This seldom can be a matter of taking decisions one at a time, according to prevalent Decision-Rules (i.e., not just a matter of working out coalitions *de convenance* for every matter to be decided). The probability that differences will be harmonized on specific issues is obviously increased if sizable groups engage in rather persistent arrangements to act in concert. The probable persistence of such arrangements, and the extent to which they operate effectively, itself depends on the extent to which they are based on petty, close calculations of the balance of benefits

the respective participants derive. In gist, the persistence and effectiveness of the arrangements is in peril insofar as they are maintained only if immediately "profitable" to the particular interests they combine. The extent to which this is the case obviously varies, in turn, with the tendency to take into account any values and interests other than narrow personal or segmental ones in decision-processes.

3. It follows that participants in decision-processes may generally act to make the outcomes difficult or easy to attain, and the tendency to do the one or the other lies at the heart of processes of collective choice. It is difficult to reach a decision if participants use competitive or downright antagonistic behavior, making no concessions except those that seem compelled or in some narrow sense "profitable." Conversely, the outcome of a decision can be facilitated by cooperative, mutually accommodating behavior, making sacrifices that entail no apparent immediate profit to the participants, except perhaps that of safeguarding harmony in a larger group (coalition, superordinate structure, or overall social unit). The more Decision-Rules approach the polycratic extreme, the larger the group whose harmony needs to be safeguarded, and the less important becomes the role of calculations of the immediate profitability of specific directives to special interests.[5]

Much if not everything that occurs in decision-processes can thus be located on a dimension that runs from *concordance* to *discordance* (see Figure 5.2). Decision-processes are concordant to the extent that supers value general harmony (consensus, mutually supportive behavior) and act in ways tending to promote or maintain it—that is, tend to make value sacrifices. Such sacrifices entail supers' yielding their own preferences to those of others or modifying them to achieve better fit with other views. Since conflicting preferences are sometimes difficult to discern because they are not allowed to emerge or are tailored to each other by anticipation, value scarifices may also be posited if supers yield any apparent "interests" to other supers—that is, simply go along with decisions clearly costly to themselves or parts of a unit with which they are specially identified. It is always better to know directly about conflicting preferences than to impute them to presumed interests; however, the more concordant the units are, the more likely it is that conflicts over alternative actions will not emerge for scrutiny by observers in the first place. Hence imputation is unavoidable precisely in the more concordant cases.

Concordance is extreme if supers always seek and attain unanimity in decisions, making all value sacrifices necessary for such outcomes. Extreme discordance involves the overriding valuation of competitive attitudes and antagonistic behavior toward fellow supers: sticking uncompromisingly to

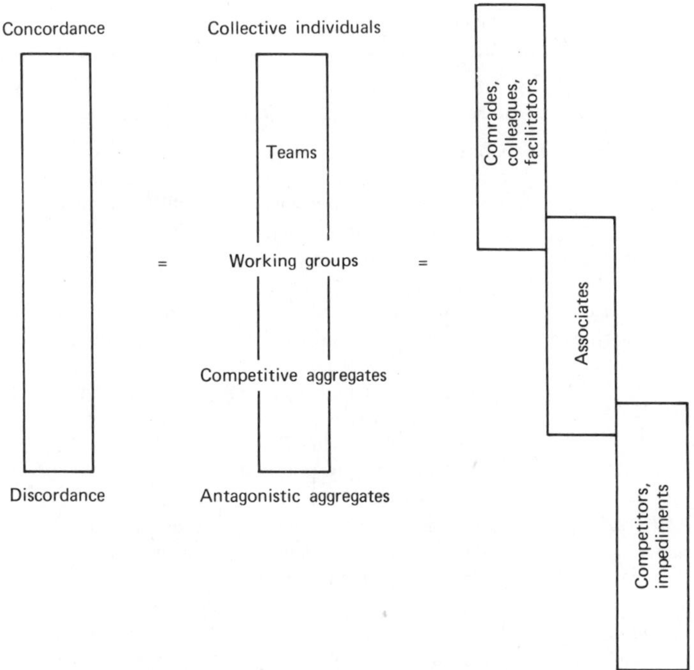

Fig. 5.2 The Decision-Behavior dimension.

one's own preferences and mobilizing all available power resources to impose them, regardless of consequences for cooperation in the social unit, its structure of superordination, or coalitions within that structure. In such cases, the resolution of conflicting preferences is always forced, not agreed. As usual, both extremes are unlikely in practice. One can indeed question whether extreme discordance is consistent with the very existence of a social unit. It resembles Hobbes' imaginary state of nature and thus may be a limiting case in the literal sense. However, actual cases that closely approach the two extremes are not hard to find.

To make the nature of the dimension more vivid, Table 5.1 lists some contrasting observations that are likely to be made in highly concordant and discordant units; the tabulation also serves to illustrate the sense in which a concordance-discordance dimension "underlies" much that is qualitatively different in decision-processes.

Table 5.1 could be extended, but the patterns mentioned should serve the purposes intended. Note particularly that although all the observations listed involve different kinds of behavior, many seem to be correlates of one

Table 5.1 Examples of Decision-Behavior

Behavior Items	Concordance	Discordance
1. *Conflict resolution*	Conflicts among supers (if allowed to surface) are resolved amicably and with dispatch, even if conflicting values or interests are far apart or deep-seated.	The resolution of differences tends to be rancorous, difficult, and slow, even if differences are petty and superficial.
2. *Decision-Rules and decision-taking*	Even highly polycratic Decision-Rules tend to produce outcomes smoothly. (And note that high concordance is clearly a functional requisite of the effective operation of highly polycratic Decision-Rules.)	Even if Decision-Rules require only narrow agreements, outcomes tend to be fewer and are tougher to produce.
3. *Stability of coalitions*	Coalitions among supers tend to be stable, even if there are major disagreements among parties.	Coalitions tend to fall apart over trifling conflicts.
4. *Amount of agreement on decisions*	Decisions tend to be made unanimously or by large majorities, regardless of what formal Decision-Rules prescribe.	Decisions tend to be made by narrow margins.
5. *Collegiality*	Supers prefer to operate as collegial bodies, even if formal rules do not prescribe collective *S*-structures.	Supers tend to operate through systems of "dispersed monocracy," to the extent they operate effectively as groups at all, even if collective *S*-structures are formally prescribed.

another. This reinforces the point that they express a common underlying dimension—that they constitute a logically coherent complex of behavior, whose various elements derive from a single general disposition.

At the high extreme of concordance, then, supers act as if they were "collective individuals"—as if literally a "unit," in the manner of close-knit families. At a point below that extreme, but above the midpoint of the continuum, they work in the manner of most "teams": there is considerable self-effacement for the sake of the harmony and efficient working of the whole, but also discernible concern with attaining individual values. At the

Table 5.1 Examples of Decision-Behavior—Continued

Behavior Items	Concordance	Discordance
6. *Divisive issues*	Issues known or suspected to be highly divisive tend to be sublimated into the realm of "nondecision-making."	The divisiveness of issues has no relation to the extent to which they are pressed; supers may vigorously press issues fraught with antagonism.
7. *Amount of conflict*	There is little conflict over issues that normally entail sharp conflicts (especially significant redistributions of values among supers or social segments they represent).	Sharp conflict visibly appears over issues that involve low personal or segmental stakes.
8. *Mutual support*	In the process of ironing out disputes, supers can often count on support from others whose values or interests are rather distant from their own.	Supers can rarely count on support from others, even if their interests or values seem close.
9. *Collective responsibility*	Supers manifest collective responsibility, in the sense of publicly supporting, or at least not dissenting from, collective decisions with which they disagree.	Supers frequently carry their disagreements into the public arena, attempting to generate pressures in behalf of their preferred positions.
10. *Collective identity*	Supers generally use the collective "we" even for the individual decisions of other supers.	Supers often disavow decisions taken by groups of which they are members, and *S*-structures are deliberately represented as units of dissociated individuals.

midpoint we can place what might be termed "working groups"; here individual preferences and the value of harmoniously and efficiently producing group results are in close balance. Between the midpoint and the discordant extreme are "competitive aggregates" (tenuous coalitions) and, at the discordant extreme, "antagonistic aggregates" (people who work together the better to do one another in, as it were).

These, however, are all arbitrary terms of convenience. Location on the dimension, which is continuous and not readily compartmentalized, is essentially determined by two related considerations: (*a*) the extent to which personal and segmental values are subordinated to larger values of the overall group, and (*b*) the level of intensity of preference at which participants in decision-processes prefer conflict, especially open conflict, to accommodation, or tenacious haggling to easy compromise. The proposed labels merely convey general impressions of what occurs in units at different points on the continuum.

For this purpose, it may also be useful to think of location on the continuum as bound up with the manner in which supers in a social unit generally perceive one another. Along the higher (concordant) span of the continuum they are likely to perceive one another as "comrades" or "colleagues": people who act as mutual "facilitators." Along the lower (discordant) span, they perceive one anothere more as "competitors": people who tend to be mutual impediments. In between, they regard and treat one another simply as "associates": co-workers having personal and segmental interests or values of nearly equal importance at stake in common tasks and the welfare of the overall group. These perceptions can, of course, be held in different degrees and mixtures, and, as Figure 5.2 indicates, they overlap or shade off into one another at the margins.

Research on Decision-Behavior is likely to produce problems in identifying the reference groups (i.e., sets of supers) in regard to whom degrees of concordance and discordance are to be gauged. The more complex a unit's conformation, the more likely it is that such problems will arise, and the more difficult they will be to solve. In highly complex units there will be a great many supers, at numerous levels of superordination (location on which may not be clearly "resolved"), specializing in different functions and/or spatially segmented, operating in parallel hierarchies and in more or less collective bodies of superordinates. In such cases it is next to inconceivable that the whole population of supers should be the reference group for determining the degree of concordance. And although the problem of defining proper reference groups arises most obviously and viciously in the most complex cases, it is likely to appear in some form in any case that is not extremely simple.

An easy solution of the problem is to treat supers at the same level as the reference group. But this is too easy—better than no solution, but manifestly flawed. The principal difficulty with this approach results from functional specialization. For example, it is unlikely that supers responsible for virtually unrelated functions (say military and "cultural" activities) will seek out mutual agreements, except perhaps on those very limited subjects, usually finances, which clearly affect them all. Functional considerations would more often lead us to expect concordant supers to work as well-oiled teams across levels of superordination in closely related functional domains than at the same level in domains only remotely related. Moreover, unless a structure of superordination is highly resolved, it will be difficult to identify supers at the same level, or indeed the levels of superordination at which decisions really are taken.

Under the circumstances, one can *begin* by considering as reference groups supers at the same level—particularly supers who constitute collective bodies as well as having separate functions. However, there are at least three other ways of defining reference groups for the present purpose that are probably better than that simple procedure and certainly useful as supplements to it.

One is to use knowledge of a unit's Decision-Rules to identify the proper reference group. Such rules generally identify at least roughly the people necessary for decisions to stand, thus also indicate the gross number required. In academic departments, for example, the typical Decision-Rule nowadays calls not only for the wide agreement of tenured faculty members on "major" issues, as was once the case, but that of junior faculty and often of representatives of students as well; the result, by our impressionistic reading, has been a considerable decrease of concordant behavior.

Second, we can try to examine concordance and discordance by emphasizing matters that clearly cut across functional specialties and spatial boundaries, and thus are unlikely to be indifferent to many supers. The matters that most obviously qualify are basic modes of material allocation, like budgeting or the assignment of personnel. In such cases one can surely assume that at least all high-ranking supers—not necessarily only those who rank highest—will be an appropriate reference group. It is probably also safe to assume that attitudes and behavior patterns displayed in regard to such matters will be typical of the "operational code" of superordinates in the unit; this is an empirical, not a logical, assertion, but the contrary seems less likely on the face of it.

A third possibility, probably the most telling, is to look for the extent to which supers seek agreements beyond what is required by Decision-Rules, even informal ones—or, much the same, the extent to which informal Decision-Rules go beyond the level of agreement called for by formal rules. In a similar vein, one can search out tendencies to seek broad agreements beyond domains that clearly are functionally related, as well as tendencies to seek agreement from people with doubtful expertise in particular matters or occupying lower positions in a hierarchy of superordination. Since the notions of concordance and discordance refer to generally preferred modes of operating, rendering them accessible for research should if possible entail looking beyond groups that might closely collaborate for pragmatic reasons only or because no alternatives exist. Therefore, the extent to which the search for agreements thus extends below particular levels of status, beyond functionally related domains, and beyond people having pertinent expertise, offers a particularly useful basis for gauging the extent and intensity of norms of concordance. In other words, we learn most about concordance, or anything else, by looking at behavior that cannot be readily explained away on grounds different from those asserted.

Illustration: Polycracy and Concordance in Norwegian Politics and Society

Decision Making in Norway. In a study of political divisions and the bases of political cohesion in Norway, Eckstein argued that a highly polycratic Decision-Rule operates on the Norwegian national parliamentary level.[6] Although majority rule ostensibly (formally) prevails, the normatively held rule for parliamentary decisions runs more like this: agree as widely as possible—if at all possible, unanimously; if wide agreement is not possible, act as if it existed or, much the same, as if there were no extensive disagreements (i.e., do not display disagreements; keep quiet about them or mute them); and if neither the fact nor the appearance of wide agreement is possible, do not bring a matter to the point of decision at all. Admittedly, this generalization was based on raw observation, not systematic data gathering. The observations, however, were extensive; and they included statements from numerous parliamentarians. No contrary statements were made; the generalization has not been criticized or questioned in Norway; and it can serve as a quite accurate predictor of specific legislative activities and outcomes. In addition, preconceptions played no role in arriving at the rule; if anything, its discovery seemed surprising and puzzling.

Obviously a Decision-Rule like this can operate effectively only if Decision-Behavior is highly concordant. If decisions conforming to the rule are to be made, it must be possible to reconcile smoothly many divergent values and interests. Value sacrifices must also be made for the sake of "nondecisions." In fact, more costly value sacrifices are entailed by these than by most decisions, for the simple reason that people who command narrow majorities must be prepared not to take advantage of them. Other things equal, it is less costly to forego an uncertain benefit than to give up a certain one. By the same token, the threshold of intensity at which participants in decision-processes prefer conflict to accommodation must be very high. This again pertains to nondecisions as well as decisions, and it pertains as much to cultivating the appearance of wide agreements as to the processes of working them out.

The Decision-Rule works effectively in Norway, and Decision-Behavior is precisely as expected in such a case. It would take much space to supply all the details, but a sample of relevant points is presented.

The Norwegian legislative process permits a great deal of sounding out of all points of view before matters are allowed to come up for debate. This is not unusual. However, the purpose of the process is not just to discover the most common preference but to find or work out the most widely acceptable policy, to adjust to any intense views, thus incorporating or placating minority preferences, and to assure that nothing that remains deeply opposed or opposed by a sizable minority comes to the point of public debate. It is noteworthy that this tendency operates when a single party has a cohesive parliamentary majority, as Labor did from 1945 to 1957, no less than when there is coalition government or government by a minority dependent on the support of excluded groups. Minorities are not ignored or discounted just because they are minorities, which is to say that it is not merely substantive outcomes that are valued but also the processes by which they are reached (concordance) and the spectrum of assents they embrace (polycracy). A condition of the self-restraint of the majority is, of course, the concordant behavior of minorities: the game is and must be one of *mutual* accommodation.

Since the game of concordant adjustment is relatively difficult to conduct when large numbers of people are involved, much of it is played on the level of legislative committees. Not only does the legislature tend to acquiesce in any recommendations by committees, but parties generally defer to the views of members who serve on legislative committees, even if these views diverge from standing party preferences and seem to go against party interests. And Torgersen points out that a crucial demand on work in committees is to be "fully agreed" (*enig:* "at one") and to iron out all disparities in positions.[7] According to Torgersen, engineering full agreement is the main function of committee chairmen, and achieving it is also a norm constantly pressing on committee members. Anything coming to the legislature from its committees thus usually has passed the crucial test of concordant harmonization to achieve near unanimity, and committee recommendations become tantamount to legislative outcomes (and, incidentally, parliamentary "debates" tend to be unexciting, technical discussions of barely divergent positions).

Most of the conditions indicating high concordance outlined in the general discussion of the dimension can be used as reliable descriptions of Norwegian politics. (1) The existence of a highly polycratic Decision-Rule does not make for notably immobilistic government. Norway in fact has "positive" government *par excellence*, although a few areas are consistently ignored in national decision making because they are subject to intensely contrary preferences (e.g., what the Norwegians call "cultural" questions: chiefly religious and linguistic ones), and there is a predictable tendency for governments to be particularly active in areas of broad social consensus (e.g., social welfare legislation). (2) Norway tends to have rather stable governmental coalitions, even among parties that are widely divided. An example is a recent coalition between urban, industry-minded conservatives and agrarians with antipathies toward industry and representing divergent interests; this coalition also included secularist Liberals and Rightists and a fundamentalist Christian party. (3) Collegiality in structures of superordination is a Norwegian way of life and implies more than collective *S*-structures. It also implies high egalitarianism among the members of the structures. The Norwegian Prime Minister, for example, is hardly even *primus inter pares* compared to his British counterpart. Only two domineering Prime Ministers are even remotely identifiable in Norway's history, and only one (Knudsen, 1908–1917) indubitably played at being boss. The rest have been chairmen, mediators, and advisers, functioning chiefly to create *enighet* by coordinating attitudes and inducing bargains and compromises. They are first among equals, but they cultivate equality more than primacy. Furthermore, collective *S*-structures tend to be used even when not formally prescribed: even before the adoption of the parliamentary and cabinet system, the king's counselors functioned as a "markedly collegial council."[8] (4) The Cabinet functions smoothly as a body having collective responsibility, in the British sense, even in the absence of a myth of it being the emanation of an indivisible body, the monarch. It is virtually unknown for ministers to air publicly their disagreements with collective decisions or to treat decisions as not their personal responsibility. Individual resignations rarely occur, since decisions that have not passed through a unanimity-seeking process are not taken.

Since the evidence on high concordance in Norwegian national government is mainly "raw" or indirect, the ability to base correct predictions—especially predictions not intrinsically likely to prove correct—on the assumption of concordance is a matter of some moment. An occasion tailor-made for such predictions occurred in 1965, when after 30 years of Labor governments, a potentially discordant coalition of four "bourgeois" parties (including, as stated, urban Rightists, Liberals, Agrarians, and the fundamentalist Christian People's Party) assumed power. It seemed to Eckstein, at the time, that four predictions about the coalition could be made on the assumption of high concordance.[9] First, it could be predicted that despite large disparities among the parties constituting it, the coalition would achieve a degree of stability, principally by avoiding potentially divisive issues. Second, it seemed likely that if divisive issues could not be avoided and differences easily resolved, the coalition would nevertheless operate smoothly by a kind of functional differentiation: special responsibilities for certain areas of policy would tacitly be delegated to members of the coalition having the most direct interests and intense preferences in regard to them (e.g., as the Agrarians did in farm policy), while the coalition would act as if collective decision making had operated and collective responsibility had been applied. Third, the postulate of high concordance entailed that the coalition would not do anything greatly repugnant to the opposition, the Labor Party. After 30 years of dominance by Labor, just the opposite might have been expected. However, two considerations made it very unlikely in this case that a substantial amount of earlier legislation would be repealed or revised or the opposition's wishes ignored in making new policy: policies made under the Labor-dominated governments generally expressed much more than preferences unique to Labor, and Labor still represented a very large minority—in fact, it remained the largest political party. Fourth, and setting a limit on concordance, if an issue arose that could not be avoided, and the preferences of the coalition diverged widely and intensely on the matter, the coalition should have been expected to fall apart.

As it happens, all these expectations were confirmed by events—the last of them by the coalition's resignation because of tensions over the proposal that Norway enter the Common Market, an unavoidable and explosive issue.[10]

Concordant behavior in Norway is by no means confined to national politics. Much the same pattern prevails in the political parties, which function as cohesive teams even more than in Britain, despite the absence of sanctions that might enable leaders to compel party "discipline," such as the unrestricted power of parliamentary dissolution to which the docility of British parliamentarians is often attributed. Similar patterns of mutual accommodation and collegial habits can be discerned in nonpolitical organizations. The typical *formenn* in Norwegian organizations function as mediators and conciliators in collective bodies, regardless of whether these are formally prescribed; and in such organizations much work is also delegated to special committees, where the fashioning of accord is eased by considerations of size. Studies of microcosmic units like families also reveal the pattern—for example, among parents and in relations between parents and children, or in peer groups formed by children. The normative valuation of persuasion and the prohibition of compulsion and sanctioning, especially violent sanctioning, also appears in such primers for parental behavior as Sundal's *Mor og barn*, which for many years has been the bible of Norwegian parents.[11]

The Bases of Concordance in Norway. How can the existence of the pattern of Decision-Behavior that prevails in Norway be explained? Obviously that pattern is highly functional to the operation of polycracy. But we already know that Decision-Behavior is not always well adapted to Decision-Rules. In any case, it seems more sensible to think of the Norwegian rules and behavior patterns as all of a piece—that is, as expressions of the same underlying conditions. What then are these conditions?

Political scientists have two favored, almost instinctive, explanations of the kind of behavior described: consensus on issues and homogeneity of a population. Neither, it seems to us, withstands scrutiny.

One problem associated with attributing Norwegian Decision-Behavior to consensus is this: although consensus obviates a need for concordance, it does not necessarily make for it. In fact, concordance logically presupposes the existence of differing values and interests. Granted, a framework of broader agreements might facilitate overcoming narrower disagreements. But it is also true that people whose disagreements seem narrow often are especially stubborn about reconciling their differences and even become violently antagonistic. The history of socialist and Marxist factions attests to that, among many other available examples. On the other extreme, Lijphart has persuasively argued that something closely resembling what we call concordant behavior often characterizes societies that exhibit high "subcultural cleavage"[12]—perhaps just because discordant behavior is likely to have especially explosive consequences in such societies. What he calls "consociationalism" obviously does not occur in all such cases. Still, it occurs in some; and since obstinate discordance can exist in the opposite case, the safe conclusion seems to be that levels of consensus and concordance are not directly related at all.

Whether there is a high level of consensus in Norway is a further problem. Sharp and persistent political divisions, as described in Eckstein's study and uncovered in much survey and other research, do exist, even if alongside areas of undoubtedly broad agreement. We do not know how to measure overall consensus and "dissensus," and neither does anyone else, including devotés of consensus theory. Even without exact measurement, however, Norway presents a clear discrepancy between level of concordance and level of similitude in values and interests. If one searches for wide and deep consensus in Norway, the area that stands out most is agreement on the desirability of observing the described Decision-Rules and Decision-Behavior. This may confirm the familiar agrument that procedural consensus promotes political stability, but it does not explain the existence of the rules and behavior in the first place. If Norwegian consensus is predominantly procedural, the argument that the procedures exist because of consensus is a transparent tautology.

If we substitute lack of objective differences (homogeneity) for lack of subjective differences (consensus), much the same arguments apply. Concordance presupposes either values or "interests" (or both) to be reconciled, and the lack of objective differences obviates any need for harmonizing "interests." Furthermore, Norwegians are very far from identical: it is not hard to find the heterogeneities that concordant behavior keeps from surfacing in overt conflict. Norwegians differ in the ways that most people in societies differ: according to occupation, education, residence, and so on—all possible, even if not inevitable, sources of political divisions. One can even find in Norway the differences that Rogowski and Wasserspring[13] call "stigmata." These are differences the authors associate with the extreme social divisions they label "segmentation" and which, according to them, make rational the subordination of individual to corporate action. An example is Norwegian linguistic differences, which have the two chief traits of stigmata: low information costs (being easy to discern) and high conversion costs (being hard to change). One also finds in Norway differences that historically have been associated with extreme, irreconcilable conflicts (e.g., rather profound religious differences between hard-core fundamentalists and religious liberals and secularists). Some heterogeneities associated with profound conflict, like racial differences, certainly are absent. However, enough others exist to fuel any amount of civic conflict. Again, Norwegian homogeneity seems to consist, not least, and maybe above all, of shared attitudes toward propriety in the exercise of authority. Thus attributing the attitudes to homogeneity also becomes afflicted with tautology.

A much more plausible basis for explaining the rules and patterns of behavior described is provided by Rogowski and Wasserspring themselves. Their arguments rest on the "rationalist" postulate that patterns of decision making will be regarded as proper if demonstrably consistent with what a society of calculating maximizers of personal utility would want. On this basis they reason, among other things, that "consensual" decision making would be considered proper in highly "segmented" societies. (The chain of reasoning is very complex; readers interested in how the premise entails the conclusion should consult the work cited in note 13.) By consensual decision making the authors mean almost exactly what has been described for Norway: polycratic and concordant decision making, not a lack of divergent interests and values in society. And they consider societies to be segmented to the extent that they consist of groups differentiated by traits easy to discern and hard to change, especially if the traits are closely related to occupational roles. Rogowski and Wasserspring also reason out that straightforward majoritarianism, in contrast to consensualism, will be associated with individualistic societies, in which a high degree of egalitarianism exists, and as a corollary of egalitarianism, a perception of persons as inherently interchangeable.

The Rogowski-Wasserspring hypothesis about the bases of consensualism is especially appealing here because it imputes the kind of decision making that prevails in Norway to some of the conditions we have used to impugn the consensus and heterogeneity hypotheses. The trouble with *their* hypothesis is that these conditions notwithstanding, Norway is one of the most egalitarian of all societies, where identification with the overall society strongly overrides segmental identifications. In most respects, Norway is precisely the kind of society in which plain majority rule should be preferred, if Rogowski and Wasserspring's reasoning holds. It is certainly not a society divided into clear-cut "corporations" resembling the corporations of traditional societies, especially European medieval society, which is the chief model for the Rogowski-Wasserspring conception of corporate segmentation. Rather, Norway exhibits the chief traits of "individualist" society, even with some dilution: equality (to an astonishing degree), open access to occupational roles, rather low differentials in honors and wealth, little association (if any) between personal traits and occupational roles, and so on.

Eckstein developed what might be called a "cultural" explanation of the cohesive forces at work in Norwegian politics and society. Such explanations are based on a postulate that is the very antithesis of that used by Rogowski and Wasserspring—namely, rather than behaving as rational calculators of maximum utility, people act as they do because of orientations they have "learned" and try to make consonant. Since Norwegian social life (even on the microcosmic levels of the family and childhood peer group, where the most basic social learning occurs), exhibits traits similar to those of political Decision-Behavior or inculcates values clearly conducive to these traits, the cultural explanation may seem clearly preferable to the rationalistic one. But it must be recognized that cultural explanations always have a flaw: they fail to explain how culture patterns that may be transmitted from generation to generation originate, unless, at some point, structural explanations are invoked. Explanations of the latter kind are needed to account not only for the origins of culture patterns but also their persistence: culture patterns are unlikely to endure unless reinforced, and an element in their reinforcement must be their suitability to the structures in which they exist. That suitability *need* not be judged by the Rogowski-Wasserspring model, but the model is attractive. Thus we may ask whether anything in Norwegian social structure can still rescue it, even if salient traits of that structure seem to contravene it.

Eckstein's study presents a possibility for doing so. He argues that polycracy and concordance work effectively in Norway at least partly because of a phenomenon that he calls functional deference, which involves acceptance of the views of people considered especially competent to have "right" views in special areas. How this facilitates polycratic and concordant decision making should be clear without discussion. Functional deference is most likely if there is a great deal of special schooling for a great many occupational roles—making occupations into professions, as it were. The Norwegians use such schooling to an extraordinary extent—even, for example, for postal or cafeteria workers. As a result, many occupations are "open" in the sense that anyone can easily become almost anything, provided he obtains the necessary training; but occupations are also "closed" in that there is also little cross-occupational mobility once an occupation has been entered—so little, in fact, that for virtually all Norwegians, occupations become a part of their names. In most countries people are identified as doctors or professors. In Norway they are identified also as lawyer, secretary, automobile mechanic, policeman, bricklayer, and so on. In that sense, occupations themselves become equivalents of "segments," without being associated with the stigmata that usually are the bases of segmentation.

Norway is a society of highly equal *but not interchangeable* people. Basing their abstract ideas on concrete examples—chiefly traditionalist Europe and frontier America—Rogowski and Wasserspring seem to have missed the possibility that their segmentation-individualist dimension may consist of quite different and only imperfectly related subdimensions. If this possibility holds, interchangeability, or lack of it, may coexist with a variety of traits in different cases.

Of course it has not yet been demonstrated whether lack of interchangeability in an egalitarian society would, on rationalist premises, yield the decision-processes characteristic of Norway. And the possibility remains that the decision-processes described rest more on cultural than structural reinforcement.[14]

Concluding Note

We mentioned at several points of this chapter that the two aspects of decision-processes—Rules and Behavior—are often related, but, in general, only imperfectly so. However, the relation is functionally and perhaps empirically close enough to have led to the use of much composite terminology for what the two dimensions denote. An example is Steiner's term "amicable agreement" as a label for the operative Decision-Rules and patterns of Decision-Behavior in Switzerland;[15] his study of that country is also a goldmine of hypotheses about the conditions of polycracy and concordance in polities. Another example is Lijphart's term "consociationalism."[16] And still another is Reich's *Konkordanzdemokratie*[17]—also intended especially to apply to Switzerland. Undoubtedly there is much to be said for collapsing the two dimensions thus, but probably more for keeping them conceptually separate, if only to permit the establishment of empirical relations between them.

Notes

1. The notion usually applies, even in such cases, to the preliminary stages of decision-processes and the succeeding stages of implementation, in which much "tacit" decision making often still occurs.

2. The term "polycratic" is deliberately used here in place of a now more familiar neologism, polyarchic. The latter is used (by Dahl and Lindblom, who coined the concept) to label *overall* sociopolitical processes, including the role of subordinates in them.

3. L. S. Shapley and Martin Shubik, "A Method for Evaluating the Distribution of Power in a Committee System," *American Political Science Review*, Vol. 48, No. 3 (September 1954), pp. 787–792.

4. Hans Tschäni, *Profil der Schweiz* (Zurich: Rascher, 1969), pp. 101, 112.

5. This does not imply that effective decision making presupposes "nonrational" behavior, in the economic sense. It may be rational to increase special personal utility by increasing general social utility and to assure the overall ability to work out directives in a social unit at the expense of certain losses of value. It is, in fact, difficult to see how any values dependent on collective actions might be maximized by making such actions difficult or preventing them altogether. The discussion therefore leaves open the question of whether collective decision making is, or may be, "rational".

6. Harry Eckstein, *Division and Cohesion in Democracy* (Princeton, N.J.: Princeton University Press, 1966), pp. 97–98.

7. Ulf Torgersen, *Norske politiske institusjoner* (Oslo: Institute for Social Research, 1964), Sec. 7.5.

8. Kristian Bloch, *Kongens råd: Regjeringsarbeidet i Norge* (Oslo: Universitetsforlaget, 1963), pp. 37–38.

9. For a partial statement of these, see Eckstein, "Norwegian Democracy in Comparative Perspective," *Tidsskrift for samfunnsforskning*, Vol. 8 (1967), p. 315. The statement was only partial because of an unwarranted but common diffidence about basing predictions on social science hypotheses.

10. To learn why this was an especially explosive issue, readers should consult *Division and Cohesion in Democracy*, Ch. 3. For ineluctable economic reasons, the issue was unavoidable once Britain decided to enter the Common Market.

11. For detail, see ibid., esp. pp. 143–144 and 160–163.

12. Arend Lijphart, "Consociational Democracy," *World Politics*, Vol. 21, No. 2 (January 1969), pp. 207–223. See also his *The Politics of Accommodaton: Pluralism and Democracy in the Netherlands* (Berkeley: University of California Press, 1968) and "Cultural Diversity and Theories of Political Integration," *Canadian Journal of Political Science*, Vol. 4 (1971).

13. Ronald Rogowski and Lois Wasserspring, *Does Political Development Exist?* (Beverly Hills, Calif.: Sage Professional Papers in Comparative Politics, No. 01-024, 1971), p. 19.

14. To make full sense of this discussion, reading Eckstein's book and the Rogowski-Wasserspring monograph is probably mandatory. The illustration is meant more to give concrete content to conceptual abstractions and to raise theoretical problems and suggest possible solutions than it is intended to settle anything. The whole problem of the origins and supports of Decision-Rules and patterns of Decision-Behavior is largely unsolved and crying for suggested solutions. The discussion of it here attempts to contribute to that enterprise by developing conceptual tools needed to state the problem and, to a lesser extent, by indicating some lines along which solutions of it might be sought.

15. Jürg Steiner, *Amicable Agreement versus Majority Rule: Conflict Resolution in Switzerland* (Chapel Hill: University of North Carolina Press, 1974).

16. See note 12.

17. Richard Reich, "Image und Stellenwert der schweizerischen Parteien in der heutigen Politik," *Schweizerisches Jahrbuch für Politische Wissenschaft,* Vol. 9 (1969), pp. 7–20.

CHAPTER SIX

The Recruitment of Superordinates

One universal, important, and highly variable aspect of authority patterns calls for separate discussion because it does not fit under either *S-s* or *S*-S relations. It involves the ways in which superordinates come to occupy their positions: the Recruitment of supers. In current sociological jargon this is a species of "boundary interchange," a matter of crossing lines between superordinated and subordinated positions.[1]

All social units that have stratiform, or asymmetric, order must have provisions (not necessarily formal) by which positions in the order are determined and recognized, just as they must have rules for recognizing that directives have been issued. In most social units, superordinates must also be replaced or replenished with greater or lesser frequency, because of natural attrition or other factors. One could, of course, simply take sets of supers as givens, ignoring the ways in which they attain their positions and dealing only with their relations to subs and among themselves. However, even ignoring that being superordinated implies a process of becoming superordinated, we have reason to think that much of importance would be missed if that process were neglected. For example, processes of Recruitment are likely to be highly interrelated with other aspects of authority patterns. Consequently, they are likely to be important in the development of synthetic (general typological) concepts for characterizing, comparing, and theorizing about the patterns.[2] Also, since processes of Recruitment, anyway certain aspects of them, are likely to be highly "visible" to members of a unit, the processes are likely to play important roles in perceptions of legitimacy, and for that reason too are likely to be important for both description and theory (see Chapter 7). These practical reasons for using a Recruitment dimension are elaborated in later chapters.

General Discussion

The broad meaning of Recruitment has already been stated. However, note that the term covers both processes by which subs become supers and those by which lower supers rise to higher positions. The processes can, of course, vary at each level of superordination and for each functional and spatial part of a segmented *S*-structure. Such variations can make simple, summary descriptions and measures of Recruitment difficult, if not impossible. On the other hand, important information is likely to be missed if only the most elementary processes of Recruitment are taken into account. For example, much about Recruitment to governmental positions in Britain may escape us if only "political" (i.e., legislative) positions are considered, and, in regard to such positions, if we consider only how people become members of Parliament, neglecting how they attain ministerial status and, beyond that, become members of the Cabinet.

The upper regions of the Recruitment dimension can be labeled *competitive* and the lower *uncompetitive*. It is unlikely that many units will fall on the absolute extremes of the dimension (although neither is, strictly speaking, a "limiting case"). The reasons for this emerge when we examine the variety of factors that should enter into any overall assessment of competitiveness in Recruitment.

As in the case of certain other dimensions of authority patterns, the extent to which competition occurs in filling superordinated positions depends on a number of distinct but often interrelated factors—subdimensions that can be treated separately or combined:

1. The extent of competition depends on the extent to which *S*-positions are *open*: that is, attainable at all by subs or lower supers.
2. Competitiveness depends on the size of the *base of eligibles* for superordinated positions: that is, the proportion and kinds of people who have the potential to attain positions of authority, legally ("formal eligibility") and/or on the basis of a unit's operative norms and practices ("effective eligibility"). This must be ascertained for a simple reason: however "open" *S*-positions may be, they are not likely to be equally open to all subs or lower supers; consequently, openness alone tells us very little about the competitiveness of Recruitment processes.
3. Competitiveness depends on *modes of boundary interchange* between subordinated and superordinated positions: the ways in which dividing lines between lower and higher positions are traversed. These variables matter because they differ in the extent to which they provide chances for rising to higher positions (opportunities for turning potential into actuality) and inherently require, encourage, or permit contention among "eligibles." Again, the variables matter for a simple reason: eligibility is not yet incumbency, nor even necessarily contention for incumbency.

In gist then, we ask the following questions in analyzing Recruitment. Are positions of authority open to competition? To what proportion of a unit's members, and what particular kinds of people? And what are their intrinsic chances for converting eligibility into incumbency? These considerations clearly are "value additive": each adds an increment to overall competitiveness.

The three aspects of Recruitment , which are discussed in more detail presently, are depicted in Figure 6.1. To understand the overall relationship schematized in the figure, note the following points:

1. The openness of S-positions is represented by the ratio between the total number of such positions S_n and the number of positions for which any subs or lower supers are eligible to compete S_e.
2. The base of eligibles is represented by the ratio between total members of the unit M_n and those who have characteristics that make them eligible to attain S-positions M_p or S_p.
3. The arrows between levels represent processes of boundary interchange, but no special graphic device is used to indicate differences in their competitiveness, which appear in the sizes of M_p and S_p in any case.

Assuming that the general case obtains and higher supers are recruited from supers at the next lower rung of the ladder, similar figures can be superimposed at each level of superordination to provide a full picture of Recruitment in a social unit. (In Figure 6.1, two levels of superordinates are assumed; one might, for example, think of them as members of Parliament and ministers.)

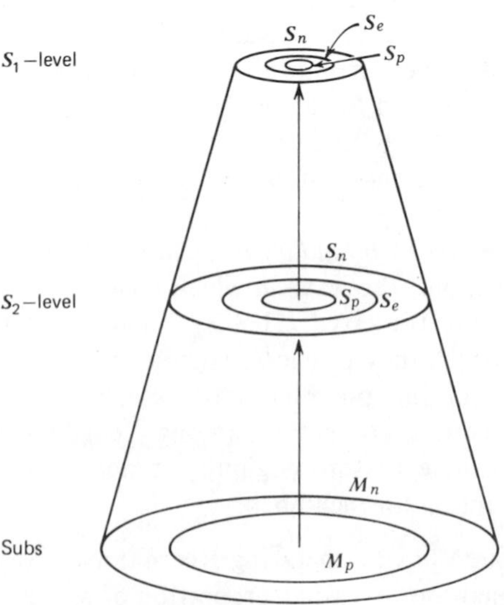

Fig. 6.1 Competitiveness of Recruitment.

Openness of S-Positions

If superordinated positions are to be regarded as competitively attainable, the minimum requirement is that the positions be open to at least some subs or lower supers in the unit. The *S*-positions are closed if one or another of three conditions obtains:

1. Supers cannot be replaced at all. If they vanish through natural causes (death or incapacity), no others take their place. Examples are parents in most nuclear families—granted that older siblings or guardians can become surrogates for them.
2. A sub cannot take the place of a super (or a lower super that of a higher one). An example is the teacher-pupil relationship. (Of course, pupils might grow up to be teachers.)
3. The successor of an incumbent super is perfectly predictable by the observer because of the operation of ascriptive criteria. Examples are monarchical succession, if strictly practiced, or any strict application of rules of seniority.

Several points about the openness of *S*-positions are apparent with little elaboration. *First,* there are unlikely to be many units in which *S*-positions are completely closed, and any such units will generally be easy to identify by their functional nature. This is the chief basis of the foregoing argument that absolute noncompetitiveness is rather improbable. Still, fully closed *S*-positions exist: being a parent, for example, is not an open position; just as obviously, there can hardly be boundary interchange between teachers and pupils (except in the trivial sense that pupils might sometimes play at being teachers).

Second, although closed superordinated positions are necessarily governed by ascriptive criteria (age, position in a lineage, etc.), it does not follow that ascriptive criteria restrict any such position to a unique eligible; they might only restrict the base of those formally and/or effectively eligible to compete.

Third, openness-closedness is best regarded as a simple dichotomous variable for any given *S*-position—a yes-no proposition—but there are two ways in which the matter can be treated as a genuine (continuous) dimension. (*a*) One can use the predictability of incumbency as a general definition of openness, in which case openness clearly becomes a continuous variable. As a simple example, in some nuclear families it may be perfectly predictable that the father will be head of the household; in others one can only predict that the head will be one of the parents. Such a general definition of openness may have a certain attraction, but it presents one problem: almost everything that affects degrees of predictability is caught by the other two aspects of Recruitment. (*b*) Predictability of incumbency thus is better regarded as a general indicator of competitiveness (see below) than as a measure of openness alone. Openness, however, unambiguously becomes a continuous dimensions if all *S*-positions in a complex unit are considered. Location on the dimension then is a simple matter of proportions of open and closed positions, complicated perhaps by weights assigned to positions according to level and type of superordination.

Bases of Eligibles

Once we know whether *S*-positions are open, we will want to know the proportion of members of a unit to whom they are genuinely open. There are two ways of restricting the base of eligibles; one is intricate to deal with in research, the other, simple and straightforward.

The straightforward factor is represented by legal or quasi-legal limitations on access to the positions. Examples are legion and familiar: at certain points in British history Catholics were legally barred from public offices; in most academic departments nontenured faculty may not hold higher administrative positions; members of the Congress of the United States must satisfy certain age and residence requirements; in countless electoral systems, property and other qualifications have legally limited the rights to vote and to be voted for. For example, the age (25+) and citizenship restrictions on our Congressmen limit the base of formal eligibles to roughly 40% of the total American population at any time; what might be called the "formal eligibility ratio" thus is .40.

Important as formal considerations are, they can be vastly misleading unless one also knows about informal norms and practices that might further restrict a base of eligibles, to much the same effect as formal limitations. Informal eligibility, of course, includes cases of groups in a unit that might be completely excluded from access to superordinated positions, despite "legal" eligibility (e.g., groups that receive only token access, to make appearances misleading, or are subjected to highly discriminatory quotas). Even if complete exclusion does not exist, moreover, there might be considerable discrimination against certain groups in regard to access to high positions—significant inequalities among groups in regard to their members' potential for achieving such positions. Blacks in the American legislature (and almost all other governmental structures) illustrate both points. Despite legal provisions against discrimination (or, at any rate, lack of legal exclusion), blacks have gradually progressed from literal exclusion, to no more than token inclusion, to highly unequal access to positions as Representatives and Senators. Considerations of the same type apply to women. And similar norms and practices restricting bases of eligibles often operate in other American institutions. In some American academic departments, for example, the chairmanship is still a male, WASP preserve; their proportion is rapidly dwindling to insignificance, but that is not equally the case in regard to deans, presidents, and trustees.[3]

As well as a ratio of formal eligibility, one therefore wants a ratio of "effective eligibility." How is such a ratio to be computed? The problem of properly conceptualizing effective eligibility seems inseparable from that "operational" question. To deal with it, let us outline a simple procedure and then, both to make the matter concrete and to justify the procedure, apply it to a hypothetical example. (In one of the illustrations used later, the procedure is applied to a set of actual cases.)

To determine effective eligibility, one should first find an overall index of inequality among members of a unit regarding their access to superordinated positions, varying between absolute inequality (unity) and none at all (zero). For this purpose, the Gini index of inequality seems suitable. The Gini index has generally been applied to the unequal cumulative distribution of highly tangible values, like land or money; however, it is also applicable to less tangible personal or group traits regarded as resources for attaining other values—in this case, advancement in a unit. By subtracting the Gini index G from 1.0, we can then arrive at a ratio of effective eligibility; the ratio will be only approximate, but it will never overstate inequalities. If a group in the unit is absolutely, or as good as absolutely, excluded by informal means, a further step is indicated: subtract the proportion of members in the group X_e or groups ΣX_e from 1.0; then find G for the remainder and further subtract that index (multiplied by the proportion not previously subtracted). Ratios of effective eligibility E_e thus may be computed either by

$$E_e = 1 - G$$

or by

$$E_e = 1 - \Sigma X_e - G(1 - \Sigma X_e)$$

To ensure that ratios thus found will have qualitative content, one also should know the particular ratios of advantage of more privileged groups in the unit as against those less privileged. This can be determined simply by dividing proportions of superordinated positions held by group members by the proportions of total members in the various groups, and expressing the results as proportions of unity.

To illustrate all this, consider a hypothetical business firm, run at the S_1-level, by a 10-man board of directors. We want to know the ratio of effective eligibility for becoming a director for all members: most entered the firm as ordinary workers, many did so as junior executives (recruited out of business school), and some started out as senior executives (nephews of directors, and the like). Suppose the composition of the firm is as portrayed in Table 6.1. A Gini index of inequality can be computed by measuring the area of inequality defined by a Lorenz curve (see Figure 6.2) as a proportion of the area defined by the line of perfect equality in the figure; an index of 1.0 would denote perfect inequality (e.g., one man or special group possessing all the money in a unit). In the present case, the index is computed thus, with the terms in parentheses representing the following areas: first term, area of s's; second term, area of S_3's; third term, area of S_2's.

$$G = 1.0 - 2\left[\left(\frac{.8 \times .2}{2}\right) + \left(\frac{.2 + .7}{2} \times .16\right) + \left(\frac{.7 + 1.0}{2} \times .04\right)\right] = .63$$

In other words, dividing members by their level of entry into the firm, we find that the firm is 63% of the way toward absolute inequality (i.e., no one able to become a director unless he started as a senior executive).

Note now that exactly the same result would have been obtained if only 37% of the members could become directors, and if their individual chances of rising were exactly equal. By subtracting the Gini index from 1.0, then, a decent estimate of the ratio of effective eligibles (.37) can be arrived at; in

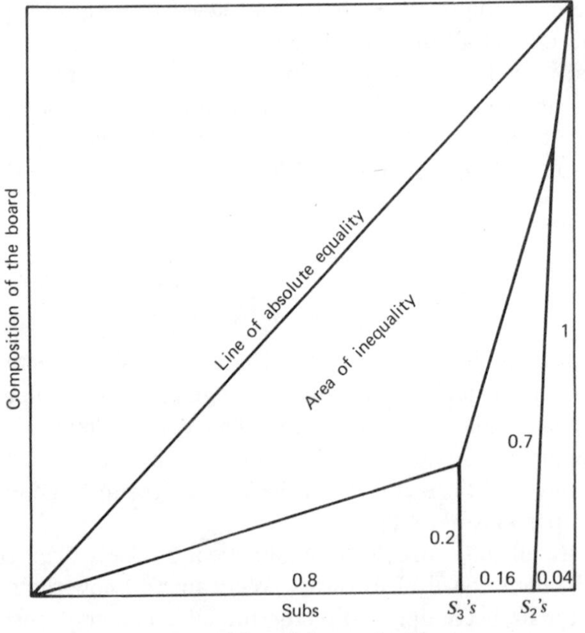

Fig. 6.2 Inequality of access to S_1-positions in a hypothetical firm.

Table 6.1 Composition of a Hypothetical Firm

Composition of Membership			Normal Composition of Board (S_1)		
Types of Members	N	%	Level of Entry into Firm	N	%
Subs (s)	400	80	As subs	2	20
Junior executives (S_3)	80	16	As S_3's	5	50
Senior executives (S_2)	20	4	As S_2's	3	30

effect, this ratio is an estimate of what would be the case if formal rather than informal restrictions were in operation. The ratio exaggerates level of effective eligibility if chances to rise are not equally distributed among the effective eligibles. At least, however, the ratio can be no higher than the level found, and it is generally likely to be lower.[4]

To introduce a social and technical complication, assume now that half the subs (40% of all members) are female and that no female has ever become a director of the firm. In that case, we should measure inequalities among males only, females being entirely out of the picture. If that is done, the Gini index is about .5—considerably less inequality than our initial finding. The overall base of effective eligibles, however, is reduced:

$$E_e = 1.0 - .4 - .5\,(.6) = .30$$

On this basis, the firm is within 30% of absolute inequality, as a result of 40% of its members being totally excluded at the start, but the remainder being less subject to discrimination than initial appearances indicated.

Ratios of advantage for groups in the firm by level of entry (but leaving the complication caused by the exclusion of females aside) can be calculated by dividing the proportion of the board who originated at the various levels by the proportion of unit members in them, then restating the results in various ways, including as proportions of 1.0. This yields the results of Table 6.2. In effect, senior executives have 30 times more potential than workers to become directors and 70% of all the "privilege" in the unit; they also have about 2.5 times the advantages of those entering the firm as junior executives.

Two sources of difficulty in making such calculations should be pointed out. One involves trends over time. Eligibility is potential, and potential lies in the future, whereas the data on which it will be calculated lie in the past and the present. In consequence, any measure of potential may err, unless

Table 6.2 Ratios of Advantage in a Hypothetical Firm

	S_2's	S_3's	Subs
Percentage of members	4	16	80
Percentage of board	30	50	20
Ratios of advantage			
% members/% board	7.5	3.1	.25
Transformed to make smallest number = 1.0	30	12.4	1
Expressed as proportion of 1.0	.7	.28	.02

always couched in the past tense. But that seems unnecessary if a clear secular trend appears over a considerable span of time. For example, one may discount (at least to a degree) disproportions between male and female academic personnel if the disproportion between male and female Ph.D.'s has been constantly diminishing, if the disproportion between male and female junior faculty members has also constantly declined (even if at a slower rate), and if the same process has also occurred at the senior levels. In such a case, disproportions may appear only because time is required, in the normal course of events, to eliminate them. The rate of change, of course, also matters. One cannot count women as fully included in a base of eligibles if their disabilities are being remedied so slowly that it is unlikely that more than a few will become incorporated in the base in a given pertinent period (in academic positions, over about 40 years—the normal span of the academic career).

A second difficulty concerns the question of how to subdivide a social unit into groups for purposes of determining informal exclusions and inequalities. Human beings vary in a great many ways, and it would be frivolous to attempt to account for them all. We might want to know about the effective eligibility of women as against men, but rarely about that of red-haired people as against blond or bald-headed individuals. In addition, the greater the number of different, overlapping groups into which units are divided, the greater the amount of inequality that will be found—some or much of it because of factors that have only an accidental relationship to privilege and discrimination. In our hypothetical firm, for example, we might find that the effective eligibles are not only chiefly male executives but among these, persons who have two or more children, play tennis, and prefer Mozart to Brahms. The obvious solution of the problem is to divide the unit according to criteria that are considered paramount by the members themselves. The hypothetical case used here assumes that level of entry and sex are (or express) such criteria, and a less hypothetical way of selecting salient criteria is provided in one of the illustrations used below to exemplify the dimension.

Modes of Boundary Interchange

As stated, we wish to know about modes of boundary interchange to ascertain the chances that mere eligibility (potential) might become actual incumbency. In the case of our hypothetical firm, the chances of the eligibles might vary between 1.0 and about .07, there being 10 directors and about 150 eligibles below them. The location of actual chances on such a scale turns on the nature of facilities for and obstacles to advancement by eligibles and the distribution of the facilities and obstacles among them—and this complex of factors depends on both formal and informal aspects of the modes of boundary interchange.

The formal aspects are explicitly prescribed methods for attaining *S*-positions. Among these are the following:

Random selection A process such as the drawing of lots, specifically designed to eliminate inequalities in attaining higher positions. (Rare)

Rotation Processes that give all or many eligibles a chance to rise as a matter of routine: for example, routine advancement into and withdrawal from higher positions according to criteria any eligible can satisfy, such as length of service. (Less rare, but still uncommon)

Periodic elections Processes by which supers attain their positions through the regularly expressed preferences of constituencies of their peers and/or inferiors. (Common)

Performance tests Processes by which supers are recruited, promoted, or demoted on the basis of scores on competitive tests, efficiency ratings, and the like. (Common)

Designation Processes by which supers at certain levels recruit lower-ranking personnel to their own or lesser levels, on the basis of criteria that leave them significant scope for choice. (Common)

Seniority Attaining an *S*-position solely or mainly on the basis of length of service, but without provisions for routine rotation that tend to equalize prospects. (Common)

Succession Becoming a super on the basis of clear ascriptive criteria that narrow eligibles for any given position to a single individual, or at most a very few members of a unit. (Common)

One rather conspicuous way in which a person can become a super or higher super has been omitted from the list. We might call this "self-designation": simply setting up shop as boss by force, trickery, or mere pretension, and trying to make the claim stick. The method is certainly not uncommon, but hardly one that will be explicitly prescribed, hence out of place here, if not elsewhere in the discussion. It should also be evident that in complex units the methods may be combined in quite intricate combinations.

The order in which the methods have been listed is probably an order of the chances they provide and the obstacles they raise for converting eligibility into incumbency—although a few ambiguities in regard to that require attention to the idiosyncrasies of particular cases. Random selection, by definition, equalizes chances. Rotation does so by specified routines, but only over the long run, not at every point. Elections, if genuine, also equalize chances (if not genuine, they are not elections); but voters' preferences may handicap some potential candidates, as may differences in resources not themselves subject to perfect competition. Performance tests equalize only to the extent that capacities to perform are equal; such tests also tend to "channel" people early in their careers, and normally those in disadvantaged streams are permanently handicapped relative to others, even if not absolutely excluded. Designation involves a more obvious ambiguity: by definition, it leaves scope for discriminatory behavior; but of course higher supers may discriminate more, less, or not at all. The seniority criterion may seem highly egalitarian, but it narrows chances of advancement to the extent that ability to stay the course is not equally distributed and the regular, frequent phasing out of higher supers is not provided for; therefore, selection based on seniority is inherently less equalizing than any method for attaining positions in which length of service is not a prerequisite for advancement (including elections and designation). Succession obviously narrows chances of advancement most of all—in fact, often (but certainly not always) it implies that positions are "closed."

One formal aspect of boundary interchange makes for greater or lesser chances to achieve incumbency, regardless of which of the methods listed is used. This is formal provisions for turnover or the possibility of turnover in incumbents. Some of the methods of interchange involve high possibilities of turnover in their very nature (e.g., periodic elections, which may, of course, occur more or less frequently). Others do not, but particular provisos may increase or lessen chances (e.g., limitations on terms of office). Such formal provisions, therefore, should always be taken into account. Turnover, however, probably depends less on formal than on informal modes of boundary interchange, to which we now turn.

Formal prescriptions provide certain intrinsic chances for achieving higher incumbency, but this condition alone does not imply that the chances will be fully exploited. Neither does the formal limitation of such chances imply that some people will not try to beat the obstacles. Informal aspects of boundary interchange therefore must be considered along with formal ones. The informal aspects can be summarized by the notion of "contentiousness": the extent to which competition is normatively approved or tolerated, and the doubtless related extent to which eligibles vie with one another intensely, stubbornly, and with all available means.

Perhaps contentiousness (as fact, if not as norm) is a constant of human nature, not a social variable, hence not worth special attention. Large edifices of social theory have been built on the assumption that everybody always wants the most he can get. (See the voluminous literature on value maximization, in politics no less than economics.) Some theories proceed from the more specific assumption that people particularly want to better their "stratificatory" positions.[6] But the position that contentiousness is invariate is dubious. No doubt there are pushy individuals in most social units. No doubt, also, there is usually a measure of intrigue, back-stabbing, or fawning on people with something to bestow. It seems, however, that "achievement motivations"—hence, one may suppose, exploiting opportunities for contention—are far from equally distributed among cultures and subcultures.[7] The proclivity to compete also seems to vary among social units within the same cultures: although the American culture encourages competition in general, there is surely a difference between behavior that is tolerated in our academic institutions versus activities allowed in politics or business—not an absolute difference, but not a negligible one either. Even if there are no large differences between what people generally want, there are surely sizable ones between what they do, and may do with social approval, in seeking betterment.[8]

Can contentiousness be ignored simply because it reflects the chances of advancement inherent in prescribed methods? Not likely. To be sure, there are bound to be relationships between formal methods and amount (and/or type) of contention. Elections require and surely encourage contention, as do performance tests; designation at least allows it; the other methods seem to make it pointless. Perhaps, then, the more scope formal methods leave for contention, the more of it there will be (which logically implies that cultural and other differences in amount of contentiousness will appear in prescribed methods of advancement). The actual case, however, is a great deal more complicated.

For one thing, contentiousness is hardly equal in all cases in which elections, performance tests, or designation are used. In some elections, for example, there are "incumbency effects": a tendency not to oppose established superordinates. Trade unions, for which solidarity is of great functional importance, furnish abundant instances. We also know that the number of candidates and the intensity of campaigns varies greatly among elections. Also variable is the extent to which people jockey for favors where designation is used.

As for the methods that seem to make contention pointless, it seems wrong to say that they necessarily prevent it. A better argument is that they either preclude contention or make for particularly vicious—corrupt or criminal—modes of it: assassinating human obstacles, rigging lots, spreading nasty scandals, and the like. These things occur and must obviously be noted if they happen frequently. Indeed, formal methods of advancement may be more highly correlated with modes of contention than with amounts of it. Although corrupt or criminal modes of contention may be associated with any formal method whatever, some such methods leave no choice but to use them. "Despotism tempered by assassination" describes the Roman Empire well—and also many other social units. And it is not only formal methods that have such effects. Regardless of formal method used, if open contentiousness is normatively disapproved, contentious people will probably not only be atypical but will tend to use grim or shady methods to get ahead.

Finally, what was earlier called "self-designation" is always available for circumventing formal methods of advancement. In some cultures it seems the rule rather than the exception (anyway for the highest *S*-positions), formal methods being either pretty (legitimating) window-dressing or simply inoperative. In such cases it is, if anything, the formal methods that should be discounted, not the informal ones. A singularly blatant case is the Roman Empire in the third and fourth centuries: in one single reign (Gallienus) more than 30 men proclaimed themselves Caesar.[9] Whether such events occur more often under some formal methods than others is an open (and not uninteresting) question.

As an informal aspect of boundary interchange, contentiousness is important to us because it bears on the purpose of the subdimension: facilities for and obstacles to converting eligibility into incumbency. We have, however, omitted the reckoning of such factors as personal capacities and ambitions. These undeniably affect personal chances for rising in a unit, but they are not attributes of social units as such and are probably rather randomly distributed among them—granted that the dividing line between social and purely personal attributes (especially ambition) is thin at times.

A notable advantage of making contentiousness a part of overall competitiveness in Recruitment is that by including it, we are less likely to commit ethnocentric fallacies. The most common of these is to associate competitiveness entirely with institutions and formal provisos developed in Western democracies, like two-party or multiparty systems and regular elections. At worst, such fallacies lead us to mistake reality; at best, they set off procrustean quests for functional equivalents of the familiar competitive institutions.

Indicators for the Recruitment Dimension

Although we are not concerned here with full "operationalization," we should anticipate two problems likely to arise in putting the Recruitment dimension to work. One is that the various aspects of the dimension will be difficult to combine in any summary measure (even aside from problems arising from complexity of Conformation). The second is that the special aspect of contentiousness will be difficult to observe and assess accurately, nonimpressionistically, and nonarbitrarily, partly because it is a subjective disposition, partly because the disposition often surfaces only in veiled behavior. Therefore, we inquire whether there might be available good, even if imperfect, "indicators" of these matters, anyway for broad measures and comparisons.

As previously argued, *predictability of incumbency,* especially early predictability, can be one such indicator. The more competitive is Recruitment, the less predictable should be incumbency. At the extreme of noncompetitiveness, we can predict what individual will hold any given *S*-position. Passing up the ladder of competitiveness, we can predict what type of person will achieve incumbency, but not precisely who; and the more limited the number of persons in the set, the less Recruitment is competitive. At the competitive extreme—say, if *S*-positions are equally open to all members and selection of supers occurs through random selection—predictability is obviously nil. Thus the degree to which Recruitment departs from *randomness,* regardless of whether formal methods of random selection are used, is an equivalent for predictability of incumbency. It should be possible to establish this degree by analysis of former incumbents, obviating the usual difficulties that arise in actual prediction, if a large span of time is used and secular trends are allowed for. (For example, the presidents of Princeton University have nearly always been Presbyterian males; this is very far from a random outcome, and it surely denotes highly limited competitiveness in Recruitment for the position.)

A second promising indicator is *turnover* of supers. Two kinds of turnover should be distinguished: *total turnover,* which is useful for gauging overall competitiveness, and *abnormal turnover,* which is useful as an indication of contentiousness. Total turnover includes all changes of supers, except those that manifestly have nothing to do with competition for places: events of nature (e.g., death or incapacity) that may befall any super in any social unit, and purely voluntary resignations, promotions, and the like—acts that wholly depend on and/or are beneficial to displaced superordinates themselves. Abnormal turnover further excludes: (*a*) changes in supers that occur through the hazards of formal modes of boundary interchange, such as passing out of power into opposition as a result of electoral processes; and (*b*) turnover that occurs through such well-entrenched conventions as phasing out people who have not progressed beyond certain levels after certain terms of service, or routine reshufflings of personnel, as in many cabinets. Abnormal turnover is, of course, always a greater or smaller proportion of total turnover.

The argument for using turnover rates as indicators rests on two simple propositions:

1. The more Recruitment is competitive, the greater total turnover is likely to be.
2. The greater is contentiousness, the more abnormal turnover is likely to occur.

These propositions are surely sensible; try to imagine their reverse. But even if they hold measures of turnover have certain imperfections as indicators that, although far from crippling, should be noted. For example, total turnover of, say, Cabinet members might be great because of the structure of a party system or particular electoral results (indecisive elections). Or it might be small because the same people keep winning fair elections. However, such circumstances either should even out over time or should be easily identifiable as structural characteristics of a unit; and not infrequently, the structural characteristics—like highly fragmented party systems, incapacity to form durable parliamentary coalitions, or just winning or losing elections—themselves reflect competitiveness. Abnormal turnover might also be misleading as a measure of contentiousness. It could occur, for example, because of the sheer incompetence of supers and concern for a unit's welfare, or it might fail to occur because of the staying powers of supers rather than lack of contention. Again, however, such considerations should operate over limited periods, not persistently. Over any long span of time, factors other than contentiousness that inflate and lessen the total should also tend to cancel one another out.

The Recruitment dimension and its subdimensions, as well as the observations that should generally indicate high or low competitiveness, are portrayed in Figure 6.3. All subdimensions and indices are continua, but one problem in putting the dimension to work has not been confronted: how (and whether) to weight the various ingredients of competitiveness in Recruitment. This problem might best be approached by empirically determining the relative roles of the subdimensions in accounting for degrees of predictability and rates of turnover. Extremely competitive cases have, of

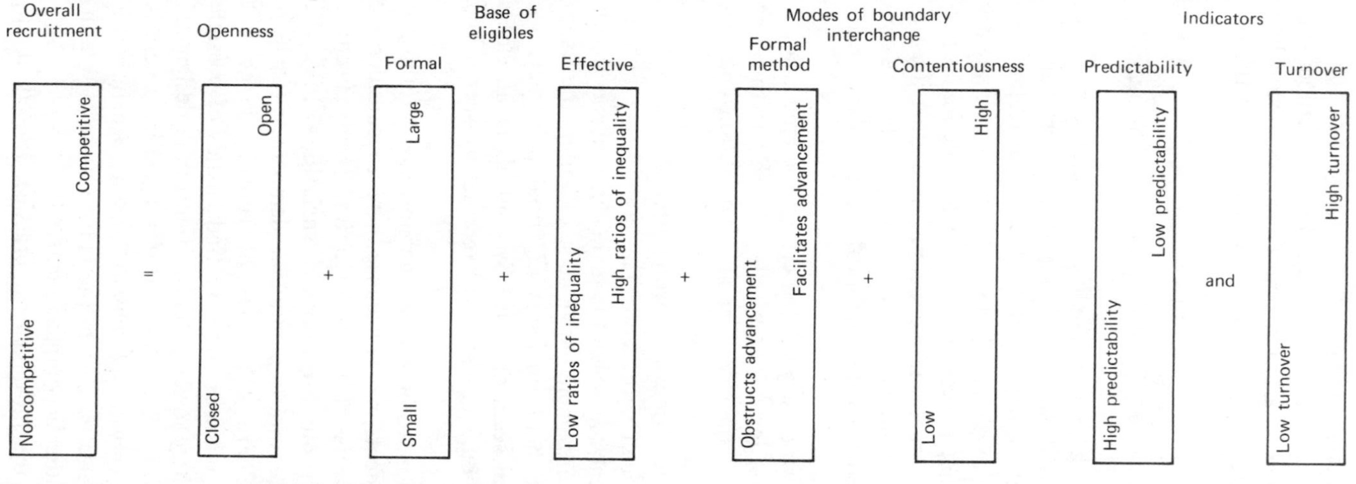

Fig. 6.3 Recruitment and its subdimensions and indicators.

course, the following cluster of characteristics: all *S*-positions are open, legally and effectively, to all members of a unit, through formal methods that highly facilitate advancement and encourage strong tendencies toward high "informal" contentiousness. Extremely noncompetitive cases have the opposite traits.

Illustration: Boundary Interchange in (South African) Tribal Societies[10]

Western political scientists often have oversimplified or flatly wrong conceptions of the politics of most tribal societies. An especially common misconception concerns Recruitment to high tribal positions—particularly the aspects of Recruitment that have to do with "informal" modes of boundary interchange. The discussion of that misconception here has the initial purpose of making an abstract conceptualization concrete. Like other illustrations of concepts, it also has larger implications—in this case, for the conceptualization of what are sometimes called political "instability events," hence for theories of civil strife.

We are concerned here with two closely related errors: the tendencies to assume (*a*) that ascriptive criteria largely or wholly close Recruitment to high tribal positions, and (*b*) that the "dead hand" of tradition and succession sharply restricts the spirit of contention.

We know that as a rule, higher tribal authorities are recruited on the basis of ascriptive criteria, through succession. This applies not only to cases—probably the most frequent—in which the higher incumbents (heads of tribes and of their segments) are single individuals, as among the Bantu tribes and Hottentots.[11] It also holds in cases of tribal polycracy: for example, among tribes and tribal segments ruled by councils of all elders (parts of East Africa) or when dual headship is exercised by sacred and secular rulers (Melanesia).

The rule of ascriptive succession, to be sure, is not universal. Nothing is really universal in tribal governments, partly because there are considerable variations in nonpolitical aspects of tribal societies, partly because nonpolitical conditions leave room for political variations. Like the Bushmen, certain tribes practice direct, communal democracy (at least among able-bodied males). There are cases of rule by large but select—generally elected—tribal councils. And we find islands of possible achievement within ascription where lower authority figures are designated by higher ones: for example, officials who perform quasi-bureaucratic duties, personal counselors, or men who hold chiefly lands as benefices. Incumbency thus can result from elections, from the judicious use of wealth, from military prowess, or from other accomplishments.

Still, ascriptive succession is the most general practice. Indeed, it approaches universality if one considers only the highest levels of superordination and does not reckon two dubious cases: societies that seem to have no clearly delimited authority patterns at all, like the Nuer,[12] and those that more resemble the far-flung feudal monarchies of the West or bureaucratic empires of the East than typical tribal societies, like the mature kingdom of Buganda.[13]

But even where ascriptive succession is the rule, Recruitment in tribal societies rarely is altogether noncompetitive, or even low on the overall competitiveness continuum. Where then does competitiveness come in? What makes for low predictability of incumbency and turnover, especially "abnormal" turnover?

Note, first, that rules of ascriptive succession need not restrict eligibility to a single, known person. More often than not we find in tribal societies a pool of eligibles for any given position, including high chieftaincy or kingship. The most obvious cause is lack of primogeniture: all sons of a chief, or all males in a "royal" lineage, may be eligible; or all sons by a "great wife" chosen for the special purpose of bearing royal children; or all sons by a chief's most nobly born wife; or all sons of a near relative, if a chief has no sons. (Females, of course, are sometimes also possible successors, but this seems exceptional.) Even if primogeniture is the official rule, related ambiguities often leave openings for incumbency. In principle, for example, succession among most groups of Bantu is by seniority; in practice, however, it is not at all automatic. The senior relatives and other important advisers of a chief constitute a kind of electoral college who "name" the successor. This often gives them considerable latitude. Among the Swazi and Venda, the "electors" do not make a successor's name public until necessary; they may keep the order of succession secret and may even conceal the fact that a chief has died until a choice has been made.[14] Obviously this practice leaves scope for competition not only among themselves but among all who might qualify for succession.

Both the common lack of primogeniture and the custom of hedging it with ambiguities are quite functional, at least in some respects. No doubt they lead to quarrels, sometimes destroying tribal cohesion. Unlike modern ceremonial monarchies, on the other hand, tribal societies cannot afford incompetent chiefs. The leaders of war societies or tribes constantly threatened by war societies must be skillful fighters and courageous. If, as is also frequently the case, chiefs are ultimately responsible for justice and the allocation of economic possessions (lands, cattle, etc.), their conduct should be equitable, generous, and punctilious. Primogeniture, strictly applied, virtually assures that leaders will often lack such necessary or desirable qualities. Since poorly qualified individuals are hard to eliminate under ascriptive criteria of incumbency, it is better to do some preliminary sorting out, even if such screening does not really prevent later crises (see below). One also ought not to assume that tribal societies, however homogeneous, have no potential for faction. Jockeying for succession provides an opportunity for that potential to surface—in current jargon, for the articulation and aggregation of interests. Thus it is likely that the risks run when ascriptive succession is not based on primogeniture are deliberately taken, and ambiguities concerning rights of succession are probably well cultivated.

Keeping successors or even occasions for succession secret is a particularly clever device for reconciling ascription with selection based on competence or factional interests. The more common practice, however, is to achieve the same end less ingeniously. For example, tribal assemblies of the Hottentots sometimes simply fail to confirm an heir who is deemed incompetent. Or, to illustrate how "interests" enter the picture, a Hottentot heir who has been bought off by one of his brothers may not be confirmed. Among the Bergdama, seniority is supposed to be the principle, but experience and ability seems generally to be the operative measures.[15]

In effect, then, incumbency is indeterminate in tribal societies not only because of the frequent existence of formally equal claimants, but, even more, because of the operation of *multiple norms* that rarely are quite consistent. Rulers are supposed to be more than people who inherit a given position; they are also expected to live up to certain ideals of conduct. Among the Bantu, for instance, the chief

> "should attend faithfully to his officials duties and not give priority to his private affairs; above all he should deal promptly with cases that come to his court and with any other matters that come to his personal attention. He should seek always to consult his councils, and seek confidential advice from men of recognized standing, not from toadies or upstarts. He should preserve law and order, and administer justice fairly and impartially; his sentences should not be unduly harsh, and he should not inflict punishments wantonly."

And so on, through a long list of expectations, including the protection of subjects against the misrule of subordinates, not meddling arbitrarily with the internal affairs of local groups, being kind, affable, easy of access, brave, wise, gentle, shrewd, open-handed, peaceable, and tactful.[16] Such qualities usually do not reside in the genes. One can try to assure that a ruler will have them by requiring service in long political apprenticeships: attendance at court, tenure as head of a district, instruction by tutors, or experience at the court of a neighboring chief. But since individuals do not always benefit by instruction and experience, a better way is to have rules that can be bent as needed. Multiple, inconsistent norms serve that purpose nicely.

An additional source of indeterminacy, and of sizable pools of eligibles, arises from the lack of exact (written) records, which leaves scope for agile memories. Tribal societies are often messy about positions of and in lineages. Jumbles about who is who result from ancient claims passed over, self-serving fictions, and vague chronologies.[17] Such jumbles, no less than inconsistent norms, probably are quite useful—life the *Schlamperei* that was said to alleviate the despotism of Hapsburg emperors.

It is true that pools of eligibles in tribal societies usually are quite small and confined to men of "royal" descent. Still, they almost always far exceed $1/n$th of total membership: Recruitment certainly is not "closed." And note that the availability of numerous "eligible" candidates always furnishes scope for factional competition—for interest mongering. Granted, such competition in tribal societies is never by organized, persistent "parties." The appearance if not the fact of tribal unity is valued highly, and ascription provides no basis for regular confrontations between rivals and periodic alternations of rule. That, however, does not rule out competition. It simply means that competition must take special forms.

Occasions for personal and factional competiton in tribal societies occur not only in connection with questions of succession. In a sense, they are ever-present—and not merely as possibility. The formal rules for boundary interchange may limit such occasions severely, but informal practices are another matter. There is, in fact, much "contentiousness" in tribal societies, and the "official" rule of ascriptive recruitment through succession leads to the use of particularly vicious means of contention. Turnover among supers thus is generally "abnormal," but far from low in many cases.

The matter is syllogistic. People eligible for succession on ascriptive bases retain at least the bases of their claims as long as they live. Even if others consider a succession settled, they themselves and their adherents may not. In practical terms, therefore, succession from pools of coequal eligibles is never finally determined. And quite apart from any intrinsic legitimacy inhering in ascriptive status, the use of multiple norms of boundary interchange provides scope for asserting rival legitimacies. But what means are available for converting eligibility into incumbency once chiefs have been designated—and (usually) possess tenure for life or as long as they can function? One can continue peacefully to press one's claim; but that is not very promising, especially if ritual sanctifies another's incumbency. One can wait for disenchantment with a ruler's qualities and for his ritual deposition—which may not occur. The practicable means then come down to assassination, organized revolt, or engineered mass secession. The choice between these is a matter of norms, taste, and opportunity. And the bloody choices are *not* evidence of savagery, in the colloquial sense. "Primitive" men are often models of gentility. Their political brutalities are, as stated, syllogistic.

According to Schapera vicious dynastic quarrels are the very essence of tribal "politics." The viciousness sometimes takes the form of tyrannicide against intolerable rulers (like the Mogôpa chief Tsoku, who slaughtered the cattle of others and had pregnant women cut open). Taboos against shedding a chief's blood are easily circumvented in such cases by strangling or poisoning the man instead (the Cape Nguni and Venda furnish examples) or tactfully abandoning him in a place infested by wild beasts; and if there is a prohibition against killing fellow tribesmen altogether, expulsion from the tribe nicely gets around that technicality. Generally, however, the distribution of powers and statuses in a tribe prevents purely "popular" actions of this kind. Rival claimants, or at least potential "eligibles," take the lead. Far more often than not, however, assassinations and tribal revolts do not represent bad efficiency reports or impeachments. Usually they result from unresolved dynastic rivalry, pure and simple.

Schapera[18] provides a set of unrelenting chronicles of such grim rivalries for eight of his South African tribes. A typical example, the case of the Zulu from 1828 to 1872, is by no means the most horrific of Schapera's recitals. In fact, we use it here because it is comparatively uninvolved and easy to follow; other cases display intricacies within intricacies—but not less grim contentiousness.

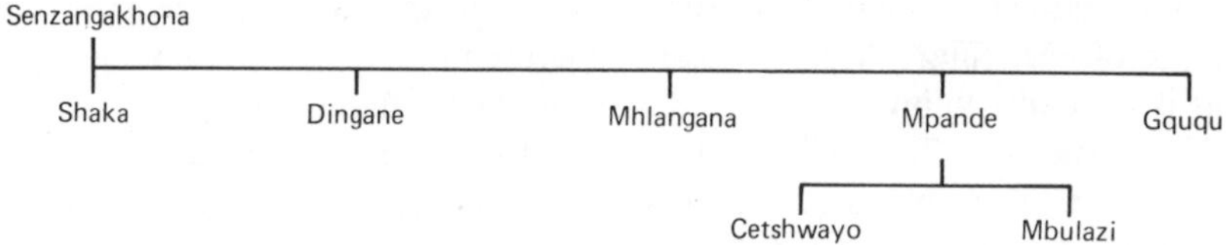

"Shaka [a chief of legendary cruelty] was stabbed to death in 1828 by his half-brothers Dingane and Mhlangana. Soon afterwards Dingane also had Mhlangana killed, and became undisputed chief. His rule was in some respects even more tyrannical than Shaka's. To strengthen his position, he set about a systematic extermination of all that remained of his family and relatives, all his friends and former comrades, the great ones of the nation. Among the few whom he spared was his half-brother Mpande, a quiet and inoffensive youth. In due course, Mpande's growing popularity turned Dingane against him. Fearing death, Mpande escaped into Natal with several thousand adherents. He soon returned, reinforced by a party of Boers. In the ensuing battle (1840) Dingane was defeated; he fled into Swaziland, where he was murdered by the local inhabitants. Mpande then became chief. Three years later he caused the murder of his only surviving brother, Gququ, a great number of whose partisans thereupon fled into Natal. Friction afterwards developed between Cetshwayo, his eldest son, and Mbulazi, son of his favorite wife, each of whom had a separate district and many followers. The rivalry between them culminated in battle (1856), Mbulazi and five brothers being among the many killed.

The remnants of the following escaped into Natal. Cetshwayo thus became unchallenged heir to the chieftaincy, to which he succeeded on Mpande's death (1872)."

To recapitulate the broad outlines of the tale: of the five incumbent Zulu chiefs in 44 years, at least four achieved their positions by "abnormal" means; not only did regicides occur, but also preventive and preemptive murders, plus one mass extermination of remote rivals or potential tyrant killers; there were escapes into asylum, a secession, battles; and each rival clearly commanded a faction of followers, even his own armies. If this is a record of noncompetitiveness, how are we to define competitiveness? Almost the only predictable variables relating to incumbency seem to be that chiefs will belong to the "royal" lineage, that older eligibles will generally become incumbents before younger ones, and that the younger are somewhat more likely to murder the older than vice versa. And this case does not include complications that often make incumbency even less predictable because of additional generations of candidates, the machinations of regents, or the ambitions of mothers for their sons.

"The king should not eat with his brothers, lest they poison him"; "princes make restless subjects"; "there cannot be two bulls in one kraal." The proverbs are only too apt. Chiefs, needless to say, learn a lot about political self-defense: they often grant "executive" positions to commoners in return for their support, frequently cementing such relations by ties of blood-brotherhood (not so different from our own forms of patronage); or they send potential rivals to remote areas; or they commit a few judicious murders; or they have rivals declared bewitched. But such maneuvers do not help much, as a rule. Nor is the carnage restricted to royal brothers and dynastic battles. In many cases, any man who acquires great wealth is regarded as dangerous because he might attract a following and turn usurper or, at any rate, tip the scales in favor of a more legitimate rival's faction. (The Nguni chiefs, for example, use the resourceful method of having diviners "smell out" a prosperous man as a sorcerer after a death or illness has occurred in the royal family; "and without further ado he is 'eaten up' and ceases to be a menace."[19]) Schapera sums it all up nicely in one deadpan passage—perhaps not intended to convey the message it contains: "Our examples show that chiefs do *sometimes* die of old age after a long if not necessarily peaceful reign."[20]

We do not generally think of persistent bloodletting as socially sensible, even if the occasional well-chosen assassination is admitted to our repertory of devices for making authority responsible. Nonetheless, theorists concerned with the sense of persistent behavior in societies—functionalists, systems theorists, or those who base explanations of behavior patterns on "rationalist" premises (calculated value maximization)—need not be stumped by the pattern we have described. (They rarely are stumped by any behavior pattern.) After all, despotism *can* be tempered by murder; sometimes social values leave no clear alternative method; and chiefs are less likely to be killed if they are able, faithful, and popular, even if these qualities are imperfect prophylactics. The informal methods of boundary interchange typically used in tribal societies allow new blood in high positions (blushes for the pun), and perhaps ensure against chiefs becoming fat and lazy with ascriptive power. If a people habitually practices war or faces warfare as a normal hazard, then, as argued, a case for the "natural selection" of its rulers can be made. Dynastic rivalries and the grim sports they engender alleviate the pervasive routines of tribal life and, apart from functions concerning power and responsibility, release frustrations and aggressions. They also make for a kind of equalization of powers: every eligible may have his turn, or at least his grisly veto or arbitrary power of impeachment.

Nonetheless, there is a remarkable lack of tension-management devices that might countervail the contentiousness surveyed. We are told, after all, that social and political compacts are entered to avoid unacceptable costs and that preserving one's own life is the minimal constant among human values. Dynastic rivalries, as we have seen, frequently involve far more people than the narrow circle of eligibles. Assassinations grow into mass exterminations and war; tribal cohesion is imperiled, and secessions occur. Yet apart from manifestly ineffectual rituals and taboos, institutional devices that might defuse contentiousness seem strangely rare.

One such device, clearly appropriate to the premises of rationalists, would be the regular rotation in office of eligibles (or, not very different, regular random selection). Although certainly not foolproof, the device at least ensures that ambitions will not be permanently frustrated and that incompetent or cruel chiefs will not have life tenure; above all, it is an apparently logical expression of coequal eligibility. But we know of only one case that even approximates the method. Among the Tsonga, a chief is followed by each of his full brothers in turn; only when the last brother dies does the chief's ascriptive successor, the "great son" of the first brother, assume office.[21] This, however, is only a rotation of regents. It assures that chiefs will not have to fend off older, more experienced men and their special followers, but it is manifestly inadequate as a tension-management device.

"Among the Tsonga, a chief, when he ascends the throne, will do his best to get rid of troublesome brothers in order to reign alone and to ensure the chieftainship to his son. This has often happened. . . . Maphunga . . . killed as many as four brothers and near relations, 'one of them by poisoning him treacherously, through the agency of a dissolute woman.'"[22]

One means that seems highly appropriate to defuse tribal contentiousness is used in a few cases: the war of succession. As practiced, for example, in the Banyankole kingdom (Uganda), the device is simple and logical. Rulers, being mainly permanent war leaders, were valued for their health, strength, courage, and cunning. Accordingly, they were not allowed to die of illness or old age. They were poisoned when signs of failing powers were detected. Successors, who had to be both in the royal line and as strong as possible, were set to fight among themselves, with no holds barred, until only one was left. The eligibles could freely recruit followers or resort to kinsmen for protection; they could fight openly or spy furtively on one another for purposes of poisoning or stabbing a rival in his sleep; mothers and sisters were enlisted to practice magic on the candidates' behalf. (Among the Banyankole, the late ruler's favorite son generally drew a bye until the final battle, being hidden until only a single challenger remained.) Meanwhile, the kingdom was ruled by a mock king chosen in mock battle, to ensure continuity of role, and the country lived in a state of chaos, with much stealing of cattle and avenging of grievances. The whole procedure was conducive simultaneously to several ends. It reconciled ascription with a particular brand of competence; it ensured prolonged incumbency and peace by eliminating potential rivals; and, for the whole society, it provided to all members a species of ritual license, over a period of several months, when free play could be given to factional preferences, private greed, and old resentments.[23]

Although not isolated, this kind of procedure is far more rare than might be supposed. The fact is that in most cases contentiousness is not even hedged by ritual or telescoped in time: warring over succession has less the traits of ritual license than those of an all-year sport.

We can proceed now to a brief examination of the broad implications of the illustration.

Clearly our discussion of boundary interchange in tribal societies has broad significance for the conceptualization of so-called political "instability events"—and, by way of their conceptualization, for theoretical explanations of such events.

The most important implication of the case is that theories of civil conflict probably ought to differ in nature and complexity because the events for which they try to account may be very different, superficial similarities notwithstanding. Normally, levels of civil strife are measured by certain raw indices (deaths, damage done, number of people involved, duration, etc.) and are considered similar if overall measures, so constructed, are similar. It is, however, likely that a difference of great potential theoretical significance will be found among cases that seem alike on the evidence of raw scores. In certain cases, the quantitative levels and qualitative types of strife will signify marked and abrupt changes from previous levels and modes of contention; in others, high levels and vicious modes of strife will simply be long-continued states of affairs. Whether the former or the latter is the case surely matters, perhaps greatly. Certain causal theories of civil conflict inherently presuppose abrupt change: for instance, Davies' theory of the *J*-curve pattern of revolution.[24] Virtually all others invoke factors that may be associated, in principle, with persistent patterns of conflict and contention, through the persistence of their causes (e.g., theories of relative deprivation or of status discrepancies) or of balances between mobilization and institutionalization.[25] These theories, however, raise fewer questions and doubts if associated with events that do not themselves constitute persistent patterns.

Cases of vicious political conflict that are persistent and patterned are usually explained in two different but not wholly dissimilar, ways. The first, as stated, is through the persistence of causes also associated with cases of conflict that deviate from "normal" patterns. The second is through the postulate of inertia in behavior: vicious conflict has its origin in some constellation of circumstances that produces an abrupt deviation which, if it persists long enough, remains in motion after the original causes have ceased to operate—perhaps through becoming a normatively expected pattern, perhaps because no new normative pattern is formed as a result of social disruption.

The case of tribal societies, however, suggests a third possibility that differs fundamentally from the others and seems particularly suitable to account for cases of patterned, continuous conflict. Suppose there are two fundamentally different types of contention, hence conflict, in politics. There is, first, contention that is "syllogistic" in regard to both modes and levels—that is, inherent in the very nature of structures (even those that are highly "institutionalized," as the term is usually understood) and not a threat to their survival. There is, second, contention that results from the failures of structures and does endanger them. These vastly dissimilar phenomena may nevertheless engender behavior that looks similar to the naked eye or index. Attempts to cover both by the same explanations are bound either to produce bad theory or, much worse (given the scarcity of good theories), to impugn or weaken sound generalizations. That is, although existing theories of civil strife are not beyond criticism, their failure to distinguish dissimilar events may make them seem worse than they are. Beyond this, it is implied that three types of civil strife theories are needed: (*a*) theories of "syllogistic" strife, which is necessarily continuous and highly patterned; (*b*) theories of "endemic" strife that is not syllogistic, but nevertheless continuous and patterned; and (*c*) theories of "discontinuous" strife (i.e., abrupt changes in levels and modes of political conflict). And still another implication is discernible. Special causes of discontinuous strife will sometimes, through their persistence, lead to strife that is self-sustaining, as an accustomed mode of behavior. If so, syllogistic strife, being inherently persistent, might also continue, at least for some time, even after the structures that made strife syllogistic have vanished, have been altered, or have been subsumed under other structures. Consequently, vicious contention in "new nations" where tribal societies play an important role—or did in the recent past—might well be explained on grounds much simpler than those usually invoked. The explanations commonly offered are models of complexity (e.g., Huntington's influential and ingenious theory of balance between mobilization and institutionalization). At least in regard to African societies, those who like to use Occam's Razor might make a splendid slaughter of such theories on the basis here provided. This, however, is only an insinuation, and it raises hosts of intricate questions (e.g., about the effects of colonialization on norms and practices prevalent in indigenous societies) that would take us far beyond our central purpose.

Illustration: Bases of Eligibles for High Positions in British Government in the 1950s

The example of Recruitment in tribal societies emphasizes mainly the role of informal modes of boundary interchange in overall competitiveness. The case of Recruitment to high governmental positions in Britain—the Cabinet, Parliament, and the higher civil service—does the same for bases of eligibles. The two cases also complement each other in that the first shows how informal aspects of Recruitment may increase competitiveness and the second how they may lessen it.

It is common knowledge that a considerable difference exists in Britain between legal eligibility for high governmental positions and citizens' effective potential, by virtue of their personal characteristics, for attaining such positions. Here we wish to give quantitative content to the words "considerable difference" and, again, to hazard some speculations about the findings that seem sensible, or at least worth pursuing further.[26]

From a legal standpoint, no Briton is barred from membership in Parliament or the Cabinet. The case of the higher civil service is a bit more complicated. The so-called administrative class—the name has now been dropped, but the thing itself continues—is entered directly on the basis of a performance test. The test is a stiff written examination (supplemented at times by such wrinkles as the bizarre country house weekend during which a candidate's personality is evaluated by unidentified observers). One is unlikely to succeed in the official examination without having a university education. No one, however, is legally barred from attending university. Civil servants are also legally able to become "higher" civil servants by promotion from lower ranks or by transfer from other services. Hence for the higher civil service, no less than "political" offices, all Britons are, legally, coequal eligibles. Entry to all high governmental offices is supposed to depend only on ability and personal inclinations.

To determine what was actually the case in the 1950s—and probably was true before and has been since[27]—we first divide the population on the basis of three variables: class, or socioeconomic status, education, and sex. We use categories based on these variables simply because Britons think of themselves as differing in these terms, just as tribal societies conceive social differences principally in terms of lineages, age sets, membership by descent or annexation, and the like. Of course, Britons are conscious of other social differences: whether a person comes from one county or another, lives in town or country, is Church of England or nonconformist, and so on. Some of these other differences (occupation, e.g., or even, in some respects, religious affiliation) are significant because of their relation to class positions; most, however, are regarded as minor traits, used only or chiefly for purposes of detailed descriptions of individuals.

Sarcastic comments to the contrary notwithstanding, Britons are as conscious as anyone of the differences between men and women. (For Recruitment to high government offices, we will see, they are sex conscious to an extreme degree.) Beyond that, the popular imagery of social categorization deals mainly with social class and education; these variables are, in fact, very highly correlated—almost interchangeable. Academic categorizations follow suit: discussions and tables of figures in social-scientific studies rarely mention other variables. Although this is not peculiar to British academics, the weight given to class and education in popular categorization is unusual. Traits associated with them are, in Rogowski's sense, *stigmata:* identifiable at low cost, through speech and other readily observable items of behavior, and costly, often impossible, to change. And the British themselves tend to be extraordinarily sensitive to them. If Americans rarely are color-blind, Britons rarely are tone-deaf even to small nuances of class accents. There are, therefore, no more basic ways to categorize British people than by the variables used.

In regard to *sex*, we can assume a 50–50 split in the population.[28] The proportion of Britons in different *social classes* is more difficult to state exactly. For one thing, the potential number of class distinctions is enormous; popular writers like H. G. Wells and academics like Dennis Brogan agree that almost everybody in England (not as much in the less class-conscious Celtic fringe) has his own "place" relative to everybody else. In addition, standard sources that assign people to broad categories—such as the national census, the London School of Economics survey of social mobility, and market research organizations—use different conceptions of the basic classes, make different numbers of distinctions, sometimes assign the same people to higher or lower strata (e.g., higher ones because they wear white collars or supervise a number of other people, or lower ones because they work for wages in factories or shops), and do not separate out certain very small groups that play a considerable role in Recruitment to high governmental positions.

We have chosen three broad categories: the *lower classes*, the *middle classes*, and the *upper classes*.[29] The lower classes include predominantly blue-collar workers of various degrees of skill, as well as groups sometimes put in the nether regions of the "lower middle class" that have more in common with blue-collar workers than with people in the solid middle class (e.g., foremen, clerks, shop assistants, small farmers). This category comprised, in our period, about 80% of the population.[30] The upper classes comprised no more than 2% of the population.[31] Of these, perhaps 1%—certainly no more—might be considered *eminent* people: aristocrats and gentry; people of great, and old, wealth; important executives; and conspicuous professionals (bishops, professors, Harley Street specialists, etc.) This leaves about 18% in the middle classes.[32] Undoubtedly, these 18% are a rather heterogeneous lot (as are the other categories), but social distances between higher and lower individuals included in the category are probably smaller than those that separate the higher middles from the upper crust or the lower middles from workers.[33]

These rough percentages, it should be noted, had not changed much over many years. Some movement upward and downward occurred, with a net gain of upward over downward mobility. Much of that movement, however, was confined to mobility within the broad categories (which, incidentally, helps justify their use): from being unskilled or partly skilled to being a skilled worker, or from being on the fringe of the "lower middle class" to being in the working class.[34] And there is some reason to think that this general pattern continues—although we can keep an open mind about that for the present purpose.[35]

In regard to *education*, we can assume that holders of high governmental offices in the 1950s went to school before 1930.[36] Slightly more than 80% of the population at that time had only primary schooling. The proportion who had attended "public schools" (private secondary schools financed by fees) was, at most, in the range of 2%; and those who had gone to the "better" public schools (i.e., boarding schools held in high esteem and/or charging rather high fees[37]) accounted for less than half of that proportion (for simplicity's sake, let us say 1%). No more than 17 or 18% then, had other kinds of secondary schooling.[38] Note the virtually exact correspondence of these proportions with those who might be considered eminent, others in the upper classes, and those in the middle and lower classes. Education attained and socioeconomic status manifestly are highly interchangeable.

The Education Act of 1944 entitled all children to some form of secondary education, and raising the mandatory school-leaving age assured that almost all would get secondary education in some form. However, the resulting changes are negligible in the light of one consideration: namely, those who used to stop with elementary school have tended to acquire terminal secondary education in "secondary modern" or "technical" schools, which are seldom more than insipid appendages to elementary schooling; they do not go to "grammar" schools (or corresponding streams in "comprehensive" schools, rough equivalents of American high schools) that prepare students for higher education. In 1951 the percentages in various secondary schools were:

Public schools	about 2%
Grammar schools (and "comprehensive" schools)	about 23%
Other secondary schools	about 75%

Clearly, then, no marked change in the distribution of schooling had occurred, just as there was no marked change in the general distribution of socioeconomic status.[39]

Using these figures, we can now calculate the proportions of the whole British population that had effective eligibility for membership in the Cabinet, the House of Commons, and the Higher Civil Service. We can also describe the composition of the eligibles by social groups and express the ratios of advantage for the groups.

Members of the Cabinet. Since the Tories were in office from 1951 on, the period 1935–1955 is especially useful for our purposes: it included Labour Party and Conservative and coalition Cabinets, in about the proportion that these have generally occurred. The Tories had a somewhat longer run than Labour during this period and, of course, a larger number of Cabinet members (62 vs. 34)—but that has usually been true in modern times. The class composition of Cabinet members was as follows:[40]

	Overall (%)	Tories (%)	Labour (%)
Aristocracy	21	32	3
Middle class	57	64	41
Working class	21	4	56

Only two (to our knowledge) were female, although a few women were junior ministers or ministers not included in Cabinets—and a female in the Cabinet still remains *rara avis*.

Figure 6.4 portrays inequalities in access to Cabinet positions by social class, overall and by part—equating "aristocrats" with "uppers," which is not fully warranted but is not overly distorting.[41] The Gini index for all members is about .64, meaning that 36% of the population (at most) had effective eligibility for Cabinet positions during the period treated. There was,

Table 6.3 Ratios of Advantage in Access to British Cabinet Positions (1935–55)

	Aristocrats	Middle Class	Lower Class
Percentage of population	1	18	80
Percentage of Cabinet members	21	57	21
Ratios of advantage			
% Cabinet members/ % population	21	3.2	.26
Transformed so smallest number = 1	83	12	1
Expressed as proportion of 1.0	.86	.13	.03

however, a vast difference between the Conservative and Labour parties. The index for the former is no less than .81, whereas for Labour it is only .24. Labour did discriminate by social class, but not much; the Conservatives discriminated to a level within one-fifth of absolute inequality.

Note, however, that these indices are for males only. Subtracting women as an excluded group, we get the following ratios of effective eligibility:

Overall membership	$E_e = 1 - .5 - .64(.5) = .18$
Tory members	$E_e = 1 - .5 - .81(.5) = .10$
Labour members	$E_e = 1 - .5 - .24(.5) = .38$

Thus at most 18% of the population had effective eligibility for positions in the Cabinet, and four-fifths of those who had such eligibility were aristocratic or middle-class males. Their advantage over others appears especially clearly in Table 6.3, which indicates that aristocrats were 83 times more likely to achieve Cabinet rank than lower-class citizens and about seven times more so than members of the middle classes; they had 86% of all the "privilege" going in regard to positions in the Cabinet.

Members of Parliament. In 1951 the strength of the two major British parties in the House of Commons was nearly even, with Conservatives slightly in the lead (321 against 304)—the general pattern since the war. In that year the composition of the House by schooling was as follows:[42]

	N	All (%)	Conservatives (%)	Labour (%)
Public schools	321	53	80	23
Secondary schools	121	20	17	26
Elementary schools	158	26	3	50

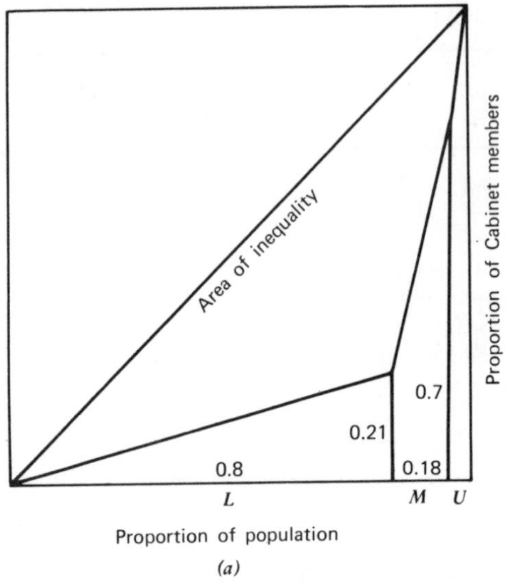

(a)

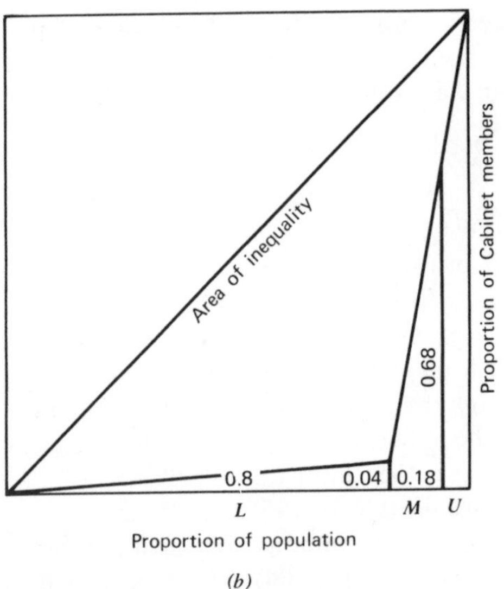

(b)

Fig. 6.4 Lorenz curves for British Cabinet members, 1935–1955 (by social class). (*a*) Total membership, (*b*) Conservative Party, and (*c*) Labour Party. *L* = "Lowers," *M* = "Middles," *U* = "Uppers."

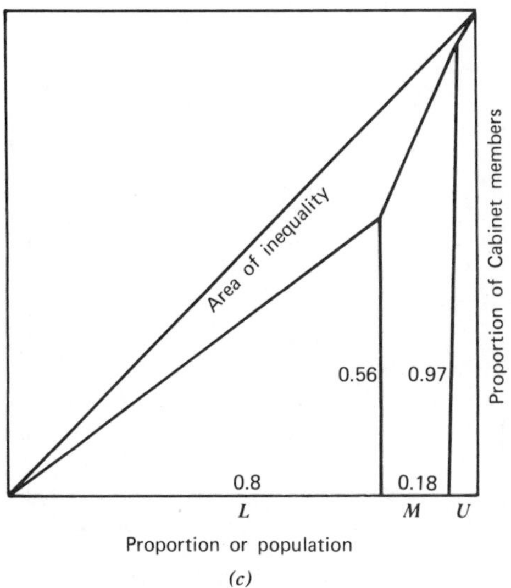

Fig. 6.4 (*Continued*)

(The schooling of 25 members was "unknown," and these individuals have been left out of the reckoning.) Females were just under 3% of the total membership (17 out of 625). Since the total proportions of the population that had attended the three basic types of schools were 2, 18, and 80%, respectively, Gini indices of inequality can be computed on the basis of the Lorenz curves in Figure 6.5. They are as follows:

All members	.63
Conservatives	.91
Labour	.33

The overall inequality for the House of Commons thus was about the same as for the Cabinet, but note that both the Conservatives and Labour discriminated more in regard to access to the House than in regard to positions in the Cabinet; the similarity in the overall index is an artifact of the condition that the membership of the House was somewhat more evenly split among the parties than was membership in the Cabinet.

Again, for all practical purposes these indices pertain only to males—although there is less (but still substantial) reason to consider females excluded by Labour (4% of Labour MP's) than by the Conservative Party (2%). Making allowances for that fact, we obtain effective eligibility ratios of about .18, .05, and .38 for all members, Tory members, and Labour MP's, respectively. About 20% of the population, at most, had effective eligibility for

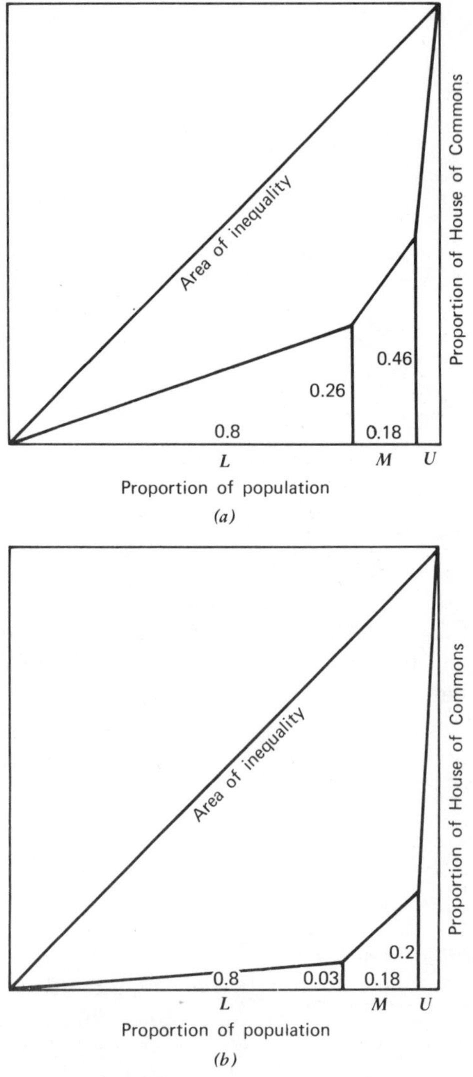

Fig. 6.5 Lorenz curves for House of Commons, 1951. (*a*) All members, (*b*) Conservatives, and (*c*) Labour.

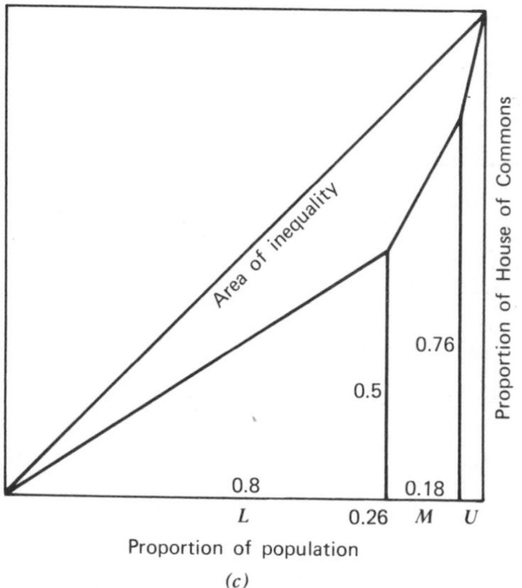

(c)

Fig. 6.5 (*Continued*)

membership in the House of Commons, but only 5% had the potential, by virtue of class and sex, to become Conservative members as against 38% for the Labour Party. Ratios of advantage by class, portrayed in Table 6.4,[43] show clearly enough the enormous advantage of having been to public school in securing a career in national politics. "Old boys" were about 25 times more likely even than those who had attended state secondary schools to enter Parliament, and they had a whopping 94% of all the privilege available.

Higher Civil Servants. In 1950 a representative group of 1045 people entered the administrative class of the civil service by all available routes: open competition, other forms of direct entry, transfer from other services, and promotion from the ranks. Only 10% were women, and the overall schooling of the entrants had been as follows.[44]

	%
Twenty "best-known" boarding schools	15
Other public schools	51
State secondary schools	25
Primary schools	8

At that time, as we saw, about 1% of each cohort of secondary school age attended "better" public schools (even if not the 20 most prestigious) and about 1% other public schools; around 23% attended grammar schools or equivalent

Table 6.4 Ratios of Advantage in Access to Parliament (1951)

	Public Schools	Secondary Schools	Elementary Schools
Percentage of population	2	18	80
Percentage of members	53	20	26
Ratios of advantage			
% members/% population	26.5	1.1	.31
Transformed	85	3.5	1
Expressed as proportion of 1.0	.94	.04	.01

streams in comprehensive schools—the category being almost equivalent to the old "state secondary schools"; and 75% attended "other" secondary schools, equivalent to primary schools under the old system.[45] Assuming no significant changes in the backgrounds of entrants into the higher civil service over the next several years—a safe assumption[46]—we can compute a Gini index of inequality on the basis of the Lorenz curve plotted in Figure 6.6. The index is approximately .82. Since sexual discrimination involved the effective exclusion of 40% of the population, overall effective eligibility was

$$E_e = 1 - .4 - .82(.6) = .10$$

This is about half the effective eligibility for the Cabinet and House of Commons.

The most important reason for the difference between the bases is apparent in Table 6.5. Although women were somewhat less underrepresented than in "politics," the advantage of having been to public school over any other kind of schooling was especially enormous. This is very odd indeed, considering that since the war, the Civil Service Commission ostensibly has made a "special effort" to recruit men and women who have *not* been to public schools, that measures supposedly were taken to guard against class bias in marking examinations,[47] and that the higher civil service was supposed to be democratized by more recruitment from outside and promotion from the ranks. Of course, the public schools provide a channel of upward mobility to those given free places or whose parents can afford the fees, as, to a much lesser extent, do the grammar schools. The bias against those of lower-class *origin* thus is less than our figures suggest;[48] but managing to attain the "better" type of schooling tends to recruit people into the higher social classes rather than to infuse lower-class people into higher positions, and for the "lower" classes the principal conduit to the administrative class is virtually closed anyway.

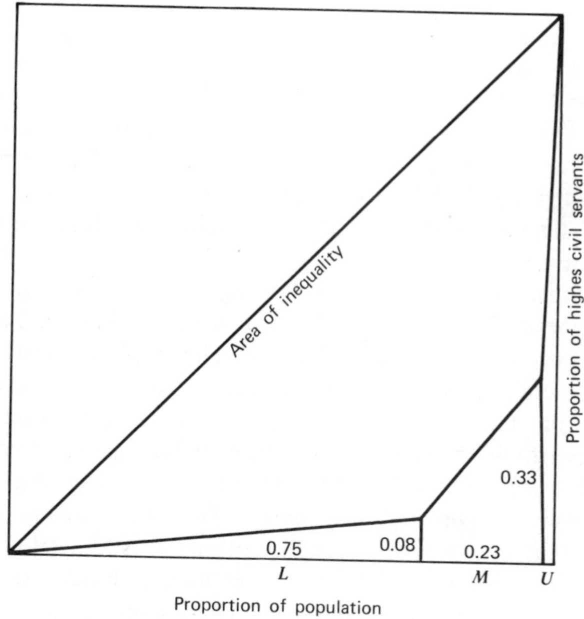

Fig. 6.6 Lorenz curve for the higher civil service, 1950.

Educational bias operated even more strongly in progress to the very highest grades of the domestic civil service (and in recruitment to the Foreign Service). In 1950 secretaries and deputy-secretaries—the equivalents in the civil service of ministers and junior ministers—consisted of more than 81% with public school background (although a sizable proportion had been to day schools, not boarding schools); about 18% were educated in state secon-

Table 6.5 Ratios of Advantage in Access to the Higher Civil Service (Based on Entry in 1950)

	Public Schools	Grammer Schools	Other Secondary
Percentage of population	2	23	75
Percentage of entrants	66	25	8
Ratios of advantage			
% entrants/% population	33	1	0.1
Transformed	330	10	1
Expressed at proportion of 1.0	.97	.03	.003

dary schools, and none at all had only primary schooling. For the intermediate grades of the service (assistant secretaries, principal assistant secretaries, and under-secretaries), the figures were about 78, 20, and 2%, respectively. These disproportions may reflect, to some extent, old biases in Recruitment, but the biases have been slow to change. By our method, the bases of effective eligibles for the higher posts come to a mere .03 and .04, respectively—figures even below those for entering the House or Cabinet via the Conservative Party.

Summary and Reflections on the Findings. A very knotty problem in political science has been *how to gauge the extents to which "ruling elites" (a) exist, and (b) are pluralistic or monolithic.* The emphasis in studies of this problem is generally put on the special influence that various social groups have on governmental decisions or within issue areas, either directly studied or imputed. No doubt the matter of influence on decisions is important. But it is also nebulous. The matters dealt with here—what overall proportion of people effectively has potential for gaining high positions in a unit's structure of superordination, and how such potential is distributed among subgroups—surely are also relevant, less resistant to exact research, and at least useful for making initial judgments. These considerations reveal with some precision something about at least one characteristic of Dahl's ideal model of a ruling elite: that it be a "well-defined minority."[49] Similarly, we are now in a position to study those whom outsiders try to influence—a factor that must surely bear some relation to whether influence is effectively exerted.

Britain, from that standpoint, clearly fits the ruling-elite model; our computations confirm and give quantitative content to the common lore about British "elitism." Overall bases of effective eligibles for high governmental positions were very small (between 3 and 19% of the population), and still smaller when one allows for the tendency of the underrepresentation of women to cut the proportions by approximately half in all cases. The composition of the bases certainly makes for a well-defined minority, consisting mainly of vastly overrepresented male "highers" or "old boys," plus a reasonable admixture of "middles." (See Table 6.6.)

The elite, however, was not altogether monolithic, except in the higher civil service. The Labour and Conservative parties differed not just in regard to preferred policies but also, perhaps more substantially, in another sense: Labour provided a channel to high governmental positions to a clear majority of the male population (and also somewhat greater chances to females), whereas the Tories provided such a channel only to a small fraction—in fact, almost the same fraction that was enfranchised before the electoral reforms of the nineteenth century.

This suggests a novel classification of political parties, perhaps pertinent

Table 6.6 Effective Eligibility for High Positions in Britain: Summary (Early 1950s)

Measures	Parliament			Cabinet			High Civil Service (Domestic)		
	Overall	Labour	Con-servatives	Overall	Labour	Con-servatives	Entry	Intermediate Grades	Highest Grades
Eligibles (whole population)	.19	.34	.05	.18	.38	.05	.10	.04	.03
Eligibles (males)	.37	.67	.09	.36	.76	.09	.18	.08	.06
Ratios of "privilege"	Uppers	Middles	Lowers	Uppers	Middles	Lowers	Uppers	Middles	Lowers
	.94	.04	.01	.86	.13	.03	.96	.03	.003
		Males	Females		Males	Females		Males	Females
		.97	.03		1.0	0		.90	.10

beyond Britain. In his classic work on parties, Duverger modified Lincoln's conception of democracy to read "government of the people by an elite sprung from the people."[50] The "popular" nature of the elite, he argued, results precisely because democratic leaders are selected by political parties competing for general popular support. In Britain, however, a choice, and competition, exists between a party that conforms to Duverger's definition and one that does not: a literally "popular" party and a highly selective one. To the extent that the parties alternate in power, the British elite has a "pluralistic" trait. But this is no synchronic pluralism of well-defined groups. It is pluralism over time, through pulsations of "popular" and "exclusive" rule.

It would be interesting and instructive to compare this situation with other countries, parties, and patterns of power over time. But we must leave the matter here as only an item worth adding to the agenda of unperformed research—also as the possibility that political parties might be usefully classified on the basis of the effective "eligibility" for high office they provide.

A further reflection prompted by the findings and the points just made concerns the *significance of legal or otherwise formal provisions in regard to overall levels of competitiveness of Recruitment*. The differences between formal and effective eligibility (100% as against 3 to 19%) might seem large enough to suggest that legal aspects of Recruitment could just as well be disregarded altogether. A case to the contrary should be made, however, especially since both the illustrations we have used emphasize informal aspects of Recruitment.

Legal provisions almost certainly make a larger difference where elitism is a less pronounced cultural trait, even if class remains a basic criterion for distinguishing groups. But, more important, legal provisions concerning Recruitment appear to make a noteworthy difference in Britain too.

Without the Labour Party, the base of effective eligibles in Britain would shrink to a tiny fraction (and party competition would be far less likely to add an element of "pluralism" to the structure of the political elite), and it is clear that the Labour Party could not exist without universal suffrage and universal legal eligibility for high office. Formal methods of boundary interchange also clearly matter apart from their effects on the party system. Recruitment by periodic elections is, as we surmised, markedly more competitive (as measured by bases of effective eligibles) than Recruitment by performance tests (19% as against 10%)—even though Recruitment by open examinations rather than connections and patronage was supposed to open up the British administrative system. And places attained by designation (the higher positions in the administrative class) are the most exclusive of all (3 to 4%), far more so even than membership in the Cabinet.[51] The higher ranks of the administrative class exhibit a pronounced measure of oligarchy in Michels' sense, which includes an "impulse toward aristocracy": the continuous hegemony of similar types of people. Performance tests and periodic elections countervail that tendency even in extremely elitist societies.

However, it is undeniable that neither the latter factor nor the former significantly compensates for the tendency toward oligarchy in Great Britain or in similar cultures. The difference between a base of .03 and one of .19 could be regarded as greater than 500%, therefore large. Nevertheless, the difference is only about one-sixth of what it could be and would be if legal provisions were all-important. Formal arrangements manifestly matter; informal norms, just as manifestly, matter more.

A century and a half of formal democratization in Britain raised bases of effective eligibles for high office by about 3 to 16% (in different categories); and these figures, if anything, overstate the case. Perhaps effects on policies were greater. But surely lack of democratization of the bases of eligibles also had effects, lending credence to the position that social reforms matter more than reforms in formal-legal arrangements.

These observations also provide additions for the agenda of unperformed research. What effects follow changes in formal arrangements regarding Recruitment in different cultures, subcultures, and social units? Is the size of the effects predictable? If not the size, can one at least predict the direction of the effects? Do expectable effects occur only after specific time lags (perhaps through the gradual modification of social norms toward consistency with forms)? And do the effects differ for groups of different kinds (e.g., does the legal broadening of competition filter down the social scale at different rates)?

The case of Britain may, of course, be untypical, and effects on national governmental levels may differ from effects on local levels or in nongovernmental units. One item among our findings, moreover, goes contrary to our initial expectations. Although performance tests overall make for less effective eligibility than periodic elections, they have the opposite effect on women: the proportion of women entering the higher civil service far exceeds their proportion elsewhere. The obvious implication is that the introduction of performance tests will particularly broaden bases of eligibility in regard to groups whose low eligibility is not associated with socioeconomic factors—factors that generally reduce competence. This apparently tautological statement also implies that lower socioeconomic groups have a stake in the less "universalistic" methods of Recruitment, as well as a greater stake in social than legal changes.

Both questions discussed thus far have to do with the extent to which "formal" democratization leads to "effective" democratization. We can also examine a perspective of political study by another question: *Do major parties* (those that compete for broad public support) *tend to tailor the com-*

position of their more conspicuous groups of leaders to the composition of the electorate? This question, like some raised earlier, is of consequence for the evaluation of the postulate of "rational" value maximization in political study—not least since the postulate was first applied in the realm of politics to voting behavior and party tactics.[52]

If the postulate held, the following logically related propositions might be expected to hold as well:

1. Political leaders prefer policies favorable to the segment(s) of the population to which they belong.
2. Voters therefore vote for leaders recruited from the segment(s) to which they (voters) belong—hence for parties that recruit heavily from their own segment(s).
3. In trying to maximize the number of votes they obtain, parties select types of leaders in rough proportion to the segmental composition of the electorate—or overrepresent the more numerous segments of the electorate.

Clearly proposition (3) does not hold in Britain, least of all in the Conservative Party. Yet the Conservatives do not suffer at the polls from the exclusiveness of their Recruitment; on the contrary, they generally do somewhat better than Labour (even disregarding the unearned profits they reap from the way parliamentary seats are allocated). This anomaly can be explained without violating the assumption of value maximization. At the same time, however, the case brings out some important limitations on the explanatory range of the postulate.

First of all, it might be argued that proposition (3) does not hold because proposition (2) is wrong: voters do not tend to prefer candidates who come from their own segment of the population.[53] This is generally supported on the basis of a "cultural" disposition to be deferential among the British lower classes—a disposition sufficiently widespread to make it safe or even advisable for "uppers," in combination with some "middles," to use elections as means for realizing their segmental values (see note 54). That argument, of course, is incongruous with the assumption of value maximization, but "rationalists" do not lack resources for more consistent explanations.

Lack of accurate and sufficient information might be one reason for the failure of "rational" voters to vote for a party that provides channels of Recruitment to their own kind. If actors do not have such information, their behavior is unlikely to correspond to that expected by well-informed theorists. From one point of view, however, that way of saving the postulate seems dubious: British voters, even if unable to put accurate numbers or indices on the matter, are surely aware that the Tories are more "blue-blooded" than the Labourites. Nevertheless, one aspect of British voting behavior lends credence to the argument of imperfect information. The people who are better educated and higher in status emerge in all studies as more informed about politics and more politically active than others. That they possess more information might account for the following behavior: they vote Tory much more monolithically than "lowers" vote Labour; in addition, their being more politically active might help explain our observation that voting favors the Conservatives far beyond the level expectable on the basis of proposition (2). These arguments, however, bring out something that "rationalists" have conceded all along: predictive theory based on their postulate will work only if information is sufficient and accurate—which does not seem to be the case for much or most of the British electorate.

Calculating voters might not vote in the manner stated for a second reason. The social characteristics of candidates might be relatively immaterial to them compared with the policy positions taken by parties. In fact, so long as these positions are "correct", voters might prefer to be represented by leaders from the higher classes who, presumably, are better educated, more worldly wise, therefore better able to accomplish public goals.

Proposition (2) could fail to hold on this ground, however, only if proposition (1) were wrong—that is, if leaders did not in many cases prefer policies favorable to their own segment(s) of the population. British political leaders often do not select policies on this basis. Both parties have pursued rather similar (although not identical) "welfare state" policies which, although they do not utterly deprive the higher classes for the sake of the lower, also stop short of the policies that would be adopted if political leaders fully exploited their positions for segmental gains.

Why, then, do leaders act contrary to proposition (1)? The common explanation hinges on the "cultural" disposition of *noblesse oblige* among the British upper classes, or paternalism, to give it a less flattering label. Again, this is not congruent with a value maximizing postulate, but once more, "rationalists" have resources for explaining the inaccuracy of the proposition. It seems clear in retrospect that the expansion of the franchise was tolerated, even promoted, by the British upper classes to ensure that lower-class voters (more deferential and/or less informed than those of the middle classes) would counterbalance the growing strength of the bourgeoisie; that, in all probability, is why Mr. Disraeli "caught the Whigs napping and stole their clothes." Once the franchise was made universal, however, the parties had substantially to adjust their programs to the electorate to win elections. There was no point acting in accordance with proposition (1) if, in so doing, preferred values would be forfeited because of lost elections. A fourth proposition thus becomes paramount: parties trying to maximize the votes they obtain select *policies* (not leaders) in a way that does not play into the hands of their opponents. Or, perhaps better, parties strike an optimum tradeoff in their selection of policies between two different imperatives: to promote their leaders' own segmental interests and to keep a sufficient hold on the electorate to retain good chances of winning elections.

Nothing in British politics is inconsistent with that position. Moreover, if the argument holds, a different face is put on the finding of "elitism" in Britain (it pertains much more to men than measures) and on the effects of changes in formal modes of Recruitment (they affect directives more than personnel).

Nevertheless, what we have explained on "rationalist" premises can also be explained, less intricately, on different premises (deferential dispositions among voters and a sense of social obligation on the part of leaders). Moreover, British patterns of Recruitment do not follow the simplest expectations derivable from rationalist assumptions, which implies limits on their parsimonious operation, or on the areas in which the assumptions might have great explanatory power.

The postulate of "rational" value maximization has been used with some persuasiveness to account for voters' preferences among parties and parties' choice of platforms.[55] The essential question is whether the postulate should also be used to account for the selection of candidates and, if so, how it can be used to account for the particular circumstances of candidate selection in Britain. Beyond this lies an even more fundamental question. If "nonrational" factors explain those circumstances better, might they not also better explain other aspects of the processes of competition among parties, in other countries no less than in Britain?[56]

Notes

1. In its broadest sense, the notion of boundary interchange denotes any transactions across real or analytic boundaries among parts of a "system." See Talcott Parsons, *Structure and Process in Modern Societies* (New York: Free Press, 1960), pp. 18, 74–78.

2. This point is considerably elaborated in Chapter 13.

3. Informal norms and practices might of course increase, no less than lessen, a base of eligibles; but the latter no doubt occurs more frequently.

4. For a discussion of conventional measures of inequality, see Hayward R. Alker, Jr., *Mathematics and Politics* (New York: Macmillan, 1965). The measurement of inequalities is one of the livelier areas of innovation in applied statistics, and the methods summarized by Alker have recently been much criticized, amended, and surpassed. The Gini index, which remains conventional, is discussed on pages 36 to 42 of Alker's book.

5. The complication in our second formula could be avoided, and a single of G calculated, by starting the curve of cumulative inequality at an appropriate point of the x-coordinate (in this case, at 40%), not its zero point. However, that would involve using one coordinate to denote two or more variables. The procedure we propose has the same result and, perhaps, more clarity, although not economy.

6. For instance, David E. Apter, "A Comparative Method for the Study of Politics," *American Journal of Sociology*, Vol. 64 (1958), pp. 221–237.

7. See, for example, D. C. McClelland, *The Achieving Society* (Princeton, N.J.: Van Nostrand, 1961).

8. Eckstein's study of Norway, *Division and Cohesion in Democracy* (Princeton, N.J.: Princeton University Press, 1966), emphasizes the extent to which "noncompetitiveness" pervades the Norwegian culture, as well as the extent to which prevalent norms inhibit using other people as mere instruments for one's own goals. As an aside, contentiousness in Norwegian academic life seemed to the author rather greater than in many parts of the polity or economy. If so, one may suspect further that contentiousness does not necessarily vary with type of social unit. In the Norwegian case, contentiousness in academic life probably results from the high prestige of academic roles, the great dearth of places, and the lack of international interchangeability of certain types of academics—notably social scientists, who were observed more closely than others. (It should be added that these are "impressions"—in no way hard findings.)

9. Jacob Burckhardt, *The Age of Constantine the Great* (London: Routledge & Kegan Paul, 1949), pp. 34–35.

10. Much of the material used in this illustration comes from the magisterial study of government and politics in South African tribes by I. Schapera (*Government and Politics in Tribal Societies*, London: Watts, 1956): the Bushmen, Bergdama, Southern Bantu, and Hottentot peoples, each of which consists of numerous tribes. Schapera considers these typical of "primitive" (non-literate) societies, and we agree. There is, however, some question about whether the conditions here described have parallels in all "tribal" societies everywhere: for example, whether they apply when bilateral rather than unilineal descent systems prevail. To avoid an argument (which hardly has importance for our present purpose), we use the qualifying term "South African" in the subtitle—but in parentheses, to signify our belief that the conditions described are widespread.

There are, of course, many books, articles, and monographs on political anthropology (see Chapter 1, note 5), and we have not relied on Schapera exclusively. But Schapera's study has two important advantages for us: it is explicitly comparative, not a superficial textbook or "overview" (like Mair), and it puts particularly great emphasis on Recruitment. Most of the other works on tribal politics we have seen give scant attention to the matter in the absence of some exotic practice, like a war of succession. Rather, they emphasize balances among or checks on political forces, the variety of functions performed by tribal authorities, and degrees of centralization. [See, e.g., the pioneering introduction in M. Fortes and E. E. Evans-Pritchard, *African Political Systems* (London: Oxford University Press, 1940). Moreover, in monographic studies broad outlines are too often lost in heaps of undigested detail, especially names and curious incidents.

11. Schapera, *Government and Politics in Tribal Societies*, pp. 40–41.

12. See E. E. Evans-Pritchard, *The Nuer* (Oxford: Clarendon Press, 1940). See also his brief summary of the Nuer "constitution" in Fortes and Evans-Pritchard, *African Political Systems*, esp. p. 296.

13. L. A. Fallers, ed., *The King's Men* (London: Oxford University Press, 1964). These societies are probably considered "tribal" more for reasons of race and geography than because of actual structure.

14. Schapera, *Government and Politics in Tribal Societies*, pp. 51–52.

15. *Ibid.*, pp. 53–54. Note that the syndrome of ascriptive expectations, pools of eligibles, expedient selection, and consequent unpredictability of incumbency is generally not confined to the highest levels of superordination but is also found at lesser levels: heads of tribal segments, advisors of chiefs, and the like.

16. *Ibid.* pp. 138–139.

17. We refer here, among other things, to "upstart" fictions about descent of an inferior lineage from a high-born ancestor, or denigration of the validity of high positions enjoyed by certain lineages. Bailey's study of Orissa (see Chapter 3, note 7) brings out that tribal life there teems with self-aggrandizing claims and malicious gossip—supporting Apter's view that the urge to be upwardly mobile may be found even in the most ascriptive societies.

18. Schapera, *Government and Politics in Tribal Societies*, pp. 157–165.

19. *Ibid.*, p. 111.

20. *Ibid.*, p. 74.

21. *Ibid.*, p. 53.

22. *Ibid.*, p. 174.

23. For a full description, see K. Oberg, "The Kingdom of Ankole in Uganda," in Fortes and Evans-Pritchard, *African Political Systems*, pp. 157–161.

24. James C. Davies, "Toward a Theory of Revolution," *American Sociological Review*, Vol. 27 (1962), pp. 5–18.

25. Ted Robert Gurr, *Why Men Rebel* (Princeton, N.J.: Princeton University Press, 1970); Johan Galtung, "A Structural Theory of Aggression," *Journal of Peace Research*, Vol. 2 (1964), pp. 95–119; Samuel P. Huntington, *Political Order in Changing Societies* (New Haven, Conn.: Yale University Press, 1968).

26. The figures used throughout are approximate, but the approximations are near enough to exact values to distort findings very little. Approximations are sometimes used for ease of computation. But they also result from the use of secondary sources that allow no other recourse; British social scientists tend to be rather rough with figures (to put it mildly), in sharp contrast to their prose.

27. We deal with the 1950s because of the availability of good, and comparable, secondary sources of data for the period.

28. Actually, in the 1950s the division was 52–48, in favor of females—a ratio that has been fairly constant for almost a century. David C. Marsh, *The Changing Social Structure of England and Wales: 1871–1951* (London: Routledge & Kegan Paul, 1958), pp. 19–21. The preponderance of females was due to longevity, and it is early age that counts in gauging "potential" for adult positions.

29. Plurals are used because each category could and for many purposes should be divided further divided into many subgroups.

30. The census of 1951 put 83% in categories that correspond roughly to conventional conceptions of skilled, partly skilled, and unskilled workers; however, the category "skilled occupations" included some rather incongruous people (e.g., actors and actresses) that certainly are not all lower class. The London School of Economics survey of mobility in the early 1950s had 70% listed as manual workers and an additional 12.5% as lower nonmanual workers. The British Market Bureau of Research, in the same period, listed 72% as "poor" or "workers" and 17% more in the "lower middle class," including a good many people almost indistinguishable from workers if rough categories are used. The figure 80% thus should be approximately right. (See Marsh, *Changing Social Structure of England and Wales*, pp. 194, 197, 198.)

31. The census of 1951 put 3% in its broad class 1 (professional and similar occupations, higher administrative and managerial staff, and large employers). All other measures of the highest categories used are about the same. But most doctors, lawyers (especially solicitors), and many business executives have more in common with the solid middle class than the undoubted upper crust. Hence the figure of 2%—which, if it errs, probably is a bit larger than it should be.

32. This is about the same as the proportion in Class 2 of the census and Class B of the British Market Research Bureau's scheme of classification by status.

33. Readers who balk at the simplicity of this threefold division of social classes are reminded that British pubs are generally divided into three bars: public, saloon, and private bars. "Highers" are the people who are not out of place in the private bars, "middles" in the saloon bars, "lowers" in the public bars. There are literal thresholds here, and they fall approximately at the points of division we have in mind. (The comparison, we might add, is seriously made: pubs are excellent sorters of class—probably superior to sociologists.)

34. See Marsh, *Changing Social Structure of England and Wales*, pp. 194 and 198.

35. Britons appear to have become more aware of social mobility and to think more of themselves as "middle class" than in the past. See Richard Rose, *Politics in England: An Interpretation* (Boston: Little, Brown, 1964), p. 19. Nevertheless, the British Institute of Public Opinion consistently finds about 75% to be "very poor" or "average minus" in regard to socioeconomic status, about 21% as "average," and only about 4% as "average plus" (sic).

36. The median age for MPs has been steadily in the 51–55 years range; see J. F. S. Ross, *Elections and Electors* (London: Eyre & Spottiswoode, 1955), p. 389. Members of the Cabinet are unlikely to be younger. And it takes from 20 to 30 years to progress to the higher grades of the civil service—the former administrative class; see R. K. Kelsall, *Higher Civil Servants in Britain* (London: Routledge & Kegan Paul, 1955), p. 198.

37. Kelsall, *Higher Civil Servants*, pp. 120–124.

38. The estimates are based on Marsh, *Changing Social Structure of England and Wales*, pp. 200–202.

39. The figures are derived from Marsh, pp. 202–203. We have doctored them slightly by distributing people in two residual categories of "other schools" (about 8% of the total) proportionately among the unambiguous categories used. "Other

schools" probably vary from fine schools (abroad, e.g.,) to ghastly ones. The figures do not imply, of course, that educational opportunities have not changed. (Note also the omission of the proportion having university education. This has been consistently in excess of the proportion in public schools, but not much: in the period 1900–1939, somewhat below 3%, and a fraction above 3% in the 1950s.)

40. W. L. Guttsman, *The British Political Elite* (London: MacGibbon and Kee, 1963), p. 79.

41. One may assume that Guttsman's "middle class" catches some individuals whom we would classify as uppers, or even as notables.

42. Ross, *Elections and Electors*, p. 405.

43. The ratio for the House as a whole is below Labour, since the Labour Party commands only a proportion of seats. Trying to enter the House (or the Cabinet) via Labour in effect itself entails a degree of "underprivilege."

44. Kelsall, *Higher Civil Servants*, pp. 124–125, and 176.

45. Estimates based on Marsh, *Changing Social Structure of England and Wales*, pp. 202–203.

46. See Rose, *Politics in England*, p. 96.

47. *Ibid., loc. cit.*

48. *Ibid.*, p. 95.

49. Robert A. Dahl, "A Critique of the Ruling Elite Model," *American Political Science Review,* Vol. 52, No. 2 (June 1958), pp. 463–469.

50. Maurice Duverger, *Political Parties* (New York: Wiley, 1954), pp. 9, 425.

51. We assume that Cabinet positions depend on party competition, hence, indirectly, periodic elections. Prime ministers, of course, are routinely "designated" by the monarch and lesser ministers by the Prime Minister. There is, however, little scope for arbitrary choice in either process, except for assignments to particular posts.

52. By "rational" value maximization we simply mean basing actions on cost-benefit calculations and always choosing the course that will provide the greatest amount of benefit to oneself.

53. Or: voters, given a choice between two candidates, will vote for the candidate more like themselves, even if from a quite different social stratum.

54. Eric A. Nordlinger, *The Working-Class Tories: Authority, Deference and Stable Democracy* (Berkeley: University of California Press, 1967).

55. By Anthony Downs, *An Economic Theory of Democracy* (New York: Harper and Row, 1957).

56. A suggestion has been made to us that candidate selection can be accurately explained on "rationalist" premises by taking into consideration two factors: that party activists choose candidates (and generally have higher status than mere voters) and that they choose them to appeal to (middle-class) swing voters in marginal constituencies. One could readily check whether Labour and Tory candidates in such constituencies tend to be respectively higher and lower in status than in safe constituencies. It seems to us difficult, however, to account for the extraordinarily high "elitism" of the Tories on that basis.

CHAPTER SEVEN

Bases of Legitimacy

Bases of Legitimacy as Aspects of Authority Patterns

In his pioneering work, *Public and Private Government,* Merriam argued that all associations (read "social units") are "governments" because, like polities, all must deal with problems of rules, leadership, and consent.[1] Concepts pertinent to two of these problem areas have been discussed. Merriam's notion of "rules" stands for directives, and, by implication, the structures and processes by which they are formulated; it thus covers the various *S-s* and *S-S* dimensions. (Merriam did not attempt systematically to distinguish such dimensions.) His notion of "leadership" is equivalent to that of Recruitment, although it may also include aspects of the *S-S* dimensions. The notion of "consent," however, reaches at an important aspect of authority not yet covered, which helps distinguish authority relations from other human relationships: their capacity to evoke perceptions of legitimacy. In this final chapter on analytic concepts we deal with that facet of authority patterns.

Three questions can be asked about perceptions of legitimacy: whether they are evoked at all; whether the sentiments evoked are favorable or unfavorable; and what bases underlie, or criteria govern, positive or negative judgments of what is perceived. Only the last of these matters concerns us here. Whether legitimacy perceptions are evoked decides whether one is dealing with an authority pattern in the first place. Whether levels of legitimacy are high or low is, properly speaking, an aspect of the "performance" of patterns of authority. Only the third consideration has to do with their "nature"—granted that levels of legitimacy necessarily depend on the bases that underlie judgments of it.

Since the very definition of authority patterns refers to the evocation of sentiments of legitimacy, no special justification for including bases of the sentiments in the scheme of analytic concepts is needed. Quite aside from the definition, however, it is hard to imagine any general theorizing about authority patterns that does not take Bases of Legitimacy into account. Since

Bases of Legitimacy are important for explaining the performance of authorities, they are bound to be of some account in regard to virtually all theoretical problems that can be raised about authority patterns (e.g., how the patterns undergo change, are dissolved, are generated or regenerated, or contribute functionally to other aspects of social units). Bases of Legitimacy may also have a more direct bearing on such problems.

The idea of legitimacy has always had a particular association with the State. But, although originally applied only to polities, the notion has been smoothly extended to the study of leadership, hierarchy, and management in social units of all kinds, especially "organizations."[2] This was clearly intended by Weber,[3] and Parsons, Weber's chief interpreter in modern sociology, came to think of legitimacy as the "primary link" between the values of individuals and their relations to all "institutionalized patterns" in societies.[4] Biographies and novels—and our own experience—make clear that sentiments of legitimacy arise even in social units where ties are intimately affective and dependency is great (e.g., in the relations of children with parents, in families). Affect and dependency in such cases increase the probability that the sentiments will be positive, but this does not imply that perceptions of legitimacy (or illegitimacy) do not occur.

Bases of Legitimacy thus belong in the scheme of analytic concepts. There is, however, one difference between them and all other concepts thus far developed. Although certainly a "variable" (they vary), the bases on which perceptions of legitimacy rest do not constitute a continuous dimension. At any rate, we have not managed to find any underlying dimension expressed in them, and it seems very doubtful that any such dimension could be found. Unlike levels of legitimacy (running continuously from absolute legitimacy to complete illegitimacy), the bases are distinct qualities that can be described but not continuously ranked. But location on a continuous dimension, or several, might itself still underlie perceptions of legitimacy; we simply point out that no single, special dimension on which Bases of Legitimacy can be ranked is available. This assertion is clarified at length after the general notion of "Bases of Legitimacy" has been defined and certain problems concerning the conceptualization of special kinds of bases have been discussed.

Definition

Bases of Legitimacy are values which govern perceptions that authority patterns are rightly constituted and therefore worthy of support—worthy, that is, of actions that tend to keep the patterns in existence and functioning effectively. The intended meaning of this definition is probably best explicated by pointing out matters to which it does *not* refer, that might easily be confused with those to which it does.

1. The concept of legitimacy bases does not apply to perceptions of particular incumbents of superordinated positions, particular directives, or any special aspects of the structures and processes by which incumbents arrive at directives. It pertains to perceptions of overall authority patterns. The literature on legitimacy often blurs or makes unwarranted equations between perceptions of whole patterns and of their parts, including incumbents and directives. Such blurring is perhaps inevitable and not altogether reprehensible. Perceptions of overall patterns of authority and of special aspects of them no doubt are interdependent, even if imperfectly so. Whether a particular superordinate is entitled to his position has to do with norms of Recruitment, and the whole pattern of authority need not be imperiled by any particular perception that a super improperly occupies his position. But should such perceptions frequently occur, spillover to the whole constitution of the authority pattern is likely, although there are probably exotic cases in which dubious incumbency is a way of life and legitimacy perceptions of the entire pattern of authority remain positive. Again, authority patterns are unlikely to be considered rightly constituted if their directives are generally perceived as improper and not obligatory (e.g., because they persistently overstep boundaries set by norms of Directiveness, or because valued Decision-Rules are regularly violated). However, the perception of any particular directive as improper need not lessen positive sentiments toward an overall structure of authority; and if an overall pattern is perceived as proper, some benefit of doubt is likely to accrue to its directives, whatever the processes (if known) by which some of them were worked out. In the same vein, people may have doubts about a particular dimension of an authority pattern—say, the amount of Participation formally permitted—without experiencing alienation from the whole. Such "differentiated" perceptions of legitimacy usually underlie preferences for structural reform rather than transformation. One may also tolerate a dubious aspect of a pattern if it is perceived as somehow functional to the existence of an approved general arrangement. But if doubts extend to a large number of dimensions, it is probable that the whole pattern will be negatively judged.

Perceptions of an overall pattern and of its constituent parts thus do not belong to altogether different universes. General legitimacy should be considered a resource for favorable judgments of particular incumbents, directives, or arrangements, and particular judgments of these can be regarded as conditions for general perceptions of legitimacy. Nevertheless, the relationship between them is far from one-to-one. And the thresholds at which judgments of the particular have significant consequences for those of the general, as well as the kinds of particular judgments that have such consequences, are probably highly variable among societies and social units.

The line between the particular and general is often hard to draw precisely because, for one reason, there will be some interplay between the two kinds of judgment. It is especially hard, and perhaps inadvisable, to draw the line in regard to overall patterns and their dimensions—a crucial point on which much of our subsequent discussion depends. There is an important and obvious difference between particular incumbents and directives as against structural and procedural arrangements on particular dimensions. Incumbents and directives generally are more easily conceived as passing accidents of a pattern rather than as lasting expressions of their essence: the possibility of unseating or unmaking them is usually more palpable. Making the distinction between an overall pattern and its particular elements at least requires more sophistication, since overall arrangements are always sums of particular relationships. This, however, does not affect the general argument here: a distinction that is hard to draw is not, by implication, nonexistent. And to deny its existence in this case leads to absurdity: for example, the position that perceiving any directive to have been improperly drawn is equivalent to a general revolutionary or alienated attitude toward the overall authority pattern of a social unit.

2. A distinction should also be made between Bases of Legitimacy and bases and amounts of voluntary compliance with directives: the former do not directly pertain to the latter. This point is important because legitimacy and voluntary compliance are commonly factors in an equation; indeed, legitimacy is often defined by tendency to comply voluntarily. No doubt there is some justification for this, but not enough. As we saw earlier, compliance and noncompliance with directives are affected by many considerations.

General perceptions of legitimacy no doubt play an important role in regard to compliance with directives. But such perceptions are certainly not the only factor involved. One may comply with a directive issued by an authority perceived as illegitimate because compliance appears to be in one's calculated interest (i.e., because the benefits of complying outweigh the costs of going against an authority pattern considered unworthy). One may fail to comply for the same reason: legitimacy may be unquestioned, but the costs of compliance may outweigh the benefits. Equally important are norms or habits of Compliance as a special dimension of authority. There are, as Eckstein has written elsewhere, "cultures in which knuckling under to authority is virtually a conditioned reflex" and "cultures in which circumventing or pulling the noses of authorities is reckoned for manly virtue or as a pleasant game."[5] However, cultures of the first kind do not automatically perceive any and all patterns of authority as worthy; nor are they always notable for lack of revolutionary activity; and in cultures of the second type the tendency to disobey certainly does not amount to permanent rebelliousness.

Since tendencies to comply may be variable in cultures, subcultures, and particular social units, we are justified in the use of a separate Compliance dimension. However, compliance that results from habits or calculations is just as "voluntary" as compliance based on legitimacy. Rates of compliance, like general levels of legitimacy commanded by authority patterns, are best considered a dimension of the "performance" of the patterns.[6] One may, of course, use uncoerced compliance as an index of positive legitimacy and as a clue to the values that underlie legitimacy sentiments; complying is one way to act out the perception that an authority pattern is worthy of support. Considerable precautions, however, are advisable.[7]

Weber's Typology of Legitimacy Bases

In attempting to specify types of legitimacy bases, we unavoidably start with Weber. His classification of polities by the bases on which their authority rests is unique; the typology he proposed was supposed to cover all types of "organizations" (however much we may know it only as a classification of States); and for many years his typology enjoyed a virtual monopoly over the characterization of Bases of Legitimacy, in strange contrast to the glut of competing taxonomies found in much of the rest of political science.[8]

Weber's classification of three broad types of legitimacy bases (traditional, rational-legal, and charismatic) is familiar, at least in a broad sense.[9] Probably less well known is how Weber arrived at the types, and how they might be justified as a good typology. In part, no doubt, empirical observation went into their construction—not least, observation of the structures and histories of the leading world religions. More fundamentally, however, the types have a quasi-logical basis. Weber held that human beings can have three, and only three, basic orientations to actions of all kinds. Their actions may be habitual (past-oriented), or rational (*zweckrational*: based on ends-means, or cost-benefit, calculations), or affective (*wertrational*: directly oriented to achieving values without calculation of costs; emotional; zealous). Weber uses these basic orientations to classify a great variety of social structures, from religious sects to administrative staffs; and although he provides no strictly logical demonstrations that the general orientations will lead to his types of legitimation (hence "quasi" before "logical"), it is implied that such demonstrations would be possible. Each type is also a logical construct in that it is a "pure" (or "ideal") type: the types do not necessarily exist in exactly the way elaborated in any actual structures, but they describe the forms that would be taken if based consistently on one mode of action or another. The types thus provide idealized standards to which actual cases can be compared, the classification of cases being determined by their approximation to the types.

Why might Weber's classifications be considered a good typology? First, because in their "idealized" form the types have characteristics that all good typologies ought to have. They seem to exhaust all possibilities, since it is hard to imagine any other basis for human action; nothing seems left to that undefined catchall of typologies, the residual category. The types also seem mutually exclusive, therefore unambivalent; no particular action (or aspect of an action) can be simultaneously habitual, rational, or affective—only separable aspects of complex actions and patterns of action can be. And the types seem unambiguous: there ought to be no problem identifying whether something is calculated or based on habit or emotional zeal. Second, Weber's typology yields two bonuses beyond what is generally demanded of typologies. It has wide applicability—not least, the capability of being applied both on the smallest social micro-level (an individual action) and the largest macro-level (societal structures). And, like any models logically developed from simple premises, the types have "heuristic" utility for theory. In its own way, each is a "formal" theory based on a particular premise; and actual deviations from the models raise questions about the premises, their elaboration, or the deviations, whereas correspondences confirm the tenets of the models.

Perhaps these attractions of Weber's typology of bases of legitimation explain the paucity of attempts to replace or revise it. But Weber has never lacked for critics, even though many objections to his typology seem petty or beside the point.[11] However, enough valid criticisms remain to warrant an attempt at an alternative approach to the subject.

The most frequent criticism of Weber's types is that since the types are "pure," actual cases almost always are mixes of them. Stated baldly, as it nearly always is, this criticism would hardly be news to Weber. He himself says the same thing, emphatically, and he has a particular rationale for using pure types as descriptive concepts: the heuristic uses summarized previously; the property of the ideal types to be used, like chemical elements, to characterize actual mixes; the ability of tensions engendered by certain mixes of different or contradictory qualities to help turn static description into dynamic theory.[12]

Nevertheless, the criticism does have merits. Pure models are certainly useful as sources of problems and of theoretical illumination. But the practice of using them as descriptive categories seems to be less advisable. If *particular* ideal types are chosen to characterize cases, questions arise about how closely cases have to correspond to the types to justify their being called one thing or another. The closer the correspondence, the less the difficulty, of course, but the door is wide open in most, or many, cases to ambivalence (almost equally warranted classification under more than one category) and ambiguity (having no idea where a case belongs). Two major attractions of the typology thus seem to vanish. No matter, a Weberian might say: cases are to be described by using the set of types to characterize their various aspects. If, however, we state not merely that cases have traits $x + y + z$ (which seems vacuous) but that they have them in particular degrees and in regard to particular aspects (which is informative), the number of potential classifications may be as large as the number of cases examined. We might, in that case, capture the uniqueness of cases, but at the obvious cost of being unable to classify them. Pure models always raise these difficulties when employed as descriptive constructs.

This leads to an important point. Weber's conceptions of the Bases of Legitimacy constitute either a weak typology or an analytic scheme (as we have used the term) for describing the elements of particular patterns of legitimacy. That scheme differs from ours in that it is not "dimensional" but identifies the different qualitative elements of which patterns of legitimation may be compounded. Weber's concepts make for a comfortable analytic scheme; an analytic scheme may in fact be preferable to a typology, or a "synthetic" typology might best emerge from the use of such a scheme (as argued in Chapter 2). But the concepts are useful on that basis only if they constitute a *good* analytic scheme. Here a second, more pointed criticism of Weber's types becomes pertinent.

The criticism is suggested but not quite rightly stated by Blau.[13] His argument is that Weber makes "force" and "legitimate authority" all but antithetical: opposites in every sense but the use of coercive sanctions by legitimate authorities. Thereby, says Blau, Weber misses the role that coercive force may play in helping to create legitimacy. And it often happens that structures of authority, subsequently legitimated, originate in force.

Thus stated, Blau's argument is also off the mark, for Weber is concerned with bases of legitimation, not with the origins of legitimated structures. Blau perhaps intended to suggest that force may itself be a value that governs perceptions of legitimacy. This may well be true, even for favorable perceptions. The legitimacy of the early feudal authorities of Western Europe seems to have rested largely on their ability to provide physical protection during a period of political disintegration and constant physical peril from bellicose princes and marauding Norsemen, Magyars, and Huns. That of the early absolute monarchies also seems to have rested on Hobbesian foundations—their ability to impose peace on warring nobles and religious sects. In more recent times, legitimacy based (anyway in part) on ability to suppress riotous behavior and compel order is familiar—and seems to be coming close to home. In gist: coercive ability, or forcefulness in a more general sense, can be highly valued; thus, like *anything* so valued, it can serve, at least potentially, as a source of positive legitimacy perceptions, under specifiable circumstances—in this case, when minimal security is lacking or when just directives are inoperative because they cannot be enforced.

What has this to do with the adequacy of Weber's types as an analytic scheme for characterizing bases of legitimation? The larger point suggested is that as an analytic scheme of qualitative elements, the types are defective on one of two grounds. (1) They are not comprehensive—they omit not only force but also many other Bases of Legitimacy: think of the notions that political philosophers have used to justify domination (e.g., the Greeks' conception of proportional justice). (2) If comprehensive, the scheme identifies bases of legitimacy only at a level of generality where important information is lost. The category of rational legitimacy is outstanding in that regard; strictly speaking, it includes absolutely anything that may be rational to use as a basis for authority under different circumstances (force, wealth, technical competence, legality, seniority and the experience that goes with it, etc.). Charismatic legitimacy also seems to be a catchall for different personal qualities that might appeal to subordinates; it includes demigods, gurus, heros, demagogues, or simply attractive personalities. Only traditional legitimacy seems to be reasonably circumscribed, but even that includes many aspects, from following brute custom in directives to hereditary succession in incumbency.

Either way, the moral, and the problem to be solved, should be evident. Apart from the general undesirability of using formal, ideal models as concepts for describing actual cases, Weber's taxonomy of the bases of legitimacy can be regarded as only a beginning. We need concepts that are more comprehensive and more discriminating. How, then, can we discover them?

"Balances of Norms" as Bases of Legitimacy

Fortunately for our search for a comprehensive analytic scheme for characterizing Bases of Legitimacy, we already have a comprehensive analytic scheme for characterizing authority patterns; and by making explicit something that has been implicit throughout the discussions of the dimensions of authority, the scheme might readily be converted for use in describing bases of legitimacy perceptions.

Throughout, the dimensions have been discussed in three modes, which are worth distinguishing explicitly because they raise different methodological issues and provide problems for theory (see chapters 9, 14–16). Sometimes we dealt with legal or other "formal" prescriptions pertinent to the dimensions, of the kind found in constitutions, charters, by-laws, or compilations of conventions treated as having a quasi-constitutional status (e.g., the prescriptions that establish formal eligibility for Recruitment). At other points we dealt with what actually occurs on the dimensions, which might or might not correspond to what formal prescriptions require, prohibit, or allow (e.g., the discussion of "effective" eligibility). Elsewhere, we referred to prevalent preferences in regard to the various dimensions (e.g., the alleged Norwegian preference for concordant Decision-Behavior). Such preferences might correspond neither to what is actually done nor to what is formally prescribed in a social unit, or they might account for differences between formal prescriptions and actual behavior.

The three modes might be labeled the *forms, practices,* and *norms* of authority. Every dimension is bound to have practical and normative aspects, except for one dimension (Distance), which is purely subjective by definition. Each dimension also may but need not be covered by pertinent forms: it would perhaps be silly to set formal requirements for Compliance (unless formal provisions for sanctions in case of noncompliance are so interpreted). Moreover, the extent to which forms are used also varies among societies and social units, as indicated in Table 7.1, which also summarizes the whole scheme of dimensions and subdimensions.

The operative point here is that the normative aspects of the dimensions are all, in the nature of norms, potential sources of perceptions of legitimacy. The norms concern conditions deemed desirable. If correspondence of practices (or perhaps forms) to norms is perceived, positive perceptions of legitimacy should occur; if not, the perceptions should be negative.

This approach to Bases of Legitimacy has obvious attractions. (1) As stated, it saves labor by obviating the need to identify special sources of legitimacy. (2) It provides a set of Bases of Legitimacy that in their own way are highly discriminating and comprehensive. (3) It allows one to give legitimacy bases content appropriate to any social unit. (4) Since the Bases of Legitimacy are themselves continuous dimensions, the approach facilitates extrapolation from bases to levels of legitimacy: depending on what is perceived as actual as compared to normatively proper, perceptions might range from absolutely favorable, through indifference, to absolutely unfavorable. (5) Most important, the approach seems defensible on the likely assumption that the legitimacy of authority patterns will depend on what they are, or at least are perceived to be, compared to what people think they ought to be.

The approach does not preclude the use of Weber's categories, or concepts like them. Their principal use would be to give additional substantive content to notions of legitimacy, or content that might differ somewhat from that provided by the dimensions and subdimensions. For example, to the observation that more or less competitive Recruitment is preferred in a unit, one might add, for additional information, that preferred processes of Recruitment are of the habitual, rational, or affective varieties, or that incumbency is approved if superordinates have traits associated with ascription, achievement, or emotional appeal. Alternatively, categories like Weber's can be used to describe recurrent or diverse themes in norms, thus the extent to which they hang together or are inconsistent.

Table 7.1 Summary of the Dimensions of Authority Patterns

Cluster of Dimensions	Dimensions	Subdimensions	Probable Significance of Modes[a] Norms	Practices	Forms
S-s relations: influence	Directiveness	Coverage	+	+	±
		Latitude	+	+	±
		Supervision	+	+	−
		Sanction threshold	+	+	−
	Participation	Channels	+	+	+
		Use	+	+	−
	Responsiveness	(None)	+	+	−
	Compliance	(None)	+	+	−
S-s relations: inequality	Distance	(None)	+	0	−
	Deportment	(None)	+	+	−
	(Proximity)	(None)	+	+	−
S-S relations: structures and processes of direction	Conformation	Stratiformity	±	+	+
		Resolution	+	+	+
		Segmentation	±	+	+
		Parallelism	±	+	+
		Type of *S*-body	+	+	+
	Decision-Rules	(None)	+	+	+
	Decision-Behavior	(None)	+	+	±
S-s boundary interchange	Recruitment	Openness	+	+	+
		Base of eligibles	+	+	+
		Mode of interchange	+	+	+

[a] The signs signify the following: + = likely to exist widely and to be important; − = unlikely to be important or to exist widely; ± = depends on variety of considerations; (0) = not applicable, by definition. Thus practices exist and are likely to be important throughout (except for the subjectively defined Distance dimension); forms are most likely to cover *S-S* dimensions Recruitment and Participation; norms matter throughout, except for certain aspects of Conformation.

At this point two matters left hazy earlier in the chapter should become intelligible. First, although perceptions of legitimacy are not reducible to a single continuous dimension, they might still be based on a unit's location on continuous dimensions. Second, lines between general evaluations of authority patterns and the evaluation of their special structures and processes might not merely be hard to draw, it might be inadvisable to make them rigid by definition.

The second point, however, suggests a possibly fatal flaw in the proposed approach. We *are* trying to make general evaluations of authority patterns, not particular judgments of their special aspects; and there is every reason to think that people have "values" that govern global, undifferentiated judgments of the worthiness of authority patterns, as well as "norms" about their special aspects.[14] Their values and norms, to be sure, are certain to be related. But there is a difficulty nonetheless associated with attempting to study general evaluations of authority patterns by way of special norms. The dimensions and subdimensions of the patterns are many, and the correspondence of norms to practices (and/or forms) is unlikely to be the same for them all. In cases of full correspondence or discrepancy—especially marked discrepancy—no difficulty would arise. Most cases, however, are not so accommodating and can be expected to exhibit irksome mixtures of correspondence and discrepancy and of degrees of them: marked and faint correspondences, extreme or moderate discrepancies.

If cases are not clear-cut, problems in arriving at overall evaluations follow not only for observers but also for actors in a unit. Is it probable that their general judgments of legitimacy will at all resemble sums of complex computations? Psychology suggests that people tend to follow lines of least calculation (as particles travel paths of least resistance). Following lines of least calculation probably occurs especially if pertinent information is inherently uncertain or hard to acquire, as it will be in regard to many aspects of authority in many social units. In this case, the "rationalists" are at one with the psychologists by holding that it "pays" to base general judgments on simple, expedient criteria—for example, judgments about whether to vote for one political party or another.[15]

There is an analogy between legitimacy and voting. One (presumably) votes for a party because he considers it worthy of support, and people accord legitimacy to an authority pattern for the same reason. How then is the decision to vote for a party and not another "calculated"—if calculated at all? Here an intriguing possibility arises for rescuing the suggestion that in their normative aspects, the dimensions of authority patterns might be treated as bases of general legitimacy.

It has been commonly held that voting decisions flow more from brute habit or the appeal of vague ideologies than from complex calculations. Kelley and Mirer,[16] however, have demonstrated all but definitively a contrary hypothesis. Voters, according to these authors, have numerous specific preferences they would like to have promoted and dislikes they would like to have hindered; the authors then show that voting decisions can be very substantially accounted for on the basis of a simple yes-no summing of perceptions that parties would or would not do what voters like or dislike. A vote thus may be considered a general judgment that flows from a "simple" balance of specific perceptions. Translated to perception of legitimacy, the Kelley-Mirer argument simply implies that members of a unit perceive gross correspondences to or discrepancies from dimensional norms, and they accord legitimacy to the unit's authority pattern if the balance is clearly favorable, illegitimacy if it is not, and are indifferent if the balance is rather even. This argument does not necessarily conflict with that about avoiding complex calculations, since the balances can be simplistically arrived at (e.g., if only yes-no judgments are made, if cumbersome weighting of dimensions is avoided, and if only glaring correspondences and discrepancies are taken into account). And the Kelley-Mirer approach has an important additional advantage: it allows the ready estimation (and explanation) of degrees of legitimacy and illegitimacy.

The Kelley-Mirer solution, however, entails difficulties of its own. The analogy between support for a party and for an authority pattern exhibits imperfections that make particularly dubious the validity of the simple transfer of the Kelley-Mirer hypothesis. Judgments of authority patterns tend to be more general, diffuse, and ill defined than those of parties: in the latter case, one chooses leaders and policies; in the former, complexes of relationships. Moreover, greater uncertainties enter into judgments of the worthiness of authority patterns. Parties publicize their leaders and positions, whereas the nature of authority relations often is highly nebulous (not infrequently, deliberately so). More important, uncertainty is greater because of the simple and crucial fact that alternatives in party systems already exist and usually have track records, whereas the alternatives to any existing authority pattern must largely be imagined. The choice of parties, in its very nature, occurs in a situation of open competition; the choice of authority patterns does not. If, as stated, uncertainty leads to the "simplification" of calculations, it follows that judgments of support for authority patterns are likely to be even simpler than those of support for parties.

Perhaps, then, the suggestion that perceptions of legitimacy express balances of norms on the dimensions of authority would be better regarded as a point from which to proceed than as a stopping point—still, however, keeping an open mind on the question of whether empirical findings might sustain the possibility.

"Salient Norms" as Bases of Legitimacy

Quite aside from doubts about the applicability of the Kelley-Mirer hypothesis to support for authority patterns as well as parties, there is a significant discrepancy between the balance Kelley and Mirer struck and that suggested here. We proposed that balances of normative perceptions on all dimensions might underlie legitimacy. Kelley and Mirer, however, did not take into account preferences on anything and everything. Respondents defined their own preferences and antipathies in answer to open-ended questions that allowed them to name only a limited number of choices. One may suppose that the respondents listed preferences they consider important rather than those of little significance to themselves.

This immediately suggests an uncomplicated way of avoiding problems posed by the conception of legitimacy bases as overall balances of norms: simply take into account only norms on dimensions that particularly matter to members of a social unit—"salient" norms. In that case, norms on a single dimension might govern perceptions of legitimacy, or the perceptions might be governed by a limited cluster of dimensions.

Common sense surely favors the assumption that the various dimensions will have different import for evaluating an authority pattern. Common sense, of course, has often been wrong. More important, therefore, we note that the use of salient norms as Bases of Legitimacy seems virtually compelled by considerations of uncertainty and simplicity of judgment. The use of only salient norms makes judgments simpler. Uncertainty also is bound to be reduced: dimensions may stand out as salient precisely because they offer small impediments to knowledge; or, if a dimension looms large, knowledge about it is likely to be intensively sought and perceptions of it are likely to be formed, even if they are misperceptions. By the same token, the acts of imagination needed to envision alternatives are more likely to be made if dimensions seem to be of great rather than small importance.

The suggestion that salient norms might govern perceptions of legitimacy retains the principal advantage of the procedure first suggested: the analytic scheme for describing authority patterns can still double as an analytic scheme for describing Bases of Legitimacy. One simply selects from it pertinent dimensions or subdimensions. An additional advantage is that it allows us to avoid distinctions (dubious, hard to draw, and, in all cases we know about, extremely nebulous) between "general" values and "particular" norms. "Values" on this basis are especially important norms, not preferences of some ill-defined higher order. Similarly, we can avoid resorting to the fuzzy notion of "ideology" in place of more definite and specific judgments.[17]

The salient dimensions of authority might always be the same, or (more likely) they might differ according to social units and circumstances. How are they to be found? Any dimension or subdimension can potentially have special import for a unit's members. The methods for finding salient dimensions thus would seem to be empirical. Reasoning, however, can anticipate results (even if always subject to being confounded by research). And there are indeed good reasons, logically implicit in the previous arguments of the chapter, for considering some dimensions stronger candidates for salience than others.

We can derive four criteria governing the likelihood that dimensions will be salient from previous arguments:

1. Because of considerations of "certainty" (having knowledge, perceptions), dimensions that inherently have high visibility—"palpable" or "tangible" dimensions, so to speak—are more likely to be salient than others. It will probably also be easier to envisage alternatives on such dimensions.
2. Because legitimacy involves perceptions by actors (numerically in the main by subs) of how authority affects their lives, dimensions that have a direct and evident bearing on their lives are more likely to be salient than nonimmediate dimensions. Although this criterion might overlap with the first, since the immediacy of effects could make aspects of authority palpable to subs, the two considerations are not quite the same.
3. Because legitimacy involves general perceptions of worthiness, consequential dimensions should be more salient than others. Dimensions are "consequential" if they might be considered to have direct and general effects on the contents of directives and could therefore be regarded as having an especially close bearing on the extent to which justice, or fairness, prevails in a social unit.
4. Because ability to draw lines between overall authority patterns and their particular aspects depends substantially on the perceived transience of the aspects, dimensions that do not seem highly mutable are more likely to be salient than others. Originally, the factor of transience was used to distinguish between judgments of particular incumbents and directives as against particular structures and processes of direction; the same reasoning used to make that distinction can also be applied, anyway potentially, to different dimensions of authority.

On these grounds, which dimensions are most likely to furnish salient norms as bases of legitimacy perceptions?

Before trying to answer the question, a difficulty inherent in the criteria should be pointed out. Being different, the individual criteria are unlikely to indicate exactly the same dimensions. Several familiar options can be used to cope with this difficulty. We can proceed on the assumption that the larger the number of criteria satisfied by a dimension, the more likely it is to be salient for perceptions of legitimacy. An alternative would be to weight the criteria (e.g., by assuming that palpability and immediacy are essential to considering anything important, therefore inherently more weighty considerations than the others). Another possibility is to use the convenient and usually sloppy *ceteris paribus* device. Still another is to make the relative significance of the criteria depend on types of units or circumstances. Since we have no firm convictions about which of these options is most defensible, what follows is a tentative first attempt to identify all dimensions likely to be salient for perceptions of legitimacy.

Personal Legitimacy: Recruitment as a Salient Dimension

Perceptions of legitimacy are concerned with superordination in a unit, and superordination involves "directors" (superordinates) using "processes of direction" to arrive at and carry out "directives" for members of the unit. Legitimacy perceptions may thus be focused on *who* directs, *how* directives are worked out and applied, or *what* they are; in polysyllables, they may be personal, procedural, or substantive. Mixes of the three are not precluded, since the categories, although different, are not mutually exclusive; but most mixes are bound to emphasize one factor more than others.

Of the three aspects of superordination, the most palpable surely is the persons who occupy superordinated positions. How directives are made and administered (especially "informally") is likely to be only nebulously grasped, except perhaps in very simple units—and this applies to lower supers no less than subs. The particular tangibility of persons no doubt accounts for the observed tendency of children to first grasp the concepts of governmental positions that can be symbolized by a particular person.[18] Processes, to be sure, are concrete too; but greater powers of abstraction are usually required to grasp them, as are greater efforts at seeking information. For example, we often find specialists in formal processes (e.g., parliamentarians) and in informal ones (e.g., lobbyists, not to mention political scientists) on whose judgments even supers frequently rely. What directives are is less enigmatic than how they are worked out, especially when they are violated. Most people, however, encounter only small slices of the whole pie of directives, even in units that are only moderately large and complex. Thus again, specialists exist whose (often very lucrative) business it is to know the substantive rules and how they work; this category includes not only lawyers, but also other inquisitive and well-informed individuals: barrack-room lawyers and the like. Who supers are thus is the most transparent aspect of superordination. In complex units, perceptions of the persons of supers tend to be confined to the highest levels of superordination (the more "decisive" actors) and to the lowest (those who are in most direct contact with subs); incumbents at the middle levels tend to be hazier figures. The point is not that all supers are equally tangible. It is that some or many of them are the most palpable aspect of superordination—hence perceptions of persons are particularly likely to enter into the general evaluation of authority patterns. This is especially likely once a certain threshold of complexity is passed. Yet even in very simple units, like families, authority is likely to be perceived first of all as personal, although for somewhat different reasons (e.g., because procedures are not defined or are poorly defined, hence also "impalpable"; because the substance of directives seems more dependent on personal whim; or because subs are the kind of people who tend, through immaturity and dependence, to personalize authority in any case).

Palpability might well be considered the most weighty of the four criteria, since perceptions are most likely to fix on matters most readily grasped (especially, of course, if certainty and simplicity of thought are major considerations). Other criteria, however, also point toward the likelihood of "personal" legitimacy perceptions. Lower supers have great "immediacy" for subs, as do supers one step removed from lower superordinates: foremen and shop stewards are in direct, continuous contact with workers, as are department chairmen with faculty, coaches and managers with athletes, policemen with citizens. Higher supers make up in consequentiality what they lack in immediacy because they hold more decisive positions and because *who* issues directives surely has great effects on *what* the directives are.

Only the criterion of "mutability" seems to downgrade the probable significance of personal legitimacy, depending, of course, on how open and otherwise "competitive" *S*-positions are. Even that criterion, however, does not entirely weigh against the argument, if the personal traits of incumbents are associated with the ways in which superordinated positions are attained. Undeniably, these ways are procedural matters, but the procedures have to do with who is superordinated, not decision-making processes. And ways of entering into high superordinated positions certainly tend to be conspicuous. In most units, the installation of supers in high positions provides the most dramatic occasions for authority to manifest itself (coronations, inaugurations, etc.). In competitive units the processes that lead to the emergence of a chief—whether general elections or wars of succession—are the occasions on which authority gains its widest attention.

Many findings are consistent with the surmise that personal legitimacy is especially important. The tendency of children to "personalize" authority, brought out in many studies of political socialization, might be left aside, children being children. Still, these findings imply that the extent to which people perceive authority in other ways depends on their level of sophistication. And there is much evidence that high levels of sophistication or ability to abstract are rather uncommon. Two examples might suffice to make the point. Almond and Verba found that in all but one of the countries they studied, many more people were able to name party leaders than were able to name ministries.[19] The sole exception was Mexico, where no competitive party system exists, and where, in any case, few people (21%) were able to name even four ministries.[20]

Peabody's study of three organizations—a police department, a welfare office, and an elementary school—revealed that in two organizations "personal" perceptions governed bases of authority: competence, in the school, and personal traits, loosely defined, in the police department.[21] The welfare office was an exception; but the largest proportion of subordinates there simply accepted the condition that someone occupied a superordinated position as a sufficient basis of authority. Procedural or substantive considerations at least did not outweigh personal ones (in fact, a personal characteristic, competence, was the one factor other than position as such frequently mentioned as a basis of authority).

All this implies that the *Recruitment* dimension is especially likely to be salient for norms of legitimacy. It is a dimension that both closely relates to the persons of superordinates and renders accessible the less mutable aspects of the personal characteristics of authorities. Perceptions of correspondence or discrepancy between normatively expected and actual levels of competitiveness thus should have much if not everything to do with the legitimacy accorded to authorities. The perceptions of actual competitiveness, needless to say, might differ from the technical, somewhat arcane measures of competitiveness suggested in Chapter 6. They can, in fact, be expected to fix largely on the more palpable aspects of the Recruitment dimension: whether positions are open at all, and the formal provisions governing eligibility and boundary interchange. Glaring discrepancies between formal and informal aspects of the dimension should, however, affect legitimacy—negatively if forms and norms correspond; positively if they do not (and if the informal expresses prevalent norms).[22]

Aspects of at least two of Weber's categories are caught under norms of Recruitment. Traditional legitimacy is associated with personal legitimacy based on ascriptive status. Such *ascriptive-personal legitimacy* would be reflected in part by the openness of *S*-positions, in part by the way bases of eligibles are defined, and in part by modes of boundary interchange (seniority and succession). In this case, Weber provides a special label for certain norms of Recruitment, but hardly much detailed information, since ascriptive bases of personal legitimacy can be extremely diverse, including the belief in an aristocracy's right to rule, basing legitimacy on a ruler's position in a lineage or age set, length of service, caste, sex, and any number of other personal traits that cannot be freely acquired. Rational legitimacy is associated with personal legitimacy based on achievement. The subdimensions of Recruitment also clarify various aspects of that; and again many kinds of *achieved personal legitimacy* might exist: physical force or strength, possessions (if really open to acquisition), technical expertise or competence, the related ability to pass performance tests, or the ability to win elections.

To fit Weber's third category into the discussion, we must mention a difficulty that would arise in identifying personal legitimacy solely with Recruitment. The importance of personal judgments of incumbents need not lead to preoccupation with Recruitment; it might result directly in the evaluation of incumbents on the basis of their personal traits. Members of a unit, that is, might not be at all concerned with how incumbents came by their positions but only with the kind of people the incumbents are; they might not even care what kind of people generally succeed through established processes of Recruitment, only with the here and now. This is what Weber's "affective" category of legitimacy, charismatic legitimacy, chiefly illuminates: legitimation by a leader's immediate emotional appeal, regardless of what qualities give him such appeal.

The criterion of mutability, however, implies that perceptions of personal legitimacy are more likely to focus on the less mutable processes of Recruitment than the more mutable personal traits of particular incumbents. Hence the direct, legitimating appeal of personality, although not precluded, ought at least to be exceptional. And so it seems to be. Weber himself stresses the transitory nature of charismatic authority: in part because charisma cannot be transmitted; in part because it seems to arise only in highly unsettled periods—in crises or in the interstices between different institutionalized patterns. Easton and Dennis also provide support for the position; the children they studied, who were surely not sophisticated, tended to personalize authority in a way that approved the incumbent because of his office, instead of vice versa. The finding of these investigators was not that unsophisticated people judge supers by personal attributes; rather, they tend to evaluate complex patterns of authority by judging institutions readily symbolized by particular persons—usually a unit's head. In that, they are, of course, at one with Bagehot.

Affective-personal legitimacy undoubtedly exists and generally involves one or more of the following perceptions:

1. That the head of a unit has *heroic* qualities—unusual capacities, particularly if associated with the resolution of a pressing crisis (think of Charles de Gaulle ending the dreadful *immobilisme* of the Fourth Republic and ending the war in Algeria).
2. That a chief has the supernatural qualities of a god or demigod (think of Mao Tse-tung).
3. That he embodies the unit in his own person (think of Jawaharlal Nehru, or, again, de Gaulle).
4. That he is a just and neutral *arbiter*, above the play of ordinary interests, especially in or after periods of great conflict.

Such perceptions are inherently evanescent, although the last three can be transformed into persistent institutionalized claims, by serving as rationalizations for the rule of ascriptively defined groups (theocracies, monarchs, castes, or estates, who by dint of genes, training, or selflessness are considered likely to rule in the general interest). More often than supplying general Bases of Legitimacy, however, the perceptions merely add increments to support for particular superordinates, supplementing less transient bases of legitimacy and heightening "incumbency effects."

Substantive Legitimacy: The Salience of Directiveness

The contents of directives are less likely on several grounds to enter into general judgments of legitimacy than are perceptions of the persons of superordinates.

As stated previously, the substance of directives is less tangible than are the persons who direct. It is true that some directives sometimes, or frequently, have high tangibility for members of social units: those that particularly impinge on them, when they impinge (e.g., traffic laws on drivers when they drive; tax laws on taxpayers when they pay taxes). Nevertheless, directives nearly always have a disembodied character, except perhaps in very simple units, like families; in such units, however, personal attributes tend to count for more as bases of legitimation anyway. High-ranking directors are always available as embodiments of superordination in its personal aspects, but it is hard to think of equivalents among directives. Perhaps constitutions are rough equivalents (where they exist), but constitutions normally specify processes more than contents. Different directives also impinge with different directness and frequency on different members of social units (especially, again, complex units). Conceivably, perceptions of legitimacy might be based on immediately relevant directives alone; more likely, however, they are based on general patterns, difficult to envisage. Not least, many directives are simply perceived as part of the given environment of one's life, rather than as tangible products of conscious will, in the way that stopping at a traffic light may seem as "natural" as having to drive up a hill. Directives may have considerable tangibility when first issued, before people become accustomed to them, but most of them, usually, exist in a disembodied state, on legal paper or in silent conventions. The will behind them surfaces when they are violated and enforced, but only for violators, not the general membership.

Perhaps more important, and certainly less subject to argument, is the great mutability of particular directives; at least this quality is likely to be perceived. It may be that the nature of directives is inherent in general structures of superordination, hence less mutable than may seem. Even if this questionable point were conceded, however, it takes extraordinary sophistication to see such a connection clearly and concretely. The particular contents of directives raise questions of whether to obey. Because of their apparent and often demonstrated mutability, however, they are much less likely to evoke more general sentiments of legitimacy or illegitimacy—issues of rebellion as against issues of disobedience. Put differently, when illegitimacy has been perceived, particular directives might be seized on to justify or rationalize rebelliousness; but the opposite is highly improbable.

Despite these arguments, it is hard to believe that what authorities do is of no consequence to perceptions of their legitimacy. Directives have immediacy for members of social units and consequentiality for their lives. But not all directives are equally immediate and consequential for all members, and the contours of the sum of directives are, as argued, likely to be enigmatic in complex units. Nonetheless, members of social units surely have a sense of justice, fairness, or equity in regard to what is demanded of them at pain of sanctions; and it is hard to believe that their sense of justice or injustice (hence also of legitimacy) will be wholly based on perceptions of the persons of supers or processes of direction.

Substantive bases of legitimacy, therefore, are not just logically conceivable but empirically likely, at least in conjunction with other bases. The problem in trying to identify them is to find norms for general, rather tangible, and persistent aspects of the substance of directives—particularly aspects that might not merely add increments to legitimacy based primarily on other considerations but will be coequal with other bases, and of primary importance.

As it happens, the analytic scheme does not allow much choice in the search for pertinent dimensions. Only two dimensions—those of *Directiveness* and *Responsiveness*—have a direct bearing on the contents of directives. Neither, it is true, denotes the detailed contents of individual directives. Directiveness involves the extent to which members' lives are covered by enforced rules of any kind; Responsiveness is the extent to which directives are based on the expressed preferences of subs. These however are matters of substance, if not of detail, and it is a decided plus that detail is not involved, since *general* aspects of directives, likely to raise questions that transcend the problem of mere conformity, are at stake.

In addition, it seems highly likely that members of units, however hazy their grasp of general policy, will have a tangible sense of the scope of authority and of expansions and contractions of that scope. They will realize how much they are controlled by authority or how much autonomy they have. Not only is that matter palpable, but it is logically prior to how domains of control are specifically covered. And on the evidence, it is capable of evoking intense sentiments. Every social unit distinguishes between what are matters of legitimate "public" as against "private" concern—where it is that authority may and may not intrude. Perceptions that these boundaries have been transgressed are inherently more likely to engender sentiments of rebelliousness than perceptions of particular directives; perceptions that a directive falling within a unit's "public" area is unwise or unfair are more likely to engender lesser sentiments and attempts at reform rather than transformation. The tendency of supers to operate within particular domains is also more likely to be perceived as less mutable than the supers' behavior itself, even granted that an occasional intrusion into private spheres might be perceived as a mere aberration.[23]

Similar considerations apply to Responsiveness. Members of units are likely to have a general grasp of the tendencies of supers to contravene, ignore, take into account, or closely follow others' preferences; and these tendencies are likely to appear to them less transitory than particular directives. It should also be evident that grievances about Responsiveness often are the basis of rebellious sentiments. Such grievances provide one theme that constantly rings in the slogans of the great revolutions: "no taxation without representation" or, still more apt, "power to the people." (A second theme, of course, is autonomy from authority.) In all likelihood, however, norms of Responsiveness are rather less salient than those of Directiveness. This is because degrees of Responsiveness are more nebulous to discern, especially if preferences diverge widely, and Responsiveness is important only to the extent that participatory norms are significant. Perhaps we can best think of the two dimensions as having a "value-added" relation: Directiveness is the more fundamental, but Responsiveness may add or subtract large increments from legitimacy based on it.

The Directiveness and Responsiveness dimensions also possess high immediacy and consequentiality. Whether directives exist at all surely has a clear and direct bearing on the lives of members of a unit. Whether superordinates take subs' preferences into account, and to what extent, surely has effects on the specific contents of directives and perceptions that they are fair. All four criteria for determining likely salience thus are met by the dimensions.

Weber's categories of legitimacy can provide useful additional information about substantive legitimacy in three ways:

1. The categories can indicate whether dividing lines between public and private domains are drawn (*a*) on traditional grounds (conventionally), (*b*) rationally (by explicit, reasoned constitutional provisions or technical judgments about what is best subjected to or exempted from authoritative control), or (*c*) affectively (i.e., through emotion-charged ideologies).
2. The categories provide information about attitudes toward new directives. These tend to be disapproved or deprived of benefit of doubt if habitual

orientations are prevalent. They might be approved or given benefit of doubt if they are considered based on technical competence (rationality) or in tune with an intensely held ideology (affectivity).

3. The categories can also tell us whether supers' discretionary powers—or lack of them—to issue directives chiefly result from convention, rational calculation (of the kind that goes into explicit constitutions or definitions of bureaucratic roles) or affective (ideological) considerations.

It should be evident that "traditional" orientations tend most rigidly to limit domains of authority, scope for new directives, and discretionary powers, whereas "affective" orientations are least restrictive.

As in the case of personal criteria of legitimacy, one type of "substantive" legitimation does not involve any of the dimensions of authority, although fortunately it can be considered exceptional. (If not exceptional, treating Bases of Legitimacy as norms on the dimensions of authority patterns would of course be suspect.) An authority pattern might be accorded legitimacy simply because it "works"—because of the perception that it is effectively pursuing, or somehow needed to attain or safeguard, goals intensely valued by a unit's members. In such a case, one might speak of "output" (or "outcome") legitimacy. Legitimacy can certainly be accorded on this basis, even to an authority pattern considered objectionable in all other respects, for more intensely valued ends can count for more than less intensely disvalued means.

Political examples of output legitimacy readily come to mind. An obvious example is the acceptance of autocrats in time of war or other grave crisis, even in well-established democracies. Less obvious is the basis of acceptance of one-party oligarchy in the American South (or, presumably, contemporary South Africa and Rhodesia). If V. O. Key[24] is right, the legitimacy of the Southern oligarchs in the eyes of many of their constituents was largely based on intense negrophobia—the perception that although not intrinsically desirable, party oligarchy has been successful in keeping blacks in their place and may be needed to maintain the status quo. It would appear that Mexico's Institutional Revolutionary Party (PRI) has enjoyed a similar kind of legitimacy (now probably waning), as do other one-party autocracies in postrevolutionary and developing nations, based both on past successes (independence, land reform, the expropriation of imperialists) and still unrealized promises.

In what senses then is legitimacy based on outputs or outcomes exceptional? First, because it is inherently tenuous and not likely to be long sustained unless strongly supported by other Bases of Legitimacy. Actual achievements, pretended gains, and the existence or fabrication of "enemies" standing in the way of achieving goals, can prolong it. But sooner or later, authorities who base their rule on success must succeed. Where output legitimacy has been longest sustained it has generally been an adjunct to personal Bases of Legitimacy (e.g., ascriptive bases sustained by color in racist societies).

Second, output legitimacy quite probably plays a regular role only in social units that exist for a purely and well-defined instrumental purpose, so that other values do nothing to offset seriously the impact on perceptions of success or failure. People belong to trade unions, for example, to secure the best obtainable working conditions; hence they often have high tolerance for, or positively value, even corrupt trade union oligarchs who appear to perform competently. Dictatorial coaches of athletic teams are also obvious examples, as are all those musical Caesars of the podium. Purely "instrumental" units certainly are numerous, but hardly the rule.

Third, output legitimacy, like authority based directly on the personal attributes of supers, is likely to occur in units of other types only in critical periods. The chief cases in point are periods of long and intense strife and interstitial periods, between disintegrated old orders and new ones not yet established.

Output legitimacy and charismatic personal legitimacy thus have more than a coincidental resemblance. They tend to arise under similar conditions, hence generally coincide, and are both hard to perpetuate. By the same token, charismatic leaders are also most likely to appear in purely "instrumental" units—think of athletic coaches or orchestra conductors—or when a goal is so intensely sought in a unit that all other considerations are outweighed. By the same token, as well, perceptions of success are less likely to supply Bases of Legitimacy than to add increments to support for particular superordinates, supplementing less transient legitimacy and heightening "incumbency effects."

Procedural Legitimacy: The Salience of Participation

The processes through which directives are worked out satisfy well one criterion of salience: they are likely to be seen as less mutable than either directives or the persons of incumbents. On the whole, however, they do not fare well on the other criteria. The relative lack of "visibility" of decision-making processes has already been discussed. It should also be evident that such processes lack immediacy for most members of social units: the majority are not directly involved (except in a special sense, to be treated shortly), and processes always work at one remove from products. The consequentiality of processes is likely to elude most subs because of the unusual sophistication needed to discern relations between the processes and substance of direction. After all, even professionals have great difficulty figuring out the substantive effects of procedural devices (say, bicameral versus unicameral legislatures, rigid versus loose distinctions between line and staff, or the use of individuals as against collectivities at S_1-levels), and most people are not even amateurs in regard to the subject. Although all these considerations matter, probably the most important is "visibility": decision-making processes, often even in simple units, tend to be arcane, by nature or design.

One dimension having to do with processes of direction, however, does measure up on all the criteria. This is *Participation.*[25] The way members participate certainly has arcane aspects (lobbying, clientele relationships), but others are highly visible. Participation is, at any rate, the one means by which subs are incorporated into decision-making processes. It also has manifest immediacy for people and is likely to be perceived as consequential, anyway by participants; if not perceived as consequential, and if participatory norms exist, perceptions of illegitimacy are likely through the potentially salient Responsiveness dimension. (Perceived consequentiality may, of course, differ from actual consequentiality, but it is perceived consequentiality that counts.) And general patterns of Participation, like other procedural aspects of Participation, are unlikely to be seen as highly mutable.

As in the case of the dimensions already predicted to be salient, the argument that Participation is likely to be such a dimension is strongly supported by its prominence in many rebellions against authority.[26]

Weber's categories can once more provide certain kinds of information additional to that furnished by the dimension as here defined (norms regarding channels of Participation and their use). His categories can tell whether such norms have a primarily conventional or rational basis and whether actual participation has its sources in traditions (e.g., tribal councils or the medieval parliaments) or calculated rules (constitutions). The category of "affective" action particularly illuminates a peculiar device often used successfully to instill a sense of participation where none exists (or, sometimes, used without intent to deceive, to open direct channels between subs and supers). This is, so to speak, "orgiastic" participation: the conduct of public bacchanalia that stir and release extravagant emotions and establish immediate bonds between rulers and subjects, thus perhaps legitimating authority in the absence of conventions or appeals to reason. In politics this occurs commonly in revolutionary regimes—and, it seems, in rough proportion to the degree of asymmetry between supers and subs, myth and reality. Brinton's description of revolutionary ritual at the height of the Jacobin phase of the French Revolution provides especially delectable examples.[27] Recent examples are the Nazis' interminable torchlight parades and *Reichsparteitäge* (among many other orgies), Castro's balcony speeches, and the Maoist orgies during and since the so-called cultural revolution. In nonpolitical life, the most manifest cases in point are found among radical sectarian religious movements, but traces of orgiastic participation (or attempts at it) are also apparent in such eminently secular structures as democratic political parties (e.g., in the uproarious blowouts that accompany presidential nominations in the United States).

The emphasis on Participation here may seem one-sided or misplaced. In view of the large role they play in recent "rationalist" writings about legitimacy or closely related subjects,[28] it appears strange that norms about Decision-Rules have not been emphasized heavily as salient procedural bases of legitimacy. There are two principal reasons for this.

The Decision-Rules treated by those who proceed from rationalist postulates often are in fact rules of Participation. Examples are the rules that decisions should be based on simple or extraordinary majorities of all members of a unit, or that they should follow from consensual agreement among representatives of the corporate segments of societies.

Even more important, the dimension of Decision-Rules (and perhaps Decision-Behavior), as here treated, is likely to have high palpability only for certain limited groups: those privy to decision-making processes and/or sophisticated enough to be able to figure out the subtleties involved. These also are the only people for whom the rules have immediacy, and only they are likely to perceive the rules as consequential for the contents of directives. It does not follow, however, that violations of Decision-Rules will not have serious consequences. Most of those included in the groups, after all, are people able to do important things. Isolated violations of the rules will probably have only minor consequences or none: perhaps a split among supers, or attempts to unmake directives or to force certain supers out of their positions. Persistent violations or violations connected with decisions regarded as having far-reaching consequences may, however, induce elite rebellions—or may lead to making public, and hence visible, matters that are generally left obscure. Thus Decision-Rules, even if not directly connected with norms of Participation, may *sometimes* become a salient basis of legitimacy for all members of a social unit. It should also be evident that the force of the arguments against Decision-Rules as salient bases of legitimacy varies with the size and complexity of units. Yet the arguments have some force even in the simplest units, if only because subs (e.g., young children) are especially likely to be unsophisticated and/or tend to derive their legitimacy perceptions from personal bases.

Conclusion

The principal arguments of this chapter can now be summarized:

1. Bases of Legitimacy are, by definition, components of authority patterns and likely to be of great importance in theorizing about them.

2. Weber's typology of legitimacy bases has many virtues but important shortcomings, if properly regarded as an analytic scheme that identifies elements in the Bases of Legitimacy.
3. These shortcomings can be avoided and labor can be saved if norms pertinent to the dimensions of authority patterns are used as Bases of Legitimacy.
4. The dimensions are not likely to be equally salient as Bases of Legitimacy owing to considerations of tangibility, immediacy, consequentiality, and transience.
5. Three dimensions stand out as especially likely to be important for perceptions of legitimacy on these criteria: one that is "personal" (Recruitment), another that is "substantive" (Directiveness), and a third that is "procedural" (Participation).
6. Responsiveness may also be a salient basis of legitimacy if strongly participatory norms exist; and Decision-Rules may be salient for a limited proportion of members or if widely publicized because of violations.

This approach to legitimacy is novel; but the case for it seems to us strong.

The approach is subject to refutation by research, particularly since it is not a mere taxonomy but contains large theoretical assumptions and assertions. It might be found after all that perceptions of legitimacy reflect simple, overall balances of norms on all or most of the dimensions of authority. Reasons have been given for considering this alternative improbable, but it is not precluded. It might also happen that the criteria that make norms on certain dimensions more likely to be salient than others have been wrongly stated or misapplied; again, this seems improbable but not impossible.

It should be noted, however, that certain possibilities that might seem to have been overlooked in the approach, or to be inconsistent with it, are not ruled out by the tack here taken, and in fact are readily accommodated to it.

First, nothing rules out the possibility that dimensions not generally likely to be salient Bases of Legitimacy might become salient under special circumstances and/or in particular kinds of units. This would not impugn the approach if exceptional conditions existed—much as the notion of output legitimacy (which has nothing whatever to do with norms on the dimensions) can be admitted as an exceptional possibility under specified circumstances. In particular, the emergence of unexpected dimensions as salient would not impugn the approach if the criteria considered to make dimensions salient could plausibly account for the role of the dimensions in special units or conditions.

As an example, consider the probable effects of persistent failures to achieve desired outputs. As well as helping to legitimate new authority patterns, such failures might direct attention to the cluster of dimensions considered least likely to be palpable and immediate, or to seem consequential, to most members of complex social units: the various *S-S* dimensions (including the most unlikely of them, Conformation). If output failures are profound and conspicuous, attention certainly is likely to become focused on structures and processes supposed to produce results. Something like this is probably going on in America now in regard to the governance of cities; the circle of people who are "sophisticated" about that subject, even if still limited, has clearly been enlarged.

More important here is the possibility that the dimensions of inequality might become highly salient Bases of Legitimacy in certain social units. For reasons discussed earlier, personal bases are always likely to be predominant; and Distance and Deportment undoubtedly refer more directly to supers' personal traits than does Recruitment. Why then were these dimensions not considered generally important Bases of Legitimacy? The reasons are several: (1) Distance, being subjective, is inherently intangible. (2) The same does not apply to Deportment, but that dimension will also lack tangibility if, and to the extent that, levels of stratiformity separate supers and their subordinates and/or if close "proximity" among them is avoided. In such cases, too, Distance will be particularly intangible, and both Distance and Deportment will lack "immediacy" for most members of social units. (3) The "consequentiality" of the inequality dimensions will generally also be rather unclear. A good deal of sophistication is required to discern connections between them and the ways in which social units are directed—not least, since distant and arrogant supers may rule in a benevolent (paternalistic) manner, leave areas of activity uncovered by directives, and tolerate or indeed respond to participatory inputs made in an appropriately obsequious manner. (4) Perhaps most important, supers who cultivate excessive (or insufficient) inequality are likely to be perceived as transient: people who can be eliminated or who will sooner or later be replaced.

These arguments, however, do not apply equally to all social units. If units are small and simple, the first three points are clearly inapplicable or much diminished in force. If, in addition, positions of superordinates are closed or perceived to be so, the fourth reason also is not applicable. Consequently, to the extent that these two conditions (small and simple units, irreplaceable supers) obtain, the dimensions of inequality are likely to be salient Bases of Legitimacy, by themselves or along with other dimensions. The social units that most obviously satisfy both conditions are families and classes in schools; both are small units lacking stratiformity, and the supers are not subject to competition and replacement.

Most often, however, Distance and Deportment are likely sources of disaffection from or noncompliance with particular overbearing supers, not alienation from overall patterns of authority. The strike at the General Gypsum plant, discussed in Chapter 3, illustrates how perceptions of inequality may disturb a social unit (in this case, one that was quite small in scale). However, the action hardly amounted to a general crisis of legitimacy in the company, or even the plant. To be sure, sentiments about equality often surface in rebellions in large, complex units, but generally in conjunction with matters of Recruitment and Participation.

Second, we do not preclude the possibility that supers' salient Bases of Legitimacy might differ in some respects from those of subs. The probability that Decision-Rules might loom large to supers has already been mentioned. The *S-S* dimensions are more likely to figure in supers' perceptions of legitimacy (especially on grounds of palpability)—and by the same token, the *S-s* dimensions are somewhat more likely to be salient for subs. To the extent that dimensions of inequality are significant, it is also likely that Distance will be of greater concern to supers and Deportment to subs, although "greater" does not mean "much greater" in this case. And although Recruitment is likely to figure as a salient dimension for both supers and subs, supers may be especially concerned with aspects of it that are different from or additional to those of subs (e.g., with the informal rather than formal aspects of eligibility and boundary interchange, particularly on grounds of tangibility and immediacy).

Some of these differences are brought out in Tables 7.2 and 7.3, which provide highly tentative rankings of the probable significance of dimensions for subs' and supers' perceptions of legitimacy and graphically display the overall argument of the chapter. These tables also seem to imply a difference of another kind between the Bases of Legitimacy of supers and subs. Supers, for whom many aspects of authority patterns are generally more tangible than to subs (or low-ranking supers), and more likely to seem "consequential" and "immediate," are more likely than subs to base legitimacy on a complex set of dimensional norms. One can thus deduce from the criteria used to identify salient dimensional norms a simple hypothesis that can serve as an indirect test of our general approach: the higher the rank of members of a social unit in the unit's structure of superordination, the more complex will be the bases on which members' perceptions of legitimacy rest. (Note that no dimension has a minus score for supers.)

Third, the approach does not preclude the possibility that dimensional norms might express deeper, more general "values." As long as such values affect legitimacy mainly through norms on salient dimensions, there is no problem. Weber's categories of action might well be taken as such general values, as might be certain ideological *Weltanschauungen*. The argument here has merely been: (*a*) if norms reflect general values (as they surely must), one can sufficiently represent the values by the norms; (*b*) the relative nebulousness of general "values" (among other reasons, because values by defini-

Table 7.2 Dimensional Norms as Bases of Legitimacy (for Subs)[a]

Dimension[b]	Criteria of Salience[c]				Probable Salience[d]	
	Tangibility	Immediacy	Consequentiality	(Non)-Mutability	Score	Rank
Recruitment	++	++	++	+	+7	1
Directiveness	++	++	++	±	+6	2–3
Participation	++	++	±	++	+6	2–3
Responsiveness[e]	+	+	+	++	+5	4[e]
Deportment	++	+	−−	+	+2	5
Distance	±	+	−−	++	+1	6
Decision-Rules[e]	−	−	±	++	0	7[e]
Decision-Behavior	−−	−−	±	+	−3	8
Conformation	−−	−−	−−	++	−4	9

[a] Rationales for considering dimensions to be more or less salient are provided in the text only for the first four listed. Rationales for other dimensions will probably be evident. Since the table is based on plausible surmise, however, there is scope for disagreement and refutation by evidence.

[b] No subdimensions are used, only overall dimensions. The Compliance dimension is omitted because it involves norms pertinent only to subs. Compliance may, however, increase or decrease probability of positive legitimacy, all else equal.

[c] The signs vary from very high (++) to very low (−−).

[d] Scores are arrived at by totaling + signs and subtracting − signs.

[e] For lower supers and knowledgeable subs, the Decision-Rules dimension will have a higher value, approximately equal to Responsiveness in units where norms of participation are high (++, +, ±, + on the four criteria, respectively). Responsiveness will tend to increase in probable salience with increasing norms of Participation. A unit with fairly high norms of Participation is assumed, as is a unit in which most subs are not highly knowledgeable about the behavior and norms of superordinates.

Table 7.3 Dimensional Norms as Bases of Legitimacy (for Supers)[a]

Dimension	Criteria of Salience				Probable Salience	
	Tangibility	Immediacy	Consequentiality	(Non)-Mutability	Score	Rank
Recruitment	++	++	++	+	7	1–2
Decision-Behavior	++	++	++	+	7	1–2
Decision-Rules[b]	+	++	++	+	6	3
Directiveness	++	+	++	±	5	4
Participation	++	+	±	+	4	5–6
Responsiveness	++	+	+	±	4	5–6
Distance	+	++	±	±	3	7
Deportment	++	+	−	±	2	8
Conformation	+	±	−	±	0	9

[a] To read the table, consult the notes to Table 7.2. Tabulations similar to those applicable to supers and subs could have been constructed for different kinds of social units. We have not presented more tables here to avoid complexity—and because both Tables 7.2 and 7.3 are highly speculative and tentative: intended more to illustrate possibilities than to settle anything.

[b] Operative Decision-Rules are considered often to be rather intangible even to most supers; hence the single + sign. (E.g., our colleagues agreed with the illustration used in Chapter 5, but while aware of the behavior accompanying it, had not been fully aware of the rule underlying the behavior.)

tion lie deep in people's orientations) makes it advisable to leave them alone, if little is lost in doing so; and (*c*) general values or ideologies can be used to provide information in addition to that furnished by the dimensions as here discussed, if additional information seems useful.

Fourth, perceptions of legitimacy may rest on certain very diffuse judgments of authority patterns, so long as salient dimensions play the vital role in the formation of such judgments. This point can perhaps be best elucidated by an example that illuminates a "synthetic," not "analytic" characteristic of authority patterns and involves the idea of liberty.

Much has been made in contemporary literature of two quite different ideas of freedom: freedom "from" and freedom "to." It seems assumed in the literature that the two types of liberty exhaust all possibilities. But there is at least one other. Southern[29] has pointed out that to medieval men liberty meant not so much the absence of directives as freedom from the *arbitrary* will of rulers. The notion had less to do with the absence of constraints on subordinates than with the presence of constraints on superordinates. Supers no doubt have varying amounts of latitude in what they do. No doubt also there are varying norms about the amounts of latitude they ought to have, or that subs consider tolerable. Thus perceptions that supers operate within or beyond expected levels of constraint can readily become a base of legitimacy or illegitimacy. This may occur in any culture, not just in those that define liberty in terms of constraints on supers. (The very term tyranny, which is the quintessence of illegitimacy, conveys mainly the notion of arbitrary authority—whether exercised by an individual tyrant, an "oligarchy," or a rampaging mob.) Constraint on supers, however, is affected objectively by most of the dimensions of authority, hence is a "synthetic" trait. The scope permitted to Directiveness operates as a constraint; so does Participation; so do expectations of Responsiveness; so does the Conformation of structures of direction; so do Decision-Rules and expected Decision-Behavior; so, in a certain narrow sense, do the inequality dimensions; so even does Recruitment (e.g., through certain modes of boundary interchange like those used to depose despotic chiefs). It may be then that diffuse perceptions about the extent to which authority is properly circumscribed will underlie perceptions of legitimacy; but this is quite consistent with the approach here taken, if such perceptions depend on the normative aspects of particular dimensions, especially salient dimensions.[30]

Fifth, and finally, a possibility should be mentioned that is consistent with our approach and cries for elaboration through voluminous reflection and research based on it. Although there is no *abstract* reason for assigning greater or lesser weights to the dimensions deemed likely to be salient Bases of Legitimacy, their relative significance, no less than their nature, almost certainly varies with the *concrete* nature of social units, conditions, and types of members. A few simple surmises illustrate how their role might thus vary:

1. In the course of personal development (maturation), personal Bases of Legitimacy occur first, followed by substantive bases, then procedural ones. The later bases do not necessarily replace the earlier but are likely to be superadded; with maturation, therefore, Bases of Legitimacy become more complex and more probably reflect balances of norms.
2. In primary social units (families), personal bases of legitimation predominate; in secondary social units (e.g., schools), substantive bases become dominant; procedural bases are important—although not necessarily all-important or even of first importance—only in tertiary units (polities, etc.).
3. In the process of social development, a similar sequence occurs. In small-scale, "primitive" societies personal bases are most important; as societies become larger, more complex, and more differentiated, substantive and procedural bases are superadded and become increasingly important.
4. In all social units and at all stages of "development," the more knowledgeable members of units (the older and more experienced, the better educated, the more involved) tend to base perceptions of legitimacy more on procedural bases and on complexes of bases than the less knowledgeable members.
5. Bases of Legitimacy vary with problems of performance and "institutionalization." More specifically, in periods of performance crises or in times of transition between one settled order and another, Bases of Legitimacy (in any social unit, at any level of development) tend to become personal; in the most severe cases, the bases tend to become divorced from the nature of authority patterns altogether, as against their ability to get jobs done. Either kind of legitimacy is tenuous and inherently short-lived; but by the same token, basing legitimacy on procedures is bound to fail in such cases.

These possibly invalid surmises certainly do not exhaust the connections that might be drawn between Bases of Legitimacy and other characteristics of people and social units. Nothing, for example, is suggested about an obvious subject: how the specific tasks or functions of social units affect the bases, independent of other considerations. The possibilities sketched should therefore be regarded as *hors d'oeuvres:* suggestions that might whet appetites for the complex researches and reflections needed to explore the subject.

A Note on s-s Relations

Before leaving the subject of analytic concepts for describing authority patterns, brief reference should be made to the omission of concepts for a set of relations that by definition (see Chapter 1) is part of any pattern of authority.

We refer to relations among subordinates (*s-s* relations) that manifestly have to do with the direction of social units. These relations are not treated separately because they are sufficiently caught in the Participation dimension—particularly the aspect dealing with types of participatory actions, and most especially by the notion of "group actions." In organized participatory groups (like parties or pressure groups), the *S-S* dimensions can also describe *s-s* relations. Such groups, being organized, have their own patterns of authority *and* try to exert influence on higher-level authority patterns.

Notes

1. See Chapter 1, note 7.

2. See, for example, Robert L. Peabody, *Organizational Authority* (New York: Atherton, 1964); Robert Presthus, *The Organizational Society* (New York: Knopf, 1962); Fred E. Fiedler, *A Theory of Leadership Effectiveness* (New York: McGraw-HIll, 1967); and the literature excerpted in Sanford A. Lakoff, *Private Government* (Glenview, III.: Scott, Foreman, 1973).

3. See Chapter 1, note 30.

4. In Carl J. Friedrich, Ed., *Authority* (Cambridge, Mass.: Harvard University Press, 1958), p. 201.

5. Harry Eckstein, *The Evaluation of Political Performance* (Beverly Hills: Sage Professional Papers in Comparative Politics, No. 01-017, 1971), p. 51.

6. This subject is discussed at length in Chapter 16.

7. For elaboration of this point and an attempt to arrive at better indices see Eckstein, *The Evaluation of Political Performance*, pp. 50–52 and 55–65.

8. Alternatives to Weber's types are only now beginning to appear: for instance, those proposed in Ronald Rogowski's *Rational Legitimacy* (Princeton: Princeton University Press, 1974).

9. For an excellent elucidation and discussion of the types, see Reinhard Bendix, *Max Weber: An Intellectual Portrait* (London: Heinemann, 1960), pp. 302–449.

10. See the discussion of criteria of "good" typology in Chapter 12.

11. For a good summary of such criticisms, see Peter M. Blau, "Critical Remarks on Weber's Theory of Authority," *American Political Science Review*, Vol. 57, No. 2 (June 1963), pp. 315–316.

12. See Bendix, *Max Weber*, p. 299.

13. See note 11.

14. Sociologists and anthropologists commonly distinguish values and norms. Values are more general, norms more particular. See, for instance, Neil J. Smelser, *Theory of Collective Behavior* (London: Routledge & Kegan Paul, 1962), pp. 24–27, and Talcott Parsons and Edward A. Shils, *Toward a General Theory of Action* (Cambridge, Mass.: Harvard University Press, 1951), p. 411.

15. For example, see Anthony Downs on the use of "ideologies" for getting votes: *An Economic Theory of Democracy* (New York: Harper and Row, 1958), pp. 96–113.

16. Stanley Kelley, Jr., and Thad W. Mirer, "The Simple Act of Voting," *American Political Science Review,* Vol. 68, No. 2 (June 1974), pp. 572–591.

17. As we saw (note 15), Downs immediately invokes "ideology" as a solution of problems of uncertainty in voting. Like other definitions of the term, however, his is a model of vacuity (p. 96): it does not even tell us the difference between ideologies and clusters of policy preferences (the phrase "verbal image of the good society" is hardly helpful.) Downs also repeatedly refers to the inherent ambiguity of ideologies. He is speaking about ambiguity as a strategy for getting votes—but one can be ambiguous about anything, including specific policies.

18. David Easton and Jack Dennis, *Children in the Political System: Origins of Political Legitimacy* (New York: McGraw-Hill, 1969), p. 199.

19. Gabriel A. Almond and Sidney Verba, *The Civic Culture* (Princeton: Princeton University Press, 1963), Table II.7.

20. A different result might also have been obtained if people had been asked to name high-level incumbents, not "party leaders."

21. Peabody, *Organizational Authority,* Table 10.

22. It is important not to commit the "liberal" fallacy of thinking that legitimacy is imperiled only if competitiveness is insufficient. Excessive competitiveness should have the same effect. It is quite conceivable, for example, that excessive turnover and unpredictability of higher incumbents counts against parliamentary systems of government—especially if, as in contemporary Italy or Weimar Germany, parliamentary *Kuhhandel* (cattle-dealing) keeps placing ephemeral, minor figures in august positions. It is also not in conceivable that a more representative Cabinet and House of Commons would count against the British system.

23. Here again avoid a "liberal" fallacy: legitimacy need not be imperiled only by the perception that authority extends too far. It may also be endangered by the perception that public matters are left to private devices. Southern whites, for example, may be alienated by the perception that the polity's attempts to regulate relations among the races intrudes on a "private" sphere; blacks are likely to have the opposite perception if left to fend for themselves. Fundamental cleavages and conflicts in any social unit often concern precisely such different conceptions of the legitimate limits of authority.

24. V. O. Key, Jr., *Southern Politics* (New York: Knopf, 1949).

25. Participation, of course, often has to do with Recruitment. But even aside from its other aspects, expressing preferences for leaders and policies are generally intertwined.

26. Once more, as in the cases of personal and substantive legitimacy, avoid the "liberal" fallacy. It is not always the more participant patterns that are perceived as more legitimate. Legitimacy may be imperiled if participation is by popular mobs, by "inferior" people, by people who have "no stake in the country," by incompetents, or (even for liberals) by people with too selfish interests at stake. And there have been many rebellions to reduce levels of participation, rather than to increase it.

27. Crane Brinton, *A Decade of Revolution* (New York: Harper & Row, 1934).

28. See especially James Buchanan and Gordon Tullock, *The Calculus of Consent: Logical Foundations of Constitutional Democracy* (Ann Arbor, Mich.: University of Michigan Press, 1962), and Rogowski, *Rational Legitimacy*.

29. Richard W. Southern, *The Making of the Middle Ages* (New Haven, Conn.: Yale University Press, 1953), pp. 107–110.

30. Here is a final "liberal" fallacy to be avoided. Illegitimacy is likely not only if lines of circumscription are overstepped, but also if authority is perceived not to perform its proper tasks: for example, if areas of activity expected to be covered by Directives are left to individual devices, or if supers fail to exercise independent judgments in regard to matters about which they are supposed to have special knowledge, competence, and duties.

PART THREE

Method: Problems of Empirical Inquiry into Authority Relations

Authority relations, as we have conceived of them, are pervasive: virtually everyone is involved, every day, in a mesh of authority interactions. One cannot fill the role of parent, teacher, worker, manager, student, or citizen and escape the onus of receiving directives—or, usually, giving them. One consequence of the property of pervasiveness is the many "obvious" manifestations that authority relations display if we but look for them. In their entirety, though, they are complex and resistant subjects of study. In this introduction we review briefly and generally how we went about organizing research on authority relations in different cultures and some of the methodological and technical precepts we tried to follow. The subsequent chapters provide more detailed answers to some of the knotty problems of empirical research on this subject. Detailed empirical studies are not reported, mainly for reasons of space, but we make frequent references to investigations completed thus far and intend to include others in a future volume.

The Organization of Research

The first task in the study of authority relations was to give substance and operational specification to the analytic scheme; the second was to apply it in field research. Both these tasks were initiated in the Workshop for Comparative Politics at Princeton University, beginning in 1966. Those who were directly engaged in this collaborative effort, in addition to the authors and several research assistants, were graduate students of the Department of

Politics at Princeton, most of whom planned and carried out their dissertation research as members of the Workshop.

Field research on authority relations was planned from the very outset of the venture, which lent a special urgency to our first efforts to make the analytic scheme operational. The task was carried out by nuclei of Workshop members, each with responsibility for one or several dimensions, in the spring and early summer of 1967. The results were summarized in a set of preliminary fieldwork manuals. Each contained a conceptual elaboration of the dimension; guidelines for documentary analysis and systematic observation, where appropriate; and specific (though tentative) items for interview and questionnaire schedules. In the process of working out and discussing these manuals, the analytic scheme itself took on new and revised dimensions (literally and figuratively); subsequent research experience in several countries and diverse social units also helped shape the scheme.[1]

The process of conceptualization, operationalization, and field research was an iterative one: each step had implications for the others which had to be worked through. Some of the conceptual implications of the fieldwork are incorporated in the discussion and illustrations of Part II. After fieldwork, as well as before and during it, we invested more collaborative work in refining the operational procedures. The following chapters report matters of general methodological prudence we learned from this process. We also include, as Chapter 10, the latest version of our operational manuals for the four influence dimensions reviewed in Chapter 2. These manuals incorporate some changes and details that have not been used in fieldwork thus far. But they should work better, by a degree, than the guidelines to research that were employed in the field between 1967 and 1970.[2]

Two Problems and a Methodological Solution

Each subject of political research poses distinctive difficulties for empirical work. The study of authority relations is exceptional only in the severity of the problems to be overcome.

One of the special problems we faced is the sensitivity of authority relations, in at least some aspects and for some members. In larger social units and many societies, more secrecy surrounds decision-making roles and practices than sexual relations. And it is very common to find subordinates afraid to have their opinions and actions fully disclosed for fear that they will be punished for violating the norms of their superordinates. Thus information that is easily available is likely to be both biased and incomplete.

A more onerous problem arises from the relational nature of authority patterns. Most analysis in political science focuses on *objects,* like political institutions and roles; on *actions,* like riots and voting decisions; or on *at-*

titudes, like political preferences and civic orientations. Authority patterns, however, comprise a network of both formal and behavioral relationships among hierarchically ordered set of roles and actors. Political institutions typically are studied using prescriptive and reportorial documents on what they are and do. Political preferences and orientations are studied by means of interviews with representative individuals *qua* citizens, irrespective of their roles or interactions with others, or by the use of techniques like content analysis. Authority patterns, though, can be described only in specific institutional contexts and by reference to formal structures plus prevailing attitudes plus the cumulation and interplay of members' decisions and actions.

Triangulation is our preferred methodological approach to the problems posed by the sensitivity and complexity of authority patterns. No single method for collecting information on the different dimensions and facets of authority is ideal or clearly preferable. Rather, all the procedures customarily used to analyze group structures and behaviors in sociology and political science are applicable: participant observation, interviewing, documentary analysis, even experimental methods. And no single source is likely to be sufficient: human and documentary sources with diverse perspectives should be consulted. The most valid generalizations about authority relations, in our view, are those which are supported by convergent evidence from different sources and methods of inquiry. Some readers will be familiar with Campbell and Stanley's prescribed "multi-trait, multi-method" strategy for measuring concepts.[3] The full description of authority patterns requires an analogous strategy: we should study dimensions of authority, using multiple research strategies and sources. Others may question our methodological eclecticism. We think there are two definitive rejoinders. What seems to be "eclecticism" is compelled by the subject matter; even if it were not, the use of multiple methods is intrinsically better than choosing any single mode of inquiry.

We also have a special though not exclusive preference for studies that deal intensively with authority in one or a few units, rather than broadly with a large number of them. This follows from the same conditions of sensitivity and complexity that dictate methodological triangulation. The more a researcher has immersed himself in material about an organization, and *in* the organization, the more likely he is to be able to characterize it on all salient dimensions, and to do so accurately and with sensitivity to intentions and behaviors that are not manifest.

Information Requirements

Our central objective was and is to *characterize authority relations,* partly for descriptive purposes, partly to identify relationships and to test causal statements. The aspects or dimensions of those relations in which we are interested are the subject of Part II; a summary list appears on page 206. The question here is how fully and precisely we want to describe the dimensions specified in the analytic scheme. The first issue is whether verbal description and categorization of how an organization is characterized on these dimensions will suffice, or whether a numerical measurement is sought. If measurement *is* required, we must ask next, what level of measurement?

We assumed the desirability of measurement from the start; the structure of the analytic scheme reflects that assumption. Our discussion of authority has referred throughout to variables and dimensions of authority located on a continuum along which individuals and groups have "more" or "less." All such statements imply measurement. Moreover, any definition of categories along such dimensions which can be applied operationally is a measuring instrument: it enables us to say where a person or group is located with respect to others along a continuum.[4] The verbal definitions of each dimension, and their ranked categories, imply at least an ordinal level of measurement. Generally, though, we sought ratio-order measurement, with specifiable zero points and equal intervals. The "zero-point" requirement posed few conceptual problems, since most of our dimensions are defined as having a "zero" origin or pole: one of the poles of Participation is "closed" (i.e., no participation whatsoever, etc.). Our approach to the "equal interval" requirement was to devise operational scales with "equal-appearing" intervals, a procedure advocated by Tukey and Tufte, among others.[5] Usually we employed five-interval scales, both for attitudinal items and for scales to be coded judgmentally by the researcher. Our model was the three-point scale used in attitudinal research which asks for distinctions among "low," "medium," and "high" (or the equivalents), expanded to allow for judgments in two intermediate categories:

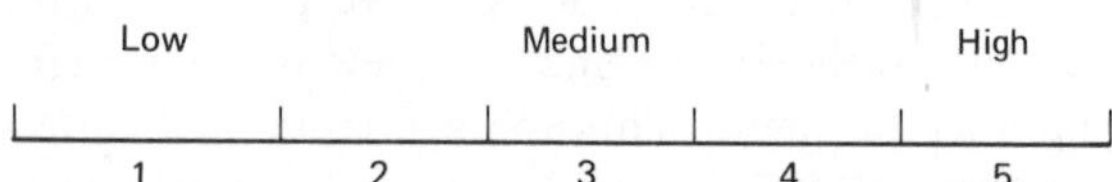

We were not ritualistically consistent in using the five-point scale. Some kinds of data—the base of eligibles for an *S*-position or number of directives issued, for example—could be estimated with much greater precision. And some attitudinal items permitted only dichotomous or trichotomous distinctions.

The "equal-appearing intervals" procedure has inherent limitations, especially for comparative research. What may appear to be "equal" intervals to one group of researchers, in one culture, may not appear at all equal to others. Cultural and related ideological distortions are especially likely to intrude. There are two malign consequences of such distortions for our kind of research. First, all the significant variation within one social unit, or society, may occur within one or two of the categories along our five-point scales: the scales will thus fail to discriminate. Some members of the Workshop, when confronted in fieldwork with evidence that the questionnaire scales failed to discriminate among their subjects, revised them to permit finer distinctions. They thereby gained more precise description, at the possible cost of reducing cross-unit or cross-cultural comparability of results. Second, we risk systematic bias (error) when correlating such data across units and cultures. A technical solution is to analyze suspect data using ordinal (rank-order) rather than interval statistics, at the risk of losing good information. The reader familiar with cross-cultural surveys will recognize that this issue is one aspect of the more general problem of cross-cultural equivalence of survey and questionnaire items.[6] We were aware of the problem but dealt with it only insofar as each researcher relied on prudence and his or her knowledge of the groups under study to adapt and supplement our common interview and questionnaire schedule and coding schema.

Measurement questions aside, detailed and insightful description of authority patterns is crucial to our recommendations for and practice of comparative research. Technically, good quantitative comparison is a function of good measurement. But not all nor even the most important characteristics of authority patterns are easily or fully measurable at this rather early stage of research on the subject. To a degree, we remain uncertain about what their "most important characteristics" are. Moreover, we are applying a new descriptive scheme to phenomena that have not, for the most part, been studied in this way before. Thus we are convinced that good measurement presupposes careful, knowledgeable observation and verbal description of authority relations. Much emphasis in our fieldwork was given to such observation and description. We hoped thereby to add to the basic stratum of information by which we and others can determine what is worth measuring, and the reliability and validity of alternative measures.

The four chapters that follow explain our solutions to many of the specific conceptual, methodological, and technical problems we encountered when applying the analytic scheme and when synthesizing the information so gained. In Chapter 8 we suggest how to deal with problems of defining and comparing social units in empirical work. The next two chapters propose operational strategies for field research (Chapter 9) and report our revised guidelines for gathering evidence on the Influence dimensions (Chapter 10). The final chapter shows briefly how such data can be combined to provide a comprehensive description of an authority pattern. These chapters are neither case histories of research nor a "cookbook," although they contain elements of both. We have concentrated mainly on recurring issues, with the purpose of summarizing our thinking and experience to facilitate and give coherence to future empirical research on authority relations.

Notes

1. The obdurate realities of diverse foreign cultures and different units of inquiry—schools, parties, bureaucracies—required many local additions to and collective revisions of the operational procedures initially devised. Many of these were worked through in a meeting of Workshop members held in January 1968. A second, smaller cohort of four Workshop members began fieldwork later in 1968, employing a more thoroughly tested set of procedures. For a full list of fieldwork studies see the Preface.

2. A revised manual also has been prepared for the Distance and Deportment dimensions. The fieldwork manuals for the other dimensions are available in the original 1967 edition, on request from the authors. Those who refer to the latter documents are cautioned about their preliminary nature: they include none of the changes that are suggested by subsequent years of conceptual revision and practical experience.

3. Donald T. Campbell and Julian C. Stanley, "Convergent and Discriminant Validation by the Multi-trait–Multi-method Matrix," *Psychological Bulletin,* Vol. 56 (March 1959), pp. 81–105.

4. The Bases of Legitimacy are a partial exception; they are not ordered categories along a single dimension. For measurement purposes we treat each legitimacy category as a separate variable whose relative importance can be evaluated, for an individual and a group, by comparison with other categories.

5. See Edward R. Tufte, "Improving Data Analysis in Political Science," *World Politics,* Vol. 21 (July 1969), esp. pp. 644–646 and the references there.

6. See Adam Przeworski and Henry Teune, *The Logic of Comparative Inquiry* (New York: Wiley, 1970), Chs. 5 and 6, and the references on pp. 138–139.

CHAPTER EIGHT

Units of Analysis: Problems of Choice and Comparability

The "unit of analysis" for studies of authority patterns is the social unit, not the individual. Often we must rely on individuals as sources of information, but the object of analysis remains the description of the authority patterns of a unit as a whole. Certain conceptual and operational problems accompany the decision of what is and is not properly treated as a "social unit" and the choice of appropriate elements for study within units. These problems and approaches to their solution are the subject of the first section of this chapter.

A second, substantial problem posed by social units arises from their sheer diversity. They vary enormously in size, function, and primacy for their members, and all these characteristics might be expected to affect authority patterns in more or less systematic ways. The characteristics also constrain the researcher's choice of information strategies. On both conceptual and empirical grounds, then, the diversity of social units raises questions about the comparability of analyses of their authority patterns. The second section of this chapter attempts to deal with this problem by identifying five dimensions of variation among social units generally, suggesting how each dimension is likely to affect their authority characteristics, and naming the probable consequences for empirical research.

Social Units and Their Elements

Five defining properties of social units are specified in Chapter 1. (1) They are collective individuals, having an identity (to members and others) independent of their individual members' identities. (2) Interactions within them are recurrent and patterned. (3) Members identify themselves at least partly in terms of their membership in the unit. (4) The collectivity has goals distinct from those of individual members. (5) There is some allocation of roles or division of labor commensurate with the attainment of the unit's goals. A number of types of social units self-evidently fit this definition. Families resident in a single dwelling or compound are "social units," and so are "households" in the aristocratic and upper-class Western sense. In non-Western societies extended families and clan groups also are likely to qualify. At the other end of the scale, industrial organizations and national governments are social units, and so are the representatives and staff of the United Nations and other international organizations. An inexhaustible roster of other kinds of social units could be cited: armies, commercial farms, guerrilla movements, guilds, hospitals, houses of prostitution, labor unions, monastic orders, municipal governments, political parties, secret societies, ships' crews, sports clubs, supermarkets, tribal associations, universities, witches' covens, *ad infinitum*. Not every organization of these types necessarily meets all five criteria of a "social unit," but most are likely to do so.

Unit Boundaries: Who is a Member?

One of the operational difficulties posed by the definition is that some kinds of units have a large class of nominal members who do not satisfy one or both of our second and third criteria. Let us consider the entity called "Estados Unidos do Brasil." There presumably are substantial numbers of people resident in Brazil (as in most national societies) who have few if any specifically political interactions with anyone. They are not taxpayers or voters; their encounters with police and officials are as infrequent and potentially threatening as lightning strikes. Some, notably Indians, may not even be aware of the existence of an entity called "Brasil," much less identify with it. But to say that "Brasil" is therefore not a social unit is to confuse a legal definition of citizenship with effective membership in a unit. *The existence of a social unit is determined by the presence of a substantial core of individuals and activities that have all five defining properties of a social unit.* There may be more or less large numbers of people who identify with the unit without having any regular interactions within it. Citizenship has this nominal quality for many groups and individuals in many states, including some in Western ones. Affiliation with religious bodies and political parties is often nominal in the same way. There also are individuals in many units who are regularly subject to its directives and agents but have no significant identification with the unit. Slaves and prisoners are extreme cases. They have more numerous counterparts in the chronically rebellious students of slum schools, as well as alienated factory workers and unwilling subjects of alien or illegitimate rulers.

A related question is where to draw the boundaries of a social unit for purposes of analyzing its authority patterns. Our conception of an authority pattern provides the answer: the unit's de facto boundaries extend to those groups and individuals who have some recurrent, asymmetric interactions with it (i.e., those who regularly take part in formulating or issuing its directives or are regularly and actively obliged to abide by them). Other people and groups may occasionally influence or be influenced by the unit, as friends, nominal members, victims, or innocent bystanders; but the study of these effects is the study of *what the unit does,* not of its authority pattern per se. The slaves in an Arab merchant's household are members of it for the purposes of authority analysis, regardless of whether they are there willingly. Dwellers in Brazil's urban *favelas* and peasant farmers in the Northeast are members of the Brazilian state so long as they are obliged to abide regularly by its laws and decrees, or at least regularly subject to sanctions when they visibly fail to comply. Urban guerrillas in Brazil are also members of the state, on two counts: they are attempting to effect systematic changes in what the state is and does (i.e., changes in its directives), and they are subject to the state's very active attention and to its harsh sanctions when caught. But many of the Indians of the Amazon Basin are not members of the state because they live almost wholly outside the reach and regulation of state agencies.

One of the characteristics of the state is that people within its geographical boundaries are at least nominal members, and whether they are "regularly and actively" its subjects is largely a function of the state's activities and resources. Membership in organizations of most other kinds is much less comprehensive. In many "private governments," including commercial enterprises and some voluntary organizations, effective membership does not extend much beyond officers and paid employees. A national organization of hobbyists, for example, is unlikely to formulate directives for or apply them to anyone other than the core of active membership and the headquarters staff. The greatest difficulties in determining the effective boundaries of the unit are likely to be posed by organizations like contemporary Western religious congregations and labor unions. In the former, effective membership probably turns not on church attendance or donations but on whether the member feels obliged to abide regularly by the church's moral and ethical prescriptions. In the latter, the test is whether the rank-and-file member assumes an obligation to abide by, say, union grievance procedures and strike calls.

Another difficult case of unit boundaries is posed by the United Nations and other international bodies. There is little question that the UN is a social unit, one whose core comprises the General Assembly, the Security Council, the Secretariat, related organs and agencies, and military forces and truce teams under UN command. The question is whether the governments or citizens of the UN's member nations are members in the sense of having recurrent, asymmetric interactions with the organization. Generally they are not. Member nations of the UN selectively abide by the "directives" that are formulated regarding finances, reporting of internal social and economic data, sanctions against members, and so forth. These "directives" mostly have the quality of agreements among equals; those who do not agree seldom accept them and are seldom sanctioned for this behavior. Thus the UN as now constituted is a head without a body, a hierarchy whose effective directives regularly apply only to those who are employed to carry them out.

It also follows from the foregoing discussion that unit boundaries do not remain constant over time but can be subject to quite rapid change. "Modernizing" nation states are generally engaged in expanding the effective scope of their activities, which generally means subjecting more people to more directives. Private governments similarly expand and contract, depending on their leadership and on political and economic circumstances. The cautionary point for the researcher is that his characterization of "the" authority pattern of a social unit may well be subject to change—especially increased or reduced variability—as the unit's effective boundaries change.

Marginal and Indeterminate Cases

For some social entities, status as social units for the purpose of authority analysis is doubtful. These are mainly of two kinds: entities that are indubitably "social units" but have little or no visible authority pattern, and entities that have some manifest authority relations but otherwise are so ephemeral or elusive that the question arises whether they exist as social units.

Units without authority patterns are uncommon but not therefore unimportant. Recall (from Chapter 1) that a great many interactions occur within social units that are not concerned with authority. We have defined an authority pattern as "a set of asymmetric relations among hierarchically ordered members of a social unit that involves (its) direction." This special subset of asymmetric interactions simply may be absent from the unit. Childless marriages qualify if decision making is absolutely egalitarian and neither husband nor wife regularly gives orders to the other.[1] Counterculture communes afford some more interesting examples: in many, the members collectively formulate minimum rules and divisions of labor that are binding on all. It seems a vacuous verbal exercise to argue that such communes "really" have authority patterns because the members occupy both sides of hierarchic asymmetries seriatim. The existence and persistence of such a pattern is of great interest for the study of authority patterns because it seems to represent the irreducible minimum of hierarchic "direction" in social organization—whether one formally calls it an "authority pattern" or something else. Similar collective procedures have been used by religious congregations—some early Christians and monastic foundations, and contemporary Friends—and by small political, labor, and other voluntary associations. If the core of political science should be the study of authority patterns (see Chapter 1), that should encourage rather than preclude the study of their minimal forms and the conditions under which they are viable.

Indeterminate entities are those which are either short-lived or defined mainly by the existence of authority interactions. The Paris Commune of 1870 (not Paris as such) is an example of the former; it lasted scarcely two months, from late March to the "Bloody Week" of May 21–28. Without question its members attempted to establish an authority pattern, and one that was highly revealing about Parisian's authority norms as well as consequential for subsequent French attempts at political engineering. Thus its authority characteristics appear well worth analysis. An example of an "indistinct" or protosocial unit is the neocolonial relationship that allegedly holds between France and her former black African territories. The outside observer cannot determine easily, if at all, whether the formal meetings of French with black African officials and the pattern of French aid, economic exploitation, and politicomilitary intervention are evidence for the existence of a social unit with an emergent "authority pattern" or a set of discrete, bilateral acts and interventions among otherwise autonomous entities. The existence of a social unit and authority pattern encompassing all the "Mafia" families in the United States is similarly problematic. In both these examples lack of information is the immediate difficulty; there might later be a need to clarify operationally what constitutes "recurrent and patterned interactions."

The Elements of Social Units

Questions about what is or is not a social unit, and whether a social unit has an authority pattern, are mainly of interest to the theorist and to those who evaluate and synthesize empirical findings. The researcher beginning a field or library study is not often or long concerned with them, for the simple reason that most decisions about research foci are made on nontheoretical grounds of personal interest, convenience, and so forth. Hard choices are likely to concern the level of generalization to be attempted and the number of elements (strata and segments) to be distinguished within units, both analytically and empirically. Consider the difficulties of characterizing "the" authority pattern of the Democratic Party of the United States. The party has a national chairman and staff, a National Committee, a Congressional Caucus, regular conventions, and a panoply of state, county, municipal, ward, and precinct organizations. One pillar of the party authority pattern, from some viewpoints its central one, is the stratified flow of inputs from the local party organizations through the state to the national level on matters of ongoing policy and operation, and the flow of directives back down the structure. Another pillar is the relationship between party organization and elected members of the party; in some localities and states we can identify patterned authority relations between the party organization and elected officials (the officials may be *S*'s or *s*'s, depending on their rank and on the locale), in others no discernible relationship exists in form or practice. With respect to both these pillars, comprehensive description would have to indicate something about the range of variation in authority patterns of the local and state organizations. Another "chapter" of description is required by the presidential election process, from delegate selection to nominating convention to the campaign. The process involves an enormous expansion and branching of party organization, hence a whole new set of authority patterns to be considered. The organizations of individual candidates for the nomination require at least a lengthy "footnote."

Admittedly the Democratic Party is among the more difficult examples that might be chosen, but if the problems it poses are not soluble in combination, solutions to them separately are only partial ones. Analytically, the problems are the following.

1. *Multiple, diverse hierarchies.* Different unit functions are carried out by different hierarchic elements, which differ from one another in structure, in their relationships to the nominal head of the unit as a whole, or in both.
2. *Autonomy.* There is a "federal" or "confederal" relationship between the layers or strata of the unit, whereby the elements of nominally subordinate strata are substantially free to operate as they choose.
3. *Diversity.* Within a given stratum of the unit there are multiple elements exhibiting wide variation in authority patterns. (This is almost always a characteristic of units that have multiple, diverse hierarchies and autonomy, but it also may be found within units that have only one or neither of those conditions.)
4. *Discontinuity.* Some of the elements of the unit have no continuous existence but are established or disestablished as circumstances require.

All four conditions hold for the Democratic Party, and in a rather extreme degree. Whether this is a "problem" for the investigator depends on his objective. If the objective is an idiographic description of one intrinsically interesting element, such as the Democratic National Committee or the Cook County (Illinois) Democratic Party Organization, it will not be a problem at all. If the objective is to describe and compare state Democratic Committees, the most casual acquaintance with the subject will alert the researcher to their diversity, leading him to study a selection or sample of all such committees. The full weight of the descriptive burden falls on the investigator who wishes to make an overall characterization of the party's authority pattern, say for the purpose of comparison with the Republican Party or some other social unit(s). A professional lifetime would be required for an absolutely thorough study; macropolitical comparisons often call for much more summary and abstract analyses.

The initial step in characterizing authority in any complex social unit is to analyze summarily its Conformation, with special attention to the nature and interrelations of its various elements. If summary analysis is required, it should focus on the unit's *central* elements, which have the following characteristics:

1. They set the unit's primary goal(s).
2. They direct or coordinate the pursuit of the unit's primary goal(s).
3. They represent the highest level of direction or coordination concerned with those goal(s).
4. They have the dominant position in determining the allocation of scarce resources within the unit.

Such "central" elements tend to have certain other characteristics as well. Historically they are usually the oldest elements in the unit. Their operation is likely to be continuous and institutionalized. Positions in these elements generally have the greatest status and visibility within the unit. When new elements are added to the unit, their formal authority patterns are most likely modeled on those of the central element(s). When the unit is in a crisis situation, the central elements are likely to be the major actors or prizes in the conflict arena. But because of the number of exceptions to the latter characteristics, they should be regarded as clues to centrality, not as definitive evidence.

Several elements in a unit may share the "centrality" characteristics just cited. In the case of the Democratic Party, a case can be made for the "centrality" of two related elements: the National Committee and the National Convention. Description of authority patterns in both—including their relationships with nominally subordinate elements of the party—should give as good a summary description of dominant party authority patterns as is possible. What this procedure does not provide is a characterization of diversity among the semiautonomous regional and local strata of the party. The distinctive characteristics of urban party "machines" and of party organization in the Southern states are widely recognized, and there is a substantial literature that could be used in the analysis of their authority patterns. The interests and resources of the investigator will determine in part how much attention is given to diverse and "deviant" elements.

One important general point about "diversity" follows from this example. In a unit that has diverse elements in lower strata, it cannot be assumed that the authority patterns of the central elements are necessarily modal patterns. They are dominant by definition, but they may be either "left" or "right" of the typical pattern at lower levels. This is especially likely in periods of organizational change. Between 1968 and 1972 the Democratic National Committee shifted from what was probably a modal position among party elements on the openness of Participation to a reformist, more egalitarian position. And after 1972 it began shifting back again. Activist elites in developing societies have characteristically established modernizing institutions, both voluntary (parties, trades unions) and compulsory (schools), which are designed to "lead" or pull more traditional sectors into the modern world. A common characteristic of these modernizing institutions is their formal reliance on Western (and Soviet or Chinese Communist) models of authority relations; a frequent result is a substantial discrepancy between "modern" authority patterns in the central elements and more "traditional" patterns among local elements. Equally or more common is the existence of a "lag" between authority patterns in central elements and those in local elements. For example, Robert Friedman suggests that in the Swedish educational establishment, the central elements (the National Ministry of Education) have authority patterns that are distinctly more inegalitarian than those of the schools themselves, because egalitarianism in Swedish schools has been a grass-roots and, to a degree, generational phenomenon to which the educational establishment has only partly adapted.[2] We suggest that *summary description of authority patterns in social units with diverse, autonomous elements should include reference to any substantial discrepancies between the central and local elements.* Greater research effort is thereby required, but anything less is inadequate as a description of "the" authority pattern of a diverse unit.

In summary, Conformation is the first dimension of the analytic scheme to be evaluated when one is dealing with a complex social unit—that is, a unit characterized to a substantial degree by many and autonomous strata, by diverse segments and hierarchies, and so forth. The initial evaluation mainly will be concerned with formal Conformation and will rely on secondary studies, organization charts, and possibly the guidance of expert informants from the ranks of superordinates. This evaluation should be conducted to provide information on the identity and nature of the unit's elements to ascertain which components require closer study. The evaluation will not ordinarily provide sufficient information on Conformation, however. Comprehensive description will later require a collection of both detailed and general information, and most important, information on organizational practices as well as forms.

Variability Among Social Units: Problems of Conceptual Equivalence and Information Strategies

We have thus far considered the general nature of social units, attempting to determine how much the enormous variability among social units constrains the use of a common analytic scheme for them, and how diversity affects the researcher's choice of information strategies. Our problem is analogous to two questions in physics. First, are analytic properties such as width, energy, and mass determinable in principle for all physical objects, regardless of their size and diversity? The answer in physics is "yes," with qualifications at the subatomic level. Such broad applicability for our analytic scheme of authority remains to be demonstrated, although we also believe the answer to be "yes." Second, what are the appropriate, and workable, approaches to measuring the basic properties of such diverse objects? Each scientific discipline accumulates a body of answers to such operational questions. Our answers for authority study are necessarily partial and tentative, because derived from our limited—but not negligible—experience.

The Comparability Problem

Survey researchers concerned with "political culture" usually treat their respondents as interchangable units; this assumed equivalency justifies the aggregation and direct comparison of their attitudes.[3] In the literature on macropolitical comparisons, by contrast, there is considerable concern about the appropriateness of equating nations as diverse as Denmark and India, or of regarding the Communist Party of the USSR as a member of the same set of entities as the Communist Party of the United States. The question is whether any significant analytic purpose is served by regarding either of these two pairs of entities as members of the same set. The answer in cross-national research is usually a qualified yes, depending on the variables under study,[4] but the problem is increased by several orders of magnitude when we include the entire gamut of human social organizations from the nuclear family to the nation-state and international bodies. It is not likely to be disputed that all (almost all) such social units have authority patterns. The question is whether their extreme diversity precludes the use of a single analytic scheme or vitiates any comparisons based on its operational use.

We concede straightaway that the type of social unit substantially influences the relative importance of some authority dimensions and that in some types of units "forms" are of negligible interest. Moreover, in a few instances authority traits of a social unit are largely determined by the nature of the unit: in the nuclear family, proximity is almost always and of necessity "close." Similarly, Directiveness is likely to be quite high for production workers in all munitions factories, otherwise output will be explosively discontinuous. But we do not think that the nature or function of any social unit wholly or even substantially determines the unit's position on all the authority dimensions. If the contrary is assumed—that is, if large classes of social units have authority characteristics largely predetermined by the traits of those units—the content-free or "analytic" status of the analytic scheme is impugned. And empirical statements about variations and covariations among units' authority characteristics will thereby be subject to systematic error or bias by the effects of the nonauthority variables. We systematically evaluate the effects of traits of social units and of societies on authority patterns in Chapter 13.

We might evaluate how social unit diversity affects the applicability of the analytic scheme by referring to concrete social units: the family versus schools versus political associations versus governments. Yet each of these types is also subject to great variation among and even within cultures. Our approach is to specify five variable characteristics of social units that can have substantial effects either on the authority characteristics of the units or on the procedures best used for studying them. The procedural question has several aspects. Some units are more appropriately or efficiently studied with one kind of technique than with another. Some are rather likely to yield biased results on some dimensions, hence require special techniques and interpretations. And some units are simply more accessible and easier to study and describe than others; thus they can be analyzed more widely and deeply than others, given a fixed level of resources.

The first of the five dimensions of social unit variation to be considered below is *scale*. The second distinguishes between large-scale *atomic* and *organic* units: that is, between those units which consist of numerous almost-identical local elements and those which—like the Democratic Party in the United States—consist of many formally and functionally different elements. The third dimension concerns the degree to which membership in a unit is *compulsory* rather than *voluntary*. The fourth is the *primacy* of the unit for its members. Finally we examine some of the special problems of studying units that are either highly *authoritarian* or highly *egalitarian*. These five dimensions are not intended as an "analytic scheme" for the study of differences among social units. They are chosen because they seem to us, on the basis of practical experience and reflection, to subsume the more substantial effects that social unit variability has on the operational use of the analytic scheme. Researchers who take them into account should thereby improve the comparability and reliability of their findings.

A prefatory note: some of the dimensions of unit variation have greater implications for authority characteristics than for operational procedures, and vice versa. But insofar as the authority characteristics of a unit are strongly influenced by its scale, primacy, voluntariness, and so on, research should be easier: a cursory research effort should indicate whether a highly probable condition is present, or an unlikely one absent. If we can expect the family to have few forms of authority, as suggested below, there is little point in investing heavily in a search for them. If voluntary units tend to have low Directiveness, as we also suggest below, then detailed questions about coverage, supervision, and sanctions need seldom be asked; brief observation should suffice. If, however, a "quick check" reveals the unexpected—extensive family "forms" or high coverage in a voluntary organization—the researcher is alerted to the need for special attention. The existence of authority characteristics that are not visibly functional to the unit should prove highly informative about the cultural context of the unit, its relations to other kinds of units, the characteristics of its members, even its *raison d'ètre.* These points about the "expected" and the "unexpected" in authority characteristics apply to all the following discussion.

Social Unit Scale

"Scale" refers to the size of the social unit, in terms of its number of active—as distinct from nominal—members. The numerical extremes in the contemporary world are 2 and 700×10^6: the childless couple and the People's Republic of China. Most research on authority patterns is on units well within the extremes, but still the effective range is substantial, from schools and local party organizations with membership in the hundreds to business enterprises and government agencies with tens of thousands of members, to national political systems with millions of citizens and subjects.

Scale and the Facets of Authority. The complexity and formalization of authority patterns tend to vary with the scale of the social unit. The scale of a unit thus has considerable influence on several specific authority characteristics. The principal ones are as follows.

The smaller the unit, the less likely it is to have fully specified *forms* of authority. Forms are almost always unimportant for the study of primary groups but are increasingly important and fully specified as scale increases. Lack of consonance between forms and either norms or practices thus is indeterminant for the smallest groups.

Among the dimensions of authority, Conformation is substantially affected by scale: the larger the unit, the greater its likely internal complexity.

Deportment also is affected in the opposite direction: the smaller the unit, the more likely its members are to interact on a familiar, face-to-face basis. Thus if we are comparing authority patterns of units of widely different scale, we would expect to discount—though not ignore—differences in Conformation and Deportment. There is also a tendency for smaller social units to have less social distance between superordinates and subordinates, with such striking exceptions as master-slave relationships. But the Influence dimensions, and the *S*-dimensions other than Conformation, are likely to vary largely independently of scale.

All these scale constraints on the variability of the authority dimensions are probabilistic only, and deviations from the presumed "functional requisites" of a social unit may be highly revealing about a society's general authority norms. A characteristic of French authority relations, for example, is *terreur* of unstructured, face-to-face interactions between superordinates and subs. The consequences include low proximity (an aspect of Deportment) even in many small-scale social units, and a proliferation of highly detailed regulations that formally constitute a very high degree of Directiveness. In Russian society, by contrast, there has been remarked a preference for face-to-face authority interactions rather than indirect ones, which in practice has dysfunctional effects on the efficiency of large-scale units. We also can cite an analysis of the "constitutional" documents of Norwegian voluntary associations. A high degree of formal complexity was found even in the smallest associations, and the same forms appeared repeatedly in associations and public bodies of vastly different scale. There is no direct, functional advantage in a local sports club having the same basic organizational forms and procedures as, say, a national organization of municipal employees. What seems to be reflected here is a societal norm about what is proper Conformation. One of the benefits of similarity, intended or otherwise, is that people who are socialized into one associational context are therefore likely to be comfortable in and function effectively in any other.[5]

Scale and Procedures. Large-scale units self-evidently require procedures somewhat different from those of small ones; we can mention questions of *access* and *technique.*

Access is the process of obtaining approval to study, observe, question the records and members of a social unit. For small units in "open" societies, access is usually rather easy to obtain. The researcher approaches the head of the organization and attempts to persuade him or her that the academic and/or practical value of the research exceeds the nuisance value of having the researcher underfoot. Effective arguments for access vary among societies. In England the introduction of esteemed mutual acquaintances is often crucial. In Latin cultures access may turn on whether the investigator is perceived as worth having in the debt of the person who can open the requisite doors. North Americans are often sufficiently inbued with the scientific ethos, or sufficiently gregarious, that they are flattered to be studied.

Larger-scale organizations pose greater difficulties, sometimes insurmountable ones, although the problems here depend as much on the kind of unit as on its scale per se. Caution tends to prevail over curiosity in business organizations and bureaucracies, unless the results of inquiry are likely to be of practical benefit for the organization. A large organization may propose that the investigator place results at the disposal of the corporation or government, which would violate the anonymity that is practically and ethically required by almost all research on authority patterns. Or it may request prior approval of interview and questionnaire schedules, as a way of preventing the release of embarrassing information. Such problems with large-scale organizations are not necessarily less severe in open than in "closed" (i.e., centralized, authoritarian) societies. In closed societies the researcher who succeeds in obtaining approval for his work from high officials may well find that almost all doors are opened, even those not formally controlled by the authorizing officials. A case in point is Robert Rotberg's research on the Haitian political elite in the late 1960s; he succeeded in obtaining favorable audiences with President François Duvalier during the early stages of fieldwork, after which he received extensive cooperation in what proved to be a highly critical study.[6] One other pervasive problem of access to large-scale organizations is the insulation of their highest-ranked supers. They are generally shielded from the impositions of "outsiders" by functionaries who typically respond to requests for access either by "no" or with a menu of misleading public relations pap. Persistence and resort to influential intermediaries can sometimes overcome such institutional resistance. We also have observed that senior research and development personnel in large-scale organizations are often more sympathetic to researchers than other officials and may be willing to use their influence to ensure access.

The most appropriate *techniques* of inquiry also vary with scale.[7] In small-scale units the investigator may be able to review all or a large portion of available records; to observe all its basic operations, including decision-making sessions; and to interview all the officials and a cross section of members. This might be possible, for example, in a small educational institution or a trade union local. For units of larger scale, comprehensive interviewing and observation are usually impracticable. It is especially important that the researcher begin with a thorough review of any extant studies of the unit, to familiarize himself with the unit generally and to glean what authority information he can on elements that he cannot study directly. Insofar as such studies provide authority data, the researcher can make initial categorizations of the unit on various dimensions as hypotheses to be tested and modified in his own research. The next step will probably be to identify and use a few expert informants, preferably unit members, who can provide supplementary information. Lower and middle supers are likely to be the most useful informants; they are likely to have broader knowledge of the unit than subordinates although not sharing all the inhibitions of top *S*'s about discussing unit affairs with outsiders.

Preliminary information gathering will be followed by intensive study. Of necessity this will require sampling, hopefully representative sampling, among equivalent units and within various groups of lower supers and subs for interview and questionnaire administration. Relatively little of a unit's activities will be subject to observation. Observation will be used proportionately less than in small units, mainly to verify or qualify the results obtained by other techniques.

Atomic Versus Organic Units

Some large-scale units are comprised of many structurally and functionally similar elements. The principal examples are the religious congregations of Western and some non-Western churches; public elementary and secondary schools in almost all contemporary nations; and local chapters of many national trades unions, political parties, and other voluntary organizations. Local and regional government units in centralized states sometimes have this characteristic, except that urban and rural governments tend to be vastly different in scale and functions. "Atomic" is the term we use to distinguish such units, comprised of similar local elements, from large-scale "organic" units comprised of structurally and functionally dissimilar elements. Examples of the latter are most large economic enterprises, all national governments and many government agencies, and quite a few voluntary associations, including the two major political parties of the United States. The differences are of degree. A national educational system, for example, will have a number of functionally specialized bureaus or inspectorates and some specialized institutions in addition to its basic stratum of similar public schools. A unit is "atomic" to the extent that its *s*- and *S*-members are situated in similar local elements, "organic" to the extent that they are in diverse elements. The distinction has few implications for the applicability of the analytic scheme but a good many for information strategies.

Facets of Authority. The Conformation of atomic units is almost by definition less complex than that of organic units. The former tend to have fewer horizontal layers and less functional segmentation (but a high degree of spatial segmentation—i.e., a wide dispersion of local elements). With this exception, we do not anticipate any functional determinacy or strong disposition between the atomic-organic dimension and the authority dimensions.

Procedures. Atomic units are generally though not necessarily easier to study. *Access* to them tends to be easier, depending on the degree of subunit autonomy. If the local elements have a moderate degree of autonomy, it is generally easy for the researcher to secure cooperation for a study at that level. If they are highly centralized, however, access to any local element is probably contingent on the approval of officials near the apex of the unit. The problems are the same as those discussed earlier with reference to large-scale organizations.

Background research on atomic units is usually simpler than on organic units because one or two extant studies of local elements permit tentative generalizations about others, whereas a preliminary picture of an organic unit requires fitting together many extant studies like a mosaic. Rather different approaches to choice of elements for study also are required. For atomic units, representative sampling among local elements is especially necessary. In organic units "centrality" considerations are paramount, and the researcher is obliged to ignore some functionally diverse elements. "Atomic" units also permit efficient procedures in the use of interview, questionnaire, and observation techniques that are not open to the researcher dealing with an organic unit. In the first few local elements that are studied, the researcher will want to invest rather heavily in all three kinds of methods, for purposes of "triangulation." But once he determines—*if* he determines—that questionnaire results are reliable, subsequent units can be studied relying more heavily on the more efficient questionnaires, with interviews and observation serving only to spot-check the results of the initial triangulation. Craig MacLean used this kind of procedure in his Workshop study of Philippine governmental bureaus, with the proportion of interviews to questionnaires declining as he moved to successive bureaus.

Voluntary Versus Compulsory Units

It is important to distinquish between units that rely on interest in unit activity rather than penalties to maintain membership, and those from which members can opt out only at heavy cost. The distinction is clearly of degree, not dichotomous. Membership in the national state tends in the compulsory direction, especially in closed societies, but many states do not actively prevent their citizens from assuming the costs of emigration or exile. Primary and secondary schools in Western societies tend to be "compulsory" units for their student members. Membership in some "voluntary" associations such as Western trades unions and Communist political parties is far from wholly voluntary; the cost of dropping membership is often loss of employment. Membership in the family (for adults, not children) and in economic enterprises is generally a "mixed" case; the costs of leaving are moderate to high, but not high enough to eliminate either divorce or heavy employee turnover rates in most Western societies. It may also be noted that no functional necessity determines that a unit performing a particular kind of activity will tend toward the voluntary or compulsory extremes. Some states imprison would-be emigrants, others provide them grants. Religious bodies have variously burned their heretics or bade them "go with God." There are few visible costs of leaving the Republican Party of the United States not even for former New York mayor John Lindsay; but backsliding members of South Vietnam's National Liberation Front were rather likely to be executed if caught.

Facets of Authority. The Influence dimensions of authority seem to be especially subject to variation with a social unit's degree of voluntarism. In more voluntary units, Directiveness—detailed orders, close supervision, quick sanctions for disobedience—is painful except to masochists and is likely to result in membership loss (or nonrecruitment). Responsiveness of *S*'s to *s*-inputs is likely to be high for a similar reason; dissatisfied rank-and-file members will probably leave. There are exceptions, of course: dedicated voluntary associations of activists, like the Salvation Army, have been established by selectively recruiting members who are willing to accept close direction because of their commitment to the goals of the group. There presumably are special, and especially interesting, circumstances that help account for such "deviant" cases.

We should note also that although low Directiveness and high Responsiveness tend to be functionally linked to voluntarism, the opposite does not hold: units in which membership is in the compulsory direction may tend to be more Directive and less Responsive, but there seem to be no strong functional pressures in that direction. There also is no functional tendency for Participation to be higher in voluntary than in compulsory units, although in Western societies there may be an empirical trend in that direction. Compliance also seems unlikely to be directly affected by the degree of voluntarism or compulsion in membership. There tend to be fewer pressures for Compliance in voluntary organizations than in compulsory ones, but this is countered by a hypothetical tendency for interest-based Compliance to be more consistent than Compliance motivated by fear.

There is likely to be a systematic functional association between openness of Recruitment (from *s*- to *S*-levels within a unit) and voluntariness. There are several grounds for such a relationship, including the relatively higher motivation and interest that characterizes rank-and-file members of most voluntary organizations (hence high suitability for *S*-positions), and the *S*-tactic of retaining competent members by promoting them rapidly. One occasional consequence of the latter practice is a proliferation of organizational substructures in voluntary organizations and a tendency toward an "all chiefs and no Indians" structure. In the campaign organizations of political candidates in the United States, for example, the lowest-ranked members may have such impressive titles as "precinct coordinator," "youth coordinator," and "office manager." The effective status of such members becomes clear when it is observed that they are principally responsible for such basic tasks as canvassing, envelope stuffing, poll watching, and running the returns. Here Conformation tends to be formally more complex than unit practices. Of course voluntary units do not have a monopoly on the efflorescence of honorific titles and offices.

Some of the emergent properties of authority patterns also tend to vary with voluntarism. Complementarity of *S*- and *s*-practices tends to be high, otherwise *s*'s find themselves in frequent overt conflict with supers and tend to leave the unit or to force out the *S*'s. Consonance of the norms of subs with those of supers is more weakly associated with voluntarism; awareness of *s*- and *S*-members that they hold mutually inconsistent norms tends to weaken the bonds of collegiality that help hold voluntary units together.

All the foregoing statements are concerned with functional tendencies, however, not with functional requisites. That is, one can conceive of and empirically find effective voluntary units that have most of the conditions that tend to be dysfunctional for voluntary units generally. We would expect to find such "exceptional" units in societies in which the prevailing authority pattern is "authoritarian" and membership ordinarily compulsory.

Procedures. We have suggested an occasional tendency for voluntary units to have deceptively high formal complexity on the Conformation dimension. The recommended approach is to rely heavily on observation and reports about activities in practice when describing organizational structure. Voluntary organizations seem to be somewhat more accessible than compulsory organizations because the former tend to maintain a studied cordiality toward nonmembers—at least in Western societies—whereas compulsory units may have fewer reasons for such attitudes. But with these two minor exceptions we know of no special procedural problems associated with degrees of voluntarism or compulsion.

Primacy of Units

Primary units are those intimate, spatially restricted groups into which one is born and lives: the family, the clan, the community. They are substantially different, in Western and other societies, from the functionally specific, rationalized, and often large-scale and remote units in which most males—other than subsistence farmers—pursue their vocations and avocations. The question here is the extent to which such units have functionally determined or functionally influenced characteristics on the authority dimensions. The prior question is whether they have authority patterns, and the answer must be "not necessarily." In most "traditional" and non-Western societies, all families and most clans and villages do indeed have heads who exercise substantial authority over the affairs of the group. In much of precolonial Africa there were no authority patterns more encompassing than these. In modernizing and Western societies, governance of the community has tended to be assumed by or brought under the aegis of national governments: community authority has changed in function and character; it is no longer "primary." Only the family remains as the primary unit—sometimes the extended family or clan, but more often only the nuclear, two-generation family. Thus the following comments apply in the West mainly to the residual primary group, the family, but in traditional societies to more numerous and varied units.

Facets of Authority. The authority patterns of primary units are seldom formally prescribed, at any rate not by or within the unit. In Western states there may be legal codes that formally limit aspects of family formation and function, and religious bodies also may prescribe about family life. The Spanish civil code, for example, stipulates that within the family "The husband must protect the woman. The latter must obey the husband" (Article 57). But this is highly abstract, scarcely more than enough to enable us to say that the Spanish family is formally stratified between husband and wife. The general lack of formal prescription does not signify that primary units are necessarily "informal" or amorphous. It is usually quite the contrary. As a rule their norms about authority are strongly inculcated in members and highly salient for their day-to-day activities. It is the daily, face-to-face reinforcement of authority norms in primary groups that makes their formal specification generally irrelevant.

Primary units tend to be highly Directive, because they are multifunctional. This is most visibly true with respect to children, who are the objects of a heavy flow of directives about a wide range of activities. The flow of directives to adults—to wives by husbands, villagers by clan chiefs and elders—is generally much smaller, not because authority coverage is any less broad but because most adult subordinates long ago internalized the relevant authority norms. The test of Directiveness norms in primary units is the extent to which *s*'s feel constrained about or obliged to engage in diverse kinds of behavior, and the extent to which they feel guilty or are subject to external sanctions when they act contrary to the norms.

The face-to-face quality of life in primary units affects a number of authority dimensions. Although Deportment tends to be "familiar" and "close," enough exceptions come to mind to preclude the assumption of a necessary relationship. In the English upper class, for example, children often have only a half-hour or hour's very formal contact each day with parents; otherwise they are under the ministrations of nurse and tutor. Close and familiar Deportment also generates pressures for greater Participation and Responsiveness. These are tendencies only, and one can cite many literary and real-life exceptions in the form of stern, remote, and unyielding fathers. But such individuals are more often denigrated than praised in Western and non-Western literature. The non-Western norm is more likely to be the patriarch who is both firm and compassionate. A widespread theme in world folklore and fiction is the absolute ruler who deals mercifully with subjects who make personal supplication to him; surely this theme is not only wish-fulfillment but an echo and projection of the Responsiveness of myriad autocratic fathers and village chiefs to personal influence attempts. Whether Distance between supers and subs tends to be less in proximate groups is more problematic. The needs of children for nurturance can be satisfied only through "familiar" interactions with some adult, usually the mother, but the terms on which nurturance is given are as likely to add to Distance between mother and child as to reduce it. And the father's role may be remote and formal throughout.

We may also mention some special characteristics of Conformation and Recruitment in primary units. Complexity is likely to be greater in primary units than in others of small scale. The nuclear family of four or five members, for example, is likely to be as complex in authority structure as an elementary school of several hundred members. In most cultures the family has two strata of superordination—husband and wife, respectively—between whom there is also, typically, a functional division of responsibility (segmentation) as well as a considerable degree of joint decision making (hence structural interconnection, and a need to evaluate Concordance as well). Whether Conformation is similarly complex in extended families, clans, and villages, is an empirical question. Recruitment within primary units in Western societies is largely but not entirely irrelevant to the description of their authority patterns. The "open-closed" continuum is not applicable to children in the nuclear family because they later establish their own units—that is, they do not "move up" in the family into which they were born. But various ascriptive and achievement criteria have some bearing on what women, and men, can marry into a particular extended family or clan, or join a village community. Moreover, these criteria affect not only outsiders' eligibility for membership but their subsequent status in the primary group, as when an immigrant's son marries into a Boston Brahmin family and is treated as a "poor relative" in family councils, or when a former slave joins an African village as a free farmer but because of his origins is accorded, along with his descendents, an inferior rank and lesser privileges in the village hierarchy.

Procedures. There are some distinctive aspects to doing authority research on primary units. Documents generated by the unit, either formal prescriptions or directives, or records, are largely absent. On the other hand, there may be a very extensive secondary literature, ranging from fictional portrayals of family life (in almost all literate cultures) to careful and numerous anthropological studies of family and village life in non-Western ones. Access normally is rather easy, though varying with the kind of study to be done. Questionnaires and interviews are easiest and likely to yield shallow information—especially in the family, where the hierarchic, directive aspects of family life are so inextricably bound to everything else that much goes unthought of and unreported. Long, careful, and especially *analytic* observation is usually necessary to draw a full picture of family authority patterns. This is clearly a case in which the observer can influence the observed behavior, but some scholars have been remarkably successful in gaining not only access but unselfconscious acceptance as a member of the family under study. Oscar Lewis' portrayal of Puerto Rican family life in *La Vida* is an outstanding example.[8] If the objective of the study is to characterize family life generally in a culture, there must be compromises between depth and breadth of study. Ideally, several families (representative of different socioeconomic classes, locale, etc.) would be intensively studied, and a much broader sample of families would be studied more summarily through interviews or questionnaires.

Authoritarian Versus Egalitarian Units

The authoritarian-egalitarian dimension underlies or at least covaries with many of the dimensions in the analytic scheme. We are not concerned here with how it relates to the analytic scheme per se but with its effects on research procedures.

The basic difficulty is that social units located near either extreme of the authoritarian-egalitarian continuum are especially likely to yield biased results. In extremely egalitarian units there may be a tendency to deny that "authority" exists at all in the unit. This will be especially likely in contemporary Western cooperative and communal organizations.[9] In authoritarian units no one will deny the existence of "authority," but it is likely to be regarded as a sensitive matter, one to which outsiders should not be privy. If the researcher is using prescriptive documents, certain questions of interpretation consistently arise. It is quite possible, not necessarily so, that the prescriptive documents of authoritarian units will be for external consumption and will have little correspondence to either norms or practices. The constitutions of the Communist states are very widely held to have this mythic quality. In egalitarian units such documents may reflect the norms of units members rather well but are likely to be seriously incomplete and to deviate in varying degrees from practices. Written accounts by unit members may well be self-censored, either because "there isn't any authority" or because one is not supposed to write about it. Informants who "tell all" are suspect because of the likelihood that their motives for confession have distorted their observations. Triangulation from diverse documentary sources may help resolve these problems.

Interview and questionnaire techniques are similarly difficult to apply. A researcher may gain access to a highly egalitarian or authoritarian unit on the pretext that he wishes to study "how the organization functions." Many of the questions we propose to ask will quickly raise doubts about his purposes, however. The overpersistent or incautious researcher may find doors shut in his face—ordinary doors in egalitarian units, cell doors in authoritarian ones. Systematic observation may be the only recourse.

In authoritarian units the norms and practices of authority are clear enough for the observer who succeeds in penetrating the cloak of secrecy. In egalitarian units there are special problems, however open and cooperative unit members may be. The distinction between *s* and *S* may be analytic only (i.e., a difference that the investigator detects, although it has no reality in the eyes of the unit members). It may be found that directives are formulated and issued in ways that are not perceived by the actors as having any hierarchic aspect at all. Recognized *S*'s may disvalue holding office, or pretend to, and Recruitment may be overtly a function of subs' "push" rather than supers' ambition or mobility. When formulating directives, *S*'s may act as though—or *think* they act as though—all *s*'s are their peers. Distinctions between Participation and Responsiveness on the one hand and Decision-Behavior on the other, may therefore be difficult to make and to a degree artificial. Statements that have the effect of directives may be regarded by one or both parties as "suggestions." All such problems can be overcome by the researcher who is sensitive to the feelings and often subtle cues of the people he is studying. He must be especially careful, though, not to make one of two kinds of error. (*a*) He should not "read" authority implications into all asymmetrical behaviors; only those which are recurrent and concern the direction of the unit are authority behaviors. (*b*) He should not accept incautiously the statements of unit members that no hierarchic distinctions are made and no orders given; such norms may be admirable, but practices are the proof of the pattern.

Notes

1. A recent study which surveys historical and contemporary evidence on roles and authority structures in families in Western societies is Michael Young and Peter Willmott, *The Symmetrical Family* (New York: Pantheon, 1973). As the title implies, the authors conceptualize the modern family as a symmetrical structure in which the husband-wife bond has become progressively more egalitarian.

2. Robert S. Friedman, "The Tension between Hierarchy and Equality in the Swedish National Board of Education." Paper prepared for the annual meeting of the American Political Science Association, September 1972; and Friedman, *Participation in Democracy: A Theory of Democracy and Democratic Socialization* (Ph.D. dissertation, Department of Politics, Princeton University, 1972).

3. Although there is relatively little concern in the literature on political culture about the matter, the orientations of specific respondents are of vastly different significance for the functioning of their political systems, depending on their roles and hierarchic position. The views of a health insurance executive or a city councilman are more revealing about the operant political culture of the United States than the responses of the average store clerk. The point is not unrecognized: in a major cross-national study of norms and practices of participation by Sidney Verba and Norman Nie, the subjects included substantial samples of both elites and ordinary citizens. See Norman H. Nie and Sidney Verba, "Political Participation," in Fred I. Greenstein and Nelson W. Polsby, Eds., *Handbook of Political Science, Vol. 4: Nongovernmental Politics* (Reading, Mass.: Addison-Wesley, 1975).

4. For some discussions of this issue see Donald G. Morrison et al., *Black Africa: A Comparative Handbook* (New York: Free Press, 1972), pp. 392–409; Adam Przeworski and Henry Teune, *The Logic of Comparative Inquiry* (New York: Wiley, 1970), Ch. 2; and Erwin Scheuch, "Cross-National Comparisons Using Aggregate Data: Some Substantive and Methodological Problems," in Richard L. Merritt and Stein Rokkan, Eds., *Comparing Nations: The Use of Quantitative Data in Cross-National Research* (New Haven, Conn.: Yale University Press, 1966).

5. Harry Eckstein, *Division and Cohesion in Democracy*, (Princeton, N.J.: Princeton University Press, 1966), Ch. 8.

6. Personal communication; also see Robert Rotberg, *The Politics of Squalor* (New York: Twentieth Century Fund, 1970).

7. Techniques of documentary and field research are reviewed systematically in the next chapter with reference to their appropriateness for different dimensions and facets of authority relations. Here we examine the situational constraints on their use.

8. Oscar Lewis, *La Vida: A Puerto Rican Family in the Culture of Poverty—San Juan and New York* (New York: Random House, 1966).

9. For a sociological study of two counterculture groups in London, see Richard Mills, *Young Outsiders: A Study of Alternative Communities* (New York: Pantheon, 1973), which touches on norms about authority.

CHAPTER NINE

Sources, Strategies, and Techniques for Empirical Research

This chapter addresses in detail some basic operational issues in the systematic study of authority relations. We have encountered many of these issues; others we anticipate as research on the subject proceeds. We do not attempt here a comprehensive or detailed survey of possible techniques, but instead suggest some of the more appropriate applications and modifications of existing approaches to the kinds of research questions posed by the study of authority patterns.

Forms, Norms, and Practices of Authority Relations

Ideally we require information on three facets of authority patterns: their *forms, norms,* and *practices.* The three concepts are defined and discussed in Chapter 7. In any one unit these facets are not necessarily similar (or *correspondent,* to use our technical term). On the contrary, we suggest as a basic precept of authority studies that *forms, norms, and practices should be assumed to be significantly and observably different unless and until proved similar.* We have read of no organizations of any size or in any culture that function entirely in accord with their formal rules or in accord with such rules alone, nor do we know of any social units that function without some "deviance" from group norms about ideally desirable behaviors. If this is true of group behavior generally, we expect it to be even more the case with authority-laden behavior, because it entails often-painful subordination and deprivation for some members. The discrepancies we have observed in our own empirical data among the three facets of authority are occasionally so pervasive and wide that the data seem to emanate from quite different social milieus.

The distinction among forms, norms, and practices poses the operational problem of how to gather reliable information on each of them. Our approach is to use multiple techniques and different sources of information, making some a priori assumptions about which sources of information are most reliable for which facets. The discussion that follows refers both to techniques that were tried in field research by members of the Workshop and to other, hypothetically relevant techniques.

Evidence about Forms

The forms of authority patterns, when they exist, can usually be determined directly and rather easily. They are to be found mainly in the prescriptive documents of the social unit: constitutional documents, legal enactments, standing orders and regulations, codes of behavior, organizational charts, and certain written orders—particularly those which give substance to more general prescriptions. In preliterate societies formal prescriptions may be embodied in ritualistic oral traditions; in literate societies we rely only on written documents for evidence about the forms of authority patterns. Formal, prescriptive documents must meet the following three criteria:

1. *They are formulated or approved by the social unit's supers.* The *S*'s under whose aegis the prescriptive documents were formulated may be past or present; they may or may not have had the cooperation or consent of *s*'s.
2. *They prescribe or proscribe authority behaviors for categories of people or for roles,* not for individuals. A statement that "Supervisors are required to . . ." may be a prescriptive document; a statement that "Obermeister Klaus Metzer is required to . . ." is a command, not a prescriptive document.
3. *They refer to persisting or recurring patterns of authority behavior,* not to specific actions. The statement that "District Chairmen shall call monthly meetings of the District Advisory Committees" is a formal prescription; the statement that "District Chairmen shall schedule the next meeting of their Advisory Committee on 5 May" is a directive, not a formal prescription.

Relatively few of an organization's documents are likely to meet all three criteria. Routine correspondence, memoranda, and most directives are ruled out. Descriptions of the ideal or actual nature of the system, by members or external observers, also are not formal prescriptions; this includes such documents as analytic studies, organizational records, memoirs, and diaries. Any such documents may contain *evidence about* formal prescriptions, and especially about how they correspond with norms and practices, but are not themselves forms.

"Conventions" may pose a special problem. Conventions are codified norms, that is, generalizations about desirable past behaviors that may acquire the force of prescriptive statements. English "case law" is an example, insofar as it relates to authority relationships.[1] The powers of the British monarch and some of the powers of the Prime Minister have been similarly defined and restrained in ways that are documented not in a written constitution or statutes but in learned commentaries that have acquired the force of law. There are equivalents in other traditional and posttraditional societies. We regard such "conventions" as forms if their codification is accepted by successive *S*'s as tantamount to prescription.

Many social units have few formal prescriptions, some have none. Families are an example *par excellence:* most modern societies make formal prescriptions about the conditions of marriage, economic and civil rights of wives versus husbands, and parents' treatment of children, but these cover only a tiny fraction of the authority relationships within the family unit. Except for those rare families which operate under "marriage contracts," family authority patterns are mostly uncodified. The larger and more complex a social unit, the more formal prescription is likely, but very few organizations approach the authority-saturated condition imagined in George Orwell's *1984:* "Everything that is not required is forbidden." The North American academic reader need only consider how few of the authority interactions between faculty and students, or faculty and administrators, are governed by formal rules, to realize how limited in coverage are the formal prescriptions of American universities. North Americans by and large lack the *horror vacui* with some European societies—notably the French and German—regard unformalized authority relations.[2] Thus formal prescriptions are likely to be limited in their coverage; and we emphasize that many dimensions of authority can be ascertained only by more intricate observation and inquiry.

This is no justification for ignoring forms, though. Nor does the likely discrepancy between forms and norms or practices justify our unconcern. If codification is highly selective—discounting dimensions that are not susceptible to codification—we have a clue about which aspects of authority are most salient in a culture or social unit and which are most likely to be the subject of conflict. Moreover, the nature and extent of discrepancies between formal prescription and norms/practices can be highly informative about the direction of change and the nature of stresses in social units. With this in mind, we discuss below some problems the researcher may face in gathering information on forms.

Forms may prove difficult to determine, when they exist, in three circumstances: (*a*) if the unit regards its formal rules to be "for members only," (*b*) if the formal rules are so irrelevant to actual practices that unit members are literally unable to locate copies or statements of them for the researcher, or (*c*) if the unit operates within formal constraints imposed by one or several outside agencies.

Rules are likely to be "for members only" in social units that generally value or require secrecy. Some diverse examples are intelligence-gathering and secret police agencies, Mafia "families," the Black Muslims, revolutionary organizations, and the elites of some traditional—and some modern—political communities. But this is seldom a real problem for the investigator, because he is unlikely to attempt to study such "closed" organizations unless he is a participant-observer. If the naïve researcher does find that a supposedly open organization resists disclosure of documents about its basic structure and operating rules, he is forewarned that getting information on any other facet of its authority patterns is likely to be difficult if not impossible.

Situation *b* is to be distinguished from the case in which the prescriptive documents of an organization are in such desuetude that they cannot even be located. Bureaucratic organizations in some non-European societies have allegedly codified structures and procedures to satisfy Western legal norms and have then ignored them with perfect nonchalance. Local and small-scale social units throughout the world often do the same, either because forms borrowed from or imposed by outside organizations are held to be irrelevant, or because "everyone knows" what is to be done so well that no one needs to refer to written documents. In such circumstances the datum of "nonavailability" is important to the researcher because of what it says about the relative importance of norms versus forms; the actual substance of the missing formal prescriptions is likely to be of peripheral interest, except for historical inquiry.

The more common difficulty for the field researcher is posed by situation *c*: the presence of subordinate units of larger organizations, which operate under a "mix" of externally prescribed and internally generated formal rules. In Western societies the problem arises with such units as public schools, local units of political parties and trade unions, and local and regional governmental organizations. An example is a branch office of a public welfare agency studied by Peabody in 1959–1960. The relevant prescriptive documents included those of the three working units of the office, the district director's office, the county welfare department, the state government's Department of Social Welfare, and the U.S. Department of Health, Education, and Welfare, insofar as its agencies impose requirements for grants-in-aid to local welfare programs. (Peabody describes this structural hierarchy but not the prescriptive documents.[3]) Not all the formal documents that are applicable to an operating office of this kind will be available there; others will be in the state or county offices. On the other hand, copies of those which are most relevant to the day-to-day authority interactions in the welfare office are rather likely to be "at hand." Thus if the researcher is prepared to trust in the bureaucratic "rationality" of the system he is studying, the immediately available documents are informative not only about forms per se but about the importance and relevance of different kinds of formal prescriptions. Similarly, the researcher may find selective communication or reinforcement of some kinds of formal rules—say, in this example, by examining a year's file of directives from the district director to the case workers. Patterns revealed may be good evidence of the relative salience of authority norms, not merely of forms.

Generally, a good deal can be learned about authority patterns from the sophisticated examination of formal documents—especially if the examination extends beyond the founding, "constitutional" documents of an organization to its "enabling" regulations, those which specify its operations and the behavior of its members in detail. Instructive comparisons also can be made within and among cultures based on the analysis of forms; much of the traditional "institutional" school of comparative politics was concerned with such comparisons of constitutional documents. Comparisons of the forms of nongovernmental institutions across nations are much more rare; a notable exception is Janda's comparative study of the structure and activities (and other characteristics) of political parties in 50 countries.[4] Comparisons of the heterogeneity or homogeneity of institutional forms within nations are also uncommon; Eckstein has pointed out the formal homogeneity of organizational forms throughout Norwegian society, arguing that this homogeneity correlates with high political performance in that country.[5]

Finally, we should remark that some authority dimensions are intrinsically more likely than others to be the subject of formal prescription. The following generalizations apply particularly to governments and associational groups in modern and modernizing societies; formal prescriptions tend to be fewer in traditional, non-Western societies and in primary groups generally. Some dimensions, like Distance and Bases of Legitimacy, are by definition normative ones, hence can have no "forms." Others, like Concordance and Responsiveness, are characteristics of elite behavior whose formal prescription most *S*'s would resist. Still others, notably Recruitment, Directiveness, and Participation, are dimensions that *s*'s have historically pressured elites in Western societies to codify, although the formal prescriptions about them tend to be incomplete. Organizational structures (Conformation) and Decision-Rules are the dimensions most likely to be fully and formally prescribed. Our judgments about the dimensions and the documentary sources of their formal specifications are summarized in Table 9.1. The judgments are of course tentative and subject to exceptions among specific social units.

Evidence about Norms

We regard the norms of authority patterns to be both more important and less easily ascertainable than their forms. Historically, "forms" are codifications of some individual's or some group's norms about how a social unit ought to function; "norms" are the attitudes held by contemporary members of the social unit about how it ought to function. (We are not concerned here with the attitudes about a social unit held by people outside it.) Note that the phrase "how a social unit ought to function" refers to the full range of structures, behaviors, and perceptions specified in the analytic scheme. That is, some or all members have views about how a unit should be structured, how members and leaders should be selected, how they should regard one another, what the relationships between them ought to be, how decisions ought to be reached, what they should be about, and whether and how they should be implemented. Whereas "forms" are usually incompletely specified, a complex social unit will have norms about almost all aspects of all the dimensions. In this section we consider some operational problems posed by the heterogeneity of norms within a social unit, and some of the kinds of evidence that may be used to evaluate them.

Formal prescriptions are usually consistent: that is, we seldom find two contradictory sets of constitutional requirements about Participation or some other dimension. But there may be as many different normative positions in a unit as there are members. The extent to which unit members hold the same views about the desirability of a particular structure or behavior is an aspect of what we call *consonance*. Perfect normative agreement is unlikely. As expected, we found a distribution of responses to almost any normative question in every social unit we studied empirically. The two important descriptive and analytic questions concern (*a*) the range, means, and distributions of normative responses, and (*b*) the extent to which these differ among the unit's distinguishable strata and subpopulations. The hypothetical distributions in Figure 9.1 illustrate some significant differences. The norms of unit A's members, taken as a group, are relatively homogeneous, especially by comparison with those of unit B. The potential for overt disagreement and friction in B is hypothetically greater, depending on the salience of the norm for the group's activities. When we compare the norms of subordinates and superordinates, we see that the within-unit differences are more striking than those between units. In A, *s*'s and *S*'s have

Table 9.1 Formal Prescriptions of Authority Dimensions in Associational Groups

Dimension	Likely Extent of Formal Prescription	Types of Documents
Superordinate dimensions		
Conformation	High	Constitutional documents, regulations, organization charts
Decision-Rules	High	Constitutional documents; legislation and rules that assign decision-making powers and require consultation and approval
Decision-Behavior (Concordance)	Low/nonexistent	Regulations about cooperative interaction among subunits; procedures for mediating disputes between them
Influence dimensions		
Directiveness	Moderate to high	Constitutional documents, regulations, negotiated agreements reserving areas of subs activity from intervention by supers; regulations, procedures for sanctioning noncompliance
Participation	Moderate	Constitutional documents, negotiated agreements, regulations for legislative and advisory bodies, grievance procedures
Responsiveness	Low to moderate	Constitutional documents, agreements about *S*'s obligation to abide by legislative decisions or to submit grievances to arbitration
Compliance	Low	Compliance is generally assumed, not formally prescribed. Noncompliance is sometimes formally acknowledged and provided for (e.g., regulations granting rights to disregard or appeal directives, or specifying permissible levels of absenteeism, mistakes)
Inequality dimensions		
Distance, bases of distance	Not applicable	Normative dimensions only
Deportment and Proximity	Low	Regulations of personal conduct of *S*'s and *s*'s toward one another
Other dimensions		
Recruitment	Moderate to high	Constitutional documents; regulations on membership eligibility, elections; personnel selection and promotion procedures
Bases of Legitimacy	Not applicable	Normative only

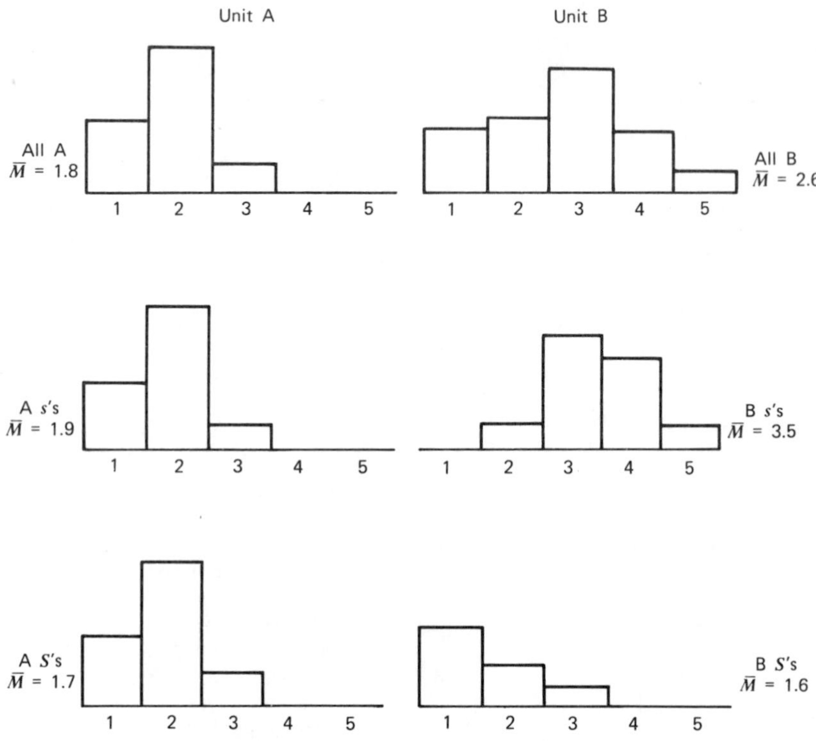

Fig. 9.1 Hypothetical distributions of authority norms in two social units. All = all members of the units, s = subordinate members of the units, S = superordinate members of the units.

maximally similar norms; they are *complementary*. In B they are sharply different and are potentially dysfunctional for the unit (again, depending on the norm's salience). Sharp normative dissonance on one dimension can be compromised or neutralized, of course, but means alone are uninformative: *a full description of group authority norms requires information on the distribution of normative positions within the group and its structural subsets.*

Another kind of operational and conceptual problem concerns what we variously called *official, dual,* or *situational* norms. Essentially, many respondents—and field researchers—commented on the applicability of alternative sets of norms to the same situation or condition. In some of these cases two "real" sets of norms seemed to be operative in people's minds: one applicable in one role or situation, a second in others.[6] It is not difficult to diagnose the general source of this problem. Many, probably most, people in complex modern societies have been exposed to diverse authority patterns and are aware that different expectations are operative in different situations, even within one unit. When we find substantial evidence that depending on the situation, two (or more) alternate sets of norms apply (alternative in the sense that the same individuals acknowledge the applicability of both), then both sets should be treated as applicable, however much it may complicate the researcher's description of "the"normative pattern in a social unit.

Another aspect of the "dual norm" problem is that some respondents, when asked to characterize "the" norms governing a particular authority practice in a unit, made an implicit or explicit distinction between "official" norms and their own. They might respond, "This is what one is supposed to do in this organization," or "That is what an (*S* or *s*) is expected to do." Or, in connection with practices, they might distinguish between the typical practice within the unit and their own. Our operational adjustment for such problems was straightforward: where possible, we asked respondents for separate characterizations of their own and others' norms and practices. Examples are given below.[7]

Interviewing and questionnaire techniques are generally used as the most direct and efficient means for assessing norms about authority. Peabody, for example, relied solely on these techniques to get information on norms about compliance and "acceptance of authority" in the organizations he studied.[8] They are not necessarily sufficient or accurate guides to norms, however, and triangulation using other kinds of evidence is necessary. The methodological approach suitable for interviews and questionnaires is to use such phrases as "should," "how adequate," and "how desirable." The following examples are from our fieldwork manuals; others appear in the next chapter:

"Are there any kinds of people you think should not become (*S*'s) in this organization?" (Recruitment)

"How desirable do you think that collective leadership bodies are, and to what extent do you prefer them to individual leadership?" (Decision-Behavior)[9]

These examples "personalize" the question: respondents are asked for their own norms. Given an adequate samples of strata members, we can estimate the actual distribution of normative positions. But if the researcher must rely on one or a few knowledgeable informants, the question should usually be generalized, as in the following example, to be asked of *S*'s:

"How do most (*S*'s of your own rank) feel about the kinds of restrictions there are on the new rules and policies they can make?

______ Most think there should be fewer restrictions.

______ Most think that things are all right the way they are.

______ Most think there should be more restrictions."

The rule of thumb is that when respondents are a "sample," personalized norm questions are best; when they are "informants," distributional questions should be used, supplemented when feasible by an inquiry about how subjects personally feel.

Some normative questions are "sensitive." Supers, for example, may be reluctant to admit that they would rather not respond to *s*'s efforts at participation. This is another situation in which a distributional question may be more appropriate than a personalized one. The assumption is that the subject will tend to give a truer account of his views on a sensitive issue if he can "bury" them in a group response. The following example, adapted from one used by Schonfeld in French schools,[10] permits teachers to characterize the norms of other teachers about Responsiveness rather precisely.

"Here is a list of five points of view that might be expressed by various teachers. How many of your fellow teachers hold each of these points of view? Check one answer for each statement.

Many	Some	Almost None	
_____	_____	_____	a. Teachers should ignore *all* attempts by students to influence them.
_____	_____	_____	b. Students occasionally have good ideas; when this occurs teachers should take into consideration the students' ideas.
_____	_____	_____	c. When teachers and students have different points of view, an attempt should *generally* be made to work out some sort of a compromise.
_____	_____	_____	d. In case of conflict between the views of students and teachers, important concessions should always be made to the students' point of view.
_____	_____	_____	e. Students should always be consulted about decisions which are to be made and the teachers should generally be guided by their wishes."

In some instances—but not as a general prescription—we suggested the use of "cross-checking" questions about "sensitive" norms and practices. For example, *s*'s might be asked what they thought their *S*'s norms were about Responsiveness to *s*-inputs, and the results compared with *S*'s own statements. When such questions reveal discrepancies, they raise interpretative problems. Are the *S*'s dissembling, or do the *s*'s misperceive them? Only careful observation is likely to provide a satisfactory answer. In either case, though, we may interpret the discrepancy as evidence of normative dissonance within the unit.

Some of the limitations of interview and questionnaire responses as reliable sources of information on authority norms have already been suggested. Moreover, some people in some situations and societies consistently dissemble or tell the outsider what they think he wants to hear. And norms about some behaviors may be so sensitive that direct questions cannot be asked about them. We therefore recommend the use of both observational cues and documentary sources to cross-check and supplement interview and questionnaire data.

Observational cues about norms are generally verbal and are likely to be suggestive rather than definitive. Praise or condemnation of unit members by other members can be especially revealing. Those who are identified as paragons by their peers and hierarchical opposites are worth careful observation. In fact, inquiries about especially praiseworthy *s*'s and *S*'s, and the reasons for such esteem, may be more informative about norms than more direct questions. Conversely, judgments that particular *s*'s or *S*'s "are doing a poor job" or that "something is wrong with that lot" are invitations to close observation and conversation about how and why the subjects are deviant. The catch to all this, of course, is that the normative standards that justify praise and condemnation may have little to do with authority behavior.

Interactions of *S*'s with *s*'s in which demands are made or criticisms expressed can also be informative about norms and normative dissonance. The researcher should be especially alert to the statements "we've always done it that way," "that's how it is supposed to be done," and their functional equivalents. But it often happens that *S*'s who exhort their *s*'s are expressing forms rather than what they themselves regard as the norms: American university professors often stipulate deadlines for student papers when in fact they hold the norm that "anytime before grades are due is okay." It also is common for *s*'s to criticize and make demands on *S*'s not on the basis of norms but simply to increase their value satisfactions.

The threat or invocation of negative sanctions is usually a strong indication that norms are being violated, hence is indirect evidence of the norms themselves. The researcher may be able to observe disciplinary actions directly, or he may obtain access to organizational records about them. But again there are cautions to be kept in mind about using negative sanctions alone as a clue to norms. And some behavior that *is* normatively proper may be subject to penalty because of the existence of dual normative standards, the idiosyncrasies of a particular *S*, or a sporadic attempt to enforce forms otherwise ignored. Probably the most serious drawback to using negative sanctions as a systematic clue to normative violations is that sanction thresholds are often so high that a great deal of deviant behavior can occur before sanctions are used or even mentioned. This is especially likely in voluntary organizations, in which positive sanctions are more functional than negative ones in keeping membership. "The carrot not the whip" is in some places a societal or subcultural style: Lois Wasserspring observed that this is characteristic of student-teacher authority patterns in the Mexican secondary schools she studied. In such units and societies, we cannot simply reverse the observational equation and say that unrewarded behaviors are contrary to the norms: in most units and societies normative behavior goes without (visible) reward most of the time.

Documents occasionally provide useful information about norms. Organizational records about "violations" and sanctions were mentioned earlier. Anecdotal accounts, correspondence and complaint files, records of meetings dealing with matters of organizational strategy or housekeeping, and memos that dispute or ask for changes in directives all may contain evidence of norms. Memoirs, diaries, and even fictional accounts of an organization may also contain such information. Most of this information will be "from the top looking down," though; it is likely to reflect the authority norms of *S*'s not *s*'s. Overt sabotage, rebellion, or sudden loss of membership may be the only documentary evidence that *s*'s norms have been seriously violated. Two other points need making about documentary evidence. First, the documentary sources are "low-grade ore"; much material usually needs to be processed to gain modest amounts of information. Second, the norms of historical social units are therefore largely unknown and not directly knowable. Ordinarily they must be inferred from the intersection of evidence about formal prescriptions and reports of actual behavior.

The Practice of Authority

Authority practices are what members of social units actually think and do in their roles as *s*'s or *S*'s. Supers who acknowledge that subs deserve a measure of respect may in fact despise them; the difference is that between the norm and the practice of Distance. Subs may strongly affirm the desirability of participating in decision making but in fact fail to use most of the channels open to them; the difference is that between the norms and the practice of Participation. As with norms, there is always a range of variation in authority practices among individuals within a social unit, and often situational variation in individuals' behavior. The same descriptive problems therefore arise. A full characterization of authority practices requires us to examine the distribution of practices within the unit as a whole, among its significant strata and segments, and by important or modal individuals over time, in different situations.

Observation is the ideal source of information about "behavioral" authority practices. These include all of the dimensions except Distance and Bases of Legitimacy. The latter two are attitudinal dimensions by definition, for which observation can suggest only clues. The practices of Concordance, for example, can best be determined by observing the interactions of *S*'s in a variety of decision-making and conflict situations. The extent of subs' Compliance with directives is ascertainable with least bias by the participant observer who can watch, day in and day out, what his co-workers do and fail to do. The practical difficulties are obvious: few researchers have the time or opportunity for long-term observation of authority practices even in one segment of a social unit, much less all of them. Thus it is not only useful but usually necessary to rely on other types of evidence. It remains highly desirable for the researcher to observe a sample of authority interactions in a unit, to acquire a "feel" for its activities, to ask sensible questions in interviews and questionnaires, and to cross-check information gathered from other sources.

The more complex a social unit and the less time available for studying it, the more the researcher must rely on interviewing and questionnaire methods to assess authority practices. The appropriate questions are descriptive (i.e., they ask people to characterize reality). Here, as with the normative questions, we can ask the respondent to tell us either what his own practices are or what the practices of people in his group are. Our recommended procedures are similar to those proposed for norms. If information can be obtained from numerous respondents in the same stratum, they should be asked to describe their own practices, subject to several qualifications. If respondents can or must be relied on to provide information about others' actions, they should be asked about the relative frequency of the behaviors in question. The latter approach is also suggested for "sensitive" subjects and for behavior that is distinctively collective. Two illustrative sets of questions about Decision-Behavior are given below; the first is designed for self-characterization, the second for describing group behavior.[11]

"Some (*S*'s) often consult with their colleagues while others prefer to rely mostly on their own judgment. Under what circumstances, if any, would you want to consult with others? For each of the following questions, please specify the alternative which you think reflects best the way you would act.

(*a*) certainly would consult (*b*) probably would consult (*c*) probably would not consult (*d*) certainly would not consult

a b c d Would you consult those (*S*'s) who would be affected by an important decision that you must make?

a b c d Would you consult other (*S*'s) on those occasions when you must make a decision and are not sure which course of action is the right one?

a b c d Would you consult other (*S*'s) on those occasions when you plan to make a proposal at a formal meeting but have no idea what will be the reaction of the other members?

a b c d Would you consult other (*S*'s) before a formal meeting to line up their support, if possible, for proposals that you plan to make?

a b c d Would you consult with other (*S*'s) about matters which are your own responsibility and about which the others have no particular competence?"

The question is worded as it would be on a questionnaire form. For interviews it would be presented in a somewhat less structured way. The following example was designed specifically for interview use.

"Suppose that one or more of your colleagues proposed a course of action about which he (they) seemed to *feel strongly,* while others *felt strongly* that the proposal was wrong or was against their own interests. Such disagreements probably occur among any group of colleagues. I would like to know, if you care to tell me, how such cases are likely to be handled here. It would be helpful for me to have examples.

Sometimes people try to avoid conflicts in such situations by *not raising their objections* or *by dropping the proposal* if strong objections are raised, for the sake of harmony in the (unit). How often does this happen here, if ever? Would you say ______ usually, ______ sometimes, ______ seldom, or ______ almost never?"

(This option is followed by a series of similar questions about other possible responses to *S*-conflict.)

Field researchers often suspected and sometimes were convinced that respondents dissembled in their answers to such questions. This was especially likely for "sensitive" aspects of authority patterns, in which "idealized practices" (norms) were more likely to be reported than real practices. We recommended and used several techniques to deal with such difficulties. One was observation, though ordinarily only spot checks were possible. A more effective technique was to ask *s*'s what *S*-practices were, and vice versa, on the same or corresponding dimensions. What the results might be is suggested by a Norwegian study in which parents and children were separately asked about whether they resorted to/received physical punishment; children reported being punished considerably more than parents' self-reports would indicate.[12] Such discrepancies raise questions about which set of responses is the more accurate. If *S*'s dissemble about their extent to punitiveness, *s*'s may exaggerate it. And if *s*'s underreport their noncompliance for fear of retribution, it may be that *S*'s do the same thing because they do not wish to acknowledge problems within the unit. But it generally is likely that real practices lie somewhere between two contrasting sets of self-reports.

Evasion in interviews was also reduced by having the interviewer illustrate his question with a specific example of the behavior in question. An *S*, when asked the foregoing question about conflict avoidance in decision making, might answer "sometimes." The well-informed interviewer could then refer to a real situation in which the situation was quite different and ask specifically about it. The technique should be used carefully and in moderation, because an interview can be "blown" if the respondent feels that he has been directly challenged. Philip Goldman's experience with the technique in interviews with Dutch administrators, though, suggests that respondents are likely to be more frank with researchers who prove themselves knowledgeable about affairs in the social unit. Alan Zuckerman similarly found that in a second round of interviews with officials of the Italian Christian Democrat Party he was able to discuss questions about party factions in the government in extremely frank terms by convincing the party members, through his comments and questions, that he was closely familiar with the subject.

All the examples just given concern authority behavior. Distance and Bases of Legitimacy are defined as attitudinal dimensions, hence have no direct behavioral manifestations. In the case of Distance we can distinguish between norms about how people should regard *s*'s and *S*'s, and the ways in which *s*'s and *S*'s actually regard each other: the latter are "practices." Our measures of Bases of Legitimacy required interviews or questionnaires, but it is possible to infer something about *s*'s legitimacy notions and how seriously they are violated, from the pattern of Compliance practices in a unit.

There also are documentary sources, sometimes quite good ones, about authority practices. If we are studying "public" units like governments and some political parties and trade unions, there are often records of authority practices among the superordinate strata. We refer to the debates and votes of legislative bodies, the actions of executives vis-à-vis their immediate subordinates and legislative bodies, reports of auditing agencies, internal studies of bureaucratic organization and "delivery systems," and hearings and findings of commissions of inquiry, administrative courts, and public trials. The Watergate investigations and trials, for example, have provided a windfall of information on authority relations in the Office of the President during the Nixon administration. These are the traditional sources of comparative political studies, for contemporary and historical governments and political parties. But we can expect these sources to provide information on only some authority practices, mainly within the upper strata of relatively few—albeit important—organizations. There are other, less obvious documentary sources for other aspects of authority practices. We can infer something about "Distance" from the differentials in pay, perquisites, working conditions, and life styles of different sub and super strata: pay and perquisites are usually matters of record. Directiveness practices can be indirectly inferred from the detail and comprehensiveness of a unit's codes, regulations, and directives; it can be more directly assessed from records of punitive actions. The same records, along with information on "performance"—attendance, productivity, output records—are instructive about

Compliance. The extent and nature of Participation can be partly estimated from complaint files and voting and meeting attendance records. Recruitment practices are probably determined more fully and accurately from (*a*) personnel selection and promotion records and/or (*b*) studies of supers' characteristics and career patterns than from any other sources. The actual structures of complex organizations—the practices of Conformation—are ascertained by examining who works with whom, who clears what with or without whom, and who directs whom to do what, not by examining organization charts. Superordinate practices of Responsiveness, Concordance, and Decision-Behavior are partly revealed in records (memos, transcripts, voting records) about how specific decisions were made.

These examples are of organizational or "public" records. Depending on the social unit, there may be many other kinds of information as well. Additional primary sources include the memoirs and diaries of unit members. Secondary sources include academic and journalistic accounts. Fiction constitutes a "tertiary" source of a kind that may be considerably more revealing about practices at the *s*- and lower *S*-levels than primary and secondary sources, which more often focus on the top *S*-levels. For example, a rather full characterization of authority practices in English public schools before World War I is provided by Rupert Wilkinson's study *The Prefects,*[13] which draws largely on biographies of "old boys" and various secondary studies.

Complementary Techniques

We have considered in some detail the relative merits of observation, interviewing, and documentary analysis for assessing the forms, norms, and practices of authority. Here we summarize and suggest some of the advantages and limitations of each of a number of techniques, drawing on our experiences in the Workshop.

Observation, Participant and Otherwise

Systematic observation by someone who is accepted at least temporarily as a member of the social unit under study potentially provides more intensive understanding of its authority patterns than any other technique. The personal views and practices of the observer's intimates are likely to be more fully understood than they could be by any external observer. The significance of subtle cues will be better appreciated—and subtle cues about authority may be crucial to its understanding, especially in more egalitarian social units. The range of permissible and impermissible behaviors, and changes in norms and practices over time, also will probably be understood more precisely by the participant observer than any other researcher. These advantages are predicated on the assumption that the observer is really making systematic, self-conscious observations using explicit, standard guidelines. Otherwise his observations have similar status to those of the writer of "Reminiscences of an Indian Police Official."

Field researchers rarely have the time or opportunity to become fully participant observers of social units in other cultures. But many of the same advantages of participant observation accrue to the outsider who carefully watches the behavior of unit members as they go about their regular tasks.[14] The evident drawback of observation is the tendency of the researcher studying authority patterns to trade away breadth of information for depth. Usually he can observe firsthand only a segment of a unit's activities. That information will be highly valuable if the "segment" is the top echelon of *S*'s and nearly as important if the segment is farther down the hierarchy but known to be "typical" of many others. Access to the first is usually difficult, however, and the "typicality" of a segment is seldom known without broad-gauged research.

A second difficulty associated with observation is that the observer is rarely anonymous. Those he is observing probably know or suspect his purpose and may alter their behavior accordingly. The reliability of observation, in short, is always problematic to a degree.

Whatever the limitations in breadth of direct observation, we have a strong methodological preference for its use in conjunction with others whenever possible. Fully *participant* observation may be out of the question in most field research on authority patterns; but some more-than-casual observation is usually possible. One of the most serious "access" problems in the Workshop's experience came in Tunisia: Donald Newman spent a year in the field before receiving approval to observe school classrooms; but in the process of seeking that permission, he became all too intimately familiar with the authority practices of Tunisian educational administrators. In the more open societies of Northern Europe, some Workshop members were able to observe classroom behavior systematically, over a longer period of time. Robert Friedman did this in Sweden, using a standardized form to record the nature and frequency of different authority interactions. In France William Schonfeld had the good fortune to be completing an intensive study of students enrolled in the elite *Ecole Nationale d'Administration* (ENA) at the time of the May 1968 "revolution"; he was able to stay on during the weeks of crisis as a fully accepted observer.[15] In England, a few years earlier, Eckstein was engaged in an intensive observational study of a regional hospital board; he acquired such expertise, in the eyes of the board members, that he was asked to register his vote on one issue being considered.[16] Our general precept is that when there are no serious obstacles to observation of authority patterns, it is indefensible for a scholar not to carry out observation.

There also is a kind of "surrogate observation" option that may be feasible even for historical or closed contemporary units. Memoirs and novels about an organization or society represent the observations of their authors, albeit with some degree of distortion. "Triangulation" using a number of such sources may provide information of greater scope and almost as much reliability as firsthand observation.

Surveys and Interviews

National surveys may be useful for determining general attitudes toward authority and also for ascertaining how citizens think and act as *s*'s in the national political system. But national surveys are not likely to be particularly informative about the authority patterns of particular social units; except possibly families. Since we are concerned with the authority patterns of particular social units, these are best studied *in situ*. Within social units we are especially interested in authoritative interactions, which means that the hierarchic and functional positions of respondents are much more important considerations than their "representativeness" in a purely probabilistic sense. Generally, the closer an individual is to the top of the hierarchy of a social unit, and the more typical his *role* at whatever level, the more probably we shall choose him as a subject. The sampling techniques used in survey research are applicable for authority studies mainly when we want to characterize the norms and practices of a large-*n* stratum of *s*'s, like secondary school students or rank-and-file party members.[17]

The interviewing techniques of survey research are more applicable to authority studies than are its sampling techniques. We recommended and used a combination of interview and questionnaire techniques in our fieldwork. An ideal-typical interview and questionnaire schedule, prepared in advance of fieldwork, was substantially modified to fit different field settings. Field researchers usually began their work in a unit by seeking informal discussions with a few "informants" about the nature of the unit and its authority patterns. Subsequent, more formal interviewing made use of some version of common interview schedules. Researchers can have others conduct interviews for them too, but this requires a thoroughly pretested interview schedule and well-trained interviewers. In his study of Swedish schools, Friedman trained 30 high-school sociology students to carry out interviews with parents (not their own) who had already indicated their cooperativeness by filling out questionnaires (see below).

A general principle governing interviewing in fieldwork was that the more knowledgeable and articulate the (set of) subjects, the greater the reliance on open-ended interview questions. A flexible interview schedule is especially appropriate for higher *S*'s, partly because they are sometimes inclined to be resentful of the constraints of a tight interview schedule. However, Alan Zuckerman found that Italian political party officials were quite responsive to highly structured interviews and so cooperative that they usually permitted the sessions to be tape recorded. Since the view "from the bottom up" can be even more revealing than that "from the top down," open-ended interview techniques were recommended and used for some *s*'s also. Parenthetically, problems of lack of interest by respondents or "no response" proved in our fieldwork to be less serious than in conventional survey research. People generally, across the diverse cultures we studied, seem to have clear views and strong opinions about many of the aspects of the authority patterns in which they work and live, once they overcome reluctance to discuss the subject with outsiders.

The retrospective interview provides a way of overcoming the time-bound nature of most information gathered in fieldwork. That is, older and former members of a unit can be asked to describe it as it was in some past era. The technique serves in historical research but has been used only occasionally and incidentally in our fieldwork thus far. It is probably more reliable when anchored to the present, by asking how attitudes and practices around, say, 1940 differed from those prevalent now. Responses will no doubt be inaccurate to some degree, on two grounds: faulty and self-serving memory, and a tendency to report things as they should have been (norms) rather than as they were—the same human disposition that has created legends of "Golden Ages." Retrospective interviews are nonetheless a valuable, independent source of information which can be used to check and supplement historical accounts.

Questionnaires

Questionnaires, compared with interviews, have the potential advantage of efficiency but at the occasional cost of respondent comprehension and the certain loss of opportunity to follow up responses with probes. Questionnaires were most often used in Workshop fieldwork when researchers had access to large, "captive" groups of *s*'s—for example, students and workers. For use in French secondary schools, William Schonfeld devised a "group interview" technique that combined the efficiency of the questionnaire with some of the advantages of interviewing: a class of students was given a questionnaire in the presence of the researcher, who explained its purpose, read the questions aloud, and answered queries about their meaning; the students then recorded their responses. Schonfeld also sent questionnaires to teachers in some of the 13 schools he studied, but only after his presence and purposes in the school were generally known; this, plus his use of a "reminder" procedure for nonrespondents, ensured a relatively high rate of return.

Questionnaires also can be used for *s*- and *S*-level respondents to whom the researcher has no direct access, and some Workshop members had no better alternatives. In Spain, Joel Prager could not have access to secondary school students directly, and he entrusted questionnaires to Spanish nationals who said that they would administer the instruments on the behalf of the investigator. The individuals so deputized failed to honor the agreement, however, thus illustrating a possible drawback of questionnaire research. In Colombia, Rafael Rivas mailed a questionnaire to a widely dispersed group of *S*'s: local and regional officials of the Liberal and Conservative parties, plus members of Congress. The returns were low—less than one-fifth—and of very questionable representativeness. In Italy, Alan Zuckerman had mixed results with questionnaires. A general mailing to party members yielded low returns. On the other hand, a few party officials who were to be interviewed could not meet with the investigator but were quite willing to write their answers to questions submitted in writing.[18] In the much different cultural setting of Sweden, Robert Friedman gave school children questionnaires about family characteristics, to be filled out by the parents. The questions were mostly but not entirely nonsensitive, and the response rate approached 80%. The technique seems to be a good one for acquiring information on families because of parents' typical disposition to help out children in school.

Interviews are generally preferable to questionnaires for securing information on authority patterns, but there are many exceptions, not only "practical" ones of efficiency and large *n*'s but also, in some settings, because they guarantee anonymity to the respondents. Note in particular that the attempts to use questionnaires by Workshop members were successful or not because of cultural, situational, and idiosyncratic factors, not because of intrinsic characteristics of the questionnaire. People in some cultures are compulsive about filling in forms, people in others are thoroughly indifferent. Obviously it helps if the respondents accept the credibility of the researcher and his objectives, but that is not always easily conveyed nor a guarantee of success.

The foregoing comments apply to studies initiated by the researcher investigating authority patterns. He may also locate relevant material for secondary analysis in others' surveys and questionnaire or interview studies. In Spain, Joel Prager found many national and regional surveys including questions that tapped general authority norms. Robert Friedman discovered that the following questions had been included in a survey of the provincial Swedish city where he studied school and family authority patterns; the responses provide information on Participation, Concordance, and Bases of Legitimacy for local government:

"How great are the possibilities for citizens to take issues to their councilmen and have them considered?" (Participation)

"Are you acquainted with any of the councilmen?" (Participation)

"Are councilmen always in agreement, or are they often in disagreement?" (Concordance)

"Are they obliged to reach agreement?" (Concordance)

"Many jobs are now done by nonelected officials that once were done by elected officials. Is this an advantage, disadvantage, or not important?" (Bases of Legitimacy)

Such studies are more likely to deal with citizens' relations to political authority than with authority patterns in nongovernmental units.

One other, distinctive kind of questionnaire, used occasionally in Workshop fieldwork, is the "self-questionnaire." That is, the investigator uses an open-ended questionnaire schedule to summarize his evaluation of a unit after a period of observation or open-ended interviews with its members. Such an exercise serves more than a recording function: it requires the investigator to do some role playing, which often helps sharpen his understanding of the unit and sensitizes him to the blind spots in his knowledge of it.

Content and Documentary Analysis

In the first part of this chapter, and in the next one, numerous suggestions and hypothetical illustrations are offered about the use of content and documentary analysis for information on authority dimensions. Little use of them was made during field research by Workshop members, for the rather good reason that documentary analysis seems to be a waste of time when one is surrounded by living evidence and voluble informants. Some pre- and postfieldwork documentary analysis was performed, however, in addition to the ordinary background reading that is part of any field research study. A number of book-length studies of social units were systematically evaluated by Workshop members for information on the authority patterns of social units as diverse as French nationalized industries (using Crozier's *The Bureaucratic Phenomenon*), Mexican rural families (on the basis of Lewis' *Life in a Mexican Village*), and villages in the traditional African kingdom of Buganda (from Fallers' *The King's Men*).[19] These were mainly intended as "feasiblity tests" of the analytic scheme, but the approach could fruitfully be extended to the analysis of any historical or contemporary social unit about which there is a substantial monographic literature. The Christian Democratic Party of Italy, for example, has been studied sufficiently to permit such analysis of its authority patterns.

Documentary analysis was used by Eckstein as part of his 1966 study of Norwegian authority patterns. He collected a sample of "constitutional" documents of diverse public and private organizations. Comparison of them revealed a remarkable similarity, which supported, at the level of "forms," one of the central arguments of his "congruence" theory about the determinants of political performance.[20]

Quite a different kind of content analysis was attempted by Ronald Rogowski to supplement his field research on West German political parties.[21] Proceedings of the Social Democrats' 1969 party congress were subject to a "General Inquirer" tabulation of authority-related concepts. The results were not very informative in and of themselves, but comparison with analyses of proceedings of other German party congresses, past and present, might be quite instructive both for descriptive purposes and to test hypotheses about changes over time in German political culture.

Another, much different kind of documentary analysis of authority is used in Gurr's historical study of authority characteristics of national political systems, 1800 to 1971. A variety of historical and a few journalistic sources were used to code the basic characteristics of each successive pattern of political authority—each "polity"—in some 90 nation-states. The coding categories were broadly defined and referred to only the most salient dimensions of authority, because for many eras and countries there was not enough information for more detailed assessment. Although for polities that have been more fully studied, much more complete descriptions could be made, we want to emphasize here that the "polity persistence" study offers evidence that our analytic scheme can be applied systematically to the traditional stuff of comparative political institutions.[22]

Semiprojective and Experimental Techniques

Other techniques, not yet used by the authors or members of the Workshop, are potentially applicable to the study of authority relations. Semiprojective testing has been successfully employed by Greenstein and Tarrow to elicit comparative information on children's political orientations: interactions between two authority figures are described or portrayed in part, and the respondents are asked to describe what else they think will happen. The coded responses for French, English, and American children reveal many juvenile attitudes toward political figures.[23] Modifications of the technique could provide much normative information about authority patterns among adults as well as children. It could be especially useful in cultures and settings in which conventional interview schedules elicit evasive or politely false responses, or none at all.

Simulated authority situations could be used to obtain some kinds of authority information, following either of two strategies. Subjects could be placed in familiar roles and their situations, *s*'s and *S*'s, varied to clarify their authority practices in circumstances that might not ordinarily be observable. But there are relatively few cultures and settings in which such an approach seems both economical and feasible. The second strategy is to train subjects in the roles of *s*'s and *S*'s as determined a priori, from fieldwork or in historical studies, then to manipulate situations or parameters and compare the responses to those deduced from theory or observed in the real world. This is, of course, an application of a common kind of simulation to authority analysis.

A Strategy for Intensive Field Research

We have discussed research techniques analytically and separately thus far. In actual fieldwork, though, the researcher is likely to use a number of approaches in sequential and complementary fashion. The "intensive" strategy we recommend is essentially a systematization of the procedures that scholars have long used when studying a single social or political entity.

Before beginning fieldwork, the researcher immerses himself or herself in available information about the entity to be studied. The object is to gain a general understanding of its primary functions; the identity of its principal divisions, strata, and members; and how it is linked to other social entities. Some documentary analysis is possible at this juncture, especially of the forms of authority relations, but this is mainly for "familiarization," not an occasion for systematic research.

In the second phase the researcher attempts to achieve full working knowledge of the entity. He needs to find out enough about its detailed structure, and how its members and subgroups interact with one another, to permit him to ask relevant and intelligible questions. This is best accomplished by firsthand observation of the unit, but observation alone scarcely suffices: it should be complemented by unstructured or semistructured interviews with knowledgeable informants, and continued reading. Structured interviews and questionnaires are developed and tried out at this stage, but not yet widely administered. Depending on the researcher's sensitivities and access, he may conclude this stage with the feeling that he "understands" the unit very well, regarding the remainder of his work as largely a matter of ratifying his hunches.

The premature certitudes of the second stage usually give way to recognition, in the third stage, that things often are not what they seem. Apparently simple statements and actions often prove to have hidden or secondary meanings. Once the researcher has acquired the sensitivities to read such cues and understand latent meanings, he is ready for the final, intensive round of information gathering: structured observation, systematic interviews, and the administration of questionnaires. It is also true that the longer the researcher stays in a unit, the more likely he is to see how the unit is affected by crises and change; authority patterns under stress may be quite different than in normal times.

The fourth stage, if all goes well, is one of analysis, reflection, and synthesis of the findings. Indeed in the final phases of fieldwork the researcher often becomes an information-gathering automaton with little occasion to see or reflect on the larger patterns and relationships inherent in the data. Therefore the postfieldwork analysis and written synthesis is often the most intellectually challenging and rewarding part of the research process.

This idealized description of one type of research on authority patterns is not far removed from the experiences of a number of members of the Workshop. There also are equivalent stages in the research process for scholars who cannot have personal access to the social entities they are studying. If the secondary accounts and documentary materials are good enough, the same basic sequence of familiarization, sensitization, data collection, and analysis can be followed.

Conclusion

It should be evident beyond doubt that no one technique or methodology is peculiarly appropriate to the study of authority relations. One of our main contentions has been that only a variety of methods and information sources will provide the "triangulation" necessary to a full and reliable description of any social entity's authority patterns. Methodological pluralism may seem so "obviously" required for the subject that it warrants no special emphasis. Still, other subjects of inquiry in political science have become unduly limited by methodological monism. Historically, the comparative study of national political institutions has become so identified with formal-legal analysis, in the minds of both its practitioners and critics, that it is still in disrepute. At present we can point to the virtual identity assumed between survey research as a method and "public opinion" and "political culture" as subjects for systematic inquiry. We regard authority patterns as a subject of study that is and should remain independent of any single technique, and we hope that we have persuaded readers of the sensibility of that view.

Although we eschew emphasis on any one research technique, we recommend one research strategy over others: the intensive analysis of one or a few units is preferable to broad and shallow comparative studies. The reason is simply that there are very few detailed morphological and physiological studies of the authority patterns of most kinds of social and political units, whereas there are quite a number of partial and superficial descriptions, and most of these employ some version of the democratic-autocratic dichotomy. One of many consequences of our ignorance about the details of authority patterns is our lack of evidence even for the common assumption that there is a regular association between the prominent features of authority patterns observed in macro-studies and the diversity of relations that becomes evident on closer inspection. A case in point is the unresolved argument about the effective differences, if any, in political participation between autocratic polities (at least some of which seem to have a considerable volume of influential Participation) and plural democracies (in which the more visible and routinized forms of political Participation often meet little Responsiveness). The whole may be greater than or different from the sum of its parts, but until more of the parts have been carefully studied, we scarcely are in a position to say.

Notes

1. An example is Sir Thomas Erskine May's compilation of the rules of the House of Commons, *Treatise on the Law, Privileges, Proceedings and Usage of Parliament* (first published 1844; 16th ed., 1957.)

2. On France see Michel Crozier, *The Bureaucratic Phenomenon* (Chicago: University of Chicago Press, 1964) and William R. Schonfeld, *Youth and Authority in France* (Beverly Hills, Calif.: Sage Professional Papers in Comparative Politics, 01-014, 1971). On Germany see Herbert Spiro, *Government by Constitution* (New York: Random House, 1959), esp. Ch. 15.

3. Robert L. Peabody, *Organizational Authority: Superior-Subordinate Relationships in Three Public Service Organizations* (New York: Atherton Press, 1964), pp. 68–69.

4. See Kenneth Janda, *A Conceptual Framework for the Comparative Analysis of Political Parties* (Beverly Hills, Calif.: Sage Professional Papers in Comparative Politics, 01-002, 1970), and Janda, *Comparative Political Parties: A Cross-National Handbook* (New York: Free Press, forthcoming).

5. Harry Eckstein, *Division and Cohesion in Democracy* (Princeton, N.J.: Princeton University Press, 1966), Ch. 8.

6. For a case study of dual orientations toward Compliance among French students see Schonfeld, *Youth and Authority in France.*

7. Some of the foregoing and following discussion is drawn from "Distribution of Responses on Continua," prepared at the Workshop Conference, January 1968, by Robert Friedman, Ted Gurr, Ronald Rogowski, and Lois Wasserspring.

8. Peabody, *Organizational Authority, passim.*

9. Most of the examples of interview and questionnaire items given here and subsequently are adapted from a general schedule developed in the early stages of Workshop fieldwork. This schedule was explicitly "paradigmatic": the questions had to be pretested and made relevant to each culture and social unit by field researchers.

10. William R. Schonfeld, *Authority in France: A Model of Political Behavior Drawn from Case Studies in Education* (Ph.D. dissertation, Department of Politics, Princeton University, 1970).

11. The first is from a working document, "Revised Concordance Continua and Questions," prepared at the Workshop's 1968 Conference by Robert Friedman and

Philip Goldman for use in their fieldwork in Sweden and the Netherlands, respectively.

12. Thomas D. Eliot et al., *Norway's Families* (Philadelphia: University of Pennsylvania Press, 1960).

13. Rupert Wilkinson, *The Prefects: British Leadership and the Public School Tradition* (London: Oxford University Press, 1964).

14. Two basic references on simple and structured observation are Claire Selltiz et al., *Research Methods in Social Relations*, rev. ed. (New York: Holt, Rinehart & Winston, 1959), Ch. 6, and Eugene J. Webb et al., *Unobtrusive Measures: Nonreactive Research in the Social Sciences* (Skokie, Ill.: Rand-McNally, 1966).

15. Schonfeld, *Authority in France*, Chs. 4 and 5.

16. Harry Eckstein, *The English Health Service* (Cambridge, Mass.: Harvard University Press, 1958).

17. All information we obtain about authority relations is a sample in the sense that it is selective rather than comprehensive. However, there are some but relatively few circumstances in which the researcher will have both occasion and opportunity to draw a probability sample of units, people, behaviors, or documents. The fundamental purpose of sampling theory and procedures is to ensure that reliable generalizations can be made from a sample to some larger population. Hence they are applicable in studies of authority relations whenever we want to generalize about, say, large numbers of similar schools, documents, or subordinates. In other instances, including most case studies, the researcher must rely on other means of assessing the reliability of his information—and triangulation is our principal means to that end.

18. Professor Zuckerman suggests (personal communication) that the return may have been low less because of the Italians' disinclination to respond to questionnaires than because most rank-and-file Christian Democrats are party members in name only, hence have little or no experience or interest in their nominal role as subordinates to party officials. Also see Alan S. Zuckerman, *Hierarchal Social Division and Political Groups: Factions in the Italian Christian Democratic Party* (Ph.D. dissertation, Department of Politics, Princeton University, 1971).

19. Crozier, *The Bureaucratic Phenomenon;* Oscar Lewis, *Life in a Mexican Village: Tepoztlan Restudied* (Urbana: University of Illinois Press, 1951); L. A. Fallers, Ed., *The King's Men: Leadership and Status in Buganda on the Eve of Independence* (London: Oxford University Press, 1964).

20. Eckstein, *Division and Cohesion in Democracy*, Ch. 8.

21. Ronald Rogowski, *Social Structure and Stable Rule: The German Case* (Ph.D. dissertation, Department of Politics, Princeton University, 1971).

22. Ted Robert Gurr, "Persistence and Change in Political Systems, 1800 to 1971," *American Political Science Review*, Vol. 69 (December 1974), pp. 1482–1504.

23. Fred I. Greenstein and Sidney Tarrow, *Political Orientations of Children: The Use of a Semi-Projective Technique in Three Nations* (Beverly Hills, Calif.: Sage Professional Papers in Comparative Politics, 01-009, 1970).

CHAPTER TEN

The Study of Influence: Sample Guidelines for Field Research

Thus far we have presented general maxims to guide empirical inquiry into authority patterns: some plain common sense, others not; all based on experience in a variety of social units in various cultures, successful and unsuccessful. The general maxims must, of course, be translated into specific research procedures for each dimension of authority, and each dimension poses certain special problems of observation and measurement. Early in our research into authority relations we therefore developed extensive "fieldwork manuals" for each dimension and subdimension; subsequently these were revised in light of experience and further reflection. Each manual covered conceptual matters, suggested pertinent sources of information, listed items for interview schedules and questionnaires (and usually rationales for them), and outlined methods of numerical scoring for aggregating and comparing findings.

As a sample of the manuals, we have selected those for the four influence dimensions: Directiveness, Participation, Responsiveness, and Compliance. The discussions expand the relatively brief treatment of the dimensions in Part II, though there is also some unavoidable repetition of basic conceptual points. The other dimensions were treated somewhat more fully in Part II, precisely because detailed guidelines for research into them are omitted here (though available).

Readers who want only a general sense of how research into authority patterns can proceed may simply want to skim or skip this detailed chapter. The manuals should have considerable value, however, for those who seek guidance in planning their own empirical work.

Note that we have reduced citations to a minimum by using names and dates only (e.g., Schonfeld, 1971) when referring to work by participants in the Workshop. Full citations to such work are given elsewhere in this book (see Preface).

Directiveness[1]

We have defined directiveness as "the extent to which activities in a social unit are . . . subject to directives, rather than being left to the free discretion of members." Since activities within units are varied and all not equally subject to regulation, we distinguish six *domains* of unit activities. An exhaustive operational treatment of Directiveness will consider four subdimensions in each of these domains: the extent to which it is subject to regulation of any kind (*Coverage*), the detail with which activities within a "covered" domain are prescribed (*Latitude*), the extent to which regulated activities are supervised (*Supervision*), and the threshold at which sanctions are invoked against noncompliant actions (*Sanction threshold*).

The relationships among the six domains and four subdimensions of Directiveness are shown graphically in Figure 10.1. The outer circle A represents everything that is done within the unit: for the individual, it symbolizes all the time he or she spends as a member. The six domains are represented as pie-shaped wedges of unit activity. Circle B represents Coverage, which is "comprehensive" to the extent that everything done within the unit is subject to regulation. Members' freedom of action is

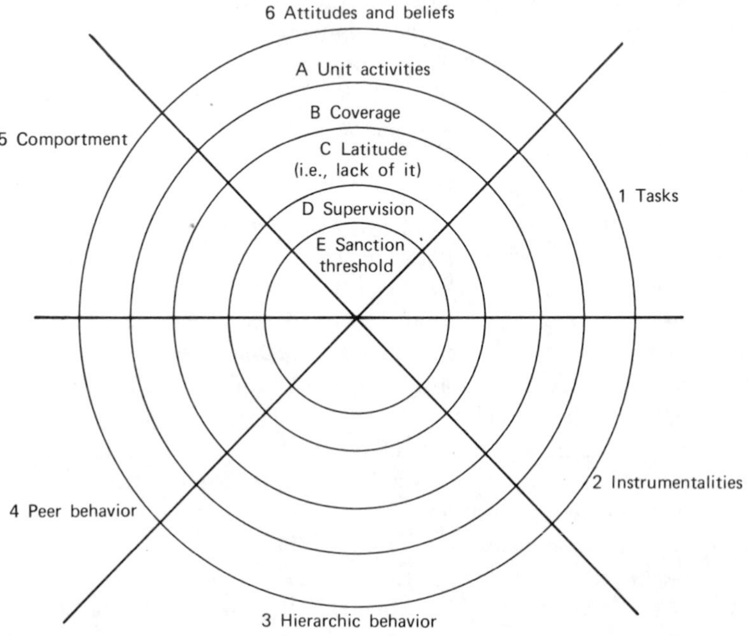

Fig. 10.1 Aspects of Directiveness.

further constrained by the extent to which the rules and directives limit their discretion; this is Latitude, represented by the third circle C. Latitude is "specific," and it coincides with Coverage, when all regulated activities are specified fully and precisely leaving the unit member no discretion in how he carries out any activity. The extent of Supervision is represented by circle D. Not all specifically regulated activities are necessarily subject to supervision; Supervision is "close" to the extent that it is systematically applied to all such activities. The innermost circle E signifies the proportion of supervised activities for which violations are likely to be sanctioned. Sanction threshold is "severe" insofar as all violations detected in supervised activity result in sanctions being meted out.

The most highly "regimented" social unit is one in which all unit activities are regulated in detail, closely supervised, and all violations penalized. Graphically, the five circles in Figure 10.1 would coincide in such a case. Mathematically, the ratio of each successive aspect of Directiveness to the preceding aspect would be 1:1 (or greater, in the case of Coverage: Unit activities, because Coverage can be extended to activities outside the unit per se). Even in formal prescription, very few units approach this extreme (e.g., some families, prisons and labor camps, a few military units, and perhaps revolutionary cells). The most "permissive" social unit is one in which little is regulated, regulation is very general, supervision is almost nonexistent, and sanctions are scarcely ever applied. Graphically, the inner four circles in Figure 10.1 would approach the central dot. Mathematically, the ratios of at least some successive aspects of Directiveness would approach 0:1. Certain families and schools approach this extreme of complete "permissiveness," and we have suggested in Chapter 7 that this level is characteristic of many voluntary organizations.

Forms, norms, and practices can be distinguished with reference to each of the five aspects of Directiveness. Specific approaches to their operational assessment are proposed below.

Coverage

Coverage is distinguished here from Latitude, but in field research carried out heretofore the two dimensions were treated without distinction under the general rubric of Coverage.

Operational Rules. Coverage is "comprehensive" to the extent that standing orders and current directives and their functional equivalents (see below) govern all domains of members' behavior during the time they spend in the social unit and in meeting its requirements when outside the unit. The approximate proportion of all activities of *s*'s and lower *S*'s during time devoted to the unit that are so governed constitutes the *scope* of Coverage.

Not all directives are explicit: *S*'s may regularly supervise *s*'s and administer sanctions even though no standing orders or current directives apply to the supervised activity. This practice is functionally equivalent to having directives and must be taken into account in evaluating the scope of Coverage.

Some or most of a unit's activities may be governed by general cultural norms or "conventions" (see Chapter 8) rather than by explicit directives. We regard general social conventions as directives if the *S*'s of a unit specifically act to ensure that they are observed within the unit, whether by reinforcing them with explicit directives or, indirectly, by using sanctions when they are violated. If, for example, a school board regularly fails to renew the contracts of teachers because of unconventional dress and appearance, we say that there is Coverage of this sector of behavior even if no explicit regulations or directives are issued. This should be distinguished in turn from community enforcement of norms, as when an atheistic teacher is harassed by his colleagues, or a peculating teacher is taken to trial. The former is pressure by peers, not Coverage; the latter is an aspect of governmental Coverage of all citizens' behavior.

"Overspill" is our term for the extension of Coverage to time and activities outside the unit per se. For example, schools in the United States have at times regulated students' behavior on the way to and from school; corporations sometimes specify where their junior executives should live, and even how; religious congregations instruct parishioners how to act toward their neighbors. Overspill requires no special conceptual treatment; the foregoing remarks about supervision and general cultural norms as functional equivalents of directives apply to overspill as well, and so do the following distinctions among "domains" of Coverage. Operationally, however, we need to give special attention to the possibility and extent of overspill. To the extent that it is present, Coverage tends to be exceptionally high.

Domains of Coverage. Units vary greatly according to whether different spheres or domains of behavior are regulated. Detailed description requires us to determine whether different domains are covered and how—by explicit rules and directives, by supervision only, or by *S*-reinforcement of general "conventions." Domains might be identified for each social unit. Reference to the following list of domains is preferable, because it seems to us both generally applicable and exhaustive.

1. *Tasks* are the "work" or functions performed by members of the social unit. Coverage is present if there is clear specification of what *s*'s and lower *S*'s are expected to do or accomplish in the unit. This is the almost-irreducible minimum of Coverage.

2. *Instrumentalities* consist of the ways in which tasks are to be accomplished. Coverage is present if there is regulation of the ways in which specified tasks are carried out. Note that instrumental coverage tends to decrease Latitude, but not necessarily: techniques may be specified in more or less detail.

3. *Hierarchic behavior* indicates the ways in which *s*'s act toward *S*'s, and vice versa. The question is not *how* *s*'s and *S*'s are expected to act toward one another, which is an aspect of the Deportment dimension. The question for Coverage is whether such behavior is subject to regulation.

4. *Peer behavior* comprises the ways in which *s*'s and *S*'s act toward other *s*'s and *S*'s in the same stratum.

5. *Comportment* includes considerations of the dress, demeanor, appearance, and so on, of unit members (i.e., all personal matters aside from those involved in interactions with other unit members).

6. *Attitudes and beliefs* are the evaluative and affective elements of members' psyches. These are intangibles, but no less subject to attempts at regultion than overt behavior. Families, schools, and religious bodies are greatly concerned with implanting and reinforcing "proper" attitudes and beliefs in their members; we can speak of the *regulation* of those attitudes and beliefs when members are explicitly required to profess acceptance of them.

One approach to the domains of Coverage is to determine whether each one is subject to regulation above a fairly low threshold. This may suffice for summary description. More complete characterization of the dimension requires us to distinguish the scope of Coverage within each domain. Are instrumentalities prescribed for all unit tasks, most of them, or only a few? Are interactions of students with one another regulated only in the classroom or elsewhere in the school as well? And so forth.

Note that concern with the domains extends beyond Coverage to the other components of Directiveness: within each covered domain we assess the degree of Latitude, the closeness of Supervision, and the severity of Sanctions for noncompliance.

Forms. The most consequential forms of Coverage are those prescriptive documents which, analogous to constitutional specification or limitation of powers, stipulate the domains of behavior of members that are subject to regulation and/or are free from regulation. Formal Coverage is a function of the number and proportion of domains of subs' and lower supers' activities that are formally subject to, or not excluded from, the regulatory power of the unit. Every formal extension of rule-making power to a new domain or type of activity in a domain is an extension of Coverage.

Norms. High Coverage is normatively valued to the extent that unit members believe that all activities in or related to the unit should be regulated. Restricted Coverage is valued insofar as members believe they should have substantial initiative or autonomy in determining what they do and think, in the unit and outside it. Coverage norms are rather likely to vary between *s*'s and *S*'s, with *s*'s tending to value less Coverage than *S*'s. Most important, norms are likely to vary greatly among the domains of Coverage. Subs and lower supers may fully accept Coverage of task and instrumental coverage but strenuously resist regulation of their comportment, attitudes, and beliefs. Special attention also should be given to Coverage overspill. Subs may be sharply resentful of attempted regulation of a domain outside the unit, even though they accept its regulation within the unit.

Practices. The practice of Coverage is difficult to judge aside from Latitude practices. The basic empirical question is the extent to which the sub and lower super members of a unit act independently (in choice of tasks and how they do them, behavior toward others in the unit, etc.) as distinct from engaging in unit-prescribed behavior. But unit behavior may be covered in such a general fashion that members "doing their own thing" in great diversity may all be consistent with formal Coverage. Some cues are relatively unambiguous. If, for example, *s*'s and lower *S*'s spend much of their time when formally in the unit at their leisure (talking, reading, engaged in personal business, lounging, sleeping) we would judge that task and instrumental Coverage in practice tend to be "restricted." Similarly, if there is great diversity in the deportment and appearance of unit members, and in their social views, but no concern to supervise or sanction any such behavior, we would judge that Coverage does not extend to these domains. On the other hand, if *S*'s regularly supervise and sanction numerous domains of behavior (task, instrumental, deportment, etc.) irrespective of formal regulation, Coverage in practice tends toward "comprehensive." Similarly, if Latitude is low by virtue of numerous detailed regulations in several domains, and unit members comply quite closely with them, we can say that Coverage in practice extends to those domains. In general, Coverage practices are best evaluated jointly with Latitude practices. If Latitude practices in a given domain are "specific" or narrow, the scope of Coverage practices in that domain is comprehensive. But if Latitude practices are "general," the investigator must ascertain whether unit members are truly acting on their own preferences or abiding by general regulations before deciding whether Coverage practices are comprehensive or restricted.

Latitude

Operational Rule. Latitude is "specific" to the extent that standing orders and current directives prescribe "covered" domains of activity in detail. The extent to which *s*'s and lower *S*'s are free to determine for themselves how to carry out prescribed activities constitues the *degree* of Latitude. As pointed out in connection with Coverage, not all directives are explicit. Regular supervision and sanctioning of the detailed activities of *s*'s and lower *S*'s, even in the absence of formal directives, reduces the degree of Latitude in practice very substantially.

Forms. There are rarely any formal prescriptions about Latitude. An exception would be "constitutional" statements that *s*'s or subordinate elements in a large-scale unit have autonomy in determining how to carry out a prescribed function. Such grants of moderate to high Latitude are characteristic of some governmental functions in federal systems. (The differential allocation of functions among national and local governments is a matter of divided Coverage; formal Latitude is at issue only when a higher level of government both directs a lower one to carry out a function and specifies the amount of discretion allowed the lower unit.)

Norms. A low degree of Latitude is normatively valued to the extent that unit members believe that all activities in the unit should be prescribed in detail. High Latitude is valued to the extent that members believe they should be given general guidelines, not petty directives, about how to fulfill unit tasks and meet other unit obligations. Precise regulation may be valued in some domains of unit activity but not in others. It is crucial to comprehensive description that Latitude norms be separately evaluated for different domains—especially those that are most "important" in terms of members' perceptions and the allocation of their time and resources.

Practices. The extent of Latitude in practice can be determined in part from whether prescribed activities are carried out in formally specified ways. What is likely to be more revealing is the range of variation in the ways similarly ranked *s*'s and lower *S*'s behave, carry out equivalent tasks, and so forth. If there is wide variation in how a particular job is done, Latitude is in practice high. If there is little variation, Latitude is likely to be but is not necessarily low; functionally there may be few ways in which a task can be carried out. Or there may be a cultural or unit-specific convention that *s*'s do certain things in certain ways, even though *S*'s have no preferences and issue no directives on the matter. The most unambiguous indication of low Latitude in practice is the coincidence of highly specific directives and homogeneous practices.

Information Sources for Coverage and Latitude

Reliable characterization of the extent of Coverage and Latitude requires analysis of unit documents, evaluation of secondary studies and sources, and, where possible, observation and interviewing. Some uses and interpretation of various kinds of evidence are suggested below.

Documents and Directives. A unit's prescriptive documents are the only source of information about its formal Coverage and Latitude. Its accumulated of standing orders and current directives are principal sources of information on Coverage and Latitude practices as well. A survey of the kinds of behavior dealt with by rules and directives indicates which domains of behavior are covered. Within each domain of behavior, the degree of Latitude is a function of (*a*) the sheer volume of directives applying to that domain, (*b*) the extent to which they are specific (i.e. limit the options open to compliant *s*'s and lower *S*'s), (*c*) the extent to which they are precise (i.e., permit no interpretation by *s*'s), and (*d*) their detail (i.e, the extent to which they govern discrete acts rather than clusters of activities). Generally, every directive that does not simply replace a previous one restricts Latitude in practice, whereas directives that leave room for interpretation and choice increase it more than those which do not.

One effective procedure for assessing Coverage and Latitude practices, therefore, is to obtain all or a representative sample of a social unit's written rules and directives and to evaluate them by reference to the foregoing criteria. Two examples follow.

1. The constitution, bylaws, and written codes of a student political association deal with such diverse matters as form and conduct of meetings, objectives of all committees and subcommittees, behavior of junior toward senior members, modes of dress, and preferred types and sites of group recreation. *Coverage is comprehensive in form and practice, and Latitude tends to be low in practice.*
2. The constitution and bylaws of a union local stipulate that periodic meetings be held and that meeting and membership records be kept. Members are required only to pay dues and to abide by strike votes. There are no instructions about the conduct of meetings, selection of officers, the obligations of shop stewards, or grievance procedures. *Formal Coverage is relatively restricted, but information is insufficient to assess Latitude* (because there may be many specific written or verbal directives to members).

Observation and Interpretation of Secondary Accounts. Direct and surrogate observation are primary sources of information about Coverage and Latitude practices. The same sources are indicative of normative standards. Some observations and reports, mostly hypothetical, are offered below, with interpretations of what they likely signify about Coverage and Latitude.

1. *Evidence about norms*

   a. Supers frequently express dissatisfaction about the idleness of *s*'s or the lack of ability of the latter to govern themselves. *Comprehensive Coverage is valued by S's.*

b. Supers state that *s*'s should take more initiative, that they "shouldn't have to be told what to do every minute." *High Latitude is valued by S's.*

c. Subs demand more "free time" while in the unit, or flout *S*'s efforts to regulate conduct and appearance. *Subs normatively reject existing levels of Coverage.*

d. Subs complain chronically about "petty interference" or ask repeatedly for more independence of action in meeting general directives. *Subs value high Latitude.*

2. *Evidence about practices*

a. Subs whose dress and behavior deviate from the unit norm tend to be passed over by *S*'s when seeking advice and deciding on raises, promotions, retention, and so on. *Coverage extends in practice to deportment and comportment.*

b. Supers repeatedly instruct *s*'s in how to carry out their activities and regularly supervise them, even though *s*'s are already familiar with those activities. *Latitude is low.*

c. Supers prescribe the goal of a novel activity without detailed instructions; if *S*'s ask for more specific directives, these are given as suggestions. *Latitude tends to be high.*

3. *Norm and practice examples*

a. In the French tobacco monopoly, workers' activities are prescribed in great detail, and the workers directly and through their union resist deviations from or attempts to change the regulations unless they initiate the changes themselves. *Low Latitude is valued by s's.*

b. The working-class English mother is reported to have specifically prescribed duties with reference to her husband's comfort, as well as generally prescribed family duties. She apparently has considerable discretion about how she organizes her time and is expected to seek entertainment on her own through conversation, shopping, and going to the cinema. Nonfulfillment of the prescribed duties, however, invites neighbors' scorn. *Coverage and Latitude norms and practices approximate the midpoint of the dimension.*

c. A teacher when giving homework assignments typically describes each step to be taken in fulfilling them, including precise topic, work procedures, outline, nature of presentation, form for submission, and time of completion. *Latitude (in this domain of behavior) is low.*

d. Elected local officials have by constitutional prescription competence for local schools, public works, welfare programs, and zoning. Grant-in-aid requirements for schools and welfare provide detailed specification of the substance of programs; in practice local officials issue implementing directives only. The same officials frequently initiate public works projects and repeatedly review and revise zoning standards. *Coverage by the municipal government is formally moderate but restricted in practice; Latitude within the domain of effective Coverage is relatively high.*

Interview and Questionnaire Items. These questionnaire and interview items were devised for use in field research by members of the Workshop. They are "paradigmatic," as are most other questions in this chapter; when used, they were altered to suit particular units.[2] Note that the items do not follow the sequence of the preceding operational discussion but, instead, the sequence most efficient and sensible for field use.

1. *Latitude: "Task" and "Instrumental" practices.* Think in a general way of the [work/tasks/duties] (*s*) perform in this unit [mention them]. In some [social units] of this type, the duties of the (*s*) are set out in considerable detail by the rules of the [unit] or the instructions of the (*S*), or by the [members'] realization that there are specific, required ways of carrying out their duties. In others, the (*s*) have to decide to a considerable extent for themselves how to discharge their duties. Which of the following most closely corresponds to what is *actually* the case in this [social unit]?

Almost all duties are prescribed in detail	*Most* duties are	*Many* duties are	*Some* duties are	*Few* duties are

2. *Latitude: "Task" and "Instrumental" norms (1).* To what extent do you think (*S*) *should* have their [duties/tasks/work] prescribed in detail by (*S*)?

Much more than now	Somewhat more	To same extent	Somewhat less	Much less

3. *Latitude: "Task" and "Instrumental" norms (2).* Are there any *particular* [types of duties, etc.] that you think should be prescribed in greater detail, or that (*s*) should be more free to decide on themselves?

   a. Should be prescribed in greater detail:
   b. (*s*) should be freer to decide:

4. *Coverage: "Deportment" and "Comportment" practices.* In some (units) only the [work/tasks] of (*s*) [is/are] covered by [directives/rules/orders]; in others there are [directives/rules/orders] about other matters as well, such as *how* (*s*) act toward (*S*), or *toward other* (*s*), or *personal matters* [like how (*s*) dress]. What is *actually* the case in regard to these matters in this (unit)?

Response options: Many rules Some Few

a. In regard to how (*s*) act toward (*S*)?
b. In regard to how (*s*) act toward other (*s*)?
c. In regard to personal matters?

5. *Coverage: "Deportment" and "Comportment" norms.* What do you think should be the case in regard to these matters?

Response Options: Many rules Some Few

a. In regard to how (*s*) act toward (*S*)?
b. In regard to how (*s*) act toward other (*s*)?
c. In regard to personal matters?

6. *Coverage: overspill practices.* To what extent do (*S*) in this (unit) *actually* try to regulate what (*s*) do when they are not in the (unit) or not doing things outside of it that concern their (unit) duties?
[Specify: e.g., homework]

To a *large* extent	To *some* extent	To a *small* extent	*Not at all*

7. *Coverage: overspill norms.* What *should* be the case in regard to such external activities?

Some regulation by (*S*)	*Little* regulation	*No* regulation

Supervision

Operational Rule. Supervision is "close" to the extent that *S*'s or their surrogates closely and systematically observe the regulated activities of *s*'s and lower *S*'s to determine whether they are in compliance with rules and directives. In most domains of behavior, supervision requires direct observation of subs' behavior. If the activities of subs and lower supers have "outputs," though—in the form of goods produced, services rendered, decisions, and so on—the output itself can be scrutinized in lieu of direct supervision. Examination of output constitutes supervision only if the results of that examination are communicated to the responsible *s*'s, of course. The *degree* of Supervision is the extent to which all regulated behavior and/or outputs of subs and lower supers is continuously scrutinized. This function is sometimes performed by *s*'s designated by *S*'s. This should be distinguished from spontaneous peer pressure on members to conform to general, societal norms or to abide by the unit's regulations; such actions are revealing about the Compliance norms of members, but they are not evidence of Supervision.

Supervision should be separately evaluated for each significant domain of unit behavior. Primary operational attention will focus on Supervision in formally regulated domains. Other domains should be examined more cursorily for evidence of de facto Coverage and low Latitude by virtue of Supervision and sanction application.

Evidence about Supervision Norms and Practices. The *S*- and *s*-norms about Supervision levels are likely to vary. It is generally likely that close supervision is normatively valued by *S*'s to the extent that *S*'s attempt to supervise more closely than forms prescribe. Close Supervision is valued by *s*'s to the extent that they seek closer Supervision than forms prescribe. It was rather widely observed in Workshop fieldwork that Supervision norms and practices are a significant facet of Directiveness—in the eyes of unit members and from the viewpoint of the outsider concerned with authority patterns—irrespective of whether noncompliance was sanctioned.

1. *Interpretations of observations*

a. Supers attempt to supervise *s*'s on a random rather than a predictable, periodic basis. *Close Supervision is valued by S's, moderate Supervision is practiced.*

b. Supers frequently complain about the inadequacy of, seek resources for, further supervisory activities. *Supers value close Supervision.*

c. Supers make special efforts to avoid the appearance of supervising *s*'s. *Loose Supervision is practiced by S's; either they value loose Supervision or they are responding to s's disvaluation of Supervision.*

d. Subs regularly ask *S*'s to examine and check their activities; *S*'s typically respond. Close Supervision is valued by s's, practiced by S's.

2. *Examples*

a. An organization has routinized procedures for inspecting all outputs, and the results are communicated daily to all responsible lower *S*'s and *s*'s. *Supervision is relatively close.*

b. All decisions of local union officials regarding wage and fringe benefit demands and strikes are submitted for prior approval to the national body. Decisions about grievances, membership gains and losses, elections, and some other local business are transmitted to the national office for information. *Supervision of the local is rather loose.*

c. A teacher requires homework assignments but seldom reads or grades them; often leaves the classroom during class, gives frequent exams, and does not monitor the class when exams are in progress. *Supervision is loose.*

3. *Questionnaire and interview items*

a. Supervision: "Task" and "Instrumental" practices. How closely do (*S*) in (this unit) check up on the way (*s*) carry out their prescribed [work/tasks/duties]?

Very closely	Rather closely	Rather loosely	Very loosely/ not at all

b. Supervision: "Task" and "Instrumental" norms. In regard to the closeness with which (*S*) check up on the way (*s*) carry out the [work/tasks/duties] expected of them, what do you think should be the case:

They should watch more closely than now	Somewhat more closely	About the same	Somewhat less than now	Much less than now

c. Supervision: "Deportment" and "comportment" practices. How closely do (*S*) in (this unit) supervise personal matters, like how (*s*) act toward other (*s*) and how they dress?

Very closely	Rather closely	Rather loosely	Very loosely/ not at all

Evidence about Supervision Forms. Prescriptive documents can be examined for evidence of institutionalized Supervision; examples include stipulations that enactments or decisions of certain kinds must be reviewed, records of the existence and extent of "quality control" and "police" units, and data on the establishment of routinized reporting, testing, or evaluation procedures. With reference to decisions, for example, formal Supervision is close if all decisions of *s*'s and lower *S*'s are subject to obligatory review by higher *S*'s; if only a few are reviewed, it is relatively loose. Two examples follow.

1. A clerical staff is required by company regulation to punch in and out and to keep time records of all activities. Supervisors are required to monitor all clerical processes continuously. All output is subject to review and checking by controllers. *Formal Supervision is relatively close.*
2. According to the articles of incorporation, a trade association was established to provide central information, research, and lobbying services for member companies. It also enforces a set of precise advertising standards, subjecting all advertising material to review prior to publication. *This does not constitute Supervision for the association*, since it does not relate to the association's own activities; it *is* relevant to the degree of Supervision of the advertising staffs of the member companies.

Sanction Threshold and Severity

Negative sanctions but not positive ones (reinforcements) are germane to Directiveness. Negative sanctions are important because "directives" without any potential sanctions do not "regiment" or direct *s*-behavior; they have the status of suggestions or negotiating positions. Positive sanctions are not relevant to Directiveness for essentially the same reason; they do not intrinsically constrain *s*-behavior but rather are a (potential) element in cost-benefit calculations. Both negative and positive sanctions are, however, relevant to Compliance, since they are among its determinants.

Operational Rule. The Sanction threshold is "severe" to the extent that negative sanctions are invoked for *any* deviations from formally or normatively prescribed activities. Sanction thresholds are relevant only to supervised activities as defined in the section on information sources; sanctions cannot be invoked for deviations of which *S*'s have no direct or indirect knowledge. But note that sanctions may be applied by *s*'s acting as surrogates for *S*'s as well as by *S*'s themselves.

By "negative sanctions" we mean all "noxious stimuli," including *S*'s expressed disapproval (when approval is valued by *s*'s), verbal reprimands, withdrawal or denial of expected rewards, and overt punishments. It is especially important in empirical research to seek evidence on the more subtle sanctions (e.g., *S*-disapproval) and on impending sanctions, (e.g., students' acceptance of classroom discipline for fear of being "flunked" at end of term).

By "deviations" we mean any discrepancy between *s*-behavior and the compliance criteria formally or normatively specified, and/or regarded as appropriate by *S*'s.

As a general operational rule, we regard the regular use of sanctions to instruct *s*'s about Coverage and Latitude to be a "severe" Sanction threshold.

The severity of sanctions should be described and taken into account in assessing this subdimension. Subs who fear loss of job or imprisonment for violation of a directive are more "regimented" than those who fear only *S*'s disapproval or loss of a holiday. But the sanction threshold per se is determined by the imposition of any kind of sanction, not by its severity.

Evidence about Sanction Forms. Prescriptive documents often specify what kinds of sanctions are to be used for different kinds of deviations, and they rule out some sanctions as "cruel and unusual punishment." The judicial codes of most governments specify sanctions for different crimes and violations in detail. They also may prohibit, as in the United States, the use of severe sanctions in other units: parents cannot brutally abuse their children, schools and factories cannot imprison rebellious *s*'s, and so forth.

But these forms all relate to *sanction severity*, not to the thresholds at which sanctions are actually applied. More precisely, formal documents that refer to sanctions almost always deal with the penalties appropriate to noncompliance but seldom if ever say when noncompliance should be tolerated and when it should be sanctioned. Sanction threshold thus is generally a matter of norm and practice, not form. As an operational convention, however, we suggest that formal Sanction threshold be regarded as "high" to the extent that constitutional documents prescribe numerous grounds or channels for appeal of decisions that *s*'s are "guilty" and subject to punishment.

Evidence about Sanction Norms and Practices. Super and sub norms about Sanction thresholds and severity probably vary, hence it is important that they be separately assessed.

1. *Interpretations of observations*

a. Supervisory activities are concerned primarily with determining whether specific forms or norms are violated; whenever deviations are found, *S*'s employ sanctions. *Supers are severe in practice and probably value severity.*

b. Supers finding deviations repeatedly warn guilty *s*'s before invoking sanctions and attempt to help *s*'s correct deficiencies. *Supers are relatively lenient in practice and probably value leniency.*

c. Supers who observe noncompliance appear to ignore it or remedy its consequences but do not warn or punish the responsible *s*'s. *Supers highly value leniency and are highly lenient in practice.*

d. Lower *S*'s are expected to report all noncompliance to higher *S*'s; in fact they report only gross noncompliance. *Lower S's value and practice leniency.*

e. Subs, in the absence of *S*'s, voluntarily impose sanctions on deviant *s*'s (not necessarily sanctions of the same type or severity as S's employ). *Subs value severity.*

f. Subs complain vigorously about imposition of sanctions on others, conceal evidence of others' noncompliance. *Subs value leniency.*

2. *Examples*

a. In an Asian village the local chief is concerned in the traditional sector, merely with determining whether a norm has been violated; if it has, sanctions are automatically invoked. *Supers practice and probably value severity.*

b. Records of punitive actions in an industrial organization indicate that almost all offenders who were reported were penalized; observation of supervisory personnel indicates that relatively few acts of noncompliance are reported. *In practice the sanction threshold is relatively lenient; lower S's value leniency, higher S's probably value severity.*

c. In Buganda in the 1950s, local chiefs were reluctant to impose sanctions. Even belated and mild application of sanctions for noncompliance (on taxation) could lead to bitter complaints by *s*'s. *Subs value maximal leniency, S's practice considerable leniency.*

3. *Interview and questionnaire items*

a. Sanction threshold: "Tasks" and "Instrumental" practices. (*s*) do not or cannot always carry out their [work/tasks/duties] as they are supposed to. When this happens, about how often do (*S*) *actually* take action against them (i.e., warn them, punish them, count it against them when considering a promotion or raise, etc.)?

Almost always	Often	Sometimes	Seldom	Almost never

Sanction threshold question used in questionnaire with German secondary school students (by Ronald Rogowski):

Pupils cannot or will not always do what teachers demand of them. In your class, how often do the teachers undertake some action against this, such as punishment, scolding, and warning?

Almost always	Often	Sometimes	Seldom	Almost never

b. Sanction threshold: "Tasks" and "Instrumental" norms. In regard to taking action against (*s*) who do not do their [work/tasks/duties] properly, what do you think *should* be the case?

(*S*) should almost always take action	Often	Sometimes	Seldom	Almost never

c. Sanction severity: practices. When (*S*) *do* take action against (*s*), is the action likely to be:

Severe	Moderate	Mild

d. Sanction severity: practices. What kinds of actions do (*S*) generally take when an important [rule/order] has not been properly carried out by (*s*)?

e. Sanction severity: norms. In regard to the severity of (*S*) actions against (*s*) who do not carry out [rules/orders], what do you think *should* be the case?

They should be *more severe* than now	About the same	Less severe

Summary Evaluation of Directiveness

Two related questions are at issue. First, how precisely can and should we estimate the different aspects of Directiveness? Second, once we have estimated these aspects, how ought they be combined in an overall evaluation or "measure" of the degree of Directiveness in a unit?

Exactitude of Estimation. The degree of precision with which Directiveness might be described has no intrinsic limits. Its dimensions and domains have clear empirical referents, which all should be ascertainable under open conditions of access—provided they exist at all, as forms of Latitude, for example, do not. High degrees of precision naturally require the investigator to make further operational assumptions. What, for example, constitute the precise gradations of Latitude? But previous information should make it possible to construct instruments yielding valid and reliable results. Our questionnaire and interview items, for example, are designed to serve as just such "instruments."

It is more likely that only approximations of authority characteristics will be possible, because the unit under study is historical rather than contemporary, because access to it is restricted, or simply for want of time and resources. It is moreover likely that information will be lacking for some aspects of Directiveness. But it is our view that the requirements of summary description and comparison can be satisfied if the more important aspects and domains of Directiveness can be characterized to a "high-medium-low" degree of accuracy. This may seem remarkably imprecise, but on reflection it should be apparent why ordinarily it suffices: gross characterization of cases on each of a large number of conceptually and operationally distinct dimensions provides for at least as much discrimination among the cases as does their precise characterization on one or two dimensions.

Summary Measurement of Directiveness. A set of scoring and weighting conventions are proposed here by which "high-medium-low" judgments about the facets of Directiveness can be converted into ratiolike scales with at least five intervals. The exercise is illustrative, not definitive; in subsequent sections of this chapters, scoring is more cursorily treated.

We assume that some subdimensions and domains of Directiveness are more significant than others. Latitude and Sanction threshold we judge to be more important constraints on freedom of action in a typical social unit than Coverage and Supervision; Latitude and Sanction threshold judgments are therefore weighted twice as heavily. The "Task" domain we regard as substantially more important than others; in most units, most members' energies are concentrated on tasks. We make the simplifying assumption that the greater the Coverage in a domain—other than "Tasks"—the greater the weight it should be given *vis-à-vis* the others. Numerical weights—admittedly arbitrary ones—are as follows

"Tasks"	×5
The two domains, other than "Tasks," having highest Coverage	×3
Remaining three domains	×1

The weights have clear implications for narrative description and analyses: work should focus on the "Task" domain and one or two others in which Coverage is relatively high, and within those domains on Latitude and Sanction threshold. The weights also serve for summary scoring purposes. If "high-medium-low" judgments can be made about aspects of a domain, they can be numerically scored as follows: high = 2 (except *low* Latitude = 2), medium = 1, low = 0.

The "directiveness" of each domain can then be evaluated on a 13-point scale:

Subdimension	High	Medium	Low	× Weight
Latitude	0	1	2	×2
Sanction threshold	2	1	0	×2
Coverage	2	1	0	×1
Supervision	2	1	0	×1

The maximum summed score, 12, is obtained by a unit that is "directive" in all four subdimensions.

The scores for each domain then can be combined using the "domain" weights, yielding a highly discriminating scale with a range of 0 to 168:

Domain	Weight	Maximum Score
Tasks	5	12 × 5 = 60
Two high-Coverage domains	3	2 (12 × 3) = 72
Remaining three domains	1	3 (12 × 1) = 36
		168

Extreme scores are likely to be rather rare; the scores so obtained for different units can be converted to a five-point scale such as the following, which attenuates raw scores at either extreme (using ratios of approximately 2.0:1.5:1.0:1.5:2.0):

"Raw" score	0–44	45–74	75–94	95–124	125–168
"Scaled" score	1	2	3	4	5

Three stipulations apply to any empirical use of these procedures. First, the weights and procedures are proposed *a priori*; we have made no calculations to determine empirical location or distribution of different units on the scales. Second, a technical point: if no judgments are possible (or conceptually appropriate) for a subdimension, it should be categorized as "medium" and scored 1, to avoid understating the summary score for comparative purposes. Third, the procedures are equally appropriate to forms, norms, and practices.

In concluding our summary description of Directiveness, we reiterate that judgments represented by numbers are no better than the information that went into the judgments: denumeration on a high-medium-low scale, or a more discriminating five- or twelve-point scale, is the final step in description, not a sufficient one. Nor do we regard numerical scoring of authority data as a *necessary* descriptive step. It is necessary for quantitative comparative analysis, but many kinds of systematic comparative analysis can be made without quantification. Finally, we stress the heuristic nature of the procedures outlined. Other, equally or more appropriate procedures may be devised.

Participation[3]

Participation refers to the diversity and extent of subs' attempts to influence the directive activities of *S*'s, that is, to influence the making and implementation of decisions about what is to be done in and by the unit. We are not concerned here with the impact of such influence attempts on *S*'s or with the *success* of influence attempts. That is partly a function of *S*-Responsiveness and partly dependent on communication channels, unit resources, and many other factors. The central operational question is the degree to which a given unit is "participant" or "nonparticipant." How this question is answered differs according to whether we are concerned with the forms, norms, or practices of Participation. The next subsection identifies four general channels of Participation, with examples of specific modes of each. Participation is *formally* "participant" to the extent that all such channels are provided for and their use facilitated by the prescriptive documents of the unit. *Norms* are "participant" insofar as members of the unit approve the regular and widespread use of all such channels. Participation is high in *practice* to the extent that all conceivable channels are widely and vigorously used. The subdimensions of the Participation dimension, then, are the openness of Channels and the extent of their Use.

There are certain conceptual and operational problems in evaluating Participation in *complex* social units. For example, in determining how to regard the participant role of lower *S*'s with respect to higher *S*'s we must be concerned with all influence attempts directed at top *S*'s, whether by *s*'s or lower *S*'s. But this makes it necessary to give special attention to the Participation channels and influence attempts of lower *S*'s, since these are likely to be rather different—and probably more "participant"—than those of *s*'s generally. A corollary problem is deciding whether to distinguish between influence attempts directed by *s*'s at lower *S*'s, and influence attempts by both toward higher *S*'s. The answer for comprehensive description is "yes": in a school, for example, the influence attempts of students on teachers should be analyzed, and so should those of students and teachers toward school administrators. If the purpose is summary characterization of Participation for a unit as a whole, it probably will suffice to examine influence attempts directed at the top-most decision makers. If questions of political socialization and experience of *s*'s are at stake, however, it will be necessary to examine all significant channels and uses by *s*'s to whatever *S*'s they are directed.

Types (Channels) of Participation

We distinguish four general types or channels of participatory action: *group, direct personal, indirect personal,* and *impersonal.* These are categories of action, not dimensions, and can be used for descriptive characterization of any unit's specific modes of Participation. The categories share at least one underlying dimension, however: the relative effort they require. Group actions generally call for the greatest effort and entail the most intense influence attempts; impersonal actions tend to be least energetic and least intense. We use the rank order of the categories to weight information on the "openness" of Channels and their Use: a unit in which group activism is the dominant mode of Participation is more "participatory" than one in which indirect personal activism is predominant.

One other introductory note should be made about types of channels. There is no question about whether each of these types is "present" or "absent" in a unit in a given time frame. Channels of each type are potentially usable at any time in almost any conceivable type of social organization. Our central concern when evaluating Participation is whether each is encouraged or discouraged, used or not used.

Group Activism. The establishment of or participation in collective action aimed at influencing *S*'s decisions and actions—that is, group activism—can be exemplified as follows:

Highly articulated (e.g., formally organized) associations of *s*'s established for the purpose of influencing *S*'s (e.g., party or pressure group politics and their functional equivalents).

Regular meetings of *S*'s and representatives of *s*'s organized groups.

Structures in which *s*'s are attached to *S*'s decision-making units, where they act as if they were *S*'s (e.g., codetermination councils).

Protest activities, such as work stoppages, rallies, picketing, demonstrations, riots, and equivalent actions, when directed at the policies of specific (groups of) *S*'s.

Terrorism and sabotage, in those relatively rare instances in which the object is to influence the policies of specific *S*'s rather than to destroy the *S*-structure.

Disruptive forms of group activism are never (almost never) normatively sanctioned by *S*'s and usually are rejected by *s*'s. But we think that they are appropriately part of the "group activism" category because they are recurrently used in many societies, they are often recognized by *S*'s as "influence attempts," and they sometimes lead to the intended changes.

Direct Personal Activism. Face-to-face, individual contacts with *S*'s, whether through institutionalized channels or on an ad hoc basis, constitute direct personal activism. Some examples are:

Opportunities for *s*'s to talk directly to *S*'s in an individual capacity (e.g., audiences with rulers, appointments with government officials, group meetings with supervisory personnel and officers).

Opportunities for *s*'s to talk directly to *S*'s privately, attempting to influence them.

Regular channels for redress of grievances (e.g., ombudsmen, administrative courts for citizen grievances, grievance committees).

Public (but not secret; see below) voting procedures.

Running for elective office and attempting to secure appointive office, to change *S*-policies (but campaign organizations and slates of like-minded candidates with such purposes constitute "group activism").

Indirect Personal Activism. We define as indirect personal activism individual contacts with *S*'s that are not face to face: for example:

Writing personal letters to *S*'s designed to influence them (in support of or against policies, or to request attention to a grievance).

Existence of channels for the expression of *s*'s opinions, such as newspapers.

Writing signed letters to such "media."

Circulation of petitions designed to influence *S*'s.

Opportunities for *s*'s to appeal to other, presumably influential, *s*'s or lower *S*'s in the hope that they will influence higher *S*'s.

Impersonal Activism. Individual actions in which the actor is anonymous to and distant from the *S*'s whom he hopes to influence are called instances of impersonal activism. Some examples are:

Voting for persons or policies under conditions of secrecy.

Use of anonymous letters, unsigned petitions and suggestions, posters and epithets.

Impersonal activism is generally the least effortful and least intense of all participatory activities, which is not to say that it may not sometimes require considerable effort and entail high risks. Campaign activities to mobilize votes for particular candidates constitute "group activism" for all those involved. Voting is "impersonal activism" only for those who go to the polls as isolated individuals. We note finally that voting is not necessarily "participatory" at all: obligatory participation in choiceless elections is not Participation.

Openness of Participatory Channels

The first subdimension of Participation concerns the extent to which any and all of the channels specified earlier are formally open and normatively approved, and their actual use not impeded by sanctions or "roadblocks" thrown up by *S*'s. Four conditions contribute to the degree of "openness" or "closure" of each type of channel.

Conditions of Channel Openness

Open (facilitated)	Closed (impeded)
Open in form ($F+$). One or more modes of Participation of a channel are formally required or provided.	*Closed in form* ($F-$). All modes of a channel are formally proscribed.
Normatively open ($N+$). One or more modes are normatively approved by *S*'s.	*Normatively closed* ($N-$). All modes are of a channel normatively disapproved of by *S*'s.
Free from sanctions (P_s+). One or more modes are tolerated by *S*'s in practice.	*Subject to negative sanctions* (P_s-). All modes are of a channel sanctioned by *S*'s in practice.
Feasible (P_f+). One or more modes are capable of being used by *s*'s (i.e., are not situationally denied them by the unit's structure or *S*'s actions).	*Unfeasible* (P_f-). All modes of a channel are effectively foreclosed by the nature of the unit or *S*'s actions.

"Free from/subject to sanctions" refers to the use of negative sanctions against *s*'s and lower *S*'s who use a particular mode of Participation. In contemporary Spain, for example, any public manifestation of political protest has been formally proscribed; occasional violations by individual picketers (a mode of "direct personal activism") have resulted in jail sentences (sanctions). In professional athletics in the United States, there generally is no formal prohibition against the formation of players' associations for the purpose of bargaining with owners (a mode of "group activism"), but player representatives to such associations run an unusually high risk of being dropped or traded by their clubs (i.e., sanctioned). Any such sanctioning restricts the use of a channel in practice; the more severe the sanctions and the more systematically they are applied to would-be participants, the less open is the channel.

"Feasible" means that *s*'s can actually use a mode of Participation with some frequency and/or without great inconvenience. For example, a professor who schedules office hours in such a way that students can see him only rarely and at considerable personal cost is, in practice, impeding opportunities. The holding of elections in which most opposition candidates are ruled off the ballot is a partial closure, in practice, of group activism channels. Any such action designed to reduce frequency or convenience of use constitutes at least partial impediment of a channel.

Information Sources for the Channels Subdimension. We determine *forms* by examining unit documents, taking account of all regulations and directives that either (*a*) explicitly state procedures and structures by which *s*'s may participate in the decision-making or grievance processes, or (*b*) explicitly foreclose certain kinds or forms of participation by *s*'s. Prescriptive documents may exist for channels of any of the four types, but they are most common with reference to *group activism* and *impersonal activism.* Direct and indirect personal activism are more likely to occur (or to be foreclosed) without reference in prescriptive documents.

Norms can be estimated from reports and observation and can be determined more directly through interviews and questionnaire items. Here are interpretations of some observations:

1. Subs make concerted efforts to organize to secure redress of grievances from *S*'s or to negotiate with them. *Subs value "group activism" at levels greater than those which prevail in the unit.*
2. Supers formally prescribe channels of group activism (formation of political parties, labor unions, and their equivalents) and impersonal activism (voting) but repeatedly restrict their use by *s*'s in practice. *Supers disvalue the formally prescribed channels.*
3. Subs attempt to discuss grievances in person with *S*'s but are repeatedly turned down in requests for meetings. *Supers disvalue direct personal activism.*

In large-scale units, proposals for reform by supers and subs and the actions of committees investigating possibilities for reform, may offer excellent sources of information on norms. Hearings held by such bodies will suggest the distribution of normative positions.

Practices may be evaluated from a combination of observation, documentary analysis, and interview and questionnaire techniques. We are concerned here with whether the channels are not foreclosed *by the S's* of the unit. This is distinct from levels of Use as such, as explained in a subsequent subsection. Channels can be formally open, not impeded in practice, and their use not sanctioned, but still be very little used by *s*'s.

Any actions by *S*'s that systematically restrict use of a formally open channel are relevant here. In example 2 just given, supers' restriction of formally open channels is a "practice" restriction as well as an indication of *S* norms. Subs who attempt to influence *S*'s in various ways may be subject to various judicial and quasi-judicial proceedings or simply may fail to be promoted or retained by the *S*'s. Thus records of sanctions against "activists" and information on their retention or release shed light on Channel openness in some kinds of units. Special note also should be given to channels that are either closed or not formally provided for, yet in fact are used and not visibly impeded by *S*'s. Two examples are supplied.

1. High elected officials in the United States are not formally obliged to meet individual constituents or respond to inquiries by mail. Yet the President and Congressmen set aside blocs of time for personal meetings and have large staffs devoted to screening and answering mail. Selected instances of Responsiveness to problems and requests that reach the *S*'s attention in these ways are widely publicized. *In practice, "direct personal activism" and "indirect personal activism" channels are open and encouraged.*
2. In this country most forms of peaceful group protest against the Vietnam War were legally acceptable. The extensive and indiscriminate arrests and detention of some demonstrators, and the use of widely publicized trials of prominent war resisters, constituted *partial closure of this mode of "group activism" in practice.*

Questionnaire and interview items are interrelated, and a set on Channel openness and the volume of Use was employed in Workshop field research. Modified forms of them are listed here; some are relevant to Use of Participation channels.

1. *Volume of Participation, practices* In very general terms, about how *often,* if ever, do the (*s* in this unit) try to influence the (S) in regard to how the unit is run?

Very often Often Sometimes Seldom Almost never

2. *Channels of Participation, Use practices* Here is a list of ways in

which (*s* in this unit) might try to influence (*S*). How often have you done each of these things, say, in the past year?

Often   Once or twice   Never

(*Alternative,* if the respondent is an "informant"):
About how many people in this unit would you say take these kinds of actions, say, in the course of a year?

Most   Some   A few   Practically none

(*Alternative,* if the respondent is a higher *S*):
About how often do you and other (people in your position) deal with or take into consideration these kinds of activities by (*s*), say in the course of a year?

Frequently   Fairly often   Occasionally   Almost never

List
(adapt to include examples germane to the unit)

a. Organize a special group for the purpose
b. Act through established groups of (*s*) and (*S*)
c. Act through a group of (*s*) alone
d. Contact (*S*) personally
e. Try to induce a sympathetic (*S*) to contact the (*S*) concerned
f. Use "third" party outside the (unit) [specify: e.g., parents] to contact the (*S*)
g. Write signed letters or notes to (*S*)
h. Circulate petitions among (*s*)
i. Write unsigned letters or notes to (*S*)

3. *Channels of Participation Openness, norms.* In your view, how adequate do you think (*s*) opportunities are for letting (*S*) know their opinions? Would you say:

Many more opportunities should exist	*Some* more	Present situation *about right*	*Fewer*	*Many fewer*
		to 6 ↓		

4. (If "Many more" or "Some more"): What specific additional opportunities should exist?

5. (If "Fewer" or "Many Fewer"): What specific opportunities should not exist?

6. *Channels of Participation Openness, practices.* Is it at all usual for (*S*) to discourage (*s*) from expressing their views about how (the unit) is run?

Very common Sometimes Rare
In what ways?

7. *Channels of Participation Openness, practices.* Do (*S*) ever in any way punish (*s*) who do so?

Often Sometimes Rarely or never
In what ways?

8. *Volume of Participation, norms.* Are (*s*), in your opinion, active enough in helping (*S*) know their views? Would you say they should be

Much more active	Somewhat more active	About as active as they are	Somewhat less active	Much less active

Summary Rating of Channel Openness. The four conditions of Channel openness and closure are a series of continua. For some purposes they are evaluated separately, for others it is desirable to reduce them to a single summary continuum. For illustrative purposes we treat each continuum as a trichotomy: + signifies a relatively "open" condition, – a relatively "closed" condition, and × signifies the *absence* of relevant forms or norms, treated as a midpoint.

Forms, norms, and practices of channel openness can be separately scored on a five-point scale using the following conventions; we assume that negative sanctions (subscript *s*) are a more effective bar to Participation then are constraints on its feasibility (subscript *f*). Since *S*'s norms and practices are not necessarily uniform, intermediate scores of 4 and 2 may be appropriate.

Open	5	$F+$	$N+$	$P_{s,f+}$
	4			
	3	$F\times$	$N\times$	P_{s+f-}
	2			P_{s-f+}
Closed	1	$F-$	$N-$	$P_{s,f-}$

Cumulative Rating of Openness, All Channels. We suggested earlier that the modes or channels of participation be weighted according to the relative effort and intensity of action they reflect. The proposed weighting used in Table 10.1 permits summary scores for each channel of participation to be combined into a summary "openness" score for Participation in its entirety.

To use this procedure, each channel of Participation is evaluated and

Table 10.1 Encouragement of Various Modes of Channels of Participation

	Group Activism	Direct Personal Activism	Indirect Personal Activism	Impersonal Activism	Summary Score for Openness
Encouragement of modes	5				(open) (10)
of each channel	4	5			(9)
		4			(8)
	3		5		(7)
		3	4	5	(6)
			3	4	(5)
	2	2		3	(4)
			2	2	(3)
	1	1	1	1	
					(closed) (2)

scored on a five-point scale according to the degree to which it is facilitated or impeded (open or closed). The score for the unit as a whole is determined by the highest score attained. For example, a social unit may encourage group activism at the 4 level but impede the other forms of activism at the 1 or 2 levels. The summary score is nevertheless 9.

Use of Participation Channels

Operational Rules. The Use subdimension takes into account both the *frequency* and *intensity* of *s*-inputs to *S*'s. It varies on a continuum from voluminous (frequent and intense) activity to none. For operational purposes we can evaluate *frequency* according to the proportion of unit members who participate in a particular way in a specified period of time, *or* according to the number of identifiable influence attempts in a time period. Our operational approach to *intensity* is to assume a relationship between the mode of participation used and its intensity: group activism is (assumed to be) most intense, personal direct activism less so, personal indirect activism still less, and impersonal activism least intense.[4] The overall intensity of Use is jointly a function of type and variety of channels used; it is greatest when all are in use.

Note that this subdimension is concerned only with inputs by *s*'s that (*a*) are directed to *S*'s of a social unit to which *s*'s belong and (*b*) deal with a subject that at least conceivably lies within the *S*'s directive-making competence.

Sources of Information. Questionnaire and interview items appropriate to determining the actual and normative level of activism were proposed previously. Some other sources of information are as follows.

1. *Forms*. Most social units are unlikely to have forms relating to levels of use of participation channels. Exceptions are prescriptions that members of organizations vote in elections or attend meetings on pain of sanctions.
2. *Norms*. One can observe or solicit evaluative remarks (e.g., at meetings and among committee members) about how the members regard the amount of participation in the social unit. Are suggestions made that are intended to increase—or decrease—the use of the opportunities available? One should also note whether there are any sanctions by subs or supers against nonparticipation. For example, are those who do not participate in prescribed ways in any way isolated or deprived?
3. *Practices*. Documentary records of the unit are a major source of information on practices (e.g., attendance records may be kept of meetings, committee meetings may have formal transcripts, the social unit may keep voting records, letters and petitions by *s*'s to *S*'s may be kept on file). Actual levels of participation at public and other meetings also can be observed.

Examination of the frequency of certain reiterative forms of participation can be examined through sampling. One might, for example, note the frequency with which *s*'s visit *S*'s who are responsible for processing subs' complaints, or *S*'s can be asked about the frequency with which *s*'s make requests of them. And the frequency of letters from *s*'s and lower *S*'s proposing reforms or expressing grievances might be determined from unit publications or *S*-files.

Frequency of Participation Practices. The possible sources of information on Participation practices are numerous. It remains to specify what constitutes relatively low and high frequencies of use with respect to the several channels of Participation. "Never" is the lowest possible frequency of influence attempts by subs and supers. It is much more difficult to make a priori specification of "high" frequencies; the highest conceivable level of Participation is that in which all members spend all their time "participating." Tables 10.2 to 10.5 suggest some approximate guidelines with which to base ratings for comparative purposes of the frequency of Use, both qualitatively and numerically. More precise rating scales would require information on the range and distribution of participation practices in a large and varied number of social units.

Note also that the volume of Participation in practice cannot always be determined accurately from study of behavior during a narrow time span. Since Participation tends to be higher in times of crisis than in normalcy, information should be sought on practices in both kinds of circumstance.

Table 10.2 Frequency of Groupist Participation

Indicator	High	Medium	Low	Nil
Voluntary membership of *s*'s, lower *S*'s in organized pressure groups, parties, and their equivalents	One-third or more of unit members	One-tenth to one-third of members	Some members but less than one-tenth	None or negligible
Sub and lower super self-reports of active participation in group influence activities during past year	One-tenth or more	3–9%	A few, up to 2%	None
Higher super reports of the frequency they have to deal with or give consideration to overt group influence attempts	Frequent	Fairly often; sometimes	Occasionally	Almost never

Table 10.3 Frequency of Direct Personal Activism

Indicator	High	Medium	Low	Nil
Activity at meetings at which *s* views are communicated to *S*'s	Consistently high attendance, high frequency of statements, demands[a]	Moderate or fluctuating attendance, *s*'s statements, demands[a]	Attendance low or apathetic[a]	No meetings held; no response to any that are held
Sub and lower super self-reports of direct personal activism in past year (speaking directly or publically to *S*'s)	One-third + of unit members report doing so	One-tenth to one-third of members	A few but less than one-tenth	None or less than 1%
Higher super reports of the frequency of direct influence attempts[b]	Frequent	Fairly often; sometimes	Occasionally	Never, almost never

[a] Assuming that regular, convenient meetings are held.

[b] Only for *S*'s who have some regular, direct contact with *s*'s; excluding *S*'s who because of their function or position have few or sporadic contacts.

Table 10.4 Frequency of Indirect Personal Activism

Indicator	High	Medium	Low	Nil
Observed frequency of reported complaints, letters, petition signatures, etc., in unit files	One per two *s* members, or more	One-fifth to one-half of members	Some but less than one-tenth of members	None or almost none
Sub and lower super self-reports of letter writing to *S*'s, signing petitions, resort to influential intermediary	More than one-third of unit members report doing so	One-tenth to one-third of members	A few but less than one-tenth	None or less than 1%
Higher super reports of the frequency of indirect influence attempts	Frequent	Fairly often; sometimes	Occasionally	Never, almost never

Political units, and some others, have regular cycles of participatory activity; the equivalent of a full cycle, from one election to the next, should properly be studied not merely because election turnout varies but because other modes of Participation also are likely to be modified with the ebb and flow of the political cycle.

Summary Assessment of the Volume of Participation. The final step in the assessment of the Use subdimension is to estimate its volume by weighting its "frequency" by "intensity." Only the information specified previously is needed for this evaluation but it must be synthesized for the purposes of summary description and, if desired, for assigning numerical scores. The following table of weights (Table 10.6) is proposed as a guide. It

Table 10.5 Frequency of Impersonal Activism

Indicator	High	Medium	Low	Nil
Frequency of secret elections in which most unit members are eligible to vote	One per year or more	One per 2 or 3 years	One per 4 years or more	Less than decennially; never
averaged with				
Turnout of eligibles at secret elections	More than 75% turnout	40–75% average turnout	Less than 40% average turnout	No elections

is constructed on two sets of assumptions. The first is that "intensity" varies according to the channel used, with group activism being the most intense channel and impersonal participation the least. Second, the frequencies of Participation in the four different channels are assumed to be "additive." Conceptually there can be little question of subs' energy and commitment; operationally, the weights shown and their sums provide only the roughest indicators of those sums. We expect that these weights will be used more as a guide to precise verbal evaluation of the volume of Participation than as scores for statistical treatment.

Responsiveness[5]

Responsiveness refers to the extent to which superordinates' decisions and actions take into account and are based on the preferences of their subordinates. The completely unresponsive *S* wholly ignores *s*-preferences. Forms, norms, and practices of Responsiveness can all be distinguished.

General Operational Considerations

It is likely that Participation and Responsiveness vary rather closely together, for two reasons. First, if Participation is low by preference and in fact, *S*'s will not have any significant number of *s*-inputs to which they might respond. Second, Participation is not likely to remain high for any length of time unless *S*'s are at least grudgingly responsive. Thus it is a general operational principle that an initial assessment ought to be made of Participation. If this dimension is low, a cursory rather than detailed check

Table 10.6 Frequency of Use of Channels of Participation[a]

Frequency of Use	Channels of Participation			
	Group	Personal Direct	Personal Indirect	Impersonal
High	9	6	4	3
Medium	6	4	3	2
Low	3	2	2	1
Nil	0	0	0	0
Summary score =	( )	+ ( )	+ ( )	+ ( )
			4	

[a] Range of possible scores = 0 to 5.5.

of *S*-Responsiveness can be made. But the empirical tendency is by no means a perfect one. The researcher should be alert to the possibility that *S*'s value Responsiveness to *s*'s who do not participate and may therefore take "soundings" to anticipate *s*'s preferences correctly, or may "overrespond" to the few inputs they do receive.

The more likely case, empirically, is that Participation is relatively high but *S*'s do not particularly value Responsiveness and practice it only at their own convenience or when compelled to do so. Hence high Participation does not necessarily entail high Responsiveness, and the latter must be independently determined.

Another general consideration is that Responsiveness is likely to be a sensitive matter for *S*'s. This is especially true if they tend to disvalue Responsiveness or are subject to *s*-inputs well in excess of what they prefer to respond to. Contrariwise, statements by subs and lower supers about the (un)-Responsiveness of top *S*'s, although freely given, are rather likely to be biased by animus and by restricted knowledge of the range of inputs to top *S*'s. These two problems arise directly in questionnaire and interview studies, and indirectly in historical inquiry or in studies based on documentary and secondary material. Sources that reflect the supers' point of view are likely to distort Responsiveness practices in the direction of *S*-norms (overreporting it if valued, otherwise underreporting it), whereas "the view from below" may well underestimate *S*-Responsiveness in both norm and practice.

Responsiveness When, and About What?

Responsiveness is not necessarily uniform. First, *S*'s may be differentially responsive to inputs about different *domains* of unit activities. They may, plausibly, respond to inputs about instrumentalities but not tasks, and to inputs about peer behavior and comportment but not hierarchic behavior. Second, *S*'s may respond selectively to inputs depending on whether they are of concern only to an individual *s* or a group of *s*'s, or to the unit as a whole. (Friedman [1972] found that Swedish teachers regarded student inputs about collective matters considerably more favorably than inputs about individual matters, although whether the teachers selectively responded to inputs on this basis was not determined.) Third, *S*'s may selectively respond to inputs depending on the mode of Participation. In some units "group activism" may have more impact than "personal activism" because the former represents more pressure, or more people. In other units the precise opposite may hold true, because *S*'s value personal supplications but fear loss of face if they give in to group pressure. Finally, inputs may be directed to and responded to at different stages in the process of making and implementing decisions.

A "fine-grained" analysis of Responsiveness should, perhaps, take account of several or all of these conditions as they affect the overall degree of Responsiveness. Only the last is elaborated here, because it is more central than the others to the "influence process." That is, if we want to understand the nexus between *s*-Participation and *S*-Responsiveness in any organization, the first thing we wish to know—once we have determined the nature of Participation—is where and how inputs impinge on the decision-making process. It may be desirable in a particular study to go beyond this and to ask: inputs about what domains? Directed through what channels?

The six analytically distinguishable points or decision-making phases at which *s*-inputs may be taken into account by *S*'s are as follows.

Definition of issues is the identification of problems or issues about which *S*'s should take action. Any group(s) within the unit may identify issues that require decision making, even groups outside the unit. Subs and lower *S*'s may pose issues by making demands, proposals, or simply suggestions. The unit is "responsive" to the extent that all issues that *S*'s consider for action are those so defined by *s*'s (including lower *S*'s).

Deliberation is the process of formulating and evaluating alternative courses of actions, and directives. The unit is wholly "responsive" insofar as (*a*) all alternatives under consideration are ones posed by *s*'s and lower *S*'s, and (*b*) the criteria used in their evaluation are those preferred by *s*'s. Stipulation (*b*) is needed to deal with the problem of "pseudo-Responsiveness" in which *S*'s make a show of considering all alternatives brought to their attention but give serious consideration only to those which they themselves have formulated.

Resolution is the process of deciding among alternative courses of action. This is "decision-making" narrowly construed: the point at which the final decision is reached. A unit is responsive to the extent that final decisions are made wholly on the basis of *s*-preferences, as in referenda and union contract and strike votes. Even if the effective range of choices at "resolution" is limited to "yes-no," this is not a constraint on Responsiveness because it is taken into account by the degree of Responsiveness at the previous two stages.

Implementation is the carrying out of courses of action, through issuing and acting on the requisite directives. Subs may have been generally satisfied with their influence on the definition, deliberation, and resolution of an issue but still take exception to the ways in which directives are implemented. They are even more likely to have articulate preferences if there has been little responsiveness at earlier stages. The unit is Responsive here to the extent that preferences of *s*'s and lower *S*'s are recognized in decisions about whether and how directives are implemented. It is a characteristic of some "autocratic" units—those in Latin cultures, for example—to manifest little responsiveness at the earlier stages of decision making but to be highly responsive at this one.

Sanctioning is the application of sanctions to those who fail to comply with directives. The most highly responsive unit is one in which *s*'s decide whether sanctions should be imposed. The trial-by-jury system, which in Anglo-Saxon countries is nominally concerned with deciding on guilt or innocence (compliance or noncompliance with directives), also has the effective function of allowing *s*'s to decide whether a noncompliant citizen *ought* to be sanctioned. The "rule of law" formally excludes citizens from influencing the administration of sanctions; the jury system lets their influence in through the back door, and the prohibition on double jeopardy ensures that *S*'s will be responsive to their decisions.

Feedback is the reception and processing of inputs about the effects of directives once they are implemented. Responsiveness is high to the extent that *S*'s base decision to retain or modify directives on feedback from *s*'s. Although this phase is analytically distinguishable from the others, it may not be worth distinguishing operationally because it is closely linked to implementation and also to new cycles of definition, deliberation, etc.

To say that a unit is relatively responsive in any or all the foregoing phases of decision making does not mean that all *s*'s will necessarily be satisfied with what is done. Since there will always be diversity of preferences among *s*'s, even the completely responsive *S* will have to make some choice among inputs. Generally, the more diverse the preferences of *s*'s in a unit, the greater the limitations on Responsiveness that *S*'s will have to practice; otherwise the unit would be immobilized by competing demands. We also recognize that there are substantial, qualitative differences among moderately Responsive units according to the stages at which supers *are* responsive. The most highly responsive units are, by definition, responsive in most of the six phases of decision, and the least-responsive ones are uniformly unresponsive. But there is substantial variation among units and political cultures in the junctures at which moderate Responsiveness is valued and practiced, and these differences in turn markedly affect institutional forms and style.

Information on Responsiveness Forms

Many social units have formal prescriptions regarding Responsiveness. The most unambiguous are provisions for referenda on decision issues. More ambiguous cases in point are: the formal participation, *with full rights*, of subs' representatives on committees and boards of management, formal provisions for *s*'s to introduce policy motions and other initiatives, regular meetings of *S*'s with *s*'s on decision issues, and grants of the right to petition. It will be evident that these are really formal prescriptions about Participation, but they may be regarded as relevant to Responsiveness if *S*'s are obliged to act on their results in some significant manner.

Note that the mere existence of a legislative body comprised of representatives of *s*'s does not constitute evidence about Responsiveness. Representatives are themselves *S*'s; their formal Responsiveness is high only if they are required to base their decisions on the views of their constituents. Legislative bodies are usually subordinated to collective or individual executives; the latter, who are top *S*'s, are formally Responsive to the extent that they are constitutionally required to take the actions legislated by representative bodies.

Information about Norms and Practices

In most social units it is intrinsically more difficult to acquire comprehensive information on Responsiveness than on Directiveness and Participation. The directives of a unit are generally a matter of record, and information on group activism and voting is also readily available, as a rule. But most of the business of decision making is conducted *in camera*, even in legislative bodies. The conventional approach to estimating Responsiveness is to compare inputs with outputs, but this is really a "black box" approach: not all inputs can be detected from outside, nor can one determine whether matchings are coincidental. The fullest information can only be gotten from "inside" the decision-making process, directly or secondhand from the decisionmakers themselves. For "practices" we recommend a case-history approach that can be applied both to "historical" (inaccessible) decisions and to contemporary decisions in units whose *S*'s are prepared to give firsthand information. For norms, some interview and questionnaire items are suggested.

Case Histories. Responsiveness practices can be discovered, even if not very rigorously, through constructing a series of *case histories of decisions* arrived at by *S*'s, either from documentary materials or from interviews with relevant actors. Ideally such case histories should comprise decisions taken at different levels within the unit and dealing with different domains of unit activity. The case histories may be used for other dimensions as well, but here the object is to determine whether *s*'s played a major role in the decision-process. It is especially important to test whether *s*'s were influential when the preferences of *S*'s were in conflict with those of *s*'s, because in such cases *s*'s influence or lack of it is most clearly discernible.[6] In constructing the histories, the phases of the decision-process can be used as a checklist and "self-answering" questionnaire (i.e., one to be answered by the researcher himself after studying the relevant material). The following is a provisional checklist:

Definition of Issues

1. What is the problem at issue?

a. Did its consideration originate with an action by an *s* or *s*'s?

b. By which mode(s) of Participation?

c. Is there reason to think that *S*'s would have preferred not to consider action on the matter?

d. Did the *s*-initiated action challenge an existing rule or order enforced by *S*'s?

2. Was "pressure" required to put the matter on the agenda?

3. Did the *S*'s originate action despite the preference of *s*'s to keep matters as they were? Did their action, in that case, challenge a rule or order in whose determination *s*'s had been influential or with which they were otherwise "identified"?

Deliberation

1. Did *s*'s participate, formally or otherwise, directly or through representatives, in the evaluation of proposed action?

2. What were the principal alternative actions considered?

a. Did *s*'s themselves propose any specific alternative actions and, if so, was there due consideration of their proposals?

b. Is there reason to think that *S*'s would have preferred no such proposals, or did *s*'s proposals run counter to those of *S*'s?

3. Were *s*'s proposals given high or low priority in the deliberative process? Much or little attention?

4. Were there any *S*'s who especially espoused the *s*'s cause, and what was their influence?

5. Was the objective of deliberation the working out of a compromise between *S*'s and *s*'s? If so, was the attitude of the *S*'s toward compromise grudging or generous?

6. Ask the questions posed in item 5 about any "mediation" between *S*'s and *s*'s.

Resolution

1. Did *s*'s or their representatives have "voting rights" (or any equivalent) in deciding on action?

a. If not, did the *S*'s decision reflect any part of the *s*'s preferences—large, medium, or small?

b. Where they did, is there reason to think that *S*'s left to their own devices would have decided in any way differently (very differently, somewhat differently, not much differently)?

2. Was there resentment of the *s*'s influence (suggesting responsiveness

in practice but not in norm—e.g., that *S*'s are responsive only because of *s*'s real or imagined powers)?

Implementation

1. Did *s*'s affect the way the implementing directives based on the decision were carried out? If so, did this in any major respect implicitly change the actions originally decided on?
2. Is there any evidence that postresolution changes were made despite contrary preference by *S*'s?
3. Did the *S*'s take pains to explain specific directives to *s*'s? Or persuade them of its advisability? If so, did they reconsider the directives in whole or part on the basis of *s*'s response to it?
4. If *s*'s opposed a directive, was it allowed to "lapse"?

Feedback

1. If *s*'s did not fully comply with implementing directives or otherwise disappointed expectations (e.g., had difficulty carrying it out), was the matter reconsidered?
2. Did the *S*'s try to ascertain the effect of directives on *s*'s?
3. Did *S*'s provide channels for complaints, and so on, against implemented directives and, if so, do they take these seriously?
4. Do *S*'s have periodic reviews of the impact of directives with *s*'s or their representatives?

This checklist is not comprehensive and is, of course, subject to modification depending on the unit and the decision. Note also that it can be used to help assess Participation by *s*'s and Decision-Behavior among higher and lower *S*'s.

Questionnaire and Interview Items. The following items can be used to indirectly study *S*-norms of Responsiveness, as perceived by lower *S*'s and by *s*'s. Other versions of the same items can be used to illuminate supers' self-reports about their norms and practices of Responsiveness. Direct questions are rather likely to be sensitive. A set of questions used successfully with French teachers appears in Table 11.1.

1. *S*-norms of Responsiveness, as perceived by *s*'s and S_2's

The previous questions asked about attempts by (*s*) to influence (*S*) in regard to how the (unit) is run. Can you *think of any cases in which they tried to do so, and in which what they wanted differed from what the* (*S*) wanted?

Yes	No
(If "yes") About how many (*s*), in your experience, hold each of the following views?	If "no," go to next subject.

a. Since it is the *S*'s job to run the (social unit), they should do what they think right, regardless of what the *s*'s think.

Almost all think so [ ]
Many do [ ]
Some do [ ]
Few do [ ]
None do [ ]

b. Running the (social unit) is basically up to the (*S*), and they should generally do what they think right, but occasionally (*s*) have good ideas, and when they do (*S*) should consider changing their minds.

Almost all think so [ ]
Many do [ ]
Some do [ ]
Few do [ ]
None do [ ]

c. Although the (*S*) are mainly responsible for the rules and orders of the (social unit), it is not good for the (unit) if they fail to satisfy the (*s*); thus when the (*s*) have different views, the (*S*) should generally try to work out a compromise with them, but not always make important concessions.

Almost all think so [ ]
Many do [ ]
Some do [ ]
Few do [ ]
None do [ ]

d. Even when their views are different, (*S*) should attach great weight to the views of the (*s*) and, in case of conflict, always should make *important* concessions to them.

Almost all think so [ ]
Many do [ ]
Some do [ ]
Few do [ ]
None do [ ]

e. (Supers) are the people who make decisions, but (*s*) know best what is good for the (social unit). Therefore the (*s*) or their spokesmen should always be consulted about decisions and the (*S*) should generally be guided by their wishes.

Almost all think so [ ]
Many do [ ]
Some do [ ]
Few do [ ]
None do [ ]

2. *s* and S_2 norms of Responsiveness

Now could you specify which one of these statements most closely represents how *you* feel (*S*) should think? (Same response options as for item 1.)

Compliance[7]

General Considerations

Operational Definitions. Compliance refers to the extent to which subordinates are disposed to abide by superordinates' directives and to the extent they do so in practice. The poles of the Compliance dimension are "submissiveness" and "insubordination," with a midpoint at "indifference." We can speak of degrees of increasing "allegiance" along the continuum from indifference to submissiveness, and of degrees of increasing "opposition" along the continuum from indifference to insubordination. The following general—not yet fully operational—definitions are suggested for the three positions along the Compliance continuum:

Submissiveness. Subs and lower *S*'s value compliance with all standing orders and directives of a social unit (generally, or within one or several domains) and believe that they should be complied with even at considerable personal sacrifice. In practice they attempt to comply in letter and spirit with all orders and directives, even when this is painful or costly; as a rule they act as best they can to secure attainment of the objectives of the directives.

Indifference. Subs and lower *S*'s believe that they should comply with standing orders and directives only when and insofar as it is in their self-interest, taking into account both their possible value gains for compliance and the sanctions for noncompliance. In practice they selectively comply, according to costs, rewards, and personal convenience.

Opposition. Subs and lower *S*'s reject compliance with any standing orders and directives of a social unit (generally, or within one or several domains) and believe that such orders should be rejected even at considerable personal sacrifice. In practice they defy directives, encourage others to follow suit, and attempt to sabotage the attainment of the apparent objectives of the directives.

Individual members of social units may be found who are entirely allegiant or opposed, but rarely are all members entirely allegiant, except perhaps in some religious orders and voluntary associations. No unit can be comprised entirely of insubordinate members because it would quickly cease to exist. There are, however, conflict-ridden units like prerevolutionary states and industries riven by labor-management disputes in which oppositional attitudes are widespread and intense, and compliance can be obtained only by high levels of coercion. (These units are to be distinguished from organized collectivities like prisons and gangs of conscript laborers, which are only "quasi-units" because few if any of their *s*'s identify with the unit. Such collectivities are held together *only* by force, and whenever it is relaxed, "members" manifest the most extreme forms of insubordination.)

Norms, Forms, and Practices. Compliance is essentially a norm-practice dimension. In most cases *forms* do not exist at all; to our knowledge, one of the rare instances of a formal prescription concerning Compliance is contained in the Uniform Code of Military Justice of the United States, which specifies the conditions under which an order may be disobeyed. But high degrees of Compliance are almost always *assumed* in "constitutional" documents. Documentary prescriptions of penalities for noncompliance are an aspect of formal Directiveness, not Compliance. The prescription of means for redressing grievances is an aspect of formal Participation, not Compliance.

Our operational focus is on the norms of Compliance rather than its practices, because there are various and important motives for high and low Compliance in practice which are not authority considerations, or part of authority patterns at all (see Chapter 2). This does not mean that the practice of Compliance is unimportant. Its observation often provides significant indications of norms, for example. Compliance practices are, moreover, an important aspect of the *performance characteristics* of any social unit: in other words, they are part of a category or variable of social unit activity that is conceptually distinct from its authority characteristics. But this is a further and persuasive reason why operational descriptions of Compliance concentrate on norms.

Sensitivity of Compliance. We found questions about the norms of Compliance to be sensitive in some units and some societies, as can be determined in pretesting, but they need not be avoided on a priori grounds.

Uniformity of Compliance. Compliance may be differentially valued and practiced among the different domains of unit activity. Where possible, empirical research should assess Compliance separately in the several domains of unit activity, distinguishing at least between the more central "task" and "instrumental" domains and the (usually) more peripheral "deportment," "comportment," and "ideological" domains.

Compliance also may be differentially valued and practiced according to the level of superordination from which directives originate. In the Spanish colonial empire, for example, it was accepted that local officials could comply conditionally, if at all, with the directives of governors-general and ministers who ranked between them and the king, but these lower *S*'s were expected to accept royal decisions almost without exception.[8] Much closer to home, the child who selectively accepts one parent's directives but more uniformly complies with those of the other is widely familiar. If such selective Compliance is observed, it is worth noting and its sources should be determined. It may be that Compliance with one source of directives is indeed more highly valued than Compliance with another; this was rather clearly the case in the Spanish colonial situation. But it seems more likely that differential Compliance is predicated on differential legitimacy and cost-benefit calculations.

Information Sources: Norms of Compliance

The principal sources of normative information about Compliance are interviews and questionnaires, where possible, and observation (directly and on the basis of others' reports and studies).

Direct and Surrogate Observation. The researcher sometimes hears or reads comments that directly reflect Compliance norms. Supers often attempt to inculcate and reinforce high valuation of Compliance in *s*'s; parents usually do so with children, military officers and noncoms with recruits, teachers with students. Strongly dissident *s*'s often exhort other *s*'s to value and practice conditional or absolute disobedience toward *S*'s; contemporary examples that come immediately to mind include British labor militants, student leaders of *chahuts* in French schools, and antiwar activists in the United States in 1965 and later. But these are mostly obvious cases: it is not surprising to find that rebels disvalue Compliance and that *S*'s highly value it. The closer one comes to the "indifference" point, however, the more subtle the cues are likely to be. Usually it will be necessary to infer norms from practices. What we suggest below are the kinds of observations about Compliance practices suggesting that *s*'s value something less than complete submissiveness or absolute insubordination.

The following *cues suggesting s valuation of opposition* are rank ordered according to what they seem to imply about the intensity of opposition; the ordering is tentative, however, and certainly no "equal-interval" assumption is made.

Mild opposition

1. Subs institute tasks in response to directives reluctantly or with displays of hostility toward (absent) *S*'s.
2. Subs respond to new directives only when supervisors are present and "on the prowl," or only when an explicit threat of sanctions for noncompliance is made.
3. Subs allow external factors to halt the implementation of directives without attempting to avoid them.

4. Subs interpret directives literally ("work to rule"), thereby undermining attainment of the goal for which the directives were designed.
5. Subs stop or botch a task for want of absolutely precise instructions, even though it is within their abilities to complete the work.
6. Subs deliberately violate what they regard as *S*-norms of proper conduct in areas of unit activity not subject to regulation (i.e., make themselves disagreeable to *S*'s whenever they can get away with it).
7. Subs refuse to comply with explicit directives even at some personal cost, such as loss of status or reduced compensation.

Intense opposition

8. Subs actively sabotage attainment of the goals of directives or of the unit generally.

Cues suggesting s-valuation of allegiance are tentatively rank ordered. Here as in the preceding and following section, such observations permit only inferences about Compliance norms, not definitive judgments. Motives and circumstances quite apart from opposition or allegiance may exist to account for them.

Mild allegiance

1. Subs respond to new directives even in the absence of supervision and without threat of sanctions.
2. Subs carry out tasks and obey directives more carefully and thoroughly than specifically required.
3. Subs respond to new directives promptly and with a show of enthusiasm.
4. Subs repeatedly refer to standing orders and directives while implementing a task, even though it is functionally unnecessary that they do so.
5. Subs act independently to achieve the objective of directives even when there are no visible rewards for their doing so.
6. Subs encourage other *s*'s to comply and bring pressure to bear on those who do not, even when there are no apparent rewards for *s*'s to act as "policemen."

7. Subs comply with directives even at considerable personal sacrifice and for no visible gain (e.g., work very long hours or with unnecessary care and effort to meet *S*-directives and suggestions).

Intense allegiance

We find in studying *cues suggesting valuation of qualified allegiance* that it is rare for any *S*'s, even of the lowest strata, to value opposition by *s*'s. When such values are held, they are likely to be strikingly manifest. The more challenging task is to determine just what normative expectations *S*'s have of their *s*'s along the continuum from submissiveness to indifference. It is by no means exceptional to find lower *S*'s—minor bureaucrats, teachers, shop foremen—who go through the motions of issuing "directives" but are content with the gesture and do not care whether their *s*'s comply. It also is not uncommon to find higher *S*'s, as well as many lower ones, who expect *s*'s to be only approximately and selectively compliant with their directives; such individuals may even be embarrassed when *s*'s comply submissively. The following kinds of observation are suggestive about *S*-valuation of Compliance:

Indifference

1. Supers issue directives with which noncompliance is significant but make no use of available means of supervision or prescribed sanctions.
2. Supers make no changes in directives issued or in their practice of supervision and sanctioning despite substantial changes in compliance rates.
3. When punctilious *s*'s call violations to *S*'s attention, the *S*'s do nothing or express disinterest.
4. Supers issue directives with which noncompliance is significant and supervise the prescribed activities, but make no use of available sanctions.
5. When *s*'s comply literally and with considerable effort to directives, *S*'s modify the directives to require less effort or less precise compliance.
6. Supers exert considerable effort in supervision and systematically impose sanctions for noncompliance.

Intense allegiance

Supers may take the actions just outlined for reasons other than qualified valuation of Compliance. It is possible, for example, that they treat noncompliance lightly because they fear loss of morale among *s*'s or outright rebellion. But even this is a telling consideration, because it suggests that Compliance is by no means an overriding value for these *S*'s; they will compromise it to achieve other ends.

Interview and Questionnaire Items. The first question below gives the respondent five response alternatives, of which the first, third, and last correspond respectively to the "submissive," "indifferent," and "insubordinate" positions on the Compliance continuum. The first question treats the respondent as an "informant," asking his opinion on *s*'s generally, because this may be a touchy question. The second question asks the respondent's own view. Following these questions are two versions of the response options used successfully in Workshop fieldwork. Finally we give the text of a paradigmatic question regarding Compliance norms in various domains of unit activity.

1. *General Compliance norms*

Which of the following statements best represents the way most (*s*) in this (unit) think about obeying (rules/orders)? If several seem true, indicate the one that represents the way the *largest number* thinks. If none seem true, provide an answer in your own words.

a. It is the duty of (*s*) *always* to obey [rules/orders], regardless of whether they seem hard or easy, beneficial or not beneficial.

b. Obeying [rules/orders] is *generally* a duty of (*s*), but they may be disobeyed where they involve great hardship and not much benefit to (*s*) or the (unit).

c. Whether (*s*) should obey [rules/orders] depends on whether it is *in their own interest* to do so, that is, whether the benefits of obeying are greater than the hardships.

d. (Subs) *should do as they like* regardless of [rules/orders] as long as they can do so without severe punishment.

e. Most (*S*) are selfish and try to exploit (*s*); thus (*s*) should *resist* them as much as possible.

f. Other.

2. *Respondent's Compliance norms*

Looking at these statements again, which most closely represents the way (*s*) *should* think, in your opinion?

3. *Compliance norm items used in interviews with German secondary school students,* by Ronald Rogowski (1971)

It is sometimes asserted that pupils have a moral obligation to obey the rules and directives of the school. So far as is possible, I would ask you to ignore the possible consequences of disobedience (punishments and the like) and to attend purely to the moral question. (Present list.) Here are five different answers to this problem. Please tell me which of these views best corresponds to your opinion.

a. A pupil is obliged to resist; if he does not want to follow a directive, he should refuse to obey even under threat of heavy punishment.

b. A pupil is not obligated to obey at all; he should follow directives only according to his own preference, so far as that is possible without heavy punishments.

c. A pupil is obligated to obey only if he can convince himself that the directive is justified beyond doubt.

d. A pupil is ordinarily obligated to obey, but he may act differently if he is convinced that the directive is completely unjustified.

e. A pupil is morally obligated to obey every directive of every teacher, regardless of whether the directive appears to be justified.

4. *Compliance norm items used with Canadian public officials,* by Gurston Dacks (1972)

a. Rules and orders should always be obeyed scrupulously, even if they seem ill conceived or arbitrary.

b. Rules and orders should be generally but not necessarily scrupulously obeyed.

c. Subordinates should obey rules and orders, but they should try, by interpreting them as freely as possible, to maximize their independence and freedom of discretion.

d. Rules and orders should be generally followed, but a subordinate should make minor deviations as he sees fit.

e. If an order seems very unreasonable or likely to cause unusual hardship, it should not be obeyed. Every effort possible should be made to shelve or sidetrack it. (Persons feeling this way may at the same time attempt to influence their superiors to change the order or policy.)

f. If junior members of the department have not been adequately consulted on a given policy or directive, they need not implement it unless they personally agree with it.

g. One should do whatever is in his own personal interest, so long as he thinks he can do without severe punishment.

5. *Compliance norms by domain*

[Rules/orders] might be concerned with the following different things:

The [tasks/work] of the unit
Behavior of (*s*) toward (*S*)
Behavior of (*s*) toward other (*s*)
Personal matters
Activities of (*s*) outside of the (unit)

How do most (*s*) feel in regard to obeying [rules/orders] about these different things?

Should always obey	Usually obey	Obey if in own interest	Do as they like	Resist

a. [Rules/orders] about (tasks) of (unit)
b. [Rules/orders] about behavior toward (*S*)
c. [Rules/orders] about behavior toward other (*s*)
d. [Rules/orders] about personal matters
e. [Rules/orders] about outside activities

Compliance Practices

Compliance practices are observed partly because of their intrinsic importance and, equally important, for the clues they provide about Compliance norms. In a cursory study we look mainly for evidence of gross, widespread acts of noncompliance; if none are reported or observed, Compliance can be judged relatively high. But a cursory look is not likely to reveal whether Compliance is equally high with respect to small matters and large, or with regard to directives in all domains of activity or only some. Compliance practices ought to be evaluated primarily by reference to currently issued and reinforced directives (meaning by "reinforced" those which are most actively supervised and sanctioned by *S*'s). These ordinarily are directives about the unit's most central tasks and activities. Compliance with "marginal" directives should be taken into account only to qualify these observations. Compliance is absolutely highest in practice if punctilious with respect to all kinds of directives in all phases of "covered" activity; it ought to be judged only slightly less high if exact Compliance is given to directives in central areas of unit activity but only approximate Compliance is practiced in other areas.

Records and Observation. Indicators and observational cues of Compliance practices are almost always specific to the social unit. Here are a few suggestions:

1. *Suggested documentary sources*

a. Turnover rate for *s*'s, either due to resignations or because of suspension, can be suggestive about Compliance, provided it can be established that there is a regular connection between dismissals/departures and noncompliance.

b. Records of supervised activities can be examined, to see to what extent *s*'s meet output norms or otherwise carry out tasks in specified ways.

c. Records of sanctions applied and/or other quasi-judicial proceedings can be used to give a general idea of the areas in which noncompliance is likely, types of directives violated, and so on.

2. *Suggested situational sources*

a. List a day's orders or instructions by one or two *S*'s and observe the degree of compliance with them during that period. Attention is particularly called to behavioral aspects indicating willingness or disinclination to comply. Such observation can be followed up by informal interviews with *S*'s.

b. Similar knowledge can be gained by studying and comparing the directives and behavior of both harsh and lenient *S*'s, with particular attention to a comparison of the behavior of the *s*'s in these situations.

c. Situations in which rewards to *s*'s vary should be sought out; what variations in compliance, if any, are noted? How are they commonly manifested?

d. Situations occasioning unusual demands in time or effort should be looked for, and compliance rates observed.

Questionnaire and Interview Items. "Practice" items were not developed for general Workshop use because of their presumed sensitivity. Such questions could readily be devised by revising item 5 on Compliance norms to inquire about the extent to which rules and orders in each of the specified domains are in fact obeyed. Schonfeld (1971) asked such questions in French schools with some success.

Bases of Compliance

If cost-benefit calculations seem likely to be of considerable importance for Compliance norms and practices in a particular unit, the researcher may want to inquire into them more closely. Earlier we suggested some observations indicating that Compliance norms approach the "indifference" point. If interview and questionnaire techniques are practicable, it is possible to inquire about the matter more directly. Two items are suggested below. Note that they are not "dimensional" in the sense that they affect a unit's rating on the Compliance dimension; rather, they provide confirming and supplementary evidence about how the unit ought to be judged. Since the items were devised after the conclusion of Workshop fieldwork, we cannot evaluate their usability.

Bases of Compliance: Practices

What do (*S*) do in this (unit) to induce members to obey its rules and regulations? Specifically, to what extent do (*S*) rely on reprimands and punishments for those who do not obey?

A great deal   Quite a lot   Some   A little   Not at all

And to what extent do (S) rely on praise and rewards for those who obey very well?

A great deal Quite a lot Some A little Not at all

Bases of Compliance: Norms
What do you think that (S) *should* do to ensure that the rules and regulations of this unit are obeyed?

Use mainly punishment and warnings
Use punishment and rewards about equally
Use mainly rewards and praise
Nothing; (s) should decide freely whether to obey

Notes

1. This discussion is a much revised and expanded version of a draft fieldwork manual on *Permissiveness* prepared for the Workshop in Comparative Politics in June 1967 by Harry Eckstein, Ted Gurr, Craig MacLean, and William Schonfeld. It takes into account numerous suggestions and proposals by other members of the Workshop; many of them were summarized by Craig Maclean in "Permissiveness/Directiveness Revisited" (1969).

2. Throughout this chapter the interview and questionnaire items are appropriate for both s's and S's, except when otherwise noted. Those which are open-ended are recommended only for use in interviews, the others are suitable for questionnaires and interviews both.

3. This is a substantially revised version of a fieldwork manual on *Participation* (Workshop in Comparative Politics, July 1967) prepared by Harry Eckstein, Robert Friedman, and Ted Gurr. A considerable expansion and elaboration of the Participation dimension is proposed and employed by Friedman, *Participation in Democracy* (1972).

4. We assume only a correlation, not a necessary connection, between mode of participation and intensity. In some cultures, and social units, group activism may be especially valued and other forms of activism disvalued, in which case group activism would not necessarily have the intensity that it has in most cultures.

5. This section is a substantially expanded version of a fieldwork manual on *Responsiveness* (Workshop in Comparative Politics, June 1967) prepared by Harry Eckstein, Ted Gurr, Craig MacLean, and William Schonfeld. It also draws on a working document on the same subject prepared by Donald Newman in August 1970.

6. See Robert Dahl's argument that the existence of a "ruling elite" can only be determined by reference to which group's preferences regularly prevail when there is disagreement over issues, in "A Critique of the Ruling Elite Model," *American Political Science Review*, Vol. 52 (June 1958), pp. 463–469.

7. This is a substantially revised and extended version of a fieldwork manual on *Compliance* prepared for the Workshop in Comparative Politics (July 1967), prepared mainly by Harry Eckstein. It draws in part on documents prepared by Ronald Rogowski and William Schonfeld.

8. See Frank Jay Moreno, "The Spanish Colonial System: A Functional Approach," *Western Political Quarterly,* Vol. 20 (June 1967), pp. 308–320.

CHAPTER ELEVEN

The Comprehensive Description of Authority Patterns

All that was taken apart in the analytic scheme and separately described by the procedures of the preceding three chapters, must be put back together for the purpose of synthetic description. The researcher's intellectual interests mainly determine which social unit's authority patterns are studied. Notions of "centrality" influence choice about which elements of the unit(s) to study closely. The dimensions of the analytic scheme, and the distinction among forms, norms, and practices, dictate the traits of authority about which data are to be gathered. The next question is, what constitutes a comprehensive description of the unit's authority pattern?

There are two facets to any comprehensive description. First is the aggregate characterization of elements of the unit, categories of members, and the unit as a whole. The second is specification of the degree and kinds of within-unit diversity. What follows is a set of guidelines for exhaustive description within the framework of the analytic scheme and its contingent distinctions. Rarely if ever are units so completely described in one study. Theoretical interests dictate a highly selective approach to description. Lack of time and resources, or a quest for breadth rather than detail, may require that only the most visible manifestations of the most salient dimensions be studied. Some of the levels of aggregation and some within-unit comparison are irrelevant to particular kinds of units. Still, it is necessary to have an ideal-typical model of comprehensive description in mind. If nothing else, it serves as a standard against which to judge how incomplete are prevailing descriptions of authority patterns.

Aggregate Description

Whatever choices the researcher made about which of several elements of a social unit to study, which of many individuals to interview, which documents to analyze, and which behaviors to observe, his observations constitute a sample. What was sampled at one level of analysis, among individuals or elements, must in studies of authority relations be aggregated or generalized to a higher level of analysis. We are less interested in the Participation practices of a particular member than in the pattern of Participation practices of the unit as a whole and of its major elements. And we are not only interested in the overall pattern of Participation but in the extent of variation in its norms and practices between subordinates and superordinates, and among other elements of the unit.

Norms and practices of authority patterns call for aggregation and comparison; forms ordinarily do not. Forms, which are specified in documents, require not aggregation but analytic interpretation and summary by the investigator. Since simple units and most complex ones have a single set of forms, within-unit comparison of forms ordinarily are irrelevant. The principal exceptions occur in complex and internally autonomous units such as the Democratic Party, some of whose autonomous but functionally identical elements may have different forms. These formal differences may be characterized in terms of synthetic concepts, such as "autocratic" or "democratic," "open" or "closed," but the problems of their comparison are a good deal simpler than comparisons involving norms and practices. The discussion below concentrates on the latter.

We illustrate the procedures of aggregation and comparison with a hypothetical school classroom and a school in its entirety. Most classrooms today have the simplest possible authority structure: a single S-level, the teacher, and a homogeneous stratum of s's, the students. The school in our example has two degrees of complexity: it is composed of multiple similar elements (different classrooms) and has at least two superordinate strata, the principal S_1 and the teachers S_2.[1] The first step in aggregation is to cumulate information on each of the dimensions of authority, separately for norms and practices and for distinct groups of unit members. The classroom is the simplest case. The teacher's norms and the students' norms on each of the dimensions of authority are separately summarized, and their practices are also separately summarized. Just what is summarized depends on the information strategies used. *Norms* mostly likely have been determined using interview and questionnaire schedules. Student norms about Directiveness, for example, are the s's mean responses to the Directiveness question(s). The range and standard deviation of their responses also is reported, as in any comprehensive report of survey-type work. And the distribution of responses should be visually inspected for evidence of bimodality. For a single teacher there is no "distribution" of norms, but a single (set of) responses.

Practices are likely to be assessed using several kinds of information: reports of teacher and students about what they actually do, plus the researcher's own systematic observation of classroom behavior. In either case the results will be summarized by reference to a standarized scale—such as our five-point rating scales—to indicate both the average tendency and the range of variation around it. Examples of two rather different but comparable kinds of aggregation are given in Table 11.1. French teachers' norms of Responsiveness are evaluated using a five-item scale, in the first column on the basis of student perceptions of what most of their teachers think, in the second on the basis of teachers' self-reports. Note that the teachers strongly disavow the "completely ignore" position, whereas students believe that it is one of the views most commonly held by their teachers.

The four basic levels of aggregation are listed in the first four columns of Table 11.2. It should be noted that all members of the unit, S and s, might conceivably hold norms about each of the dimensions. Only some of the dimensions have a "practice" facet, however. Compliance and Participation, for example, are attributes of subordinate behavior; there can be no S-"practice" of them (except with respect to higher S's, in which case the

Table 11.1 Examples of Aggregation of Questionnaire and Interview Responses from French Secondary Schools: Responsiveness of Teachers to Student Influence[a]

Normative Position	Percentage of Students Reporting that most or some Teachers Hold this Position (n = 1187)	Average Teach Agreement wit Position[b] (n =
Teachers should completely ignore the students when the students try to exert an influence on them.	66	6.54
From time to time the students have some good ideas. When this occurs, the teachers should take these ideas into account.	75	1.14
When the students and teachers have different views, the teachers should generally try to make a synthesis.	46	2.52
In the case of conflict between the students' and teachers' point of view, important concessions should be made to the students.	33	5.14
The students or their representatives should always be consulted before any decision is taken, and the teachers should generally be guided by and follow the wishes of their students.	27	5.73

[a] From Schonfeld, *Youth and Authority in France*, pp. 20–24. The data are from second- and fourt year students (aged 12–15) and a sample of their teachers in a stratified sample of French secon ary schools.

[b] 1 = complete agreement, 7 = complete disagreement.

Table 11.2 Authority Aggregation Matrix for a Social Unit with Simple Structure[a,b]

Dimension of Authority	Superordinates		Subordinates		Total Unit	
	Norms	Practices	Norms	Practices	Norms	Practices
Superordinate dimensions						
Conformation	$\bar{M}$ resp	Σ obs	$\bar{M}$ resp	Σ obs	$\bar{M}$ S, s resp	Observed flow of directives and influence attempts
Decision -Rules, -Behavior	$\bar{M}$ resp	Σ obs	($\bar{M}$ resp)	—	$\bar{M}$ S resp	Observed S-interactions
Boundary exchange						
Recruitment	$\bar{M}$ resp	Σ obs	$\bar{M}$ resp	—	$\bar{M}$ S, s resp	Observed s, S mobility in unit
Influence dimensions						
Directiveness	$\bar{M}$ resp	Σ obs	$\bar{M}$ resp	(Σ reports)	$\bar{M}$ S, s resp	Σ observations of S
Compliance	$\bar{M}$ resp	(Σ reports)	$\bar{M}$ resp	Σ obs	$\bar{M}$ S, s resp	Σ observations of s
Participation	$\bar{M}$ resp	(Σ reports)	$\bar{M}$ resp	Σ obs	$\bar{M}$ S, s resp	Σ observations of s
Responsiveness	$\bar{M}$ resp	Σ obs	$\bar{M}$ resp	(Σ reports)	$\bar{M}$ S, s resp	Σ observations of S
Inequalities						
Distance	$\bar{M}$ resp	$\bar{M}$ resp	$\bar{M}$ resp	$\bar{M}$ resp	$\bar{M}$ S, s resp	$\bar{M}$ S, s resp
Deportment	$\bar{M}$ resp	Σ obs	$\bar{M}$ resp	Σ obs	$\bar{M}$ S, s resp	Σ observations of S, s interactions
Bases of Legitimacy	$\bar{M}$ resp	—	$\bar{M}$ resp	—	$\bar{M}$ S, s resp	—

[a] Levels at which data should be aggregated for units with a single superordinate stratum and a homogeneous subordinate stratum. See text.

[b] Symbols: $\bar{M}$ resp = mean (and distribution) of responses to interview and questionnaire items about the dimension; *or* researcher's rating based on observation and documentary evidence. Σ obs = summed observations of researcher, whether based on direct observations or documentary analysis *or* summed self-reports of behavior by members of the unit. Σ reports = summed reports by members of unit about behavior of their hierarchic opposites (*S*-reports about *s*-behavior; *s*-reports about *S*-behavior). *S* = superordinates, *s* = subordinates, — = not applicable; parentheses indicate aggregations of questionable relevance or reliability.

lower *S*'s are analyzed as subordinates; see below). Decision-Behavior and Responsiveness are among the dimensions that refer only to *S*-practices; subordinates may report information on how the *S*'s practice them, but that information is used, if at all, for triangulation.

The next level of aggregation is to the unit as a whole. Here the unit norms are some weighted average of the norms of subordinates and superordinates. Three alternative treatments are to weight *s*- and *S*-members of the unit (*a*) according to their relative number, (*b*) equally, or (*c*) disregarding *s*-norms and characterizing the unit according to *S*-norms exclusively. We recommend alternative *b* not only because it is the "middle" one but because it seems to be consistent with the general nature of social organization. Whether and how a social unit functions depends in significant part on both its "leaders" and "followers." If it is objected that the *S*'s are paramount, one need only point out the frequency with which *s*'s rebel against, sabotage, or abandon units whose *S*'s violate their sense of what is tolerable. And if the objection is that *s*'s are paramount because of their sheer numbers and their capacity to overthrow *S*'s the answer is that in almost all social units we know about, in any culture, *s*'s most of the time do more or less what they are directed to do.[2]

Practices pose fewer problems of unit-level aggregation than norms. The practice aspects of dimensions refer either to practices that are intrinsic to one stratum, *s* or *S*; or to interactions between two strata. The study of practices of Directiveness in the classroom as an entity is therefore the study of what the teacher instructs the students to do and how they are supervised and sanctioned when doing it; Compliance practices reveal how well the students abide by those instructions.

The more complex the social unit, the more numerous the aggregations to be performed. In the school as a whole, with two levels of superordination, an exhaustive description requires us to aggregate norms at least at four rather than two levels:

1. Norms of the principal as S_1.
2. Norms of teachers as subordinates of the principal.
3. Norms of teachers as S_2's.
4. Norms of students as subordinates.

And if the principal has any substantial direct dealings with students, a fifth level of description is needed, of his norms in that role. Practices similarly would have to be aggregated at five levels. Generally, the number of levels of aggregation is twice the number of *S*-strata distinguished in a unit (if each has authoritative interactions only with the two immediately adjacent strata), or more.

In addition to aggregation of authority data by level, it may be advisable to aggregate the data separately for different segments within a level. In the school, for example, the simplest aggregation would be to pool all classrooms and teachers, thereby characterizing "the" norms and typical practices of all teachers and all students. The most complex aggregation is classroom by classroom, although this seldom would be desirable. It is quite likely, however, that classes might be categorized by grade, as a preliminary to testing for age differences in authority norms and practices. Figure 11.1 provides an illustration, showing how Participation and Responsiveness be-

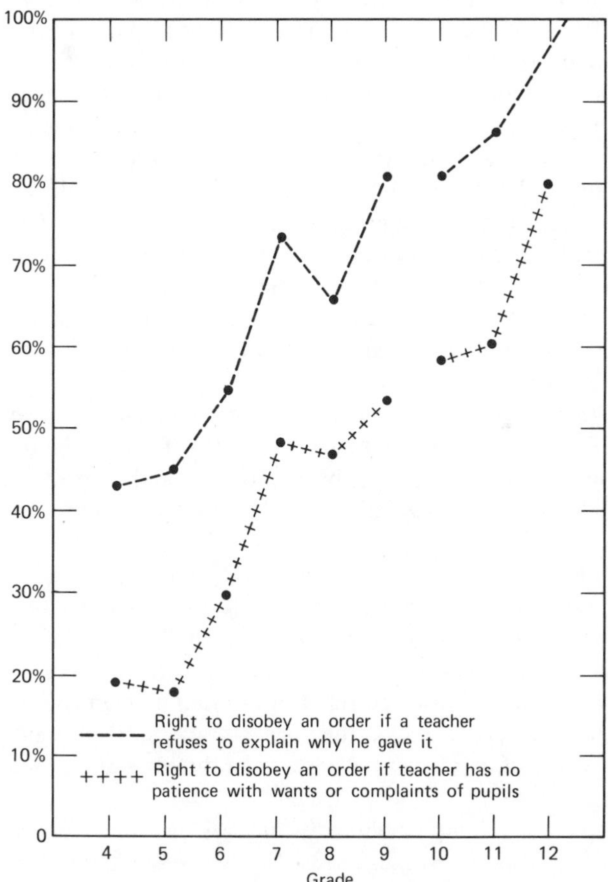

Fig. 11.1 The growth of participation and responsiveness as bases of legitimacy in Swedish schools, by grade. From Friedman (1972), *Participation in Democracy,* Ch. 4. The basic question is: "assume that the class has received an order of which you do not approve. Do you think that the student who does not follow the order acts rightly or wrongly if . . . ?" The graph shows the percentages agreeing with two of the "if" statements that tap what we originally referred to as "consensual" legitimacy. Respondents are students in the schools of a provincial city, *n*'s varying from 46 to 82 in the lower grades and from 19 to 42 in the upper grades.

come increasingly important as Bases of Legitimacy in successive grades of Swedish elementary and secondary school students. The general principle is that authority data from a complex unit should be aggregated within levels along whatever functional or ascriptive lines are thought to make a difference.

Description of Variations Within Units

Aggregation is a necessary prelude to the within-unit comparisons that are an essential part of the description of an authority pattern: the study of its "configurative" traits, so to speak. The question is whether and to what extent authority norms and practices are internally consistent, or "consonant." One of its aspects is *consistency*—the extent to which attitudes and behaviors in a unit are uniform or unimodal.[3] Within a simply structured unit this can be determined by inspection of the means, distributions, and standard deviations of the aggregations per se; the question is whether *S*-norms, *s*-norms, and total unit norms (and practices) about each dimension are closely grouped on a five-point scale. Consistency is low to the extent that norms are widely or bimodally distributed. Three other aspects of consonance can only be determined by comparing aggregates; they are listed in Table 11.3 and discussed below.

Normative complementarity is the extent to which the norms of subordinates agree with those of their superordinates. This can be determined on a dimension-by-dimension basis, by comparing and testing for significant differences between aggregated *S*- and *s*-norms (Table 11.1). For full characterization of authority patterns, such comparisons are most appropriately made at low levels of aggregation, for groups of *S*'s and *s*'s that directly interact. In the school, for example, the appropriate comparisons probably are of teachers of lower grades with their students, teachers of higher grades with their students, and principal with teachers. For summary characterization of authority patterns, it is often enough to pool the norms of all *S*'s for comparison against the norms of all *s*'s. (Representative sampling of *S*- and *s*-norms is assumed here, as in the foregoing discussion of aggregation.)

An example of a Complementarity comparison from Robert Friedman's data on Participation in Swedish schools is given in Table 11.4. The norms of teachers and students about appropriate circumstances for students to make influence attempts are compared across several grades. The norms of students and their teachers are increasingly complementary as students move up through the grades, with the exception that students come to value protest on purely personal matters more than do teachers.

Practice complementarity is the extent to which superordinate practices

Table 11.3 Comparison Matrix for Authority Characteristics of a Social Unit with Simple Structure[a,b]

Dimension of Authority	Complementarity of *S*- with *s*-norms	Complementarity of *S*- with *s*-Practices	Correspondence of Norms and Practices
Superordinate dimensions			
Conformation	×	0	×
Decision-Rules and -Behavior	×	0	×
Boundary interchange			
Recruitment	×	0	×
Influence dimensions			
Directiveness	× }		×
		×	
Compliance	× }		×
Participation	× }		×
		×	
Responsiveness	× }		×
Inequalities			
Distance	×	×	×
Deportment	×	×	×
Bases of Legitimacy	×	0	0

[a] Basic types of aggregate comparisons that should be made of facets of authority patterns, for units with a single superordinate stratum and a homogeneous subordinate stratum. See text.
[b] 0 = comparison not possible, × = comparison feasible.

match with related practices of subordinates. As Table 11.3 shows, there are only four direct practice complementarities among the authority dimensions. Three are self-evident. The first concerns Distance. If *S*'s and *s*'s each perceive the other as near equals, *or* if each group perceives the other as moderately or highly distant, these shared perceptions constitute complementarity. Unmatched perceptions pose difficulties, as when *S*'s think much more highly of themselves than do their subordinates. Second, Deportment involves matching sets of behavior of *s*'s toward *S*'s, and vice versa. Arrogant *S*-behavior complements obsequious *s*-behavior, familiar *S*-behavior complements familiar *s*-behavior. The uncomplementary, stressful patterns are those in which *S*-arrogance is met by *s*-familiarity, and *S*-familiarity by *s*-obsequiousness. The dimensions of Participation and Responsiveness are complementary or not in comparison with each other; in a complementary pattern, high *s*-Participation is matched by high *S*-Responsiveness, or low

Table 11.4 Complementarity of Swedish Teacher and Student Norms About Participation[a]

Q. to Students. If something happens in school that you do not approve of, would you complain to the teacher (or rector)?	*Q. to Teachers.* In which of the following situations do you think a pupil ought to be able to attempt to influence those with authority? Percentage Agreement			
	Fourth Graders ($n = 82$)	Ninth Graders ($n = 82$)	Twelfth Graders ($n = 24$)	Teachers
When the matter directly concerns (the pupil himself) (yourself) [e.g., grade on a test].	28	80	79	42
When the matter concerns many pupils [e.g., date for a test].	34	83	100	93
When the matter concerns not only (the pupil himself) (you) but the whole school [e.g., the time the school day begins].	48	52	67	76

[a] From Friedman, *Participation in Democracy,* Chs. III-42 and V-18. See legend to Figure 11.1. Note that the question to students appears to be a "practice" question but is not; it asks what they *would* do in a hypothetical situation, and we regard these responses as normative, in contrast to what students might report when asked what they *have* done in real situations.

Participation by low Responsiveness. The "dissonant" patterns, especially high Participation and low Responsiveness, are dysfunctional. The fourth complementarity is between Directiveness and Compliance, where "complementarity" is less clear-cut than previously. Since high Compliance is more functional for any unit than low Compliance, the pattern of high Compliance and high Directiveness is most complementary. The opposite pattern, low on both dimensions, does not promise much about the efficiency of the unit, but at least it minimizes intraunit conflict between groups of *S*'s and *s*'s. It also is more functional than the uncomplementary pattern in which Directiveness is high and Compliance low. In a unit so characterized, much energy is expended and friction generated by *S*'s issuing directives and supervising subordinates who systematically ignore or resist the directives.

Correspondence is the extent to which the forms, norms, and practices of the unit match one another. Correspondence of norms and practices is assumed to be of universal significance for how social units function; people who are frequently obliged to act against their preferences or to work with or for others who violate their norms, are not likely to be either content or effective. It is problematical, though, whether correspondence of *forms* with norms is as significant as correspondence of forms with practices. In some cultures and social units, forms are taken quite seriously, whereas in others they are blithely ignored. Exhaustive description requires all three "correspondence" comparisons; in actual field research the "form" comparisons may often be ignored.

There are special methodological problems of norm-practice comparisons that seldom arise when assessing equivalence of norms between *S*- and *s*-groups. When norms are assessed by means of interviews and questionnaires, the responses to identical items can be assumed to be comparable for both *S* and *s*. But precise norm-practice comparisons can be made directly only if norms and practices are rated on the same or conceptually equivalent scales. This is possible if the investigator applies the same rating scale to both, or if the basic sources of information are informants' responses to identical questions about norms and practices. Otherwise the investigator must rely on more impressionistic judgments about the extent to which and the direction in which unit norms differ from modal practices. Evaluation of form-norm and form-practice correspondence poses the same problems. We cannot specify the degree of correspondence unless a common measurement scale is used.[4]

Toward Simpler Description

Full characterization of an authority pattern, in brief, requires a set of aggregations or summary ratings of information on different parts of a unit and a series of within-unit comparisons of these aggregates.[5] It is apparent that a forbidding number of aggregations and comparisons is required for exhaustive description of the overall "configuration" of authority patterns, especially as the complexity of units increases. In practice the researcher usually finds it necessary or desirable to reduce the number of separate aggregations and comparisons. This can be done in any of several ways. The *dimensions* may be reduced in number, either by elimination or by constructing conceptually justified composite dimensions from some of the Influence or Superordinate dimensions. Similar *elements* may be combined, or some eliminated, to reduce the number of interelement comparisons. In his study of Dutch secondary schools, Philip Goldman summarized information not by individual school but by sociopolitical orientation of school: data on Catholic, Protestant, and nondenominational schools were separately aggregated. The justification in this instance was the investigator's concern with authority differences among the three major "pillars" of Dutch society.[6] Finally, adjacent *strata* may be combined, to reduce the number of aggregations by level and the number of cross-level comparisons. Different levels of superordination are most readily combined, though in complex units it is almost always advisable to distinguish between higher and lower *S*'s. Occasionally the lowest level of *S*'s may be combined with *s*'s, especially if the lowest *S*-level engages in relatively few authority interactions as *S*'s. Student monitors in a classroom are an example.

The means of simplification chosen depends, of course, on the purposes of the researcher. If his objective is hypothesis testing about, say, the relations between influence dimensions and the Bases of Legitimacy among subordinates, only these dimensions and unit members will be studied. If his purpose is to identify a modal authority pattern, he will focus on the central or typical elements of a complex unit. Within them, he will concentrate on the most frequent or salient authority interactions. In the school, for example, the great majority of authority interactions occur between teachers and students, not between teachers and the principal or principal and students. The classroom authority patterns are thus the modal ones, and two levels of aggregation probably will suffice.

The most efficient kind of summary description requires a detailed, carefully worked out typology, in which an authority pattern can be pigeonholed according to its more basic authority traits. But such typologies are not yet available, as we point out in Chapter 12, and their construction depends on the collection and evaluation of much more, and more detailed, information on authority relations than is now available. The crux of the matter is that it is premature to rely exclusively or mainly on brief summary descriptions of authority patterns. Summary description always proceeds at the cost of detail, and we know too few of the details or their effects to warrant assumptions about their inconsequentiality. However, the arguments about likely "salience" of dimensions in Chapter 7 point toward a defensible approach to simplified description—provided our speculations about salience are borne out by research. As we show later, the systematic use of "salient" dimensions can also help in the construction of methodical typology (i.e., "synthetic" concepts). Questions about what is or is not salient for members of social units among the facets of their authority patterns thus deserve special priority in research.

Concluding Comment

Part III has laid down a number of rather detailed guidelines for the methodical analysis of authority patterns. Though few data are reported, we have taken pains to demonstrate that the guidelines are not solely the result of desk-bound speculation. The members of the Workshop in Comparative Politics put many of them into practice when conducting and reporting their field research, with what we judge to be more than modest success.

The reader may observe that the guidelines are rather tedious to contemplate and arduous to implement. If so, we ask him to consider the alternative to niggling concern with the nature of social units and their elements, narrow distinctions among the aspects of authority, and detailed specification of authority characteristics at different levels of aggregation and comparison. That alternative is broad-brushed impressionism and a decided lack of comparability and cumulativeness, which is to say, precisely the conditions that characterize the literature on authority. We acknowledge that the guidelines are onerous and not always practicable. It also is recognized that the conceptual distinctions may not all be suitable or pleasing to others. But we think that there is little point in doing further empirical studies of authority that do not use greater conceptual precision and strive for more empirical rigor than have characterized earlier efforts. This contention applies not merely to nongovernmental entities. Many, perhaps most aspects of authority in the polity have been studied with relative lack of concern for detail and imprecision that are grounds for professional embarrassment.

Notes

1. S_1 is our notation for the top stratum of superordinates. Secondary and tertiary superordinate strata are denoted S_2, S_3, and so on, for as many distinct strata as are appropriate to the research question and unit. It is demonstrated below that each additional stratum that is analytically distinguished increases the aggregation and comparison task by an order of magnitude; thus it is generally advisable to combine adjacent strata for comparative purposes.

2. Another approach to characterizing "the" norms of a unit is to weight them according to the unit's general type (see Chapter 13) or to the prevalent orientation toward authority in the culture of which it is part. "The" norms of a closed or *S*-dominant unit might therefore be heavily weighted toward the norms of *S*'s and "the" norms of an egalitarian unit weighted according to the relative numbers of *s*'s and *S*'s.

3. For a more complete discussion of the dimensions of consonance see Chapter 13, and also Eckstein, "Authority Relations and Governmental Performance," pp. 300–307.

4. An interview and questionnaire approach to assessing norm-practice differences is to ask a "practice" question first, followed by a norm question about how widely the practices of the unit differ, and in what direction, from the respondent's normative ideal. If the "practice" question is anchored precisely to a conceptual dimension, norm-practice correspondence can be estimated with a degree of precision.

5. Some such comparisons can be made among units as well. Aggregate norms and practices of one unit can be compared with those of another. Though there are seldom reasons for comparing, say, *S*-norms in one unit with *s*-norms in another, the extent of normative consistency is directly comparable among units. Degrees of complementarity and correspondence are also comparable among units, provided similar yardsticks have been applied to all the units being compared. Possibilities and rationales for such comparisons within and among nations are far too numerous to consider here.

6. Philip Goldman, "The Congruence of Authority in Dutch Secondary Schools." Paper given at the Annual Meeting of the American Political Science Association, September 1972.

PART FOUR
Typology

The subjects treated thus far—descriptive concepts and methods of observing and reporting pertinent phenomena—are obviously fundamental for all inquiries into patterns of authority. Usually, though, they are themselves tools for a larger purpose: the theoretical solution of general substantive problems. Major issues for theory about authority patterns, and possible solutions, are taken up in Chapter 14 to 16. First, however, we deal with a subject that links description and theory and also analysis and synthesis. That subject is typology.

Political scientists have used many inadequate typologies because most apparently are unaware of the characteristics of good schemes of classification and of appropriate ways of constructing them. Undoubtedly our suggested typology has its own shortcomings, but for a different reason: because good typologies, like good theories, can hardly be fully and conclusively constructed on the first attempt, given the need for constant interaction between the development of theories and taxonomies.

Our discussion of the subject is divided into four parts. First we state the senses in which typology links theory and description, synthesis and analysis. Next, major shortcomings in existing "political" typologies are pointed out. Procedures and criteria for improving on these typologies are then suggested—this being the main purpose of Chapter 12. Finally, in Chapter 13, we use these procedures and criteria to begin classifying authority patterns. In that last, most important part of the discussion (as also in parts of Chapter 12), we see how the construction of adequate typology depends on solving certain intricate theoretical issues, most of which remain quite unresolved in the study of authority patterns.

This part of the book provides a transition and connection between the descriptive and procedural concerns of Parts II and III and the speculative, theoretical concerns of Part V. Also, we see it as an, alas, novel attempt to build "political" typology thoughtfully.

CHAPTER TWELVE

Foundations for a Typology of Authority Patterns

Nature and Uses of Typology

The problem of constructing typology is, of course, to discover the more and less general (inclusive) classes to which particular cases belong. Such classes most often are used for purely descriptive purposes. If so used, the labels for the classes, appropriately defined, serve as shorthand descriptions of the traits of cases that fall into them. The amount of information furnished by such descriptions depends (as pointed out in Chapter 1) on the level of inclusiveness of the classes. The statement that an organism is an "animal," for example, provides several items of detailed information; the statement that the subject belongs to the "order" of carnivora tells much more: it says summarily that the organism is an animal that is multicelled, has bone structure, has a supporting rod of backbone, nurses its young, breathes through lungs, and eats other animals. Political typologies are (or should be) similar; for example, the classificatory label "democracy" provides (or should provide) several points of information, but less than the label "parliamentary system" as a subtype of democracy.

Although most often used for summary descriptive statements about more or less similar cases, well-constructed typologies also have important theoretical uses. Among these are the following:

1. A set of classificatory categories may itself suggest theoretical generalizations. For example, a classification of organisms by complexity of structure, joined to the discovery of certain distributions of simpler and more complex organisms in geological strata, suggested a theory about evolutionary development. Similarly, typologies of complex phenomena may suggest generalizations about the tendency of particular elements or dimensional traits to occur conjointly in stable or unstable compounds.
2. Typological classes may be used in theorizing, as either dependent or independent variables. In the examples used in Part II to illustrate the

analytic concepts, we chose only particular dimensional traits as grounds for theoretical speculation; however, it should be obvious that the same can be done with concepts that stand for general contours of sets of authority patterns. Political science teems with cases in point: for example, Almond and Verba's attempt to explain the origins and consequences of what they call parochial, participant, and subject cultures. Each of these is a category that labels the general nature of political orientations, not any single attitude.

3. Every typological class is susceptible to distinctive theoretical explanations, which are usually but not necessarily derived from more general theory about more inclusive classes.

4. Testing theories about sets of cases requires precise criteria for determining whether particular cases belong in the set, hence typology. If, for example, a theory of the etiology of "revolution" is to be tested by examining the American War of Independence, one must be assured that the case is in fact a member of the set "revolutions." If not, a good theory might be refuted by an irrevelant case.

There are especially close links between typology and theories about combinations of authority traits that are particularly viable (persistent and able to work effectively) and combinations that are particularly ineffective and short-lived. The most common combinations of authority traits, hence the most common "types," presumably have some inherent coherence and probably are more effective and persistent than uncommon combinations. That, however, is only a hypothesis worth testing. It may be that evanescent or volatile combinations frequently occur, in which case there are three important subjects for theoretical explanation: what accounts for their occurrence, what causes their instability, and what are the likely directions of their subsequent transformation? It is an open question whether especially unstable combinations of authority traits ought to be considered types in their own right. If they prove empirically to be regularly occurring transitional forms, ones that typically develop from and change to more coherent types, they surely warrant consideration as distinct types.[1]

Typologies also direct theoretical attention to the conditions of change, especially if there is empirical evidence that cases of one type are frequently transformed into another type. If typology is constructed on the principle of progressive differentiation, as in biology and in our own essay (below) at constructing a typology of authority patterns, specifically evolutionary or developmental questions are raised. One can scarcely avoid speculating about the circumstances under which "new" or more complex types have emerged, which types have declined in number or effectiveness, and whether there is any directionality in the process.

Typology is a matter of "synthetic" inquiry at all levels except the most inclusive and heterogeneous. At that general level typologies are constructed by dichotomizing or more finely categorizing a single variable—for example, distinguishing biological entities according to number of cells, or social entities according to whether they have hierarchic asymmetries. Synthesis is not involved here, but further discrimination permits one to identify classes by compounds of elements or traits. And always implicit in classificatory constructs at any but the most primitive levels is a set of "synthetic" and theoretical assertions: that such-and-such a combination of traits is at least possible, occurs frequently, and is not inevitably evanescent.

Any typology of authority patterns thus makes theoretical assumptions, raises theoretical questions, shapes the process of observation and analysis, and is—or should be—subject to revision and refinement on the basis of observed empirical patterns. How best to classify authority patterns thus is a question that affords no easy answers. Before suggesting a solution, we examine critically some typologies of authority patterns now in use in political science, to clear ground for an altogether new attempt—tailored, of course, not just to "politics" but to all kinds of authority patterns.

A Critical Review of Typologies in Political Science

Political scientists have always dealt with patterns of governmental authority that vary widely on the dimensions identified in Part II. Unfortunately the classificatory categories they have used afford scant help in our attempt to construct a typology applicable to any and all patterns of authority; their typologies, in fact, are mainly instructive about what to avoid. The difficulty certainly is not lack of alternative typologies. If anything, the discipline offers an embarrassment of classificatory riches. Curiously enough, the more concerned political scientists have become with the systematic integration of their field, the more classificatory schemes have multiplied in number and diversity.[2]

Authority types may be subject to a process of "natural selection;" typologies of them are not—anyway, not yet. The real difficulty is that extant typologies of political systems are ill constructed in one or more ways that we now review.

Unidimensional Categorization

One of the most pervasive shortcomings in the construction of political typologies has been the use of single variables to distinguish cases that differ on many. Any one such typology is almost sure to be unsatisfactory because the most heterogeneous cases turn up as categorical bedfellows. The profusion of such typologies infinitely complicates matters. If units of analysis vary in a great many ways, the potential for diverse typologies based on single aspects of the units obviously is vast. And if typologies are highly diverse, the comparison and cumulation of empirical findings is seriously impeded. The diversity of typologies that can result from the use of single variables is illustrated by the following, partial catalog of bases on which political scientists have classified political systems.

1. *The number of those who participate in ruling.* The classic distinction, first advanced by Herodotus, was among three pure forms of government: monarchies, aristocracies, and democracies, based respectively on the rule of one, few, and many. This was long the dominant typology of political science, with revisions: Plato differentiated moral and corrupt forms of each type, Polybius added the idea of a "mixed" constitution, and Montesquieu reduced the typology to two classes: the rules of one and of many.
2. *The social characteristics of dominant elites.* This basis for typology developed concurrently with the view that all polities are oligarchic. Mosca, for example, classified polities according to whether their elites were military, theocratic, aristocratic, plutocratic, or meritocratic, arguing that political evolution involved a progression from the first through the last.
3. *The bases of the legitimation of regimes.* We referred to Weber's classification of polities by bases of legitimation in Chapter 7.
4. *The extent to which authority in polities is integrated (centralized) or dispersed.* This variable gave rise, for example, to a distinction between polities that exercise "sovereignty" and those in which only "dominium" exists.
5. *Whether a polity governs a culturally homogeneous or heterogeneous population.* The distinction here is between "states" and "nation-states"; the latter have in common not only a structure of authority but also such characteristics as a common language and ethnic homogeneity.
6. *The number of political parties found in a polity.* Duverger, for example, has proposed that the most telling distinction among polities is that between single-party, two-party, and multiparty systems.[3]
7. *The balance of flows of influence between subs and supers.* Kaplan,[4] for example, distinguished between "system-dominant" and subsystem-dominant" polities. Another such set of categories is Dahl and Lindblom's[5] distinctions among "price systems," "hierarchies," "polyarchies," and "bargaining systems." These distinctions, however, can be called multidimensional, since each category is defined in terms of a set of required or disposing conditions on numerous variables.
8. *The nature of a polity's political culture*, with particular emphasis on attitudes toward participation. This is the basis of Almond and Verba's dis-

tinction between parochial, subject, participant, and "civic" cultures—which in some contexts serves them as a typology of polities.

9. *The extent of competitiveness in polities.* An example is Coleman's distinction between competitive, semicompetitive, and authoritarian polities.[6]

10. *The nature of characteristic goals pursed by polities.* Apter[7] distinguishes (*a*) revolutionary polities that seek large-scale, rapid transformation from (*b*) the gradual and limited reforms of *progressiste* polities, from (*c*) conservative and (*d*) revivalist polities, which seek, respectively, the maintenance of the *status quo* and a return to a *status quo ante.*

11. *The basic economic characteristics of societies.* A case in point is Sutton's[8] distinction—also used by Riggs—between agrarian and industrial systems, which doubles as a typology of societies and of their polities. The frequently used distinction among underdeveloped, developing, and developed polities also often rests on economic criteria, although more often it stands for a variety of traits.

Using a single variable to construct typology is not necessarily reprehensible. It makes obvious sense if one is only interested in theorizing about a special aspect of cases. Single variables also can be used as points of departure for constructing "pure" types, though this exercise requires much thought about and study of the properties that are "logically" entailed by the master variable.[9] It also may be sufficient, for some kinds of empirical analysis, to make only the broad and undiscriminating distinctions among cases to which one is usually restricted by a single variable. In all these instances of a univariate approach to categorization, though, it is essential that scholars not use the typology to summarily represent other aspects of the cases. Such claims can be made only on the basis of good theory that corresponds to wide empirical knowledge, and it is very doubtful that we have such theories about the ways in which characteristics of political systems affect one another. We are in fact unlikely to attain such theory if we fail to recognize a number of traits and their interactive effects when making distinctions among cases.

Nonpolitical Bases of Classification

A second difficulty associated with many political typologies is their use of traits that have nothing directly to do with authority as a basis of classification. Some choice examples are the classification of polities by their mode or level of economic production, geographic region, and cultural homogeneity of their members. This practice might be justified if it were demonstrated that such nonpolitical traits regularly determine political traits. Even if true, however, one wonders why the nonpolitical traits should be used rather than the political ones. It is surely safer to classify cases according to some of their essential properties than according to contextual ones. What the essential traits or properties of any unit of analysis might be is initially a matter of definition, but those who would classify polities according to economic, geographic, cultural, and similar contextual criteria do not define their subject in terms of such properties. It is clear enough that they usually regard the contextual properties as causes of or correlates of political traits, in which case our criticism has even more force: the causal dependence of political types on social, economic, or cultural traits cannot even be demonstrated unless political types are defined and identified independently of those traits.

These criticism apply equally to most synthetic typologies of polities—those which define their categories in terms of a number of traits rather than a single variable. Some of the principal synthetic typologies in use are at bottom societal or economic. This was true of Comte's distinction among military, feudal, and industrial regimes, and Marx's distinction among feudal, capitalist, and socialist ones. The trend continues in contemporary distinctions among traditional, developing, and developed polities, or between agrarian and industrial, military and civilian ones.

Imprecision

Shortcomings due to imprecision reflect in part a third, more fundamental difficulty: the tendency to be extraordinarily casual in working out political typologies. Classifications are "casual" if no systematic method of classification is used to arrive at them. The ultimate index of casualness in classification is the tendency first to label classes and only then to ask what traits the labels identify. Perhaps the most pointless and embarrassing exercise that fills the writings of political scientists involves attempts to discover content for the names authors use. What, they keep asking, is it to be democratic, or totalitarian, or developed, or bureaucratic? Labels like these might in fact be useful. But it is absurd first to posit that objects identified by them exist and then to ask what they are. Inevitably, the labels mean many different things to different people. This is especially regrettable because attempts to find contents for names are particularly common in regard to manifestly synthetic concepts that stand for compounds of traits. The concepts just cited are examples.

Even if casualness does not take such an extreme form, it tends to occur in other ways. An example is Janowitz's[10] distinction between five types of polities: authoritarian-personal, authoritarian-mass party, democratic-competitive or semicompetitive, civil-military, and military oligarchies.

These labels do have content; however, Janowitz simply thinks on the basis of wide knowledge (but no discernible method) that the world is somehow divided along such lines, and that thus sorting it out is helpful to his special interest in the role of the military in developing nations.

The Basis of Methodical Classification

Criteria of Good Typology

Classifications of polities tend to be casual partly because typological constructs often are used chiefly for rhetorical, propagandistic purposes—in fact are often directly imported from the real world of political rhetoric. It is hard to give precise content to pejorative terms like totalitarian or imperialist, simply because they are intended to induce a mood more than to furnish information. The same applies to laudatory terms. However, a more important reason for being offhand about political typology is the common belief that classification can be no more than arbitrary—that there are no criteria by which the adequacy of typologies can be judged and, consequently, no proper methods of classification either.

Surely this view is wrong. One classifies for purposes, and from purpose follows method. As Stephen Toulmin has forcefully argued, where there are purposes there also are criteria, deducible from the purposes, for evaluating actions or arguments, as well as appropriate methods, deducible from (or at least experientally suited to) the criteria.[11] We began this chapter with a list of the objectives of typology, and at various points we have mentioned characteristics desirable in taxonomy. We now schematically relate these matters.

Typology, at a minimum, has the purpose of sorting particular phenomena into more or less populous and homogeneous sets. However, this function is not always fulfilled: for example, the classic typology of polities according to whether rule is by one person, or some, or all, probably leads to the placing of virtually all cases into the middle set. A related problem arises when a classificatory scheme leaves residual cases. The larger the number of cases in a noncategory, the less adequate is classification. Typologies can therefore be judged by how close they come to being "exhaustive." It should be noted in this connection that the existence of a large miscellaneous category is often concealed by the use of "negative concepts" that seem to mean something but really leave cases residual. An example is the term non-Western, which, of course, simply means "situated somewhere, but not in the West." The terms Western and non-Western classify about as much as a division of occupations into plumbers and nonplumbers.

Typologies have the purpose of providing descriptive information in shorthand ways. They can hardly achieve this goal if the classes of which they consist do not have precisely defined traits—that is, are "ambiguous." If the definitions of types make it difficult to determine whether a case belongs to one class or another, which is the essence of ambiguity, describing cases by the names of classes conveys more noise than information. The distinction between two-party and multiparty systems generally entails this problem at least to a small degree: the reason is that most two-party systems consist of more than two parties, and the threshold of support below which "minor" parties are to be disregarded is seldom specified.[12]

Residual classes also fail to provide descriptive information. They tell what a case is not, rather than what it is. Lerner,[13] for example, says that "modern" societies have literacy, urbanism, media participation, and empathy. This is informative; but he also defines "traditional" societies as those in which the traits just named are absent—which says nothing about what is present, leaving us guessing about the nature of the vast majority of societies that have existed. Furthermore, Lerner's conception of a third, "transitional" type of society involves three different compounds of traits, present or absent (actually, there are 14 logical possibilities). Consequently, to call something a "transitional" case amounts to no more than saying that it lacks something or other, but not everything, present in modern societies. This hardly tells exactly what the case *is*.

Typologies are supposed to provide more or less inclusive sets of cases to which more or less general theories apply. Obviously nothing theoretical can be said about residual or empty categories (except why they are not something else); and if a descriptive category is ambiguous, theory about it cannot be precise. From this objective of classification it also follows that classes in a good typology must not be "ambivalent." If a case can, for equally good reasons, belong to two or more classes on the same level of inclusiveness, then two or more different, perhaps even contradictory, same-level theories should apply to it. But then the failure of a case to fit a pertinent theory becomes meaningless, and the most important theoretical value of classification is forfeited.

The objectives of typology thus imply a number of criteria for judging the adequacy of classifications. The most basic are: (*a*) that typology sort phenomena into classes that all include some (preferably many) cases, (*b*) that the classes be as exhaustive as possible, (*c*) that they be unambiguous, and (*d*) that they be unambivalent.

Systematic Methods of Classification

Proper procedure in classification is whatever yields results conforming to the foregoing criteria. We have already suggested that the criteria will not be satisfied if cases are characterized "negatively" or, usually, by any single variable deemed strategic. This, though, is only prudence about what to avoid; we still have options about what to do.

Whatever other options might be available, the method of progressive differentiation, by which we delimited authority patterns as a subject matter, is well suited to all the criteria of good typology. Used as described in Chapter 1, the method can hardly fail to yield distinctions that (*a*) distinguish, (*b*) are exhaustive (at any given level of generality), (*c*) provide unambiguous information (less at higher levels, more at lower), and (*d*) avoid ambivalent overlaps. In addition, the method—as its name suggests—leads to the construction of a hierarchy of more and less inclusive classes; hence it allows for precision about the homogeneity of cases in a class (the number of traits they share), as well as precision about the levels at which more general theories apply and more special theories are needed.

Despite these virtues, the method of progressive differentiation poses difficulties. The most obvious and important of these is the selection of traits by which to distinguish types at successive levels of the "tree" of progressive differentiation. What ought to be used initially to divide authority patterens into highly inclusive, heterogeneous classes? What traits can sensibly be used to make each subsequent distinction into less inclusive, more homogeneous classes? Choices of variables for these purposes will be arbitrary to a degree, and subject to modification as our empirical knowledge increases and our theoretical interests change. Still, there are some plausible points of departure.[14]

The problem of selecting traits to classify authority patterns can be somewhat reduced by including only those variables that involve authority (i.e., those which figure on the scheme of analytic concepts). We thus exclude variables that are structural or functional traits of the social units in which patterns of authority exist (e.g., their size or autonomy, or their functional concern with educational or economic tasks). Such traits might define areas of special interest in the study of authority patterns, like the study of "polities" or of authority in families or schools, but that is clearly not the same as constructing a typology of authority patterns. The types or functions of social units may tend to coincide with particular types of authority patterns, but we cannot determine any such coincidence empirically if we treat it as an assumption on which to base typology.

The analytic scheme leaves many alternatives at each level of differentiation, however. It has 10 dimensions, and each could provide a basis for differentiation—as could each subdimension. The first question, then, is which dimension or subdimension should be used to make the initial differentiation. The only way to avoid answering this question and still be systematic is to use a "matrix" or "clustering" procedure—which is what has been done in the few political typologies that are based on more than a single variable or an ad hoc concatenation of several variables. The matrix procedure can be illustrated by Apter's classification of polities[15] based on their structural and attitudinal attributes. He dichotomizes these two variables (hierarchial vs. pyramidal structures, secular vs. sacred attitudes), uses them to generate a 2 × 2 matrix, and thus obtains four compounds or clusters that logically exhaust all the possibilities in his analytic scheme. This classificatory scheme has most of the traits of good typology; it does not tell whether certain combinations actually exist, but this question can be left to empirical research.

What Apter does in a simplistic way with two dichotomized variables could also be done in principle with a much more complex analytic scheme like ours. We have identified 10 dimension (plus a qualitative variable) on which patterns of authority may have different traits. Their traits on these dimensions can be combined in a finite number of ways and the resulting clusters used as a preliminary classificatory scheme. Each cluster would differ from every other in a precisely defined way, and together they would cover all possibilities. The most obvious disadvantage is the sheer number of categories thus generated. Even if we dichotomized the 10 dimensions, the matrix would consist of 2^{10} (i.e., 1024) categories. Even if we then eliminated the combinations that are logically impossible or empirically nonexistent, the scheme would be far too cumbersome for use as a typology. Such an exercise suggests the potential of our analytic scheme for providing highly detailed descriptions of particular cases, and in this respect the analytic scheme clearly has advantages over those, like Apter's, whose dimensions provide few and simplistic distinctions. But that very detail makes straightforward clustering almost impossible as a basis for typology: the gain in ability to "particularize" is outweighed by the loss of capacity for generalized descriptions.

The use of matrices to generate typologies has a sedutive simplicity but does not avoid the problem of choice. The only way to avoid a paralyzing proliferation of categories is to make careful selection among the variables used to generate a matrix. Either variables so used will themselves be synthetic clusters of traits—which we believe to be the case in Apter's reduction of all political variety to two dichotomized variables—or they will require selection of traits that are deemed particularly important. And the second requirement is the one that applies to the use of progressive differentiation. We thus opt for the method of progressive differentiation to construct an initial typology of authority patterns, for which we need first an ordering of dimensions according to a criterion of importance.

The Case for Progressive Differentiation by Salient Authority Traits

The basic criterion we propose for choosing dimensional traits to progressively differentiate authority patterns is the same as that used to identify Bases of Legitimacy: the probable salience of dimensions (and subdimensions) to members of social units. This is not a mere criterion of convenience; it has a solid rationale.

First, and probably most important, we expect a typology of authority patterns to be useful for developing more and less general theories about those patterns. It seems likely that the problems that are subjects for general theories will be concerned with the most salient authority traits. The problems include: (*a*) the general conditions of the persistence and change of authority patterns, (*b*) the general sources of cohesion and conflict within them, (*c*) the general conditions of their capacity for carrying out their functions, and (*d*) problems of etiology. All these problems lead to a primary emphasis on salient authority traits because—almost truistically—the traits of authority that members of social units think of as most important are those which most determine how and whether members comply, cooperate, resist, or work for transformation.

Persistence and change depend on the salient dimensions because dimensions important for legitimacy substantially determine members' level of support and compliance with an authority pattern, old or new, and support and compliance are primary determinants of persistence. Problems of conflict and consensus similarly depend on salient authority traits in several ways. Conflicts over authority itself are usually most intense when they involve the bases on which legitimacy depends; we pointed out in Chapter 7 that it is the "salient" aspects of authority that chiefly figure in revolutions. Conflicts over other aspects of authority are less likely to occur, tend to be less intense, and usually involve fewer members of social units. Similarly, people are more likely to fight bitterly over matters that are highly consequential and have immediacy for them than over those they see as being remote and insignificant. If conflict does arise about less salient aspects of authority, consensus on more salient traits is likely to temper its acerbity.[16] The effectiveness of a social unit depends very largely on whether its members comply with directives; we showed earlier how salience and compliance are linked.

The problems of etiology lead to a primary concern with salient authority traits in a more circuitous manner. Old patterns of authority may disappear and new ones emerge in two ways: spontaneously or by institutional "engineering." In either case changes in salient dimensions tend to have more general and quicker repercussions (consider, e.g., the likely effects of a change in form from uncompetitive to highly competitive Recruitment).

Moreover, changes in other dimensions tend to have significant general effects only through their impact on the most salient dimensions, rather than directly (e.g., a change in Decision-Rules through its impact on Recruitment and/or Participation).

Emphasis on salient traits thus seems to be justified by the theoretical purposes that are served by classification. The arguments just reviewed also have a broader implication, pertinent to the descriptive purposes of typology. In Chapters 2 through 6 we simply dealt with all dimensions on which authority patterns vary and which might be used in detailed, systematic descriptions. On the basis of the present discussion we are able to arrange the dimensions in order of their likely general significance for perceptions of legitimacy, for the probable import of their congruences and incongruities, and for identifying coherent and incoherent compounds. Their order of significance is highly useful for descriptive research, since it suggests what to emphasize when we make limited inquiries into authority patterns—and virtually all inquiries are limited rather than exhaustive.

The order of salience among dimensions of authority varies, according to arguments in Chapter 7, between supers and subs. If we simplify, combine, and focus only on the most salient dimensions, we obtain the following rankings:

S only	*S* and *s*	*s* only
	Recruitment	
Decision-Behavior and -Rules		
	Directiveness	
	Participation	
	Responsiveness	
	Distance, Deportment	
		Decision-Behavior and -Rules

The logic of progressive differentiation thus indicates that the most general distinctions among authority patterns are to be made on the basis of Recruitment. We make such a distinction, in the next section, between patterns in which supers are drawn from a "closed" line of succession, caste, or age-grade, and those which are effectively "open" to subordinates. At the next level of differentiation, though, we propose to use different dimensions. "Closed" authority patterns are likely to be *S*-dominated, which suggests that they be differentiated at the second level according to Decision-Behavior and Decision-Rules. In "open" authority patterns the perceptions of salience held by subordinates are probably more consequential, hence the second-order differentiations in such units ought to be based not on Decision-Behavior or Decision-Rules, but on the influence dimensions. A systematic application of this approach is offered in the next chapter, but there are several other topics to be dealt with first.

One special virtue of basing the progressive differentiation of authority patterns on salient authority traits is the probability that the types, like biological types, will correspond to an order of development, or "evolution." We suggested hypotheses to that effect at the end of Chapter 7. The proposed order of differentiation certainly seems to correspond to the sequence in which aspects of authority become significant in the life cycle of individuals. The young child first becomes aware of the simple fact that his world is inhabited by powerful beings—parents or their surrogates—who issue directives and use rewards and deprivations to back them. For this there is abundant evidence in the literature on children's attitudes toward authority. It is likely that shortly after children discover supers, they become aware that some of their own actions are regularly subject to directives (and/or supervised, and/or sanctioned), while others are not. The discovery that one can affect the formulation of directives—can participate—seems to occur at a still later stage. Before Participation can occur, children must develop confidence in their own judgments and a sense that parents and other figures of authority are fallible, accessible, and susceptible to influence attempts. Concomitantly, the figures of authority must show evidence of Responsiveness to children's judgments and requests: we have made the point elsewhere that Participation is not likely to occur in any regular and recurring way unless superordinates practice minimal Responsiveness. It is not nearly so plausible that children next become self-conscious about Distance and Deportment, however. What is more likely is that perceptions of inequality, and the modes of behavior reflecting those perceptions, are essentially a function of the apparent powerfulness of the authority figures and whether and how they respond to influence attempts.[17] The elements of authority patterns that next become salient for children, once they have become aware of the perils and payoffs of participation, probably are Decision-Rules and Decision-Behavior. If and when parents and other authority figures are observed to be responsive, the rules by which they decide matters become increasingly visible and important to children. There may be considerable mystery about these matters, especially in autocratic families and in all kinds of large organizations whose superordinates are remote from subordinates. But once subordinates become aware that superordinates are responsive to their demands in anything more than the most whimsical and paternalistic way, Decision-Rules and Decision-Behavior become distinctly salient. They also may become the objects of intense efforts at codification (for predictability) and formal revision (to enhance Responsiveness); but that is another subject.

Thus our proposed order of differentiation among authority patterns is likely to correspond to the ontogeny of an individual's awareness of facets of authority. The causal argument is that ontogeny is itself a primary determinant of salience, and since we intend to rely on salience for successive differentiations, those differentiations should recapitulate ontogeny. The argument is based more on reasoning than empirical evidence, but relevant evidence can readily be gathered. A question of larger scale, and import, is whether the social phylogeny of authority patterns corresponds in any degree with the same developmental sequence. If so, the primal social units—extended families and hunting bands—would be expected to differ mainly in openness of Recruitment. Units with more open Recruitment would tend to become more functionally specific in their Directiveness. Later some units would develop regularized means of Participation, and Decision-Rules, some of them ordaining Responsiveness, would be established. Any such developments in human history writ large are beyond the reach of scholarship, because the oldest documentary and legendary evidence we have about patterns of authority—in the Semitic and Indo-European traditions, anyway—suggests that 3000 years ago there already existed a great diversity of open and closed, functionally diffuse and functionally specific, participant and nonparticipant patterns.[18] If there is a general developmental pattern, though, it ought to be manifest to some degree in the ontogeny of any social unit that is established de novo, like the first industrial organizations and autonomous former colonies. Of course, the members of such units bring cultural baggage with them that will confound any "natural" developmental patterns. In any case, the progressive differentiation of authority patterns along the lines we have sketched has high potential for stimulating theories and research about personal and social developmental sequences. Moreover, as we have seen, typology and theory are, at many points, interwoven.

Criteria for Differentiation

Also to be decided before proposing a typology are the number and kinds of distinctions that should be made at each level of differentiation. We propose to follow several principles.

First, even the more salient dimensions, like Recruitment, have more tangible and more arcane aspects. If the salience of authority traits is selected as the basis of progressive differentiation, the more tangible aspects of such dimensions should be used. Unless there is compelling logical argument or empirical evidence to the contrary, the less tangible aspects of authority are better reserved for the detailed description of individual cases, not for defining types.

Simple distinctions also are preferable to complex ones at each level of differentiation. Two practices that contribute to simplicity are (1) to make few rather than many distinctions at each level of differentiation, and (2) to base those distinctions on differences in kind rather than degree. The simplest possible distinction is a dichotomy, and many of the dichotomous distinctions we might make using the dimensional traits of authority are indeed differences in kind (e.g., between "closed" and "open" patterns of Recruitment to superordinated positions). We suggest three reasons for aiming at simplicity in differentiation at any one level. First, simple distinctions in the construction of typologies are analogous to parsimony in theoretical explanation: the fewer the variables needed to explain a phenomenon, the more powerful the theory; the fewer the distinctions needed to divide subjects into meaningful sets, the more powerful the descriptive generalizations. Second, the smaller the number of distinctions made at each level of differentiation, the less the proliferation of categories as we move down the hierarchy of salience of authority traits. This is especially important for our typology of authority patterns because, even after combining related traits, we have seven levels of differentiation to take into account. Detailed differentiation based on only the two or three most salient traits would almost surely ignore empirically consequential distinctions that ought to be made on the basis of traits that are only moderately less salient. Finally, typological distinctions based on clear-cut differences in kind facilitate unambiguous classification—and as we have argued earlier, ambiguity is one of the bugbears of most classificatory schemes in social science.

Salience and simplicity are prudential guides to differentiation, not absolute criteria. They do not always point to the same distinctions, either. We propose a third principle that provides a further check on the reasonableness of each classificatory distinction: whether it divides authority patterns into sets that are distinctly different in complexity. We use "complexity" here in a way that extends its technical meaning for Conformation (see Chapter 4): the more complex authority patterns are those having relatively complex decision structures *and* complex (numerous, diverse, interdependent) patterns of influence relations and boundary interchange. The chief reason for taking complexity into account is our conclusion, from diverse evidence and speculation, that virtually every dimension of authority patterns in our analytic scheme discriminates, at least at its polarities, between patterns that differ systematically in overall complexity.[19] If this statement is empirically true—even in a probablistic sense—the condition should be reflected in any typological distinctions we make. We might also posit (by analogy with biological differentiation, and in conformity with the arguments of social evolutionists) that successive branchings in the historical development of authority patterns ought to be associated with an increasing complexity of pattern—though this hypothesis remains to be tested by comparing a typology of the patterns with actual evolutionary sequences.

Notes

1. "Pure" or "ideal" types are typological constructs that refer to especially coherent combinations of traits. Such constructs are coherent in one of two senses: either they all logically express a single underlying principle, or they are what would be expected to follow from a particular starting point, such as Recruitment by succession, which generally should entail great Distance between *S's* and *s's*, which further entails closure of Participation, and so on. Whatever the shortcomings of such types for purposes of description, they certainly are useful in theorizing, and they raise the issue of coherence in its most stringent form.

2. A brief sample of political typologies is presented in Harry Eckstein and David E. Apter, Eds., *Comparative Politics: A Reader* (New York: Free Press, 1963), pp. 3–4. It could have been much expanded, even in 1963, and since then the number of typologies of authority patterns has greatly increased.

3. Maurice Duverger, *Political Parties* (New York: Wiley, 1954), p. 393.

4. Morton Kaplan, *System and Process in International Politics* (New York: Wiley, 1957).

5. Robert A. Dahl and Charles E. Lindblom, *Politics, Economics, and Welfare* (New York: Harper and Row, 1953).

6. In Gabriel A. Almond and James S. Coleman, Eds. *The Politics of the Developing Areas* (Princeton N.J.: Princeton University Press, 1960), p. 532 ff.

7. David E. Apter, "A Comparative Method for the Study of Politics," *American Journal of Sociology*, Vol. 64 (1958), p. 227. (Apter also uses four other typological categories—of "representativeness"—in this essay.)

8. Francis X. Sutton, "Social Theory and Comparative Politics," in Eckstein and Apter. *Comparative Politics*, pp. 67–81.

9. "Pure types" have heuristic and descriptive uses that are independent of their (non)correspondence to empirical reality; but their construction entails much latent theorizing about what empirical conditions are dependent on what others.

10. Morris Janowitz, *The Military in the Political Development of New Nations* (Chicago: University of Chicago Press, 1964), p. 5.

11. Stephen Edelston Toulmin, *An Examination of the Place of Reason in Ethics* (Cambridge: Cambridge University Press, 1950), p. 84.

12. Data handbooks—like Arthur S. Banks and Robert B. Textor, *A Cross-Polity Survey* (Cambridge, Mass.: M. I. T. Press, 1963) and Charles Lewis Taylor and Michael C. Hudson, *World Handbook of Political and Social Indicators*, 2nd ed. (New Haven: Yale University Press, 1972)—do employ precise but generally arbitrary thresholds when dealing with this and similar typological problems. In view of the imprecision of most typological exercises in the literature, one probably ought not to cavil at a measure of arbitrariness here.

13. Daniel Lerner, *The Passing of Traditional Society* (New York: Free Press, paperback ed. 1964), p. 71.

14. This problem may seem similar to that of selecting a "strategic" variable for classifying complex cases. Because the problem arises not just once but at each step of differentiation, it might in fact seem greater. This should not be true, though, since we do not claim that the primary (i.e., most general) differences on a single variable can represent all significant differences among classes. At each successive step of differentiation an increasingly large combination of variables is used to characterize types, whereas in classification by a strategic variable one always stops with a single variable.

15. David E. Apter, *The Politics of Modernization* (Chicago: University of Chicago Press, 1965), p. 24.

16. Important conflicts can and do arise over policy, incumbents, and nonpolitical matters without conflict over what used to be called political "fundamentals." Our argument is that disputes over fundamentals are more likely to be projected on "circumstantials" than the reverse. The distinction between fundamentals and circumstantials originated with Oliver Cromwell; for an elaboration see Herbert J. Spiro, *Government by Constitution: The Political Systems of Democracy* (New York: Random House, 1965), pp. 211–213.

17. Perceptions of inequalities tend to change as a child matures; however, the change occurs as the child becomes increasingly aware of the nature and behavior of superordinates with respect to himself. The implication of this point for construction of a typology is that the inequalities should not be used as a basis for differentiation among authority patterns. Rather, they tend (hypothetically) to vary systematically with the other properties of the patterns.

18. The earliest evidence about authority patterns relates mainly to political and religious organizations—not surprisingly, since they were the units whose members had need and occasion to make records and inscriptions. For summaries of evidence about authority patterns of polities before 500 B.C. see chapters in Mason Hammond, *The City in the Ancient World* (Cambridge, Mass.: Harvard University Press, 1972), on Mesopotamia (Chs. V and VI), archaic Greece (Ch. XIV), and Etruscan Italy (Ch. XVIII). There also are fascinating clues about guild structure and the relation of guilds to the state in Mesopotamia in the eighth to sixth centuries B.C.; see David B. Weisberg, *Guild Structure and Political Allegiance in Early Achaemenid Mesopotamia* (New Haven, Conn.: Yale University Press, 1967).

19. The "complex" polarities of the dimensions are open Recruitment; regimented Directiveness; facilitated Participation; alterocratic Responsiveness; indifferent-to-insubordinate Compliance; polycratic Decision-Rules and, usually, discordant Decision-Behavior (*some* patterns of concordance can be very "complex"); complex Conformation; and arrogant/obsequious Deportment (which entails much more complex behavior than is found when everyone treats everyone else the same). Whether Distance and Bases of Legitimacy can be said to have more or less complex polarities or facets is largely irrelevant, since these dimensions denote perceptions rather than behavior.

CHAPTER THIRTEEN

A Tentative Typology of Authority Patterns

There is nearly always slippage between figuring out how to do something appropriately and actually doing it. Readers may have to content themselves with the thought that getting to this point has been more than half the fun, because the typology sketched in this chapter is less satisfying than our criticisms of others' typologies and our reasoning out of principles for developing a classification of authority patterns. The cause is innocent enough: good typologies are not just logical exercises but must be grounded on a great deal of empirical information. Contemporary polities aside, we lack the necessary data. As a result, our typology is like a preliminary set of hypotheses needing validation and revision.

Primary Types: Recruitment

Regulated Versus Unregulated Recruitment

In considering Recruitment, we must first determine whether there are any established modes at all by which superordinates are chosen. This may not seem to be a particularly significant distinction in Western societies, where Recruitment is generally "regulated," but it surely was a fateful watershed in the historical development of complex patterns of authority. Even now there are some few entities in Western societies that meet all criteria for "social units" yet lack routinized means for the selection of leaders. Most are so-called informal groups, including some—not all—cliques, factions, and gangs.[1] Leadership in such groups is usually accorded to those who flaunt their prowess—sometimes influence, sometimes sheer aggresiveness. Such leaders retain their positions until an ambitious subordinate successfully vies for other members' support or violently dispossesses the incumbent. The phenotypical origin of groups so characterized can be seen in bands of higher primates, which are led by the strongest and most aggressive male—until he is successfully challenged. Recruitment in such units, in other words, is intensely competitive but not regulated: one cannot tell when or whether a super will be challenged, nor what, other than power, will determine the outcome.[2] The distinction between "unregulated Recruitment" and "regulated Recruitment" is simple and generally unambiguous. The two types, moreover, vary in complexity, which is generally greater in patterned behavior. In fact, if Recruitment is not regulated, little else is likely to be regulated either, hence the distinction divides authority patterns into two classes that differ fundamentally in respect to almost all characteristics of authority. We suspect also that the distinction is historically a very important one, in that more and more social units have shifted from unregulated to regulated Recruitment, as a concomitant of development. In non-Western societies, unregulated Recruitment may still be more common and influential in economic and political affairs than is recognized by outsiders. In the West, though, it has largely been supplanted by patterns with regularized Recruitment.

Closed Versus Open Recruitment

To say that Recruitment is "regulated" is to say nothing about how regulation is accomplished. We therefore propose two additional levels of differentiation according to the ways in which Recruitment can be routinized. Two generically different alternatives exist to the vicious competition and dysfunctional unpredictability that frequently result from unregulated Recruitment. One is to predetermine who becomes a superordinate according to a highly exclusive ascriptive criterion that is universally recognizable. In such "closed" patterns of Recruitment, supers are drawn from a single family or caste, and the choice usually is further circumscribed by other immutable factors, like sex, primogeniture, and age. "Open" patterns of Recruitment, in contrast, are those in which there are regularized competitive procedures by which a significant proportion of a unit's members has the opportunity to achieve superordinated positions. It is not necessary that all or even most of the members be eligible for superordinated status for a pattern to be classified as "open"; the exclusion of some groups on ascriptive grounds, like sex and race, does not make Recruitment absolutely "closed" either. The criterion is whether eligibility for incumbency is limited, for each *S*-position, to one person or a handful of individuals who share highly exclusive ascriptive traits.

The distinction between "open" and "closed" Recruitment is dichotomous and distinguishes between more and less complex cases. It is not entirely unambiguous, however. There is, first, a problem in dealing with cases in which some *S*-positions are open and others not. Hereditary monarchies often have relied on competitively chosen commoners to carry out the affairs of state, for example. For our purposes, it seems defensible to classify patterns according to Recruitment to the higher, hence more decisive, *S*-positions: operationally this ordinarily means the top two *S*-strata (e.g., king and council, president and congress, headman and elders, chairman and board). We do not thereby discount the opening of lower *S*-positions to competition; historically that has been an important step in transforming closed polities into open ones. But it does not seem to be a characteristic suitable for clear-cut typological distinction at a very general level of analysis, whatever might be its role in explaining changes from closed to open patterns.

Ambiguity also arises in attempting to classify cases like the tribal societies discussed in Chapter 6, where a set of potential incumbents fight it out for supremacy. Since the pattern has characteristics of unregulated Recruitment and of open and closed Recruitment, one might suspect that it is transitional between unregulated and regulated Recruitment. But it endured for centuries. Perhaps, then, for functional reasons, an aspect of unregulated competition, of ancient origin, survived within a closed and otherwise highly regulated pattern. It is noteworthy that in such societies eligibility was very sharply restricted by ascriptive criteria; and competition among contenders, although violently contentious—as is more typical of the primeval band than, say, the negotiations by which village headmen were more typically chosen in African societies—was nevertheless subject to clearly defined rules.[3]

Many arguments could be advanced to justify using openness and closure of Recruitment as a fundamental distinction between broad classes of authority patterns. The most compelling evidence for it would be a demonstration that cases in either class, however heterogeneous, have more in common together than with cases in the other. One major contrast of this kind is that closed patterns generally occur in "primary" social units, whereas open patterns prevail in "secondary" social units. Primary units are nuclear groups, that is, groups on which other groups are based and in which relations are personal and diffuse: face to face, intimate, and not between specialized role players, like buyers and sellers, doctors and patients. The prototypical primary group is the family; the typical secondary group involves a specialized functional relationship that is not "intimate." Beyond both primary and secondary groups are the "Great Associations," including the polity itself, that subsume and integrate numerous smaller groups.[4] Closure of Recruitment is not exclusive to primary groups, but other groups in which such patterns occur closely resemble primary groups. Secondary groups having closed patterns generally are concerned with instruction, protection, or provision of the means of subsistence—which are the major functions of the family. Supers in "closed" secondary groups are persons who, like parents, are presumed to have special skills and the function of instructing subs in them, as in master-apprentice or teacher-pupil relations; or they are thought to have unique means for providing physical protection and subsistence, as in lord-serf or patron-client relations. Such secondary units are functional analogues of families and generally seem to have emerged as specialized surrogates for them.

If closed patterns are also found in the Great Associations of society, one can be almost certain that the bonds of society are exclusively or chiefly primordial ties of kinship and/or simple dyadic relations, like patronage. In such societies bonds between supers and subs are highly diffuse; the functions of supers are conceived in terms of tutelage, physical protection, and resolving problems of subsistence; and relations between high chiefs and lesser rulers, and the latter and subjects, tend to have a high degree of personal intimacy. Such societies can be regarded as primary units writ large, both in their structural and functional aspects.[5]

We can suggest other substantial differences between closed and open patterns. Social units that have closed authority patterns tend to be much smaller in scale and less complex in structure than those that have open ones, although this is of course a "statistical" difference.[6] They tend to perform little "innovative" direction: directives tend to be regarded as parts of a fixed natural order, not as products of will and contrivance. They also tend to differ systematically in regard to dimensions of authority other than Recruitment. Closed patterns generally make little or no provision for routinized Participation by subs; where there is little innovative direction, there is little or nothing to participate in. Beyond this, if people cannot think of themselves as potential supers, they are less likely to think of themselves as qualified to participate in the work of superordinates. Low Participation in closed units is reinforced by the existence of an ineluctable basis of Distance in them. Recall, in this connection, the high Distance between teachers and younger pupils, parents and children, in Sweden, despite high egalitarianism elsewhere in Swedish society (Chapter 2).

From all these points of view, then, closed and open patterns seem to be quite different universes within the still more inclusive universe of "regulated" authority patterns: they occur in substantially different kinds of social units and tend to be associated with different functions; they also differ, to a degree, in other characteristics of authority.

We continue, below, to make finer differentiations among types of authority patterns on the basis of other traits without offering such extensive justifications (chiefly out of considerations of space). The same kinds of criteria used previously are applicable, though some of the distinctions we propose rest on less weighty arguments than those justifying the closed/open distinction, thus are more likely to suffer revisions as research unfolds.

Modes of Boundary Interchange

In the contemporary world, virtually all secondary units except schools (*in loco familias*) have open patterns of Recruitment, and we have mentioned evidence that the earliest records of polities on several continents indicate the parallel existence of both open and closed patterns. The modes of boundary interchange whereby subs can become supers in open patterns provide the obvious basis for further differentiation among the very large set of "open" units. The distinction we suggest is between Recruitment by *selection* and by *election*. By "selection" we mean procedures by which incumbent supers themselves choose their successors and/or peers. "Election" signifies procedures by which a substantial proportion of subordinates determine the final choice of top supers. The distinction is more general than the procedures of boundary interchange described in Chapter 6, but it subsumes them. Two of the seven modes there listed are characteristic of "closed" Recruitment: attainment of top *S*-positions by *succession* or *seniority*. The modes of Recruitment by "selection" are *designation* and *performance tests*. Performance tests are more regularized than designation and generally involve a wider base of eligibles, but the two modes have one fundamental characteristic in common: the incumbent superordinates set the criteria to be met by would-be superordinates. The typical modes of election are *periodic elections, rotation in office* (which is rare and found only in small units), and the equally rare procedure employed by ancient Athenians, the choice of superordinates by *lot*.

The distinction between *selection* and *election* is likely to be about as salient for members of open authority patterns as the distinction between open and closed patterns.[7] It also meets our criterion of simplicity: it is dichotomous and should permit unambiguous classification. The criterion of differential complexity is also satisfied by the distinction, though probabilistically rather than in an absolute way. That is, selection of supers generally involves fewer structures and less involved (and "involving") procedures than does election.

Sometimes subs can choose only among candidates for *S*-positions named by other supers, which is a potential source of ambiguity between patterns of election and selection. The choice that subs have, even if only between Tweedledum and Tweedledee, is the touchstone of the difference—which is important because Dum and Dee are thereby obliged to vie for subs' support. A more general and serious potential ambiguity arises from another source: how to classify patterns in which top supers are chosen by a mix of succession (a defining characteristic of closed patterns), selection, and election. We suggested earlier without elaboration that open and closed patterns should be differentiated on the basis of Recruitment to the top *S*-stratum or strata. Here we propose some more precise rules:

1. If the S_1 (individual or collectivity) is purely monocratic (not obliged to take the preferences of others into account), classification is based solely on the Recruitment of the S_1.

2. If S_1 is in any degree obliged to take account of preferences of an S_2 body (e.g., a council, assembly, advisory board, or spouse), classification should be according to the following principles:

a. If S_1 and S_2 attain positions by the same means, classify on that basis (closure; open: selection; or open: election).

b. If S_2 positions are closed and S_2's choose the S_1 from among themselves, the pattern is *closed.*

c. If the S_1 position is closed and the S_1 selects S_2's, the pattern is *closed.*

d. If the S_1 position is closed or open: selected and S_2's are elected, the pattern is *open: elected.*

Other combinations are possible but implausible. The rules are mainly self-evident, and only the last requires explanation. The assumption is that any significant element of subordinate involvement in who decides on directives at the top-most levels should be reflected in classification. To put it more bluntly, representation of subordinates in decision making, however indirect, is the thin edge of a powerful wedge to (ineluctably) expand representation. In polities, anyway, combinations of variety 2,*d* are likely to prove unstable in the long run and to generate pressures either for the election of S_1's or the elimination of their power; thus they become nominal and replaced by (some of) the S_2's as de facto and de jure S_1's. A number of European monarchies became parliamentary democracies by this process. If legends are a guide, the king-ruled tribes of archaic Greece so also became the democratic or tyrannical city-states of classical Greece.[8]

The distinctions we have made thus far constitute a fourfold differentiation of authority patterns, as sketched in Figure 13.1. This typology permits the categorization of authority patterns into very broad groupings. The patterns of some kinds of social units fall almost entirely into one category: families and schools are "closed," large business enterprises (and armies, bureaucracies, and churches) are "open: selected." Only modern associational groups[9] and polities are distributed among the categories, mainly between "open: selected" and "open: elected." More detailed differentiation among these types should be made on the basis of other authority traits.

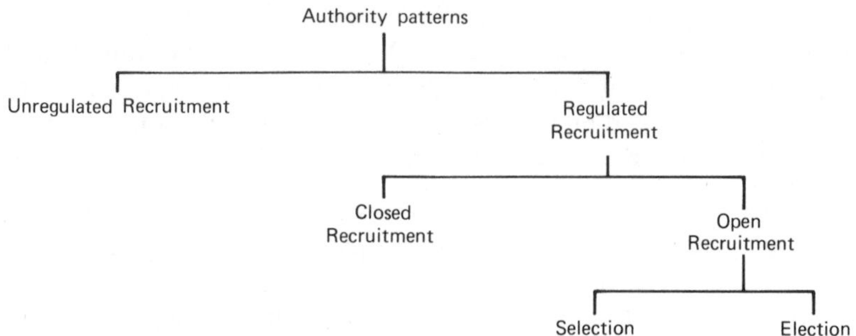

Fig. 13.1 Basic differentiations among authority patterns, based on Recruitment.

Decision-Rules and Decision-Behavior

Decision-Rules and Decision-Behavior probably are considerably more salient for superordinates than for subs (see Chapter 7), because supers are directly involved in them; subs' direct involvement in them is not unknown, but rare. Supers also are more consequential in some of the authority patterns differentiated earlier, on the basis of Recruitment, than in others. If Recruitment is closed, one of the principal avenues of subs' involvement in the direction of the unit is closed off, and Participation also is likely to be low. The same characteristics are likely to be found in units with unregulated Recruitment, at least when challengers to chiefs are not in the arena. We conclude that patterns with either closed or irregular Recruitment ought to be differentiated next on the basis of the processes of direction. But for units with either type of open Recruitment, the influence dimensions provide a basis for more consequential distinctions.

Decision-Rules (to recapitulate) vary from "monocratic," in which a single *S* decides all consequential matters, to "polycratic," where unanimity among supers (typically S_1's and S_2's) is required for directives to take effect. Majority rule among supers occupies the midpoint of the Decision-Rules continuum. Decision-Behavior refers, essentially, to the extent of cooperative versus contentious activities among supers in the process of working out directives. The former dimension, Decision-Rules, is more suitable for making generic differentiations among authority patterns at a high level of abstraction, for two reasons. First, Decision-Rules tend to be embodied in the forms or highly conscious norms of units, hence are both more visible and enduring; Decision-Behavior is more likely to vary according to when and how closely a unit is examined. Second, although there are modal differences among units in the relative concordance of Decision-Behavior, the differences are of degree rather than kind and thus impede precise categorization (but not detailed description).

The simplest and sharpest distinction we can make is between patterns in which monocratic (one-man) rule prevails and those in which some kind of assent is required, whether by especially prestigious minorities of supers, numerical majorities, or virtually all of them. We label the latter "concurrent" patterns, to distinguish them as a group from "monocratic" ones. This distinction certainly has been salient in Western societies. The prolonged struggles of the European nobility to require monarchs to consult them on issues of war and finance are cases in point. The transition of the modal Western family from father-dominated monocracy to a pattern in which concurrence of the spouses, and sometimes children, is sought on many issues has been equally fundamental. One can also distinguish among groups with irregular Recruitment according to whether the leader works with a council for decision making, a common feature of American youth gangs and of the Mafia, or exercises unqualified power, which seems to be a characteristic of many patron-client networks, particularly in Asian nations.

The differentiation between monocratic and concurrent patterns is simple and generally unambiguous.[10] It also distinguishes between patterns of substantially different complexity: decision making is a much more involved and taxing process for supers who depend on assent of their peers (regardless of numbers) than for monocrats. We could also further differentiate among authority patterns depending on how wide the assent for directives must be. The most obvious dividing line is between patterns in which a majority or more of supers must assent and those in which less than a majority suffices. But we suspect this is not even determinable for many if not most units in which assent is required. In African village councils and American departmental faculties, what is really important is the sounding-out of opinion. Some opinions count for more than others (as in the Congress of the United States, viz. those of committee chairmen), and headcounts, when used at all, are employed to resolve only certain relatively unimportant or uncertain issues or to ratify decisions reached by other means. The difference between polycracy and specially empowered minorities is certainly an important one. Nevertheless, it does not seem unambiguous enough to warrant a typological distinction at a still broad level of differentiation.

Further Differentiation by the Influence Dimensions

The overall typology, as far as we propose to carry it here, is portrayed in Figure 13.2. The first, most inclusive, six categories have been discussed. It remains to explicate and justify the ways we further differentiate them by use of the influence dimensions.

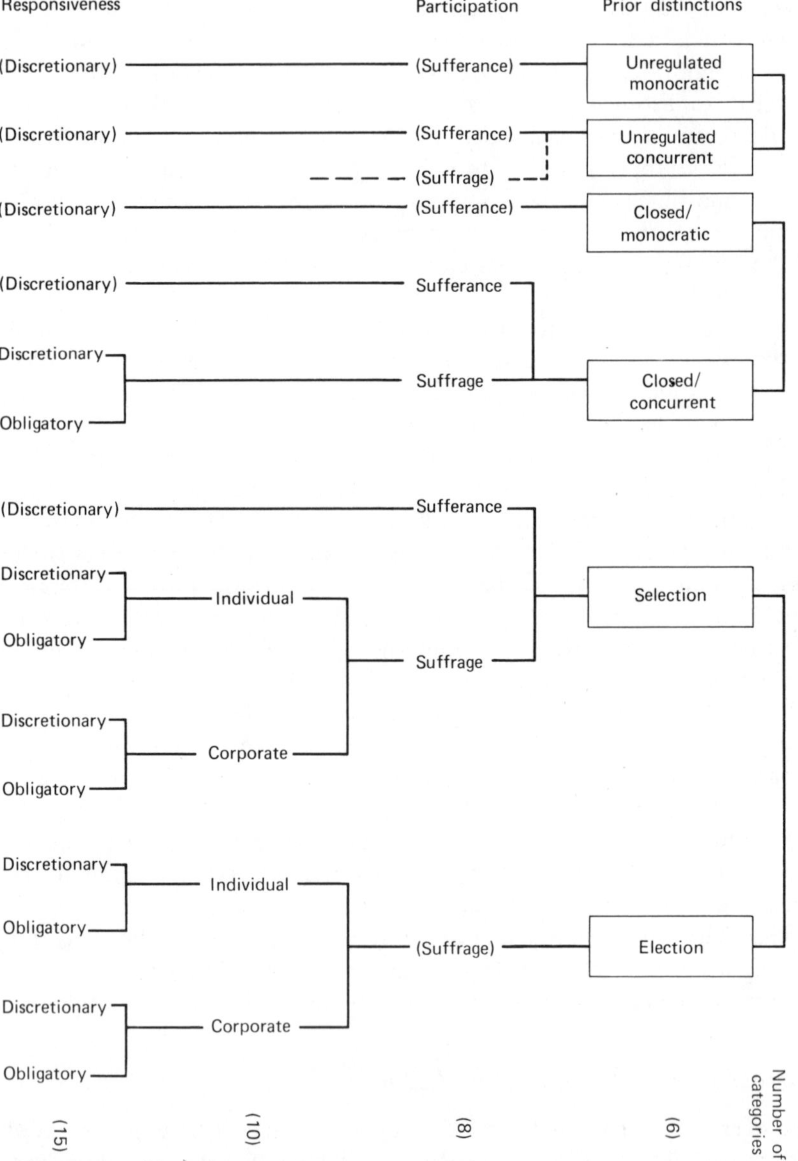

Fig. 13.2 The overall differentiation of authority patterns.

Directiveness

The most salient dimension of influence probably is Directiveness. However, several problems make it inadvisable to base differentiation at a high level of generality on that dimension. One has to do with the logic of differentiation: specifically, the requirement that types distinguished at one level be substantially different in characteristics at subsequent levels of differentiation. We used this kind of argument to help justify the distinction between closed and open Recruitment. In the case of Directiveness, on the other hand, it would be hard to argue that differences between broad and narrow coverage, or close and loose supervision, or high and low sanction thresholds lead to sharp differences in, say, patterns of Participation or Responsiveness. On the contrary, casual consideration of the finer differentiations we make among types of authority suggests that Directiveness can and does vary widely within each. If degrees or aspects of Directiveness are highly salient to unit members but do not predetermine other authority traits, the conclusion must be that Directiveness should be used to distinguish among patterns of authority at a rather low level of generalization.[11]

Two other considerations support this conclusion. One is an empirical observation about the social phylogeny of authority types in Western societies during the last few centuries. There has been a close chronological and causal connection between the development of patterns characterized by open Recruitment and the development of greater Participation and Responsiveness. This has been true of diverse social units, including polities, parties, businesses, and schools, which vary widely among and within themselves in Directiveness. There also has been a tendency within specific social units for Directiveness to decrease as Participation and Responsiveness increase, because subs often use the latter means to reduce the onerousness of directives, and especially to increase their supers' tolerance of noncompliance. What these historical sequences suggest, then, is that types devised on the basis of Recruitment be differentiated next according to their patterns of Participation and Responsiveness, and only then according to Directiveness. It is also especially difficult to make simple, unambiguous distinctions among authority patterns on the basis of their Directiveness. The most salient aspects of Directiveness are the breadth of coverage of the activities of members, and the amount of detail and precision characterizing the rules within each regulated domain of activity. These, however, are inherently differences of degree, not kind, and categorical distinctions among them, though possible, pose relatively numerous empirical instances of ambiguous classification.[12]

Participation

Participation varies among social units in overall levels—how many participate, how often—but factors that are probably more consequential for subs than the volume of activity are whether Participation is generally facilitated or impeded, and what modes of Participation are most common and efficacious. One broad, unambiguous basis for distinction is between patterns in which supers are accessible to the expression of preferences and those in which they are wholly inaccessible. We suspect that the latter is virtually an empty category, though. Even gods are believed to be swayed by propitiation and prayer, and the most imperious human rulers—whether fathers, entrepreneurs, or emperors—are virtually always susceptible to some kinds of influence attempts from their subordinates. What seems to distinguish "absolute" rulers from others is that they "suffer" their subjects to petition them, rather than making themselves accessible as a regular right accorded the subjects.

Our first distinction, then, is between patterns in which Participation is a matter of *suffrage*, one that subs hold and use by right, and those in which Participation is by *sufferance* of the supers. This distinction does not turn on whether superordinates take subs' preferences into account; that is a question of Responsiveness. The crux of the suffrage/sufferance distinction is that, in the former, supers are regularly obliged to expose themselves to expressions of subordinates' preferences, whereas in the latter they do so only when, where, and if they choose.[13] The specific channels of "suffrage" can vary widely, from mass assemblies and representation in councils to grievance procedures and rights of petition. If channels exist at all for any substantial class of subordinates, we categorize the pattern as one of "suffrage."

The distinction is dichotomous (though of course there are larger and smaller suffrages), and it differentiates patterns that vary systematically in complexity: other things equal, units having regularized means of Participation are structurally more complex than those which lack them. The distinction also is unambiguous in most instances. Operational problems are most likely to arise when classifying small units that have no formal structures and a high degree of face-to-face interaction. A great deal of observation, as well as information on the norms of the members, may be required to determine whether subs in such units have regular rights to express their preferences. If they speak their minds frequently, the answer is clear enough, but if they do so rarely it may be because they lack the motivation rather than the right. Nonparticipation due to apathy is another recurring characteristic of many large-scale social units, but the presence or absence of formal channels for Participation, combined with evidence of their occasional use, should suffice for classificatory decisions.

We suggested at several points that patterns of Recruitment have a bearing on patterns of Participation. Thus some of the types distinguished at the top of Figure 13.2 are unlikely to vary with respect to the sufferance/suffrage distinction. On the extreme right-hand side of the "tree" of differentiations are patterns characterized by election of superordinates. This is by definition a form of suffrage, hence no suffrage/sufferance distinction can be made. On the other side of the "tree," both logical argument and empirical evidence suggest that subordinates are unlikely to be enfranchised in authority patterns having monocratic Decision-Rules. Real-world attempts to combine absolutist decision making with regularized Participation are likely to be ephemeral: either the participatory rights soon lapse into desuetude or monocratic Decision-Rules give way to concurrent ones. Only three of the top categories in Figure 13.2 remain for subdivision using the suffrage/sufferance distinction: two characterized by concurrent decisions and one by selection of supers. And one of these is dubious. We suspect that few cases will be found of social units with irregular Recruitment, concurrent Decision-Rules, and Participation by suffrage. When such combinations do occur, they probably portend a change from irregular to regular Recruitment, or from suffrage to sufferance.

In Figure 13.2 we symbolize the unlikely but not inconceivable combination with dotted lines and suggest no further differentiation of it. It is, in a way, our typology's equivalent of an "extinct species" in the biological world. Such claims are of course subject to empirical verification. If a specimen of the Loch Ness monster is captured, zoologists will probably have to admit a novel species to the *Ichthyosaurus* genus of reptiles; and if patronage networks in Southeast Asia frequently produce self-anointed leaders who reach concurrent decisions with the regular participation of clients, a category we consider fanciful will gain substance. The same empirical means can be used to breathe life into any other combination of traits that we exclude here on grounds of implausibility.

The suffrage/sufferance distinction refers to the "facilitation" aspect of Participation. We also propose a subsidiary distinction based on channels of Participation. Just as there is a large qualitative distinction between supers' toleration of participatory acts and their recognition of such rights, there is also a qualitative difference between *individual* and *corporate* suffrage. By "individual" suffrage we mean that regular Participation is restricted to channels through which only individual preferences can be expressed. "Corporate" or associational suffrage is characterized by the regular, approved use of collective Participation by organized subgroups. The difference is quantitatively important because the existence of participatory associations, like parties and interest groups, is likely to mobilize Participation. It is also quantitatively important because groups are likely to exert more effective influence than atomized individuals. And it is qualitatively important because the regularized formation of participatory groups implies and leads to the formation of oppositions to established ruling groups, which formulate whole programs of action rather than merely expressing particular preferences.

The dichotomous distinction between individual and corporate suffrage differentiates between authority patterns of lesser and greater complexity. It does pose two kinds of ambiguity, however. One is the common co-occurrence of individual with corporate channels (e.g., voting and rights of petition along with party activity). Conceptually, we regard any regular departure from purely individual Participation as signifying a change of type—because of its implications for the level and consequentiality of participatory acts. The second ambiguity arises with respect to relatively small and "informal" social units, in which there is seldom any occasion for "groupist" Participation. Units of this type should not be differentiated on this trait, and any further distinctions among them should be made at lower levels of the typology.

The typological distinction between individual and corporate suffrage provides a basis for differentiating authority patterns with elected supers, a category we could not differentiate on the basis of facilitation. We also can distinguish between the two patterns of suffrage in "open/selection" and "closed/concurrent" patterns. The question is whether this is worth doing. In the class "open/selection" it surely is: this category includes a very large and diverse set of "modern" organizations ranging from corporations and churches to bureaucracies and polities. Probably most of them recognize some kind of suffrage, but not all are characterized by organized group Participation. The "closed/concurrent suffrage" category on the other hand, will probably be only sparsely represented by some modern families, schools, and universities (units of nurturance), but few units of any other kind. Little seems to be gained by making a categorical distinction between such patterns according to channels of Participation; the more consequential difference between them probably resides in the Responsiveness of their ascriptively chosen superordinates. American academic departments, for example, are "closed" with respect to undergraduates but generally practice concurrent decision making at the faculty level and, in recent years and in some universities, have acquiesced to a form of suffrage whereby students are represented in all or some departmental councils. The most salient current issue is not whether the subs can organize but how responsive the supers are to their Participation.

The preceding argument is summarized in Figure 13.2, where we subcategorize only two of the more general categories according to the "individual/corporate" distinction.

Responsiveness

We cannot conceive of any enduring authority pattern that has regularized Participation without some *S*-Responsiveness. The lack of responses will eventually extinguish attempts at Participation; the structural channels may remain and convey occasional bursts of protest or outrage, but neither constitutes Participation in the present sense. There is, however, an important qualitative difference in Responsiveness that is analogous to the distinction between sufferance and suffrage. In some authority patterns the supers are obliged to incorporate some preferences of subordinates into decisions, in others they need only consider them. Most ruling Communist parties follow the latter pattern: there are regular (even if limited) opportunities for party members to express their views on matters of party policy, but ordinary members seldom are empowered to make choices among alternative policies. Most political parties in Western democracies, and some labor unions, have institutionalized the provision of choice for at least some kinds of policies. Our tentative terms for the two modes are "discretionary" and "obligatory" Responsiveness.[14] Regular choice by popular voting, such as referenda, is probably the most common way in which supers are obliged to be responsive to the preferences of subordinates; regular choices among policy-making officials are a kind of functional equivalent, provided the *S*'s appeal to their "constituencies" for support principally on the basis of clear proposed policies.

Any procedures requiring supers to submit some types of decisions to referenda or veto by subs constitute obligatory Responsiveness. So does the empowering of certain classes of subordinates to negotiate with supers in the formulation of directives or to veto unsatisfactory ones. Decision making in Mexico's ruling Institutional Revolutionary Party (PRI), for example, is said to involve just this kind of regularized negotiation among the principal party sectors, including workers, farmers, businessmen, and the military. The bargaining rights of unions vis-à-vis employers are a more familiar example of the same collective negotiation of policies.

The threshold between discretionary and obligatory Responsiveness occurs at precisely the point that supers concede an obligation to accept subs' views or negotiate agreements with them on any recurring and consequential issues, however narrow. As with the sufferance/suffrage distinction, crossing that boundary substantially alters the role of subs in the unit and opens up possibilities for binding supers' decisions more and more to subs' preferences. This does not mean that the expansion of Responsiveness is inevitable once that threshold is crossed: supers may and do resist further infringement on their "prerogatives" and may even reverse the entire process. It is virtually certain, though, that transitions from obligatory to discretionary Responsiveness will be more rare and will occasion more conflict than transitions in the opposite direction.

The difference is clear in the abstract and should be unambiguous in large-scale social units. It will be more difficult to make in small and informal units, but this does not mean that the difference is any the less consequential in them. It makes a very real difference whether supers and subs believe that the former have an obligation to be responsive in certain domains of issues. We also can readily specify what information is required to make a definitive categorization of the authority patterns of such units. Responsiveness is "obligatory" if most supers *and* subs agree that some specific obligation exists; otherwise it is "discretionary." Such information is not always obtainable, but that is a data-gathering problem, not a function of any intrinsic ambiguity in the distinction.

The last question is whether *all* the categories already distinguished ought to be subdivided on the basis of Responsiveness. Since it is virtually certain that supers who follow monocratic Decision-Rules with respect to lesser superordinates will not acknowledge any obligation to be responsive to subs, no subdivision is appropriate here. Supers who listen to subs only when they choose are also highly likely to exercise personal discretion about whether they respond. No "obligation" here, except perhaps as a historical residue or future hope. The distinction only makes sense in patterns which have suffrage, and we so apply it in Figure 13.2. We expect that obligatory Responsiveness will be found to be more common in social units that practice corporate suffrage than in those with individual suffrage: subs in the former are more likely to be influential enough to secure obligatory Responsiveness from their supers. But this should be no more than a tendency; hence the distinction seems equally appropriate for patterns of "individual" and "corporate" "suffrage."

Directiveness Again

Fifteen types of authority patterns have been differentiated thus far, each of them a distinctive compound of authority traits. We have also explicitly identified a number of compounds that are implausible or likely to be unstable; many others are implicit in the distinctions we chose *not* to make. The types are all susceptible to further division according to how "directive" they are. In the extreme right-hand category, for example, which is more purely democratic in the Western sense than any other type, are social units as diverse as Sweden's social-welfare state, the United Mine Workers of America (UMW) (post-1972), and the American Political Science Association (APSA) (post-1969). Some of their diversity is due to their different functions, but much of it can be characterized in terms of differential Directiveness. There are four subdimensions of Directiveness (see Chapter 2), on which we might differentiate these three units in the following manner:

Coverage	Latitude	Supervision	Sanction Threshold
(*Comprehensive*)	(*Specific*)	(*Close*)	(*Severe*)
Sweden	UMW	UMW	UMW
UMW	Sweden	Sweden	Sweden
APSA	APSA	APSA	APSA
(*Restricted*)	(*General*)	(*Loose*)	(*Lenient*)

If these rankings are roughly accurate, we can say that the UMW is relatively the most "regimented" of these "democratic" units and the APSA by far the most "permissive." The object of this exercise is not invidious distinction but to indicate that Directiveness may be best assessed using several qualitative variables that do not readily lend themselves to categorical distinctions. Some such distinctions are possible (e.g., between coverage that is restricted to the primary task(s) of a unit and that which extends to most or all the members' activities, including their deportment and beliefs[15], but no one such distinction seems to be as clear-cut as others we have made. A rather feeble solution is to sketch a distinction into our typology between patterns that are relatively Regimented and those which are relatively Permissive. Others may want to try their hand at elaborating the typology at this juncture; but identifying 15 types at specified levels of generality, and in conformity with the criteria of classification developed in Chapter 12, is certainly a large beginning.

Some Residual Dimensions and Ideas

The inequality dimensions are next in the order of salience and therefore might be used to make the next level of differentiation among authority patterns. The most persuasive argument against using them would be evidence that inequalities between subs and supers vary systematically among the categories already proposed: if so, differentiation on the basis of "inequalities" would add little to the capacity of the typology to convey information. We already have suggested that patterns with "closed" Recruitment are likely to manifest greater inequalities than "open" ones. Within each major branch of the "tree" of differentiation, inequalities ought to decline as lower supers and subs gain more influence in decision-processes. Thus inequalities will (tend to) be greater where Decision-Rules are monocratic, less where they are concurrent; greater where Participation is by sufferance than by suffrage. Inequalities should also be greater in more "regimented" social units than in "permissive" ones, because of the relatively greater influence supers in the former have over the lives of subs. These are hypotheses that are well worth testing. If they hold up under empirical scrutiny, they justify a decision (already taken here) not to use inequalities as a basis of categorical distinction.

Some pages ago we proposed that Decision-Behavior and Decision-Rules are so important to subs that in units with "open" Recruitment they might provide grounds for finer categorical distinctions. The distinction we employed for other units was between decision making by "monocratic" S_1's, who were under no obligation to consult with other supers, and concurrent decision-making. As with inequalities, however, distinctions already made on the right-hand side of the "tree" are likely to subsume the monocratic/concurrent distinction. If supers are obliged to respond to inputs from subs, almost surely they are also obliged to take into account the views of lower-order supers. On the other hand, if they have discretion about responding to subs they probably have the same discretionary rights with respect to other supers. Admittedly, empirical evidence might invalidate these assumptions, especially the second. If so, some or all of the "discretionary" and "obligatory" orders on the right-hand side of the tree might be dichotomously differentiated further.[16]

Conclusion

Each successive level of differentiation has increased the number of categories in the typology. Depending on the fineness with which one wishes to distinguish among cases, as few as 2 or as many as 15 (or 30) types can be identified. *Which* level of generality is used depends partly on the purposes being pursued (whether descriptive or theoretical) and partly on the types of units being categorized. The vast majority of families probably can be classified as one of two types: closed/monocratic or closed/concurrent. Virtually all commercial organizations can be classified among the types that descend from Recruitment by selection. On the other hand, classification of contemporary polities probably would require all types but those in which Recruitment is unregulated, and classification of the authority patterns of all kinds of social units in all societies would necessitate using the entire typology.

Compared with other typologies in political science, this one has a precision that leaves relatively little to the imagination. Each of its types is defined in terms of a distinct and generally unambiguous compound of traits. Below its first level, it is a genuine work of "synthesis." Still, the typology is surely incomplete and inadequate in a number of respects. The types lack evocative labels. No concrete applications are reported (nor have any yet been attempted) except by way of casual illustration. We have not demonstrated, only suggested, that each more general type permits distinctive but not exhaustive generalizations about all dependent cases. It is also virtually certain that three other criticisms will be leveled against the typology as it stands. Those who are especially concerned with authority patterns in social units of one particular type, such as parties or polities, will no doubt find that our distinctions are not detailed enough to discriminate satisfactorily among their subjects. Others will fault the scheme because its differentiations almost surely are influenced to a degree by our selective, culturally influenced perceptions of what are the "important" differences among authority patterns. Still others will criticize us for not making distinctions of special contemporary "relevance," in the manner of Apter or Janowitz, or for failing to take account of the characteristics of social units when classifying authority patterns.

We do think that the typology is useful for classifying polities (which cannot be said about many "political" typologies) and that types of authority patterns probably vary systematically with types of social units (see Chapter 15). But we admit that there is room for improvement—especially on the basis of empirical information now lacking. Repeatedly we have remarked on the requirement that good typology be based on good empirical generalization. Those who find this prototypical typology inadequate to their subject matter or cultural perspectives may well have some of the empirical information necessary to revise and expand it. When enough applications, revisions, and extensions are in hand, it will be time to think out succinct identifying labels—the *last* thing that matters in classification, although too often the *first* thing done. And, most important, we claim that our typology, although a "prototype," is the result of reasoning about the principles of good classification and their application as best we are able at the present stage.

Notes

1. See James A. Bill and Robert L. Hardgrave, Jr., *Comparative Politics: The Quest for Theory* (Columbus, Ohio: Charles E. Merrill, 1972), Ch. 4, on the types and prevalence of informal groups. In Western societies they are often assumed to be ephemeral, hence not "social units." In non-Western and Latin societies they are not only common but sometimes quite durable.

2. Although the principal contemporary examples are informal groups, there are others, including some polities that have a high incidence of *coups d' état*.

3. A typology of political systems based on the openness of Recruitment to elite positions is proposed by Peter C. Lloyd, "The Political Structure of African

Kingdoms: An Exploratory Model," in Michael Banton, Ed., *Political Systems and the Distribution of Power*, (London: Tavistock, 1965, for the Association of Social Anthropologists of the Commonwealth). The empirical existence of what seems to be a transitional type (not necessarily the African case discussed in the text) does not warrant a separate category unless cases so characterized prove to be both numerous and relatively durable. If they are numerous and durable, however, this raises serious doubts about whether they ought to be thought of as "transitional" at all. The use of categories like "mixed" and "transitional" in typologies is often a way of ducking the obligation to state precisely the defining "mixture" of traits.

4. These characterizations of primary and secondary groups and the notion of (tertiary) "Great Associations" are from R. M. MacIver and Charles H. Page, *Society* (London: Macmillan, 1962), pp. 218–229.

5. See, for example, the discussion of the activities of African tribal governments in I. Schapera, *Government and Politics in Tribal Societies* (London: Watts, 1956), Ch. 3; and Lucy Mair, *Primitive Government* (London: Penguin, 1962), pp. 148–151. The empire of the Incas was similarly characterized, even at its greatest extent; see Garcilaso de la Vega, *The Royal Commentaries of the Inca* (various editions), especially the first halves of Books 2 and 4. It is noteworthy that although the Inca kings inherited their positions, de la Vega remarks that among some conquered but quasi-autonomous "nations" within the empire, leadership passed to a ruler's most preferred subject, "which meant succession by election rather than by inheritance" (Book 4, p. 135, in the Avon, 1964 edition). Thus it seems that there were "open" and "closed" polities in the Amerindian as well as the Indo-European tradition long before the "modern" era.

6. The Inca Empire, with 10 to 20 million subjects at its greatest extent, represents a class of imperial exceptions. As in most empires, though, Recruitment at lower levels of the bureaucracy was open to talented men. Moreover, the Inca Empire, though superbly organized and administered, was so focused on the deified person of the Inca that when 180 Spanish adventures captured and executed the incumbent, the empire collapsed abruptly and with scarcely any resistance.

7. It is likely to be more salient than the size of the base of eligibles, which is an aspect of Recruitment we do not use as a basis for typological differentiation. There are at least three good reasons for neglecting this aspect. One is that, except at the "closed" extreme, size permits only distinctions of degree not kind. A second is the empirical difficulty of determining actual bases of eligibles, as is evident from our calculations of ratios of advantage in Chapter 6. Finally, the effective size of the base of eligibles has been of relatively little concern to most subs in most social units that we know much about. For example, the burning issue in the political suffrage movements in the West during the past two centuries was not whether ordinary citizens were eligible for high office (a question of the size of the base) but rather whether they could have a voice in the election of supers (a question of the mode of boundary interchange).

8. The typical sequence was a gradual one, from kingship to aristocracy or oligarchy (via a broadening of the base of the economic or military elite), to popular democracy, and sometimes to tyranny. The tyrants were rarely aristocrats but rather

men active in democratic politics who found it necessary or convenient to retain and monopolize power rather than yield it to successors. Among many sources, see the classic work of Alfred Zimmern, *The Greek Commonwealth*, (London: Oxford University Press, 1911), especially Ch. III and VI, and Mason Hammond, *The City in the Ancient World*, (Cambridge, Mass.: Harvard University Press, 1972).

9. "Associational groups" are the good end of another bad typology, since categorizing a group as "nonassociational" says only what the entity is not.

10. The existence of a collective S_1 raises some complications dealt with in Chapter 5.

11. This argument obviously introduces a slight inconsistency in regard to the position that typological differentiation should follow the order of salience sketched in Chapter 7. But the word to be emphasized here is "slight," since we follow that order in all other respects.

12. See, however, note 15.

13. In any social unit, subordinates often resort to *force majeure* as a way of letting supers know their preferences. Assassinations, riots, sit-ins, and tantrums are functionally equivalent—but they are rarely "regularized" means of Participation. Thus their occurrence, even if frequent and influential, does not constitute grounds for classifying the authority patterns in which they occur on the "suffrage" side of the distinction.

14. This is rather different from the polar distinction, in Chapter 2, between "autocratic" and "alterocratic" Responsiveness. "Autocratic" practices are implied by patterns characterized by monocratic Decision-Rules. "Alterocratic" Responsiveness is almost surely obligatory, in norms even if not forms. But in the great middle ground between these extremes, differences in degrees of Responsiveness provide no basis for clear-cut typological distinction, whereas the obligatory/discretionary distinction does. We do expect, empirically, that "discretionary" Responsiveness will tend to be toward the autocratic pole, "obligatory" Responsiveness toward the other extreme. And in social phylogeny it has often been observed that subs who exacted from their autocratic supers the obligation to be responsive in some limited domain of policy have used it as a lever to expand the overall degree of Responsiveness.

15. Schonfeld in *Youth and Authority in France: A Study of Secondary Schools* (Beverly Hills, Calif. Sage Professional Papers in Comparative Politics, No 01-014, 1971), p. 14, distinguishes among the kinds of activities of members that can be covered by directives. These include *task* coverage, referring to the nature of the tasks to be undertaken; *instrumental* coverage (how the tasks are to be carried out), *comportmental* coverage (how members should behave while in the unit), and *ideological* coverage (what ideas and attitudes should be held). The distinctions are precise enough to provide the basis for a categorization of the extent of Directiveness. However, they do not take into account the very substantial differences among authority patterns on the other subdimensions of Directiveness (i.e. Latitude, Supervision, and Sanction-thresholds). They probably also apply only in certain kinds of social units, like schools, that have elements of both functional-task specificity and "diffuse" relationships based on ascriptive differences among subs and supers.

16. Readers should avoid confusing two quite different arguments. If cases in one class have more in common than with cases in another, a typological distinction among them is justified, *at the same level*. However, if they are homogeneous in respects not used to characterize them in the first place, further differentiation by use of the dimensions concerned obviously is gratuitous—though the other dimensional characteristics can then serve as further defining traits of the classes.

PART FIVE

Substantive Problems in the Study of Authority Patterns

CHAPTER FOURTEEN

Authority Patterns as Dependent and Independent Variables

We began with the basic contention that the central subject of political inquiry should be patterns of authority—any and all such patterns, not just those of states (or their supposed functional analogues where fully developed state-organizations do not exist). We then presented at length a set of concepts for "systematically" describing authority patterns in considerable and precise detail, as well as tentative concepts for summary, typological description. The ability so to describe cases surely is necessary for the scientific exploration of a subject matter. But as previously pointed out, the description of particular cases in systematic inquiry is a means to the "nomothetic" end of working out valid generalizations (laws) that assert universal or probabilistic links—generally causal, sometimes merely functional—among variables. Such laws serve three closely related purposes: to "explain" specific observations by subsuming them under general rules; to "predict" from knowns to what is not yet known; and to help "engineer" desired conditions or discover determinants of, and remedies for, undesired ones. Thus we turn, in the last part of this book, to that ultimate end of inquiry.

There is more than one route toward the attainment of nomothetic knowledge. The accumulation of data may suggest general links among variables that have prima facie validity, or at least that merit testing. Such links will become apparent, of course, only to the extent that descriptions really are cumulative—that is, not idiographic but rendered in a standardized manner, using variables and types applicable to all, or many, cases of the kind here developed. Another source of insight about links among variables is the imaginative interpretation of particular cases. Consequently, the cases with which we illustrated the dimensions of authority patterns were used not only to make conceptual abstractions vivid but also, in each instance, to indicate likely generalizations about a large variety of issues. Pure deduction is a third source of nomothetic propositions: a set of conceptual "primitives" is defined and used in axiomatic statements from which theorems are logically derived—theorems that are considered to fit experience.

Methodologists differ about the relative advantages and pitfalls of the ways in which nomothetic propositions may be worked out. We do not propose to join in their debates here. Suffice to say that nomothetic propositions are always solutions, good or bad, of "substantive" problems—problems concerning the ways in which aspects of phenomena are actually related. Such problems differ from the "conceptual" (how to describe experience) and the "methodological" (how to observe experience and make sense of data yielded by observation)—although, in the final analysis, the solution of substantive problems also requires that of conceptual and methodological issues.

In illustrating the dimensions of authority patterns we raised a great many substantive problems, but in an ad hoc, disorganized manner. We now wish to discuss more schematically the principal substantive problems that arise in the study of authority patterns. We also want to indicate possible solutions of the problems, or useful ways of going about the search for solutions—but this much more provisionally, precisely because the working out of solutions of substantive problems is the end (usually remote) of the whole process of systematic inquiry. In any event, problems must be formulated before solutions are advanced, and tentative solutions have to be considered before definitive ones are found.

Types of Problems in the Study of Authority Patterns

The most fundamental and obvious distinction among substantive problems arising in the study of authority patterns is between problems in which properties of the patterns are dependent and independent variables.

In treating authority patterns as *dependent* variables, we generalize about the determinants of some or all of their characteristics: why the patterns are what they are. Several examples, interpreting particular cases but entailing broad generalizations, were used in Part II. A case in point is our speculation about the causes of the high degrees of polycracy and concordance that characterize decision making throughout Norwegian society. We suggested a "cultural" approach to explanation, in which a crucial variable was the "functional deference" that Norwegians accord to one another's subjects of expertise (leaving aside here the question of the more remote conditions that have generated such functional deference). An alternative explanation is provided by Rogowski and Wasserspring, who argue from rationalist premises that consensual decision making is likely to typify highly "segmented" societies. This is not the place to debate or test the merits of the competing explanations, "functional deference" versus "segmentation." They serve here to illustrate that questions about the "why" of particular characteristics of authority patterns can quickly lead to fundamental theoretical confrontations—in this case, whether human behavior in political contexts (and others) is most usefully and accurately regarded as based on calculation about the maximization of utilities, or whether it is the manifestation of cultural orientations implanted in the process of socialization.

In treating the properties of authority patterns as *independent* variables, we generalize about how they account for a wide assortment of political (and other) conditions—for example, the ability of the patterns or the social units in which they exist to persist, to command allegiance, to manage conflict, or to function efficaciously. The majority of illustrations in Part II fall into this category. Recall that we cited a study of a wildcat strike in an American factory which was evidently caused by a change in the deportment of supervisors—changes seen by the workers as evidence of an unjustified attitude of arrogance (high Distance). In a much more speculative illustration of the complexity of conformation of authority structures, we suggested the broader proposition that the scions of bourgeois and upper-class families in nineteenth-century Europe were not so much "born to rule," as they maintained, but "raised to rule" by virtue of the complex structures of their family establishments. From the nursery onward they were accustomed—certainly more than the sons of workers—to deal with a multiplicity of authority relations that foreshadowed their experiences in larger social entities later in life.

These two examples are oversimple in that they attribute a social outcome to a single authority variable, when others were probably applicable as well. We can offer another and more complex example, using some of the characterizations drawn in Part II of authority relations in British society. These are some of the descriptive generalizations offered there, on the basis of evidence of varying quality:

1. Recruitment to the upper strata of British politics and administration is very sharply restricted; thus males of upper-class origin and/or public school training vastly outnumber persons with other characteristics.
2. The very high degree of Compliance demanded in English public schools is enforced by punitive sanctions but achieved mainly by securing students' absolute acceptance of the legitimacy of the purposes and practices of the school and their schoolmates as a collective entity.
3. Family life in the English working class tends to be highly regimented for wives and—most important in the present argument—for children.

One interpretation of this set of conditions (and others not reviewed here) is that the vaunted stability and effectiveness of British democracy depend on conditions of authority that are neither particularly democratic nor palatable. On this argument, British society consists at bottom of people who are raised in an "authoritarian" setting and therefore make malleable citizens—if ruled "authoritatively." The elect of British society are a class of men trained in unswerving loyalty to their peers and the institutions they staff. And the pattern of Recruitment to elite positions ensures that these men operate the institutions of government with only a small leaven of men—occasionally women—of less exclusive backgrounds. The actions and policies of this elite have a decisiveness and convey a general unity of purpose consonant with ordinary citizens' expectations that their leaders will be highly directive and will demand close compliance. Elements of this argument are not unfamiliar in intellectual and Labour circles in Britain, but its originality is not at issue here. Neither is its accuracy. (If the argument is essentially accurate in the political realm, how can we account for the low legitimacy and lack of compliance accorded by many British workers to their employers?) However, the argument demonstrates that explanations of the sources of and constraints on democracy in polities generally can fruitfully be sought in authority relations far removed from what is conventionally considered political. This, of course, does not preclude the possibility that characteristics of authority in polities might also help explain traits of lesser units.

When traits of authority patterns are treated as dependent variables, two different tacks can be taken. The first is to emphasize factors *extrinsic* to the patterns, such as nonpolitical aspects of the social units in which the patterns exist. Both we and Rogowski and Wasserspring did this in our proposed explanations of high polycracy and concordance in Norwegian patterns of authority: social segmentation and functional deference are both aspects of the context or environment of authority patterns. We also suggested that lack of Responsiveness in German families during the Imperial and Weimar periods was largely a consequence of the industrialization of German society.

On the other hand, certain aspects of authority patterns might be used to account for other aspects of the patterns. On this tack, factors *intrinsic* to authority patterns serve as both independent and dependent variables. Our assertion that some aspects of authority are more fundamental (salient) than others, presented in our discussion of Bases of Legitimacy and used again in constructing a basic typology, makes it particularly likely that causal relations will exist among properties of authority relations. From that assertion it is only a short step to arguments that some authority traits will be epiphenomenal functions, not of extrinsic conditions but of characteristics of authority patterns per se. For example, Distance may be epiphenomenal in this sense. Such arguments can also be sustained on the "systemic" assumption that any consequential change in a trait of authority will have repercussions on others—although the saliency argument is still useful in identifying sensitive dimensions that might have especially pronounced effects on the overall patterning of authority.

A simple example of the interaction among aspects of authority is provided by the illustrations of Participation and Responsiveness in Swedish schools, in Chapter 2. We saw from Friedman's data that Swedish schoolchildren develop a high valuation and practice of Participation, especially collective participation. This is closely—we are tempted to say reciprocally—related to the norm and practice of high Responsiveness by Swedish teachers. They seem not only highly responsive in general, but especially so to collective participation by students on matters of concern to the group. A contrasting case is provided in Schonfeld's study: in French schools, teachers do not place a particularly high value on Responsiveness; the students claim to value both Participation and Responsiveness, but in fact they participate very little, except in a disruptive way when they perceive the teacher to be ineffectual. The behavioral differences in Participation between schools in the two societies, then, seem to be markedly influenced by teachers' attitudes toward and practice of Responsiveness.

The uses of extrinsic and intrinsic variables to explain the nature of authority patterns are not mutually exclusive. One reason is that conditions extrinsic to authority patterns might affect certain aspects of the patterns only by way of other circumstances. A strong possibility is that extrinsic forces affect overall structures of authority only if they first affect one or more of their salient dimensions. If this is true—even if changes in scale and complexity, for example, are capable of affecting decision-making performance—they are less likely to change overall authority relations than changes in, say, Recruitment. (We realize that the argument is tendentious at this stage—but it may be valid.) Second, an extrinsic force, like industrialization, might have—in fact, probably ought to have—dissimilar effects on different patterns of authority. Industrialization is an "initial condition" from which effects follow, but so are the arrangements on which industrialization impinges. In the case of German families, for example, the lack of Responsiveness associated with industrialization manifestly could occur only because of the preindustrial patterning of authority. This in turn does not rule out the possibility that some extrinsic conditions might have universally similar effects on authority, regardless of other initial conditions.

The possibility that aspects of authority might determine others suggests a set of problems worth mentioning separately, which are of the essence in "synthetic" study (e.g., in chemistry). These problems concern the *interactive effects* (or "reactions") that occur when different elements of authority or authority traits are conjoined. What may occur, of course, are highly stable, or gradually decaying, or explosively disintegrating compounds; some compounds of authority traits may also be capable of doing efficient work while others are sluggish or inert. For example, the compound of high Participation and low Responsiveness that apparently existed in German families during the initial period of industrialization would seem to be inherently subject to decay, if not indeed explosive disintegration. It seems clear as well that an authority pattern characterized by high polycracy cannot do efficient work unless supers value and practice high concordance, as in Norway. Most questions of interactive effects, however, are far more problematic. One might propose that high concordance among supers would fit uneasily with low Responsiveness on their part; after all, concordance involves a tendency of supers to respond to other supers, and it might be weakened by contrary norms and practices toward subs. On the other hand, the ability of supers to act concordantly might presuppose a great deal of insulation from pressure by supers' "constituencies." If special groups are represented by supers, if the groups are highly participant, and if values of both high concordance and high "alterocracy" prevail, the resultant compound may well be highly inert: the traits might be accommodated only by many "nondecisions," and even then only uneasily. The Norwegian governmental system thus perhaps works efficiently only because concordance is a general social value, even more strongly held by subs than values of Responsiveness.

The study of interactive effects is not primarily concerned with explaining why authority patterns have particular characteristics. In studying "reactions," the independent variables are combinations of authority traits; the dependent variables are chiefly differences in the "performance" of the patterns—whether they can persist, effectively do any kind of work, or do effective work of particular kinds. Theories about interactive effects thus belong to the study of authority traits as independent variables. At one remove, however, interactive effects may also account for the nature of authority patterns. If some compounds of authority traits are inherently evanescent, we know at least that they will change, if we cannot tell precisely how.[1] Perhaps (although the notion is subject to disproof) patterns of authority have a short-run or long-run tendency to assume stable and efficient forms; in this case, the existence of any trait of authority might be "explained" at least partially by the argument that it fits well with others. All such explanations, of course, beg the question of why trait *y* changes to fit trait *x*, not *x* to fit *y*, or both to fit each other.

In raising the last question, we come on still another set of substantive problems. These concern the *normal sequences* that occur in changes of authority patterns. Two general subtypes of this set of problems can also be distinguished.

The first involves issues like those just raised. What is the relative malleability of authority traits; or, which dimensional changes tend to initiate particularly far-reaching changes on other dimensions, hence in the overall characteristics of authority patterns? Our previous arguments suggest that the more salient dimensions should be particularly consequential. Whether this is true surely provides a good test of the whole argument about saliency and of whether we have identified correctly more and less salient dimensions.

Equally or perhaps more interesting are questions about whether there are "normal" developmental sequences in the evolution of patterns of authority. Such sequences have sometimes been considered to exist in general social evolution or in that of polities (e.g., continuously greater functional differentiation, rationalization, centralization of governmental authority, or the expropriation of "private" spheres of control by public ones). The cases discussed in Part II provide some raw material for identifying developmental sequences in authority patterns. Friedman, for example, found that as Swedish children became older, they tended to use a greater variety of participatory styles, and particularly to increase the use of group actions (Chapter 2). Is this pattern peculiar to Sweden? Or is it a normal (typical) mode of development in the life cycle of individuals? Probably it is a "normal" pattern, for the obvious reasons discussed in the section on Participation, at least in cultures where group actions are widely used. But a more important question is whether changes in authority traits associated with individual maturation have analogues in general social development and/or the genesis of particular authority patterns. Is there a general tendency in authority patterns toward greater Participation over time? Toward a shift from individual to group actions? Toward more and more variegated Participation as development occurs (if it occurs) in the general societal context?

We think there probably is a general relation between social development and greater Participation, for several reasons. Development, in the sense of man's growing mastery over his environment, requires that at least some people acquire greater and more diverse knowledge. This means that they are more likely to see needs to participate and to acquire the skills necessary to form and use organizations for that purpose. Empirical evidence for this hypothesis is the universal finding that "political" Participation tends to increase as formal education increases. Recall also Almond and Verba's finding that groupist Participation increases with levels of educational attainment. Moreover, some moderate levels of Participation—and also Responsiveness and concordance—appear to be functional requisites of complex and diverse organizations. Without them, the steady flow of reliable information on which managers of complex organizations depend will be impeded, bad decisions will be made, and the organizations will decay to lower levels of complexity and efficiency—those requiring the lesser flows of information that are consistent with nonparticipant and "autocratic" patterns of authority.[2]

The nature of authority patterns is primarily explained, in a particular way, by propositions about normal developmental sequences in the evolution of such patterns. In these explanations, the initial conditions (independent variables) that explain consequences are either the developmental level of the (exogenous) social context or, if patterns of authority have developmental dynamics of their own, the previous state of the (endogenous) patterns. In the latter case, we would want to have nomothetic propositions about the "stages" through which all patterns of authority, or patterns in particular kinds of social units, "evolve." But propositions about normal developmental sequences could also be used to explain aspects of the performance of authority patterns: their ability to endure, command allegiance, and function efficaciously. Patterns of authority might be tenuous and inefficacious simply if "ripe" for change, in transition from stage to stage, or out of phase with the developmental context in which they operate. The argument about Participation sketched in the preceding paragraphs is a point of departure for one such set of propositions. On this or a similar basis we would expect the developmental stage attained by patterns of authority to account, as an independent variable, for traits of social units as dependent variables (e.g., their level of internal conflict and capacity to manage it, and their ability to attain particular goals).

What Is Variable in Authority Patterns?

The foregoing discussion merely outlines and illustrates the basic problems for nomothetic generalization that might be raised in studies of authority patterns. In the chapters that follow we treat these problems more schematically and in more detail, dividing the material into treatments of the role of authority traits as dependent variables (conditions to be explained, predicted, diagnosed, and engineered) and their role as independent variables (conditions that explain, allow predictions, and allow the engineering of effects). Both sets of problems, however, can be tackled only if another preliminary question has been clearly answered: What is variable in patterns of authority?

Empirical investigations and nomothetic propositions are likely to focus on six analytically distinguishable kinds of variation in the authority patterns of different social units or the same units at different times.

Variations in Particular Dimensions of Authority

On the basis of the inquirer's interests, convictions regarding salience, or assumptions about the significance of particular dimensions for solving particular problems, one can ask whether and how authority patterns of social units differ on the 10 discrete dimensions (and Bases of Legitimacy) specified in Part II. Friedman's study of Swedish schools, for example, is one of many political studies that deal almost exclusively with Participation. The animus behind the author's emphasis was largely normative: Friedman was committed to participant values and was interested in finding out conditions that in his terms "subsidize" participant activities. He also assumed that Participation in schools is critically important for extent and kind of Participation in adult contexts; thus he used Participation in one type of social unit as an independent variable that explains Participation in others. Beyond this, Friedman wanted to examine the widely held nomothetic assertion that very high, no less than very low, Participation lessens the performance (viz., stability) of democratic polities. Consistent with his normative predisposition, he found this assertion to be false, or at least of dubious validity; thus his study also illustrates how independent authority variables might help explain dependent performance variables. We also mentioned before that he discovered a particular temporal sequence in rates and types of Participation, which may be generalizable.

Variations in Clusters (or Compounds) of Dimensions

One can be concerned with particular combinations of dimensions, no less than traits on single dimensions. This is normally the case if one is interested in such intrinsically multidimensional considerations as the extent to which influence in a social unit is weighted in favor of superordinates, or how supers work out directives. It will also be the case if one wishes to examine the effects of one authority trait on others, or if a dependent variable (e.g., the stability of an authority pattern or social unit) is presumed to depend on a set of initial authority traits. The clusters of dimensions chosen may be whatever inquirers please; however, they are likely to be dimensions considered closely related causally or because they are aspects of a general dimensional cluster like influence relations or superordinate structures and processes. Schonfeld's study of French schools, for example, gives nearly equal emphasis to all four dimensions of "influence." Schonfeld does this because he wishes to explain general orientations among Frenchmen toward the authority of polities and their consequences for the ways and effectiveness of French rule at the national level—and also because he assumes that the general orientations useful for this purpose are compounds of all the influence dimensions. By way of contrast, a study by Gurston Dacks[3] of the ways in which attitudes and practices of authority affect national-provincial relations in the Canadian federal systems emphasizes the *S-S* dimensions: the actors involved are all superordinates, and the dependent variables are the ways in which federal-provincial negotiations are conducted and the effectiveness with which the work proceeds.

Variations in General Types of Authority Patterns

Typological differences among patterns of authority have been defined by us in terms of clusters of authority traits (except, of course, at the first, most inclusive level of progressive differentiation). Inquiries into typological differences are nonetheless different from inquiries of the kind just listed. Rather different empirical and nomothetic questions are likely to be addressed when we deal with summary types instead of specific dimensions. If, for example, social units are large and complex, economies of inquiry (imposed by the investigator or by research grants) may lead to summary typological characterization, rather than the intensive investigation of clusters of variables. Similarly, if authority patterns overall, not in any particular aspects, are subjects of investigation, summary characterization is generally chosen. Similarly again, very wide-ranging comparative treatments of authority patterns are likely to focus on typological traits—that is, traits that define types at highly inclusive levels of differentiation. (In this connection, it is an unintended bonus that the traits defining the most inclusive types can be identified without large investments of research resources—*if* our suggested typology has merit.) In addition, variations in specific dimensions of authority are likely to be seen as incremental change and explained in terms of other incremental changes. The study of "types," and especially of changes in type, more often than not directs attention to the nature and causes of "step" or "threshold" changes. To put the distinction somewhat differently, studies of changes *in* particular dimensions of authority relations probably deal with a set of extrinsic variables and types of nomothetic statements different from those of studies of changes *of* type. And Grand Theory is likely to be concerned with evolutionary changes in authority types, whereas "diagnostic" studies of contemporary institutions are more likely to deal with progressive (or regressive) changes or lack of change on particular dimensions. (Even radicals generally simplify the world in the latter manner, to make radical transformation seem to be a manageable enterprise.)

Variations in Formalization and Institutionalization

Norms and practices are always found on all dimensions of authority patterns. The extent to which explicit formal rules exist is highly variable, however, in regard to both overall patterns of authority and particular aspects of them. The authority patterns of certain small-scale social units, like families, are almost never formalized, but in other kinds of social units wide variety exists in regard to whether formal rules are used at all, what they cover, and how detailed they are. Spiro, for example, considers "legalism"—one aspect of which is to prescribe constitutional rules in great detail—a "style" of particular political cultures; his chief case in point is

Germany, and he attributes the German penchant for detailed formal rules to the influence of the Roman law, as against the common-law traditions of other countries.[4] Weber, on the other hand, did not consider the high formalization of politics culturally peculiar; rather, he looked on it as part and parcel of a general bureaucratization of political life accompanying social and political development. Both Spiro and Weber were only or chiefly concerned with polities; but clearly, widely varying degrees of formality are also found in less inclusive patterns of authority. Eckstein has pointed out, for example, that formality is pervasive in virtually all Norwegian authority relations:[5] Norway appears to be a thoroughly legalistic "political" culture even within our broad conception of politics. Norwegians seem generally to dislike implicitness, ambiguity, and scope for arbitrariness in social relations; therefore they tend to "constitutionalize" virtually all authority relations, often in elaborate detail. In the same vein, contemporary academic departments in America, judging by our experience, have also tended to proliferate procedural (and substantive) rules regarding matters once left mainly to implicit conventions.

Although norms and practices are always found on the dimensions of authority patterns, an important general difference exists in regard to them too: they are more or less changeable over time. This variation in authority patterns we term their "institutionalization". Though that concept is used in altogether too many senses in sociology and political science, the notion of relative fixity or flux in norms and behavior seems to be its common denominator. The variation can again be exemplified (imperfectly) by Friedman's and Schonfeld's findings. Friedman observed only minor changes, by age, in the norms of Swedish pupils—and, in that sense, a highly institutionalized pattern. Schonfeld, however, found much more considerable change in the norms, and still more considerable modifications in the practices of French schoolchildren. It may be, of course, that the pattern of change discovered by Schonfeld is itself regular from cohort to cohort, from generation to generation; but it may also be that rapid socialization to different sets of norms and practices at an early age lays a basis for fluctuating behavior and expectations in later life. (Here, of course, we begin to touch on the explanation of variations in authority patterns, as well as the nature of the variations themselves.)

Variations in the Consonance of Authority Patterns

Authority patterns have varying degrees of internal homogeneity or "fit," so to speak, among their elements. Our technical term for this is "consonance." The notion of consonance, in turn, has four distinguishable connotations. Three of these were mentioned before, as "configurative" characteristics of authority patterns, in the section on method (chapter 11); but brief recapitulation, with illustrations, is in order here.

Consistency in an authority pattern refers to the extent to which attitudes and practices in a pattern are uniform rather than distinguishable from one subgroup to another. Schonfeld found fairly consistent norms among pupils in French schools, especially at the same class levels, but also some noteworthy inconsistencies—for example, in pupils' attitudes toward teachers whom they perceived as valuable utilities for scoring well on critical examinations versus teachers not so perceived. It is, of course, extremely unlikely that all members of a social unit will display exactly similar attitudes and practices of authority, but there is a vast difference between a unimodal distribution with low standard deviation and, say, a polarized bimodal distribution. (The term "institutionalization" is sometimes also used to denote consistency in the foregoing sense.)

Complementarity refers to the extent to which norms and practices of different strata of members (especially supers and subs) are in agreement or otherwise mutually compatible. Schonfeld, as we saw, found a notable lack of complementarity between the norms of French pupils and those of their teachers. This lack of agreement constitutes inconsistency of a particular kind: that which results from disagreements or agreements among subs and supers. These probably are especially fateful; in any case, they are different from others mentioned here and probably have different causes and effects. Furthermore, since supers generally are only a small proportion of a unit's members, lack of complementarity is unlikely to appear as a marked inconsistency.

Correspondence refers to the extent that norms, forms, and practices in a unit are in harmony. A typical example of lack of correspondence was brought out in the discussion (in Chapter 6) of Recruitment to high governmental positions in Britain. The case involved discrepancies between forms and practices; to what extent it signified a discrepancy between practices and norms is much harder to determine. Note also the peculiar discrepancy discovered by Schonfeld in regard to norms and practices of Participation in French schools; arguably, such a lack of correspondence is far more likely to engender dysfunctional consequences than one that pits forms against either norms and practices.

Coherence refers to the interactive effects of compounds of authority traits. The term is used here in its strict dictionary sense: the tendency of parts to stick together or to have harmonious connection. Unlike the other aspects of consonance, coherence can be discovered only by empirical study informed by theory; as stated in the previous section, it is itself a large subset of the substantive problems posed by authority patterns. It is, however, clearly something variable in patterns of authority that calls for explanations and is capable of leading to fascinating ones.[6]

Variations in these four aspects of consonance are surely influenced by conditions extrinsic to the authority pattern per se, in addition to being generated by the internal dynamics of the unit. Equally important in the study of theoretical linkages are questions about the effects of changing consonance on the performance of the social unit and its adaptation to changing circumstances.

Variations in the Congruence of Authority Patterns

Congruence is a "relational" property of a set of authority patterns. It denotes the extent to which the authority patterns of different social units resemble one another. Hence it can vary (*a*) among distinguishable segments of a society (e.g., between the Protestant and Catholic "pillars" of Dutch society), (*b*) from one society to another, and (*c*) within any segment or society over time. In the conceptually simplest sense, congruence is an aggregate of the similarities among different social units on specific dimensions of authority. Thus we could distinguish a large set ($n = 11$, or more if subdimensions are separately considered) of congruence dimensions. We might also have reasons for distinguishing congruence of forms of authority in different patterns, or of their norms and practices: these reasons might be theoretical, or considerations of convenience might have been responsible. For example, Eckstein's argument that authority patterns in Norway are highly congruent, while making impressionistic reference to norms and practices, was chiefly based on an intensive examination of organizational forms. The principal reasons were the ready availability of documents setting forth formal rules and lack of large research resources; a better reason would have been that Norwegian forms of authority seem generally to "correspond" to norms and practices.

The notion of congruence as an aggregate of similarities and differences on all dimensions is conceptually simplest, but it is also operationally difficult to handle—and it is suspect if dimensions differ markedly in salience. An alternative conception of the term, less difficult to manage, is to consider authority patterns congruent if they are similar on dimensions revealed by preliminary research to be particularly important in the general perceptions that unit members have of authority patterns. Another possibility, though somewhat less satisfactory, is to assess congruence with respect to the dimensions that have been assumed a priori to be most salient. In studies encompassing a large *n* of cases, the second approach may be the only feasible one.

The variable properties of authority patterns are diverse and numerous. In the next two chapters, we refer to them summarily as "authority variables." We discuss the extrinsic conditions that might affect them and what variables they in turn may affect. These chapters, even more than those on typology, are tentative in a way that Chapters 1 through 11 are not. The problems of description dealt with in Part II are substantially solved, so far as we are concerned, and we have had sufficient experience with empirical work to be confident about most of the methodological precepts of Part III. The final two chapters are much less conclusive. They are intended chiefly to make plausible suggestions and to place items on the agenda of research: to provoke thought rather than to settle any debates.

Notes

1. We mentioned some compounds that tend to be unstable in Chapter 13, to rule out logically conceivable but empirically unlikely types of authority patterns.
2. For a discussion of growth of Participation in the life cycle of individuals (which may be analogous to its increase in social development), see Chapter 13.
3. See Part II, Introduction, note 1.
4. Herbert J. Spiro, *Government by Constitution: The Political Systems of Democracy* (New York: Random House, 1965), Ch. 15.
5. Harry Eckstein, *Division and Cohesion in Democracy* (Princeton: Princeton University Press, 1966), p. 171.
6. The various aspects of consonance were elaborated in Harry Eckstein, "Authority Relations and Governmental Performance," *Comparative Political Studies*, Vol. 2 (October 1969), pp. 300–315, with a discussion of how consonance in authority patterns might be used as an independent variable.

CHAPTER FIFTEEN

Authority Variables as Effects

The general kinds of extrinsic conditions that might affect the authority variables are readily identified. Three classes of variables cover the main possibilities:

1. Authority variables might be conditioned by the *traits of the social units* of which they are a part. (Authority in a large factory, e.g., might reflect the fact that the unit is a factory or that the factory is large.)
2. The authority variables, even of subsidiary social units, might be conditioned by the *traits of the societies* in which they occur. (Authority in a Norwegian factory might reflect the fact that the factory is a part of Norwegian society, no less than—or more than—the fact that it is a factory.)
3. Authority variables might be conditioned by the *dynamics* of societies and/or social units—not so much, or just, by their structural or functional traits as by kinds of change they are undergoing, such as rate of change or whether society is in process of being "modernized." (Authority in a factory might reflect the fact that rapid, modernizing change is occurring in the unit or in the society.)

Factors of two other kinds also can impinge on authority patterns, though we do not examine them here. One is the possibility that some authority variables might be conditioned by other authority variables—especially by the most "salient" variables. (Factory workers might, e.g., be highly participant because Distance between subs and supers is slight; and Distance might be slight because supers are recruited chiefly from among subs.) We concentrate only on extrinsic factors for two reasons. First, even if the more salient authority variables affect less salient ones, we still need to know what extrinsic conditions affect the salient variables. Second, we have already identified in passing some interactions among authority variables, but we have not systematically speculated about their extrinsic causes.

The other general influences on authority patterns that we choose not to examine further are contingent situational influences: that is, forces exerted on authority patterns by unusual, contingent conditions in the "environment" of social units and societies. (Authority in a factory, e.g., might reflect the fact that there is a depression or a period of special scarcity of the commodities on which operation depends.) We do not treat these forces here for several reasons. They often have only temporary effects or explain only deviations from modal patterns. The most dramatic "situational" changes in authority patterns are those imposed after conquest or in attempts at revolutionary engineering. These subjects for policy analysis are hardly appropriate for general, explanatory theory about the causes of authority relations. The major questions that require theoretical generalization in situations of imposed change in authority concern how new patterns work and what support or opposition they inspire; these questions are on the "effects" side of the ledger, which is examined in the next Chapter.[1]

Under each of the three main categories just listed, a large number of possibilities exists and might affect any of the authority variables given in the previous chapter. Three general problems for research into authority patterns arise from this. (1) What conditions, in any of the classes of extrinsic variables, are worth exploring in the first place? (2) In relation to which authority variables? (3) Much more intricate, what is the relative significance of particular conditions and classes of conditions relative to others? As stated, we do not have settled answers to these questions, each of which is potentially a rich, perhaps inexhaustible, subject for theorizing and empirical inquiry. But we can list major possibilities and offer tentative suggestions to guide theory and research.

Characteristics of Social Units

Social units differ markedly in composition and the activities in which they engage. What aspects of their composition and activities might have significant consequences for the authority variables? Which are likely to have the more important consequences? And, in general, which matters more—aspects of the composition or of the activities of social units?

Scale

The most obvious differences in the composition of social units are those of scale: numbers of members, distinct subgroups, and, usually related to these, geographic extensiveness. Some effects of scale on authority were mentioned in Chapter 8, in connection with procedures of inquiry into authority in different social units. These points, however, referred to "negative" consequences: what will not occur in units of a certain size. More important problems arise, of course, in regard to "positive" consequences.

Scale has been widely used as an impressionistic explanatory factor in studies of polities and has recently been treated systematically by Dahl and Tufte.[2] Studies of bureaucracies and industrial organizations also make frequent reference to the variable. That scale is closely related to complexity of Conformation seems truistic; it also seems reasonable to expect that large-scale units will generally be more highly formalized than small ones and that Distance will be less in the latter than the former; similarly, consonance, at least in the sense of consistency, probably varies inversely with the scale of units. There is, then, a case for relating most of the authority variables to the scale of units.

The relative importance of scale as a variable, however, is not so readily apparent. At least two apposite tests are available for attempts to determine its significance. If scale is a major determinant of clusters of authority dimensions, salient dimensions, or general type of authority, one should expect considerable incongruence between large-scale and small-scale units. Similarly, one would expect units of similar scale to resemble one another between societies in important respects, and perhaps more than they resemble units of different scale within societies. We suspect that these tests will not be passed with flying colors. We are impressed by the range of differences on authority variables that appear cross-nationally in units of quite similar scale: compare, again, Friedman's and Schonfeld's findings in regard to schools. We are also impressed by the differences that emerge when similar-scale units, like families, are compared, even in regard to Conformation. It is true that patrician and plebeian families tend to differ somewhat in scale, and even in patrician families scale constrains complexity—but the differences in scale are much less, and seem less consequential, than the great differences in complexity between such families. It follows (if these generalizations hold) that there is no necessary incongruence among units of quite different scales.[3]

Homogeneity of Members

A second manifest difference in the composition of social units involves the homogeneity of their memberships. Members are more or less different in regard to mutable characteristics (traits of achievement) like education, skills, or social class; they also differ more or less in immutable characteristics (traits of ascription) like age, sex, ethnicity, or caste. This factor, even more than scale, has been widely used to explain the "performance" of polities. A prima facie case for a relationship between the two variables can certainly be made: homogeneity of personal traits may be considered to entail similarity of interests and purposes, hence to reduce conflict, and through that to enhance the possibilities of orderly political competition and rule and the ability to arrive at governmental decisions. By the same token, homogeneity of members ought also to be a determinant of the authority variables—most obviously of consistency.

Actually, there are reasons to doubt that the "obvious" relationship between homogeneity and governmental performance holds, however plausible are the arguments in favor of it. The relationship (to our knowledge) has not been systematically tested, and Eckstein has argued extensively against it elsewhere, on grounds that large-scale units like polities are almost never homogeneous in any significant sense.[4] Social units of smaller scale can be homogeneous, of course, but there are other, compelling reasons against thinking that their homogeneity dictates their authority patterns.

Consider two dimensions of authority that might be expected on a priori grounds to be closely affected by homogeneity. Recruitment in homogeneous units might be expected to be particularly "competitive": *S*-positions should be uniformly "open," the bases of formal and effective eligibles large, and methods of Recruitment used which facilitate advancement. It seems that it could scarcely be otherwise, since homogeneity of membership precludes the identification of distinct groups that can readily be excluded from bases of eligibles. Or could it? In fact, the effect of homogeneity on Recruitment might well be just the opposite. If conflicts of interests and purposes are minimal, there is little reason, save honor, to compete for superordinated positions. There ought also to be little pressure to open channels of Recruitment; some limited group (e.g., a particular lineage) might "represent" the collectivity well enough. Still, not *all* kinds of Recruitment are consistent with homogeneity. If a unit's membership is highly homogeneous, Recruitment is likely to be either narrowly restricted to one ascriptively characterized group, or entirely open to members, by way of regulated or (in some "primitive" units) unregulated competition.

Decision-Rules might also be thought to depend on homogeneity. A high degree of homogeneity among supers certainly facilitates polycracy. On the other hand, extreme homogeneity should obviate polycracy, since the collective will ought to be conceivable as embodied in the will of any monocrat. Here again we conclude that both extremes, polycracy and monocracy, are equally likely.[5] In fact polities having highly homogeneous "citizenries" have frequently resorted to one or the other of these extreme options: consider the common appearance of consensual democracy in the polities of some Greek city-states and monarchy (or tyranny) in others.[6]

Homogeneity of membership does appear likely to promote the consistency of authority patterns, as well as their correspondence: those who are alike in objective and subjective characteristics are likely to act and think alike in authority relations. Thus we cannot write off homogeneity as simply irrelevant to authority patterns. But we have shown that extreme homogeneity is equally consistent with traits that are polar opposites on particular dimensions. Moreover, the substantial majority of social units are significantly heterogeneous in membership—a condition that tells us nothing about the dimensions of authority and only raises the possibility, not the certainty, that members will think and act inconsistently in authority relations. We suggest, then, that homogeneity/heterogeneity is a relevant but not highly consequential determinant of the authority variables.

Binding and Voluntary Membership

The composition of social units also varies in regard to the role of choice as to membership and roles in the units. Some units and/or roles in units are entered without any choice or on the basis of an initial voluntary decision that subsequently is irrevocable; this is true of families in all societies and, in many societies, also of other social units. In other cases, both initial and subsequent choices are open, but the latter are severely restricted (by high cost or by more direct limitations on range of open alternatives); this is generally true of occupational units. In still other cases, recurring choices among numerous options are possible, including the choice of no membership at all; this is typical in voluntary associations: hence their name.

Little has been made of these distinctions in political studies, no doubt because political scientists have conventionally concentrated on social units that are highly similar in regard to the variable of choice.[7] Given our broader conception of the scope of political science, the potential significance of the variable at once seems apparent: it may be presumed to affect most of the authority variables. The greater the element of choice, the more likely (it would seem) are: (*a*) high consonance, (*b*) low asymmetry of influence (relatively low Directiveness, relatively high Participation, Responsiveness, and Compliance), (*c*) low inequalities, (*d*) polycracy and concordance in *S-S* relations, and (*e*) open Recruitment from large bases of eligibles. We suggested in Chapter 8 why some of these hypotheses ought to hold, or, more precisely, why alternatives should not.[8]

Since patterns of authority are orders of direction and constraint, the element of choice in joining and leaving a unit surely will have important effects on most of the authority variables. Nevertheless, the two main arguments made about homogeneity also seem to apply to choice. First, choice, like homogeneity, will probably reduce alternatives on certain variables, without having precisely predictable effects on them. Voluntary associations, for example, frequently have been found to have very low rates of Participation. The reasons probably are that supers in them can be relied on to do what members want in any case (because of shared interest, and for fear of losing members) and, more obviously still, that dissatisfied members can simply terminate membership. For much the same reasons, Compliance may be either very high or low—the latter because sanctions are easily avoided by leaving the unit, the former because of commitment to the unit. Second, the tests we suggested for hypotheses that relate homogeneity to the authority variables may readily be used to test hypotheses about the effects of choice—and will probably yield similar results. Clearly, units like schools whose members lack choice have markedly different patterns of authority across societies. Moreover, units within societies that involve different degrees of choice can be substantially similar. As one consequence, units that are very different with respect to choice are not necessarily or even probably incongruent. We suspect, however, that in one respect the variable of choice will prove more consequential than homogeneity. Large variations in authority seem to occur mainly in units in which choice is slight (schools are cases in point—and so, of course, are polities). Where the element of choice is large, however, the range of tolerable variation in authority patterns seems to be much more constrained.

Functional Specificity

Social units vary greatly in the functional specificity of their activities. Some social units have a single, well-defined function (religious worship or industrial production) whereas others are more or less multifunctional (clans or, perhaps, universities). Yet the composition of social units is not necessarily associated with functional specificity or diffuseness. Schools, for example, can be highly specific or diffuse in function. Instruction in academic subjects is an irreducible function in them (Ivan Illich might not agree), but others certainly can be superadded or indeed loom more important. The same is true of industrial firms, political parties, or any number of other social units.

Functionally specific units seem, prima facie, more likely to be consonant than those that are diffuse—*if* one may assume that structures tend to be attuned to functions and that different functions entail different structural arrangements. As for the dimensions of authority, "specific" units are likely to have less directive (more "permissive") authority patterns because directives need not extend beyond coverage of the special tasks of the unit. At the same time, functionally specific units may involve greater *s-S* Distance, since supers in them tend to be functional "experts."

Are there, however, any reasons to think that the variable of functional specificity makes a large, fundamental difference in the nature of authority patterns? Functional diffuseness does not rule out consonance in any of its senses, nor does it necessitate high Directiveness, certainly not low *s-S*

Distance. Still, functionally specific units can reasonably be expected to have rather similar typological traits. Recruitment in them is unlikely to be unregulated or closed and is far more likely to be by selection than by election because of the need for special expertise in supers. Participation in such units may be by suffrage or sufferance, individual or corporate; but Responsiveness is likely to be anything but discretionary. And as noted previously, functionally specific units are rather likely to be more "permissive" than others. Hence specific units are not likely to occur frequently in more than three of the types suggested in Chapter 13. On this basis, the variable of specificity substantially constrains the potential variation in authority patterns but does not determine details.

Unit Goals

Specificity (or diffuseness) conveys nothing about a unit's particular goals. Schools, governmental bureaucracies, and armies all tend to be functionally specific, but surely the goals they seek to attain are sufficiently different to influence the authority characteristics of the units. Thus degree of specificity is at best a weak explanatory condition, unless one also knows what goals or sets of goals are pursued.

Goals, of course, are extremely various, and we know of no summary way to classify them appropriately. Goals are also qualitatively discrete, not continuous variables like scale or degree of functional specificity. Hence we can give only illustrations of how goals might be related to authority variables. As a very simple example, we observe that an army's goals do not permit leaving as much discretion to subs as, say, those of a skiing club or even a school. Neither do an army's goals permit subs to divide into competitive factions. (Supers are another matter, of course.) Armies, therefore, are bound to be highly directive (hence the literal appropriateness of the term "regimented" for that condition) and to have highly one-sided flows of influence. Much the same probably holds for any social unit whose very survival depends on the effective attainment of a particular goal, especially a competitive goal—as, for example, the survival of business firms depends on making profits. (It is in such units, we think, that Michels' iron law best applies; Michels' crucial test cases for the law, the Social-Democratic parties, thus were probably not crucial at all, despite their formal structures and "democratic" aspirations.) As a less obvious example, consider social units in which the principal goal is the "nurture" of subordinates—tutelage, protection against physical danger, and/or provision of subsistence. As earlier stated, this is the goal, or goal set, that parents typically pursue vis-à-vis children; it also prevails in the master-apprentice relationship and in that between lords and serfs. Where nurture is a unit's principal goal, authority patterns can be expected to be highly consonant, especially in the sense of consistency and complementarity. One may, for example, expect to find a tendency toward high Directiveness by supers and high Compliance by subs, as well as rather high perceptions of Distance on both sides, for supers will be considered to possess special attributes indispensable to subs. Consistency and complementarity will also be promoted because the goal of nurture generally involves a symmetrical exchange relationship between subs and supers (not to be confused with symmetry of control): compliance and deference are exchanged for instruction, security, and subsistence. This, of course, tends to change when impersonal institutions, like schools, polities, or markets, assume the traditional responsibilities of parents, masters, and landholders (i.e., when the intimate personal association between nurture and authority is dissolved).

If the arguments sketched here hold, then, *to the extent that the authority variables are conditioned by the characteristics of social units at all, they should reflect more the activities of units than the units' composition.* In regard to activities, goals seem to explain more than functional specificity or diffuseness; and in regard to composition, the element of choice of membership seems to be more consequential than homogeneity, and the latter more than scale. By the same token, the weaker of these variables may have indeterminate effects because of variations in the stronger ones. It remains distinctly possible, however, that unit traits affect the authority variables mainly through their interactions with societal characteristics, and it is also possible that the latter alone explain more than the former.[9]

Characteristics of Societies

As stated in Chapter 1, we think of "societies" as the most inclusive social units with which individuals identify.[10] Societies are, of course, the "social units" of polities. As such, their characteristics should affect polity traits in the first instance. A very large literature exists to explain how they do so, and we referred to some of these works in the preceding section. Societies, however, are also large-scale networks of relations in which "lesser" social units play a part. Consequently, it is likely that the general characteristics of societies will also affect authority relations in the lesser units.

Traits of societies may affect patterns of authority in the subsidiary units of society in three ways, portrayed in Figures 15.1 to 15.3. In Figure 15.1 societal traits are simply parts of the overall "field" of forces affecting authority relations among members of social units; as such they may reinforce, modify, or offset the effects on authority of unit traits. In Figure 15.2 the effects of societal traits on authority in lesser units are indirect: characteristics of societies affect those of polities, but there is also a greater or lesser tendency to replicate the traits of polities in the lesser units. In Figure 15.3 societal traits have both direct and indirect effects on authority traits. A fourth possibility is that traits of societies affect those of social units, which in turn affect authority patterns within them. We have already examined the last stage in this causal sequence: the ways in which unit traits affect authority. And most of the indirect effects of societal by way of unit traits should be accounted for in what follows.

The relative significance for the authority variables of general societal traits, versus those of lesser units, is itself a significant problem for theoretical inquiry. So also is the extent to which, and conditions under which, lesser units replicate the traits of polities, or polities those of lesser units. The solution of these problems, however, presupposes a more prosaic exercise: identifying societal traits that condition the authority patterns of polities and, by any of the paths depicted in Figures 15.1 to 15.3, other patterns of authority. In one sense we have already done this: like other social units, societies vary in regard to the conditions discussed previously. They differ vastly in scale (from tiny village societies to the ancient "universal" empires), in homogeneity of their members, and in their principal goals. These conditions need not be discussed again: there is no reason to think that their effects on the societal level differ from those they have on lesser levels. Our special concern here is with conditions that characterize societies *qua* societies.

"Societal" traits may be conceived in two ways. Most simply, they are traits that cut across most or all of the units that constitute societies. An example is language: the members of most societies speak or at least understand a common tongue. Less simply, societal traits are those peculiar to large, complex macrounits. An example is the very differentiation of

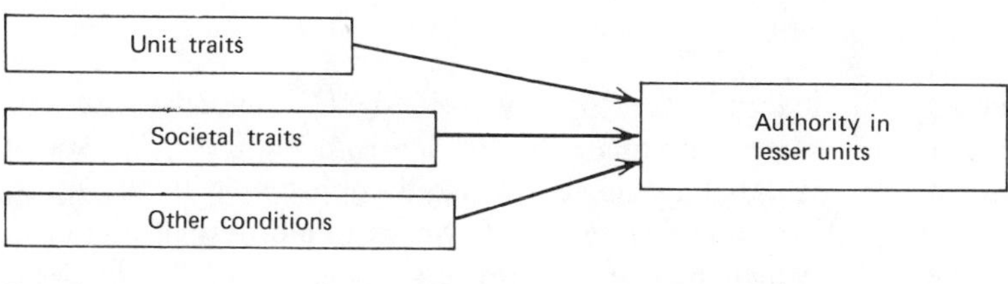

Fig. 15.1

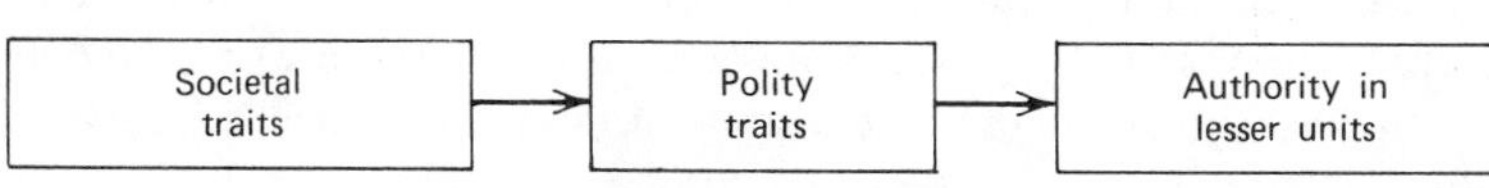

Fig. 15.2

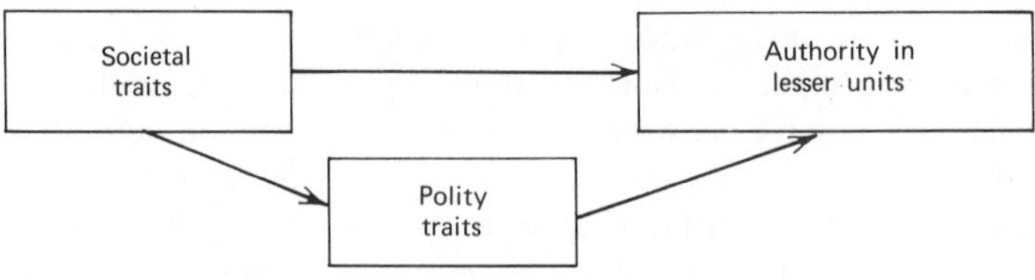

Fig. 15.3

members into numerous and diverse subunits and the concomitant use of coordinating and unifying mechanisms to bind them together.[11]

A great many traits cut across the constituent units of societies. Those which are most likely to affect authority relations can be identified in a preliminary way by reference to the intrinsic nature and tasks of authority patterns: they are networks of relations among hierarchially ordered segments that perform the task of fashioning and maintaining unity out of diversity. Those tasks include the definition of common goals and of conduct appropriate to their attainment, the harmonious allocation of tasks and duties, the prescription of a measure of uniform conduct, coordination, and the minimization of conflict. This particularly directs attention to factors of two kinds: general patterns and sources of *division* in societies (including the division of members into "ranks") and general patterns and sources of societal *cohesion*. These sets of factors should also capture much of what is "peculiar" to the larger, more complex macrounits: the existence in them of intricate, variable balances of centrifugal and centripetal forces. And, as subsequent material indicates, general factors of societal division and cohesion are also those most often used in the existing works relating societal characteristics to government and politics.

Stratification

Earlier we used the term "stratiformity" to designate the division of a social unit's structure of superordination into levels. The term, as stated in Chapter 4, was deliberately chosen to avoid confusion with the more familiar concept of stratification, by which we mean a different kind of ranking: the ways in which people in a society are horizontally divided into higher and lower strata in terms of prestige, respect, worthiness, and dignity. Stratification always involves an element of invidious ranking; stratiformity may not. Since both involve ranking, there are bound to be relations between them which are discussed later. But since different kinds of ranking are involved, the relations may be complex and difficult to ascertain: a higher-level super, for example, may come from a lower social stratum than a subordinate, in which case "distance inversion" is likely to be perceived by the latter and "complementarity" in perceptions of Distance is unlikely.

The modern and premodern literature relating social stratification to politics is enormous. Little in the field has been investigated more voluminously or intensely. Almost without exception, however, the literature deals with the nature of, and the relative success and failure of strata in, political competition, and with the ways in which stratification affects governmental performance; the effects of stratification on the *nature* of authority patterns are slighted. The recurrent themes are stratification and conflict, stratification and the distribution of political influence, stratification and the composition of political elites, stratification and the stability of types of governments (chiefly "democracies").[12] No doubt there is a strong case for relating such variables to stratification. But there surely is a case that equally or more manifestly encourages relating stratification to the authority variables as such.

A few words on how patterns of stratification differ. Volumes have been written on that subject, but we need only three sets of distinctions here. *First*, and most basic, there are differences in degrees of stratification. These vary in at least four ways:

1. *The number of stratificatory distinctions*. A great many stratificatory distinctions have existed, for example, in modern, especially early modern, Britain. As Denis Brogan has remarked: "The observer may come to the conclusion that the English class structure consists of forty-odd million classes, which have nothing more . . . in common than an unconscious acceptance of this odd state of affairs as right and natural for Englishmen."[13]

2. *The degree of invidiousness or psychic distance among the strata*. In Britain this distance has been great, even if not as great as in caste systems. H. G. Wells wrote (in *Tono-Bungay*) that the "head and centre of our system was Lady Drew, her 'leddyship,' and . . . Miss Somerville, her cousin and companion . . . when I was a boy I used always to think of these two poor old creatures as superior beings living, like God, somewhere through the ceiling."

3. *The salience of stratification* or, more exactly, the degree to which stratification enters into identifications of the self and others. In Britain this factor apparently was also great; see Wells again: "In that English countryside of my boyhood every human being had a 'place.' It belonged to you from birth like the colour of your eyes, it was inextricably your destiny."

4. *The physical distance among strata*, in the sense of the frequency and proximity of their interactions. Brogan testifies about the width of this gap

in Britain: "The classes that in a crisis trust each other cannot in fact speak to each other. Even if their language is mutually intelligible (which it is not always), they have little or nothing to say to each other."

Second, systems of stratification differ according to the principal bases of stratification. The chief distinction here is between systems that rely on ascribed, immutable bases (e.g., kinship position, hereditary estate or caste, membership in ethnic or racial groups) and those using achieved, mutable bases (e.g., skills, knowledge, and possessions). *Third*, there are differences in mobility among strata, including variation in the opportunity and risk structures by which people rise to higher positions or fall from them, and variation in the actual rates of upward and downward movement.[14]

Both the common use of stratification as an explanatory condition in regard to politics, and the central role assigned to it by theorists as diverse and separated in time and experience as Marx and Apter,[15] seem to be warranted. It is in fact more difficult to think of an authority variable that is not likely to be affected by stratification than of variables that are. However, the effects of stratification are unlikely to be equally great for all authority variables. Since stratification involves a kind of hierarchic ordering, based on diffuse social superiority, its strongest effects are probably on the inequality and influence dimensions; consequently, we discuss them first and in more detail than the other variables.

Inequalities and Influence. The nature of the effects of stratification on influence and inequalities can be illustrated by Friedman's work on Swedish schools. The society, in this case, is one with generally low stratification, in which the principal basis of ranking (occupation) is highly subject to open achievement; consequently, mobility is considerable. Verney,[16] for example, speaks of a gradual "merging" after 1921 of the former Swedish middle, lower-middle, and working classes into a single mass—which implies both low stratification and high mobility. Prior to that time an amalgamation of the old upper class (nobles, clergy, holders of large estates) with the new entrepreneurial middle class had also apparently occurred.[17] An indicator of Sweden's current low stratification is the distribution of the country's very high per capita income (second only to Switzerland among industrialized nations): it is "probably more equal than in any other developed country in the world."[18] Since this is largely the result of deliberate governmental policies of income redistribution, and since the polity is characterized by what Rustow[19] calls the politics of compromise (and consensus), it is more likely that low differentials in income are caused by social egalitarianism than vice versa. The most prestigious and best paid large group is that of professionals; this is significant because the specialized professions are inherently categories in which membership is achieved and highly mutable from generation to generation, and because entry into them in Sweden is through a highly egalitarian system of publicly financed education. A somewhat exotic but telling indicator of low stratification in Sweden is that some of the best studies of Swedish government and politics make only the most casual and cursory references to the subject.[20]

This pattern of stratification has a series of correlates in the authority patterns of Swedish schools that are just what one would expect if stratification is an important determinant of authority variables. (*a*) *Distance* between subs and supers declines very steeply as children mature and is already quite low by the time they are in sixth grade (e.g., less than half of the children studied by Friedman "looked up" to teachers in sixth grade and only about one quarter of them did so in the two most advanced grades). Over the same time, norms of *Deportment* become highly familiar: (e.g., similar proportions of pupils "would not disapprove of calling teachers by their first names"[21]). (*b*) Both norms and practices of *Participation* are extremely high in ways described at various points previously, and the norms are almost equally high for pupils and teachers. (To add a datum not already mentioned, the great majority of teachers considered "suitable" every item on a long and diverse list of methods of participation—only 26% disapproved even of the least-approved method: participation through the intervention of a parent). (*c*) *Compliance* becomes increasingly "conditional" (less "submissive") rather than "absolute"; that is, pupils increasingly say that they will disobey directives they consider improper or unwise, or question the wisdom or propriety of directives in the first place. (*d*) Friedman mentions no survey findings on *Directiveness*, but we know from other sources that the Swedes have been pioneers in "liberal" methods of pedagogy, in regard to the content of pupils' studies as well as behavior in schools. And Friedman does report direct observations relevant to the point: for example, "there is an overall liberality in the classroom atmosphere . . . very little behavior in the classroom is punished. . . . An observer in a Swedish classroom sees students talking to one another, walking in and out of the classroom, and evincing all the time no fear of punishment."[22] (*e*) *Responsiveness* is simply assumed by Friedman to be high, as a logical correlate of the other conditions. It is hard to imagine that it might not be, and one fact indirectly bearing on the point is probably significant: most teachers approved of pupils going to the rector (principal) if teachers are unresponsive to their complaints.[23]

In contrast to Swedish schools, consider those in Britain. Recall Wilkinson's discussion of "conformity" in *The Prefects*, and his linkage of the tendency to conform in elite schools at least in part to pupils' awareness of being trained for superior positions in later life. Almond and Verba provide a further piece of evidence that fits in nicely.[24] Regrettably, they only report on Participation in schools, not any other aspects of authority, but what they report is exactly what one would expect: only 16% of their British respondents stated that they could and did participate in school discussions, whereas 68% said that they could not. And Almond and Verba further remark that only Americans in their five-nation study had generally felt free to complain about school matters and actually voiced complaints.

In sum, then, low stratification based on achievement (as low stratification usually is) tends to be associated with low Distance, familiar Deportment, high Participation and Responsiveness, relatively low Directiveness, and unsubmissive Compliance (although not outright insubordination). High stratification, especially if substantially based on ascriptive considerations, should of course have the opposite effects.

The appearance of these relationships between stratification and authority variables in schools suggests that, although certainly no more than "statistical," they are probably very strong. Schools are units whose special characteristics we would expect to limit, not enhance, the effects of low stratification on authority patterns. Schools join people who are inherently unequal in knowledge and experience, and schools always have goals—instruction per se, and preparation for competitive access to highly rewarded roles—that make subs highly dependent on supers. Hence schools ought to be among the units that least reflect egalitarian stratification. Yet the extent of egalitarianism in Swedish schools is quite remarkable. Perhaps one could argue the case away on the ground that Swedish schools have adopted a rather unusual set of educational goals. But it is also possible, and more likely, that their deemphasis of competitive performance and lack of concern with instilling conformity to a hierarchic order are themselves products of the general pattern of low stratification.

This is not to say that stratification controls all the effects of specific unit traits on dimensions of authority. For example, in most societies the family seems to be a more restrictive context than schools. Despite the intimacy of family relations, Friedman found consistently greater Distance toward parents than teachers and a lesser tendency for Distance in families to decline with age. In the same vein, Almond and Verba report only petty differences in "remembered influence on family decisions" among the five nations they studied—although the differences run in the expected directions.[25] One might also expect the hypothesized effects to be diminished in units that join people of homogeneous social rank in highly stratified societies (e.g., upper-class clubs and lower-class churches or trade unions in Britain). And there is reason to think that some types of "achievement," characteristic particularly of functionally specific units, make for high Distance rather than low, as well as for low Participation and high Compliance. The perception of special functional "expertise" seems to have such effects;

Friedman, for example, establishes that as inequalities and influence decline in Swedish schools, so do perceptions of teachers as people possessing esoteric expertise. These qualifications, however, are small hedges of otherwise strong relationships. At the very least, we ought to be able to hypothesize that even if units are substantially similar in composition and activity across societies, differences in stratification will make for major differences among them on the inequality and influence dimensions.

Recruitment and Bases of Legitimacy. Our "boundary interchange" dimension, Recruitment, is also likely to be strongly affected by stratification, for reasons that should need no spelling out. The stubborn resistance of the British polity to "effective" eligibility consistent with "formal" eligibility for high positions is a case in point. The other authority variables, being less immediately tied in with social ranking, are probably less closely and obviously affected by stratification; but even in regard to them we can discern likely, if less strong and direct, relations to stratification.

It seems probable, for example, that "personal" Bases of Legitimacy will play a larger role in societies with high rather than low stratification. Most of all this is likely if the bases of stratification are ascriptive, as they generally are where stratification is steep: in the social units of such societies, the first and sometimes only condition of legitimacy for supers is that they have the requisite family, "estate," or caste origin. In societies with low stratification and high mobility, the openness of Recruitment is likely to be a dominant basis of legitimacy, since high mobility, by achievement, creates strong expectations about the competitive openness of authoritative positions. A widely familiar instance is the marked difference between socioeconomic (especially economic) mobility in the French *ancien régime* and the resultant discrepancies between "power" and "status" that obsessed the bourgeoisie on the eve of the Revolution.

Other Effects of Stratification. The high mobility that is usually associated with low stratification is also likely to have important effects on consonance, if it is true (as we argued in Chapter 3) that lower-class and upper-class units tend to have rather different authority patterns and that new norms and practices are not easily learned. In cases of high mobility, consequently, attitudes toward authority are likely to be confused within individuals and dissonant among them. Mobile individuals who achieve *S*-positions are also likely to display lack of correspondence among norms and practices. Dissonance, in the particular sense of inconsistency, is especially likely to exist, in situations of high mobility, among superordinates who come from different formative backgrounds. By the same token, if the class backgrounds of supers are divergent, the probability of concordant Decision-Behavior should also be diminished. High mobility may, for similar reasons, create strong pressures for the formalization of authority relations—in the case of Recruitment, to guarantee channels for advancement on the ladder of superordination; in the case of decision-processes, to provide external guides to behavior where internal norms diverge or have been disoriented. (Note, in this connection, that the formalization of governments—constitution making—largely coincided with the industrialization and, in other senses, modernization of Western societies, and their attendant rates of unprecedentedly high mobility.) An even more likely consequence of high mobility is low institutionalization, at any rate for the more mobile elements of society. The various effects of mobility, however, are bound to differ with the extent of stratification that exists in the first place. Rising or falling from one rank to another does not always imply traversing the same stratificatory distance. Finally, if degree of stratification is in fact an important determinant of the authority variables, and if it is also true that the location of social units in a scheme of stratification has effects on authority in them, cases of low societal stratification should also have a higher potential for congruence than cases of high stratification. This, perhaps, explains the remarkably high congruence among authority patterns Eckstein found in Norway (although the case of Britain suggests that the condition is not a "necessary" one).

We do not mean to imply that authority relations are nothing but superstructure on underlying phenomena of class, even just on the level of polities—certainly not on evidence now available. We do suggest that there is a prima facie case for holding (*a*) that stratification has likely effects, worth intensive investigation, on all aspects of authority, (*b*) that the strongest, most direct effects of degrees of stratification are (not surprisingly) on the aspects of authority patterns that most directly involve interactions or interchanges among hierarchic levels, (*c*) that bases of stratification are (also not surprisingly) most likely to affect bases of legitimacy, and (*d*) that social mobility has its main effects in relation to formalization, institutionalization, aspects of the *S-S* dimensions, and consonance. More important, we argue that the Marxian perspective (or, better, neo-Marxian perspective, since we say nothing about the causes of stratification) is worth extending—as hypothesis, not dogma—from the state to authority in all social units, and from the study of who dominates, to the ways in which direction and subordination are conducted.

Differentiation

Societies have vertical as well as horizontal divisions: different degrees and kinds of differentiation. The term "social differentiation" refers, in essence, to the number and nature of the distinct subunits of which societies consist (and also "groups" that share traits—other than those that differ in all societies, like age or sex—without being full-fledged social units). Most "societies" have a quantitatively high degree of differentiation: a large number of distinct social units. More consequential for the authority variables probably are certain qualitative variations in the characteristics of differentiation—although these are often associated with quantitative differences.[26] The vertically differentiated parts of societies may be functionally specific (e.g., specialized occupations) or functionally diffuse (e.g., "ethnic" groups or communal and regional units). They may also be functionally diffuse units organized around some special core function, like the "corporations" (churches, guilds, merchant companies, etc.) of traditional Western society. Or they may be what the Dutch call social "pillars": diffuse units sharing cultural traits (e.g., religion), each further divided into a comprehensive set of functionally specific units. The quantitative and qualitative aspects of social differentiation can be combined in the notion of societal complexity. The more complex societies have large numbers of distinct subunits, much functional specialization, and a mix of specific and diffuse units as strong foci of identification.

Much is made in the literature on polities of the differentiation of societies, no less than their stratification: political studies that can trace their ancestry to Durkheim are hardly less voluminous than those that stem from Marx. When social differentiation has been used as an explanatory variable in political studies, however, the stress again has been overwhelmingly on the effects on political competition and performance. Ethnicity, for example, has been used chiefly to account for difficulties in "nation building" and other tasks and problems associated with political modernization. Such aspects of differentiation as religious or regional divisions have been invoked mainly to account for patterns of cleavage and partisanship, and these to explain political stability and instability. Occupational differentiation has also been linked mainly to partisan activities, like voting. These are all important concerns; ours, however, is with the effects of differentiation on authority patterns per se.

Social differentiation is, of course, most likely to affect the authority patterns of the subsidiary units of societies: it determines their scale, homogeneity of membership, goals, and other unit traits discussed earlier, which in turn affect their traits of authority. The society-wide pattern of differentiation is likely to affect only the traits of polities and the relational variable of congruence—unlike societal stratification, which affects most of the aspects of authority. On the level of polities, consonance is the property that seems most manifestly dependent on differentiation. A simple, general, and important proposition seems compelling: the more complex is differentiation, the less likely should be high consonance. Since specialized units have different goals, their members may be expected to have significantly different norms and practices of authority; the division of societies along communal, ethnic, or other diffuse lines is perhaps even more likely to introduce elements of dissonance at the overarching polity level; and the division of society into odd mixes of specific and diffuse parts, along parallel lines or in corporations or pillars, will probably introduce the greatest dissonance of all. This should be most obvious in regard to consistency; but if governmental leaders are drawn from special parts of society—as they usually are—complementarity should also be compromised; and if governmental authority requires uniform kinds of behavior from citizens, correspondence also will be reduced. By the same token, the differentiation of society into units with different specialized tasks, or into different diffuse segments, ought also to lessen congruence among the units.

Here an important puzzle emerges, and it is critical for assessing the significance of differentiation as a variable affecting authority. How is it possible for any complex society to have a significant degree of consonance in its more inclusive authority patterns, or high congruence between such patterns and others? This problem pertains not just to polities. It also arises in regard to any social unit that draws members from diverse segments of society (e.g., many or most political parties), and it arises, as well, in regard to social units, such as modern industrial corporations or indeed most other units distinctive to modern societies, that have their own complex patterns of internal differentiation.

The problem is greatly compounded by a further probability: that complex differentiation ought to have quite different, even downright antithetical, effects on the authority patterns of societies and their units. Consider, for example, its effects on Directiveness. The more a society is differentiated into specialized or culturally diverse parts, the greater the need for coordination and integration by societal authority. Even if we grant that some mechanisms, functioning like a "hidden hand," might help coordinate the segments of complex societies, the problems of general coordination in complex societies surely must be greater than such problems in simple cases. Similarly, there should be greater need in complex societies for the authoritative definition and pursuit of societal "collective goods." Even if we grant with Olson[27] that all social units have a need for the coercive definition of common goods, the problem of arriving at such a definition is magnified, as Olson realizes, at the societal macrolevel, where quite different social units, rather than just individuals, are the component parts. Hence Directiveness should be high or should have an ineluctable tendency to increase, in polities that direct the more complex societies. Within the specialized units of societies, however, just the opposite is likely—only what Schonfeld called "task-coverage"[28] is likely to be attempted; and within culturally distinct, internally homogeneous segments, the sharing of norms should obviate high Directiveness by superordinates. Similarly, supers in functionally specialized or culturally distinct subunits of societies should tend to be either monocratic or highly concordant and polycratic, by virtue of shared expertise and/or outlook (see our prior agruments about the effects of homogeneity on Decision-Rules and Recruitment). In the more inclusive units, on the other hand, supers' behavior should be competitive and governed by arithmetic Decision-Rules like majoritarianism. It is possible that the ability of the segments to paralyze one another might lead to arrangements whereby each of them has a veto; but in that case discordant nondecisions rather than concordant decisions are likely to be the rule.

Thus we see that in highly "complex" societies there are theoretical reasons for expecting congruence and consonance to be low, or anyway lower than in simpler societies. And if the performance of social units depends on the congruence and consonance of their authority patterns,[29] we are led to speculate that there are "natural" limits on the complexity a system may achieve before deterioration sets in. Before we settle on Spenglerian conclusions about the decline of complex civilizations, though, we must consider that there are glaring cases to the contrary. Norway is a very complex society whose authority patterns are highly congruent and consonant; Britain also seems to be a case in point;[30] and so, it seems, is Sweden.[31] Such cases need explanation, even if they deviate from what is usual—which is by no means certain. What might explain them?

One possibility is that all the cases mentioned are societies that have a high degree of functional specialization. This would solve the puzzle if the pursuit of specialized goals is more consequential than the nature of the goals. If this is a tenable argument, even the authority patterns of "pillarized" societies might be congruent and their polities consonant—although the association of specialization with diffuse cultural differences might well have distinctive effects of its own (like those described by Lijphart[32]). If so, we would also have to modify slightly our earlier arguments about the significance of unit goals: it would then be certain general characteristics rather than specific contents of goals that count for most. The difficulty inherent in that solution is, of course, how to demonstrate that specialization has uniform results and greater consequences than what is specialized in.

There are alternative ways of handling the problem. Each, however, poses further puzzles. It might conceivably be the case that societal complexity has consequences for authority on the polity level similar to those produced by other forces in functional or cultural segments of society. But if so, how? And why does this happen in some highly complex societies and not in others? Another possibility is that social units might sometimes "replicate" the ways in which polities exercise authority. This is especially likely when an emerging elite—whether early British entrepreneurs or modernizing Tunisian politicians—"engineers" authority patterns to permit social units to interact harmoniously. But if so, under what conditions do these social experiments become sufficiently institutionalized to offset the countervailing pulls toward diversity? A third possibility is that the intermediate units of society—those above the basic microlevel but not as inclusive as the largest macrolevel—might have internal patterns of differentiation similar to the societal pattern, hence also similar patterns of authority. The validity of that argument is somewhat dubious because no social unit can include such a number and diversity of subunits as society, and most include far less; still, the argument has a certain elegance that makes it advisable to return to it later. The most obvious alternative of all is that factors other than differentiation, cutting across the segments of societies, have more powerful effects. Stratification itself might be such a factor, but so perhaps are the general sources of societal cohesion that have not yet been discussed.

In general, these arguments imply that differentiation is not as powerful a determinant of authority relations as stratification or other factors to be considered. Not only is its impact on authority likely to occur only or chiefly on the level of polities, but even on that level it seems to raise more problems than it solves. The discovery of interesting problems may in fact be the chief utility of the variable. Since interesting theory presupposes interesting problems, that is not a negligible utility. Nevertheless, it is clear that we must look elsewhere or to inobvious forces generated by differentiation itself for solutions.

Interdependence

It is only a slight exaggeration to say that the two seminal figures in modern social macrotheory are Marx and Durkheim: the first obsessed with forces of social division and conflict, the other with forces of cohesion and solidarity—most of all with the problem of how it is possible for highly complex societies to operate smoothly as units at all. In his *chef-d'oeuvre* on the division of labor, Durkheim[33] identified two basic sets of forces that may solidify societies. One he called *mechanical solidarity*, which results from social resemblances, especially collective "sentiments" (norms). The other he called *organic solidarity*, for reasons of presumed analogy to the structure of higher biological species; this set results from social divisions themselves. Both sets of forces operate in every society—more or less effectively, and in varying combinations. Durkheim's treatment of these forces can be distilled in two propositions. (1) The more complex are societies, the greater the cohesive force generated by their divisions. (2) The more complex a society, the less its reliance on a certain type of Directiveness ("repressive," or criminal, law that enforces communal standards of moral conduct) and the more its reliance on "cooperative" (civil) law that prescribes rules of interaction among persons in their various roles.

Without commitment to the intricate body of theory Durkheim generated, we can certainly employ his admirable taxonomy of cohesive forces and speculate about their probable effects on the authority variables. Consider first *cohesive forces generated by the divisions of societies themselves*. The divisions of society can generate forces of solidarity in three ways.

1. One source of solidarity particularly stressed by Durkheim is *interdependence:* social differentia cannot do without one another; or at least they have important effects on one another. Interdependence operates mainly through differentiation but can also work through stratification: in feudal society, for example, the landowning aristocrats depended on the labor of their serfs and the latter on the physical protection and meting out of justice of their masters.

2. "Organic" solidarity may arise from *cross-cutting (or multiple) memberships:* as societies become more fragmented into specialized units, particular individuals tend to have roles in many units. Empirically this is particularly true of "elites," that is, people likely to occupy *S*-roles. Such memberships can also link specialized and diffuse units, as when people who are members of different diffuse groups (e.g., ethnic or religious groups) perform similar technical roles in the same specialized units. Although such links may be imperfect and few, it is equally obvious that technical and administrative roles in industrialized societies are filled by people of ever more diverse ascriptive traits and social origins.

3. A third solidifying force within social division is *interconnection*: members of social units may have profound affinities, such as ties of family and kinship, of common educational background, or simply of frequent social interaction. An example is the widespread network of kinship relations that links town and country—hence also occupational, religious, and cultural differences—in Norway.[34] Interconnections are probably most likely in elite groups because of the affinity of common status, intermarriage, and frequent "socializing" among top dogs. Southern,[35] for example, thought that the chief bonds of early medieval Europe were to be found in the aristocrats' interconnections by kinship and social intercourse. The much-discussed and often condemned "old boy network" or "Establishment" in modern Britain is a contemporary version of the same phenomenon.[36]

These three types of solidifying forces are not mutually exclusive: they probably reinforce one another, although their relative significance is likely to vary with level of social development and degrees of stratification and division along diffuse lines. We suspect that interdependence and cross-cutting memberships increase with development, whereas interconnections are generally strongest in cases of steep stratification and the persisting significance of diffuse segments.[37] In what ways can they be expected to condition authority?

Interdependence is bound to have a pronounced effect on numerous aspects of polities. It is a term virtually synonymous with the economic notion of "externalities." These arise when the actions of particular units entail costs for others over which the latter have no direct control (industrial pollution is an obvious example) or provide to them benefits to which they make no proportionate contribution. To the extent that externalities arise and have wide effects, there is bound to be pressure for their fair regulation by overarching authority. Consequently, as Durkheim foresaw,[38] the march of social differentiation, and with it the growth of "individualism" (the emergence of people not wholly submerged in "collective identities"), does not lead to the kind of laissez-faire polity that Spencer envisioned nor to any other withering of the State, but rather to much increased Directiveness by the polity. Durkheim also foresaw correctly that greater social complexity and interdependence would lead to increased formalization:[39] the greater use of explicit "abstract" rules, perhaps to make mutually impinging conduct more predictable. Two correlates of these tendencies appear to be the greater functional segmentation of societal structures of direction and their greater "resolution." Furthermore, the increased significance of polities in regulating externalities is likely to increase Participation to achieve favorable allocations of costs and benefits—especially Participation of the "groupist" variety (pressure-group politics). Not least, the interdependence of groups (hence their ability to paralyze or damage one another by "irresponsible" actions) exerts pressures toward polycracy in Decision-Rules and concordance in Decision-Behavior—or, failing these, toward the monocratic rule of an arbitral figure. Consensual rule (real or the result of hard bargaining) or dictatorship seem to be the principal possibilities at the *S-S* level in highly interdependent societies.

Interdependence thus can potentially explain a great deal—but only at the level of the polity. It also seems to leave unsolved the problem of how congruence might be possible in highly complex societies. No obvious reason compels mutually dependent units to resemble one another on dimensions of authority by virtue of such dependence, or to be like the overarching structures that regulate them. It is plausible to expect that, at the level of the polity, interdependence will lead to consistent norms, hence practices, of Directiveness, Participation, Decision-Rules, and Decision-Behavior. But we have not yet identified any forceful reason for normative expectations and practices at the level of the polity to resemble those in lesser units. It may be that psychological factors prevent individuals from compartmentalizing their norms and practices according to the contexts in which they act; hence perhaps they behave in "political" roles as they do in "nonpolitical" ones. But if so, how can interdependence at the polity level generate internally *consistent* authority patterns there? What explains consonance leaves congruence puzzling, and vice versa.

It has already been suggested that men may, by conscious design, attempt to engineer the convergence, over time, of the authority patterns of polities and adjacent units. After all, the basic principles of our congruence theory of political performance may not be unknown to elites. Moreover, if they are engaged in "institution building" they may unselfconsciously work to the same end by replicating familiar patterns of authority when they establish new units. Not all elites in modernizing societies—historical or contemporary—have had such objectives, and not all have had the social engineering capacities to attain them, which may account for the relatively small number of complex societies characterized by high congruence. Unfortunately, "conscious design" is not intrinsically a convincing kind of explanation for structural social phenomena: the more convincing theoretical arguments are those which show how general structural and situational factors dispose men to take particular kinds of decisions.

Cross-cutting memberships and interconnections provide alternative structural solutions of the problems of congruence and consonance. If roles in varieties of social units are performed by the same people, by people with common background, or by people who frequently interact, the chances that norms and practices of authority will be substantially similar are obviously increased. (So too, of course, is the probability of concordant Decision-Behavior.) But here again the assumption of a psychological tendency toward uniform rather than compartmentalized norms and actions must be invoked. There are psychological theories that point toward the tenability of that assumption: we have in mind theories of the effects of "strain"[40] and of "cognitive dissonance."[41] Nevertheless, the explanation of congruence—and to a lesser extent consonance—rests somewhat uneasily on factors of "organic" solidarity, however much can be explained by these factors on the polity level alone: an assumption that may or may not hold is required to make the explanation work. Moreover, multiple memberships and interconnections seem to occur with great frequency only among elite groups, not among the rank-and-file members of social units. Consequently, they might explain resemblances in *S-S* relations but can explain others only if it is further assumed that elites impose similar types of *s-S* relations within the social units they dominate. The notion that social differentiation might generate its own unifying and homogenizing forces is intriguing and elegant, but what we seek to explain is probably better accounted for by forces of "mechanical" solidarity which, like stratification, cut across the principal segments of societies.

Shared Societal Norms

The "shared sentiments" that explain congruence most directly are, of course, norms about authority relations themselves. The literature on authority abounds with references to societal "styles" of authority (e.g., the supposed authoritarianism of Germans—anyway in the past—or the libertarianism of Scandinavians). But explanations based on that notion are clearly flawed. Most important, they are circular, the condition to be explained also being the condition serving as explanation (unless shared norms are used to explain similar forms and practices—which is a little, but not much, better). If tautology is to be avoided, the sharing of certain norms, like norms of authority, must manifestly be explained by other shared factors. Unfortunately, societies having complex differentiation are not likely to exhibit many other shared factors. In simple societies, especially "primitive" ones, it is easy enough to find "objective" conditions that appear to account for the origin of shared sentiments: the members of such societies are placed in substantially similar life situations. But more developed, complex societies are characterized by great differences in their members' life situations. Hence all "mechanical" forces of solidarity should operate much less in them. From this arises a problem worthy of a Durkheim: whether and how societies, despite great complexity of differentiation, can retain elements of commonality that might account for similar authority relations across their units.

We have as yet no Durkheimian solution to this problem. Our puzzlement is intensified by the suggestion of Durkheim himself that "mechanical" forces of cohesion continue to operate in highly complex societies, although he did not say how, or what the forces might be. Moreover, deductions of authority relations from objective social structure thus far apply only to polities, and only to particular dimensions of authority, such as Decision-Rules or Bases of Legitimacy.[42] But we can offer some very tentative hunches for further exploration.

First, we return to the possibility that the structural modality underlying resemblances in authority relations in quite different units might be stratification, which proved to be a powerful explanatory variable in regard to virtually all dimensions of authority. If so, stratification should be regarded both as a force dividing societies and as one that makes them cohesive: the first in regard to competition for authoritatively allocated values, the second in regard to the valuation and conduct of authority relations. This possibility, however, entails a problem. How, in highly complex societies, can patterns of stratification themselves be uniform? Perhaps solutions of this problem can escape circularity more easily than solutions of the same problem in regard to authority relations directly, but it remains a question unsolved in the literature on stratification.

Second, it is possible that complex societies retain modal preferences for kinds of social interaction that do not directly involve authority but might have important effects on it. Preferences for hierarchic or egalitarian interactions themselves are cases in point, but other possibilities exist as well (e.g., preferences for "dyadic" vs. "collective" relationships, or "clientelistic" vs. "contractual" obligations). Here again, however, we face the problem of how such modal preferences can exist despite great differentiation.

We might attempt to extract an explanation from the notion of "social ethos"—the notion that societies have general culture types like those identified by Sorokin: ideational, idealistic, or sensate cultures.[43] But here once more the problem of how commonality survives in complex differentiation is simply pushed back a step. In addition, notions of social ethos have invariably been extraordinarily vague and linked, as by Sorokin, to historical progression, not to the explanation of differences that can exist despite similar levels of development.

A better "mechanical" approach to the problem may be that in complex societies, congruence can be high only among the few authority patterns that are structurally similar. More specifically, it may be that the polities of the more complex societies can be congruent only with social units that are themselves complex macrounits differentiated into many parts. What MacIver and Page called the Great Associations are such units: the State itself, political parties, occupational associations like trade unions and professional societies, other large-scale voluntary associations, churches, and the like.[44] It might be objected that such units hardly differ in complexity (or other structural traits) from one society to another. But this is by no means necessarily so; Kornhauser, for example, detects a great deal of difference in their development. Thus high congruence, even if not absolute identity, might exist regardless of complexity of structure, between any set of units not greatly different in structural traits; polities are unlikely to be congruent with authority patterns in other social units if large intermediate associations are not highly developed; and between the most and least inclusive units of societies might run a series of "graduated resemblances."[46] This explanation fails to account for one critical fact, though: in the Scandinavian countries, in Britain, and perhaps elsewhere, there is high congruence between the authority patterns of small units like schools and those of much larger units, including polities. Perhaps the only solution to this obdurate condition is to invoke again the structural trait of stratification or policies deliberately established by elites to mold schools to the patterns of national authority (or vice versa).[47]

Problems in Search of Theory

Through our discussion of unit traits, we were able to arrive at a tentative ranking of the probable significance of the traits. Our discussion of societal traits as causes of authority variables has a different outcome: it has identified four major problems for theoretical interpretation. Although we have suggested solutions to these problems, outlined below, they deserve more rigorous specification and empirical study than can be given them here.

Which are more important for explaining the authority variables, unit traits or societal traits? On the level of the polity itself, societal traits are obviously of utmost importance, since they are also the pertinent unit traits. But we suggest further that traits of authority in the social units of at least *some* societies will be inexplicable unless societal characteristics are taken into account: the characteristics of Swedish schools on the influence and inequality dimensions are an example. And we also suggest that some authority variables will be inexplicable in *any* society unless societal variables such as stratification, interdependence, or multiple memberships are taken into account. Chief among these, of course, is the relational variable of congruence. However, the relative significance of societal traits is itself likely to vary among societies and to depend on intricate considerations (e.g., on the extent to which interdependence exists or the extent to which identifications with the "society" are stronger than those with lesser units).

What is the relative importance of the societal traits themselves? The trait that has posed least difficulty throughout is stratification. It seems to be applicable to units of all levels of inclusiveness; it helps explain problems left unresolved by other variables, chiefly that of congruence, but also that of consistency of norms among supers in complex units; it may also be the ultimate basis of such matters as "social ethos" or "modal preferences in interaction." This does not rule out the possibility that other societal variables also furnish substantial explanations of some of the authority traits of polities, like Directiveness, "groupist" Participation, or structures and processes of direction.

By which of the paths identified at the outset do societal traits affect authority in lesser social units? The answer probably depends on which societal traits we are talking about. Stratification, as stated, seems to have quite direct effects on authority in most social units. So, obviously, would variables like "social ethos" or "modal preferences in interaction"—if indeed such variables exist and are not just epiphenomena of stratification. On the other hand, differentiation and the forces of "organic" solidarity it generates seem only to affect polities directly. Note, in this connection, that we had difficulties throughout in generating explanations of congruence between polities and lesser authority patterns on the basis of these variables, except by postulating a somewhat nebulous, certainly inobvious, tendency to "replicate" polity traits in lesser units, to "homogenize" norms and practices of authority.

How then can congruence among the authority patterns of complex societies be accounted for, and how also explain consonance among the members of their more inclusive units? This seems to be the most difficult problem of all, and perhaps a key to solving all the others—for the solution of the problems of congruence and consonance is bound to shed light on whether societal traits matter more than unit traits, which of them are of special import, and through which paths (and mechanisms) they impinge on authority in lesser units. We suggested several possible explanations. All, however, were themselves sources of additional puzzles or dependent on still untested assumptions. We speculated further that congruence might exist only among units not very different in structural complexity; but although this argument may apply in many societies, it certainly is not true for all—there are cases of congruence that extends to a much wider range of units. Perhaps, then, we are compelled to resort to some form of the "replication" hypothesis, after all. At least two other approaches, however, seem to be more persuasive and less anticlimatic, and these are developed in the next section.

Characteristics of Social Development and Change

Thus far we have considered only "static" structural and functional traits of societies and social units in relation to the authority variables. Explanations of "dynamics" (viz., change) in authority can certainly be derived from such traits: if an authority variable is conditioned by a particular social trait, a change in that trait should lead to a change in the authority variable. But societies and their units also have characteristics that are intrinsically dynamic. In the literature on polities two such processes of change are discussed especially often: the effects of processes and "levels" of development, and the effects of rates of change, regardless of whether these are developmental.[48] In such studies, competition, conflict, and performance remain the chief dependent variables, although there is also a modicum of concern with the effects of processes of social change on the nature of authority (e.g., the likelihood of "democratic" and "authoritarian" rule or the growth of "bureaucratic" institutions). What then are some of the effects of development and rates of change on the authority variables we have identified, and how significant are these factors for explanations of the variables?

Societal Development

The notion of *development* is not among the clearer, more settled concepts used by social scientists. Varying definitions are coupled with dispute about whether "general" processes and levels of development can be talked about at all, as against development in the analytic "subsystems" of societies and the concrete units associated with them (the economy, the educational subsystem, etc.). The evidence that processes and levels of development in the subsystems are interrelated is, however, impressive.[49] There is also substantial agreement that these interrelations result from certain common underlying factors: above all, changes in technology, communications, literacy, and social mobility. There is also wide agreement that development entails the growing "rationalization" of life (the waning of custom, myth, and magic), the growth of "associational" groups (*Gesellschaften*), and increased functional specialization. "General social development" does seem to occur, with fateful consequences.

Since development generally entails increasing differentiation, particularly increasing specialization and, therefore, interdependence, much that can be said about its effect on authority has already been mentioned. We have more to say, however—particularly about the effects on authority of factors commonly considered to be the underlying motor forces of development.

One concomitant of development is the growth of all facets of communication: the number of senders and receivers, and the volume and complexity of messages transmitted. This motor force of development provides a possible explanation of congruence and consonance in complex societies that seems "obvious" and simple. The solution resembles Durkheim's in that the forces that create the problem also solve it; it differs in that the solution flows not from the structure of developed societies but from factors that underlie their structure. In a nutshell, development breeds complexity, hence the likelihood of incongruence and dissonance. But in compensation, development provides a countervailing capacity to "homogenize" norms and practices, through the increasing exposure of members of societies to mass communications, whose high-volume content can also provide standard, reinforcing stimuli. Development similarly supplies elites with the means to increase the uniformity of socialization, by creating and controlling agencies of socialization—chiefly schools. An equilibrating principle thus seems to operate in the process of development, as Durkheim thought:

as the life situations of members of society become more fragmented, the forces that mold their attitudes become more uniform.

This argument, though neat and plausible, raises some difficulties of its own. First, there are cases that do not quite seem to fit. Societies notable for high congruence and consonance (e.g., Norway) are not always equally distinctive in the uniformity of their mass communications[50] nor their controls over agencies of early socialization.[51] In a more general vein, a question is begged about what molds attitudes most: the life situations in which people find themselves (as Marxists, among others, would argue) or early socialization and/or the stimuli provided by printed and electronic communications.

It also is evident that highly developed societies are not similarly high in congruence and consonance. Both those variables seem, on impressionistic evidence, to be distinctly lower in the United States than in, say, Britain or the Soviet Union. The differences are no doubt attributable to the different uses made of the media of communication and/or socialization. The messages that flow through highly developed networks of communications may not be uniform or mutually reinforcing; rather, they may themselves reflect the fragmentation of societies, as is generally true in "libertarian" polities. Similarly, there is no reason for agencies of socialization to inculcate the same norms in highly developed societies, unless closely controlled by an "authoritarian" polity—or unless norms are uniform at the start. Thus the argument that development "homogenizes" even while it fragments is helpful, but we still need light on the conditions (other than authoritarian control) under which socialization and communications are in fact highly uniform.

This argument also implies that the process of development does not have highly determinate consequences for the authority variables, but rather opens possibilities previously closed. If so, there should be statistical relationships between certain authority variables and a particular kind development: a necessary but by no means sufficient condition for a particular authority trait will be development above a specified threshold. We can illustrate this argument by discussion of several of the dimensional traits of authority patterns.

As development occurs, the increased availability of physical, human, and organizational resources makes possible increasing influence over the behavior of members of societies and social units: the capacity for *Directiveness* increases. Surely this is why the most "regimented" social units—the so-called totalitarian polities—are found mainly in societies of relatively high development. Certainly there is a vast difference in Directiveness between totalitarian polities of the twentieth century and earlier modern autocracies—which, as someone put it in reference to the despotism of the

Hapsburgs, were substantially mitigated by *Schlamperei.* Yet the more highly developed polities, and their social units, are far from uniform in that respect. Permissiveness seems to have increased no less than regimentation; and, not infrequently, both regimentation and permissiveness seem to increase within the same societies and social units, in regard to different domains of activity or functions. Thus it is not true that Directiveness becomes greater with development—only that it may.

The spread of literacy, the proliferation of media of communication, and the development of organizational resources make possible increasing *Participation,* by more people, more continuously, through more numerous channels, and in a greater variety of ways. The more extremely participant societies thus seem also to be the more highly developed; and what applies to societies also seems to apply to their social units (e.g., schools). Yet highly developed societies are sometimes also notable for the extreme repression of genuine participation; the "totalitarian" polities again are manifest examples.[52] These generally use directed shows of allegiance in which nonparticipation is the only way of registering preferences. And even where Participation is not repressed, participatory activities, such as voting or activism in parties, seem to vary considerably among polities that are hardly distinguishable by general level of development. So too, apparently, do participatory activities in subsidiary social units, like schools or universities.

As development occurs, *Recruitment* appears to become more competitive. Bases of eligibles grow and boundary interchange occurs increasingly through elections and competitive tests of performance. Forces that push in that direction during the process of development are readily identified: they include the spread of literacy and of higher forms of education (which reduce one basis for the restriction of eligibility), increased organizational capacity throughout society (which adds force to pressures for "civic incorporation"), and perhaps also the increased interchangeability of people (which weakens the case for the existence of some highly exclusive political class). We saw, however, that patterns that are highly competitive in a formal sense may be quite exclusive in regard to effective eligibility—even in a society highly developed by any conceivable indicator. And, again, in "totalitarian" polities, contentiousness may be extreme but other aspects of Recruitment may seem highly exclusive.

This line of argument should not be taken to imply that authority becomes *more* indeterminate as development occurs. Although some options are opened or facilitated in the process of development, others no doubt are progressively closed or impeded. For example, succession as a method of Recruitment and "ascriptive-personal" Bases of Legitimacy seem to disappear; so probably do fully polycratic Decision-Rules, given the increasing variety of interests that supers in complex patterns represent. Instead, the feasible alternatives become redefined, with factors other than development per se deciding which ones actually occur in particular cases. And this point raises a further intriguing possibility. In the course of development, the likely alternatives, at least on some dimensions of authority, seem to become increasingly extreme, antithetical, or polarized. In highly developed societies, for example, alternatives seem to exist between extreme Participation and "permissiveness" on one hand, and extreme regimentation and suppression of participant acts, on the other. What makes this growth of antinomy likely is the tendency of development to increase both the capacities of supers to control and those of subs to influence—just as it seems both to fragment and to generate forces of cohesion.

Rates of Change

Rates of social change vary in two ways: how rapidly change is occurring, of course, and whether change is "even" or "uneven" among different components of societies or of the same social units. The chief authority variables likely to be affected in either case clearly are congruence and consonance. Slow and even change may not guarantee that congruence and consonance will be high; but rapid and uneven change are bound to increase greatly the likelihood of incongruence and dissonance. Examples of both rapid discontinuity and uneven change are provided by the "forced-draft" institution building that has occurred on the governmental level in many "new nations," and in some old ones as well. In these cases, it is hard to see how the polity's authority pattern could be congruent with others, and equally hard to see how there might be consonance in the sense of consistent political norms and practices or correspondence between forms, values, and actual behavior. Cases in point are many and familiar. Much the same outcomes are likely if the rapid discontinuities occur in, say, the economic realm of society or in its educational system, without corresponding changes in the polity or in other social units. In cases of rapid change of any kind, dissonance is particularly likely to arise between older and younger members, and between the norms of older people and the behavior exacted of them in unaccustomed roles.

All these points have been much discussed in the literature (even if not in the terminology we use), and elaboration is unnecessary. We should add, too, that rapid and uneven change are likely to have consequences, through their effects on incongruence and dissonance, for some of the "dimensional" variables. For example, if norms are highly dissonant within or among units, explicit directives are likely to be used as substitutes; what might otherwise be left to "inner-direction" will probably be covered the "other-direction" of superordinates; thus Directiveness is likely to expand. By the same token, the probability of widely divergent participatory inputs, made irreconcilable both by divergence itself and by intensity, is likely to engender a tendency toward the suppression of Participation. Since rapid change tends to produce sharp conflict and frustration, as well as inordinate "expectations,"[53] it is also likely that periods of rapid change will be associated (for reasons discussed in Chapter 7) with a "peculiar" kind of substantive legitimacy—output or outcome legitimacy—and a peculiar kind of personal legitimacy, that of charismatic leaders.

The general conclusion suggested by this discussion is that *factors of development and change matter, but only in a limited sense. Rate of change can help account for incongruity and dissonance, but it is far from the only valid consideration, and it cannot account for congruity and consonance at all. Levels of development do not have determinate effects but only define sets of likely alternative conditions on the authority variables.* Therefore we conclude that, in the dynamic study of authority relations, greater emphasis should probably be given to specific changes in the traits of societies and their units than to the general characteristics of change going on in the societies.

Conclusion

Although we have been selective about the factors considered in this chapter as possible "causes" of the authority variables, we are aware that many such factors are listed. They could in fact have been still more numerous if we had also schematically treated the effects of "situational" factors and the very complex subject of how particular authority variables tend to affect others. Perhaps it is inevitable that a numerous, unwieldy, and logically unrelated set of explanatory conditions should be discerned when first inspecting the messy networks of causal relationships in societies and their units: initially, almost everything seems to affect everything else. Still, simplicity and unity of explanation (parsimony) are an overriding end in the construction of theory. Usually the most parsimonious theory emerges from theory that was once complex and disjointed. In conclusion to this initial exercise we therefore ask how such theory might be distilled from the many factors we have treated.

One way to work toward parsimonious theory is by attempting to weight the causal factors. This we have done throughout, at least in a tentative manner. A more drastic way is to single out, at an early stage, a particular factor that seems to have uniquely great and broad explanatory potential for all dependent variables. Obviously, this is much more risky, but ultimately perhaps also more rewarding. Does our discussion point to any factor that might have such potential? *We suggest that the most potent explanatory factor to emerge is the societal variable of stratification.* The reasons for this position are numerous. Most were earlier brought out, but a few were not.

(1) Recall that we could relate stratification to virtually all the dimensional variables and, by way of mobility, to dissonance, formalization, and degree of institutionalization. No other factor seemed to have equally broad explanatory powers. (2) Recall also our demonstration that some social units have traits that can be expected from stratification but not from their activities or memberships. Moreover, as our discussion proceeded, it became increasingly evident that the most consequential and vexing problem we had to solve was that of congruence and consonance in complex societies; surely that problem would dissolve if it could be shown that stratification is decisively important in determining the nature of authority relationships and that other factors account for only minor variations. In that case, the existence in society of a uniform, unambiguous, unambivalent, and integrated pattern of stratification would account, simply and directly, for congruence and consonance, and the opposite conditions for incongruence and dissonance.[54] Marx's variable would solve Durkheim's problem.[55] (3) Still further, if stratification were a critically important variable, other problems raised at the end of our discussion of societal traits also would largely dissolve: we could specify conclusively the paths that link the structure of societies to authority in their subsidiary units, arriving at a definitive judgment of the relative significance of societal and unit traits. (4) Finally, we could readily account for the conditions under which the communications media of society have or do not have reinforcing content, and those under which a society's specialized agencies of socialization inculcate similar or dissimilar attitudes; it would also be easy to relate the factor of stratification to the effects commonly attributed to different rates of change among and within societies.

At some points in our discussion we raised problems about using stratification as a basis for explaining authority relations; but these problems seem far from insurmountable. Two of them were particularly stressed:

1. How, we asked, could the kind of stratification we linked to congruence and consonance exist in highly complex societies—how could uniform, unambiguous, unambivalent, stratification survive in the face of galloping social differentiation? Two quite different answers seem plausible. (*a*) Stratification might retain its uniformity (despite changes in its degrees and bases) if the process of development and the attendant increase in complexity were gradual and even among the sectors of society. Britain seems to be an apposite example. And stratification appears to become most messy

wherever social change is very rapid in only limited social sectors, like the economy. (*b*) If a "premodern" pattern of stratification is rather egalitarian (and there is no absolute reason for it not to be), even rapid and uneven change might not spoil the pattern. Egalitarianism clearly makes it easier to absorb social change without muddle about who is up and down in the scale of status, simply because people concern themselves less about the question. Cases of premodern egalitarianism may be rare and of course are never absolute, but they do seem to exist (e.g., in Norway). Immigrant societies also tend to be egalitarian, depending on who arrived in the area first: New Zealand and Australia are quite egalitarian, and so is Israel; the United States is less so, but much more than the immigrant societies of Latin America, which were founded by those who brought with them the virus of Spanish class distinctions.

2. We also pointed out that low stratification seems to have less impact on authority in the family than in other social units. Families, however, seem to be very distinctive institutions, anyway in regard to relations among parents and children. Parents are not only different from children in experience and expertise, but also are usually linked to them by a peculiarly close "empathy" rarely, if ever, found outside the family. There generally are bonds of affection, attachment, and intimacy of knowledge between parents and their children that seldom are characteristic of other authority relations;[56] we saw in Chapter 3 that the discernment of such empathy underlay the continued perception of Distance in Swedish families, despite lessened perceptions of parental "expertise." There is a simple way to test the merits of this theory-saving argument: if it is valid, then authority in the family should diverge from what stratification leads one to expect only in relations among parents and children, not in those between husbands and wives. Clearly the use of stratification as a critical variable does not explain absolutely everything, but the exceptions it leaves unexplained do not seem difficult to account for.

Some of our arguments for singling out stratification as a "decisive" explanatory variable are, admittedly, wishful: *if* stratification were the critical determinant of the authority variables, such-and-such problems *would* dissolve. Others involve speculations, supported by limited evidence, about the effects of stratification on variables that also are likely to be affected by other factors. The arguments thus are not yet compelling enough to justify ignoring other possibilities. They only make it advisable to give stratification an especially prominent place in the study of the causes of the authority variables. No other factor we have considered seems to have equal potential to explain traits, to dissolve problems, to avoid question begging, and to obviate hypothesis saving. And, after all, none is so intimately bound up with the notion of "asymmetry," which figures critically in the very definition of authority patterns.

Notes

1. Another contingency that may affect authority involves the personal quirks of particular leaders (e.g., a factory's managing director); such factors, however, are obviously short-lived and not to be captured in theoretical generalizations. Their significance, which we consider slight in most cases, can easily be checked by determining whether authority patterns tend to change with changes of top supers. The cases in which such personal factors may play a relatively important role are, of course, small-scale units and monocratic ones. But even in these, *general* relations throughout societies (e.g., in their families) probably do not much depend on contingent aspects of leaders' personalities.

2. Robert A. Dahl and Edward R. Tufte, *Size and Democracy* (Stanford, Calif.: Stanford University Press, 1973).

3. This contention weakens somewhat an argument Eckstein advanced in an earlier work (Eckstein, *Division and Cohesion in Democracy,* Princeton, N.J.: Princeton University Press, 1966). It goes as follows. (*a*) Stable democracy requires congruence between governmental and nongovernmental authority patterns. (*b*) Units like families and schools cannot be highly democratic in structure. (*c*) Therefore, stable democracy—since cases of it exist—depends on authority patterns in adult organizations (which typically are larger in scale). (*d*) Because families and schools socialize individuals, "impure" democracies that have substantial nondemocratic elements are more likely to be more stable than pure democracies. It is true that this argument rested chiefly on considerations other than scale; nevertheless, it would be stronger if scale were an important cause of variable authority relations.

4. Eckstein, *Division and Cohesion in Democracy,* pp. 51–64.

5. This point should be distinguished from that of Ronald Rogowski in *Rational Legitimacy* (Princeton, N.J.: Princeton University Press, 1974) who associates the high "interchangeability" of individuals, by deduction from rationalist premises, with majority rule. Interchangeability does not mean homogeneity, but the easy change of occupational and other personal traits.

6. Alfred Zimmern, *The Greek Commonwealth* (London: Oxford University Press, 1911), Ch. 6. The large city-states of classical Greece were scarcely homogeneous, but the small city-states and tribes of preclassical and classical Greece probably qualify—and they divide mainly into those ruled by assemblies of all arms-bearing males and those ruled by monarchs.

7. The variable has, however, been accorded much attention by sociologists. It seems crucial for their distinction among primary, secondary, and (sometimes additionally) tertiary units. Much confusion of meaning, incidentally, afflicts these widely used terms. For some typically ambiguous definitions, see R. M. MacIver and Charles H. Page, *Society* (London: Macmillan, 1962, pp. 218–229). A good way to distinguish them is on the basis of choice of membership, at least as a major ele-

ment in the definitions. In primary units, membership is wholly involuntary; in secondary units, only initial choice is possible or subsequent choice highly "expensive;" in tertiary units choice is recurrent and cheap. This set of definitions fits quite well the concrete units we have referred to at numerous points by these labels. We suggest the definitions here only as a way of overcoming persistent ambiguities in the use of the labels, even by fastidious sociologists.

8. These hypotheses, linked to congruence theory, furnish a much simpler rationale than is usually offered for the proposition that the stability of "democratic" governments is associated with the proliferation of voluntary associations. By Kornhauser's "mass society" argument, voluntary associations provide a necessary "buffer" between popular movements and democratic institutions. See William Kornhauser, *The Politics of Mass Society* (New York: Free Press, 1959). By our hypotheses and congruence theory, voluntary associations provide both models and training grounds for effective democratic polities.

9. The significance of the unit traits might conceivably vary from one type of social unit to another. Considerations of parsimony suggest a contrary assumption, however. Parsimony also dictates that we evaluate the relative significance of causal conditions, as we have done.

10. Inclusiveness may be thought of as numbers of members but is probably more appropriately defined by number and variety of subsumed social units. Numbers of members and of social units no doubt are closely related. Sometimes, however, a social unit whose members are widely dispersed (e.g., the Catholic Church) is more populous than an independent society—in the conventional sense—under which parts of it are subsumed. We realize that particular individuals or groups may be ambivalent about what they consider their "ultimate" unit of membership; some Dutchmen, for example, are probably as much Catholic as Dutch, or more. Here we prefer to skirt that difficulty—while acknowledging that it is itself a fascinating subject for research and theory, and a familiar source of intense social conflict.

11. Granted, the difference between "societies" and some other social units in this regard is not altogether clear-cut. The micro-macro distinction is not dichotomous but continuous. Many units that constitute societies are themselves large aggregates of subunits, and there are small-scale societies that have fewer constituent units than some units in large-scale societies. In any given case, however, societies, by definition, are the *most complex* macrocosms; and societies particularly differ—at least in considerable degree—from other macrounits in the *diversity* of the units that constitute them (e.g., the subunits of General Motors or the Democratic Party are far less diverse than those that make up the United States).

12. Note that these are the only "political" questions treated in such overviews of the literature on stratification as Reinhard Bendix and Seymour Martin Lipset, Eds., *Class, Status and Power* (New York: Free Press, 1953) and Bernard Barber, *Social Stratification* (New York: Harcourt Brace Jovanovich, 1957). A possible exception is Barrington Moore, *Social Origins of Dictatorship and Democracy* (Boston: Beacon, 1966). Moore, unlike virtually all political scientists, is principally concerned with the genesis of kinds of rule—a problem that seems prior to, or at least on the same level with, problems of performance, conflict, and success in

political competition, which are the "popular" subjects for empirical political theory. Moore's central explanatory variable, however, is the historic process of commercialization, and only indirectly the effects on authority of patterns of stratification.

13. Denis Brogan, *The English People* (London: Hamish Hamilton, 1943), p. 27.

14. David E. Apter, in *The Politics of Modernization* (Chicago: University of Chicago Press, 1965, p. 124) also distinguishes overall patterns of stratification into three general types, comparable to the more inclusive types of authority patterns we defined: caste, class, and status systems. We consider his typology clear and useful—perhaps especially useful for his own purpose: the discovery of relations between stratification and the process of modernization. However, we also think that his categories are caught sufficiently by the variations in stratification sketched here.

15. *Ibid.*, Ch. 4.

16. Douglas V. Verney, *Parliamentary Reform in Sweden: 1866–1921* (Oxford: Clarendon Press, 1957), p. 223.

17. *Ibid.*, p. 221.

18. Martin Schnitzer, *The Economy of Sweden* (New York: Praeger, 1970), p. 245.

19. Dankwart A. Rustow, *The Politics of Compromise* (Princeton, N.J.: Princeton University Press, 1955).

20. An example is Rustow, *ibid.* "Class" is given three references, spread over five pages, in his study. Compare this with any comparable study of Britain—for example, Samuel H. Beer, *British Politics in the Collectivist Age* (New York: Knopf, 1965). Beer lists references to class on 56 pages, about one out of every six in his book.

21. Robert S. Friedman, *Participation in Democracy: A Theory of Democracy and Democratic Socialization* (Ph.D. dissertation, Princeton University Department of Politics, 1972), p. IV-28.

22. *Ibid.*, p. V-6.

23. *Ibid.*, p. V-14.

24. Gabriel A. Almond and Sidney Verba, *The Civic Culture: Political Attitudes and Democracy in Five Nations* (Princeton, N.J.: Princeton University Press, 1963), p. 276.

25. *Ibid.*, p. 275.

26. Vertical divisions may, of course, overlap or coincide with horizontal (stratificatory) ones. We do not examine here the effects of authority of such overlaps, treating the two variables separately. The subject is not, however, devoid of interest. Rogowski (in *Rational Legitimacy*), for example, treats societies in which stratificatory and certain vertical divisions coincide—"segmented" societies—as a special, broad type, and he argues that only certain patterns of decision making can "rationally" command legitimacy in these societies.

27. Mancur Olson, Jr., *The Logic of Collective Action* (Cambridge, Mass.: Harvard University Press, 1965).

28. See note 15, Chapter 13.

29. See Eckstein, "Authority Relations and Governmental Performance," and the next chapter.

30. Eckstein, *Division and Cohesion in Democracy.*

31. We grant that the evidence that these countries are cases in point is still largely impressionistic. More systematically gathered data might refute our assertion; but the impressionistic evidence points overwhelmingly to its validity.

32. Arend Lijphart, *The Politics of Accomodation: Pluralism and Democracy in the Netherlands* (Berkeley, Calif.: University of California Press, 1968).

33. Emile Durkheim, *The Division of Labor in Society* (New York: Macmillan, 1933).

34. Eckstein, *Division and Cohesion in Democracy,* Ch. 7.

35. R. W. Southern, *The Making of the Middle Ages* (New Haven, Conn.: Yale University Press, 1953), pp. 76–80.

36. See, for example, Tom Lupton and C. Shirley Wilson, "The Social Background and Connections of 'Top Decision Makers,'" in Richard Rose, Ed., *Policy-Making in Britain* (London: Macmillan, 1969), pp. 5–25. It might be argued here that we have put the effect before the cause, that social interconnections persist despite social differentiation, rather than being generated by it. We believe, however, that a good many foci of interconnection are in fact generated in complex societies—whether for the "manifest" purpose of integration or otherwise: examples are elite clubs and professional organizations. We would guess, for example, that there is a good deal more clubbery and cocktail partying in Washington now than in the (simpler) past. And one special type of interconnection clearly is principally generated by high social fragmentation along specialized lines: the *interchangeability* of persons having skills transferable among many units (e.g., administrative skills, secretarial skills). People who have such skills are not tied to particular units or even types of units and may, through horizontal mobility, generate at least indirect connections among the units.

37. Here we can suggest an addendum to Durkheim's theory of social solidarity. In "primitive" societies, he argued, the dominant solidifying force is *mechanical* (shared norms), whereas in "developed" societies *interdependence* is most consequential. We suggest that cross-cutting is equally important in developed societies. More important, we suggest that in "semideveloped" societies *interconnections* will be most significant, due to the persistence of strong diffuse ties and high stratification. Much the same point can be made without the use of these taxonomic terms: there should be a historical progression in the relative significance of the different cohesive forces.

38. Durkheim, *The Division of Labor in Society,* Book I, Ch. 6.

39. *Ibid.,* Book II, Ch. 3.

40. See the discussion in Eckstein, *Division and Cohesion in Democracy,* pp. 253–262.

41. Leon Festinger, *A Theory of Cognitive Dissonance* (Evanston, Ill.: Row,

Peterson, 1957) and J. W. Brehm and A. R. Cohen, *Explorations in Cognitive Dissonance* (New York: Wiley, 1962).

42. An example is Rogowski, *Rational Legitimacy*.

43. Pitirim A. Sorokin, *Social and Cultural Dynamics* (New York: American Book Company, 1937–1941).

44. Note that this argument is consistent with Eckstein's position that congruence depends on the "adjacency" of social units—although the notion of adjacency has other connotations as well.

45. Kornhauser, *The Politics of Mass Society*, especially Ch. 3.

46. Eckstein, *Division and Cohesion in Democracy*, p. 239.

47. Although difficulties arise in explaining the existence of high congruence (or consonance) among any given set of authority patterns, this does not preclude the use of the congruence variable to explain others (e.g., the stability or other performance traits of governments, as by Eckstein.) Like other independent variables, one can simply take congruence and consonance as found, without pushing explanation further. Theory, however, obviously gains depth and plausibility if one can account for an explanatory condition whose existence itself seems highly problematic.

48. Some examples, among many, are: James S. Coleman, "The Political Systems of the Developing Areas," in Gabriel A. Almond and James S. Coleman, Eds. *The Politics of the Developing Areas* (Princeton, N.J.: Princeton University Press, 1960); Seymour Martin Lipset, *Political Man: The Social Bases of Politics* (Garden City, N.Y.: Doubleday, 1960); Karl W. Deutsch, "Social Mobility and Political Development," *American Political Science Review*, Vol. 55, No. 3 (September 1961), pp. 493–514; D. J. McCrone and C. F. Cnudde, "Toward a Communications Theory of Democratic Political Development," *American Political Science Review*, Vol. 61, No. 1 (March 1967), pp. 72–79; Phillips Cutright, "National Political Development: Social and Economic Correlates," in Nelson Polsby, Ed., *Politics and Social Life* (Boston: Houghton-Mifflin, 1963), pp. 569–582; D. E. Neubauer, "Some Conditions of Democracy," *American Political Science Review*, Vol. 61, No. 4 (December 1967), pp. 1002–1009; and Raymond Tanter, "Toward a Theory of Political Development," *Midwest Journal of Political Science*, Vol. 11 (May 1967), pp. 145–172. See also the readings and general reviews in Robert J. Jackson and Michael B. Stein, Eds., *Issues in Comparative Politics* (New York: St. Martin's, 1971), Ch. 1; Lee Sigelman, *Modernization and the Political System* (Beverly Hills, Calif.: Sage Professional Papers in Comparative Politics, No. 01-016). The political consequences of paths, rather than rates, of change are also sometimes, but much less frequently, discussed—as by Moore, *Social Origins of Dictatorship and Democracy*.

49. For a good summary, see Sigelman, *Modernization and the Political System*.

50. The Norwegian press is extremely fragmented (along local and party lines); the electronic media, however, are uniform and highly centralized.

51. Norway has a highly uniform school and university system, under state auspices, but the system leaves much scope for variety and experimentation.

52. We distinguish "genuine" participation from the symbolic or ritualistic participation that autocratic polities often foster.

53. For a discussion of these consequences, see Mancur Olson, Jr., "Rapid Growth as a Destabilizing Force," *The Journal of Economic History,* Vol. 23, No. 4 (December 1963), pp. 529–552. See also, Lipset, *Political Man,* and Kornhauser, *The Politics of Mass Society*.

54. A pattern of stratification is "uniform" if a single pattern of stratification exists in a society, which, of course, may not be the case: there may be considerable differences by region, ethnicity, age, and so on. Stratification is "unambiguous" if the criteria of status are clearly defined, permitting people readily to "place" one another; this may or may not be the case, regardless of degree of stratification, but it seems most likely to occur in very inegalitarian or very egalitarian situations. Stratification is "unambivalent" if the criteria of stratification rule out the possibility that a single individual might occupy quite different statuses according to different criteria. It is "integrated" if something like complementarity in authority patterns exists in stratification: uppers and lowers have the same perceptions of who has higher and lower status.

55. The existence of uniform, unambiguous stratification in society would not, of course, absolutely guarantee congruence between the polity and other social units. Through constitutional engineering, especially under foreign influence, a polity might be created that is out of tune with other patterns of authority. If so, however—and if the other patterns reflect a decisive force like stratification—one should expect the polity to be short-lived. Perhaps the Weimar Republic is an example of the point; its sad and brief history might, however, also reflect a highly ambiguous and unintegrated pattern of stratification itself.

56. Relations among elders and other members of primitive societies probably do have these qualities, but they often rest on kinship anyway. Master-apprentice and lord-serf relations may also have these traits to some extent.

CHAPTER SIXTEEN

Authority Variables as Causes

Authority and "Performance"

We consider now the role of authority variables as factors that affect other aspects of social units. Here again our objective is to place major questions and plausible but tentative answers on the agenda of research. It is especially important to be selective about problems because on casual inspection (and much social theory), it is hard to think of any aspect of social units, or of their members, institutions, and subgroups, that is not likely to be affected by authority relations. The illustrations in Part II should give some inkling of the large variety of considerations to which the authority variables can be causally linked: they range from traits of personality to the representation of large social categories in a society's ruling elite.

There will be considerable differences in the extent to which other variables are affected by authority variables and in how directly they are affected by them. There is, however, one class of variables that seems prima facie to be especially closely and distinctively dependent on the nature of authority relations. We mean, in broad terms, political "performance" variables. Such variables simply indicate how well social units operate in regard to matters that usually are explicit, and always implicit, tasks for their patterns of authority. They include:

1. The extent to which social units and their authoritative institutions obtain and retain the allegiance of their members.
2. Their success in managing internal conflicts.
3. Their ability to formulate binding policies about how to pursue the goals of the unit and how to cope with acute difficulties confronting it ("crises").
4. Their efficiency in actually achieving the goals of a unit and its members.
5. Their capacity to adapt and persist in response to changing external conditions and the shifting interests and demands of members.[1]

These are the considerations we emphasize below, relating structures to functioning. Thus we return, in this last chapter, to the most basic issue that inspired the first. There we argued for a structural, as against a functional, conception of the subject matter of political inquiry. That argument does not imply that functional considerations should be ignored. Rather, it implies that structural traits should be related to functional ones by way of theories about performance variables on which they have important effects, especially theories about the effects of structures on conditions critical for the viability and effective operation of social units and their special institutions.[2]

Before the "performance" variables are treated in detail, we should note that performance certainly does not wholly depend on the nature of authority relations, nor in all cases to the same extent. For example, allegiance to a unit's institutions of authority is obviously governed by their nature, but allegiance to a social unit as such (and its special institutions) also depends perhaps even more on such other considerations as early socialization experiences, in which the evaluation of authority plays little or no role. Still, it should be evident that allegiance to social units may be imperiled, weakened, or forfeited through inappropriate or inefficacious authority patterns; and it is also evident that authority patterns invariably have the task of maintaining social loyalties. Again, authority patterns, no matter how appropriate or efficacious, may not be able to manage all conflicts in a social unit or to achieve all goals. All do attempt to achieve unit goals, and all attempt to suppress, mediate, or adjudicate conflicts. But some goals may be unrealized less for want of appropriate directives than for want of adequate resources, and conflicts may be too intense to permit resolution or may have intractable sources. In general, the role we assign to the authority variables is that of necessary but not sufficient conditions for good performance in the senses listed. They are especially important factors in complex networks of causation.

The performance variables are treated here only in highly general terms. We are not concerned with the attainment of particular goals but with general conditions of attainment of whatever collective goals unit members set. Particular goals (or conflicts, or external stresses) are far too varied for treatment in an introductory discussion. One of the more exciting future tasks in the study of authority patterns, though, will be to explore the relations between authority variables and special social objectives. On the basis of pertinent special theories, it should be possible to specify what arrangements of authority are optimally conducive to the attainment of any given unit goals. Adapting authority relations to special goals has in fact been tackled frequently by constitution makers, experts in industrial relations, and "educationists." More often than not, however, their efforts have smacked of *bricolage,* for want of the special theories necessary for systematic social engineering. The development of such theories clearly is a large task for many specialists, and too intricate to be tackled here. But we can say a good deal about performance variables like goal attainment or conflict management on a general plane.

Our exploration of the five general performance variables remains squarely within the concerns of traditional political science. The explanation of allegiance, effective policy making, and so on, in specific instances and in general, has been a long-standing objective of political scientists. These matters are the subject of a great deal of theoretical work, and characteristics of authority patterns often have been cited among their causes. The alleged effectiveness of competitive democracy in securing legitimacy of polities and ensuring the longevity of governmental institutions is a familiar case in point. This principle—sometimes invoked as an empirical truth, sometimes as an article of faith—has been challenged repeatedly in the experience of the Third World (and some Western polities), and its failure as a universal explanatory principle has spurred the search for economic, social, imperalist, cultural, and even psychological explanations for the successes and failures of new nations and old. In recent years "participation" has gained fresh favor as a cureall for the frequent inefficiencies and occasional paralysis of Western institutions. Its advocates, while seeking explanations of political performances in political structure, say remarkably little about the complementary need for Responsiveness by superordinates, or appropriate changes in Decision-Rules, or effective eligibility in the Recruitment of official elites. Thus "participation" too may be less effective as an explanatory principle than supposed, perhaps giving way to the advocacy and study of still other variables. We are not proposing a "new departure" in the study of linkages between authority and performance, but we are convinced that past investigations have been incomplete and imprecise. As a first step, we advocate that the "authority" side of the equation be analyzed with the preciseness of the distinctions proposed in this study. As a second step, the theoretical linkages to performance require fuller and more subtle specification and testing.

Another general argument about the "performance" variables is probably less tendentious: they are conceptually distinguishable, like the dimensions of authority, but they are closely interrelated. Effective management of conflict and the formulation of binding policies, for example, require substantial allegiance of members to the institutions that carry out these functions. Efficiency in achieving the goals of an entity is dependent on all the foregoing aspects of performance. Efficiency, in turn, vitally affects the adaption and persistence of institutions. It is likely, though, that the different variables of authority patterns have differential effects on the performance variables. Hence a wholly satisfactory theoretical formulation of linkages between authority and performance must distinguish among the performance variables and must deal with their interrelationships as well.

The foregoing paragraphs could be taken to imply that performance depends only on the authority characteristics of the particular units or institutions under study. They also could be taken to apply only or mainly to national polities. Neither implication is intended. First, the performance of any unit or set of authoritative institutions depends in part on the authority patterns of units that impinge on it. If a unit draws its members from similar or less inclusive units, the members will bring with them norms and behaviors already acquired. If the unit is dependent on similar or more inclusive social units, it may be required as a condition of that dependency to adjust its forms and practices of authority in directions they dictate or in directions that facilitate interaction. Any primary school in an urban American ghetto provides concrete examples. Poor black children's norms about authority are visibly different from those of their college-trained, mostly white, middle-class teachers, and results include chronic conflict, disciplinary problems, and ineffective teaching. Moreover, the school requires a minimum of acceptance by the community, it must satisfy the requirements of higher-level administrative agencies, and it may be subject to constraints imposed by a teachers' union. These other units not only have expectations about what the school should do but how it should go about it (i.e., what some of its authority practices ought to be). When those expectations diverge, as they often do, the school is subject to cross-pressures that may drastically detract from its capacity to carry out the "simple" function of instruction. Second, as this illustration demonstrates, the performance of units other than the nation-state is affected by authority variables. These units, too, face problems of allegiance, of conflict management, of goal attainment, and of adaption.

The following general assertions may serve as summary and introduction to the more detailed discussion that follows:

1. Performance in primary, secondary, and tertiary social units is affected by (*a*) the dimensions and types of their authority patterns, and (*b*) the internal consonance of their authority patterns.
2. Performance in secondary and tertiary social units is affected also by the congruence of their authority patterns with those of parallel and less inclusive social units.

We now proceed to suggest some of the authority variables likely to condition each of the five dimensions of performance listed at the outset.

Allegiance

"Allegiance" refers to extent of legitimacy. In regard to social units, it involves commitments to keep the units in being and to maintain memberships in them. For the particular institutions of social units, like their authority patterns, allegiance involves the sentiment that the institutions are worthy of support and should not undergo major change. Allegiance is probably the primal dimension of performance, since without it a social unit can function only by coercion or bargaining. The first being costly and the second tenuous, it is unlikely that social units that must rely on these options will rank high on other performance variables.[3]

The commitments and perceptions that denote allegiance may, of course, be more or less intense, more or less conditional. For the sake of units and their institutions, extremely allegiant members are willing to suffer considerable value deprivations or to perform faithfully their roles in the units. Downs' voter is a case in point. He knows that his vote will make only an infinitesimal difference to an electoral result, and it is costly for him to make a choice and act on it; nevertheless, he votes out of a sense of "social responsibility" as a democratic citizen.[4] Extremely nonallegiant members, on the other hand, opt out of or try to destroy social units or their institutions even if the personal benefits of doing so seem to be disproportionate to costs. Allegiance may, of course, result from perceptions of benefits obtained or from sheer habituation to a unit and its arrangements; the willingness to suffer costs out of proportion to personal benefits only indicates the intensity of the feeling.

The extent to which habituation or utilitarian calculations govern allegiance no doubt has much to do with the nature of social units. In the case of families, habituation surely plays a major role. Allegiance to units that provide one with a living surely depends heavily on claculations of utility. In most cases, though, certain authority variables have a marked effect on whether allegiance is granted and on its intensity. Units that supply persons with their basic affective ties and their means of living may be able to retain loyalties beyond a point at which less essential or accustomed units forfeit them, but people sometimes forego income to escape tyrannical employers, and children and spouses have been known to decamp for reasons of intolerable authority.

By definition, *Bases of Legitimacy* are the authority variables most relevant to extent of allegiance. They make for it, or against it, through three aspects of *consonance*. Ordinary members of social units are likely to withhold allegiance in some measure if they perceive that on the more salient dimensions, the norms and/or practices of their supers diverge from their own (i.e., if they perceive lack of complementarity). The same is likely to occur if members perceive a serious lack of correspondence between professed norms and practices on such dimensions. And allegiance is likely to be imperiled if members perceive general divergence (viz., inconsistencies) on highly salient dimensions within a unit—although inconsistencies seem less obviously dysfunctional than differences among strata or hypocrisies about professed norms. The identity of the dimensions that are "more salient" varies from one group, unit, and culture to the next; we suggested in Chapter 8, though, that Recruitment, Directiveness, and Participation generally play the most important roles, and Responsiveness and Decision-Rules sometimes also count in specified cases and for specific groups of members.

Schonfeld's study of French schools provides examples, even if somewhat indirectly (since conditions of allegiance were not his principal subject). Only 6% of the pupils he examined had "high positive affect" for their schools; 21% exhibited "high negative affect," and another 23% "low negative affect." Something between indifference and antagonism seemed to be the modal pattern. No fewer than 43% of the pupils said they would not care if they had to leave their schools for others—and another 21% said they would be happy or very happy if forced to do so. Furthermore, such alienation grows as students age, despite increased concern with education as a "utility." These findings fit nicely with those on Directiveness and Participation. (Recruitment, of course, is not a live issue in the case of schools). Pupils wanted much more of the latter and much less of the former, especially in the higher grades.[5]

Congruence of authority patterns among social units is crucial to allegiance in secondary and tertiary units because it is, in effect, the most potent determinant of correspondence, consistency, and complementarity. These three aspects of consonance are likely to be high to the extent that all members of a social unit are socialized in and recruited from units that have authority patterns similar to those of the unit entered later. There is a significant and obvious qualification, however. Congruence on all dimensions between the units in which people are socialized and those in which they act later in life is not essential for high allegiance; what is important is, of course, congruence on the most salient bases of legitimacy. A commonsense example: a young schoolchild will be very aware of the leadership style and Directiveness of his teacher in comparison to his home experience but will scarcely be aware of differences between home and school decision making. The former, then, should have much greater effect on his feelings of allegiance toward the school than the latter.

If our line of speculation is accurate, it may help explain the anomalous results of the few studies that have attempted to link childhood experience of authority with attitudes toward authority in later life. A relationship has been found in some instances and not in others. If the studies had focused on dimensions of authority most salient to the respondents, rather than those determined a priori by the investigators, the results might have been more consistent (and, by our hypothesis, positive). Here in any case is a crucial and neglected area of research on political socialization: the influence of childhood experience of authority in the family on attitudes about and practices of authority in later life. William Gouge, writing in early seventeenth-century England, described the family as:

> "A little Church, and a little common-wealth, whereby triall may be made of such as are fit for any place of authoritie, or of subjection in Church or common-wealth. Or rather *it is as a school wherein the first principles and grounds of government and subjection are learned:* whereby men are fitted to greater matters in Church or common-wealth."[6]

The assertion is as plausible as it is ancient, yet the solid empirical evidence required to test and qualify it remains, with few exceptions, to be gathered.[7]

The Management of Conflicts

Conflict is a pervasive feature of social life in large groups and small, because there are few earthly utopias with unlimited resources and no societies with an unlimited set of high-status positions.[8] Many theories identify such related conditions as scarcity, inequity, and the ascendancy of one group over others as causes of various forms of conflict. One of us has proposed such a theory[9] and we both have reviewed others' theories.[10] All but the most simplistic of these theories, however, name conditions other than deprivation and inequality which affect the seriousness or intensity of conflict: some social units are much more effective than others in resolving and managing conflict. Their success is not measured solely by their ability to keep themselves from self-destructing, either. Within the broad limits of survival, some units keep conflict to lower intensities and achieve this by more humane and less costly means than others. Clearly, some are more favored than others with resources; but characteristics of authority also have much influence on the effectiveness with which conflict is managed.

Allegiance itself is critical for the management of conflict within social units. Allegiant members obviously are much more likely than alienated ones (*a*) to accept the inequities that are an all but inevitable concomitant of hierarchy, and (*b*) to accept the judgments of superordinates in resolving "private" conflicts. Accepting such judgments and inequities are the most obvious "costs" paid by members of social units to maintain social units and to play out their allotted roles in them.

The *influence dimensions* also have considerable independent effects on the control of conflict. On balance, "authoritarian" characteristics minimize the intensity and range of conflicts. Social units that are highly regimented, nonparticipant, and autocratic tend to have less overt conflict than those which approach the permissive/participant/alterocratic extreme, since of course their members have less opportunity to clash. This is the situation in political dictatorships like those of the Communist world and South Africa, in many schools in more "democratic" countries, and in "authoritarian" families. The "peacefulness" of these social units cannot be attributed to lack of issues for conflict. The lie is given to that interpretation by the intense conflicts that occur on the rare occasions when control is relaxed, as in China during the Cultural Revolution, or in South Africa during the recent (1973) loosening of controls on black industrial workers, or in French classrooms in the presence of ineffectual teachers.

The foregoing argument may seem inconsistent with empirical evidence that the most autocratic contemporary nations have as much or more manifest internal conflict ("civil strife") than do plural democracies. Gurr has reported quantitative evidence for 1961–1965, showing that "polyarchic" (democratic) nations have somewhat more turmoil, proportionately, than do "centrist" (autocratic) nations, but distinctly less conspiracy and internal war.[11] Two factors probably account for the difference, by reducing conflict in the plural democracies. One is that contemporary democratic nations as a group are more wealthy and less afflicted by internal cleavages than the autocratic nations. The second is that legitimacy tends to be higher in the older, democratic nations than in the autocratic ones. Under *ceteris paribus* conditions, though, we would predict autocracies to be less manifestly conflict-ridden than democracies. The risk of chronic low-level conflict is one of the prices democrats should expect to pay for freedom from regimentation by the state—or by authorities in other social units, whether industrial establishments, trade unions, schools and universities, or families.

The influence dimensions are major conditions of the conflict behavior of subordinates: children, rank-and-file workers, ordinary citizens. Similarly, the *dimensions of superordinate relations* (especially Decision-Rules and Decision-Behavior) sharply affect the intensity of conflicts within elites. If the operative Decision-Rule is monocratic, there will no doubt be much jockeying for position to influence the monocrat, but there will be fewer structural opportunities for organized conflict than in the case of polycracy, in which many individuals and groups are expected to have a say in decisions. Polycracy does not inevitably fuel intense elite conflict, however; conflicts may be moderated by concordance in Decision-Behavior—very nearly by definition of "concordance."[12] In general, we suggest that both concordance and monocratism tend to reduce the intensity of intraelite conflict;

but concordance is the more consequential of the two. If the variables are dichotomized, their suggested joint effects on intensity of conflicts can be summarized by Table 16.1.

The relations of certain aspects of *consonance* to conflict and its management should be obvious. Conflicts arise over the nature of authority relations no less than "substantive" issues. Thus to the extent that norms and practices of authority are consistent and complementary in a unit, potential sources of conflict are diminished. Lack of correspondence among norms and practices may also be a source of conflict, as may wide discrepancies among practices and forms. No less important, conflicts are more likely to be resolved if there is wide agreement on procedures for collective action—especially agreement among supers and subs. Less obviously, *congruence* (and, in that sense, homogeneity) in authority relations can reinforce basic social bonds or even create them, thus make complex units like nations into "communities" imparting to their members a sense of "we-ness" that mutes conflicts or leads to their resolution by mutual give-and-take among the members themselves. Eckstein has argued elsewhere that homogeneity in regard to authority has precisely this effect in Norway, where the sense of "community" seems to be extraordinary, open conflicts are comparatively slight, and nothing else seems to explain these circumstances equally well.[13]

Decisional Efficacy

Efficacy denotes the extent to which subordinate bodies can make and implement prompt and relevant decisions in response to internal demands and external challenges.[14] The capacity to take relevant decisions does not always mean that those decisions can in fact be carried out or that, put in practice, they will have intended effects. A number of extraneous factors—extraneous to efficacy, anyway—affect the ultimate outcomes of policy decisions, including compliance, the closely related extent of alle-

Table 16.1 Joint Effects on Conflict Intensity of Decision-Rules and Decision-Behavior

	Decision-Behavior	
Decision-Rules	Concordant	Discordant
Monocratic	Low	Medium–high
Polycratic	Low–medium	High

giance commanded by the unit and its special institutions, resources, and the unintended consequences that often accompany attempts at social contrivance. But if a unit's authorities are unable to make prompt and relevant decisions in the first place, nothing at all is likely to be accomplished—certainly nothing new; nor is the unit likely to endure in the face of critical stresses. Decisional efficacy thus is a necessary though insufficient condition for almost any concerted action that requires more than routine operation.

Among the authority variables, *S-S relations* clearly matter most for decisional efficacy; and among these a high degree of concordance in decision making is probably the key condition. If decision makers are accustomed to compromise personal preferences for the sake of collective decisions, policies are likely to be made smoothly and quickly. If they regard fellow decision makers as opponents and are accustomed to serving "number one" first, collective decisions not only become difficult to arrive at but units may collapse, to everyone's disadvantage, through attempts to impose particular wills. It is not unknown for labor unions and management in the United States to permit a business to cease operations permanently rather than compromise their respective bargaining positions. Coalition partners in multiparty democracies often behave similarly, because of calculations about the advantages to be had out of the coalitions, because of long-run electoral considerations, or for reasons of ideological inflexibility; sometimes the result is only the replacement of one coalition by another, but it may be a dangerous drift during critical conditions that imperil the regime as such. The relevance of conflict management for efficacy is evident in these examples; it should also be evident that strong allegiance to a unit and its special institutions may serve as an important cement in slippery policy-making situations.

The Decision-Rules of units play a self-evident role in regard to efficacy. We pointed out when illustrating the dimension that polycracy intensifies the need for concordance and cases of very high polycracy are notable, despite contrary cases (like Norway), for their ability to prevent decisions from being taken. Monocrats can override squabbling subordinates and force decisions on them, whereas in cases of polycracy particular individuals or groups can similarly enforce inaction. Here, incidentally, is another reason for not confusing "efficacy" in decision making with "efficiency" in achieving intended outcomes. Polycratic decisions may be difficult to achieve, but once made they are likely to be implemented. Whether monocrats can secure the compliance of subordinates needed to carry out their dispositions, however, is an open question.

The *influence dimensions,* especially Participation and Responsiveness, also are bound to have effects on efficacy in decision making. Policies on major issues are seldom made only within the top-most echelon of superordination. Generally, it involves several strata of superordinates and, almost as frequently, inputs from subordinates. We suggest three broad relationships between decisional efficacy and relations of influence.

1. The greater is Participation (up to a point), the more likely it is that supers will make prompt and relevant decisions, because they have adequate information about the existence of demands and stresses calling for action. In cases of low Participation, the very existence of stress often is not perceived, or incorrectly or insufficiently perceived, until some cataclysm occurs—as in the recent overthrow of the Portuguese regime by its own military. The "relevance" of decisions also often depends on kinds of expertise with which the higher leaders are inadequately supplied and on special, direct knowlege of situations they cannot themselves acquire. Hence, perhaps, the tendency of some autocrats to open participation channels when under a diffuse sense of stress—as in China's One Hundred Flowers period, or the fitful attempts at liberalization from above in Franco's Spain, or, closer to home, the admission of students to departmental councils in American universities. The parenthesis that qualifies the general proposition denotes the existence of an upper limit (not easily defined a priori) on the volume of Participation that is functional: in times of critical stress, a very high level of Participation tends to overload communication channels. When everyone is shouting, no one is clearly heard; leaders tend to tune out and follow their own bents—or to react by obstructing Participation below a functional level. The suggested contribution of Participation to efficacy in times of critical stress is represented graphically in Figure 16.1.

2. As a second general principle, the Responsiveness of decision makers in times of high stress also contributes to efficacy—again, up to a point. Supers who are entirely unresponsive to inputs from their subordinates run the double risk of grossly misjudging a situation and alienating their erstwhile supporters. On the other hand, those who attempt to respond to a great many inputs are likely either to vacillate or to be paralyzed. The

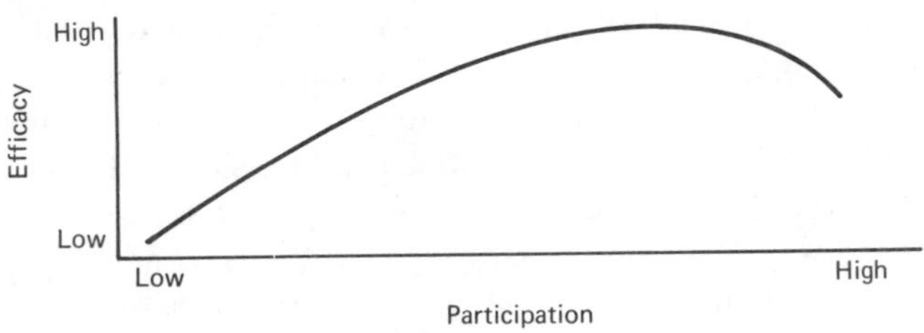

Fig. 16.1

proposed relation is similar to that depicted in the Figure 16.1, with Responsiveness substituted for Participation.

3. The matching of Participation by subs and lower supers to the Responsiveness of the decision makers is a third variable that affects efficacy. Whatever the absolute level of Participation (in norms and practice), a lack of equivalent Responsiveness by Supers has the same effect as no Participation at all—and will exacerbate stress. Participant subs who face unresponsive supers are likely to turn nasty, the more so if the crisis is their own doing or their responsibility. Also deleterious for efficacy is the less common tendency of supers to wait for inputs that never come—that is, to confuse quietude with a lack of problems for decision making.

The foregoing suggestion relates an aspect of *consonance* ("coherence") to efficacy in decision making. *Congruence* among the authority patterns of social units is at least equally important and has been related to overall political performance by Eckstein in two earlier publications.[15] The central hypothesis is that the performance of inclusive "tertiary" units—those involving adults in nonoccupational milieus that are relatively large in scale and complex—depends on degrees of resemblance between their authority patterns and those of less inclusive units, particularly those which socialize people into roles in the more inclusive units and from which elites are recruited. The argument is, of course, equally applicable to secondary units. One effect of congruence on efficacy is through allegiance, which we have discussed. But congruence is likely to have direct effects on efficacy as well, with an important difference: whereas allegiance will be affected by congruence on dimensions salient for legitimacy, the dimensions referring to relations among superordinates, especially Decision-Rules and Decision-Behavior, will be most weighty for efficacy. The rationale for this is evident in the set of learning-theory assumptions on which congruence theory rests. People who have learned how to make and carry out decisions in certain social units according to particular rules and behavioral imperatives will perform decision-making functions in other units most satisfactorily if the rules in the other units are the same—because the subjects thereby experience least dissonance, strain, or sense of anomie.

This argument has some ramifications that extend beyond the earlier statements of congruence theory. There are, in effect, alternatives that can enhance efficacy despite a lack of congruence among the authority patterns of social units. One is selective recruitment to decision-making positions. A contrast between Norwegian and Tunisian society is instructive on this point. In Norway decision making apparently is conducted by similar procedures in virtually every kind of unit, except possibly the family.[16] Whoever the governmental supers, and however selected, they are likely to be familiar with the decision procedures of the polity. In Tunisian society and in other modernizing countries, it is evident that few institutions outside the public sphere have structures and procedures of decision making that resemble those of the government. Those which do are mainly the modern schools and associations set up under the government's aegis.[17] In this situation selective recruitment can compensate in large measure for an overall lack of congruence: supers can be deliberately drawn only from the small pool of properly socialized people. Although efficacy, at least, should benefit, some other consequences may be less salutary: class and status divisions may be accentuated, and rulers and their directives may be seen as alien and "inappropriate" by ordinary citizens. Thus, again, there may be "efficacy" without "effects," or the effects may be destructive.

A second qualification to the simple congruence argument has to do with the *consistency* of authority norms and practices within an inclusive unit. The superordinates of a tightly knit organization can ensure such internal consistency in the practice of authority that new recruits, however diverse their backgrounds, are socialized to leadership roles *within* the institution. Armies are a good case in point. Most officers of most modern armies are graduates of military academies—elite training schools. But most noncommissioned officers and a leaven of commissioned ones are recruited at the lowest levels. Given early entry, a sufficiently long apprenticeship, and the consistency of authority practices through all ranks, the talented recruit can rise to high *S*-positions and perform very well. The principal characteristic of military authority structures that makes this possible is consistency, and reinforcing this trait is the broad scope of such structures: they regulate virtually all phases of their members' lives. Social units that are both highly regimented and internally consistent are likely to have a high degree of efficacy—and, partly as a consequence, great durability. Examples are not limited to armies: the Roman Catholic Church and numerous other religious orders share these characteristics.

Even in such units, however, there is at least this much to be said for congruence theory: particular leadership styles and procedures of direction within armies and religious orders, although determined to a great extent by their functional nature and goals, often differ in ways that make them to some extent analogues of more general social authority patterns. It has been argued that new religious orders (e.g., monastic orders in the Catholic Church) generally model themselves on established secular analogues and that only the ones that follow this pattern persist over a considerable time.[18] The argument does not rule out the possibility that the orders, once firmly established, may successfully do their own distinctive internal socializing. But again, recent pressures for reforms in Catholic Church governance are evidence of a need for minimal congruence between religious and secular arrangements. Conflicts about the subject, as one would expect on the basis of congruence theory, are largely between older and younger groups; and decisional efficacy has certainly suffered from the conflicts—alleviated, as we surmised, by the Church's formally monocratic Decision-Rule. Through that rule, the church is still "efficacious;" whether it can remain "efficient" is another matter.

Efficiency

By "efficiency" we mean the extent to which the authority patterns of social units actually attain the goals they pursue. Efficiency, in this sense, should not be confused with efficacy, although the latter is obviously a necessary condition for it. There are two major reasons for distinguishing the two terms. One is that a decision on policy may not be what systems theorists call an "output" except in a trivial and misleading sense. A decision can hardly be considered a full-fledged output unless properly implemented and enforced: unless needed resources are provided to carry it out, supervision carried out to detect noncompliance, and sanctions wielded at a level that deters failure to comply. The erratic history of American constitutional and statutory provisions regarding discrimination by sex, creed, or race provides cases in point. Second, decisional outputs, even if properly implemented, do not always have determinate "outcomes"; and outcomes ultimately count in gauging the efficiency of goal attainment. Again, American laws against discrimination furnish examples: their enforcement in one section of the country or in center cities may simply shift the problem elsewhere, thus even exacerbate it.

Of all aspects of performance, efficiency is probably most directly dependent on factors other than the authority variables. In regard to outcomes, there is the ever-present problem of unintended consequences, especially through insufficient knowledge about how to achieve social ends properly. In regard to outputs, lack of resources as well as bad faith can make decisions inoperative; the requisite resources include levels of technology and communications and skills in creating and operating complex, coordinated organizations. Efficiency also manifestly depends on the performance variables previously discussed—thus indirectly depends on authority variables. Apart from efficacy itself, some degree of civil order obviously is required for efficient goal attainment; units split by intense, persistent conflict have scant capacity to pursue any objectives other than the maintenance of order. The same clearly applies to units that must devote inordinate efforts to the building of fundamental allegiance—although efficiency in pursuing goals may itself help in that. But there are certain more direct relations between efficiency and the authority variables as well.

Among the dimensions of authority, the extent and nature of *Compliance* undoubtedly has the greatest and most immediate effects on efficiency. The relation may seem, but is not quite, tautological. Social units can probably function almost equally well at various points along the Compliance continuum from "submissiveness" to "indifference." The breaking point comes when members generally tilt toward insubordination. There are some insubordinate members in almost every kind of hierarchic institution, and they often have some creative value in forcing authorities to accommodate change. Moreover, if they are few in number and not strategically placed to sabotage other people's activities, they can be neutralized by expulsion, isolation, or coercion (to ensure compliance). A certain measure of noncompliance may also help keep administrative and enforcement machinery in being and supplied with adequate resources. Thus, over the long run, it may make overall adherence to directives more faithful. Still, although there may be a kind of indifference curve in the relation of Compliance to efficiency, extreme insubordination is tantamount to extreme inefficiency.

Just because of this, the issue of how insubordination becomes a general pattern in social units that have established patterns of authority bears some discussion. Insubordination by individual members may, of course, occur for any number of reasons: genetic factors, inadequate socialization to a unit's authority pattern (or any authority whatever), or resistance to particularly onerous directives. More widespread insubordination in regard to particular policies and/or in particular situations may result from many contingent factors difficult to generalize, like those that operated in the General Gypsum plant discussed in Chapter 4. General insubordination toward new authority patterns imposed by, say, conquerors or innovating leaders, can readily be explained on the basis of inadequate socialization. The theoretically difficult and socially critical issue is how to account for the development of general insubordination toward established authorities that previously commanded compliance or at least indifference.

We suggest that such changes generally are the results of processes of positive feedback. In these processes illegitimacy, which is largely the result of the authority variables, and value deprivations, which at least in part result from inefficiency, augment each other's effects over time. Neither condition alone can sufficiently explain widespread insubordination. Illegitimacy does not suffice because an illegitimate entity that provides material goods and services, security, or other values not easily obtainable by other means, can command compliance on sheer ulititarian grounds. Deprivation by itself cannot generate widespread resistance to authority, since as already argued, allegiant people will accept some costs for the sake of maintaining units and institutions that they value (with the proviso that great and prolonged deprivation may eventually erode legitimacy). The interactions of the two over time, however, can provide sufficient explanation.

The argument is quite simple. In any social unit there are likely to be members whose allegiance is relatively fragile, in that it is dependent mainly on the particular value satisfactions derived from it, or generally on the efficiency of goal attainment in the unit. This is particularly true of institutions in the "modern" world, whose members typically have partial, role-specific commitments to many units but total commitments to none. If efficiency declines substantially for any reason, their allegiance is likely to be forfeited; if this occurs, the members will contribute less, efficiency will be impaired further, and some less fragile allegiances of others imperiled; thus an inexorable train of forfeiture of allegiance can be set in motion. The process can also start with a shift from firm to soft allegiance in any group of members for reasons other than inefficiency; on the argument of the previous chapter, a common extrinsic source of loss of group allegiance is change in stratification not yet matched by concomitant changes in patterns of authority. Where this occurs, efficiency ought to be increased to retain tenuous allegiances, but just the opposite is bound to happen. The speed of the process probably depends largely on the nature of the groups in which allegiances are fragile; the insubordination of lower superordinate strata, often recruited from special subgroups of a complex unit, clearly has more far-reaching, destructive consequences than that of ordinary members.

This line of argument prompts two further observations. First, any vicious circle can also be made virtuous. In the present case, a process that generally is inexorable (especially in small-scale units, where blame cannot be diverted conveniently to peripheral segments or strata of the unit) may be reversed by providing favorable values to strategic groups—"important" groups with tenuous allegiances—and/or by changing an aspect of authority that is an especially strong object of oppositional sentiments. This way of defusing potentially explosive situations, the strategy of "reform" or "concessions," is familiar to students of incipient revolutionary situations. Second, our reasoning also provides an alternative to, and in certain respects reconciles, the views of two groups of theorists who have studied the origins of revolutionary violence. For one group, such violence is due to "abnormal" conditions and a kind of cessation of "normal" politics. The other regards it as politics continued by other means, as war has been considered a particular form of diplomacy. The second group's position rests largely on the observation that revolutionary violence is preceded in many cases by the use of less egregious, more routine means to pursue political objectives and is chosen as a last resort if all else has failed, or by groups that have no less risky means for achieving satisfactions at their disposal. In essence, their case rests on the observation that revolutionary outbreaks rarely occur abruptly but rather seem to be the culmination of a process of escalation over a greater or lesser span of time.[19] On our argument, though, the gradual generation of revolutionary violence is just what would be expected; yet the process *originates* in conditions by no means inherent in politics as such. In effect, this is a third view, drawing on the first to explain how revolutionary processes are set in train, and on the second to show how they develop. It remains, of course, in the realm of speculation. But it would surely be fascinating to test the three models against one another in the same cases. And nongovernmental structures of authority can serve as cases for that purpose no less than polities, often with fewer difficulties in regard to performing appropriate research.

Most social units that have authority patterns do not have many intensely insubordinate members, yet they vary greatly in the efficiency with which they provide justice, produce and allocate goods, socialize new members, or otherwise contribute to human survival and satisfaction. Their efficiencies depend significantly on the other influence dimensions as well. Probably the most important, after Compliance, is *Directiveness*. With some notable exceptions, the most efficient organizations tend to be rather highly "regimented." Farms, factories, schools, and bureaucracies all appear to function best if there are precise and detailed instructions—preferably internalized in members—about how the central tasks of the organization are carried out. Readers may have normative objections to this assertion. There certainly are exceptions to it. Some kinds of tasks require a high degree of autonomy for those who carry them out. Superordinates often have to be more free of detailed regulations than subordinates, the better to deal with exceptional problems. Extreme regimentation probably has a paralyzing effect on efficiency in almost any organization. Still, these are exceptions and extremes. The basic principle remains that the ordinary person who must grow vegetables in the Matanuska Valley, calculate social security payments, make a chair, operate a computer, or bring up and teach a child, must act according to *some* precise rules about how these things are done, if they are to be done well or even at all. The "democratic" principle can hardly obviate the need for appropriate, sufficient direction. "Democratic" authority is not to be confused with indolent authority. Rather, it requires limits on coverage, supervision, and sanctions, and above all, it prescribes certain norms and practices of Participation, Responsiveness, Recruitment, and, perhaps less obviously, distinctive kinds of Decision-Behavior. Understood as process rather than lack of output, it may in fact contribute much to efficiency. For example, open Recruitment to *S*-positions tends to enhance efficiency because it allows the maximum use of talents of members. There is one serious qualification, though: namely, that those recruited must be familiar with, thus able to perform, the roles they occupy. This leads to a consideration of the effects on efficiency of consonance and congruence.

The efficiency with which an authority pattern operates is likely to be reduced by any internal "contradictions"—by lack of *consonance.* The most deleterious probably are lack of complementarity and lack of coherence. If the norms and practices of subordinates are not similar to those of their supers, especially with respect to inequalities and influence, antagonisms between the two tend to impair efficiency. An illustration, used in Chapter 4, was the effect of a new mine foreman's "distant" behavior and attitudes on miners who are accustomed to familiarity and parity. We also would predict low efficiency where Participation and Responsiveness are incoherent, especially if subordinates substantially exceed in Participation the Responsiveness of their supers. Such a situation provides incentives to resist directives or to comply only at a minimum level. Lack of correspondence between norms and practices also tends to undermine efficiency; subs and supers will not carry out tasks enthusiastically if asked to do them in ways deemed improper. Problems will be especially serious where Directiveness is concerned. We suspect, for example, that many of the inefficiencies and conflicts in contemporary American institutions are the result of people being directed to carry out tasks with either greater or lesser regimentation than they regard as proper. Contemporary American university teachers certainly are aware of the divergent complaints of students—some want more autonomy, and some grumble if left too much to their own devices.

Congruence, at least on the *S-S* dimensions, has a more manifest impact on efficacy than on efficiency but is relevant to the latter precisely because of its effects on consonance. Continuing the example just begun: we know that there are substantial differences among American families and schools in regard to degrees of Directiveness (and also on other dimensions of authority). Small wonder then that some young people have difficulty adjusting to highly permissive schools and colleges or to perceived permissiveness in political life, and others have problems with the regimented life of the military, bureaucracies, or industries. The results include frustration and anomie for individuals, fragile allegiances to secondary or tertiary institutions, and chronic inefficiencies in goal attainment. Several tests of congruence theory are suggested by this line of argument. Among them are the following.

1. Children from relatively regimented family backgrounds (e.g., on the argument of Chapter 3, children from poor segments of the population) should have more difficulty adjusting to permissive schools than those from different backgrounds.

2. Permissive schools should be relatively ineffectual—not least in attaining their educational objectives—when pupils are drawn from relatively regimented family milieus. (In areas of poverty there are many variables other than those involving authority to explain low educational achievement, but in almost all cases these can readily be held constant to detect the particular effects of congruence.)

3. Members recruited from permissive institutions should have special difficulty in accepting the regimented life of bureaucracies and industries.

4. Since family and educational authority have become generally more permissive in many societies (not least American society, and most of all in American universities), there should be a general decline in the efficiency of secondary and tertiary units—most of all in those that have not significantly loosened Directiveness or cannot do so because of functional considerations.[20]

Because both Directiveness and congruence affect efficiency, highly modern societies seem to confront a dilemma of efficiency in critical economic and bureaucratic institutions. As permissiveness in formative units increases (as seems to be the case), congruence requires lesser Directiveness in others if efficiency is not be be impaired; but the same units are also unlikely to work efficiently without considerable regimentation. In fact, the tasks and bureaucratic structures of highly modern societies seem to compel a general growth of regimentation in their secondary and tertiary segments, just when congruence requires the opposite. In form, this is a "contradiction" in the genuine Marxist sense: an inexorable tension that grows worse; but it is Dahrendorf's revision of Marx that supplies its content.[21]

Modern societies have means to escape this dilemma or to keep tension within tolerable bounds. Increasing Participation and Responsiveness, instituting more broad-based Recruitment, and revising Decision-Rules can help maintain considerable congruence on salient dimensions. And in regard to Directiveness itself, an intriguing possibility exists. It involves increasing diversity of social institutions and growing social mobility. To the extent that institutions are diverse and people mobile, there may be a tendency for organizations to attract and retain a significant number of members whose norms and practices correspond to those of the organization: a tendency of like to gravitate toward like. Determining whether this occurs should lead to a pertinent and challenging test of congruence theory.

A point made in the first section of this chapter should be briefly reiterated here, because of its special pertinence. We have not touched on the fascinating question of whether some characteristics of authority are particularly, even uniquely, suitable to the efficient attainment of particular goals of social units. Certain patterns of authority in instruction, for example, may be especially conducive to the goal of preparing pupils for higher education or entry into prestigious occupations; quite different ones may be suitable for cultivating students' spontaneity, self-assurance, or capacity for good citizenship. At the level of the polity, it may be that authority relations that are conducive to goals such as "mobilization" of citizens are different from, even antithetical to, goals such as "national unity" and the reduction of inequalities. Here again, dilemmas (for "social engineers") appear in both developing and highly developed societies, not just because of diverse values calling for different authority patterns but also because formative units have the task of preparing people for dissimilar roles in units having a great variety of tasks and goals.

Persistence and Adaptation

The "stability" of polities has attracted much attention from political scientists. It is seldom clear whether this is due to the intrinsic fascination of the subject, to normative preferences for stability, or to fear of the disorders and inefficiencies that accompany instability. What is evident is that the ability of authority patterns to endure is a fundamental attribute of good performance by them. This is not to say that one should invariably "like" stable patterns; morally repulsive patterns are made all the more objectionable by their persistence.[22]

To make sense of the term "stability," some basic conceptual distinctions must be stated and the dichotomization of stability and instability avoided. Stability, of course, means nothing if not persistence over time. But there are two quite different ways in which institutional arrangements can persist: (*a*) through adaptive, incremental changes in institutional arrangements, as responses to new conditions, demands, and functional requirements; or (*b*) without such changes. In the latter cases, one might speak of *stagnant* institutions, in the former of *durable* ones. The labels are value-laden by design: new conditions, demands, and functional requirements confront virtually all human orders, and patterns that are highly resistant to adaptation are in consequence likely to suffer explosive disruption sooner or later. Cases in which major, abrupt changes *of* arrangements occur may be called *volatile*: such changes often follow long periods of stagnation.[23] A series of adpative changes *in* institutions may eventually add up to change *of* the institutions; but this kind of evolutionary change is fundamentally different from major, abrupt change, both in the perceptions of members of the unit and in its effects on other aspects of performance. Ironically, over the long run, patterns that suffer disruptive change may not have changed much at all, or may oscillate between two opposed patterns, as the French polity is often said to have done since the Revolution—itself a kind of stagnation. Still another possibility is long-run change accomplished not incrementally, but by a series of periodic convulsions.

The particular kind of "stability" we regard as a manifestation of high performance, then, is that which involves the demonstrated capacity to adapt more or less gradually in response to internal and environmental stress. Our term for the distinguishing property of institutions which both persist and adapt is *durability*. The concept combines and reconciles two separable but related aspects of good performance—preserving old patterns and meeting new requirements.[24]

One beginning point for an analysis of the conditions of durability and change in authority patterns is an examination of changes in authority patterns in Western societies. It is commonly said that the basic institutions of Western societies are undergoing unprecedented mutations. On further inquiry, however, changes in authority now occurring seem in the main to be continuations of changes long in process. Indeed we suspect that they are manifestations of lines of "development" in authority relations that are not at all peculiar to the West but "normal" sequences of the kind mentioned in Chapter 14. Certainly ours is not an era in which new kinds of social units are being established. The principal social experiments in the West during the past 30 years are the movement toward cooperative living and the establishment of transnational bodies like the Common Market; both are derivative of older models, not original, and the former already seems to be in eclipse. The changes have occured *in* existing social units, and most of these continue changes that began before or during the Industrial Revolution. The family has long been declining in size and durability; the much-touted increase in childless, ephemeral couplings is simply an extension of a trend. The state long ago supplanted the Roman Catholic Church as the most inclusive social unit in the West; the power and respect commanded by the state have continued to grow while those of organized religions have at best remained static. Economic enterprises have grown more rapidly in scale, complexity, and productivity than any other sets of social units, but they have not changed their fundamental nature, only shifted—in some countries—from private to state control. Educational institutions have gradually grown to their present condition of almost Byzantine complexity to meet the constantly increasing requirements of economies and governments for people with specialized skills.

These long-term tendencies have been accompanied by and in some degree have depended on changes in patterns of authority. The complexity of Conformation of almost every type of social unit except primary ones has increased, through increased differentiation and specialization. Recruitment has become increasingly open and competitive (even if not as much, in certain cases, as formal rules imply) because of the requirements of larger, more specialized units for ever larger cadres of skilled personnel. Ordinary men and women have demanded greater Participation in the direction of social units, and hierarchs have become obliged to be more Responsive. The distinctions between "better" and "inferior" classes of men which were pervasive in past European societies are being continuously attenuated. Distance between strata in social units has for a long time been shifting toward parity, and its counterpart, the Deportment of supers and subordinates toward one another, has become increasingly familiar. The processes of direction also have shifted. Contemporary Western institutions are likely to be more polycratic in their Decision-Rules than their predecessors, partly because there are more interests and inputs to be reconciled in decision making in complex organizations, partly because of the extension of the norm of Participation. Whether concordance in Decision-Behavior has also increased is more problematic, though one suspects that many of the highly discordant elites of past eras have been selected out of existence. There have been changes in Directiveness also, although these are too complex and varied to be summarized as a simple shift along the continuum from regimentation to permissiveness. "Coverage" of human activity by the state evidently has increased; but in most other social units it has decreased. Neither families, nor schools, nor industries attempt to regulate the lives of their members as comprehensively as they once did. The most uniform trend in Directiveness seems to be that the severity of sanctions for disobedience has decreased in virtually every type of social entity.

No doubt one can find exceptions to these generalizations, but close empirical inspection would almost surely reveal that every major type of social unit in Western societies has changed substantially on every dimension of authority over the last century—generally in the ways sketched.

This, though, says nothing about whether the changes have been accomplished adaptively or disruptively—only that our sense of novelty is much exaggerated and that similar changes have occurred widely in response to similar stimuli (and to some extent by diffusion). Which type of change has characterized which type of social entity, and under what conditions, largely remains a subject for speculation and research. On the basis of the study cited in note 23, we can generalize with some confidence about changes in polities since 1800. Almost all contemporary Western polities (and polities elsewhere, for that matter) have attained their present form not by gradual "evolution" but by a series of abrupt and substantial changes in their patterns of authority. More specifically, in all of Europe and the European-settled regions of the world (including Latin America) it was possible to identify only eight nations established before 1870 whose polities had undergone no "major, abrupt" changes as of 1971; in contrast, 48 others had experienced one or more abrupt transformations, or dissolution as nations. The eight "adaptive" cases are Belgium, Canada, Great Britain, Luxembourg, Switzerland, the United States, Costa Rica, and Ecuador.[25] The abrupt changes were not always unidirectional either. More typical has been the oscillation of nation-states between "autocratic" and "democratic" patterns of government, with the democratic features becoming increasingly dominant in Western Europe and autocratic features prevailing in Eastern Europe. In Latin America the oscillations continue, though the autocratic pattern now seems to be ascendant.

It may be that in other kinds of social units—especially small-scale primary units—evolutionary patterns are the rule. But theorists can hardly postulate that such patterns are more "normal" than others—as do social "systems" theorists who assume inherent tendencies toward homeostatic adaptation. Revolutionary (especially violent) changes undoubtedly warrant the wide, intense attention recently lavished on them;[26] but modifications due to evolution warrant as much.

There is evidence for secular trends and for "development" in specifiable directions, but not for inherent adaptation. What conditions, then, promote persistence with adaptation? The most immediate conditions are all the other "performance" variables we have examined. The allegiance of most members of a social unit to its authoritative institutions (and/or the unit itself) surely comes close to being a necessary condition of "durability." If allegiances are mainly fragile, or members alienated, authorities are likely to resist changes altogether (as opening doors to transformation, raising expectations of change), and patterns will stagnate or be disrupted, or both conditions will occur seriatim. The decision merely to tinker with existing arrangements in response to new conditions, demands, or needs implies, in any case, a commitment to the arrangements in their essence.[27]

A substantial capacity for managing conflicts also seems to be presupposed. There is always potential for conflict in hierarchically ordered social units. Even if the members of a unit are highly homogeneous in ascribed characteristics and in wide agreement on goals, conflict can arise from the very existence of hierarchy, as well as the differential allocation of values that seems to be ubiquitous in social life and usually accompanies differentials in authority and power.[28] If such conflicts are not to disrupt institutions, they must necessarily be "managed"—or coercively suppressed, which, again, is likely to entail stagnation and postponed explosion. The management of conflict in return requires efficacious decision making, as does the process of adaptation as such (itself a means for managing conflicts). Stagnation is not always the result of repression but often simply the outcome of the *immobilisme* of authorities—the French word is perhaps better then "inefficacy," and it is probably no accident that the apt term is French. Efficacious decision making and efficiency also generally are needed to achieve high levels of whatever values a unit provides its members and to help them achieve goals—which, in turn, helps firm up allegiances and reduce conflicts. Efficiency also is needed to supply higher strata with resources for maintaining a unit and its institutions.

All the performance variables probably have effects on one another (including the probability that "durability," if achieved, will itself tend to increase allegiances, efficacy, and efficiency). But we propose that in most complex units some of the causal linkages are stronger than others and that the dominant causal paths are those portrayed in Figure 16.2.[29]

This leads to a final question: Do any of the authority variables appear to have particularly strong effects on durability, thus on "performance" in a general sense? We can approach an answer in two ways: by listing the authority variables that appear to affect the other performance variables more or less strongly, to see which ones appear recurrently, and by referring again to the authority variables that affect allegiance, since that aspect of performance has consequences for all the others. These two procedures yield substantially similar results, which are apparent in Table 16.2 and can be summarized in two broad propositions.

1. *The two "configurative" authority variables on which durability depends most are congruence and complementarity.* If both are high, durability should be high. This broad assertion calls for two qualifications, though. First, all aspects of consonance other than complementarity have some lesser effects on performance. The correspondence of norms and practices is particularly likely to affect the performance variables that involve relations between supers and subs (allegiance and the management of certain kinds of conflicts). Coherence among different dimensional aspects of authority impinges particularly on aspects of performance that involve mostly supers (efficacy and efficiency), whereas consistency has some direct effects (on conflict management) but affects performance mainly through its consequences for other configurative variables. The proposition, con-

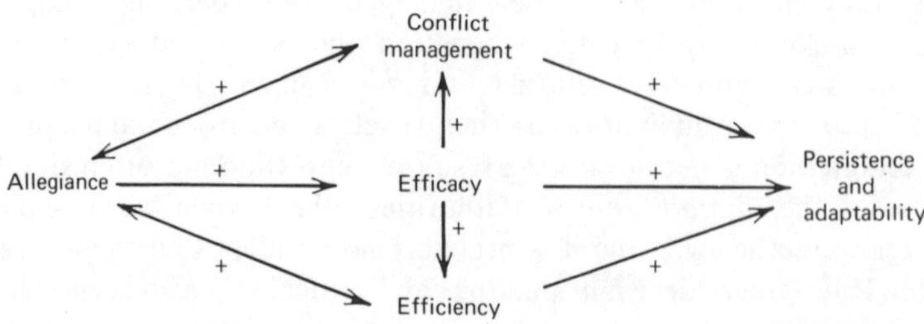

Fig. 16.2 Interrelations among the performance variables.

Table 16.2 Performance and Authority Variables: An Overview[a]

Performance Variables	Dimensional Authority Variables	Configurative Authority Variables
Allegiance	BASES OF LEGITIMACY	CONGRUENCE
	Hence: (RECRUITMENT)	COMPLEMENTARITY
	(DIRECTIVENESS)	CORRESPONDENCE
	(PARTICIPATION)	(Consistency)
	(Responsiveness)	
	(Decision-Rules)	
Conflict management	DECISION–BEHAVIOR	CONGRUENCE
	DIRECTIVENESS	COMPLEMENTARITY
	Decision-Rules	CORRESPONDENCE
	Participation	CONSISTENCY
	Responsiveness	
Efficacy	DECISION–BEHAVIOR	CONGRUENCE
	DECISION–RULES	COHERENCE
	RESPONSIVENESS	Consistency
	PARTICIPATION	
	(Recruitment)	
Efficiency	COMPLIANCE	CONGRUENCE
	(BASES OF LEGITIMACY)	COMPLEMENTARITY
	Directiveness	COHERENCE
	Recruitment	

[a] Terms in capitals denote stronger effects, terms in lowercase letters denote weaker effects, and parentheses denote indirect effects through other variables.

sequently, is a "statistical" law, by no means a "universal" one; but the statistical relationship should be strong. The second qualification is that the effects of congruence pertain to secondary and tertiary units only. The reason, of course, is that congruence theory is largely based on assumptions about the importance of learning, especially early learning in primary units. In these units, therefore, consonance is the governing considerations—although we do not categorically rule out the possibility that incongruities among primary and other units may deleteriously affect performance in the former.

2. *The dimensional variables that most strongly affect performance are those singled out as especially likely to be "salient" for members, hence to figure importantly as Bases of Legitimacy.* These dimensions are by definition important determinants of allegiance, but they also appear recurrently as determinants of performance in other senses. A significant qualification is that concordance in Decision-Behavior, though it may not loom large in general perceptions of authority relations, has a very significant impact on

efficacy and the management of conflicts.[30] In addition, Compliance was assigned a critical role in regard to efficiency; but high compliance depends substantially on high allegiance, thus, by way of Bases of Legitimacy, on the salient dimensions.

In several cases we left open the question of what specific conditions on the dimensions are conducive to durability. High concordance and compliance aside, we only mentioned that relatively open Recruitment, monocratic Decision-Rules, and a certain minimum level of "regimentation" had mildly salutary effects on the performance variables. In general, specific conditions on the dimensions seem to be less significant for durability than how these conditions affect the "configurative" traits of authority: congruence among units and consonance within them. Yet at the same time, by virtue of the second general proposition, attempts to test the congruence and complementarity theories of durability should emphasize the most salient dimensions. The two propositions thus can be combined in a single powerful hypothesis: *durability (hence also overall performance) depends principally on congruence and complementarity on the most salient dimensions of authority.*[31] If clearly contrary results are found, most of the preliminary speculation pursued in this chapter can be dismissed.

By the same token, the most critical problem in treating authority variables as effects is to explain how congruence and complementarity on the more salient dimensions come to exist, or fail to appear, particularly in more complex social units like polities. Over the last century there have been large and rapid changes in patterns of social stratification in most Western societies and many non-Western ones. If the arguments of the preceding chapter are correct, those changes are likely to have reduced markedly and at least temporarily the homogeneity or fit of norms and practices of Recruitment and Participation. Therefore long-lasting congruence and complementarity should be rare in the recent political history of most of the world. A fascinating question, then, is whether the few polities that were durable throughout the period underwent changes in stratification that themselves were unusually gradual, or alternatively had their effects moderated by highly concordant norms and practices of elite Decision-Behavior. The empirical answers to that question should provide one more test of the causal arguments posed in this chapter.

Notes

1. For a general conceptual and theoretical discussion of these "performance" variables, see Harry Eckstein, *The Evaluation of Political Performance: Problems and Dimensions* (Beverly Hills, Calif.: Sage Professional Papers in Comparative Politics, 01–017, 1971).

2. Such a theoretical treatment of "functions" seems to us more faithful to the original nature of "structural-functional" analysis in biology and social anthropology than the use of functional categories to define objects of study. See, for example, Ludwig von Bertalanffy, *Modern Theories of Development* (New York: Oxford University Press, 1933), pp. 9 ff, 184 ff; and Robert K. Merton, *Social Theory and Social Structure* (New York: Free Press, 1949), pp. 23–81.

3. For a more elaborate discussion of these points, see Eckstein, *The Evaluation of Political Performance,* pp. 50 ff.

4. Anthony Downs, *An Economic Theory of Democracy* (New York: Harper & Row, 1957), pp. 265–271.

5. William R. Schonfeld, *Youth and Authority in France, A Study of Secondary Schools* (Beverly Hills, Calif.: Sage Professional Papers in Comparative Politics, 01-014, 1971), pp. 23, 43–44, 58–61.

6. *Of Domesticall Duties* (1622), quoted in Carl Bridenbaugh, *Vexed and Troubled Englishmen 1590–1642* (New York: Oxford University Press, 1968), p. 32. Our emphasis.

7. The argument bears on a general and important methodological problem: how to measure overall "congruence" among patterns as multidimensional as those of authority. The problem arises simply because resemblances on some dimensions may differ, even extremely, from those on others, and because a mere summing of degrees of resemblance on all dimensions and subdimensions seems on the face of it of dubious validity. The obvious solution is to consider only salient dimensions, or indeed a particular dimension that seems highly significant. (Dimensions can also be weighted by established saliency.) The sure way to determine which dimensions are significant for subjects of study is by appropriate empirical inquiry (e.g., by survey questions). Such inquiries can also be used as checks on the reasoning about the saliency of dimensions in Chapter 8. That reasoning, though, seems to us sufficiently persuasive to permit using resemblances on the dimensions there stressed, singly or in combination, as proper, simplified measures of congruence.

8. The reference is to Raymond W. Mack and Richard C. Snyder's observation that all conflict arises from scarcity of either resources or valued positions, in "The Analysis of Social Conflict: Toward an Overview and Synthesis," *Journal of Conflict Resolution,* Vol. 1 (June 1957).

9. T. R. Gurr, *Why Men Rebel* (Princeton, N.J.: Princeton University Press, 1970).

10. Harry Eckstein, "On the Etiology of Internal Wars," *History and Theory,* Vol. 4, No. 2 (1965), pp. 133–163; T. R. Gurr, "The Revolution—Social-Change Nexus: Some Old Theories and New Hypotheses," *Comparative Politics,* Vol. 5, (April 1973), pp. 359–382.

11. T. R. Gurr, "A Comparative Study of Civil Strife," in H. D. Graham and T. R. Gurr, Eds., *Violence in America: Historical and Comparative Perspectives* (New York: Praeger, 1969), pp. 580–582.

12, Complexity of conformation, a third aspect of *S-S* relations, is not likely to have consistent effects on the intensity and amount of conflict. An organization with many segments and strata does provide structural opportunities and incentives for intra-unit conflict behavior (note, e.g., the conflicts among the branches of American government). However, "stratiformity" and segmentation may keep potential conflict groups within the social unit insulated from one another, possibly even unaware of objective conflicts of interest between them, each with its own special domains of authority.

13. Eckstein, *Division and Cohesion in Democracy,* Chs. 8, 9. Denis Brogan, in *The English People* (London: Hamish Hamilton, 1943), makes the same point in regard to (of all things) shared norms and practices of social stratification, despite the invidiousness of the British class structure—which one might expect to be more a bone of contention than a source of solidarity.

14. The concept is explained, with special reference to politics, in Eckstein, *The Evaluation of Political Performance,* pp. 65–78.

15. Eckstein, *Division and Cohesion in Democracy,* pp. 225–288; and "Authority Relations and Governmental Performance."

16. Eckstein, *Division and Cohesion in Democracy,* Chs. 8, 9.

17. This assertion is based on the work of Donald Newman, who based fieldwork on authority in Tunisia on our conceptual scheme. We are responsible for generalizing and encapsulating his observations.

18. Michael Sheeran, "Church Governance: How and Why?" (Unpublished paper).

19. The first view is represented by James C. Davies, "Toward a Theory of Revolution," *American Sociological Review,* Vol. 27 (September 1962), pp. 5–18; and Ivo K. and Rosalind L. Feierabend, "Social Change and Political Violence," in Graham and Gurr, Eds., *Violence in America,* Ch. 18. For the second, see Charles Tilly, "Revolutions and Collective Violence," in Fred S. Greenstein and Nelson W. Polsby, Eds., *Handbook of Political Science,* Vol. 3 (Reading, Mass.: Addison-Wesley, 1974); William Gamson, *Power and Discontent* (Homewood, Ill.: Dorsey, 1968); and H. L. Nieburg, *Political Violence: The Behavioral Process* (New York: St. Martin's, 1969).

20. A partial test of several such hypotheses is being conducted by Kenneth Barry, using interview data from high school and college students of lower- and middle-class origins, and Catholic and public school backgrounds. The specific question is how their self-reports of family and school authority practices, on key dimensions, affect their current norms and practices of Participation and Compliance in school and polity. A preliminary report is Barry, "Authority Relations in a Democratic Society" (unpublished first-year paper, Northwestern University Department of Political Science, 1974).

21. Ralf Dahrendorf, *Soziale Klassen und Klassenkonflikt in der Industriellengesellschaft* (Stuttgart: Enke, 1957). Dahrendorf stresses differential authority as the basic source of class conflict in industrial societies. Our argument, of course, differs from and expands on his; the resemblance is in the use of authority as the crucial consideration.

22. Note that we are concerned here in the first instance with the "stability" of authoritative institutions, not that of social units. Some kinds of social units (families, religious orders, nations) endure—in the sense that members continue to identify with them—irrespective of change in their particular institutions. Nonetheless, the survival of social units and the survival of their authority patterns are related. Change in patterns of authority often signals the dissolution of social units, and the dismantling of all hierarchic relations generally means the death of a unit.

23. For evidence of lack of adaptability among traditional states and empires before their dissolution see T. R. Gurr, "Political Persistence and Change, 1800–1971," *American Political Science Review,* Vol. 68 (December 1974), pp. 1482–1504.

24. For a discussion and operational definitions of what constitutes "major" and "abrupt" changes, with special reference to polities, see Gurr, "Political Persistence and Change." The study also examined the effects of various authority variables on the stability and adaptability of polities.

25. For details, and for the operational distinctions on which the findings were based, see Gurr, "Political Persistence and Change."

26. For useful compendia of relevant studies, see Ivo K. Feierabend, Rosalind L. Feierabend, and Ted Robert Gurr, Eds., *Anger, Violence, and Politics: Theories and Research* (Englewood Cliffs, N.J.: Prentice-Hall, 1972) and references in Douglas A. Hibbs, Jr., *Mass Political Violence: A Cross-Cultural Causal Analysis* (New York: Wiley, 1973). Of course violent means may sometimes be used to accomplish adaptive changes.

27. The arguments do not rule out the possibility of tinkering to disarm opposition and make allegiances more firm. They also do not rule out the possibility of alienated members opting for minor adaptive changes for strategic reasons: as steps that make disruption more likely to succeed. But we are concerned here with continuous patterns of adaptation; tactical adaptations, on the record, do little to promote such patterns—an object lesson being provided, among many other cases, by Bismarck's policies.

28. Here again Dahrendorf's revision of Marxism (see reference in note 21) is to the point. If "class conflict" is, at bottom, conflict among any superordinates and subordinates, then such conflict potentially exists, by definition, in all patterns of authority. Tilly's approach to civil violence, in "Revolution and Collective Violence," is based on a similar premise: the universal tendency of "outs" to want be be "ins" and to use more costly means to improve their status if less costly ones are unavailable or ineffective.

29. The causal model is based partly on evidence collected in T. R. Gurr and Muriel McClelland, *Political Performance: A Twelve-Nation Study* (Beverly Hills, Calif.: Sage Professional Papers in Comparative Politics, 01-018, 1971), and partly on a rethinking of the subject that is reflected in the arguments of this chapter. We judge the measures and small sample of cases used in the above-mentioned study to be too partial to permit its results to be accepted as definitive.

30. Note also that we argued (in Chapter 8) that Decision-Behavior was highly salient for supers.

31. A highly desirable first step toward testing this proposition would be to determine empirically which dimensions loom largest for members of the units or cultures being studied.

Conclusion

In recent decades, the study of politics has been a field of proliferating approaches to empirical inquiry and theory—a field increasingly divided by the search for a unifying "paradigm." Emphasis on the formal rules of governmental organizations provided a unifying focus during the field's early decades of academic autonomy. But for many reasons that focus came to seem increasingly insufficient and barren. Among the candidates for succession to formal-legalism have been the power-elite apporach and its cousins, group theory and class analysis; functionalism, and its more general version in political systems theory; and, most recently, the political-culture and "rationalist" approaches, the one treating political behavior as governed by learned orientations, the other treating it as reflecting an inherent propensity to maximize political utilities, in the manner of theories in economics.[1]

This book was not begun as a self-conscious attempt to propound yet another candidate paradigm. Inevitably, however, it touches on a number of paradigmatic issues. Holt and Richardson have identified six elements of a paradigm, and we shall briefly survey the extent to which four of them are and are not dealt with in this work.[2]

The *conceptual* element of a paradigm is very substantially represented by our notion of authority relations, in both their "dimensional" and "configurational" aspects (Parts I, II, and III). In addition to analytic concepts, we proposed in Part IV a set of synthetic ones to be used for systematic classification. We began with what we regard as the first question of political inquiry: how its subject matter ought to be conceived. The answer is not altogether novel, but it is much different from and broader than that of other new perspectives of inquiry that have recently appeared in political study. These have entailed rebellion against the emphasis on "forms" in studying the governance on nations but not really against the preoccupation with state-organizations. Some of them, as we saw in Chapter I, led to attempted redefinitions of the subject matter of political inquiry, but only as a kind of by-product; at any rate, the ramifications of the redefinitions were little explored. Thus earlier redefinitions generally proved to be only radical introductions to reformist treatments of conventional subjects.

The *theoretical* element of a paradigm consists of its basic postulates: loosely, its hypotheses; more rigorously, its fundamental axioms and the theorems deduced from them. Some other approaches to systematic political study that have been advanced in recent decades, notably the "rationalist" approach, are statements and elaborations of postulates deemed fruitful for making sense of a conventionally defined subject matter. Our work, on the other hand, leaves open the question of what basic postulates of inquiry may be most fruitful for making sense of authority, public and private. By emphasizing asymmetrical relations in hierarchically ordered units, our view of the nature of what is "political" has obvious affinity with power-elite studies; but we do not proceed from assumptions about the universality of oligarchy, the ubiquity of the desire for power, and the like. Similarly, we recognize the structural existence of superordination and subordination in virtually every social unit, but without making Marxian assumptions about the motivations of superordinates or the inevitably exploitative distribution of benefits between supers and subs. It also might seem that by juxtaposing asymmetrical and symmetrical relations as separate (though intersecting) subjects for inquiry, we stack the cards against "economic" theories of politics; but the possibility that political actors, supers or subs, behave to maximize their utilities, is not precluded. We distinguish relations of direction and relations of exchange, without however postulating that "rational" behavior prevails in the latter and "irrational" behavior in the former. There is, of course, a significant theoretical element in this work, but it is best discussed in connection with "puzzles" below.

The *rules of interpretation* of any scientific enterprise are the methods prescribed or commonly accepted for observing or otherwise assessing phenomena and their interrelations. We have dealt with this issue abstractly by specifying general strategies for studying authority relations empirically, in Part III. We also have dealt with it concretely, first by presentation of specific operational guidelines (also in Part III), second and throughout by reference to the results of studies—by ourselves and our students—that employ such diverse methods as documentary content analysis, survey research, and systematic observation. Our principal thesis has been that the study of authority relations ought not to rely on, or be associated mainly with, the use of a single, sovereign method. At the same time we have aimed at something more than eclectic empiricism. Complete observation and description of the forms, norms, and practices of authority relations is not merely facilitated by but requires *triangulation*—the coordinated use of a variety of methods.

The principal *puzzles* to be solved within this framework for research have to do with (*a*) how authority patterns develop (*b*) what social conditions they most directly depend on, and (*c*) what consequences authority patterns have for how well or badly institutions function. Numerous hypothetical answers to these questions have been posed, mainly in Part V, but it would be mistaken to take what is sketched here as a fully worked out theory. We have stated what we believe to be the principal, most interesting, and most socially critical puzzles that arise in the study of authority relations. Eckstein has proposed a precise theory with some deductive elements that links the configurative authority variables, congruence and consonance, to performance.[3] These efforts, though, are only suggestive of what remains to be done by way of fully specified substantive theory.

In sum, this book directly addresses three of the major issues encompassed by a scientific paradigm and touches on at least one other. Yet it would be folly to pretend that we have constructed anything more than a partial intellectual structure. Paradigms are brought to life and maturity only through the efforts of the scientists who choose to work within them.

The most immediate challenge facing any new approach, then, is achieving acceptability. Political scientists, out of unchanged subjective interests, may be reluctant to recognize the field we have delimited as theirs. If so, we ought perhaps to suggest a new label for it, of the kind generally used to identify special academic subjects that are not wholly within the province of any one conventionally defined discipline. *Archology* seems to be apropos, and *politology* (a term increasingly used in some countries as a substitute for "political science") may be considered one of its subdivisions, concerned with polities.[4]

Our attempt to map the field we have delineated is only a first try, although an elaborate one. Ultimately, the mapping done here will no doubt resemble those early drawings of unfamiliar continents: useful and perhaps ingenious, but incomplete, fanciful, and often mistaken—provided systematic further exploration is in fact undertaken. We have at least tried to do much of the needed initial exploration ourselves, rather than merely inviting others to do so, as seems customary in political science. Still, our chief hope is that these explorations will make further investigation seem worthwhile to others, as well as providing useful groundwork in all necessary respects.

The case for pursuing systematic "archology" rests on numerous claims. Having begun with them, let us also end with them.

First: the subject seems to cover a numerous set of substantially homogeneous cases whose study is now scattered dysfunctionally, even ludicrously, among a variety of special disciplines. The constant intermixture of illustrative materials from units as diverse as families, schools, economic enterprises, and polities should reinforce the abstract case for "archology" as a unified field. However different the units, similar general dimensions of authority can be identified, similar general problems raised, and similar general solutions proposed.

Second: the subject is fascinating and appears to be highly consequential. We have tried to convey some of its flavor through diverse illustrations, speculations about what they imply, and preliminary flings at solving general theoretical problems. The consequentiality of the subject, of course, arises from the critical effects of authority relations on the attainment of social goals, as well as matters as diverse as the formation of personality, educational achievement, industrial relations, and governmental performance. Since authority surrounds us from cradle to grave and guides our interactions in virtually all contexts, surely nothing is more consequential for human beings. For most of us, in any case, the impact of "private" authorities far exceeds that of "public" ones.

Third: to political scientists still mainly interested in the state, we address three arguments. (*a*) To understand how, and how well, nation-states are governed, it should be useful to know how their subsidiary units are governed. If congruence theory is accurate, such information is necessary. And even if the theory is wrong, it seems wildly improbable that the attitudes and behavior of "public" citizens are entirely unaffected by their relationships in "private" contexts. (*b*) The exploration of authority in private contexts can furnish useful tools and insights for those whose concerns are more conventionally "statist," including useful analytic and synthetic concepts. (*c*) Most theories about polities and political behavior, as conventionally conceived, can be tested in less inclusive units within nation-states—units that are often more accessible to intensive investigation and less expensive to study than polities. This point applies not least to "rationalist" theories of politics (e.g., theories about how winning coalitions are formed or the conditions under which different Decision-Rules are adopted). Inasmuch as testing theories, especially on the macrolevel, has not been a notable activity of political scientists, anything that might make such testing more likely to be undertaken is desirable.

Fourth: for other social scientists, we simply point out the manifest importance of authority variables for many of their concerns, as copiously illustrated in this book. A unified study of authority relations can also do much to furnish interdisciplinary bridges for the sister disciplines of social study. All social scientists ought to care about the subject, all can contribute to it, and, exploring it, all can learn from one another, across conventional disciplinary boundaries.

Not least, the subject of authority relations has special significance for any one mainly concerned with moral questions. At the core of all ethical systems and commitments are questions of autonomy and obligation: what we may choose and be obliged to do, on the basis of what procedures, by whom, and on pain of what sanctions and other consequences. Surely any ethical speculation and rational planning about desirable balances of choice and direction in human affairs should be informed by knowledge—better than we have—about what balances prevail in contemporary institutions, about what balances are possible, and about the social means to their practical realization.

Notes

1. For overviews, see Roland Young, Ed., *Approaches to the Study of Politics* (Evanston, Ill.: Northwestern University Press, 1958); Oran Young, *Systems of Political Science* (Englewood Cliffs, N.J.: Prentice-Hall, 1968); and James A. Bill and Robert L. Hardgrave, Jr. *Comparative Politics: The Quest for Theory* (Columbus, Ohio: Charles E. Merrill, 1972).

2. Robert T. Holt and John M. Richardson, Jr., "Competing Paradigms in Comparative Politics," in R. T. Holt and J. E. Turner, Eds., *The Methodology of Comparative Research* (New York: Free Press, 1970), pp. 21–71. The two elements not discussed here, because not touched on in any substantial way in this book, are what Holt and Richarson label "criteria of admissible solutions" and the "ontologic-predictive" element. (The latter, though, clearly depends on the solution of the substantive problems treated in Part V.)

3. Harry Eckstein, "Authority Relations and Governmental Performance," *Comparative Political Studies,* Vol. 2 (October 1969), pp. 269–325.

4. This suggestion of labels is somewhat playful; labels, in any case, are of no great consequence in and of themselves. But we infer from comments on Chapter 1 that many readers have admitted the force of its argument while remaining reluctant to extend the boundaries of what is conventionally labeled "political science." Names and their customary denotations do seem to matter to them.

INDEX